Menus for Movieland

The publisher gratefully acknowledges the generous support
of the Ahmanson Foundation Humanities Endowment Fund
of the University of California Press Foundation.

Menus for Movieland

Newspapers and the Emergence of American Film Culture, 1913–1916

RICHARD ABEL

University of California Press

University of California Press, one of the most distinguished university presses in the United States, enriches lives around the world by advancing scholarship in the humanities, social sciences, and natural sciences. Its activities are supported by the UC Press Foundation and by philanthropic contributions from individuals and institutions. For more information, visit www.ucpress.edu.

University of California Press
Oakland, California

Several chapters and entr'actes are revised and expanded versions of conference papers and earlier published essays: "From Pathé to Paramount: Visual Design in Movie Advertising, 1905–1914," Domitor Conference, Northwestern University, June 25, 2014; "'Daily Talks by Mary Pickford': Who Was That 'Smiley, Golden-Haired Girl'?" Critical M.A.S.S. symposium, Michigan State University, April 19, 2014; "'A Great New Field for Women Folk': Newspapers and the Movies, 1911–1916," Women and the Silent Screen conference, Melbourne, Australia, September 30, 2013; "'What Cinema Was' in the Newspapers, 1914–1915," SCMS Conference, Chicago, March 8, 2013; "Edna Vercoe's 'Romance with the Movies,'" Women and the Silent Screen Conference, Bologna, June 24, 2010; "Zip! Zam! Zowie!: A New Take on U.S. Cinema's Institutionalization," *Historical Journal of Film, Radio, and Television* 20, no. 4 (December 2009): 421–32; "The Movies in a 'Not So Visible' Place: Des Moines, Iowa, 1911–1914," in Kathryn Fuller-Seeley, ed., *Hollywood in the Neighborhood: Historical Case Studies of Local Moviegoing* (University of California Press, 2008), 107–29; "Trash Twins: Newspapers and Moving Pictures," *Americanizing the Movies and "Movie-Mad" Audiences, 1910–1914* (University of California Press 2006), 215–27; "Fan Discourse in the Heartland: The Early 1910s," *Film History* 18, no. 2 (2006): 140–53.

Library of Congress Cataloging-in-Publication Data

Abel, Richard, 1941–.
Menus for movieland : newspapers and the emergence of American film culture / Richard Abel.
p. cm.
Includes bibliographical references and index.
ISBN 978-0-520-28677-1 (cloth : alk. paper)
ISBN 978-0-520-28678-8 (pbk. : alk. paper)
ISBN 978-0-520-96188-3 (ebook)
1. Motion pictures—Press coverage—United States—History—20th century. 2. Newspapers—Social aspects—United States. 3. Motion pictures—United States—Marketing. 4. Motion pictures—United States—History—20th century. I. Title.
PN1993.5.U6A676 2015
384'.80973—dc23 2015011451

Manufactured in the United States of America
24 23 22 21 20 19 18 17 16 15
10 9 8 7 6 5 4 3 2 1

In keeping with a commitment to support environmentally responsible and sustainable printing practices, UC Press has printed this book on Natures Natural, a fiber that contains 30 percent postconsumer waste and meets the minimum requirements of ANSI/NISO Z39.48–1992 (R 1997) (*Permanence of Paper*).

For Barbara, the "Divine Ms. B"

"Oh! Piglet," said Pooh excitedly, "we're going on an Expedition, all of us, with things to eat. To discover something."

"To discover what?" said Piglet anxiously.

"Oh! Just something."

"Nothing fierce?"

. . . .

"Oh, Pooh! Do you think it's a—a—a—a Woozle?"

A. A. MILNE, *Winnie-The-Pooh* (New York: E. P. Dutton, 1926)

Contents

Illustrations

Reproductions of period newspaper pages, columns, and ads often lack clarity because they survive on microfilm or in digital files drawn from microfilm. I have selected some illustrations to give an idea of different newspaper page designs and others from newspapers that are the most legible.

Acknowledgments

I am deeply grateful for the sustained encouragement and support received during the long period of this book's writing.

Several institutions provided crucial funding for the extensive research required: a 2011–12 National Endowment for the Humanities fellowship as well as the Collegiate Professorship and other funds from the College of Literature, Sciences, and the Arts at the University of Michigan.

The readers of a draft manuscript for the University of California Press offered invaluable assistance. Mark Garrett Cooper was especially generous in his recommendations and suggested several good ideas for reorganizing the prologue and introduction as well as writing concluding paragraphs to several chapters and entr'actes. Though less generous, the second anonymous reader did prod me to make my objectives and arguments more clear and consistent throughout and clarify critical concepts at certain points, particularly in the context of recent scholarship.

Sincere thanks are due to the staff and facilities of numerous archives and libraries: Barbara Hall, former research archivist at the Margaret Herrick Library; Julia A. Johnas, director of adult services at the Highland Park Public Library; the Periodicals Room of the U.S. Library of Congress; the Research Center of the Chicago History Museum; the Michigan Historical Society Library; the Historical Society of Iowa Library; the Minnesota Historical Society Library; Special Collections at the UCLA Library; the Rubenstein Library and University Archives at Duke University; the University of Pittsburgh Library; the Heinz Research Center, Pittsburgh; the Cleveland Public Library; the Toledo Public Library; the Buffalo Public Library; the New York Public Library; the Baltimore Public Library; the Stark County District Library, Canton, Ohio; and, of course, the Hatcher Graduate Library and Inter-Library Loan Services at the University of Michigan.

The book also could not have been written without the important online sites of the Media History Digital Library, Chronicling America (U.S. Library of Congress), newspaperarchive.com, geneaologybank.com, and Proquest.

So many colleagues and friends shared source material, helped locate new resources, posed crucial questions, raised counterarguments, and pushed me to develop several lines of analysis that I apologize in advance if some are neglected in the following. Paul S. Moore generously shared a great number of materials, sources, and concepts from his own research on early-twentieth-century newspapers, motion picture pages and columns, and local newsreels. Besides his close friendship, Giorgio Bertellini offered crucial ideas for framing the book's overall argument. Other support of one kind or another came from Diane Anselmo-Sequeire, Jennifer M. Bean, Stephen Bottomore, Scott Curtis, Monica Dall'Asta, Leslie Midkiff DeBauche, Victoria Duckett, Kathryn Fuller-Seeley, Donan Galili, Hilary Hallett, Charlie Keil, Martin Johnson, Jan Olsson, Shelley Stamp, Gregory Waller, and Jennifer Wild. At the University of Michigan, Screen Arts & Cultures doctoral student Nathan Koob helped greatly by traveling to distant libraries to compile digital newspaper scans and photocopies, as did another Screen Arts & Cultures doctoral student, Ben Strassfeld, at the New York City Public Library, and the Romance Languages & Literatures doctoral student Roberto Vezzani at the Library of Congress.

At the University of California Press, Mary Francis offered her usual strong support of this project, tirelessly shepherded the manuscript through several stages of writing and evaluation, and negotiated our contract with gracious patience. Bradley Depew skillfully managed the arduous task of collecting digital files; Chalon Emmons and Jessica Moll efficiently oversaw the multiple phases of production; and the press's art department did excellent work with the cover design and illustrations. Lindsey Westbrook handled the copyediting with admirable speed and meticulous expertise.

My greatest debt, as always, goes to Barbara Hodgdon, who has done so much to shape and refine my writing and, despite illness, has continued to do so while steadily completing her own book project, investigating and analyzing the archival remains of late-twentieth-century and early-twenty-first-century Shakespeare productions from the Royal Shakespeare Theatre, the National Theatre, and the English Shakespeare Company.

Prologue

Research is formalized curiosity. It is poking and prying with a purpose.

ZORA NEALE HURSTON

The Tribune places before you an exceedingly appetizing MOTION PICTURE MENU every day in the week—a menu that gives you the widest possible range of choice, with something in it to suit every fancy and every mood.

Chicago Tribune, April 24, 1915

"Zip!-Zam!-Zowie! That's How They Stage a Movie Play." So goes the title of a story published in the *Chicago Sunday Tribune* on March 22, 1914. The writer was Mae Tinee, one of several newspaper journalists writing about the movies, either weekly in Saturday and Sunday pages or daily in local or syndicated columns. Over the past few years, my research has drawn on early instances of this and other kinds of newspaper discourse, most recently in order to reconstruct and reimagine movie exhibition and moviegoing within everyday life in the United States in the early 1910s.[1] This book greatly expands that research to encompass an even wider range of discourse and extends its reach to 1915–16, when reports claimed that the motion picture business "occupied fifth place among American industries in point of volume"[2] and that "movie-mad" audiences' appetite for anything "newsworthy" about stars, series, serials, and feature-length films was becoming insatiable. At the start, however, perhaps it is best to address an obvious question: Why should anyone take seriously this sometimes flip, readily trashed, but widely read ephemera?

In the early twentieth century, motion pictures and newspapers were prime examples of the ephemerality, the disposability, of modern industrial culture in the United States. As motion pictures became an increasingly popular "cheap amusement," the emerging industry slowly came to realize that it had to do more than promote the circulation of films through a national trade press that targeted exhibitors and rental exchanges—that it had to develop efficient, effective means to shape and sustain a mass public through local and regional newspapers. At the same time, newspapers found that "movie madness" could be exploited to generate advertising revenue and increase circulation. Between 1913 and 1916, the reciprocal and profitable alignment between these "trash twins" produced something like what Yvonne Spielmann, Ursula Bertram, and others have called a "normative structure" of "intermedial fusion" that blurred technological, social, and cultural boundaries.[3] For the cinema historian, the detritus from this alignment has turned into a treasure trove of discursive material on the promotion, exhibition, and reception of the movies, material that still remains relatively unexamined. I began to appreciate this material's value in writing *Americanizing the Movies and "Movie-Mad" Audiences, 1910–1914,* which, in research gleaned from newspapers in selected regions of the upper Midwest and Northeast,[4] analyzed popular representations (genre stories and stars) on screen and strategies of marketing and programming through the frame of Americanization. The following work both extends and departs from that book.

Menus for Movieland assumes that, at the turn of the last century, the primary function of a newspaper was to offer "menus" or maps by which readers could make sense of the complexity of modern urban life, with its increasingly vast array of options and choices (some of them threatening), and imagine how to order and interpret their own daily lives.[5] That function was crucial to the "social imaginary," as Charles Taylor writes, meaning, "the way a given people imagine their collective social life."[6] A newspaper, according to John Nerone and Kevin G. Barnhurst, "looked like an authoritative representation of the social world . . . streamlined in appearance and displaying clear hierarchy and segmentation," which worked, as Benedict Anderson earlier argued, "to enable groups of people to live together as a community (if not actually, then at least in their imagining)."[7] Among those newspaper menus or maps in the early and mid-1910s were formats that mediated the interests of motion picture manufacturers and distributors, local exhibitors, and the rapidly expanding audience of fans.[8]

The four-year span from 1913 through 1916, therefore, arguably constitutes a crucial moment in the American cinema's transformation—that is, the formation of a popular American film culture. As others have rightly argued, that transformation involved the institutionalization of cinema as a mass entertainment through newly standardized practices in film production, distribution, and exhibition as well as the development of large and luxurious theaters, feature films, and a star system. Even more crucially, however, it depended on the emergence of weekly newspaper pages and amusement sections (often in Saturday or Sunday editions) as well as daily columns on the movies that encouraged audiences of frequent, regular spectators quite different from those of the nickelodeon period. In negotiating among national, regional, and local interests during this transformative period and the "transfiguration of one culture of circulation to another,"[9] this newspaper discourse played a significant, yet previously unrecognized, role in shaping audiences' ephemeral experience of moviegoing, their repeated encounters with the fantasy worlds of "movie land," and their attractions to certain stories and stars. This overall argument proffers a substantial revision of what the movies and moviegoing could have meant, and for whom, in the transition to what we now think of as Hollywood. The book's relatively "thick descriptions" invite present-day readers to experience imaginatively the discursive world hailing those early-twentieth-century moviegoers.

Although the parallel should not be overstated, this newspaper discourse on the new medium of motion pictures offers a prototype of sorts for the far more extensive current discourse on a much broader spectrum of intermedial fusion, with the web increasingly at its core. Somewhat like the web, newspapers constituted a discursive space, with their menus of weekly pages and daily columns, for companies and publicists to reach fans of the movies directly, and vice versa. Not only did those pages and columns provide a regular diet of information and gossip to feed fans' desires and longings, they also seemed to offer fans an "interactive" forum for giving voice to their pleasures and displeasures, questions and anxieties. However diverse was the spectrum of their menus and changing menu items, newspapers served, then, as invaluable nodal points or networks of interconnectivity that were as crucial as monthly fan magazines, if not more so, in creating and sustaining the emerging public space of American film culture.

Menus for Movieland examines the formation of this film culture from the perspective of historical groups and individuals, from manufacturers, distributors, and exhibitors to newspaper journalists (a surprising number of them professional women) and young movie fans.[10] This popular film culture predates Vachel Lindsay's *The Art of the Moving Picture* (1915) and Hugo Münsterberg's *The Photoplay: A Psychological Study* (1916)[11] and likely provoked the initial stirrings of an academic film culture at Columbia University.[12] Equally significant, some of the film review discourse broaches concepts that soon would be elaborated and extolled, and eventually contribute to what would become the discipline of cinema studies.

Extending the work of early cinema historians, including my own, this book addresses two sets of related questions in order to advance its arguments. First, to what extent did those in the industry seek to act as "gatekeepers," exerting some measure of control over what should be included and even highlighted in this newspaper discourse (for their assumed readers/spectators), and how did their promotional strategies change as cinema programs came to show not only single-reel films but also series, serials, and feature-length films? And to what degree, by contrast, did newspapers and exhibitors also attempt to control this discourse (for their readers/spectators), and how did their efforts shift with changes in cinema programs? In other words, was film promotion largely a national phenomenon of "social engineering"—while allowing for a limited number of niche markets—that produced a more or less homogeneous film culture? Or was it just as often local or regional—assuming that a newspaper's "reading field" could differ from one city to another and be specific to certain social groups,[13] with the result that film culture and the alleged interests of "actual" moviegoers could be equally heterogeneous?

Second, what implications can be drawn from the fact that a good percentage of this newspaper discourse was written and edited by women? To what extent did they share the industry's efforts to expand audiences well beyond those of the nickelodeon era and include more and more middle-class whites?[14] And if they tended to target women readers, who exactly were those readers, and how might they differ in class and age, depending on a newspaper's "reading field"? Finally, along with other women finding professional and white-collar work in the industry (as Mark Cooper and Hilary Hallett have shown),[15] could these writers and editors be seen as exemplary figures of the "New Woman," that "paradigm of liberation and agency," in Linda Nochlin's words, who would not be denied "achievement through career and work outside the home"?[16]

Since beginning research on this newspaper discourse at state historical societies and public libraries, I and others have benefited greatly from new online sources—for instance newspaperarchive.com, genealogybank.com, and chroniclingamerica.loc.gov (Library of Congress)—which have revealed a wealth of material well beyond my initial geographical range. To some extent the search functions of those online databases have circumscribed the large photocopy and digital collection I have amassed, excluding many newspapers that could enhance that collection. Yet the data I do have suggests that certain papers were especially important, not only in major cities—Chicago, Cleveland, New York, Philadelphia, Buffalo, Pittsburgh, Minneapolis, St. Louis, New Orleans, and Washington, DC—but also in smaller cities and towns such as Seattle, Portland (Oregon), Toledo, Atlanta, Syracuse, Birmingham, Omaha, Des Moines, Fort Worth, Augusta (Georgia), La Crosse (Wisconsin), and Waterloo (Iowa). In order to better contextualize this discourse, I have turned to histories of early-twentieth-century newspapers and their partners in communication as "cultures of circulation,"[17] and investigated publicity strategies within the motion picture industry, both in the trade press and in archival collections such as the

Margaret Herrick Library in Beverly Hills, California. Moreover, I have extended the scope of this research to include a rare set of scrapbooks compiled by a teenage movie fan in the Chicago area (also housed at the Herrick Library). That said, my research hardly can be considered exhaustive. As more newspapers are digitized and other discursive materials turn up in online sites such as the Media History Digital Library and elsewhere—from industry documents and house organs or theater programs to scrapbooks, high school "memory books," and even diaries—the following historical analysis of "movie menus" inevitably will require some modification or even correction, particularly by those "on the ground" in local cities or towns. But, then, one always has to keep in mind that if the history one writes has to have an end, the writing of history never ever ends.

Introduction

The Newspaper, a Cultural Partner of the Movies

"Taking a paper" became a standard rite and daily routine for the American family [in the late nineteenth century].

RICHARD L. KAPLAN, *Politics and the American Press* (Cambridge University Press, 2002)

He who is without a newspaper is cut off from his species.

The Life of Barnum, the World-Renowned Showman (1899)

AN INFRASTRUCTURE OF SUPPLY

In early December of 1911, readers of the *Cleveland Leader*'s Sunday edition might have been surprised or even excited to find a new weekly page headlined "Photo-Plays and Players" devoted to "news of Cleveland's leading picture theaters" and short "reviews of the feature films of the week."[1] More than a year later, readers of weekend editions in a number of smaller cities—Fort Wayne, Indiana; Hamilton, Ohio; San Antonio, Texas; or Ogden, Utah[2]—would have felt the same on finding at least a half page headlined either "Motion Picture News" or "News of Photoplays and Photoplayers" supplied by Syndicate Film Publishing in acknowledgment that "the motion picture theatre has won its way to a position of primal importance in the life of the people." Within another year, other newspapers, most notably the *Chicago Tribune,* were editing their own weekly Sunday pages devoted to motion pictures, and especially movie stars.[3] Over the course of the next two years, these Sunday or weekend pages, often along with syndicated weekly or daily columns, proliferated across North America, aligning motion picture audiences and movie fans ever more closely with the mass "reading public" of the newspapers. This more or less standardized form of newspaper discourse followed and clearly was predicated on the standardized practices recently put in place by the new industry. None could have developed, however, without a stable infrastructure to support motion pictures as both an efficiently organized form of mass entertainment and a burgeoning film culture. If General Film, Universal, and Mutual, for instance, depended heavily on the national network of interconnected railroads to deliver their numerous film prints according to a predictable schedule to exhibitors, local and regional newspapers relied no less heavily on a national network of telegraph lines (usually paralleling railroad lines through exclusive right-of-way contracts)[4] linking most urban areas of the country in order to receive features, novelties, and a variety of news items, just as predictably, from one or more press associations or syndicated services, especially for their increasingly profitable weekend editions.[5]

As the first electrical industry, James Carey writes, "the telegraph, in conjunction with the railroad, provided the setting in which modern techniques for the management of complex enterprises were first worked out."[6] As a major innovation in communications, the telegraph made available simultaneously all manner of information, with the effect, Carey adds, that it "even[ed] out markets in space."[7] By the turn of the twentieth century, the network of telegraph lines stretching across North America covered a total of 237,990 miles[8] and had become a more or less unified system, dominated by Western Union (with its largest customer, the press),[9] linking disparate population centers from metropolises to rural small towns into the "imagined community" of a modern mass public.[10] Crucial to that public was the modern ritual of "taking a newspaper." Moreover, the daily newspaper was "read by every member of the family," claimed Guy S. Osborn in 1911, because it "respond[ed] to every daily want of the home."[11] According to a key 1923 essay by the sociologist Robert E. Park, for its readers, a newspaper made any city "habitable, [made] it feel local and coherent," but also made "vast metropolitan regions seem like sensible entities with knowable orders of place and histories."[12] In short, a newspaper helped "communities form and sustain themselves."[13] National industries gradually would come to view not only mass magazines but also regional and metropolitan newspapers, supported by the telegraph's system of transmission, as a further means of realizing a vision, in Richard L. Kaplan's words, of "American society made uniform and harmonious through standardized mass production and consumption."[14] At the local level, however, "the particular combination of reporting and advertising," Paul S. Moore argues, "characterized any specific readership as a public in relation to other publics, able to recognize themselves and their everyday life, but precisely in connection to knowledge about others and elsewhere."[15]

Taking advantage of this extensive telegraph network were what Richard T. Schwartzlose has called "newsbrokers" or wire services, that sought through syndication to regularize and control the flow of information to newspapers large and small throughout the country.[16] Newsbrokers such as the American Press Association, Irving Bacheller Syndicate, and S. S. McClure Syndicate, in Alice Fahs's words, had long "provided 'ready-plate' material or readymade sheets," especially short stories or serialized fiction, "that could simply be inserted in local papers."[17] Partly due to its early alliance with Western Union, the Associated Press (formerly Western Associated Press) was prominent in the dissemination of syndicated news and features—until, after the panic of 1907, AT&T acquired control of Western Union, modernized the company's equipment (e.g., a multiplex printing telegraph), and increased its leased excess circuit capacity (fig. 1).[18] In 1907, E.W. Scripps established the United Press Association, anchored by the Scripps-McRae chain of Midwest newspapers, which soon proved one of several formidable competitors to the older wire service.[19] Whereas the Associated Press had targeted morning papers, the United Press set up an afternoon service aimed at the growing number of evening and Sunday papers.[20] Although both wire services distributed proof sheets, feature mats, photo mats, comics, and news items, the United Press was distinctive for its "colorful, readable copy" and "short, punchy lead paragraphs."[21] And some of that copy originated in the *Chicago Day Book*, Scripps's experiment with an "adless" newspaper.[22] In 1910, William Randolph Hearst combined his syndicated American Sunday Magazine and comic strip features into the International News Service and three years later founded King Features to distribute some of the best Sunday comic pages.[23] At the same time, the Central Press Association, focused on the Midwest, appeared as a smaller regional service, and several metropolitan newspapers also began to sell their syndicated features: the *Chicago Record-Herald* (through the Associated Sunday Magazine) in 1902, the *Chicago Tribune* in 1910, the *New York Tribune* in 1914, and the *Philadelphia Ledger* in 1915.[24] Overall, what emerged from the daily output of these syndicated wire services was a distinctively American style of journalism marked by standardization, brevity, and fragmentation.[25]

As Schwartzlose suggests, Sunday newspaper editions became increasingly reliant on newsbrokers and (obviously) advertisers, who quickly realized that they were the best venue for advertising because they entered so many homes and appealed to every member of the family.[26] Initially called "supplements," they more than doubled in number between 1889 and 1899 (from 257 to 567) and also expanded in length.[27] By 1910, the estimated circulation of all Sunday editions matched that of all daily evening newspapers: fifteen million copies.[28] According to a British commentator, Sunday editions were a uniquely American phenomenon: "at once a newspaper and a literary miscellany, a society journal and household magazine."[29] As a leisure-reading supplement, they used the newspaper's "vast economies of scale and circulation" to deliver the equivalent of a mass magazine more frequently and at less expense.[30] By the early twentieth century, many of

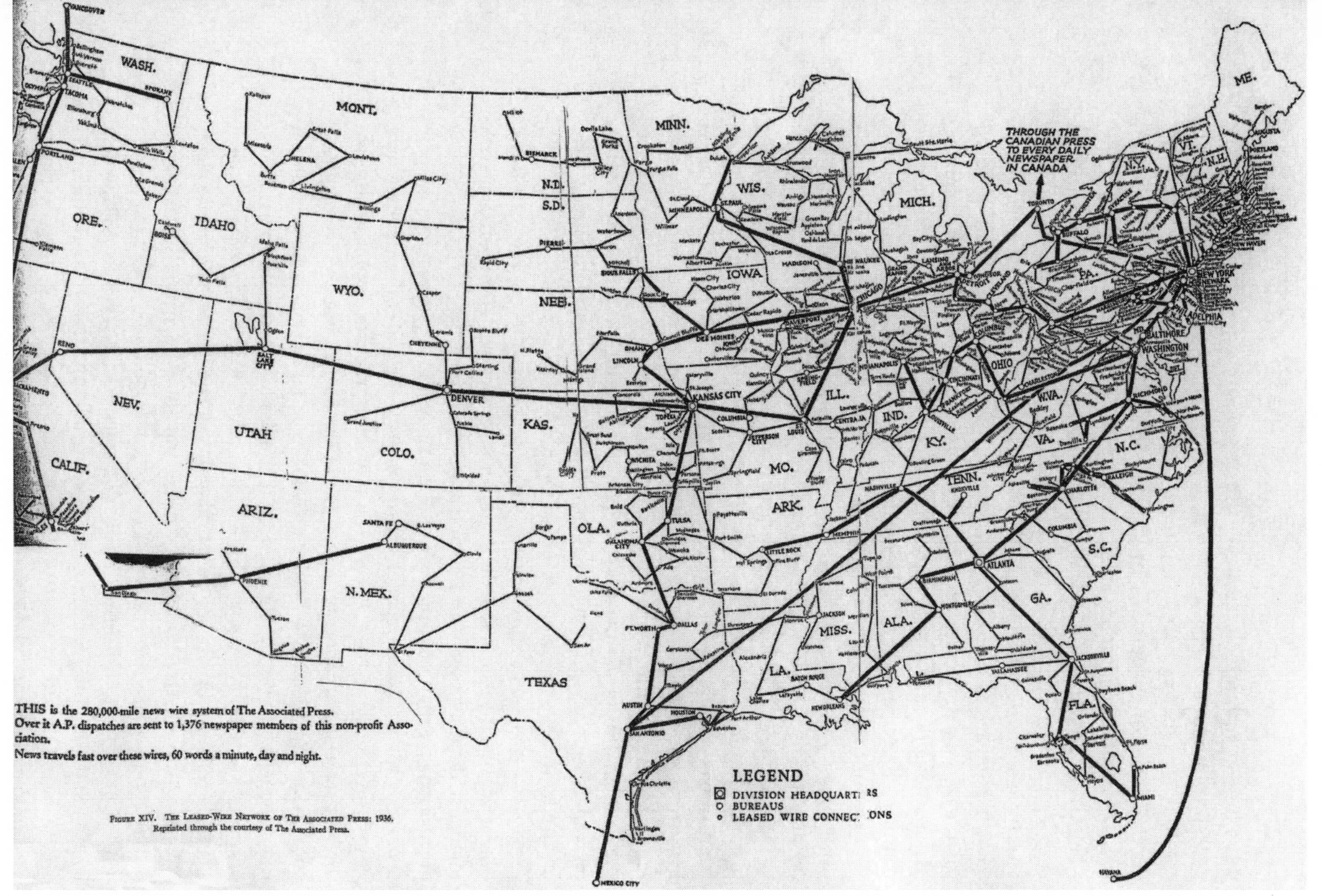

FIGURE 1. Associated Press telegraph lines map, 1936, insert in Alfred McClung Lee, *The Daily Newspaper in America: The Evolution of a Social Instrument* (New York: Macmillan, 1947).

them bulged with largely local ads, illustrations (eventually photogravure pages), color comic strips, and "magazine" sections, as well as numerous columns, all aimed at a broad spectrum of readers whose assumed interests differed according to gender, class, and age. The *New York World*'s "Sunday Magazine" and its "Funny Side" comics offer rare surviving examples— "The Great Airship Races at the St. Louis World's Fair" (January 31, 1904) and "Fire at the Funny Side Hotel" (May 22, 1904)—of the wonderments attracting so many readers.[31] Sunday editions looked and functioned somewhat like department stores, and a version of the "display" ads that lured customers into the stores soon filled whole newspaper pages, becoming a major source of revenue.[32] At the time, an advertising man confirmed the analogy: "85 per cent of the advertising in newspapers and magazines, with the exception of the classified and financial, is dedicated to women and articles women purchase."[33] For Scripps, the Sunday edition "was a great big restaurant, filled with bustle and noise, and tantalizing customers with a jumble of smells."[34] His analogy was particularly apt for many newcomers to larger cities—whether migrants from the countryside or immigrants from abroad, whether white-collar workers or skilled laborers—whose need for information and a new sense of place and identity the Sunday paper might begin to fulfill. Moreover, in the timing of their delivery as well as the social and cultural range of so much of their content, for whatever class of readers, Sunday editions, in Gunther Barth's succinct phrasing, "gave leisure legitimacy in a work-oriented world."[35]

Just as department stores systematized retailing into discrete categories (and spaces) and restaurants, on a smaller scale, did something similar with menus, so did newspapers have to find a way to manage an ever-growing flow of information that continually had to be turned into "news." The answer: departmentalize the newspaper into separate pages, often with their own heads for ease of access. "The sections of news reports, editorials, human interest stories, and advertisements," Barth writes, "imposed a rational order on a chaotic urban life," whether directly experienced or, as in small rural towns, viewed from afar.[36] Moreover, if the "amusement and sporting columns helped schedule leisure time," Moore adds, all that "advertising helped schedule consumption."[37] In the Sunday or weekend newspaper those pages expanded into discrete sections, printed and folded separately, that could number more than half a dozen. A typical metropolitan Sunday paper such as the *Chicago Tribune* or the *Cleveland Leader* would have sections devoted to national and international news, editorials and local news, business and real estate matters, society events, women's activities, children's games, arts and amusements, and sports, along with a magazine and comics. This departmentalization may have allowed for a high degree of selective reading defined by gender and age, but the Sunday edition *in toto* contained those differences within the greater mass reading public, "all the while implicitly or explicitly," writes Charles Johanningsmeier, "measuring their practices against the yardstick of civilized, urban, middle-class America."[38] Interestingly, most of these discrete sections were in place well before the turn of the twentieth century. If a new section on automobiles emerged with the rapid growth of that industry between 1905 and 1910, the only other, on motion pictures or photoplays, appeared just a few years later, also in conjunction with that industry's equally rapid development.[39] Whereas the newspaper section on automobiles targeted men, the one on motion pictures tended to cater more to women, and sometimes was aligned with other sections of particular concern to them, for instance the women's or society sections, or those devoted to arts and amusements.[40]

If perhaps half of these Sunday newspaper sections were full of "women's-interest" material, they also often were written or edited by professional women.[41] In 1892, Foster Coates, the city editor of the *New York Journal,* wrote in *Ladies' Home Journal:* "The young woman with a good constitution, who knows how to write good English and is willing to work hard has as good an opportunity as any man similarly equipped to succeed in journalism.[42] "Newspaper women," writes Fahs, "were closely linked with several newly developed genres of popular writing, including interviews, advice columns, and urban 'sketches,'" as well as "'sensational' exploits."[43] Nellie Bly (Elizabeth Cochrane), for instance, quickly became famous not only for her exposés in the *New York World* but also for stunts such as her 1889–90 adventure circling the world, in far fewer days than Jules Verne had envisioned.[44] At the *San Francisco Examiner,* Annie Laurie (Winifred Black) embodied the figure of the "girl reporter" who would cover any kind of news story in a style of "vivid, personal writing that was highly charged with emotion" and marked by "short sentences and paragraphs with hard jolts."[45] Some became popular for their daily advice columns in Hearst newspapers, for instance Beatrice Fairfax (Marie Manning) in the *New York Journal,* and Dorothy Dix (Elizabeth Meriwether Gilmer), first in the *New Orleans Picayune* and then in the *Journal.*[46] A few others were well known as drama critics (e.g., Amy Leslie of the *Chicago Daily News* and Leone Cass Baer of the *Oregonian* in Portland) or press agents (e.g., Nellie Revell for Percy Williams's vaudeville circuit).[47] In all, by 1910, according to Marion T. Marzolf, more than four thousand women held writing and editing jobs, largely at newspapers.[48] "Their work," Fahs argues, "shaped new public spaces for women within the physical pages of the newspaper, while also writing into being a far-flung new public world for women."[49] With this kind of professional precedent, perhaps it is no wonder that so many young women entered the motion picture news field, from Gertrude Price writing a movie star column for the Scripps-McRae papers to Mae Tinee (Frances Peck) editing the Sunday motion picture page and Kitty Kelly (Audrey Alspaugh) penning daily film reviews, both for the *Chicago Tribune.*

MENUS IN THE MAKING, AND FOR COLLECTING

A young movie fan, in the spring of 1911, could be hard pressed to know what was playing at her neighborhood picture theater or even at a larger one downtown. She might glean something from the "vast quantities of literature" that motion picture manufacturers allegedly were shipping "free to every exhibitor" (see chapter 1) and that a manager could be passing out as handbills or posting around a theater's sidewalk entrance.[50] She might also have learned to expect a certain brand of movie on a certain night of the week at a downtown first-run theater, because both General Film and Sales by then were distributing a standardized weekly schedule of new releases. But she probably would have little notion of what specific films would be screened or who among the emerging stars she might chance to see. Instead, she would be going to the movies with girlfriends, a boyfriend, or family members to enjoy, once a week or even more frequently, what was fast becoming a ritual as regular as going to school, church, or work. Whenever she "dropped in" to the continuous programs that nearly all picture theaters still offered, her moviegoing experience could be familiarly satisfying, pleasantly surprising, or unexpectedly disappointing. What she could not count on from a local newspaper was any information other than perhaps a regular theater ad (in some small towns), because the daily press, as a *Moving Picture World* editorial moaned, was "woefully ignorant of the doings in the moving picture world."[51]By 1914, all that would radically change (fig. 2). The change would be evident not only in metropolises such as Cleveland, Pittsburgh, Buffalo, Chicago, or New York, but also in smaller cities such as Seattle, Toledo, Atlanta, Fort Worth, Ogden (Utah), or Portland (Oregon). Reading a local newspaper in any of these cities, the same movie fan now could find a wealth of information and gossip about the movies, and probably learn which particular films and stars would be appearing in at least some specific picture theaters any day of the week. And her reading could range over a weekly or even daily variety of menus on the movies: Sunday pages, syndicated "personality sketches," industry ads and other publicity material, local columns and reviews, exhibitor ads, and "answers to fans."

Making "Movie" History

The Romance of an Idea That Fired a City's Enthusiasm

FIGURE 2. "Making 'Movie' History" ad, *Chicago Record-Herald*, February 16, 1914.

Although it now reads as little more than a puff piece, Mae Tinee's story does mark an important phase in the explosion of newspaper discourse between 1913 and 1914. But despite the ephemerality of motion pictures, pressure had been building toward that eruption since at least 1911. Before then, the practice of frequently changed programs of short films and drop-in moviegoing fostered during the nickelodeon period gave few exhibitors the incentive to spend money on advertising in local newspapers.[52] However, now that 1) the industry had established a system-wide form of standardization (in production, distribution, and exhibition), 2) purpose-built, larger, even luxurious picture theaters and neighborhood houses were fast replacing nickelodeons or storefront theaters, 3) movie stars were beginning to lure fans as much as manufacturer brands, and 4) longer, imported films such as *The Fall of Troy, Dante's Inferno,* and *Temptations of a Great City* (all 1911) could be treated as "special features," new movie audiences and moviegoing practices were emerging. The following pages offer a "tasting" of the menu items that will be the subject of much more thorough analysis in chapters 2 through 5.

The first full buffet menu for motion pictures appeared as a regular feature in the *Cleveland Leader.* In early September 1911, the *Sunday Leader* announced a "Special Arrangement [with] Photoplay Theaters in Ohio and Pennsylvania cities," urging its readers to cut out five-cent coupons that would admit them to one of a "select circuit" of dozens of picture theaters.[53] These coupons comprised half of the page bannered "In the Moving Picture World," and the other half included a list of the week's licensed and independent film releases, brief notes on certain theaters, and snippets of information about specific films, companies, and people in the industry—initially in a column called "Calcium Flashes." Within a month, in its city edition the *Sunday Leader* was including a full page bannered "Feature Photo Plays of the Week Edited by Ralph P. Stoddard" (a reporter and former theater manager in Sandusky, Ohio, who also edited a weekly column dealing with real estate and building construction).[54] Small photos of some thirty "Leader chain houses" framed this page, within which readers could find a single coupon to cut out and use on one of those theater's "acceptance days" that week. The rest of the page complemented this promotional scheme but with snippets of industry news and gossip, columns of local news about "picture fans," synopses of a few theater programs, and two or three production stills.[55] In the regional Sunday edition, Stoddard added a column on "New Educational Films," soon followed by select film reviews reprinted by permission from the *New York Morning Telegraph*.[56] Later that month, now in both editions, Stoddard profiled Mary Pickford, the first in a series of photo stories on movie stars.[57] Finally, in early December, every edition of the *Sunday Leader* began offering the same page, now headlined "Photo-Plays and Players" and devoted to "news of Cleveland's leading picture theaters" and to Stoddard's "reviews of the feature films of the week" (fig. 3).[58] This new Sunday page now was supported by ads for those thirty picture theaters in Cleveland (a quarter of the city's total number), several regional film rental exchanges, and manufacturers who provided production photos of their new films. In return, as a "guide to fans," Stoddard edited a column that listed, and briefly commented on, certain Sunday or weekly programs, allowing readers to plan their moviegoing in advance, for selected theaters located downtown or in half a dozen secondary commercial districts. Not until early 1913 (see chapter 2) did several other papers adopt the *Cleveland Leader*'s model, and it took another year for some key papers—most notably the *Chicago Tribune*, with editor Mae Tinee—to lead a surge in weekend pages.

Earlier, however, the Scripps-McRae newspaper chain, through its United Press service, introduced a more singular menu item, and on a less regular basis. In late 1911, the Frederic J. Haskin newspaper syndicate (Washington, DC) had compiled a twelve-part series on various phases of the motion picture industry allegedly "printed in forty newspapers of the first class" across

6 B THE CLEVELAND LEADER, SUNDAY, OCTOBER 1, 1911.

Feature Photo Plays of the Week

Edited by Ralph P. Stoddard

CRESCENT | MALL | PRINCESS | DREAMLAND | CAMERAPHONE | BRONX

A NICKEL THAT GROWS BIGGER EVERY WEEK

Never Before Did a 5 Cent Piece Buy So Much

See List of New Theaters Where Sunday Leader Coupon is Good

MR. READER, be sure you get all you are entitled to. The nickel you paid for this paper is still working for you. Read conditions for its use as ticket of admission to Cleveland's best photo-play theaters. It's all on the coupon in this page.

FILL IN NAME OF THEATER YOU ATTEND THEN SEE THE SHOW AS LEADER GUEST

FIVE CENTS 5¢ 5 5¢

It Means Shows Without Cost if You Get the Sunday Leader Every Sunday

MORE HOUSES JOIN LEADER'S BIG CHAIN

DEVIL MOVES TO EUCLID FOR WEEK

At the Leader Chain Houses This Week

FEATURE CHAIN HOUSES; THEIR ACCEPTANCE DAYS

St. Louis Organizes.

FIGURE 3. *Cleveland Sunday Leader* photoplay page, October 1, 1911.

the country.[59] But the United Press series was different: it took a major attraction of monthly fan magazines such as *Motion Picture Story Magazine* and made it a special, more frequent newspaper feature. This was a syndicated column of short "personality sketches" or star profiles that, beginning in early November 1912, could be picked up by UP clients as well as subscribers. The writer was a pioneering journalist located in Chicago, Gertrude Price, "YOUR 'MOVIE' EXPERT," who entertained readers with stories about the "MOVING PICTURE FOLKS" because "'the movies' are the biggest, most popular amusement in the world."[60] Price wrote in the colloquial language of UP's distinctive "colorful, readable copy," with "punchy" headlines, and consistently used the slang term "movies" rather than "photoplays" as a direct appeal to the "bright youngsters [who] gave moving pictures an apt, vivid name." Almost exclusively focused on American actors, her stories were illustrated by one or more halftone images (drawn from publicity photos) that usually emphasized the stars' faces. Appearing frequently, if irregularly, often at the top of one page or another, her stories circulated as mass culture commodities, much like the movies. And they always could be tweaked for local consumption. An added line in the *Des Moines News,* for instance, read, "You have seen this actress at: The Colonial, the Lyric, and the Family." For more than a year, before others (e.g., Mae Tinee in the *Chicago Tribune,* Mary B. Leffler in the *Fort Worth Star-Telegram,* Britt Craig in the *Atlanta Constitution,* or even Mary Pickford in "Daily Talks" in dozens of newspapers) began to follow her precedent (see chapter 3), Price's column was one of the most widely read sources of gossip and information on the movies' emerging stars.

Before 1914, if newspaper movie pages offered anything labeled "film reviews," they were brief and usually lifted from trade press or manufacturers' publicity material, whether reprinted directly or rewritten to be linked to local picture theaters (see chapter 1). Perhaps the earliest reviews evidencing a degree of independent judgment—what was to become a crucial menu item—appeared in the *Chicago Tribune* in February 1914, within a daily column titled "Today's Best Photo Play Stories."[61] This anonymous reviewer had a keen interest in the choice, construction, and tone of a film's narrative and, much like a book critic, deployed those as principles to evaluate the "artistic" worth of a film. Reliance's *The Green-Eyed Monster,* for instance, won this praise: "This compact and well acted play is pitched in exactly the right key to interest the great mass of photoplay patrons. The characters are types from everyday life. Jealousy brings them to the very edge of tragedy. The motive recurs constantly throughout the story. The denouement is natural and satisfying."[62] Lubin's *The Weaker Brother,* by contrast, was chastised for lacking such, clear, efficient storytelling: "This film of the civil war involves so much disguising, spying, and traitor turning that it is a bit difficult to be sure which side is which and who is on it."[63] Two contrasting examples in late March also depended on the choice and construction of a film story, but one added another basis for evaluation. American's *The Turning Point* came in for criticism because it "is a striking and an unpleasant picture of crime and high society," but Éclair's *Adrift,* set in Canada, received a different kind of praise: "Some splendid photographic work . . . brings the observer into the atmosphere of the snowy woods and icy streams with a convincing directness."[64] Personal genre preference also played a role in this appraisal of Éclair's *The Price:* "In this film drama—not melodrama, please—there is a real artistic emotional achievement which glimpses a day when the customary long chase, enhanced by frequent somersaulting falls, will not be the chief occupant of millions of feet of film."[65] Only on July 1 was the reviewer identified as Kitty Kelly, the pseudonym of young Audrey Alspaugh, and her column now began to single out one film each day.[66] Within less than a year, Kelly's lead was followed by others, including Mary B. Leffler at the *Fort Worth Star-Telegram,* Ruth Vinson at the *Cleveland Plain Dealer,* "Wid" Gunning at the *New York Evening Mail,* and Louella O. Parsons at the *Chicago Herald* (see chapter 4).

But how did movie fans use one or more of these menu items? Determining what of the little information still extant might be reliable is notoriously difficult. By the early to mid-1910s, there were columns recording the "voices of fans" (ventriloquized or not) in early fan magazines and Sunday newspaper pages such as the *Chicago Tribune.* But can these "voices" be considered sufficient indicators, if not evidence, of how fans read these pages and columns and what they really thought about the movies? In early February 1914, one can find the *Tribune* floating an intriguing idea for its readers of "Today's Best Moving Picture Story": "If the story interests you so that you want to see it in the pictures, put it in your scrap book. Then when it comes to your neighborhood you will have it."[67] Within four months Edna Vercoe, a teenager in Highland Park, north of Chicago, was engaged in far more than simply cutting out such stories when she began composing the first of what would become six large scrapbooks (160 pages each), all of which miraculously survive at the Margaret Herrick Library (see chapter 5). The contents of these scrapbooks offer a clear sense of what attracted Vercoe, along with her girlfriends, to the movies and made them ardent fans. So obsessed was she with the serials that synopses and photos of Pathé's *The Perils of Pauline* as well as Universal's *Lucille Love* (both 1914) take up more than half of the first volume's pages. Her other obsession, not unexpectedly, was with movie stars. Their photos, line drawings, gossip items, and other ephemera, together with her own marginalia, fill nearly half the pages in all six scrapbooks. The number of stars included is huge and diverse, and they range from well-known figures such as Mary Pickford, Mary Fuller, and Francis X. Bushman to others now largely forgotten. Her favorite stars appear in the serials she followed so closely; prominent throughout are Pearl White and Crane Wilbur, as are, at least initially, Grace Cunard and Francis Ford.[68] Overall, these scrapbooks give the impression of one teenage movie fan's intent to compose her personalized version of a monthly fan magazine.

This survey of initial menus and menu entries should already suggest tentative answers to the questions raised in the prologue, answers that will be extended, modified, and complicated in the following chapters. Syndicated press services such as the United Press, Syndicated Film, and McClure's Syndicate were involved, however differently, in promoting movies as a *national* phenomenon. And the industry itself (see chapter 1 as well as the final two entr'actes) sought to make that film culture as homogenous as possible—and increasingly defined, ideally, as white and middle class—for its own benefit, of course. Newspaper editors and writers from the *Cleveland Leader* to the *Pittsburgh Leader, Toledo Times, Chicago Tribune, Chicago Herald,* and *Washington Times,* by contrast, engaged in promotion that was often equally local or regional in character (see the first and second entr'actes) and seemed to support or even encourage the alleged interests of specific, yet diverse, exhibitors and moviegoers, producing a relatively more heterogeneous film culture. Moreover, whether they were editing weekend movie pages, penning columns of information and gossip, or writing columns of independent film reviews, many of these newspaper editors and writers were young women just entering the profession of journalism—and, consequently, at the forefront of the emergence of a popular American film culture. Finally, among the growing mass of moviegoers were other, even younger women such as Edna Vercoe and her girlfriends, near Chicago, who were collecting ephemera from industry sources, fan magazines, and local newspapers to create an idiosyncratic, personalized film culture in their own scrapbook fan magazines.

A personal postscript. My maternal grandparents—Clyde Wolfe, a department store window dresser, and Lillie Melcher, a stenographer for a paving brick company—were married in Canton, Ohio, on June 22, 1915.[69] In *Americanizing the Movies,* I imagined Lillie a year or two earlier, in an audience listening to Clyde playing the clarinet as part of the quartet that accompanied the movies in the city's Odeon Theater and Grand Opera House. Sometime before their marriage, Clyde dropped out of the quartet, Lillie left the brick company, and they may have had less time for moviegoing, as they eventually had six children. Yet they likely subscribed to or at least read the *Canton Evening Repository,* and there they could hardly have failed to notice an important long-lived column that began running less than five months after their wedding. Although the *Repository* may not have had a Sunday movie page, it did carry Mary Pickford's "Daily Talks," beginning with a full-page ad on November 7, 1915.[70] And I imagine, once more, Pickford's column piquing Lillie's interest in particular and luring her into regularly scanning the *Repository*'s daily "Women's Page," because there she would find that "the most popular girl in the world . . . talks [directly] to you."

DOCUMENT

ADVERTISEMENT, *CHICAGO TRIBUNE,* MAY 22, 1915

TOMORROW'S SUNDAY TRIBUNE

WAR—A striking story without words—reproduced in four colors.

RIGHT OFF THE REEL—Movie page edited by Mae Tinee, with "Shep," late little friend of millions of little ones in The Frame of Public Favor.

Third chapter of "THE DIAMOND FROM THE SKY"—Two full pages, with large striking photographs illustrating McCardell's famous novel.

"WITHOUT THE FOOTLIGHTS"—Another Thomas T. Hoyne story of city life.

YOUNG AMERICANS—"The Trail of the Boy Scouts," continuation of Baden-Powell's "My Adventures as a Spy"; Popular Science and Interesting Boys—a page for real boys, not namby pambies.

The Dunce goes boating on a clothespin and almost floats into the sewer, but is rescued just in time by the Cowboy with his lasso. A thrilling incident in the career of The Teenie Weenies, the world's littlest and most popular little people.

Der Captain, with the aid of Hans and Fritz, learns the best thing to do with a fresh monkey; Mamma's Angel Child plays circus; Bobby Make-Believe catches a whale; Doc Yak's protégé takes on all comers—four pages comprising the best comics in the country.

THEY SHOULD BE ON THE FIRING LINE IF WE EVER HAVE A WAR—Don't miss this McCutcheon cartoon.

"FIRST AID OUTFITS FOR SCHOOLS"—Read this article by Dr. W.A. Evans.

THE HIGHBROW PAGE—Articles by Robert Herrick, Edward Goldbeck, Robert R. McCormick, Claude Grahame-White—no better reading in any magazine.

THE DAYS OF REAL SPORT—Young Hopeful is told he should begin to do something—a characteristic Briggs cartoon.

PERCY HAMMOND in Chicago, BURNS MANTLE in New York—the country's leading dramatic critics.

RING LARDNER—the sport humorist everybody's reading.

FRANK KING, cartoonist, breaks into society for a half page.

THE EXTREME 1915 BATHING SUITS—Written about by Louise James and pictured by Maude Martin Evers.

PATTERNS BY CLOTILDE—Summer blouses to please the practical woman.

"THE TERRIBLE TURK"—Picture and sketch of Enver Bey, that curious mingling of modernism and the dark traits that have given Turkey an age-old spell of terror—one of eight pages of unusual pictures in the rotogravure section.

ALL THESE AND HUNDREDS OF OTHER FEATURES IN

TOMORROW'S SUNDAY TRIBUNE

1. The Industry Goes to Town (and Country)

The moving picture film manufacturers are anxious to popularize their industry, and they very shrewdly know that there is only one big medium of publicity—the newspaper.

New York Morning Telegraph, June 4, 1914

Sing a song of photoplays
Best that can be had!
To find out what and where they are
Read a Tribune ad!

Chicago Tribune, April 4, 1915

As early as spring 1911, *Moving Picture World* claimed that motion picture manufacturers were shipping "vast quantities of literature free to every exhibitor" throughout the country.[1] Relying on theater managers to serve as unpaid publicity agents, such a strategy was little more than an uncoordinated attempt to promote moviegoing in a very piecemeal fashion. The trade press did suggest all kinds of ideas and share others sent in by contributors—from entrance or lobby decorations and "house organ" formats to handbills and stunts—that exhibitors could devise by drawing on that "literature," specifically in columns such as Espes Winthrop Sargent's "Advertising for Exhibitors" in *Moving Picture World*.[2] At the same time, trade writers complained that exhibitors could not see the benefit of advertising in local newspapers and that, reciprocally, newspapers "were woefully ignorant of the doings in the moving picture world."[3] Labeling newspapers as ignorant, however, was hardly helpful for inducing cooperation. In the *New York Dramatic Mirror*, the "Spectator" offered several good reasons why both exhibitors and newspapers took the attitude they did, even when the trade press was reviewing films regularly. "The large number of new pictures produced each week, their ephemeral character and the brevity of nearly all of them . . . precludes the possibility of general press review of average motion picture productions."[4] If newspapers rarely reviewed vaudeville acts or short stories (unless in book form), why should they be expected to review films? Nor should exhibitors be expected to quote from a trade press review in any advertisement they did place in local papers. By the time such a review reached a theater manager, often "the picture [was] no longer a fresh feature," "Spectator" added, and "however favorable . . . of no use," except in unusual circumstances.[5] This last comment ignored the fact that lots of films would not reach managers in many cities and towns until weeks or even months after their release.

By 1913, not only had exhibitors in some cities undergone a change of attitude and expanded their promotional schemes to include newspaper advertising, but also the latter medium, "which but yesterday would not even deign to admit the existence of the motion picture, [now was] eager to learn and print all the important news in the motion picture field."[6] As early as the year before, the *New York Morning Telegraph* boasted that its motion picture department had "a right to claim a large share . . . in the different tone now generally adopted by the press," but some credit also was due to *Moving Picture World* and the *New York Dramatic Mirror*.[7] An equally important reason was that manufacturers and distributors had established publicity departments to produce and supply motion picture news in a more systematic way. Although Robert Grau attributed these departments of "men, and not a few women" to "the advent of the feature film and the coming of the majority of the best-known players of the speaking stage" (which the *Mirror* had signaled even earlier),[8] there were other plausible causes: the emergence of unusually popular movie stars, many of whom had been only minor stage performers, and the attraction of particular kinds of films, even one- and two-reelers, especially in series and serials. Yet newspapers had to ask (again as the *Mirror* had):[9] when would manufacturers and distributors, in league with exhibitors, take on the responsibility of turning a greater share of their publicity—"the backbone of every industry," as Vitagraph publicity director Philip Mindl admitted, "the product of which depends on the patronage of the million"[10]—into paid advertising rather than either ads or copy that exhibitors had to pay for, or free press matter that someone locally had to pick through? Moreover, one also now has to ask, when and how would the industry exploit what Pamela Walker Laird and others call the most current advances in advertising at the time: the "suggestive psychology" of "eye appeal," as the most strikingly effective sign of modern "good taste"?[11]

Whatever the convergence of factors, the industry only gradually saw local newspapers as a potentially *homogeneous*, if not quite simultaneous, market—paralleling that of picture theaters—for promoting its products, the movies, and the moviegoing experience itself as a *national* pastime. Building and sustaining such a market went through several sequential, but overlapping, stages, or what Janet Staiger has categorized somewhat differently as innovations in advertising strategy.[12] The initial strategy[13] was to establish a trade press devoted primarily to motion pictures, which began in 1906 with Pathé-Frères and Vitagraph sponsoring *Views and Films Index* and continued in 1907 and 1908, respectively, with *Moving Picture World* and *Motion Picture News*—one favoring the "licensed" MPPC (Motion Picture Patents Company) companies, the other the "unlicensed" so-called Independents.[14] Their chief function was to serve as a means for manufacturers and rental exchanges to inform and influence exhibitors. A second strategy, mentioned above, had many manufacturers in both camps shipping publicity material, beginning with bulletins, directly to exhibitors or indirectly through rental exchanges.[15] That, of course, assumed that exhibitors would be only too happy to act as unpaid publicity agents.[16] But once manufacturers made publicity departments a crucial part of their operations, around 1913, another more nationally oriented strategy emerged. This involved the industry supplying film stories to newspaper chains and newsbrokers as a form of paid advertising to promote their new film releases and stars. The stories of series and serials, as is well known, quickly proved successful in turning newspaper readers into regular movie spectators, and vice versa. For a short time in 1914, a few companies also filled newspapers with a daily diet of stories of single-reel, multiple-reel, and early feature-length films. Eventually, major corporations such as Mutual, Universal, and Paramount embarked on national publicity campaigns that targeted hundreds of newspapers and selected mass magazines on a weekly or bimonthly basis. Those campaigns now not only sold individual films, usually features, and specific movie stars, but, more importantly, also sought to systematically circulate the corporation's trademark as an increasingly consistent guarantee of moviegoing pleasure, supposedly for everyone.

INDUSTRY PUBLICITY FOR INDIVIDUAL FILMS I: CASE STUDIES OF SELIG POLYSCOPE AND KALEM

In summer 1912, Sargent offered some advice to exhibitors who subscribed to *Moving Picture World*. First, he admonished them to advertise in their local newspaper, especially to promote the growing number of longer films. Second, he outlined how they should write such ads. "Read up what this paper has said about the story. Digest the manufacturer's bulletin and then bring out the best points of the argument, but leave just a little unsaid. . . . Make it crisp and interesting."[17] What exactly exhibitors received from the manufacturers and gleaned from the trade press in the early 1910s, what they thought of it, and, especially, what they did with it has been difficult to determine, and until now of little concern to cinema historians. Most of those ephemera—from "the vast quantities of literature" to managers' house organs—have not survived, nor have the business records of company publicity strategies. Moreover, cinema historians have been slow to explore whatever forms of contractual relations and even partnerships were emerging between newspaper editors and the industry, from manufacturers and trade journals to exhibitors. Tidbits of information do crop up in the trade press. In fall 1912, Sargent singled out a newspaper editor who also was a picture theater manager in Jefferson City, Missouri.[18] Shortly thereafter, another *Moving Picture World* column praised William Clune, a major exhibitor in Los Angeles, for hiring "one of the snappiest newspaper reporters in town" to manage publicity for his chain of picture theaters.[19] A little more than a year later, in the *Mirror,* F. J. Beecroft described how "the wonderful growth of the film business" had recruited "a bright-eyed, keen-minded set of young men [some proved not so young], mostly trained in the newspaper field, to take charge of the advertising and publicity of the manufacturers."[20]

At least two sets of ephemera, however, do survive and offer, along with trade press discourse, some tantalizing evidence of how exhibitors and newspaper editors could have mined manufacturer publicity between 1911 and 1913, before the industry began to develop more systematic promotional policies. The rarest ephemera can be found among the hundreds of folders in the Selig Polyscope collection at the Margaret Herrick Library: namely, what were called "press sheets," "electrotype ads," and "cuts" that Stanley Twist, Selig's first publicity agent, probably prepared for individual films.[21] Although highly selective, this collection does include material on a dozen wide-ranging titles, many of them especially important examples from the company's jungle and cowboy pictures. Newspaper ads and "fillers" for one of the earliest jungle pictures, *Captain Kate* (released July 13, 1911), present at least four "mining" options available to exhibitors and editors. The *Anaconda Standard,* for instance, played up the Montana origins of the film's star, "Katie Williams, known personally to half of Butte's population."[22] Just days apart, the *New Orleans Item* and the *Oregonian* (Portland) printed brief plot synopses that so closely resemble one another, they likely came from the same unknown source.[23] The biweekly *Enquirer* of Columbus, Georgia, by contrast, apparently had a copy of Selig's press sheet, for it reprinted almost verbatim the five-paragraph plot synopsis that Twist had written for the film.[24] The *Herald* of Bellingham, Washington did something more unusual: It reprinted a short review that appeared in the *New*

York Morning Telegraph, and, unlike the *St. Louis Republic,* acknowledged the source.[25] Along with several reprints of other films, also acknowledged, in the *Cleveland Leader* later that fall,[26] this is one of the few references that confirm the New York newspaper's surprising claim that others were "republishing our critical reviews of films and our stories about moving pictures and moving picture people."[27]

The newspaper ads and "stories" for four more Selig releases from September through December provide similar examples but also different parallels between the trade and public press. Released on consecutive days in late September, *Two Orphans* was the company's first three-reel title, although some exhibitors (even in small towns) seem to have shown it as a single film on their programs.[28] In late October, the *Alton Telegraph* (Illinois) reprinted, with slight variations, the entire plot synopsis from the Selig press sheet for a screening at the Lyric theater.[29] Both the *Jonesboro Sun* (Arkansas) and *Titusville Herald* (Pennsylvania), however, reprinted most of the text from the company's trade press ad, which boasted that Kate Claxton (the original play's author) supervised the production and that "no expense" was spared to make "every detail . . . historically correct."[30] The press sheet plot synopses of two single-reel cowboy pictures, *Western Hearts* and *A Romance of the Rio Grande,* also made their way into, respectively, the *Fort Wayne Journal-Gazette* and the *Atlantic Telegraph* (Iowa).[31] Even more interesting is how Selig's third jungle picture that year, *Lost in the Jungle,* was represented in several small-town newspapers. Because no press sheet for the film survives at the Herrick Library, one cannot determine whether any of the ads and stories drew on text the company distributed. But two exhibitor ads printed very similar short plot synopses that stressed Kathlyn Williams's bravery in "this startling and phenomenal animal masterpiece."[32] Most unusual is a large ad for the Cosy Theater in Aberdeen, South Dakota, which includes silhouetted stick figures of a leopard and a human confronting each other.[33] Much of the text for this "real thriller" closely matches that published in an anonymous exhibitor's review in *Moving Picture World,*[34] but the Cosy's manager could not have been the source of that review (his ad appeared a day before the *World*'s publication date), nor could the review be the source of the theater's ad (unless the manager subscribed to the *World,* and that issue arrived before its stated date).

Two slightly later, multiple-reel films introduced other means by which Selig exerted some influence on exhibitors and editors. One was *Cinderella,* a three-reel retelling of the well-known fairy tale, released on January 1, 1912. Surviving company publicity includes trade press ads and a rare booklet, "Complete Lecture and Manual or Instruction on How to Exhibit Selig's Cinderella";[35] no press sheets seem to survive. As before, several exhibitors, in Seattle and Anaconda, respectively, either reproduced the design and text of a Selig ad or turned some lines of that text into a promotional story.[36] At least two exhibitors, in Wilkes-Barre, Pennsylvania, and San Jose, California, drew on either a trade press ad or the Selig booklet to highlight the "great dramatic star" Mabel Taliaferro and the expense of producing the film's ninety-nine scenes.[37] Another exhibitor in Toledo, Ohio, added a composite image of Taliaferro to its brief ad copy, which set on the tiny drawing of a servant girl figure a publicity photo of her head topped by a cocked hat pinned with a bouquet of flowers.[38] Indeed, the Empire Photo Theatre, in San Jose, paid for three separate newspaper ad/stories, along with free-admission coupons, in a promotional scheme to have "children 12 years of age or under" attend one of two weekend matinee screenings. One ad/story included a plot synopsis of each of the film's three reels, likely taken from a Selig press sheet, as was done earlier for *Captain Kate* and *Two Orphans*.[39] Another invoked a little-used advertising strategy (for motion pictures) by claiming to summarize "a recent full page article on the Cinderella production" written by "Ashton Stevens the eminent Chicago dramatic critic."[40] Finally, the New Boz Theatre in Boise, Idaho, paid for an attractively designed ad taking up nearly half a page that combined text from a trade press ad, a profile photo of Taliferro that also had appeared on the cover of Selig's booklet, and four production stills, one of which had been used in an equally large ad for the Mission theater in Salt Lake City.[41] This was just the kind of ad that Sargent later would call exemplary.

Selig mounted perhaps its most extensive publicity campaign for a historical epic, the three-reel *Coming of Columbus* (released in May 1912). According to a large trade press ad, that publicity included posters, electrotype ads, cuts, a press sheet, a piano musical score, full-page feature stories, and even "Columbus Busts."[42] Although none of that material survives at the Herrick Library, it had to have informed the lengthy, pre-release articles that both *Moving Picture World* and *Motography* published, giving production details, a plot synopsis for each reel, and favorable reviews.[43] And one feature story (whose text framed nine photographs) did appear in a few metropolitan and small-town newspapers, including the *Chicago Inter-Ocean*, the *Baltimore American*, the *Canton News-Democrat* (Ohio), and the *Muskogee Times-Democrat* (Oklahoma).[44] Surprisingly, the Colonial in Des Moines (Iowa) used two different electrotype ads . . . on the same day. In one, a column surrounded by white space shows the image of a sailing caravel framed by a rising sun atop a block of copy that repeats the film's title and "Selig's Greatest Masterpiece," with a tiny trademark insert (fig. 4). In the other, a line drawing of Columbus posed on the seashore like a Christian missionary, with two caravels in the distance and two watchful Native Americans crouched in the nearby reeds (left and right frame), tops a different text of no-less-celebratory language enclosed by a heavy link chain (fig. 5).[45] The *Lowell Sun* (Massachusetts) as well as the *Iowa City Press* even reproduced photographs (also likely drawn from the press sheet) of the caravel replicas originally built in honor of the 1893 Exposition and secured for the film by the Knights of Columbus.[46] Perhaps assuming the interests of the town's textile factory workers, the *Sun* also reprinted most of another *Moving Picture World* article on a Father Tonello's interview with Pope Pius X, who had endorsed the film after a special private screening.[47] Finally, Sargent came up with a promotional scheme that the Selig company first may have floated: "To interest the school teachers and pupils, have a prize contest for the best essay on Columbus, offering one prize of tickets for each grade and letting the various schools compete for the same prize . . . [and] give a special matinee for the schools."[48] Among an unknown number of exhibitors that picked up on this idea, the manager of the Orpheum in Canton arranged a special children's morning matinee two weeks before the film's scheduled weekend run.[49]

Fortunately, press sheets, lithographs, and electrotype ads survive for no less than four Selig multiple-reel films from 1913. *The Cowboy Millionaire* (early February), a remake of the company's popular one-reel title of 1909, provides a good example of how Selig's publicity found its way into a host of newspapers (fig. 6).[50] The Grand Opera House in Canton used two electrotype ads to promote this film. The first had a cowboy lassoing a cowgirl, both mounted on horses galloping at right angles just behind a large black trademark "branded" with the film's title, with severely reduced copy (fig. 7); months later the second reproduced another electrotype in its entirety that featured a single galloping horse and rider (with two others behind him) atop a rope-bordered block that included the title against a different background, copy that listed several sensational scenes, and oval portrait drawings of a cowgirl and cowboy anchoring the bottom corners.[51] Two other theaters, in Ogden and Anita (Iowa), redesigned an electrotype ad by substituting for its graphic figure, respectively, a bronco rider painting and two production stills from Selig's press sheet.[52] In their ads and "stories," other theaters either reproduced text from one electrotype ad or else combined text from two of them. The Princess in Aberdeen and the Grand in Jonesboro reprinted text from the same electrotype: for instance,

FIGURE 4. Selig's *The Coming of Columbus* ad, *Des Moines News,* May 19, 1912.

WHERE THE BEST IN MOTION PICTURES ARE SHOWN
COLONIAL
OFFERS MAY 19-20-21 AND 22
THE COMING OF COLUMBUS
SELIG'S GREATEST MASTERPIECE
IN THREE PARTS
The World's Greatest Motion Picture
The Sensation of the Film World
Selig's "Coming of Columbus" stands Paramount, Supreme, Unapproachable among Motion Picture Productions. A Masterpiece of Masterpieces
Endorsed by Educators, Press, Pulpit, Historians and Public
¶A magnificent visualization of the historical incidents in the life, and discoveries, of Christopher Columbus, told in vivid, thrilling, all-absorbing dramatic reality---inspiring in its indescribable grandeur and elegance---heart-rending in its pathetic appeal.
¶The one story that is known to everyone, is that of Columbus and his discovery of America
¶The production that cost $50,000.00 and took three years to make. 350 people in the cast. The cost to you is next to nothing.
Don't Fail to See This Great Feature
S
10 A. M. CONTINUOUS 10:30 P. M.

FIGURE 5. Selig's *The Coming of Columbus* ad, *Des Moines Register and Leader*, May 19, 1912.

"A thrilling, vivid, and humorous comedy drama in cowboy life. . . . Broncho busting, bucking horses, expert roping, reckless riding, steer throwing, cowboy sports."[53] The Columbia in Toledo, the Alhambra in Wilkes-Barre, Pennsylvania, and the Royal in Mansfield, Ohio, by contrast, lifted and spliced text from that and a second electrotype.[54] In a lengthy column, the *Colorado Springs Gazette-Telegraph* reprinted the press sheet's paragraph

"COWBOY MILLIONAIRE" ELECTROTYPE ADS.

3-Column Ad. Electro

ANOTHER GREAT SELIG INNOVATION

Prepared at Great Expense for Exhibitors' Use

Your Publicity Campaign will not be Complete Without a Set of These Electrotype Ads.

Start Your Campaign Now

Order Today from Your Exchange, *or from*

THE SELIG POLYSCOPE CO.

20 East Randolph St.
CHICAGO, ILL.

2-Column Ad. Electro

ELECTROTYPE ADS
for use in connection with
SELIG'S
The Cowboy Millionaire

One year ago **The House of Selig,** realizing the needs of the exhibitor, started the practise of getting out series of striking electrotype advertisements on each special feature released. Selig's Electrotype Ads are now used by all discriminating showmen who exhibit Selig features. They have proved to be unparralleled as box office magnets.

On this page are shown three advertisements which we have prepared for use in connection with **"The Cowboy Millionaire."** These ads are one, two, and three columns in width, and are designed primarily for use in newspapers, but they can also be used to excellent advantage on bulletins, heralds, dodgers, tack cards etc. If used properly they are sure to bring the crowds to your theater. These ads were designed by an expert and the initial cost of preparing them was unusually heavy. Notwithstanding this fact they are being sold to exhibitors at a price which places them within reach of all. The one column ad sells at $0.90; the two column ad at $1.25; and the three column ad at $1.50. When all three ads are ordered at one time the price will be $3 40 for the entire set.

The ads are so designed that you can set up your theater name, date line, admission price etc. on an attached panel as per illustration on this page.

ORDER TODAY

1-Column Ad Electro

FIGURE 6. Selig's *Cowboy Millionaire* electrotype ads. Folder 557, William Selig Papers, Margaret Herrick Library.

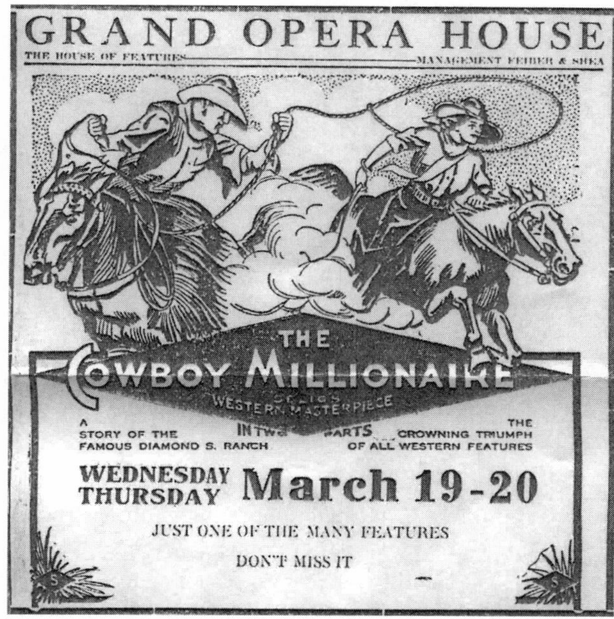

FIGURE 7. Grand Opera House ad, *Canton News,* March 16, 1913.

on the earlier film's "immense popularity" and the detailed plot synopsis (including several telegram intertitles) of the new film's two reels.[55] Other papers published short pieces that may not have come directly from Selig. The *Seattle News* told the story of how William Selig purchased Clyde Hoskins's oil painting of a bucking bronco, similar to Frederick Remington's more famous one, to hang in the cowboy hero's Chicago mansion, an "inspirational" memory image that he turns his back on at the end of the film.[56]

A press sheet and two electrotype ads also exist for *Pauline Cushman, the Federal Spy* (late March 1913), a two-reel Civil War drama based on the well-known actress who, as a spy for the Union, was arrested twice and escaped death both times.[57] Although exhibitors may not have reproduced either of Selig's electrotype ads or had local newspapers print any production photos, several did draw on the text of one of those ads. Whereas the Casino Theater in Des Moines, the Lyric in Corning, Iowa, and the Ideal in Stevens Point, Wisconsin, all highlighted the descriptive spectacle of "undoubtedly the most timely, remarkable and elaborate war time masterpiece ever produced," the Orpheum in Titusville and the Royal in Mansfield condensed the ad's rhetorical flourishes into one or two sentences.[58] The Oakland Photo Theatre reprinted the first part of Selig's press-sheet plot synopsis—drawing attention to the famous scene in which, performing Camille at Wood's Theater in Louisville, Cushman toasted Jefferson Davis and the Confederacy in order to gain passage across Confederate lines—and then briefly summarized her bravery as a spy.[59] As signs of their audiences' interest in movie stars, both the Princess Theater in Anaconda, Montana, and the Plaza in Montgomery, Alabama, featured Miss Winifred Greenwood, the actress playing Cushman, in their newspaper ads.[60] Moreover, for a return screening of the film in Corning, Iowa (soon after Decoration Day), the Lyric reproduced in its entirety one of the cuts from Selig's press sheet, telling the story of how Greenwood was chosen for the role because she so closely resembled a photograph of Cushman found in the Chicago Public Library.[61]

A pair of Selig two-reel films released in June 1913 reveal the extent of Selig's dissemination of publicity material by that summer. The press sheets for *Alone in the Jungle* provided a variety of texts for more than half a dozen exhibitors.[62] To promote the film's screening, the manager of the Dreamland in Oelwein, Iowa, got his local newspaper to reprint the full plot synopsis in a page-long column.[63] From the seven "press stories" offered by the company (none featured the film's star, Bessie Eyton), exhibitors picked out different texts to lure audiences. For the Ark in Logansport, Indiana, it was "Did you ever see a Lion Swim?"[64] For the Majestic in Sheboygan, Wisconsin, "The Leap of a Lioness in a Death Flurry."[65] For the Lyric in Portsmouth, Ohio, "Wild Animals Rampant."[66] For the Gaiety in Fort Wayne, "The Call of the Wild."[67] The Idle Hour in Ada, Oklahoma, took a double-barreled approach, filling its local newspaper with both the "Lion" and "Lioness" stories.[68] A trade press ad for "Selig's Sensational Western Feature," by contrast, complemented the press sheets for *The Law and the Outlaw*.[69] Several exhibitors—the Oakland Photo, the Alcazar in Anaconda, the Palace in Cedar Rapids, the Majestic in Ada, and the Ideal in Stevens Point—borrowed the trade press ad language verbatim or revised it slightly for their own ads.[70] This time, in Oelwein, the Gem had its local newspaper reprint an edited version of the company's plot synopsis.[71] From the six "press stories" distributed by Selig, the Acme in Olympia, Washington, chose "The All-Round Champion Cowboy" featuring Tom Mix, the film's star, while the Empire in Lima, Ohio, opted for romance in "All the World Loves a Lover."[72] Indeed, the growing popularity of Mix led the Isis Theater in Ogden to twice use his press-sheet photo as a newspaper promotion for its three-day screening.[73] Finally, a second ad for the Majestic in Ada concluded with a quote from the *New York*

Dramatic Mirror review—one of the earliest instances of that kind of promotional strategy.[74]

A second set of ephemera also survives at the Herrick Library: scattered issues of the *Kalem Kalendar,* the company's biweekly bulletin announcing new film releases. By 1913, the *Kalendar* had a column, running several pages, of "press notices" for individual films that exhibitors were encouraged to send to their "local papers." One of those films is especially noteworthy: *Shenandoah,* a three-reel adaptation of Bronson Howard's Civil War drama.[75] Within the first three weeks of the film's release in July, at least three exhibitors—the Tokyo in Logansport, the Grand in Fort Wayne, and the Princess in Aberdeen—reproduced the *Kalendar*'s full press notice in their ads for this "special" film, which concluded with "one of the most striking effects . . . a battle at midnight."[76] Weeks later, while the American Theatre in Columbus, Georgia, excerpted most of the first paragraph from George Blaisdell's review in *Moving Picture World,* the Hippodrome in Gulfport, Mississippi, got its local newspaper to reprint, without attribution, that review in its entirety.[77] Just days apart, two other small-town newspapers, the *Rockford Republic* and the *Anaconda Standard,* recycled from the same unknown source a "filler" paragraph of information on the film's production: scenes were shot on "authentic" locations, using thirty thousand rounds of small-arms ammunition, five thousand rounds from twenty cannon, and several original Confederate and Federal flags.[78] Finally, in his "Motion Pictures" page in the *Waterloo Reporter,* Arthur Stolte published a story about the "private exhibition of 'Shenandoah'" that Kalem arranged for the playwright's widow, and the Family theater in Adrian, Michigan, filled its ad with her expressed admiration and gratitude.[79]

Most manufacturers sent out bulletins and other press materials on individual films well into 1915, and exhibitors, especially in small cities and towns, continued to find them useful for placing ads and story "fillers" in local newspapers.[80] This was certainly the case with the *Kalem Kalendar* press notices for the company's Alice Joyce and Helen Holmes series in late 1914 and early 1915.[81] The Star Theatre manager in Chillicothe, Ohio, for instance, reproduced most of the press notice (except the brief plot synopsis) for *The Price of Silence* (December), "a two act feature of the Alice Joyce series."[82] The managers of the Ray in Olympia, Washington, and the Orpheum in Fort Worth excerpted similar material from the press notice for an episode in the *Hazards of Helen* series, *The Flying Freight's Captive,* in which Holmes, as a female railway telegraph operator,[83] is "possessed of an unusual amount of daring and nerve."[84] So did the managers of the Colonial in Rockford and the Bon Ton in Jackson, Michigan, in their story ads for another in the series, *The Black Diamond Express*.[85] The manager of the Grand in Reno ran a prominent column in his local newspaper, clipping the entire press notice for *The Stolen Engine*, in which "Holmes leap[s] from a locomotive going at high speed, into the cab of another engine, running on a parallel track."[86] While the Ray's manager repeated the same tactic, excerpting much of the press notice for *The Escape on the Limited*, papers in Fort Wayne and Santa Fe published the exact same publicity column, likely also supplied by Kalem, that included not only a lengthy plot synopsis (in prose with "punch") accompanied by a production photo, but also an admiring profile of Holmes in a film that gives her the chance to "display . . . her varied dramatic talents, to say nothing of exhibiting her skill as pilot of a handcar."[87]

PUBLICITY STRATEGIES FOR INDIVIDUAL FILMS II: "READ THIS STORY TODAY—THEN SEE IT IN MOVING PICTURES"

Alongside this barrage of press sheets, electrotype ads, and cuts shipped to local exhibitors, manufacturers also engaged in a second strategy for publicizing individual films that targeted newspapers more directly. Perhaps spurring this strategy was the rapid success of *Motion Picture Story Magazine*, whose monthly issues throughout 1911 were full of fictional versions of MPPC films. From November 1911 to April 1912, for instance, the *Chicago Sunday Tribune* printed "a Photoplay in Story Form" in its "Features" section.[88] Unlike the short stories and serialized fiction commonly published in mass magazines and Sunday newspaper magazine sections, this was an early version of the fictional tie-in—in this case, a one-page text based on a film about to be released by the Chicago manufacturers Selig or Essanay—in which each photoplay story seemed designed to instill in readers the desire to experience the same story at a local picture theater. For a brief period in early 1912, the *Boston Evening Traveler* also printed each Saturday a fictional tie-in from one of the MPPC companies as "The Traveler's Moving Picture Story."[89] Also briefly if irregularly, American Film tried a similar strategy of single photoplay stories that, according to a trade press ad, went out to sixty newspapers nationwide.[90] The most successful fictional tie-in that year involved Edison's popular monthly series *What Happened to Mary?* (first released in July 1912). But a mass magazine, not one or more newspapers, was the medium of circulation. Each story of the film's twelve episodes was published simultaneously in McClure's *Ladies' World*, with its nearly one million readers, largely working-class and rural women.[91]

In the films, Mary Fuller, Edison's top female star, plays a stenographer in New York, a "modern girl" who voluntarily uses her skill and cunning to aid strangers in need. Whereas the films highlight Mary's athleticism and agency, Shelley Stamp argues, the magazine stories show her "preoccupied with romance and beauty."[92] As the series drew to a close in summer 1913, Edison plotted a second monthly series, *Who Will Marry Mary?*, which aligned its heroine more closely with the Mary of *Ladies' World*.

What led the fictional tie-in to become such an immensely influential publicity strategy was the deal that Selig worked out with the *Chicago Tribune* in late 1913 to jointly produce and promote *The Adventures of Kathlyn*, a serial of thirteen two-reel episodes. The trade press quickly recognized the Selig-*Tribune* strategy as an innovative "campaign of motion picture advertising" because it guaranteed the biweekly publication of a full-page "installment of [the] serial story," written by Harold McGrath, in fifty Sunday newspapers—many of them contracted with the *Tribune*'s syndication service—soon after the showing of a new film episode.[93] Throughout much of December, the *Tribune* ran "teaser" ads, initially on the daily "Women's Page," to whet readers' curiosity about who was "Kathlyn." Women readers were warned, for instance, that their "husbands" or "sweethearts" might find Kathlyn too "dangerously beautiful."[94] In later ads that moved closer to the front page and targeted a broader readership, Kathlyn was threatened by jungle-picture stereotypes (in image and word): first, a "man-eating tiger" and then a scowling, knife-wielding "Hindu chief."[95] The "teasers" culminated in large ads that ran on the daily *Tribune*'s second page: one was a profile halftone of Williams, identifying her as the serial's star; the other, a full-page ad announcing the first film episode that could be seen at ten Chicago picture theaters (fig. 8).[96] What seems a widening appeal across gender in these ads also complemented an overall cross-class appeal that Barbara Wilinsky found in her analysis of the Selig-*Tribune* enterprise.[97] Whereas Selig had a core audience assumed to be working class and white collar, the *Tribune* had a "largely white, native-born, middle-class readership."[98] The story installments and film episodes, Wilinsky argues, together allowed the two partners to "blend their class-based audiences to attract *men and women* from all classes [my emphasis]."[99]

The publicity campaign for *The Adventures of Kathlyn* had at least three new components that would soon become characteristic. The most important was McGrath's fictional tie-in—"never been printed before" and illustrated with production stills—the first installment of which appeared in the *Sunday Tribune* on January 4, 1914.[100] The newspapers that ran these installments, in conjunction with film episodes, were unusually widespread, from major cities (for instance the *Salt Lake Telegram*, *Buffalo Times*,

FIGURE 8. Selig's *The Adventures of Kathlyn* ad, *Chicago Tribune*, January 6, 1914.

Detroit Free Press, New Orleans Item, Syracuse Herald, and *Cleveland Plain Dealer*) to smaller cities and towns (*Fort Worth Star-Telegram, Youngstown Vindicator, Hamilton Republican-News, Lima News*), making the campaign nearly nationwide.[101] Even exhibitors in cities such as Des Moines, Fort Wayne, and La Crosse, Wisconsin (where installments did not appear) told customers to "read the stories . . . printed every two weeks in the *Chicago Sunday Tribune,*" implying that the edition circulated far beyond the metropolis.[102] A second component was special ads in certain papers that repeatedly called attention to both the serial and its fictional tie-in. The *Tribune* adopted this practice, immediately following the initial installment with a different large ad each day of the week, boasting of the film's production cost, its "most beautiful moving picture actress," "love and danger and intrigue," and "biggest thrills to come."[103] In mid-March, it even printed a full-page ad for "Kathlyn's Own Story," appearing in the April issue of *Photoplay* "now on sale at newsdealers' and moving picture theaters."[104] A third, which the *Tribune* also put in practice, was a listing of the picture theaters where fans could see *The Adventures of Kathlyn* that day or any day during the week.[105] Following the *Tribune,* other newspapers combined these latter practices with large ads that included appeals to read McGrath's latest installment and listings of where the latest serial episode would be shown. The *Detroit Free Press* highlighted "McGrath's latest and greatest novel" in its Sunday edition, compiled two small columns of picture theaters (extending from Detroit to Toledo and other Michigan towns from Grand Rapids to Saginaw) and the dates of the film's screenings (through February 15), as well as a production still of "Kathlyn's father chained in a dungeon."[106] Along with its appeal to readers, by contrast, the *Cleveland Plain Dealer* printed large graphed columns noting exactly when during one week each serial episode could be seen, and where, in nearly fifty cities and towns from Corry, Pennsylvania, to Columbus and Bowling Green, Ohio.[107]

Seizing on *Kathlyn*'s unexpected success, another MPPC company, Pathé-Frères, quickly teamed up with the Hearst newspaper chain to produce and promote *The Perils of Pauline,* which became even more popular with audiences. One reason was that Hearst's News Service was extensive enough to publicize this twelve-episode serial and its stars, Pearl White and Crane Wilbur, coast to coast.[108] Beginning in mid-March 1914, Charles L. Goddard's fictional tie-in appeared in Hearst newspapers from the *New York Sunday American* and *Atlanta Sunday American* to the *Los Angeles Examiner,* but it also ran in others contracted with the Hearst service, for instance the *Pittsburgh Leader, Detroit News and Tribune, New Brunswick Times, Columbus Ledger* (Georgia), *Cincinnati Enquirer,* and *Cleveland Leader* (the latter not until early June).[109] Some Hearst papers and exhibitors even found ways to advertise in unaffiliated papers. Ads in the *New York Journal* enticed readers to look for Goddard's story in the *New York American,* and, according to an ad in the *St. Paul News,* at the Blue Mouse theater moviegoers could pick up copies of the *Chicago Sunday Examiner* (from which Edna Vercoe would read and clip Goddard's story for her scrapbook; see chapter 5).[110] The *Pittsburgh Leader, Detroit News and Tribune,* and *New York Journal* all ran Pathé ads that listed when episodes of *Pauline* could be seen, and in which picture theaters, during the course of a week. At least sixty theaters featured the serial's first episode in Detroit and its suburbs, and a lengthy column listed another fifty-five doing the same in Pittsburgh and surrounding cities and towns (from western Pennsylvania to northeastern Ohio and West Virginia).[111] As if acknowledging the serial's popularity, the *Cleveland Leader* even printed weekly ads inviting readers to "Follow the Crowds" (illustrated by a line of mostly women at a box office) to a score of theaters in the city and nearby towns.[112] Despite not printing Goddard's story, the *New York Journal* ran weekly ads informing its readers "where Pauline's reels can be seen" in nearly one hundred picture theaters not only in New York City but also in cities and towns from New Jersey to New York state and Connecticut. Most of those included an illustration depicting the crowds lined up to see *Pauline,* but one illustration had a well-dressed couple in front of a theater, with the man pointing his cane at the film's title.[113]

When, in April 1914, Universal joined the rush to release its first serial, *Lucille Love, the Girl of Mystery,* starring Grace Cunard and Francis Ford, Joe Brandt hired A.P. Robyn Syndicate in Chicago to get at least forty newspapers to publish the serial story, written by the "Master Pen" (that is, Cunard).[114] Within two weeks, between mid- and late April, the first story installment—subtitled "A Soul Thrilling Story of Love, Devotion, Danger, and Intrigue" and illustrated with a line drawing of the heroine piloting an airplane and threatened with drowning at sea—appeared in newspapers from Chicago, Cleveland, and New Orleans to Omaha, Lexington (Kentucky), and Duluth (Minnesota).[115] In fact, in Cleveland, for whatever contractual reasons, Universal muscled *Lucille Love* into one newspaper and dozens of picture theaters two months before Pathé could arrange for the first episode and installment of *Pauline* to appear. In several major cities, Universal followed Selig in promoting both story and film in advance, with full-page ads in the *Cleveland Leader, Atlanta Constitution,* and *Chicago Herald,* or with full-column ads in the *Syracuse Herald* and *Omaha World-Herald* (fig. 9).[116] The line drawings in those advance ads all whetted audience interest in the heroine: Cunard slightly slouched in a slinky gown; Lucille protecting her lover from her father, captioned "Her Father's Honor! Her Lover's Peril!"; and the sensation scene of her rescue at sea. Again, metropolitan newspapers such as the *Cleveland Leader* and *Chicago Herald*—and even the *Chicago Tribune,* which did not run story installments—sought to sustain interest in the serial by combining weekly lists of where and when fans (again, Edna Vercoe was one) could catch an episode with either a printed installment or a large ad for the film.[117] At

"Lucille was pleading for the honor of the man she loved—pleading as only a woman can plead. There at the water's edge a soul stirring tragedy was enacted. The aviator—a man among men, was being asked by the girl he loved to risk her life, and his own, to save the name of his strongest rival. Torn between conflicting emotions, he stared at her, half unbelievingly, as with appealing intensity she pointed wildly out across the bright blue water to where the majestic liner was steaming rapidly towards the horizon. Lucille hung breathlessly on the aviator's every action. His lips opened for protest, but there was something in the entreating eyes he could not resist. Breathlessly she watched him, awaiting his decision. There was a curiously twisted smile upon his lips when he faced her again. 'Get in' he m tioned. She had won her appeal."

—Extract from the first instalment of "Lucille Love, the Girl of Mystery."

Startling the World in Its Thrilling Intensity

THE FASCINATING NEW SERIAL STORY

"LUCILLE LOVE, THE GIRL OF MYSTERY"

BY "THE MASTER PEN."

It Stands Pre-eminently a Literary Masterpiece and an Assured Dramatic Triumph

To make this wonderful production still more captivating and interesting to the reader, it has been dramatized by

The Universal Film Manufacturing Company

and will be exhibited at all leading motion picture theaters in this city, and vicinity supplied with their service. Remember, you can read this great story of "Lucille Love, the Girl of Mystery," in this paper and see each dramatic situation reproduced on the screen at your favorite moving picture theater.

Read the Opening Chapters in THE CONSTITUTION, Sunday, April 12th,

FIGURE 9. Universal's *Lucille Love* ad, *Atlanta Constitution,* April 5, 1914.

least three times during the serial's run, the *Leader* also printed large graphed columns, much as the *Plain Dealer* had for *Kathlyn,* listing when and "where you may see 'Lucille Love'" (whichever of its episodes) in seventy theaters throughout northern Ohio.[118]

So successful were these publicity strategies that Thanhouser adopted them—probably with the support of Mutual and, apparently, Syndicate

Film—to promote a fourth serial, *The Million Dollar Mystery,* starring Florence LaBadie and James Cruze. Joining the *Chicago Tribune* to publish story installments of this serial (written by McGrath again) were supposedly two hundred newspapers, many of which may have been doing this for the first time.[119] The first installment initially appeared on June 29 in dozens of papers, from the *Tribune, Buffalo Courier, Baltimore News,* and *Washington Times* to the *Canton Repository, San Antonio Light,* and *Ogden Standard.*[120] Within another few weeks it had reached others, including the *Cleveland Plain Dealer, Tulsa World,* and *Macon Telegraph* (Georgia).[121] A day or even a week before the first episode's release on June 22, Thanhouser followed Selig's model by inserting teaser ads in several city newspapers. Initially these not only displayed the title in boldface but also a line drawing of a magic lamp emitting a plume of smoke curling into a question mark enclosing a woman's face with a black mask over her eyes, the mask indistinguishable from her hair.[122] A later teaser spelled out the mystery: "One million dollars disappears [when a] balloon is wrecked and drops into the ocean."[123] On the day of the film's release, something novel enticed readers and movie fans: a contest with a prize of "$10,000 for 100 words" that solved the mystery (fig. 10).[124] The *Tribune* made an extra effort to sustain interest in the serial in early July by carrying an ad that encouraged readers to pick up the latest issue of *Movie Pictorial,* where Detective Wm. J. Burns offered clues to the mystery's solution, and later printing an interview with McGrath by the Sunday movie page editor, Mae Tinee.[125] Whereas ads in the *Tribune* and *News* included a list of the theaters showing the first episode, the *Plain Dealer,* in conjunction with McGrath's first installment, printed a graphed column of when and where in northeastern Ohio any of the first three episodes could be seen that first week. The Cleveland paper then kept tracking the circulation of the serial for fans, almost week by week, through October.[126]

Universal's second serial, *The Trey O' Hearts,* confirmed the industry's success in its efforts to establish something like a nationwide publicity campaign, although still tied to a single film and one or two stars. Again, A. P. Robyn arranged for Louis Joseph Vance's story installments to appear in early August (just as those for "Lucille Love" were ending), in papers from the *Cleveland Leader* to the *Iowa City Press* and *Richmond Times-Dispatch* (Virginia); by late August, this list included the *Atlanta Constitution, New Orleans Times-Picayune, Augusta Chronicle* (Georgia), and *Aberdeen American* (South Dakota).[127] Interestingly, Universal and its regional exchanges gave much more attention to Vance than to the film's stars, George Larkin and Cleo Madison (Edna Vercoe would favor the stars).[128] As

SUNDAY, JUNE 28, 1914.

Harold MacGrath's Latest Novel Starts in Today's Repository

The Sunday Repository offers its readers one of the most expensive works of modern fiction as a part of its regular Sunday Edition—AT NO EXTRA CHARGE. The Million Dollar Mystery, the latest and most interesting novel from the pen of Harold MacGrath, famous author of "Kathlyn," "The Man on The Box," etc., will be presented free to readers of the Sunday Repository in weekly episodes STARTING TODAY, in this issue. Thanhouser's million dollar motion-picture version of this story is now appearing at the theaters.

The Million Dollar Mystery is entirely new; it has never before been published. Into this thrilling story Harold MacGrath has brought more feverish action—more unique adventure—more exciting romance—than have ever before appeared in his novels. His beautiful heroine, Florence Gray, will command your admiration by her daring deeds. His extraordinay climaxes are bound to grip you. Read this startling story—the greatest novel ever written by Harold MacGrath—starting in this issue of the Sunday Repository.

Appearing in TODAY'S REPOSITORY—the First Episode of

THE MILLION DOLLAR MYSTERY

By Harold MacGrath

Thanhouser's Million Dollar Motion Picture Production

$10,000 for 100 Words

If you've ever read any of Mr. MacGrath's novels you'll be sure to read The Million Dollar Mystery. But, as you read this wonderful, new novel, bear in mind that $10,000.00 will be paid for the best 100 word solution of the mystery. $10,000.00 for 100 words—the highest price ever offered! Everybody is eligible to compete for the $10,000.00. Clews to the mystery will be given in each episode. Full details of the $10,000.00-for-100-words-offer will be found on page 17 of today's Repository. Begin this great story TODAY.

Turn NOW to the Blue Section of Today's Repository for the First Episode of This Stirring Story by Harold MacGrath

See the Motion Pictures at These Theaters

Orpheum Theater—Canton—Every Friday and Saturday

Dreamland Theater—Massillon—Every Mon. & Tues.

FIGURE 10. Thanhouser's *The Million Dollar Mystery* ad, *Canton Repository,* June 28, 1914.

before, Universal placed advance ads to promote both the story and "the pictures." Some exploited the playing card in their design and posed this question to readers: "Could a Woman Love Her Father Enough to Kill Her Sister?"[129] At least one offered a new variation on *The Million Dollar Mystery*'s puzzle contest, asking moviegoers to identify those situations in the film that "the producer . . . claimed could not be portrayed in pictures. But they were."[130] Once again, several newspapers carried ads that let fans know where and/or when they could catch an episode. The *New Orleans Times-Picayune* printed a listing of more than twenty picture theaters in the city and surrounding area that would run the serial and connected that listing to the first story installment.[131] The *Cleveland Leader* repeatedly ran weekly graphed columns that, in mid-August, included twenty-one theaters in northeastern Ohio, and, by mid-September, had expanded to nearly fifty.[132] The *New York Evening Mail,* which printed Vance's story installments daily, listed more than forty picture theaters in a four-state area that would be screening *The Trey O' Hearts* each day of the week.[133]

Shortly after Selig and the *Tribune* launched their campaign to promote *The Adventures of Kathlyn,* the industry initiated a second fictional tie-in strategy involving many more films. Further research may determine who came up with this strategy and how it was coordinated, but it was relatively widespread in metropolitan and big-city newspapers by early February 1914. With "half of Cleveland's entire population attend[ing] moving picture shows at least once a week," the *Cleveland Leader* was one of the first to "publish each day a short story of one of the best films now being shown in the city or about to be shown."[134] Bannered as "Today's Best Moving Picture Story," this daily column initially printed the single story of a multiple-reel film such as Edison's *An American King,* Pathé's *In the Mesh of Her Hair,* or Selig's *Reconciled in Blood* (along with a halftone of each film's star), then shifted to shorter versions of two to four films of mixed reel length from General Film, Universal, and Mutual.[135] The first Mutual story, "Withering Roses," includes this tantalizing note: "Storyized by Helen Bagg in Photoplay Magazine."[136] Very few foreign features found their way into the column, and when those such as Pathé's *Germinal* or Messter's *The Life and Work of Richard Wagner* did, they never enjoyed top billing—but, then, neither did American features such as Famous Players's *Tess of the Storm Country* (with Mary Pickford) or Selig's *The Spoilers* (with Dustin Farnum).[137] In early June, the *Leader* printed an ad promising that "a complete new story of the best motion picture film released by the producers for the day will appear every morning in The Leader";[138] that promise, however, soon gave way to a greater interest in promoting *The Perils of Pauline* and *Lucille Love.*

Among other newspapers that quickly joined the *Leader* within the next few weeks in February, I want to single out half a dozen.[139] Heading its column bannered "Here's Today's Best Moving Picture Story," the *Toledo Blade* announced that it had assigned a newspaper man "to view the films in advance of their release, and to write for Blade readers short stories of what he considers the best films shown."[140] But the first story of Edison's *Rorke's Drift* belied that claim, for it was exactly the same as the one printed that day in the *Leader*.[141] In each column the *Blade* also printed several stories of mixed reel length—again like those in the *Leader*—initially favoring releases from General Film and then including those from Universal, Mutual, and Famous Players. Yet there was a difference. The column appeared only once a week in the Saturday edition and soon was subsumed within a larger bannered group of columns and accompanied by a brief star profile and photo—from G.M. Anderson to Lillian Gish—not connected with any of the stories.[142] Although the *Blade*'s stories ran until mid-July, they became fewer and shorter, finally reduced to a single column.[143] Two weeks after the *Blade*, the *Philadelphia Times* and *Washington Times* were no less forthright in announcing their stories' publication. In almost simultaneous ads printed a day or two before the first story, both reported having "just completed negotiations for the daily publication of the stories of the best moving picture films," stories that "cover all the best films, whoever makes them."[144] Although they too claimed their own "representatives" as authors, stories like that for Edison's "Sophia's Imaginary Visitors" had the same format, text, and halftone of a film's star (in this case, Mac MacDermott), whether in the *Leader*, the *Blade*, or either *Times*.[145] Much like the *Leader*, the *Washington Times* continued its column of stories into early June; in Philadelphia, by contrast, the stories disappeared from the *Times* sometime in March, only to reappear in the *Philadelphia Telegraph* in early April under the banner "Best Photoplay Stories of the Day," where they were replaced in late June by installments of *The Million Dollar Mystery*.[146]

Finally, two big Chicago newspapers adopted different fictional tie-in strategies, only confirming Paul Moore's point that "the mass audience for moviegoing was . . . an extension and supplement to the readership of popular print culture."[147] The bannered column found in the *Cleveland Leader*, "Today's Best Moving Picture Story," also appeared in the *Tribune* two days earlier, on February 5, 1914. Like the *Leader*, the *Tribune* justified the column with the claim that "moving picture plays present the drama of daily life . . . to more than a half million Chicagoens"; but, like the *Philadelphia Times* and *Washington Times*, it attributed the daily short stories to its own newspaperman "assigned . . . to view the films in advance of their release."[148] "The story may be read in the morning," the *Tribune* added, and "the picture may be seen in the afternoon or at night." This column initially printed single stories of feature-length films, with exactly the same text as in the *Leader* but in a different order; in less than a week, it too was including up to half a dozen stories of mixed reel length, again from General Film, Universal, and Mutual. At the same time, an added notice alleged that the newspaper employed "a staff of trained story writers . . . instructed to look at ALL of the films and write the stories of the best ones."[149] This probably was an empty boast meant to get readers to think the *Tribune* was one up on all other newspapers and nearly on a par with the trade papers. More interesting, however, is a gradual shift in the language of the stories that, unlike those in the previous newspapers, faintly at first and then more strongly read like reviews. Here is the opening assessment of Vitagraph's *Lost in Mid Ocean*: "This is a three reel feature film that heaps up more horrors on a lone woman's head than one would expect twenty of even the strongest feminine examples to endure."[150] Or this initial sentence of Rex's *The Babies' Doll*: "The pathos of this sad little story is relieved somewhat by the exceedingly charming acting of the two children."[151] This sounds less like a publicity man and more like a critic—and a woman at that—as chapter 4 will explore.

Slightly late in publishing such fictional tie-ins, the *Chicago Record-Herald* took a rather different route from most other newspapers. First, it bannered its daily column "Read This Story TODAY—See It in Moving Pictures" and boasted that its stories came exclusively from "the Universal Film Manufacturing Company, which represents the ten foremost American film producing companies."[152] Second, each column included only one story of a two- to three-reel film, beginning with IMP's *The Marine Mystery* (in the *King, the Detective* series) and Gold Seal's *The Leopard Lady,* starring Grace Cunard and Francis Ford.[153] For at least a few weeks, each story was copyrighted by Henry Barrett Chamberlin. Third, Universal placed a small ad on the same page with the column, listing two dozen theaters in Chicago and the surrounding region where the motion picture of that particular day's story could be seen over the next two weeks—and encouraged readers to "cut this out and save it."[154] Although the column's banner soon changed to simply "Today's Picture Story," these Universal stories ran well into August; then, on August 11, under a new contract and banner, "In the Picture Playhouses," the *Herald* started printing daily stories from all of the American manufacturers, beginning with Essanay's *Topsy-Turvey Sweedie,* starring Wallace Beery as a "giant servant girl."[155]

Universal, however, continued placing its small ads for where and when fans could find that day's film release at least through the month of September.[156] One of the few newspapers that seems to have kept to the strategy of printing a daily story, the *Herald,* maintained the practice until mid-March 1915, just days before its initial daily review column, "Seen on the Screen," appeared, soon to be signed by Louella O. Parsons.[157] By then, a much more intensive nationwide publicity campaign was well entrenched.

NATIONAL PUBLICITY STRATEGIES FOR TRADEMARKS AND BRANDS

During the first decade of motion pictures' emergence, trademarks and brand names had become part of the industry's overall marketing effort to both stimulate and control the consumption of motion pictures.[158] In amusement trade papers such as the *New York Clipper* and *Billboard* in the early 1900s, ads ballyhooed the "good will value" of company names such as Edison, Lubin, and AM&B. At the same time, Pathé-Frères initiated the practice, soon followed by others, of "branding" the titles and intertitles of its film products with its trademark Gallic cock or red rooster. One aim of these marks was to limit the widespread duping of film prints, and most manufacturers, well into the early 1910s, also stuck their trademark or brand name, often conspicuously, on the background element of an interior set and occasionally even posted it somewhere in an exterior scene. The primary purpose, however, was what Susan Strasser has called "product education," an essential component of the new system of mass marketing exemplified by Quaker Oats, Ivory Soap, Kodak, and others at the turn of the twentieth century.[159] That "education" involved a process of "*incremental* repetition," writes Richard Ohmann, connecting consumers' expectations about a product with recurring symbols.[160] Indeed, an early treatise asserted that the very foundation of American business was "built upon the significance and guaranty conveyed to the purchasing public through the medium of those particular marks, names, and symbols."[161] Through the nickelodeon period, film manufacturers relied on the repetition of such marks for moviegoers at two different points: nationally in the ads regularly placed in trade press issues mailed to exhibitors, and locally in the posters displayed at picture theaters' entrances, in house organs handed out to customers, and in the films' title cards and intertitles. Only in the early 1910s did manufacturers hesitantly seek to exploit their trademarks and brands in local or regional newspapers, and it took several years for the strategy to gain traction on a national scale.

Perhaps the first to test this strategy was Pathé-Frères, in early 1910, with its "national" advertising campaign in Sunday newspapers in such metropolitan centers as Chicago, Cleveland, Detroit, and Baltimore.[162] The initial ad reminded moviegoers that "the Rooster trademark means quality," which the company's short yet influential dominance of the American market had once guaranteed, and appealed to women and their "little daughters." Subsequent ads targeted every member of the family by promoting a different one of Pathé's wide range of "genres" each week: comedy, tragedy, travel pictures, educational pictures, juvenile pictures, and historical pictures.[163] Although this campaign lasted only two months, it made the bold claim that a motion picture company (even a French one) might have a status similar to those like Kellogg's, Coca-Cola, or Kodak, that advertised their products nationally in magazines and newspapers. Within another year, several American companies tried out variations on this strategy, but still in a limited way. In late 1911, the General Film Company began placing an ad on each "Photoplays and Players" page of the *Cleveland Sunday Leader.*[164] Once the distribution system of "Independent" films underwent a radical restructuring in the summer of 1912, Universal and then Mutual also enlisted in the practice, but initially, like General Film, through one of their regional rental exchanges. By November 1912, the *Leader* also was printing large ads for the Victor Film Service, exclusive distributors of Universal films in northern Ohio; within another month, it was taking similar ads for Lake Shore Film & Supply and its "unexcelled Mutual Service."[165] By mid-March 1913, in the *Cleveland Sunday Plain Dealer,* not only was the name of Universal now much bigger than Victor Film in the latter's ads, but also a nearby column listed "advance releases for the week" from General Film, Universal, Victor, and Lake Shore Film (Mutual).[166] At the same time, the *Buffalo Times* also began to place ads from regional exchanges for General Film, Mutual, and Victor Film Service.[167]

As manufacturers and distributors set up publicity departments the following year, their brand names and trademarks cropped up in more newspapers, in even smaller cities. In April, the *Ogden Standard* began to accept small strip ads from Universal, Mutual, and Famous Players, each of which prominently displayed its trademark.[168] But those same ads also soon appeared in other papers, from the *Des Moines Register and Leader* to the *San Antonio Light.*[169] Similar strip ads for Universal, Mutual (now without the mark), and Warner's Features (rather than Famous Players) continued to run in other papers such as the *Plain Dealer* well into 1914.[170] In the *Ogden Standard,* they also were joined briefly by ads for Kinemacolor and World Special Films.[171] It seems quite plausible that these companies had a financial arrangement with Syndicate Film Publishing, because their ads often appeared alongside the "News of Photoplayers and Photoplayers" columns shipped by Leslie's syndicated service. In late September, one block of ads in the *Standard* even claimed that they were "published in other newspapers throughout the United States" and read by "thousands of exhibitors."[172] It was also in early 1913 that certain local picture theaters became identified with a single brand. In late January, Mutual combined with the Unique Theatre to place in the *Des Moines News* a half-page ad that celebrated their "alliance" within a "frame" of ten Mutual stars.[173] A week later, the *Cleveland Leader* began referring in its columns to "Mutual houses" and theaters showing Universal films in the city.[174] Four months later, the New Royal in San Antonio was promoting its "Mutual Program—'Few as Good, None Better.'"[175] By late 1913, more theaters were closely allied in their ads with one of the three major distributors. In the *Buffalo Times,* Mutual began running a full column ad listing thirty-five theaters in the region where moviegoers could "look for the Mutual Trade Mark."[176] In Cedar Rapids, Iowa, the Columbia Theatre was now the "Home of Mutual Movies."[177] In Janesville, Wisconsin, the Royal was the "Home of the Mutual Movies," while Myers Theatre was "The Home of the Universal Program" and the Lyric-Majestic showed only "licensed photoplays" from General Film.[178] In December, while a Dream Theatre ad in Columbus, Georgia, depicted a medal won by Universal, a Gamble Theatre ad in Altoona, Pennsylvania, displayed a clock logo over a new slogan, "Mutual Movies Make Time Fly."[179]

In *The Theatre of Science* (1914), Robert Grau claims that Philip Mindl, who headed Mutual's publicity department, was the first to inaugurate a publicity campaign that was truly "national in scope and directed to the attention of the general public."[180] The claim seems well founded, especially in that Mutual's campaign aimed to promote the company's trademark and slogan in a range of metropolitan newspapers. The General Film publicity department, headed by Chester Beecroft, had set a precedent of sorts by launching a short series of ads illustrated with half a dozen people posed at different moments of attending a generic picture theater, but those ads had run solely in the *New York Morning Telegraph*'s Sunday supplement.[181] In late 1913, the Mutual campaign, by contrast, placed unusually large ads in Sunday newspapers such as the *Kansas City Star, St. Paul News,* and *Chicago Tribune.* The earliest was a full-page ad that heralded the new trademark of a winged clock (set at 8:00) framed by "Mutual Movies Make Time Fly" as the sign that "you" should look for before entering a picture theater because it "Marks the Very Best Motion Picture Entertainment in the World!" (fig. 11).[182] More

FIGURE 11. Mutual Film ad, *Kansas City Star*, November 9, 1913.

prominent was the line drawing of an imagined audience around the opulent lobby box office of a palace cinema (fig. 11). Among the crowd are two well-dressed young women, an elderly rural couple, several young children, and a single dapper young man—most of their clothing suggestive of white middle-class or at least white-collar patrons. This ad clearly asked readers to see themselves in those moviegoers, find the nearest theater brandishing the

Mutual trademark in the extensive list of more than one hundred in the region designated the "home of Mutual Movies," and "get the habit and go every night." Other, smaller ads depicted a mother sending her three excited children off by themselves to a neighborhood theater (with this caveat: "but be sure it's [to] the 'Mutual Movies'"); a satisfied group of patrons exiting a similar theater lobby, with one man crying out to a couple (as well as the reader) that it was "The *Best* Show I Ever Saw"; and a fashionably dressed woman urging her husband, "Let's See the Mutual Movies"—concluding with this advice: "Take HER to See MUTUAL Movies Tonight!"[183] A singular Mutual ad in the *Chicago Tribune,* in early January 1914, featured a mid–close-up of Ford Sterling hailing readers, like a demonic Uncle Sam, to enjoy his Keystone films as the "greatest comedies."[184]

In the summer of 1914, Mindl himself summarized the principles behind the publicity machine he had created at Mutual. "Having something to sell which the American people want, the Mutual believes in letting them know about it. To do this effectively, organized, systematized and intelligently directed publicity is necessary."[185] Mutual publicity, consequently, took a range of forms. There was the usual weekly news sheet, "Mutual Movie Fillers," along with "a cut and matrix service" sent to "6,000 editors of daily and weekly newspapers to clip from."[186] Supposedly, it was one person's job in Mindl's department to read through "the sixteen hundred newspapers" on Mutual's exchange list for how much material actually was being clipped.[187] There was a forty-four-page weekly magazine called *Reel Life* that provided advance information on upcoming film releases and promotional items, presumably shipped to exchange offices and exhibitors, "with a constantly increasing circulation" that allegedly reached thirty thousand.[188] Perhaps most interesting was the sixteen-page magazine *Our Mutual Girl Weekly,* published in conjunction with weekly episodes of the company's fifty-two-reel series starring Norma Phillips and showing off "the very latest fashions in gowns and hats and furs and shoes and lingerie."[189] Although special ads for *Our Mutual Girl* did appear in small-town newspapers such as the *Sheboygan* [Wisconsin] *Press* (the source of that quote), Mutual arranged for only a few of the episodes' stories to appear in the "Today's Best Photoplay Stories" columns. Instead, according to *Reel Life,* the magazine was available free wherever the series was shown—and thus targeted moviegoers directly.[190] Mindl claimed that one hundred thousand copies of the first issue had been printed in January, and that the number was closing in on one million that summer.[191] At least one house manager in Lancaster, Pennsylvania, suggested that the figure may not have been the usual hype: in order to give the magazine "to each lady who buys a ticket" at his theater, he had to increase his own weekly order to one thousand copies.[192]

Just as Mindl was launching Mutual's publicity campaign in late 1913, either Robert H. Cochrane or Joseph Brandt came up with a parallel national campaign for Universal's publicity.[193] In early November, Laemmle announced that he planned to expend $250,000 "to teach the people of the United States and Canada to patronize the theaters that exhibit that Universal program. . . . We are going to make that Universal Program a household name."[194] The Universal campaign differed, however, in that it continued to ask exhibitors to pay for publicity materials. Those included weekly "Moving Picture Stories" that cost exhibitors "$1.75 per hundred, postage paid"; they could then sell them for five cents each or "give them away as souvenirs."[195] More interesting was the early 1914 offer of electro cuts (twenty cents each) of the Universal trademark (in various sizes), along with smaller marks of the company's contracted manufacturers, that exhibitors could use to brand either their local newspaper ads or house organs.[196] Also available were electro cuts of Universal stars (twenty-five cents each) that could illustrate ads and stories. The success of this campaign is difficult to determine, although at least a few picture theaters were willing to spare the expense. In January, the Universal trademark took a prominent central position in a Red Moon ad in Baltimore; six weeks later, it appeared in a Myers Theatre ad in Janesville.[197] At the same time, the Hippodrome in Lebanon framed an ad for *The Leper's Coat* with oval portraits of Philip Smalley and Lois Weber, and weeks later the Faurot Opera House in Lima, Ohio, anchored its ad for *The Triumph of Mind* and *Lucille Love* with four star photos framed by the Universal "U" shaped like a lucky horseshoe.[198] By year's end, Laemmle still was exhorting exhibitors to "advertise, and keep advertising [because] shrewd business men understand the power of daily advertising—that never ceasing, constant force that compels trade."[199] To make their work easier, Universal also now offered four stock electros of bordered ad templates (from thirty to sixty cents) within which an exhibitor could add his theater's name and, in the two largest, his current motion picture program.[200]

The most systematic and expensive of these national publicity campaigns quickly emerged from the formation, in the summer of 1914, of Paramount Pictures Corporation. That too had a precedent in what Famous Players Film, a major partner in the new firm, already had been doing.[201] In the summer of 1913, as Michael Quinn first argued, Famous Players set up five state rights companies—in Boston, New York, Pittsburgh, Minneapolis, and Chattanooga—to both distribute and help finance an expected "30 Famous

Features a Year."[202] The company also contracted with half a dozen other exchanges—in New York, Detroit, St. Louis, Kansas City, San Antonio, and San Francisco—to extend the distribution of its features, especially in the West. Not only was this strategy a success, partly due to a series of Mary Pickford films, but either Al Lichtman or B.P. Schulberg also organized a publicity campaign to place ads for the company in several metropolitan newspapers, with an especially large one in the *Boston Journal* that listed a circuit of nearly forty theaters in New England contracted to screen Famous Players films.[203] Many exhibitors—often managing the most prestigious theaters in a city—also were induced to highlight the company's name in their local ads. Those included the Knickerbocker in Cleveland, Saxe's Lyric in Minneapolis, Gordon's Olympia in Boston, Talley's Broadway in Los Angeles, and Grauman's Imperial in San Francisco.[204] Finally, in late March 1914, in parallel with many newspapers' "Today's Best Picture Stories" columns, Famous Players announced a deal made with the *Boston Journal* to publish daily the "illustrated stories of all . . . Famous productions, the most instructive and interesting reading for the whole family," beginning with "The Pride of Jennico."[205] Those stories seem to have run for only a few weeks,[206] because either the *Journal*'s circulation was less widespread than was hoped in New England or else negotiations that would lead to Paramount's formation were far advanced.

The announcement of the alliance among Famous Players, Jesse L. Lasky Feature Film, and Bosworth Inc. that established Paramount Pictures as their "big distributing company" came in late May 1914.[207] Paramount's president and general manager was William W. Hodkinson, formerly a newspaperman and picture theater manager in Ogden, Utah, and later a major distributor of General Film releases in the West.[208] Thorough planning for a systematic schedule of feature film production and distribution, of course, was essential to the new corporation's success,[209] but so too was the unusual publicity campaign launched that fall. Hodkinson spelled out the stages of that campaign in a July 2, 1914, letter to Herman Wobber, his principal exchange man in San Francisco.[210] Much like Laemmle, Hodkinson aimed to invest in a level of advertising over several years that would "make Paramount Pictures a household name." To that end, he planned to "register our name and trademark in each and every state" in order to promote the Paramount name in "the papers of the big cities throughout the country." "The opening gun about September 1st" would be "preliminary announcements filling billboards all over the United States and allowed to stand for a month." At the same time, a two-page ad would be placed in the *Saturday Evening Post,* followed by several more ads over the next few months.[211] When that ad appeared, it included an image of the billboard, photos of the corporation's officers and producers, a "Paramount Theatre standard," and the Paramount trademark.[212] Within a week of that first ad in the *Post,* another Paramount ad covering two pages in *Moving Picture World* reproduced letters of endorsement from William Fox, Stanley Mastbaum (head of the Stanley theaters in Philadelphia), and S. L. Rothapfel (director of the Strand in New York), along with fifty exhibitors "contracted for the Paramount Service," most of them in New England, the mid-Atlantic, the Midwest, and the far West.[213]

As Hodkinson promised, Paramount carried through on its plan for monthly full-page ads in the *Post,* with illustrations that stressed its seriousness. The second filled a screen with photos of thirty contracted authors and playwrights; the third was framed by photos of an equal number of actors and actresses; the fourth had three lines of film stills (with sprocket holes) emanating from a corner trademark; the fifth was dominated by the centrally positioned trademark; and the sixth reproduced the fronts of a dozen Paramount theaters across the country.[214] But Hodkinson also expected exhibitors "to do special advertising" of their own in local newspapers—and they did. In September alone, at least twenty picture theaters, not only in metropolitan cities but also in small towns—from the Knickerbocker in Cleveland, the Studebaker in Chicago, the Lyric and Wm. Penn in Pittsburgh, and Tally's Broadway in Los Angeles to the Ogden (in that city), the Crystal in Cedar Rapids, the Kozy in Ludington (Michigan), and the Broadway in Muskogee (Oklahoma)—were running ads promoting their exclusive Paramount Pictures.[215] In advertising lengthy screenings of *The Virginian* (with Dustin Farnum), the Knickerbocker featured the *Paramount Pictures* brand in its serif font, while the Wizard in Baltimore may have been the first to display the Paramount trademark: a sunlit mountain and darkening sky encircled by small stars that evoked the sense of "endurance and protective strength" long characteristic of the Rock of Gibraltar in Prudential Insurance ads.[216] During the next three months, another twenty theaters, especially in relatively small cities and towns—from Lowell, Williamsport (Pennsylvania), and Massillon (Ohio) to Oshkosh (Wisconsin), Moberly (Mississippi), and Colorado Springs—brandished the Paramount name in their ads.[217] In Washington, DC, Tom Moore took out an unusually large ad in the *Washington Post* for the "inauguration" of Paramount Pictures at his downtown Strand and Garden theaters.[218] And the Bijou Theatre in La Crosse celebrated its exclusive contract with Paramount by reproducing the screen image of the thirty authors and playwrights that appeared just weeks before in the *Saturday Evening Post.*[219]

By early 1915, Paramount boasted that it was "the only organization in the industry which co-operates with its exhibitors and assists them to build their business by a national advertising campaign, and by other efficient co-operation."[220] That campaign continued in the *Post* with another full-page ad featuring the large, centered *Paramount Pictures* trademark surmounted by its named producers and with a complementary ad for Mary Pickford's tied-in story in the January issue of *Ladies' Home Journal*.[221] More picture theaters bannered their ads the "Home of Paramount Pictures," from the New Theatre in Portsmouth (New Hampshire) to the Grand in Centralia (Washington) or Grogg's in Bakersfield (California) and from the Regent in a major city such as Syracuse to the Plaza in the small town of Waterloo (Iowa).[222] Certain theaters also branded their ads not only with the company's trademark but also its name in script, for instance the Faurot Opera House in Lima, Wigwam #1 in San Antonio, and De Luxe in Hutchinson (Kansas).[223] The New Davis in Pittsburgh even "cooperated" with Paramount on a full-page story promoting the company's "extraordinary feature moving pictures" and its "handsome new theatre."[224] Besides "spread[ing] the gospel of 'Better Pictures' through the pages of leading magazines and newspapers," the company launched a magazine in parallel with *Paramount Progress*, a weekly mainly intended "to assist each Paramount exhibitor and exchange."[225] This was the monthly *Paramount Magazine*, whose aim was "to reach the public directly" with contents "bristling with interest for picture goers."[226] Very few copies seem to survive, but its sixteen pages included articles about the "development of motion picture art" and producers' "experiences in picture making," stories of current and forthcoming releases, profiles and photos of "favorite stars," and "novelties of interest to women" such as "the latest fashions."[227] In an attempt perhaps to emulate Mutual's *Our Mutual Girl Weekly*, Paramount shipped the monthly directly to exhibitors so they could distribute issues as free souvenirs at performances. This strategy apparently met with such success that, according to *New York Dramatic Mirror*, at least three hundred thousand copies of *Paramount Magazine* were being published and, by late May 1915, issues were "now sold on news stands throughout the United States."[228]

Confronted with the enviable success of what Paramount called its "efficiency system," other major distributors of feature films had to consider investing in their own publicity for moviegoers.[229] In late December 1914, the World Film Corporation's trademark elephant head appeared in an ad for Schanze's in Baltimore, but paired with Paramount's mark because that theater became an exclusive venue for both in early January 1915.[230] Shortly thereafter, Fox Film (William Fox's former Box Office Attractions) had its exchange offices in Cleveland and Pittsburgh stamp their ads with its distinctive new trademark: the brand name in modernistic bold block letters.[231] The exception was Mutual, once the corporation's producers—American, Majestic, New York Motion Picture, Reliance, and Thanhouser—agreed to cooperate and guarantee the release of two Mutual Master-Pictures per week. Mutual challenged Paramount directly with a series of "Mutual Master-Picture" ads (signed by its president, Harry E. Aitken) in the *Saturday Evening Post,* beginning in March 1915.[232] Those ads highlighted D.W. Griffith, Majestic's "chief director" (as might be expected), but even more so its authors-turned-scriptwriters, Richard Harding Davis and Thomas Nelson Page.[233] Unlike Paramount, Mutual continued the practice of featuring individual films and their stories and de-emphasized stars such as Robert Herron and Mae Marsh. And it hedged its bets by including among those ads two for Reliance's serial *Runaway Jane,* written by George Randolph Chester.[234] Simultaneously with these magazine ads, picture theaters in several metropolitan centers began advertising their programs of "famous Mutual Master-Pictures," for instance the Alhambra and Quality in Pittsburgh, the Dreamland and Alhambra in Cleveland, and the Strand in Atlanta.[235] But the brand name also appeared in small-town theater ads, whether misspelled (deliberately?) as "Mutual Masterpieces" by a theater named Mutual in Harrisonburg (Virginia) or boldly bannered in half-page ads by the Odgen Theater (where Paramount Pictures earlier had been featured).[236] And both theaters noted that, as the Ogden put it, these "superb, thrilling, artistic photoplays [were] advertised each week in The Saturday Evening Post."

In August 1915, Paramount upped the ante against its competitors with trade press ads announcing that it was expanding its publicity campaign to newspapers in order to target moviegoers more directly—a campaign that *Motion Picture News* celebrated for "acquainting the press and the public with the true status of the present-day motion picture, its artistry, its educational force and purpose, its appeal to all classes."[237] From September through at least May 1916, as many as three dozen major newspapers arranged to carry a "goodly sized Paramount advertisement," usually on the same day each week.[238] The campaign began with a quarter-page ad highlighting a halftone close shot of Mary Pickford, together with her signature (for added authenticity) that also encouraged moviegoers to "ask your theatre for a free copy" of one of the Paramount magazines (fig. 12).[239] For several months, these weekly ads promoted a spectrum of Paramount stars in halftones (mostly women), and only occasionally their new films, for example Charlotte Walker, Elsie Janis, Hazel Dawn, Blanche Sweet, Pauline Frederick, Geraldine

FIGURE 12. Paramount Pictures ad, *Detroit Free Press*, September 2, 1915.

Farrar, Marie Doro, and Marguerite Clark.[240] Some papers also ran a contest asking readers to name the greatest number of unidentified Paramount players' photos inserted in a specific picture theater's ad.[241] In December, "incremental repetition" became the determining principle, and the ads now trumpeted a recurring refrain of what the "TRADE MARK means to *YOU*": it "stands for quality" (fig. 13).[242] What evidence was offered for that "quality" or superiority? The corporation's "high class" producers and "celebrated" stars in the "best theaters," the shorts (newsreels, travel pictures, cartoons) filling out its programs, its role in supporting the shift from nickelodeons to picture palaces as the primary venue of exhibition, and its contract with Pickford (for $500,000) guaranteeing her performances in Paramount pictures throughout 1916.[243] In May 1916, it launched an ad campaign against "sensational and suggestive pictures"—asking moviegoers to sign "protest" cards at their theaters—a campaign that actually promoted Paramount's "better pictures."[244] New theaters continued to adopt the name "Home of Paramount Pictures"—for instance the Bijou in La Crosse, the Lyric in Atlanta, the Star in Sandusky (Ohio), the Colonial in Oelwein (Iowa), and the Iowa in Emmetsburg (Iowa)—whether they showed those pictures

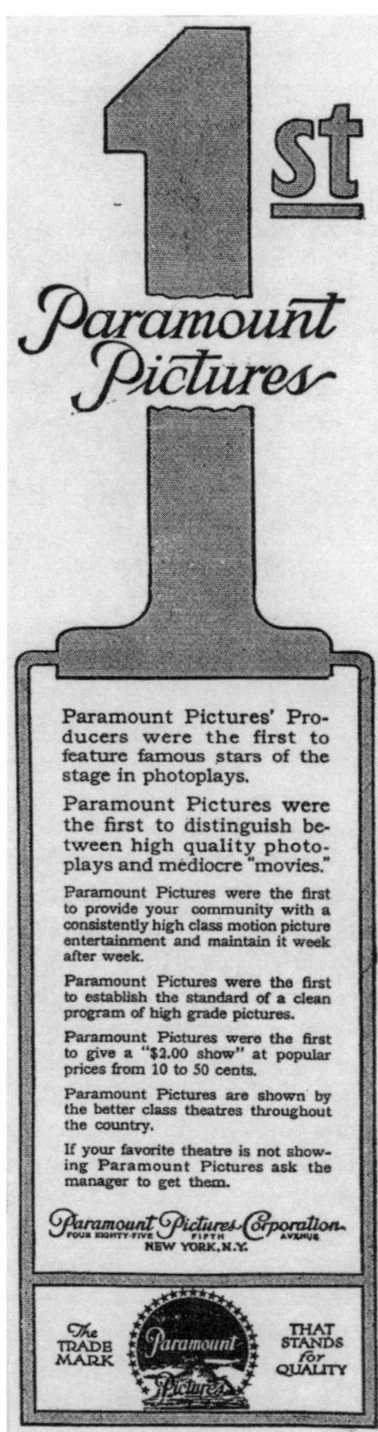

FIGURE 13. Paramount Pictures ad, *Denver Post*, December 10, 1915.

FIGURE 14. Strand Theatre ad for *Carmen, Elyria Chronicle,* October 31, 1915.

exclusively or in combination with others.[245] And Paramount started acquiring or leasing a few downtown theaters, from Chicago and Toledo to Newark and Logansport, making the brand name and trademark a permanent part of a theater's design and decor.[246]

Mutual and Fox could hardly match this 1915–16 ramping-up of Paramount's publicity campaign. Mutual, for instance, cooperated with the Lyric in Atlanta on a rare half-page ad for William Russell in *The Thoroughbred,* a "Mutual Masterpictures De Luxe Edition."[247] To compete with Paramount's *Carmen,* starring Geraldine Farrar, Fox sponsored unusual full-page ads for its own *Carmen,* starring Theda Bara, to promote the film's week-long run at the Standard Theatre in Cleveland and a three-day run at the Palace Theatre in Cedar Rapids, Iowa.[248] The company also ran two half-page ads displaying a challenging poster of Bara and an interview with her by Archie Bell of the *Cleveland Leader* for a short run at the American Theatre in nearby Elyria, Ohio (fig. 14).[249] Surprisingly, Fox joined Paramount to place a full-page Christmas ad announcing three weeks of their films, with small photos of their stars, at the New Rex in Bluefield, West Virginia.[250] One of two new major distributors, Metro Pictures, also placed very few newspaper ads, such as those extolling its own stars in the *Detroit News-Tribune* and *Buffalo Times,* although certain theaters highlighted Metro features on their programs, from the Paris Theatre in Santa Fe to the Strand in Atlanta.[251]

The only distributor to mount a competitive national publicity campaign was the Triangle Film Corporation, which Aitkin founded after leaving Mutual in June 1915.[252] The initial plan was to release each week, through its own film exchanges, two features (supervised by D.W. Griffith and Thomas Ince) and a Keystone comedy, charge $2 a ticket to play them at several leased "model theaters" (in New York, Chicago, and Philadelphia), then let other exhibitors show them at regular prices.[253] From September through December, Triangle placed an expensive series of lengthy ads, with lots of fine print about its stars and directors, in "163 newspapers," including the *Chicago Tribune, New York Tribune, Syracuse Herald,* and *Omaha World-Herald.*[254] Smaller ads soon followed from picture theaters contracted with Triangle, ads branded by its trademark and often bordered by thick geometrical "chains" of triangles in papers from Cleveland, Buffalo, Kansas City, and Fort Wayne to San Antonio, Salt Lake City, Alton (Iowa), and Kennebec (Maine).[255] When the model theater policy went bust by early 1916, rather than distribute its films individually on the open market, Triangle adopted a block booking policy,[256] promoted each week by large ads imitating those of Paramount that focused on a single star—for instance Mae Marsh, Billie Burke, Lillian Gish—along with a recent film release.[257] In Chicago, the company introduced a variation on the earlier ads for serials by listing nearly forty theaters within the city where "Triangle Plays," supervised by D.W. Griffith, Thomas Ince, and Mack Sennett, could be seen that week.[258] As Rob King argues, those that could afford to brandish the Triangle trademark in their local ads—from the Colonial in Chicago, which opened in February 1916 as "the Western home of Triangle films," and the Liberty in Pittsburgh to the Foto Play in Grand Forks, North

Dakota[259]—rarely included smaller neighborhood houses. Ultimately, that policy also proved much too risky for the company.[260]

Paramount's boast, in early 1915, that it alone was supporting exhibitors with a national advertising campaign actually ignored one scrappy competitor, perhaps because the latter was less committed to feature films. That was Universal, which, also in February, announced its own "tremendous national advertising campaign."[261] This advertising would complement the free "press stuff" and "at cost" electros of its seven weekly "multiple reelers" (two or three reels each) now available to exhibitors.[262] In contrast to the earlier electro cuts, these were heavily bordered and tended to promote a single film and its stars, along with the Universal trademark.[263] The national campaign, however, involved contracts for placing large ads weekly in more than sixty newspapers, from metropolitan centers such as New York, Chicago, and Los Angeles to small towns like Bangor, Maine, and Butte, Montana.[264] What may have been trial runs for these appeared in December and January and promoted individual feature-length films such as *Damon and Pythias* and *Williamson's Submarine Expedition Ninety Miles Under the Sea*.[265] Some of the weekly ads that began running in February singled out, in line drawings, specific Universal stars such as Cleo Madison, Billie Richie, Mary Fuller, Bob Leonard, Warren Kerrigan, and Francis Ford.[266] In early May, one ad even depicted line drawings (in three rows) of these and other "players who make pictures for Universal" and asked readers to "Pick 'Em Out"—that is, match each of those faces to one of the scores of "top-notchers" listed in the fine print below.[267] What was especially unique about these national ads—which may well have spurred Paramount, in fall 1915, to undertake its own national newspaper campaign, distinguished in part by halftone photos of its stars rather than line drawings—was the celebratory opening of Universal City, the corporation's new manufacturing facility in the Los Angeles area.[268]

In late September 1914, in a six-page ad in *Moving Picture World*, Universal first announced its investment of "a million dollars" to construct this "entire city," from studios, a laboratory, carpentry shops, and a zoo to a villa of cottages, a school, a hospital, and police and fire departments.[269] In early February 1915, the initial newspaper ad had Carl Laemmle lording over the land (like the figure of Science in a then-current AT&T ad),[270] striking "a strong personal note" that made "reader[s] feel on intimate terms" and welcoming them as potential tourists to the dedication of his city on March 15 to see "how the movies are made [and] all your favorite screen stars at work" (fig. 15).[271] The weekly ads that followed singled out one spectacular attraction after another, highlighted by sometimes-vivid

FIGURE 15. Universal ad, *Chicago Tribune*, February 10, 1915. David M. Rubenstein Rare Book & Manuscript Library, Duke University.

line drawings and "plain speech" copy colored by slang: "They Ain't No Place Like It Nowhere," "a roaring, tearing, smashing, dashing flood," blown-up scenery, buildings with a "different architecture on the four sides," a menagerie of "every kind of animal from the ookyzook to the filmazee," and a "trio of actorines" (referring to Grace Cunard, Marie Cahill, and Lois Weber).[272] Universal also syndicated full- and half-page stories in many small-town newspapers, from Elyria (Ohio) to Galveston (Texas) and Albert Lea (Minnesota).[273] It even arranged to have Universal City included in many railroad tours of the Pacific coast.[274] The *Atlanta Constitution* was one of more than thirty newspapers to join the corporation in sponsoring a beauty contest whose winner would receive "a luxurious trip" to the San Francisco Exposition, San Diego Exposition, and Universal City.[275]

Finally, Laemmle organized a special Santa Fe train of four coaches and a dining car to leave Chicago for Universal City with a big party of industry people and others from New York and the Midwest; among them was Kitty Kelly, the *Chicago Tribune*'s young film critic, who will be a central figure in chapter 4.[276] On the trip, between March 6 and March 15, Kelly posted a series of four "Flickerings From Filmland" columns: one profiled Laemmle; the last reported from "Hollywood, Cal." (one of the word's earliest appearances).[277] Having reached Universal City in "filmland," Kelly was there "when amidst music, gun salutes, and cheering, the flag went up, the Universal banner swept the air, and the gates went open" and crowds poured in to marvel at the city's "wide open" buildings.[278] She also reminisced about the conversations and amusements she witnessed during the special train trip and (after visits to various sites in Los Angeles) interviewed Universal City's chief of police, Laura Oakley, perhaps "the only woman in the world holding that office."[279] Distributed in other Midwest newspapers through the *Tribune*'s syndicated service, Kelly's columns served, much like later industry-sponsored junkets, to repeat and thus accentuate the Universal brand name. And one of those visits involved executives from Western Union and AT&T, whose telegraph networks made that and other syndicated services possible.[280]

By 1915–16, industry publicity was heavily invested in the daily smorgasbord of newspaper discourse about motion pictures, directly or indirectly, in advertisements, syndicated stories about stars and serial installments, electro cuts and other "press stuff," and recurring brand names and trademarks. That investment arguably proved crucial to making a *national* pastime of "going to the movies," a pastime that engaged more than half the American population in attending downtown, suburban, or neighborhood picture theaters once or sometimes several times a week. Industry publicity also may have helped to create the "information environments"[281] of what now might be called niche markets, defined according to whether a moviegoer was especially attracted to certain movie stars, one or more brands of films, or even specific theaters. This was as true of small-town newspapers as it was of metropolitan ones. In early September 1915, in Grand Forks, North Dakota, a movie fan could indulge her or his taste for Paramount Pictures at the Grand (e.g., Mary Pickford in *Rags*), Universal "features" at the Theatre Royal (e.g., Harry D. Carey in *Just Jim*), Mutual Master Pictures, Metro Pictures, and World Film features at the Foto Play (e.g., Bessie Barricale in *The Mating*), and/or Pathé serials and other

General Film releases at the Met (e.g., *Who Pays?*).[282] Three months later, in Cleveland, another moviegoer could devour the initial installment of *The Girl and the Game* and a week later rush to see Mutual's first serial episode, starring Helen Holmes, at the downtown Bijou Dream.[283] In early March 1916, in Chicago, a third movie fan could savor a Paramount Picture at the downtown Studebaker, La Salle, or Castle (e.g., May Murray in *To Have and to Hold* or Marie Doro in *Diplomacy*), a Mutual Master-Picture at the Strand (e.g., Crane Wilbur in *A Law Unto Himself*), or a Triangle Play at the Colonial (e.g., Frank Mills in *The Moral Fabric*).[284] That publicity as a whole—its incremental repetition in newspapers paralleling that of the films and stars on screens—encouraged the growing sense of a *homogeneous* American film culture, now defined to include the target audience that Paramount revealingly assumed: "native white families."[285] Wherever such movie fans lived, on whatever day or night of the week, they could feel bound together with millions of others through their shared reading of what newspapers were writing about the movies and moviegoing.

DOCUMENT

RUSSELL E. SMITH, "BEST FILM AD MEDIUM," *EDITOR AND PUBLISHER AND JOURNALIST*, SEPTEMBER 6, 1913

Many business men for years fought shy of the newspapers as a medium for their advertising, and only lately have they appreciated the service they render. Among those who seem blind to the advantages of newspaper advertising may be found the manufacturers of moving-picture films. The latter advertise almost exclusively in trade papers, weekly and monthly, and in the Sunday edition of a New York paper that runs a motion-picture news section. This policy is a big mistake, and the manufacturers of moving-picture films are beginning to realize it.

In advertising in a trade paper they naturally reach one class of people—the exhibitor. But it is not the exhibitor who goes to see the pictures in the various picture houses all over the country, but the public—and the public is what the film manufacturers should try to reach—and this can only be done by the use of the daily newspaper as an advertising medium.

The public is, of course, reached indirectly through the exhibitor who acts as a sort of censor and, like a theatrical manager, attempts to give the public "what it wants"; but, like the theatrical manager, the exhibitor does not always strike the mark straight in the center.

Then, why not give the attending public a chance to pick the pictures they want to see? This can be done in various ways, but only through the daily newspaper. People who go to picture shows do not read the trade papers, but they are voracious readers of the daily papers all over the country. Through them alone they can be reached.

[. . .]

The film manufacturers ought, by this time, to realize what a chance for advancing their own interests they are missing, and they should get into line as the manufacturers of other staple products have done. The low cost of newspaper advertising, as compared with magazine advertising space, is another big factor in determining the medium used in such advertising. Newspaper advertising is to-day the best proposition for the film manufacturers.

ENTR'ACTE Local and Regional Newsreels

> Every page of the printed newspaper will have its equivalent in some feature to be found from time to time in the pictorial publication.
>
> *Chicago Sunday Herald*, July 5, 1914

By 1914, major manufacturers and distributors had devised a strategy—through indirect publicity and then direct advertising—to make newspapers a crucial venue for their efforts to create and sustain a national mass audience for motion pictures. This strategy involved not only fiction films, from single reels and serials to features, but also nonfiction films, particularly newsreels. The first of the latter to become a popular staple of General Film programs, by early 1912, was *Pathé Weekly*, and for several months, ads for its weekly lineup of short subjects enticed moviegoers in newspapers from Cleveland to Des Moines.[1] Soon Universal and Mutual were distributing their own newsreels as part of a weekly package of releases and prodding exhibitors to promote them in their newspaper ads. These weeklies may have satisfied what the *New York Dramatic Mirror* called a "public craving for illustrated news" about national and international events, but some papers decided that such "public craving" might extend to news about local and/or regional events.[2] This led them to experiment with producing or sponsoring weekly newsreels within the area of their circulation. On the one hand, just as the daily newspaper sections devoted to local and regional news extended those given to national and international events, a local newsreel could serve as a tasty side dish complementing the national newsreel. On the other hand, because the "reading field" (and readers) of a newspaper could vary from city to city, this local newsreel strategy initially contested the industry's attempts to construct a more or less *homogeneous* film culture across the country and instead served to ensure, in part, the *heterogeneity* of that film culture.

Early menu references to local newsreels seem quite few and scattered. For several months in spring 1912, several picture theaters in Cleveland included the *Cleveland Animated Weekly* on their advertised programs.[3] In late 1913, the California Motion Picture Company was supplying a "topical reel" called the *Golden Gate Weekly* to the "Sullivan-Considine theaters" on the West Coast and those on the Pantages circuit that stretched into western Canada.[4] What topics were judged newsworthy? A light-harness horse race in Woodland, California, and a motor trip through Alameda County. In February 1914, the *New Orleans Item* announced the production and distribution of its own *Item Animated Weekly*, focused on "current news events of New Orleans and the surrounding county."[5] From "the top floor of The Item annex building . . . converted into a modern factory with the very latest devices," John W. Boyle and Van Buren Harris were responsible for putting out the newsreel's single thousand-foot reel of film each week. Topical subjects ranged from those expected in national newsreels—American troops leaving for the border from Texas City, just as peace with Mexico was being negotiated; a Cleveland-versus–New Orleans baseball game; the annual Southern Amateur Athletic Union track meet; and Carnival festivities—to those of more local interest, for instance "Tulane and Newcomb students practicing for their Tulane Night 'stunts,'" and the annual police festival, in which a hundred youngsters sneaked in behind the embarrassed police chief posing for the camera with his family, a "family . . . that must have made the shade of Brigham Young grow green with envy."[6] At least through June 1914, Boyle and Harris arranged for the *Item Animated Weekly* to run for several days each week at downtown theaters such as the Tudor and Trianon, smaller houses owned by Josiah Pearce such as the Grand and the Bijou Dream, and the Princess, Felicity, and Dryades in the suburbs.[7]

In early July 1914, the *Chicago Sunday Herald* took the unusual step of devoting a full-page story to "the city's debut as a film star" in the first issue of its own *Herald Movies.*[8] The story named exhibitor H. P. Wayman as head of this weekly newsreel's department, and Harold P. Brown (veteran reporter and photographer) and George W. Peters as chief cameramen. It also tantalized moviegoers with how difficult it had been to capture on film a newborn zebra at the Lincoln Park Zoo, the flight of a dirigible airship over Lake Michigan, and images of the city taken from "Harold McCormick's hydroaeroplane." Imagining the discovery of footage of "old Chicago" before the 1871 fire, it also expressed the intriguing hope that these weekly films, "stored away in the *Herald*'s library," would be of great historical interest for future generations.[9] Through the next month, the *Herald Movies* featured nine or ten stories each week, covering sports events ("Portage Ten-Mile Marathon Race," "Tennis on Top of Loop Department Store"), ceremonies ("The impressive funeral of Mayor Busse"), summer leisure ("Happy young people enjoying the Lake at a North Side beach," "25,000 'kids' have free picnic at amusement park"), and political news ("Governor's Day at Fort Sheridan," "New suffrage shop opens in the Loop").[10] Others promoted the movies in the city, such as "Orphans' Day at Prominent Downtown Theaters" and "Francis X. Bushman and other Essanay stars in leisure hours in Sheridan Park Studio."[11] Apparently, the *Herald Movies* was a hit. The downtown Orpheum released a photo of its entrance with a "big display" advertising the newsreel looming over a crowd of people.[12] Frequent ads listed the moving picture theaters where issues of the newsreel were playing each day or night, a marketing strategy similar to that for the popular serials (see chapter 1).[13] By early August, the *Herald* boasted that "one million people" were viewing its newsreel in "over 100 theaters" throughout the Chicago area.[14]

The outbreak of war in Europe may have contributed to several changes in the *Herald Movies.* No longer were there half-page ads boosting the newsreel, as there had been in late July and early August. During the next few months, ads grew smaller—only two took up a quarter page—and eventually less frequent. Just days after the declaration of war, however, several revealed how caught up Chicagoans were in "war fever," especially "the hundreds of foreign-born citizens" and, specifically, "German-Americans, Servian-Americans, and British-Americans . . . wait[ing] for news from the front."[15] One story in issue six even recorded "a delirious crowd of patriotic Teutons" receiving bulletins from the *Staats Zeitung*'s regional office and then "march[ing] over to the German consulate on Michigan avenue singing 'Die Wacht am Rhein!'" (fig. 16).[16] Yet subsequent issues of the *Herald Movies* paid little attention to the war, unlike the national newsreels; instead, among the usual local news events, they began following "Madelene Bode, Herald Movie Girl," and her electric perambulator in what turned into a weekly series of stories, *Adventures in a Perambulator,* which seemed to borrow ideas from Edison's *Dolly of the Dailies* and *Our Mutual Girl.*[17] By mid-September, interest in the *Herald Movies* was flagging: if issues supposedly were "better every week," they now were "viewed weekly by half a million patrons"—half the figure ballyhooed just two months earlier.[18] To buttress its circulation at least through December 1914, the newspaper teamed up with Essanay to involve the *Herald Movies* in the contest of "Who Will Be Sue?" for a local short film (see the next entr'acte).[19] The newsreel's last three issues that month each featured a group of the forty successful "Sweet Sue" contestants and promised to present the winner with a "$200 dollar diamond ring"—whether or not it was one of the gems worn earlier by the Herald Movie Girl.[20]

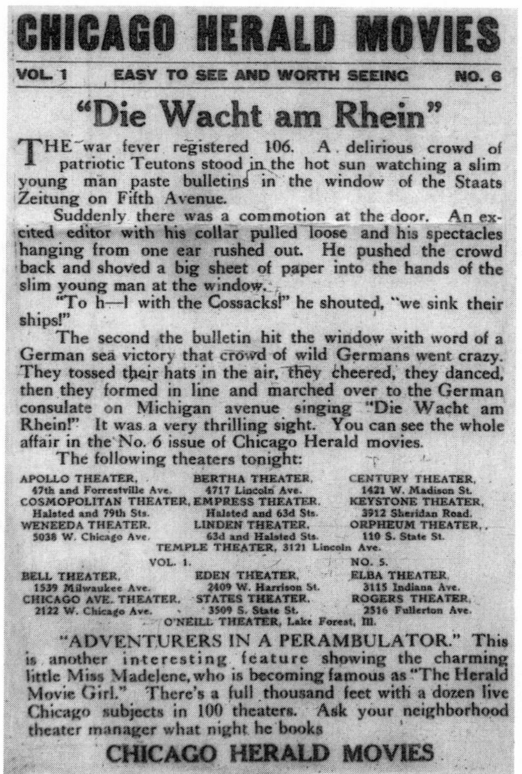

CHICAGO HERALD MOVIES

VOL. 1 EASY TO SEE AND WORTH SEEING NO. 6

"Die Wacht am Rhein"

THE war fever registered 106. A delirious crowd of patriotic Teutons stood in the hot sun watching a slim young man paste bulletins in the window of the Staats Zeitung on Fifth Avenue.

Suddenly there was a commotion at the door. An excited editor with his collar pulled loose and his spectacles hanging from one ear rushed out. He pushed the crowd back and shoved a big sheet of paper into the hands of the slim young man at the window.

"To h—l with the Cossacks!" he shouted, "we sink their ships!"

The second the bulletin hit the window with word of a German sea victory that crowd of wild Germans went crazy. They tossed their hats in the air, they cheered, they danced, then they formed in line and marched over to the German consulate on Michigan avenue singing "Die Wacht am Rhein!" It was a very thrilling sight. You can see the whole affair in the No. 6 issue of Chicago Herald movies.

The following theaters tonight:

APOLLO THEATER, 47th and Forrestville Ave.	BERTHA THEATER, 4717 Lincoln Ave.	CENTURY THEATER, 1421 W. Madison St.
COSMOPOLITAN THEATER, Halsted and 79th Sts.	EMPRESS THEATER, Halsted and 63d Sts.	KEYSTONE THEATER, 3912 Sheridan Road.
WENEEDA THEATER, 5038 W. Chicago Ave.	LINDEN THEATER, 63d and Halsted Sts.	ORPHEUM THEATER, 110 S. State St.

TEMPLE THEATER, 3121 Lincoln Ave.

VOL. 1. NO. 5.

BELL THEATER, 1539 Milwaukee Ave.	EDEN THEATER, 2409 W. Harrison St.	ELBA THEATER, 3115 Indiana Ave.
CHICAGO AVE. THEATER, 2122 W. Chicago Ave.	STATES THEATER, 3509 S. State St.	ROGERS THEATER, 2516 Fullerton Ave.

O'NEILL THEATER, Lake Forest, Ill.

"ADVENTURERS IN A PERAMBULATOR." This is another interesting feature showing the charming little Miss Madelene, who is becoming famous as "The Herald Movie Girl." There's a full thousand feet with a dozen live Chicago subjects in 100 theaters. Ask your neighborhood theater manager what night he books

CHICAGO HERALD MOVIES

FIGURE 16. "Chicago Herald Movies" ad, *Chicago Herald*, August 11, 1914.

Evidence of other local newsreels during this period is hard to come by,[21] but in early June 1915 the *Chicago Tribune* announced that it would be releasing its own *Animated Weekly*, as if to replace the *Herald Movies*.[22] Distributed each Monday by the Central Film Company, this newsreel included a unique special attraction: an animated film of the *Sunday Tribune*'s well-known comic strip starring Old Doc Yak (fig. 17). This seems to have been a smart move by the newspaper, given the appeal of Sidney Smith's cartoon figure, as Kitty Kelly made abundantly clear in her column reviewing the first *Animated Weekly*.[23] An image of Old Doc Yak headed this column, and she spent eight of nine short paragraphs describing and lauding the cartoon. *Animated Weekly* ads appeared in the *Tribune*'s "Movie Directory" almost daily, yet remained very small, and only listed the theaters in which

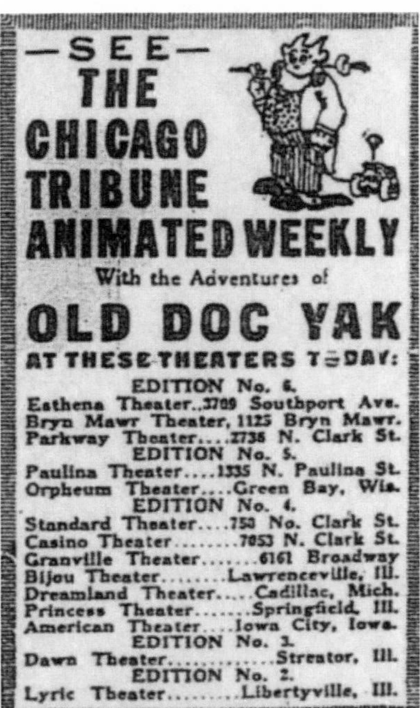

FIGURE 17. "Chicago Tribune Animated Weekly" ad, *Chicago Tribune*, July 16, 1915.

an issue of the newsreel was playing.[24] Within weeks, moviegoers could find each Monday's release in at least ten Chicago theaters, including the Colonial and the Studebaker downtown.[25] From there, each issue traveled, often for a month or more, not only to dozens of Chicago-area theaters but also to others within the newspaper's circulation: for instance the Kimmel in Cairo, Illinois; the Bijou in Fond du Lac, Wisconsin; the Lyric in Decorah, Iowa; the Princess in Huntington, Indiana; the Dreamland in Traverse City, Michigan; and the Idle Hour in Kenton, Ohio.[26]

Unlike the *Chicago Herald*, the *Tribune* rarely advertised the eight to eleven individual stories in each issue of the newsreel. Kelly mentioned a few in her column, and the topics resembled those in the earlier *Herald Movies*, except for several that highlighted military preparedness. A few scattered larger ads did offer full menus, revealing that the *Tribune*'s *Animated Weekly* sometimes resembled a national newsreel. First, certain issues included excerpts from Edwin Weigle's feature-length war pictures produced and distributed by the newspaper—for instance "Thrilling Russian war pictures," "Germany and her efficiency machine," "Scenes of the battlefields in Germany"—scenes that enlarged the audience for the features and/or served as "trailers" to promote their screenings in other cities and towns.[27] Second, other issues collated stories from across the country: number nine, for instance, had "beautiful pictures of the Panama Exposition," "giant locomotives" colliding "at the Frisco Fair," strikes at "the Remington Arms Factory in Bridgeport, Conn." and "the Standard Oil plant in Bayonne, N.J.," inspectors searching for bombs on "Europe bound vessels . . . in Boston harbor," and motorcycle relay races in Washington, DC.[28] However, the *Tribune* could exploit, in a full-page ad, the newsreel's capture of a local disaster—the wreck of the Eastland ferry on the Chicago River—and the heroic efforts to rescue most of the twenty-five hundred passengers.[29] To soften any sensationalism, it also promised to donate "every cent of the profit" to "The Tribune's Relief Fund for the families of the Eastland victims." Ads for the *Animated Weekly* seem to have disappeared in mid-October, but that simply may have masked the *Tribune*'s plans for a successor that was even less local, and coproduced with a major film company.

That fall, a competing regional newsreel came on the market in the upper Midwest. This was the *Northwest Weekly*, headquartered in Minneapolis and distributed through contracts with cosponsoring newspapers, usually to a single motion picture theater in dozens of small towns and cities in Minnesota, North Dakota, and Wisconsin (fig. 18).[30] William A. Lochren served as the chief executive of the newsreel company; Charles C. Brenham ran the Minneapolis office; among the cameramen recruited were Fred C. Place, Charles C. Brenham, and Harold P. Brown, who had worked on the *Herald Movies*.[31] As a promotional strategy, Brown wrote articles printed in several newspapers on "How 'Movies' Are Made," especially outdoor movies at night.[32] The *Northwest Weekly*'s topical subjects were decidedly local, and the stories often documented a particular town and its surroundings. Place, for instance, accompanied a St. Paul Credit Men's junket to La Crosse, Wisconsin, to create one story out of "500 feet in film-portraits of beauty spots about the city."[33] Separate issues included different scenes in Albert Lea, Minnesota: a high school football game, the Inter-State trail (from Kansas City to the Twin Cities) passing through the town, and patently promotional images of the local newspaper office and the Royal Theatre where the newsreel was shown.[34] *Weekly* cameramen occasionally caught catastrophes such as the grandstand collapse at a Minnesota-Wisconsin football game, and they could range beyond the region to film "famous cowboys and trick riders . . . at the Idaho Falls frontier day celebrations."[35] Finally, some kind of arrangement (yet to be found) must have linked the *Northwest Weekly* with the *Chicago Tribune:* Ads for both the Royal in Albert Lea and the Orpheum in Bismarck sometimes listed an Old Doc Yak cartoon among the newsreel's subjects.[36]

FIGURE 18. "Northwest Weekly" ad, *Bismarck Tribune,* November 9, 1915.

At the same time that the *Northwest* Weekly was having a modicum of success through its network of small-town sponsors, at least one major film company moved to co-op such local or regional efforts. In the late summer of 1915, Universal began contracting with certain city newspapers to have "stringers" supply stories that could be added to issues of its *Animated Weekly.* The *Charlotte Observer,* for one, assigned a staff photographer, F. L. Plaisance, to film local as well as state events for the national newsreel.[37] If the *Observer* never mentioned what events were filmed, the *New Orleans Item* did. The hundred and fifty feet of film it supplied Universal each week included scenes of hurricane damage in southwestern Louisiana and a local Orange Day parade "passing through the streets and being reviewed by [the] Mayor and other officials."[38] As part of this contractual arrangement, each newspaper attached its name to the newsreel that Universal distributed in its area: a Midwest example was the *Indianapolis Star–Universal Animated Weekly.* In New Orleans and Indianapolis, these doubly-named newsreels had a relatively limited circulation. Small ads in the *Star* mentioned only half a dozen theaters showing "the news of the day in pictures";[39] a rare ad in the *Item* listed a total of twenty-eight theaters, all within the city.[40] Yet the circulation of the *Charlotte Observer–Universal Animated Weekly* was more extensive. Repeated ads included thirty-four theaters in the same number of cities and towns throughout the Piedmont region of North Carolina.[41] The *Observer* also claimed that issues of this *Animated Weekly,* with its local stories, "were shown all over the entire country," strongly implying that certain newspapers saw this arrangement with Universal as an innovative form of boosterism, giving their city or region "some fine publicity."[42] If, by early 1916, issues of the *Animated Weekly* had dropped these newspaper names, just as the *Northwest Weekly* also seems to have run its course, that summer the *Philadelphia Evening Ledger–Universal Weekly* was still showing at up to fourteen theaters.[43] By then, of course, Paramount had entered the newsreel business with "Paramount Pictographs,"[44] and the *Chicago Tribune* also had launched an ambitious new project.

This was the *Selig-Tribune,* a twice-weekly newsreel "under the direction of Lucien 'Jack' Wheeler, former star of the United States Secret Service," and the newspaper's own Edwin Weigle, editor in chief for "a hundred photographers" throughout the country and beyond.[45] Twice a week the *Tribune* prominently advertised what it described as "the world's greatest news film" in a quarter-page vertical column comprised of frame stills from four or five of an issue's menu of a dozen or more stories, accompanied by brief synopses (fig. 19).[46] Only occasionally were any of these stories local, and those fit conventional categories: for instance, feeding time for a boa constrictor at the Lincoln Park Zoo or the sale of the Chicago Cubs baseball team.[47] Selig may have produced the *Selig-Tribune* in its Chicago facilities,[48] but the *Tribune* handled the distribution of the Sunday and Thursday releases, and that distribution was extensive enough to compete with national newsreels, at least in the region of the newspaper's circulation. If the *Selig-Tribune* appeared at twenty picture theaters in Chicago (showings continued daily at the downtown McVicker's and ran several days at a few others), it also filled out the programs of a hundred picture theaters outside the city.[49] Those ranged across the Midwest, from Ohio, Indiana, Michigan, and Illinois to Iowa, Wisconsin, Missouri, Nebraska, and Kansas. Especially intriguing was the *Tribune*'s claim that the newsreel's titles (or intertitles) were printed "in three languages: English, German and Italian."[50] This may offer unique evidence that the *Selig-Tribune* could be modified, if only to a minor extent, in order to target different ethnic theater audiences. If, by 1916, newsreels were tending to participate in the industry's construction of a homogeneous film culture,[51] the *Selig-Tribune*'s strategy implied a slight degree of heterogeneity, at least at the level of exhibition. Whether other newsreels assumed this kind of lingual multiplicity remains to be investigated. And would they have shared the *Tribune*'s boastful, aggrandizing appropriation of "Bill Shakespeare": "ALL THE WORLD IS STAGED TWICE WEEKLY IN The Selig-Tribune"?[52]

SELIG-TRIBUNE SHOWING TODAY

THE WORLD'S GREATEST FILM NEWS.

HERE are presented flashes from the SELIG-TRIBUNE bi-weekly Animated World News Service, under the direction of Lucien "Jack" Wheeler, former star of the United States Secret service and personal aid of three presidents. The bi-weekly embraces smashing war pictures by camera men under the direction of Edwin F. Weigle and a hundred photographers over America and the rest of the world. The first release is now showing.

Frozen Russia offers small inducement for active campaigning and the German reserves are hurriedly "holeing in" for the winter. The trenches they are digging will be their homes and firesides for many icy and isolated weeks.

—

"Kewpie," the baby elephant at the Selig zoo, is a spoiled child raising a veritable "rough house" until taken to breakfast. This is the meal now being served by Old Nurse Elephant.

—

At Aetna, Ind., workmen in the war munitions plants have been armed. Here is the only girl in several thousand employes to carry a weapon. And—to observe her menacing attitude — she knows how to "get the drop."

—

There may be freedom in suffrage, but Savannah, Ga., women find a greater freedom in overalls, which are more economical than dresses and permit of a bigger day's work.

—

Secretary Daniels says the California is the last word in big battleships. Here is where the camera man looked straight into eternity. A larger ship than this could not pass through the Panama canal, and Selig-Tribune film shows why.

FIGURE 19. "Selig-Tribune" ad, *Chicago Tribune,* January 3, 1916.

2. "Newspapers Make Picture-Goers"

The newspaper has come to the realization that it needs the picture quite as much as the picture needs the newspaper, that the two mediums of expression are closely allied.

Motion Picture News, October 16, 1915

The people who get the keenest enjoyment for Motion Picture shows are those who select their entertainment as discriminatingly as they select their food or clothing, making their selections from the choicest offerings to be had.

Chicago Tribune, April 24, 1915

One can determine with relative certainty when and where newspapers first experimented with, and then instituted, a weekend page devoted to motion pictures. Less easy to explain is *why* some editors and reporters came to think that their readers would be interested in having a weekly menu of news and information in the local newspaper they subscribed to or bought at a newsstand. Did they recognize a growing demand from readers now that motion pictures were more established as an increasingly popular venue of entertainment for millions of people? If so, did that demand arise from the attraction of regularly recurring brands of films, the frequent presence of early movie stars, or even the appearance of more and more multiple-reel films? Could just enough local exhibitors have concluded that jointly sponsoring such a page through their program advertisements would have a payoff: not only repeatedly drawing confirmed movie fans to their picture theaters, but also, and perhaps more importantly, continually luring new customers? In certain cities and towns, did a reciprocally beneficial relationship develop between an editor or reporter and one or more exhibitors, even to the extent that one could wear two hats simultaneously—in effect, acting as both an advertiser and publicity agent? Whatever the likely combination, the initial impetus for weekend newspaper pages devoted to motion pictures probably came not from the companies producing and distributing films but rather from a local nexus of editors, reporters, exhibitors, and moviegoers. The formats of these weekend pages varied in their selection and composition of texts and images and in their reliance on the trade press, manufacturers' or distributors' bulletins, and other press material. That is, the menu that a page displayed could depend on how it seemed to address a convergence of local and regional interests.

ON FIRST OPENING A WEEKEND PAGE

The initial signs that newspapers were beginning to take stock of motion pictures as a new mass culture phenomenon came in the fall of 1911.[1] In the *Seattle Times,* the daily "Amusements Today" column written by J. Willis Sayre frequently added short program notices for several of the city's picture theaters.[2] In the *Minneapolis Journal,* a twice-weekly theater column included brief local reviews of featured films at the Lyric, likely due to the promotional tactics of manager S. L. Rothapfel.[3] In the *Youngstown Vindicator* (Ohio), a Sunday column, "Week in Moving Picture Theaters," summarized manufacturers' film synopses, probably supplied by exhibitors. In nearby Canton, each Sunday the *News-Democrat* offered separate columns of similar synopses for several theaters.[4] In Toledo, the *News-Bee* printed a daily column, "At the Photo-Plays," with this local insert: a small graphic image illustrating one film currently in exhibition.[5]

Most newspapers, however, were hesitant to do more. One reason perhaps was the legal trouble that the *St. Louis Republic* ran into by reprinting without permission short reviews from the *New York Morning Telegraph.*[6] Another was the misconception, later lamented by Vitagraph's publicity manager, Sam Spedon, that newspapers expected the industry to offer advertising revenue before they would publish motion picture information.[7] As William A. Johnston pointed out, the industry advertised at the national level only in the trade press, and the trade press rarely reached the public at large. "The newspaper, being a *local* medium," he added, "logically expects the exhibitor [to do] *local* advertising."[8] The *Chicago Sunday Tribune* did offer a column of gossip and information, "In the Moving Picture World," beginning in November 1911.[9] But that column enjoyed a unique advantage and possible, if indirect, industry support. The only manufacturers mentioned—Selig, Essanay, American, Pathé-Frères—had production and/or distribution facilities in or near the city. Consequently, the column took a local angle, for instance, announcing the opening of American Film's new printing plant in Evanston; interviewing celebrities such as Mabel Taliaferro, who visited Chicago for the premiere of Selig's *Cinderella* (in which she starred); or summarizing the annual police report on motion picture censorship in the city.

Moviegoers apparently first encountered a full page devoted to motion pictures when the *Cleveland Sunday Leader* transformed its "In the Moving

THE CLEVELAND LEADER, SUNDAY, DECEMBER 24, 1911.

PHOTO-PLAYS AND PLAYERS

News of Cleveland's Leading Picture Theatres

REVIEW THE FEATURE FILMS OF THE WEEK

The Mall
PHOTO-PLAY THEATER
Finest and Most Select
MOVING PICTURES DAILY

The King Of Moving Pictures
ZIGOMAR
Thrilling Detective Play.

Cedar Theatre

The Daylight House

"THE PRINCESS"

Doan Theatre

CLARK THEATER

AVENUE THEATER

LORAIN THEATER

THE MARVEL THEATRE

REX THEATER

THE FULTON THEATRE

PARK NATIONAL THEATER

THE COZY THEATER

EUCLID THEATER

A Beautiful Moral Picture
LOVE AND AVIATION
Full of Excitement.

UNWISE INVESTORS FAIL AS MAGNATES

Many Lose in Picture Business by Not Knowing Trade.

EMPEROR SEES FILMS

AT LEADING THEATERS

TWO SPECIAL HOLIDAY FILMS TO ENTERTAIN OLD AND YOUNG

AT LEADING THEATERS

IS BOYS' FAVORITE

HELP SHOWS SUCCEED

FILMS WORTH SEEING.

SUPPLIES LATEST SONGS

DREAMLAND

Bijou Dream

BRONX THEATER

A Beautiful Moral Picture
LOVE AND AVIATION
Full of Excitement.

The Daylight Theater
"CAMERAPHONE"

EZELLA THEATER

LIBERTY THEATER

ENJOY U THEATER

BROADWAY THEATER

PENN SQUARE THEATER

THE TABOR
Xmas Special Program.

IMPERIAL THEATRE

The King Of Moving Pictures
ZIGOMAR
Thrilling Detective Play.

HOUGH AVE. THEATER

SUPERIOR THEATER

M. A. WALTERS SONG SLIDE RENTAL CO.

MOVING PICTURE SUPPLIES
LATEST AND BEST FILMS
THE LAKE SHORE FILM & SUPPLY CO.

Earn a Good Salary
OPERATORS MAKE FROM $16.00 TO $32.50 PER WEEK.
Write Today for Full Information
MOVING PICTURE MACHINES AND SUPPLIES
J. B. FELBER'S MOVING PICTURE SCHOOL

MAJESTIC THEATER
West 25th St. RE-OPENS TODAY
Under New Management.
THE BEST SHOWS IN CLEVELAND
Today THE VERY LATEST FEATURE PLAYS. PICTURES THAT WILL SURPRISE YOU.
Xmas THREE VAUDEVILLE ACTS. THREE REELS OF PICTURES.
5c AND 10c ADMISSION

GENERAL FILM CO.
THE LARGEST RENTERS IN THE WORLD OF LICENSED FILMS
Moving Picture Machines, Supplies and General Accessories
414 Superior Ave. N. W.
101 Century Bldg.

FAIRYLAND THEATRE
1884 W. 25th St. W. C. KASPER, Proprietor.
TODAY—Extra Good Feature Plays.
XMAS—Extra Features for Matinee and Evening.

A MERRY XMAS
and
PROFITABLE NEW YEAR
TO ALL EXHIBITORS
The Victor Film Service Co.

To Our Friends and Patrons
We take this opportunity to thank you for the many favors we have received during the year 1911 and extend to one and all our very best wishes for
A MERRY CHRISTMAS and
A HAPPY NEW YEAR
MR. EXHIBITOR—
OUR NEW AND ORIGINAL IDEA—
Photo-Play Advertising & Specialty Company (Inc.)

FIGURE 20. "Photo-Plays and Players" page, *Cleveland Sunday Leader,* December 24, 1911.

Picture Field" page of coupons into a "Photo-Plays and Players" page in early December 1911 (fig. 20).[10] Beneath a banner backed by a beam of light from an old-fashioned projector, editor Ralph P. Stoddard filled this new page with an assortment of ads, columns, brief articles, and photos. The Sunday edition of February 4, 1912, was typical.[11] The ads that framed both margins of the page came from sixteen picture theaters, four regional distributors, several equipment suppliers, a company buying scenarios, a school for projectionists, and *Pathé Weekly* (listing eight news items that week). One column consisted of single-paragraph descriptions of those sixteen theater programs; another had capsule reviews of fourteen films, including Kalem's *Two Spies,* Éclair's *Alcohol,* and Pathé's "scientific picture," *The Carrot Caterpillar.* Three photo stories formed a balanced triangular composition in the center: two contrasting Lubin films, *Zigomar* (Feature and Educational Film's "great detective picture"), and Miss May Buckley in the "Leader's Gallery of Photoplayers." For several months, the basic format of this Sunday page remained unchanged, except for the addition of more and more articles of potential interest. Some reported on either general or specific news about the industry: motion pictures were the fourth most popular amusement, according to a Presbyterian Church survey, after baseball, socials, and pool; American films, especially "Cowboy and Indian Pictures," were becoming ever more popular abroad; Reliance was offering $50–$75 for scenarios or picture stories; and Kalem had six production companies at work in New York, California, Florida, Alabama, and Egypt.[12] Others featured more local items: the Crescent Theater had exclusive rights to the *Cleveland Animated Weekly* newsreel; and on the city's west side, the Gordon Square (with twelve hundred seats) opened to a "Big House."[13]

From May through October 1912, the *Sunday Leader* reduced the space allotted to motion pictures to no more than a half page, perhaps because fewer picture theaters advertised. In early November, however, the full-page format returned, sponsored by small ads from fifteen theaters, larger ads from regional distributors, and a new ad from *Motion Picture News.* Stoddard introduced more columns devoted to local exhibitors and distributors—Samuel Bullock (an early exhibitor in the city), C.E. Thompson (the Victor Film Service manager for Universal), Edwin Kohl (owner of seven theaters and manager of Mutual Film Supply), and E. Mandelbaum (the city's most prominent exhibitor and distributor, who later founded World Special Films)—as well as specific theaters, from the new Manhattan (six hundred seats) to a redesigned Superior (nine hundred and fifty seats).[14] During the 1912–13 holidays, the *Sunday Leader* published a "Theatergoers Section" that included two pages on motion pictures,[15] but the single-page format quickly returned, and, with a new column written by Stoddard, a short history of motion pictures that ran for seven consecutive weeks.[16] During its first two years, this page shifted among various sections of the Sunday edition—News, Sports, Metropolitan, Women's, and even Classifieds—until, in November 1913, it settled, renamed, in the Society section, either before or after the page devoted to drama.[17] This was a clear sign that, for the *Leader,* readers strongly attracted to motion pictures were like those long interested in the "legitimate" theater, and that "photoplays" had become a reputable form of entertainment for the newly emergent middle class: the educated, the professional, the social elite. William Lord Wright of *Motion Picture News* called attention to the *Leader*'s "Photoplay page [as] the first of its kind to be instituted."[18]

For another year or more, the *Sunday Leader* kept the format that Stoddard had created, although his name disappeared and the banner went through changes before sticking with "What Cleveland's Photoplay Theaters Are Showing."[19] Support from local picture theaters and rental exchanges increased, particularly when the page shifted to the Metropolitan section during the latter half of 1914, and peaked with thirty-eight theater ads in October.[20] Consequently, local and regional news remained prominent: predictions that exhibition had a "rosy future" in the city, reprinted photos of scenes cut from two films by the Ohio censors, and the Majestic Theater's showing of Mutual's *Sapho,* describing its screen framed with artificial flowers, geometrically arranged and illuminated in changing colors.[21] Yet the *Sunday Leader* page did not neglect broader issues, such as experiments, especially in France, with recording human movement in order to aid the training of athletes; Stoddard's own editorial claim that "sugar-coated" literary adaptations encouraged young boys and girls to read; and Harry Aitkens's corresponding plans for Reliance to "produce great dramas by authors."[22] At the same time, several new columns took up the interests of more and more fans—"Gossip of the Players In and Out of the Studio" and "What Do You Want to Know?"—and photos of "favorite players" began to appear in the Sunday rotogravure section, which the paper then made available for separate purchase.[23] Complementing this attention to stars, as the page shifted back to the Society section, was a special magazine story, "How the Movie Queen Makes Up," which revealed another "magical trick" of filmmaking, describing in some detail (with accompanying illustrations, likely in color) how screen makeup differed radically from stage makeup.[24]

Hardly any newspapers seem to have taken the *Cleveland Sunday Leader* as a model until nearly a year after the inception of its "Photo Plays and Players" page.[25] An intriguing exception was the *San Francisco Bulletin,* which, in late December 1911, suddenly introduced a full Saturday page bannered "In the Land of Photoplays and Players."[26] The writer /editor, Ona Otto,[27] so tightly packed this page that readers must have had trouble ingesting the wealth of information. As a *flaneuse,*[28] Otto was taking note of an unfamiliar phenomenon, so her tour of this new "land" included short interviews with the city's picture theater managers and a local column of "Flashes," and her "editorial" focused on observing an audience, whose anxious outbursts and hearty laughter made her want "to find out more about these pictures." Summarizing moving pictures' progress, she singled out several actresses (Sarah Bernhardt, Mabel Taliaferro) and costly films (*Passion Play, The Fall of Troy, Dante's Inferno*). These led her to shift from *flaneuse* to social reformer at the editorial's conclusion, commending the city's exhibitors and envisioning a future when "Moving Picture houses" will be accepted "on the same scale as legitimate theaters." In the half page Otto wrote and edited each Saturday through January 1912,[29] she listed a directory of sponsoring rental exchanges, added a "Who, Why, What" column that offered answers to readers' questions, and promoted moving pictures and picture theaters for children, promising to print selected brief stories from children under age fourteen about pictures they especially liked. She also followed the earliest fan magazines in highlighting one large star photo each week. In later editorials she interviewed the city's earliest moving picture entrepreneur, suggested improvements in lobby displays, and warned that the chance of any girl or boy becoming a movie actor was very slim. Puzzlingly, this half page disappeared after January,[30] but Otto continued writing a "Window Shopping" column and then turned her attention to real estate, photography, automobiles, farming, gardens, and architecture.[31]

MOVIE PAGES PROLIFERATE, WITH THE MIDWEST IN THE LEAD

By early 1913, moviegoers were reading weekend motion picture pages in more and more city newspapers.[32] But those pages could be quite different, according to where they appeared in a newspaper, how they gained local financial support, how they were organized, and what characterized their content. Much as in the *Cleveland Leader*, pages often shifted from one Sunday section to another, suggesting that the newspapers were uncertain about how best to categorize motion pictures or whether their popularity would last. They could have the strong support of local picture theaters and rental exchanges, but not always. Menu items could be arranged to produce either a sense of familiarity—that is, a reader could find the photos, ads, and stories in relatively the same position on the page each week—or playful diversity. Pages could differ greatly in whether their readers' assumed interest was industry news and gossip, local information and programming, or a balance of these. And they could differ in terms of an assumed interest in the moviegoing experience, the films themselves, or the stars they featured.

While some newspapers modeled their motion picture pages on the pioneering work of the *Cleveland Sunday Leader* and others joined Syndicate Film's telegraphic network (see "Motion Picture News in Syndication" later in this chapter), the *Seattle Times* developed its own distinctive menu format, and later boasted it had "establish[ed] the first daily photoplay department."[33] In late January 1913, J. Willis Sayre's daily amusements column began to include a section, "In the Film World," that collated short items of industry news and gossip (likely drawn from the trade press) and brief program descriptions for up to four picture theaters advertising on the page.[34] Sayre quickly expanded "In the Film World" into a half page in the Sunday edition while continuing the separate section on motion pictures in his daily column.[35] Each Sunday's column now featured a specific news story—for example, that schools in Wichita, Kansas, were screening films—and photo profiles of stars and local movie men such as theater owners/managers Eugene Levy and Albert Meydenbauer.[36] From early March through early April, George H. Bellman edited this section, then Sayre took over once again, heading each week's Sunday half page with a different banner.[37] The general format remained the same, with specific industry stories—that educational films had doubled in number, or that feature films such as *Quo Vadis?* were earning fortunes—and brief program descriptions linked to picture theater ads.[38] Yet there were more photo profiles of stars, and the separate list of "feature" film titles at selected theaters now highlighted two or three "scenic or educational" films.[39] By September 1913, the *Seattle Times* was printing a full page of motion picture news on Sundays and a half page on weekdays, with an expanded series of brief industry news items, lengthier program descriptions, and sometimes large theater ads from the new Colonial, Alhambra, Melbourne, and Class A.[40] For the next two years, with the financial support of the city's major picture theaters, Sayre's editorial agenda apparently assumed that Seattle-area moviegoers were most interested in learning what feature films, nonfiction films, and stars were appearing in local theaters, while keeping abreast of a limited number of industry events and issues.[41]

Perhaps provoked by the *Cleveland Leader*, in mid-February 1913 the *Cleveland Plain Dealer* began printing a Sunday half page of industry news, primarily descriptions and listings of weekly General Film, Universal, and Mutual releases.[42] Initially supported by ads from the city's major rental exchanges, this half page had no named editor and often changed its banner—"The Picture Theatres," "The Movies," "Photo Plays"—but quickly settled into the paper's Editorial/Dramatic section. In the fall, a block of production stills replaced a few star photos in the upper-left corner of the page, an increasing number of city picture theaters paid for small ads, and brief synopses of those theaters' current films filled a new column, "At the Local Picture Theaters."[43] This shift from industry-wide promotion to more information of local interest culminated in late November with a contest in which readers were invited to explain "what movie you liked best last week."[44] Yet, as local theater ads and news items decreased, short pieces on the industry gradually filled the columns and now shared the page with local news about the "Boy Scouts."[45] Throughout most of 1914, as its banner shifted between "Photo Plays" and "Motion Pictures," the Sunday half page remained in the Editorial/Dramatic section, which occasionally featured a front-page piece, for instance on Gabriele d'Annunzio and *Cabiria* (playing at Keith's Hippodrome) or the comedian John Bunny.[46] While readers frequently found large ads, printed episodes, and program listings for serials such as *The Adventures of Kathlyn* and *The Million Dollar Mystery,* they also encountered, from February to October, several "review" columns (see chapter 4). When, in mid-October, the *Plain Dealer* reestablished a full Sunday page, major picture theaters resumed advertising, and on a larger scale. Filling the page now was a mélange of industry and local news and gossip: articles on home moving picture machines replacing family albums, on the unusual importance of movie actors' faces and hands, and on how "hard [it is] to be a film actress," according to Mary Fuller.[47] Yet even more items focused on industry personnel in the city: scenario writer Daisy Mayer, managers Joseph Groppman (Standard) and Fred Brandt (Alhambra), violinists at the Alhambra, and the Knickerbocker's "movie fan" cat.[48]

In late February 1913, the *Pittsburgh Leader* also established a Sunday motion picture page that, much like the *Cleveland Leader* at first, arranged with local picture theaters to redeem ticket coupons collected by its readers.[49] This arrangement, however, encompassed a far greater number of theaters: a dozen within the city, nine on the "North Side," another dozen in outlying neighborhoods, and nearly forty in towns throughout western Pennsylvania.[50] Moreover, the Pittsburgh paper supported those theaters with redeemable coupons far longer, for at least six months.[51] Instead of offering ads, a dozen or more managers supplied the unnamed editor with a paragraph or two that described their theaters and/or the films on their programs. Filling out the initial page were small photos of four movie stars, five local theater managers, and five picture theaters. A "Notes of Plays, Playhouses, and Players" column also took up one bottom corner, and three stanzas of doggerel, "Those Enterprising Motion Picture Men," the other.

During the summer months, this format remained typical, although longer columns now featured programs at the downtown Columbia, Cameraphone, and Olympic. Among occasional columns of news and gossip about either movies or stars, a unique example of movie lore was a reprint of "The Movie Lorelei," in which a "moving picture actress" responds to the proposals of a "German count," matching his three stanzas of doggerel with four of her own, ending with "And let me add, the next time you propose / Enclose a stamp or I won't answer."[52] Much as in the *Cleveland Sunday Leader*, this regularly recurring page shifted among various sections of the paper—Classified, Sporting, Theatrical & Society[53]—then settled in "Theatrical News" throughout much of 1914.

In early March, the *Buffalo Sunday Times* announced that a special department (no editor was named) would edit a "Motion Picture News" page to "further the nation wide movement for the moral and educational perfection of motion picture plays."[54] A horizontal series of line drawings made up the initial banner for this page, depicting what look like shots from an Indian picture.[55] For several months the format stayed relatively the same, with each side of the page framed by columns of ads from nearly twenty picture theaters and three branch offices of the major film rental exchanges. Filling the page's center were program listings or brief film synopses supplied by the advertising theaters, along with at least one article on an industry issue and several photos—either one local manager, a movie star, a theater facade, or a production still.[56] The *Times*'s coverage also ran onto a second half page containing a few more theater program listings, several star photos, at least one article, and a short column of synopses for half a dozen films not summarized previously.[57] Within weeks, there was enough material to fill this second page—bannered more simply "Motion Picture News"—with more articles, program listings, photos, ads from theaters and rental exchanges, and a large ad listing the three dozen picture theaters belonging to the local Motion Picture Exhibitors' League of America.[58] Sometime that summer, the simpler banner also came to headline the first page, and in September a new column appeared, "The Movie Editor," with the writer identified only by the pseudonym "Raye."[59] Appearing in the Telegraph section and then, alternately, in the Local News section, these pages served, like the *Cleveland Sunday Leader*'s, as a regular channel of information from the "Photo-play Industry" and the local "Exhibitors' Organization" targeting current and potential moviegoers and promoting "the movement for elevating the [motion picture] business to the highest plane."[60]

In early 1914, the format of the *Buffalo Times*'s Sunday pages underwent some changes, but the insistence on linking the industry and local exhibitors remained strong. Initially the first page was bannered "With Film and Screen" and, thereafter, "The Silent Drama." During that time, picture theater ads shifted almost entirely to the second page and then decreased once the "The Silent Drama" was condensed into a single page.[61] Industry news and gossip continued to come in short "filler" pieces or, less frequently, in star photo profiles for "Our Mutual Girl" and Lillian Gish.[62] The most prominent stories and illustrations, however, were devoted to local interests, which ranged from full-page "promotions" of new picture theaters to reports on the role that Buffalo exhibitors played in the annual exposition of the International Association of Motion Picture Exhibitors in New York City.[63] Moreover, they included claims not only that *The Adventures of Kathlyn* was a "big drawing card" in Buffalo but also that serial films overall were the most popular part of programs.[64] And they revealed an unusual commitment to non-theatrical exhibition: five churches were projecting motion pictures to Bible students, and the newspaper joined with Pathé to stage a contest to award a dozen Pathéscope machines to Buffalo-area schools.[65] In the "The Movie Man Says" column, the editor reiterated some of these commitments and accompanied city exhibitors to the New York exposition.[66] In December 1914, the *Buffalo Sunday Times* considered motion pictures widely enough accepted to integrate them with stage plays in a single page, and with an equal number of ads.[67] While "Buffalo News" stories largely comprised the page's content, the paper warned its readers that disillusionment awaited those who wished to become stars.[68]

The only other city besides Cleveland and Pittsburgh with two papers sporting weekend pages was Toledo. The *Toledo Blade* was the first, in mid-May 1913, with a Saturday page rather presumptuously headlined "Toledo to Be Picture Play Authority of Middle West."[69] The format of this page drew elements from several already established: half a dozen or more local theater ads lining the sides of the page, a clutch of movie-star photos centered under the banner headline, brief descriptions of the weekly program listings of those sponsoring theaters, articles on local or regional issues and events (for instance, a congratulatory story on Toledo's fifty-three picture theaters and their "public patronage of 21,000 a day"), and short pieces on industry news and gossip (for instance, an item on the hope or fear that the motion pictures' influence soon "may exceed that of the pulpit, newspapers, and legitimate stage").[70] That the page's banner changed slightly each week suggests that the unnamed editor may have reworked news stories and gossip items culled from the trade press or other sources. Soon, the page shifted from Saturday to Wednesday and remained there through early October.[71] Then, it just as inexplicably disappeared, only to reappear on Saturdays starting in early January 1914, now as a half page with hardly any ads, just one or two photos, and a few pieces about industry news.[72]

During those months, moviegoers also could read a Sunday page in the *Toledo Times*.[73] Despite the banner "News of Photoplays and Photoplayers," it shared many features of the *Buffalo Sunday Times*. Two columns of picture theater ads lined the sides of the page and others crossed the bottom (a dozen in all, downtown and in outlying districts), creating a U shape that evoked Universal Films, whose rental exchange, Toledo Film Exchange, posted a large ad.[74] Photos of movie stars, industry figures, and current films ran under the banner, and the rest of the page consisted of plot synopses of the sponsoring theaters' weekly programs. The *Times*'s coverage, like the Buffalo paper's, also ran onto a second page, with more program synopses and another photo story of a star or a current film.[75] Within a month, brief stories of industry news or gossip appeared, sometimes as "filler": Universal's *Samson and Delilah* would climax in a spectacular temple collapse; the famous Yiddish actor Jacob Adler would perform in a Ruby Feature Film; Mutual cameramen were filming the Federal Army's preparations for battle in Mexico.[76] Unlike the *Blade*, the *Times* remained focused on moviegoers' interest in local weekly programs. That orientation intensified when the banner changed that summer to an original, if roughly drawn, panel in which a strip of film spooling from one reel to another arched over the title "Reel News of Photo Plays and Players."[77] From then on, hardly any industry material disturbed the almost exclusively local interest.

Deserving brief mention is the *St. Paul News* for a Sunday column devoted to motion pictures, which first appeared in late October 1913.[78] The reason: The column was bannered "In Movie Land," perhaps the earliest use of the phrase that Mae Tinee and others later would make their own. Initially, the banner covered the weekly publicity supplied by half a dozen local exhibitors, synchronized with the small ads they placed on the page. Within two months, the column added to its short film synopses one or two star publicity photos that soon turned into brief, detached star profiles, likely syndicated material from the United Press service, because several were signed by Gertrude Price (see chapter 3).[79] By early March 1914, however, the *St. Paul News* simplified and downsized the banner, returning the column to its original format: brief synopses of that week's movies at the three to six theaters that continued to pay for ads.[80] Ignored were at least half of the theaters that sponsored an ad for the local Motion Pictures Exhibitors' Association, which always anchored the bottom-right corner of that Sunday page.[81]

MOTION PICTURE NEWS IN SYNDICATION

Almost simultaneously with the Sunday pages that emerged in 1913, Syndicate Film Publishing began to operate as a press service specializing in motion picture news. This company was an affiliate of Syndicate Publishing Company (founded in New York in 1900),[82] best known for selling dictionaries, encyclopedias, histories, song collections, and even fiction by mail order, often in conjunction with newspapers.[83] The owner-manager of this new syndicated service was Arthur Leslie, a grandson of Frank Leslie, the famous nineteenth-century magazine magnate, whose will Arthur later contested with outrageous accusations against Mrs. Frank Leslie.[84] Leslie used the connections he had built up with newspapers to begin distributing motion picture material for a far less local kind of weekend page. His staff culled items from a variety of industry sources (the trade press, manufacturer bulletins, and fan magazines) and offered them by wire as a sheet of "Motion Picture News" to newspapers in small and medium-size cities. The initial plan, announced in April 1913, was to supply "60 newspapers" across the country with a weekly template of columns, stories, photos or line drawings of stars, and "'roasts' on films."[85] This template could be reproduced in its entirety or cut up and "pasted" into different weekly formats, surrounded by picture theater ads and program descriptions. Whether bannered "Motion Picture News" or "News of Photoplays and Photoplayers," the initial syndicated material highlighted a short text promoting the newspaper as the first in the city to print "the latest photoplay news of interest" to "patrons of motion picture theaters." Jas. S. McQuade, for one, was dubious that Leslie, an industry outsider whom he labeled a "scandalmonger," could succeed—yet he did.[86]

In February 1913, the *Des Moines Register and Leader* and the *Columbus Enquirer* (Georgia) were among the first to contract with Leslie, and their initial Sunday pages offer examples of how differently papers could handle this syndicated template.[87] Both featured a rectangle comprised of a dozen movie stars (in line drawings) framing the boldface text "FAMOUS PLAYERS NOW IN MOTION PICTURES." Both also included a column of texts with subheads—the first of which listed the new films of those dozen stars—and a second column of numerous, miscellaneous brief texts. Whereas the Columbus paper bannered its page "Motion Picture News," the Des Moines paper titled its half page "At the Moving Picture Playhouses." The Columbus page also printed five additional texts in that first column—for instance, one on cameramen recording news events, and another on new ways of enhancing picture theater acoustics—and a separate interview with

Thomas Edison (in wide circulation) on how motion pictures could "revolutionize" education. The Des Moines half page, however, added several short texts in its second column, including a snippet of a much longer one on the varied salaries of child players that had appeared in the other paper's first column. Only the *Columbus Enquirer* had the announcement that its "department [would] contain all the latest photoplay news of interest" and serve as an exclusive "medium for motion picture theatres in this city and vicinity." Absent that announcement, the *Des Moines Register and Leader* gave the impression that it was offering readers this motion picture news all on its own.

At the same time, readers found a second template of Syndicate Film material in at least three more papers: the *Fort Worth Star-Telegram* (fig. 21), *Ogden Standard,* and *Hamilton Journal* (Ohio). At first, all three printed the same texts and line drawings in a block filling five columns of a seven-column page.[88] This block not only had the "MOTION PICTURE NEWS" logo and announcement but also included new material: a row of five star images, a miscellany of a dozen short texts (several linked to images of Mary Pickford, John Bunny, and King Baggot), a column on "How To Write a Photoplay," and a gossipy "Sidelights on Photoplayers." The most important text, however, was a long column signed by Leslie himself claiming that "the motion picture theatre [had] won its way to a position of primal importance in the life of the people," and therefore the newspaper should acknowledge the influence it could wield "in photoplay matters." In March, a third template appeared almost verbatim in the Ogden and Hamilton papers as well as the *Fort Wayne Journal-Gazette* and *Minneapolis Tribune.*[89] This slightly shorter block of items included a star photo of Alice Joyce, a long article on Detective William J. Burns (now starring in a motion picture), four stills from that picture, another on cameramen filming the uprising in Mexico, and "Notes from the Studios." While the Ogden and Hamilton papers printed the same block of "Photoplayers in Next Week's Pictures" along with paragraphs on each of the seven stars pictured, the Fort Wayne paper did not, having already reproduced that very block a week earlier.[90] In line with the Cleveland, Pittsburgh, and Buffalo papers, the *Minneapolis Tribune,* by contrast, included program listings from a dozen theaters whose ads (plus others from General Film, Laemmle Film Service, Mutual, and Feature Film) helped to sponsor the page.

The *Ogden Standard* and *Waterloo Reporter* (Iowa) offer good examples of what a movie fan could find in a full page of this syndicated material throughout 1913. The *Standard*'s Sunday page came in a regularized format that granted striking compositional flexibility. A consistent pattern of 1-, 2-, 1-, 2-, 1-column article heads ran just under the banner; often

Copyrighted, 1913, by Syndicate Publishing Co.

MOTION PICTURE NEWS

Important Announcement To All Patrons of Motion Picture Theatres

This department will contain all the latest photoplay news of interest and will be kept thoroughly up-to-date. Scenes from the more important forthcoming photoplays will be shown in advance of their presentation and a synopsis of their plots will be given. Photographs of photoplay actors and actresses will also be published, together with the latest news concerning them.

THE MOTION PICTURE STANDS NOW IN THE FOREFRONT OF AMUSEMENTS AND INDUSTRIES

Arthur Leslie

HOW TO WRITE A PHOTOPLAY

MAUDE ADAMS IN PETER PAN

SIDELIGHTS ON PHOTOPLAYERS

FIGURE 21. "Motion Picture News" page, *Fort Worth Star-Telegram,* February 14, 1913.

topping the page was a narrow graphic in which a projector beam streamed over the heads of a small audience to fix two figures in a cowboy picture on screen.[91] The photos of stars, industry figures, and production stills could be varied in size, shape, and placement. One week they ran in a staggered line across the page; in another they formed a centered block or articulated V; in a third they created the impression of descending notes or artfully scattered high and low notes on a musical staff.[92] Articles featured several producers and their films, initially linked to the industry strip ads at the bottom of the page (see chapter 1), one or more stars, and occasionally more general industry news. The *Waterloo Reporter* began with a Saturday half page (featuring Alice Joyce and Detective Burns) that, in two months, turned into a full page bannered "Motion Pictures";[93] by late June the editor was identified as Arthur C. Stolte.[94] Stolte's page was more full of industry news and gossip that focused on new films (at first the MPPC's) and included fewer star profiles with widely dispersed publicity photos. Occasional articles leavened this diet on issues such as censorship or a series that promoted Kinemacolor.[95] Perhaps because the small town's few picture theaters rarely advertised, Stolte offered hardly any local or regional news. Exceptions were a piece on Julius Singer's Capital City Film Company in Des Moines, a long article on his own visit to Essanay's Chicago studio, and a report on the annual meeting of Iowa exhibitors.[96] The lack of nearly anything in either paper with a local or regional angle is telling.

Perhaps sparked by the material that Syndicate Film supplied to dozens of newspapers, in April 1913 the *Washington Herald* announced its own "Motion Picture News" column, not as a weekly but as "a daily feature."[97] Attributed to an anonymous "Motion Picture Editor," this column often ran on the "Herald Want Ads" page and was decidedly local in orientation. The first column praised "the gentlemen" who managed the city's "sixty-five moving picture theaters" and estimated their weekly attendance at half a million.[98] The second extolled a film scenario written by that "Washington girl," Mary Fuller;[99] others highlighted films of regional historical interest such as Kalem's *Shenandoah*, the Saturday-morning screening of an educational film written by local school teachers and acted by their pupils, a new ordinance requiring exhibitors to display posters "flat against the walls," and complaints about projectionists not using "more judgment in regulating the speed of their machines."[100] Much like other newspaper pages and columns, this one offered advice on writing movie scenarios and encouraged readers to submit drafts, typewritten only, for review.[101] Several major Washington picture theaters seem to have fed promotional information to the *Herald*'s editor about their programs, but rarely resorted to paid advertising. Still, a half dozen claimed, in small ads, to offer only photoplays "presentable to men, women, and children"; some of the same theaters even sponsored a full page that printed a laudatory sermon written by a local Presbyterian minister.[102] As a further sign of cooperation between exhibitors and the paper, among the advertising slides shown at the downtown Virginia was one asking moviegoers to "Read the Washington Herald."[103] At the same time that some newspapers were ending their contracts with Syndicate Film, the *Herald* began reducing the size of its column from late May 1913 on, and seems to have dropped it entirely in mid-July.[104]

With further research, one might track how far the Syndicate Film service network extended, for how long it operated, and what material newspapers chose to use and what not.[105] For now, one has to rely on the practices of perhaps a dozen papers. Those in Des Moines and Minneapolis (as well as San Antonio) honored their weekly contracts for no more than two to four months.[106] This may also have been true of the *Duluth News Tribune,* whose ornately bannered "Motion Pictures" page, edited by a B.V. La Frances, ran from late April to early June 1913.[107] At the same time, others—from the *Milwaukee Sentinel* and *Pittsburgh Post* to the *Lexington Herald* (Kentucky) and *Frederick Post* (Maryland)—signed on with Syndicate Film for either a full page of "News of Photoplays and Photoplayers" or several columns under the heading "Motion Picture News."[108] And those papers, along with others such as the *Ogden Standard* and *Waterloo Reporter,* held to their arrangements with Leslie's service well into 1914,[109] although the latter ended in March, perhaps because of Stolte's impending marriage and move to Chicago.[110] As late as January 1914, a small mining-town paper in Montana, the *Anaconda Standard,* even started printing a full page of Syndicate Film columns and photos (similar to that in the Ogden paper) that continued uninterrupted for the next two years.[111] Although impossible to verify, in late 1914 Leslie himself boasted, with some exaggeration, that his service was the first not only to introduce a sustained flow of motion picture news but also to extend its reach to "a hundred or more newspaper editors."[112]

By early 1914, moviegoers in dozens of cities and towns would have become familiar with one of at least three formats, with variants, typical of newspaper motion picture pages. The first, created by Stoddard in the *Cleveland Sunday Leader,* integrated industry and local or regional news and was sponsored by local picture theater and regional rental exchange ads. Other newspapers, such as the *Seattle Times* and *Toledo Blade,* adopted a similar kind of page but gave as much attention to movie stars as to manufacturers and their films—in the case of the *Times,* even to nonfiction films. A second format was more characteristic of the *Pittsburgh Leader,*

Buffalo Times, and *Toledo Times*, whose pages were sponsored by local and/or regional ads and whose texts and photos almost exclusively addressed local interests in picture theater programs—including, in the case of the Buffalo paper, non-theatrical exhibition—and initially showed less interest in stars. A third format came from Syndicate Film Publishing as a template (in texts and line drawings) of industry news and gossip, often featuring stars (perhaps taken from fan magazines). Small-town newspapers as different as the *Columbus Enquirer*, *Fort Worth Star-Telegram*, *Ogden Standard*, and *Hamilton Journal* printed the material verbatim. Others, such as the *Des Moines Register and Leader* and *Waterloo Reporter*, selected material to set up their own weekly columns or pages. Again, variants occurred in the *Minneapolis Tribune* and, briefly, the *Duluth News Tribune*, both of which apparently took a limited amount of industry news from Syndicate Film, the trade press, and/or producers and integrated it into columns more focused on issues of local interest, especially weekly theater programs.

MOVIE MENUS MUSCLE INTO CHICAGO, "THE MIRROR OF A NATION"

Until the publicity campaign for Selig's *The Adventures of Kathlyn*, only the *Chicago Tribune*, among that city's newspapers, seems to have shown the slightest interest in motion pictures.[113] That began to change in early February 1914, when the *Chicago Daily News* introduced an unsigned column devoted to the movies.[114] This column featured some of the same menu items that had characterized earlier weekend pages: short pieces of industry news, one or more photos of "movie favorites"[115] or production stills, and brief plot synopses of films currently in circulation. What was different? First, with rare exceptions, the column ran daily, not weekly, and adopted the term "movies" for its subject rather than "photoplays" or "motion pictures." Second, the top stories focused on either a local industry figure (such as George Kleine) or a particularly important feature-length film (such as *The Squaw Man* with Dustin Farnum or *Hearts Adrift* with Mary Pickford).[116] Third, only multiple-reel films were worthy of plot synopses. At least once a week those synopses took up the entire column, but never was there any mention of where and when the films were playing in the city's picture theaters.[117] The *Daily News* column, then, seemed to promote not local moviegoing but rather the industry in general and the movies overall as a popular, legitimate entertainment, much like Syndicated Film. Although this column became a regular feature of the *News*, not until

March 1916 was the writer identified (whether or not he was the original columnist), as W.K. Hollander.[118]

Simultaneously with the initial *Daily News* column, the *Chicago Tribune* printed its first "Today's Best Moving Picture Story." Two weeks later, the paper introduced a half page of program listings for "High-Class Moving Picture Theaters." Twice weekly, thereafter, this half page comprised seven columns of small ads for approximately sixty theaters organized into downtown, north side, west side, and south side sections of the city, with special prominence given to the first two.[119] The "guaranteed" revenue from these ads, along with that from *The Adventures of Kathlyn,* very likely led the *Tribune* to initiate a Sunday page devoted to "Photoplays and Players." First advertised on February 22, 1914,[120] introduced one week later, and quickly bannered "Right Off the Reel,"[121] this page featured a centered column, "In the Frame of Public Favor," with an exceptionally large publicity halftone (in a gilded frame) and profile of a current player (fig. 22).[122] Much like the huge close-up of a movie star on screen, this image could be said to enact what Susan Stewart has called the "gigantic" in the period's advertising[123]—and was perfect in size (see chapter 5) for a movie fan to cut out and paste into a scrapbook. The initial choice, Kathlyn Williams, was obvious, especially as the page appeared in the colored Sunday Magazine, just before McGrath's latest installment of Selig's serial. From the start, moreover, the *Tribune* asked readers to mail in ballots with the name of their "favorite player" and promised each week to print a "photo" (and brief profile) of the player who received the most votes.[124] Their choices suggest what stars Chicago's movie fans favored from late March through early May: Mary Pickford, J. Warren Kerrigan, Alice Joyce, Florence La Badie, Earle Williams, Mary Fuller, King Baggot.[125] Most of these stars worked for companies that had originated in Chicago or New York, and many still acted in films produced there. Except for Pickford, nearly all still performed chiefly in one- or two-reel films, which meant that they were seen frequently in the weekly releases from General Film, Universal, or Mutual.

The *Tribune* claimed that it would answer readers' questions with "inside facts about photoplays and players," but the space allotted to anything other than stars at first was minimal. A column titled "Gossip of the Silent Players," probably culled from the trade press and/or fan magazines, supplemented the photo profile; otherwise there was room for only a short column on "Notes of the Motion Dramas" and a pair of production stills, one in each page's lower corner. In mid-April, two new columns replaced the latter two items, both of which signaled that the page now would be devoted not to "photoplays" but "movies." One was "Answers to Movie

Chicago Sunday Tribune.

Right off the Reel

Notes of the Motion Drama.

In the Frame of Public Favor

Gossip of the Silent Players.

"LITTLE Mary" Pickford, termed the Maude Adams of the moving picture stage, was born in New York state nineteen years ago. She attended an exclusive girls' school in New York City. She was known to film patrons the country over before she ever appeared in important parts as a real actress, and as "Little Mary" she was idolized by her audiences.

It was as an actress for the films that she came to the notice of David Belasco. The producer was attending a moving picture show when he was struck by the childish beauty and sweet personality of the girl. He investigated, with the result that Miss Pickford soon after made her first appearance in the leading feminine role of "A Good Little Devil."

The actress scored a great success in the part, but apparently she cared little for the stage for early in the winter she signed a contract with Daniel Frohman's Famous Players' company, and will be seen, for the present, only in their photo play productions.

Automobiling takes up much of Miss Pickford's leisure time. She is married to the popular photo play actor, Owen Moore.

Vote for the Picture of Your Favorite Player.

THE BALLOT

M__________
requests the pleasure
of seeing
the photograph of
____
appear
In the Frame
of
Public Favor
on April fifth
Nineteen Hundred and Fourteen

Inside Facts About Photo-Plays and Players.

What is it that you want to know about the motion picture world?

Do you want to know something about the life of your favorite actor and actress outside the films?

Do you want to know how the play that particularly thrilled you was produced?

Whatever your questions concerning photoplays and players, address "Right Off the Reel," in care of this paper. Answers to such questions will be given on the next page.

SCENE FROM "THE DREAM WOMAN" ADAPTED BY BLACHE FROM WILKIE COLLINS' NOVEL

WILD SCENE DURING THE DOCTOR'S VISIT IN THE SELIG COMEDY, "WHILE WIFEY IS AWAY."

THE CHICAGO SUNDAY TRIBUNE.

FIGURE 22. "Right Off the Reel" page, *Chicago Sunday Tribune,* March 22, 1914.

Fans," which purported to address readers/fans directly, most of whose questions, unsurprisingly, dealt with stars.[126] The other was a series of columns from Mae Tinee (described as an "inimitable interviewer"), written in the breathless tone of "Zip! Zam! Zowie!," that recounted her experience playing a small role at Essanay's Chicago studio, interviewing William Selig in Chicago, and talking with actors at studios around New York City, from Vitagraph and Edison to Éclair and Thanhouser.[127] These stories differed from Louis Reeves Harrison's earlier "studio saunterings" in *Moving Picture World* because they brought to life, however fancifully, what it felt like to live and work as a movie actor. Over the summer, "Right Off the Reel" relocated twice—first to the "Theater, Music, Literature, and Auto" section and then, strangely, to "Society, Movies, and Churches"—before it returned to the Sunday Magazine. Mae Tinee was identified now as the writer of "Answers to Movie Fans" (she warned that fans' queries were too many for her to address in toto), and her column (after she returned to Chicago) was renamed "Gossip of the Movie Plays and Players."[128] The page also ran a serial story about Peggy, a young woman who becomes a movie actor, and readers were asked who might play her.[129]

By late September 1914, "Right Off the Reel" was not only doling out "inside facts" and gossip (probably gleaned from industry publicity) but also including a small block of ads from five to ten picture theaters and offering a weekly forum for letters titled "Voices of the Movie Fans." These voices, named only by initials, often registered fans' complaints, from censors' lack of concern for "the physical abuse of women by men" or the vulgarity of Keystone comedies to objections to lengthy kisses and unrealistic hairstyles.[130] By now Mae Tinee's gossip column also had a significantly new title, "In Movieland," which circulated even more stories than before about movie stars' hard work, unexpected escapades, and fan tributes, from doting doggerel to a hotel special, "Omelette à la King Baggot."[131] In December, slipped into a bottom corner of the Sunday page was Quin Hall's comic strip *Adventures of the Silly Gallillies in Movie Land*, which each week lampooned the experiences of a pair of "girl extras" (see the third entr'acte).[132] Not until January 1915 did Mae Tinee sign, with a cursive flourish, the "Right Off the Reel" banner as editor and author of the entire Sunday page.[133] Earlier that same month, in what likely was a promotional stunt, the *Sunday Tribune* editor "surreptitiously . . . and without her knowledge" put "Miss Mae Tinee" in "The Frame of Public Favor" as that week's most "popular player" (fig. 23).[134]

Throughout 1915, "Right Off the Reel" held to a relatively standardized format: a prominent movie star "close up" and profile framed by familiar

FIGURE 23. Mae Tinee, *Chicago Sunday Tribune,* January 3, 1915. David M. Rubenstein Rare Book & Manuscript Library, Duke University.

columns on three sides, a bottom-corner comic strip, and an appeal to fans to vote for their "favorite player." And readers were kept pleasantly surprised by extra added attractions. In April, allegedly responding to fans, the *Tribune* relocated one Mae Tinee column to the "Drama Section," now renamed "Latest News from Movie Land." In that first column she amusingly threatened to sue Ring Lardner, in his own slangy idiom, for stealing her banner for a recent column, "Right Off the Bat."[135] She also promoted the *Tribune*'s "motion picture advertisements" and "world's greatest motion picture directory" with two full-page stories targeting middle-class adults: in one, a waiter advises a luncheon club of businessmen where to find the best picture theater information; in the other, a businessman's wife gets similar advice from her women neighbors about how to treat a visiting school friend.[136] Recognizing Mae Tinee as a valuable asset, the paper's Sunday edition ads listed "Right Off the Reel" as the second of the top weekly features.[137] Perhaps because she judged national contests soliciting the best solutions to several serials—Thanhouser's *The Million Dollar Mystery* in 1914 and American's *The Diamond in the Sky* in 1915[138]—and because her "Right Off the Reel" page circulated through the *Tribune*'s syndicated service to distant newspapers such as the *Buffalo Courier,*

Augusta Chronicle, Oakland Tribune, and (probably) *Fort Worth Star-Telegram,*[139] Mae Tinee very likely was the first well-known and influential "movie menu" editor/writer in the country.

Given this competition, the *Chicago Record-Herald* soon turned its attention to motion pictures. In late March 1914, it too began printing a half page of block ads from Chicago-area picture theaters, along with "Today's Picture Story." But this "Movie Directory" appeared daily, and its eight columns of tiny strip ads listed nearly three hundred theaters, encompassing, in order, the downtown, south side, north side, west side, northwest side, and suburban areas.[140] As with the *Tribune,* the "guaranteed" revenue from all these exhibitors likely prompted the *Record-Herald* one week later to introduce its own Sunday page, under the banner "Reel Drama."[141] Initially, this page (again, no editor was named) combined industry stories (but fewer on stars) with others of local interest, in items such as how *The Spoilers* and *The Drug Terror* were made, or when the downtown La Salle and Studebaker (nine hundred seats each)[142] switched to motion pictures; it also featured a regular column titled "Gossip of the Photoplay Theaters and Occupants."[143] In late May, the page adopted a new banner, "In the Picture Playhouses," and, after an article in imitation of Mae Tinee's experience as an "Extra Girl,"[144] took a more exclusive interest in industry news and gossip: how movies aided art, religion, and other causes, for instance, or why "You Just Can't Kill a Movie Actor."[145] Throughout the summer, "In the Picture Playhouses" shrank to half a page on Sundays, but the banner broadened to cover what had been "Today's Picture Story," which continued as a daily column.[146] Just before Labor Day, the full page returned and gradually showed more interest in local film matters, for instance several "Extra Girl" articles and the photo of a George Ade photoplay being shot in Essanay's Chicago studio.[147]

By early 1915, the *Herald*'s Sunday page was competing with the *Tribune*'s on nearly equal terms. A scriptwriter for Essanay, Louella Parsons, began writing an unusually detailed weekly column, "How to Write Photoplays," which included a rundown of the "market" for scenarios at half a dozen film companies.[148] Soon, Gene Morgan was writing a breezy column of interviews with picture players, the first of which featured Chaplin, "just annexed by the Essanay Company."[149] The page tried out several banners before choosing, in early February, "From Filmland," with bold white capital letters on a solid black background, flanked by small drawings of stereotypical movie characters (fig. 24).[150] It also acquired several new items: Rosemary Grey's short star profile; a column of news and gossip and another of answers to queries; an unsigned comic strip depicting the humorous things that befell certain movie personnel; and Morgan's column of industry lore.[151] By April there was further evidence that movie stars were assuming more importance for the paper's readers, just as they were for the *Tribune*. "By arrangement with Essanay," the *Herald* began running a daily comic strip called *Charley Chaplin's Comic Capers* in addition to an earlier Sunday strip, "Haphazard Helen," in honor of Kalem's popular series (see the third entr'acte).[152] Caroline Carr introduced a prominently centered, illustrated star profile (rather like that of Mae Tinee) and initially focused on female stars such as Ruth Roland, Grace Darmond, and Beverly Bayne.[153] A few morsels remained for readers less interested in stars: a new column of comic stories from Morgan about a character named Jitney Jim brazenly trying to break into the movies, along with an unsigned column, "What the Fans Want to Know," offering even more answers to queries from fans. The following page now hosted another unsigned column listing and briefly describing the films to be released next week in Chicago.[154]

The *Sunday Herald*'s menu options having to do with stars, however, continued unabated through the summer and fall of 1915. In June, Carr's profiles gave way to a prominent weekly column, "The Story of My Life," allegedly written by stars such as Kathlyn Williams, Edna Mayo, and Marguerite Clark. These culminated in an exclusive series devoted to Chaplin (signaling his unusually swift rise to popularity) that ran for six weeks beginning in early July, and each profusely illustrated "installment" took up more than half of the "From Filmland" page.[155] Along with these "stories," the Sunday edition introduced in its Rotogravure section a weekly "gallery" of movie star photos.[156] After wrapping up her column on scenario writing in late June—which she soon collected into a book[157]—Parsons took over the task of interviewing well-known stars or personalities for prominent photo profiles, beginning with Lillian Gish and Clara Kimball Young.[158] In September, these profiles turned into a series titled "How to Become a Movie Actress," which may have seemed a rather dubious enticement to young female readers but actually, more benignly, offered "behind the scenes" stories, supposedly for "the first time," of how "the most well-known moving picture stars won success."[159] As before, each installment included a large halftone of that week's star along with a "brief personal narrative" from such figures as Anita Stewart and Mae March.[160] Two weeks later, Parsons gave her weekly profile an even more provocative title, "How to Become a Movie Star," and her choices (except for Crane Wilbur) were exclusively women, from Ruth Stonehouse, Marguerite Courtot, and Norma Talmadge to Helen Holmes, Beverly

FROM FILMLAND

Thrill of Battle Is Experienced At Movie Targets

By GENE MORGAN.

A Wreck of Nerves.

Old-Time Gallery Gone.

How Could He Miss Such a Target?

Your Favorite Pastime.

Ruth Roland Breezily Mixes Tea and Business

RUTH ROLAND

BY CAROLINE CARR.

Her Favorite Color.

Brief Vaudeville Career.

Her Hobby

Dorothy Gish—She Loves Books.

BY ROSEMARY GREY.

Lessons for the Ambitious Young Photoplaywright

By LOUELLA O. PARSONS.

The Old Ideas.

Avoid White Slave Stories.

FIGURE 24. "From Filmland" page, *Chicago Sunday Herald,* April 18, 1915.

Bayne, and Clara Kimball Young (fig. 25).[161] Unlike the *Tribune,* the *Herald* seems not to have thought "From Filmland" and Parsons's columns all that significant for readers, at least according to a single full-page ad for the *Sunday Herald* that ranked them low in a list of features.[162] Yet, based on the circulation of "From Filmland" in newspapers from the *Oakland Tribune* to the *Idaho Statesman* throughout 1915,[163] no doubt Parsons was

How To Become A Movie Star —

By Louella O. Parsons

Is There Money in the Movies? Yes. Mary Pickford Is Paid $104,000 a Year and Many Other Stars Receive Salaries Equal to Those of Bank Presidents and Corporation Lawyers—How They Spend Their Money and Why They Must Save a Part.

Expensive Clothes Necessary.

Jack Kerrigan walked off the speaking stage one night and met a tempting offer to appear in movies. He signed a two-year contract the next day and has won a high place in filmland.

Most Stars Live Simply.

How Jack Kerrigan Entered the Movies

IT WAS the fond hope of my mother that I should some day grace the ministry. This, however, I realized almost from the first was a forlorn hope. My father, who occupied a lucrative position as superintendent of a large warehouse, resolved that I should follow in his footsteps. After my graduation from school I became a clerk in his business.

How I hated figures and all things commercial. In short, I was a failure. If I hadn't at that moment decided upon becoming an actor I might have surrendered to the pleadings of my elder brother and become a prize-fighter.

My first stage experience was under the direction of Clay Clement, my brother-in-law. The play was "Sam Houston," and I was given the juvenile lead. We opened in New York and started out on the road. I was only 18 at that time and continued playing on the legitimate stage for several years.

When we were playing "The Road to Yesterday" in Chicago a member of the Essanay company saw my performance and after speaking of the matter to my manager made me a flattering offer to join his company. I visited the Essanay plant the following day and before leaving signed a two-year contract.

Long before I became identified with them my interest in motion pictures amounted to almost a fascination. I used to stand on the curb and fight against the "call" of the 5-cent theater. I was upstage with regard to motion pictures in those days.

I left the Essanay to join the American. I was the first member engaged when the company was formed. I was later drawn into the Universal company on account of bigger inducements in every direction. I am still with the Universal.

And now for the benefit of a great number of my friends who may have read these lines and who have had ambition to enter the motion picture field I am not going to say "Keep away from it" or "You're bound to fail" or "The business is overrun with more men and women than there are vacancies." This would be unjust.

There are always openings in the picture world, as there are in the legitimate drama and every other walk of life, for the man or woman who is adapted to any chosen field.

JACK WARREN KERRIGAN.

FIGURE 25. "How to Become a Movie Star," *Chicago Sunday Herald*, January 2, 1916.

becoming nearly as well known as Mae Tinee and her fellow writers at the *Tribune*.

NEWSPAPERS MAKE PICTURE-GOERS FROM COAST TO COAST (1)

Up to now, movie fans in the Midwest, especially in large cities, had a unique opportunity to read weekly pages or even daily columns about the "moving picture field" and its bounty, sometimes complemented by weekly or daily program listings, in at least one major newspaper. Those in smaller cities or towns could savor weekly industry news and gossip, sometimes combined with local news, supplied by Leslie's Syndicated Film Publishing. Awakening to the potential benefit of their readers' fascination with motion pictures, especially in the East and South, other papers finally felt compelled to establish their own columns and pages in the remaining months of 1914 and early 1915.

THE BEST Photoplay Department in WASHINGTON

PHOTOPLAYS AND PHOTOPLAYERS

By GARDNER MACK.

What the Photoplay Department of The Times Supports

Within the last two or three days there have been several inquiries received by the Photoplay Editor of the Times that indicate a misapprehension among the exhibitors of Washington as to just what this department represents. In order that there may be no such misapprehension in the future the exact position of the editor in this connection will be reiterated:

The motion picture as represented by the photoplay, the educational and industrial films form today the greatest medium for educating and amusing the public in the civilized world.

The development of motion pictures, their betterment and the widening of their scope should be encouraged and supported by every intelligent man and woman.

The showing of cheap, clap-trap, blood and thunder films that serve no useful purpose and tell no interesting story should be condemned and made impossible.

The exhibition of old, "rainy" films, the bad projection of films should be prohibited by law.

The maintenance of stuffy, unventilated theaters and the crowding of theaters should be prohibited by law.

The exhibitors should understand that they occupy a position of responsibility toward the public, in a broad general sense, in the same class with the teacher, the minister, and the newspaper editor, and should govern themselves accordingly.

LILLIAN WALKER, WHO APPEARS IN "CUTEY'S WIFE," AT THE PICKWICK TODAY.

The Treasure Ship. (Kalem).

The Range War. (Warner's Features). Featuring Josephine West and Joe Ryan.

Francis X. Bushman Wins Ladies' World Contest

Love's Long Lane. (Lubin).

900 DROPS

FIGURE 26. "Photoplays and Photoplayers," *Washington Times*, May 26, 1914.

Published just two weeks after the first "Right Off the Reel" page, the *Washington Times*'s "Photoplays and Photoplayers" column could hardly be more different (fig. 26). Although it too included publicity images of movie stars appearing in picture theaters in and around the nation's capital, this was a *daily* column, like those earlier in the *Washington Herald* or *Chicago News*. From the start, the column was written and edited by Gardner Mack, who claimed that his was "the best photoplay department in Washington," with the aim to "represent the public."[164] To find out what "Mr. and Mrs. Public and all you little Publics" really wanted to see, he solicited readers' letters—"we don't care who you are or where you live"—to report what they wanted shown at their "favorite photoplay house" so "we can tell the exhibitors through our comments on their films." However, as a presumed spokesperson for Washington-area moviegoers, unlike Mae Tinee, he would not focus on stars. Mack's column appeared in the "Daily Magazine Pages for Everybody," although women were presumably his principal readers and letter writers. To an extent, he gave voice to their concerns, as evidenced by letters preferring travel films or "good society plays and simple homely love stories" over "blood and thunder stories."[165] And he did often address women directly. In early June, one column described how films often served as a "style show" of the latest fashions for "women photoplay enthusiasts."[166] In late December, another reported on the convergence between motion pictures and shopping: Downtown Washington exhibitors now did their best business in the afternoons because their programs "appeal to the intelligent class of women that constitute the large body of shoppers."[167]

Mack's real objective was to improve exhibition conditions by assuming the vocal role of the "intelligent" moviegoer.[168] He likened exhibitors to teachers and ministers and urged them to recognize that they had a special responsibility to their community because "more children go to the photoplay theater than go to church or to school [and] more grown people attend the performances at the photoplay theaters than go to church or to libraries or to lectures or to regular theaters."[169] He repeatedly offered advice to exhibitors, especially in neighborhood theaters: be courteous to patrons, think of their comfort and convenience, and carefully select photoplays that fulfill their interest in "the faces of certain players and the appearance of certain brands."[170] Careful selection meant choosing films for their quality and reliability, just as manufacturers, he said, had come to realize with respect to their automobiles.[171] He offered the Virginia Theater as a model when, in late March, it contracted to screen Famous Players feature films exclusively.[172] A week later, he noted its success: eight thousand people had attended the two-day run of *In the Bishop's Carriage* (starring Mary Pickford) and another two thousand were turned away, so the theater decided to extend the run of each future Famous Players film to four days.[173] Mack also praised his own neighborhood theater, which ran a variety program of MPPC films, as one of twenty-five to thirty venues in the city that took its reputation seriously.[174] Finally, for his well-to-do women readers, he floated the idea of a "photoplay tea house" for the city's shopping districts where patrons could sit at forty to fifty tables, order light luncheon dishes, drink free tea, and watch motion pictures accompanied only by the "respectable" music of a piano and violin.[175]

Throughout 1915, Mack's column continued to focus on a single subject each day, along with his signed list of "Today's [Dozen] Best Films." The subjects, as before, were initially local: Marguerite Snow had acted on city stages before becoming a movie star; area scenario writers had formed an "inquest club"; a local girl, Elsie Woodward, was a "wild riding cowgirl" at Lubin.[176] He conducted new surveys of what children wanted to see and how long "Mr. and Mrs. Public" preferred their films to be.[177] In May, he floated another elitist idea: a "progressive motion picture party" of friends could dine together and "take a run around the city," by auto or streetcar, to view a particular star's film or catch consecutive serial episodes in one theater after another.[178] That summer he promoted the National Press Club's "first showing of [Weber's] *Hypocrites*" and lauded the Crandall for adding Department of Agriculture films to its programs.[179] Mack gradually began serving more as an industry spokesman.[180] Subjects that could have a local angle now did not: for instance Universal's special service targeting schools and churches, and efforts to show free films in city playgrounds.[181] He devoted many columns to the "battle between the stage and screen," favoring those who became stars with either no stage experience or only stock company "training."[182] He offered advice on scenario writing, quoting pros such as Epes Winthrop Sargent and others.[183] Film stories, he argued, ought not to "explode" with "punch"; thrills and "hair-raising feats" belonged in the circus.[184] Taking readers behind the scenes, he named what a good film needed: editors, apt props and costumes, and actors speaking their dialogue.[185] Like Gertrude Price, he praised the industry for the opportunities it afforded women.[186] Finally, he was acutely aware of the European war, noting the importance of military training films, the dangers of wartime filming, and the lack of animosity to cameramen from all sides.[187] In February 1916, the *Times* introduced a weekly Saturday motion picture half page that featured industry articles, but Mack's name was attached only to "Today's Best Films," and in late May it disappeared.[188]

In early May 1914, the *Pittsburg Dispatch* began offering that city's second, rather different, Sunday page, "In the World of Films."[189] An initial column from George M. Downe (apparently the editor) announced that he wanted to link local "movie men" with moviegoers who had made the city "a center of motion picture enthusiasm."[190] That first page had ads from two regional exchanges (George Kleine and Pittsburg Photoplay), three companies selling theater accessories, and just three downtown theaters. It also featured a column listing eight theaters' weekly programs, with four related production stills and a photo of the newly opened, north-side William Penn. Over the next few weeks, more industry news slipped onto the page, as new exchanges (World Film, Warner's Features) and theaters began to advertise, along with Fort Pitt Film (a local production company). Most of that news, as well as Downe's column, focused on exhibition issues and upcoming films, and rarely on stars.[191] Reduced to half a page that summer, "In the World of Films" returned to a full page in the fall, with more exchange ads (Box Office Attraction, Feature Film & Calcium—Universal), a "Gossip of the Studios" column, and fewer theater program listings.[192] Soon a "With the Local Film Folk" column joined "Gossip of the Studios," complemented by articles on local "movie men" such as A.A. Weiland and Sydney E. Abel.[193] Unlike others, the page gave equal attention to both American and foreign films (*The Virginian, The Wishing Ring, Atlantis, Love Everlasting*).[194] Only once did the *Dispatch* feature "stars" (in photos of previous stage performers), just before Charles B. Frost took over in November as "moving picture editor" and columnist.[195] Frost made few changes, retitling the two industry columns, slightly increasing the number of theater program listings and current film promotions, and, in his own column, taking a somewhat broader interest in the industry (its history, censorship issues, the labor involved in producing "big films"), all of which remained characteristic well into 1915.[196]

Almost simultaneously, a second newspaper on the West Coast, the *Sunday Oregonian,* added a half-page column devoted to motion pictures. First appearing in the Women's or Society section in April 1914, this unsigned half page had a relatively consistent format: a block of five halftones (production stills and star photos) followed by brief items of industry news and gossip, mainly about stars.[197] In early May, a young journalist, Mary Anne Smith, signed the column as editor, filling it with items culled (sometimes attributed) from the trade press.[198] Smith addressed her readers informally—"Well, well, everyone can't expect to be a scenario writer, I suppose"—and spoke of visiting half a dozen downtown theaters to find that the current "war talk, baseball talk, and Evelyn Thaw talk" was having no effect on "movie fans."[199] If she assumed fans most wanted to read about stars, Smith also tossed in unexpected tidbits: the Columbia University Journalism faculty was using news films to teach reporting techniques; Union Pacific was projecting films at the end of a Pullman car during night travel; in Tacoma, "the depiction of crime on the screen or stage" was "punished by 30 days in jail or $100 fine or both."[200] In October, the *Sunday Oregonian* turned over a full page to motion pictures, soon headlined "At the Photo-Play Theaters," with sponsoring ads for half a dozen theaters taking up half the space.[201] The page now largely served to promote local interests, with film synopses supplied by those theaters, which Smith supplemented with a bit of industry news, for instance that companies were shooting scenes at night with artificial light, or an exhibitor in Lexington was holding Saturday-morning shows for children.[202] A rare personal note aligned her with suffrage issues: she praised the suffragette film *Your Girl and Mine,* recently screened in Chicago.[203] In the spring of 1915, this page abruptly disappeared, and the *Sunday Oregonian* began subscribing to the *Chicago Sunday Tribune*'s "Right Off the Reel" page.[204] The possible reason: Smith had married a fellow reporter, but within months she became the downtown Majestic Theater's publicity manager.[205]

In June 1914, after ending its contract with Syndicate Film, the *Fort Worth Star-Telegram* introduced a regular column, "Flashes from Filmdom," edited by another young woman, Mary B. Leffler. Identified as the "circulation bragger" of the paper's "Sunday Sandwich" (four columns of miscellany on the editorial page),[206] Leffler created a relatively standardized half-page format that was typical fare for the rest of the year: a list of four or five picture theater programs for the following day, synopses of their pictures, "Comments and Criticism," and "Gossip of the Film World."[207] But there was no support from any local publicity ads. In late October, perhaps following Mae Tinee's precedent, as part of her Sunday half page, Leffler initiated a "Moving Picture Answer Column."[208] At the same time, she also began including one or more star photos with her synopses and gossip.[209] By late December, the *Star-Telegram* was printing a full page each Sunday covering "theaters and picture houses," with the latter most prominent, while "Flashes from Filmdom" continued on most weekdays.[210] The Sunday page now featured more photos of stars and current films, most of the previous menu items, and occasional articles, for instance one on Marguerite Courtot and another on *Tillie's Punctured Romance*.[211] Soon Leffler was writing special pieces on stars such as Mary Pickford, asking movie fans whether they preferred single- or multiple-reel pictures (voters heavily favored the latter), and claiming "photoplay serials" would reach their apogee in Vitagraph's *The Goddess*.[212] In May 1915, Leffler's editing efforts culminated in a Sunday page bannered "In the Photoplay World" that, along with her daily "Flashes from Filmdom," would be a special feature of the *Star-Telegram* for several years.[213]

Beginning in late August 1914, the *Atlanta Constitution* may have been the first newspaper in the Deep South to have a Sunday "Moving Picture Page" (fig. 27).[214] Although bits of industry news and gossip cropped up as filler texts,[215] this page was quite local in its orientation. Large ads from the major picture theaters (the Grand, Savoy, Montgomery, and newly opened Strand) and several exchanges (World Film, Warner's Features, Consolidated Film & Supply—for Universal) took up half of each page; synopses of films (and their stars) currently playing in those theaters occupied much of the remaining space; and local news pieces sometimes matched the broader industry items, for example a report of a local film production in which the mayor appeared, or brief items on the managers of local rental exchanges

Page Twelve M. THE CONSTITUTION, ATLANTA, GA., SUNDAY, DECEMBER 13, 1914.

THE CONSTITUTION'S MOVING PICTURE PAGE

GRAND THEATER OFFERS BIG PICTURE DRAMAS

"The Marked Woman" and "Julius Caesar" Secured for This Week.

THE MASTER KEY

SERIOUS ACCIDENTS AVERTED IN FILMING "THE MASTER KEY"

The Second Episode Furnishes Thrilling Scene at Savoy and Alpha Monday.

CAVALIERI IS COMING IN SEASON'S BIGGEST PICTURE ATTRACTION

MARGUERITE CLARK AT THE MONTGOMERY

Fascinating Actress in Strong Photo-Play on Monday and Tuesday.

How Cupid Won.

The Alpha

Monday, December 14

The Master Key

(Second Episode)

With Robert Leonard and Ella Hall in leading roles.

A beautiful story of love, romance, mystery, hate, intrigue, failure, success and human sacrifice.

ALL WEEK.

Charles La' Ford in Character Songs.

5c—Always—5c

STRONG SELIG DRAMA AT VAUDETTE TUESDAY

"Unrest" With Leading Selig Players in Cast Full of Intense Moments.

MAKOTO INOKUCHI IN "OFFICER 666"

Answers to Movie Fans.

Lloyd Has Grudge.

LILLIAN RUSSELL TO APPEAR ON SCREEN

Violet Mersereau.

EXPENSIVE DECORATIONS IN KLEINE FEATURE

TOMORROW

"The Master Key"

(2nd Episode)

With Ella Hall and Robert Leonard in the leading roles.

AT

THE SAVOY

Smiles, Tears, Sorrow, Joy

Every one of these emotions of human life vividly portrayed in this greatest and latest Universal Serial Drama.

Would YOU Have Parted From Her?

Would YOU have left the girl you loved if you were convinced her father was a murderer? What would YOU have done, if, on one side stood blighted love, lost hope and a black future, while on the other side were wealth, position and the realization of true love?

That's the terrible problem John Dore faced. It's a supremely tense situation, only to be conceived and answered by such a master mind as John Fleming Wilson, author of the "MASTER KEY."

See it tomorrow.

5c — Admission — 5c

THE Vaudette

Monday, December 14.

The Greater Love (Vitagraph.)

"The Sheriff of Willow Gulch." (Biograph.)

Hearst-Selig Weekly (No. 83.)

Tuesday, December 15

"Unrest" (Two-Reel Selig.)

"The Vanishing of Olive." No. 4 of Olive's Opportunities.

All Week

Return of the Atlanta Favorites

Jack Lamey & Joe Combs

5c—ADMISSION—5c

THE MONTGOMERY

Monday and Tuesday, December 14 and 15.

The Fascinating, Irresistible

MARGUERITE CLARK

—in—

"THE CRUCIBLE"

A stirring portrayal of an agonized soul's triumph.

ADMISSION 5c and 10c

Monday, Dec. 14th

ZUDORA

(Fourth Episode)

AT

THE STRAND

The stupendous enthusiasm that has greeted the first three installments throughout America stamps this newest Thanhouser production a phenomenal success.

Extra Attraction

Tuesday, Wednesday, Thursday, December 15, 16, 17

The Incomparable

LINA CAVALIERI

The World's Most Famous Beauty

and

LUCIEN MURATORE

The Great French Tenor and Lyric Actor

In a Superb Production of

MANON LESCAUT

Abbe Prevost's Immortal Story of Love and Romance

300 Scenes — 300 People — 6 Acts.

FIGURE 27. "Moving Picture Page," *Atlanta Sunday Constitution*, December 13, 1914.

and theaters.[216] Two things were unusual about the *Constitution*'s "Moving Picture Page." First, as if responding to readers/fans, the page gave surprising attention to current serials. Both the Savoy and Alpha promoted screenings of Universal's *The Trey O' Hearts*, and the *Constitution* offered coupons as tickets; in advance of Universal's next serial, *The Master Key*, at the same theaters, the paper also printed a long story on its writer, John Fleming

Wilson.[217] Second, borrowing a menu item from the *Chicago Tribune*, in early November the *Constitution* opened an "Answers to Movie Fans" column with similar warnings about limited space.[218] In February 1915, the Sunday page acquired a new banner, "News and Notes of the Film World," and finally named its editor, L. E. Winchell.[219] Large ads continued to support the page (Universal ballyhooed another serial, *The Black Box;* Hesser Motion Picture opened an Atlanta branch of its "School of Motion Picture Acting"), but movie star photos and profiles now gained more prominence.[220] The most important change was Britt Craig's lengthy column, "Behind the Screens," which is taken up in some detail in chapter 3.[221]

MOVIE MENUS FINALLY REACH NEW YORK AND PHILADELPHIA

Not until October 1914 did a newspaper in New York City finally join the rush to institute motion picture pages.[222] This was the *Evening Mail*, which formed a special department to publish every Saturday a column ironically titled "Motion Picture News by THE CENSOR." That column's overall objective would be "a complete review of all that is interesting and important in filmdom," and its editor would "personally visit the leading houses from time to time . . . [and] write an unbiased opinion of the merit of the various features, without fear or favor" as a service not only to "the general public but to producers and show people as well."[223] For the benefit of readers, as had the Chicago papers, the *Mail* also promised "each Monday [to] publish a complete daily programme of the leading picture houses in every district of the city." Sounding rather like Mack in the *Washington Times*, the editor meant the column to "assist theatres in choosing better programmes and directly offer more pleasing bills to the movie followers."[224] Within weeks, several New York rental exchanges and production companies began to support the column with ads: World Film, William Fox, Famous Players, Alliance, Alco, and K.C. Booking. The editor's writing style was no less colloquial and readable than Mae Tinee's, but breezy, even snappy, addressing readers directly and inviting them to share his "comments of the lighter kind": "Do you remember the 'Biograph Blonde' back in the day?"[225] He chastised the industry's unwillingness to use (and pay) newspapers to promote films in advance and ignore modern advertising principles: "All great business is built around psychology, and the average moving picture man knows as much about psychology as a cat does about operating the Cameragraph."[226] He even took Paramount to task for adding "Broadway favorites of the legitimate stage fame to their roster of stars . . . disregarding their qualifications for the screen."[227]

For several weeks in November, the *Mail*'s column not only acquired a new banner, "News and Comments of the Motion Picture World," but also lengthened to include more and more news of a broad spectrum of industry personnel.[228] In early December, it turned into a full page, retitled "The Films and Film Folk," supported by larger ads from more companies: United Film Service, Kinetophone Feature, Nicholas Power, and Universal (fig. 28).[229] Most important, THE CENSOR was identified as "Wid" Gunning, "a well known film man, who has held responsible positions with prominent motion picture companies," and who quickly began writing a daily column of local news and gossip.[230] Perhaps as expected, "Wid" made sure that he lauded advertisers such as World Film and Nicholas Powers (the latter's Cameragraph made projection booths more safe).[231] More often, however, he showed unusual interest in general issues, offering an informed summary of the current industry (including why the state rights system of distribution was ending) and criticizing the continuing practice of having moviegoers read detailed film synopses in advance.[232] Yet he did not ignore local news and comments: praising the Regent Theatre for a series of "educational matinees" organized for area public schools, chastising local musicians for inappropriate music, and refusing, on ethical grounds, to help letter writers get local industry jobs.[233] Especially significant were his attempts to influence film production: arguing that "bringing the characters so close to every one in the audience" in "close ups" was an important reason for motion pictures' popularity, criticizing films that were "too understandable" due to so many lengthy intertitles, and wondering why circulating prints had so many errors.[234] From very early on, "Wid" also picked "worth-while feature films" to review, evaluating three to six features each week according to their acting, settings, photography, story, and stars (see chapter 4).[235]

In late February 1915, "Wid" shortened the Saturday page banner to "The Films," but, perhaps to placate some readers, added small star photo profiles and kept the full banner "The Films and Film Folks" for his daily columns. The chatty, comradely patter that defined his writing style remained his strong suit, as did his undiminished interest in industry issues. Weary of spectators criticizing "little errors," he joined "a pretty party of pencil pushers—s'cuse me, most of us now use typewriters" on a tour of World Film's studio in Flushing to report more accurately on production practices."[236] That didn't stop him from keeping up a steady stream of critical remarks aimed at industry insiders, from admonishing stage actors who failed to make an effort when acting for the screen to wishing that manufacturers would quit adding "a long 'cast' at a film's beginning" or the name of a character to a dialogue intertitle, and asking why "title writers" couldn't have their characters speak in "a

SATURDAY THE EVENING MAIL DECEMBER 12 1914

THE FILMS AND FILM FOLK

by "WID"

FAVORITES OF THE FILM FANS.

REVIEW OF PHOTO-PLAY FEATURES

MUSIC NOTES.

Was There a Reason? Just Think It Over

Anthony P. Kelly New Universal Scenario Chief

Lubin & Laemmle Secure Clara Kimball Young

FIGURE 28. "The Films and Film Folk" page, *New York Evening Mail*, December 12, 1914.

natural conversational style."[237] His typewriter could crank out words of praise, too, now that "the 'feature' has arrived," as in certain Paramount films playing a full week at the Broadway Theater.[238] Perhaps his industry connections let "Wid" argue that three production personnel were most responsible for a film's success: the producer (that is, the director), cameraman, and editor.[239] Anticipating Andrew Sarris by nearly half a century, he even listed his top thirty American directors, beginning with D.W. Griffith, Herbert Brenon, Ralph Ince, Maurice Tourneur, Mack Sennett, and Lois Weber.[240] Given his earlier experience in sales and advertising for Éclair, he also lauded publicity men such as Joe Brandt (Universal) and Harry Reichenbach (Metro/Equitable).[241]

"Wid" blew hot and cold in his observations about theater programming and audiences. He advocated a "'locked reel' booking plan, or booking by personal representative" to ensure a "balanced bill"—by which he meant "a feature film, a short drama, a short comedy, a news film, and an educational or travelogue"—selected by the exhibitor.[242] To counter "fool" projectionists, he argued for "a law regulating the speed at which films should be projected," with the added need for a "regulator placed upon all projection machines."[243] He rapped the knuckles of drummers who "'horned in' at the wrong time with an 'effect'" and called orchestras that "got in wrong" with their music "decidedly 'off key.'"[244] Especially catching his eye were the girl ushers at the Brighton Beach Music Hall, whom the manager chose by means of a beauty contest.[245] Ignorant remarks by wealthy spectators especially offended him: after watching three reels of *Keeping John Barleycorn Off the Trains,* one businessman said to another, "I don't see anything in this about keeping tramps off the trains"; viewing a "news film of the burning of oil tanks in Sebastopol," a woman piped up, "Oh, that is faked! Don't you remember when we came through all of that country?"[246] Again like Gardner Mack, he took pains to respect "all you fans" of neighborhood theaters—which "belong to you"—and prodded them to "make a kick" when they saw something they didn't like.[247] Any contradictions aside, "Wid" still believed that the cinema was unique because it could bring together all classes of people (previously separated according to different attractions) into a single mass audience.[248]

In August, Gunning left the *Mail,* eventually to launch *Wid's Daily* in 1917, and George F. Worts took over as motion picture editor, at least for the next nine months.[249] His signed column, however, often appeared under the larger "Drama" column edited by the theater critic Burns Mantle.[250] Worts followed Gunning's practice of reviewing new film titles (see chapter 4), occasionally included stories about the more popular stars (see chapter 3), and took positions on industry issues, sometimes through a local lens. His advice to would-be scenario writers could be ambiguous. Lasky supposedly no longer read "amateur" work, and, "in desperation," Universal had turned to professionals; yet a young woman he knew in the city was earning "$200 a reel for her scenarios."[251] He summed up what scenario editors wanted—"ideas worked out in terse . . . sentences that 'pack the punch'"—and bluntly warned all to avoid "schools which teach photoplay writing by correspondence."[252] Would-be-actors, likewise, he said should shun correspondence schools, citing the fictional example of a deluded "little fifteen-year-old girl."[253] And he joined those who protested the Knickerbocker's strategy, after the success of *The Birth of a Nation,* of adopting an admission price of two dollars for the new Triangle features.[254] Perhaps most intriguing was Worts's far-from-impartial reporting on the audiences for "German war pictures."[255] In September, at the Forty-Fourth Street Theatre, police were called to bring order to a veritable "Teuton army" of moviegoers viewing *The German Side of the War,* who roared their approval and, in the end, were "grimly enthusiastic."[256] Two months later,

"Three battalions of war pictures took up their position on Broadway": *Fighting for France* at the Cohan, *Fighting in France* at the Fulton, and *The Battles of a Nation* at the Park.[257] In January 1916, at the Park, an allegedly impartial *Europe's Reign of Terror,* sponsored by the *Mail,* led Worts to claim that "Americans as a whole are neutral."[258] That did not stop "a Frenchman and a German" in the audience from getting into their own "hand-to-hand conflict."[259]

Shortly after the *Mail* introduced the "Motion Picture News" column in late 1914, a similar Saturday column bannered "Photo Plays" appeared in the *Philadelphia Evening Ledger.*[260] This column first gained the advertising support of local theaters rather than exchanges: the Chestnut Street Opera House screening of *The Spoilers;* the Palace, of *Cabiria;* and Loew's Knickerbocker, episodes of Thanhouser's serial *Zudora.*[261] Although relatively unconcerned with news or gossip about stars, the *Ledger* did follow most other papers in catching readers' eyes each week with a few large publicity photos at the top of each page. As it gradually increased in length to half a page, the column adopted familiar menu items from the Chicago papers: a calendar of additional theaters showing a feature or serial episode that day and a request for questions from readers that could be addressed in "Answers to Correspondents."[262] In line with the ads and theater listings, local or regional news was prominent: brief stories on Henry H. Hoyt's early projector invention; Thomas Edison's "Black Maria" (with a photo); an inmate's letter extolling the effect of *The Sign of the Cross* shown in his prison chapel; and World Film's *Your Girl and Mine,* a suffrage film, booked at the Victoria for a full week."[263] Yet news of a broader interest was hardly excluded: the French government's contract with Pathé-Frères for "official" war pictures, some taken by "camera women"; statements by industry figures such as Adolph Zukor, Thomas Ince, and Samuel Goldfish; and a nationwide effort by "mothers societies" to have theater managers organize special "children's matinees," especially in neighborhoods where schools and churches were beginning to exhibit motion pictures.[264]

Perhaps spurred by large ads for the "prominent personalities" and "photo plays" of the city's Lubin Manufacturing Company, in late March 1915 the *Ledger* expanded its coverage of motion pictures to a full page.[265] Half of that page soon filled with industry ads crowding out those of the picture theaters, both from major companies (Lubin, Vitagraph, Edison, World Film) and local firms (Feature Film Exchange, Eclectic Theatre Supply, Foreign Film, Art Film). There were even ads for a local weekly, *Photo-Play Review,* once specially featuring Victor Eubank's *Charlie Chaplin's Life.*[266] As a consequence, industry news loomed larger, from interviews with Mack

Sennett, Blanche Sweet, and D.W. Griffith to ads for James Cruze's guidebook on acting and Epes Winthrop Sargent's *Technique of the Photoplay.*[267] In contrast to "Wid," the *Ledger*'s unnamed editor also singled out the artistry of the "playwrights of the moving pictures," perhaps in response to recent books on scenario writing or to Louella Parsons's column in the *Chicago Herald,* and he was one of the first to cite the U.S. Census Bureau as ranking the motion picture industry the fifth largest in the country, based on its annual production of "10,000 separate reels of negative film, from each of which reels 55 copies of 'positive' film, on an average, are made."[268] A few local news items did make it into the page, for instance motion pictures as a teaching aid for nervous diseases at the Philadelphia College of Osteopathy.[269] Finally, in mid-June 1915, the *Ledger* published a special sixteen-page "Photoplay Section" that celebrated local luminaries such as Siegmund Lubin and Stanley Mastbaum (owner of fifty area picture theaters) and named Edgar Mels as "Photoplay Editor," assisted by Kenneth Macgowan, its "Dramatic Editor."[270] This "experiment," as described by the *Ledger*'s later photoplay editor, P.R. Plough, however, did not have immediate consequences.[271]

It was not until late October 1915 that the *Ledger* introduced a special Saturday "Amusement Section" covering "photoplay, dancing, theatres, and music" in its dozen pages, with photoplay articles, ads, and photos usually comprising half of those pages (fig. 29).[272] The initial week's section established a format and set of contents that would distinguish the newspaper for the rest of the year. A featured photoplay article took up half of each first page: for instance an argument by the "Ledger's critic" countering Walter Prichard Eaton's attack on the photoplay in the *Boston Transcript;* a report on the scenario-writing course at Columbia University; or an article on painter C. Allan Gilbert's plan to produce a "silhouette movie."[273] Photos dominated the second page, half of them depicting current productions; others (of actors as well) were scattered throughout. Industry news articles filled some pages and slipped into others: "Tully Marshall on the Movies," "Sing Sing Convict Wins Photoplay Contest," and "The New Broadway of the Movies" (meaning, Los Angeles).[274] One regular column, "Theatrical Baedeker," listed "new feature films" at major picture theaters; another was a collective ad for dozens of current programs handled by the Stanley Booking Company.[275] The photoplay editor also offered jottings in an irregular column, titled either "The Photoplay Man-About-Town" or "With the Exhibitors."[276] All of this was supported in part by ads from Lubin and Pathé Exchange, several small exchanges, and a few prominent picture theaters, for example *The Birth of a Nation* at the Forrest, *The Battle Cry*

Evening Ledger

PHOTOPLAY DANCING | AMUSEMENT SECTION | THEATRES and MUSIC

PHILADELPHIA, SATURDAY EVENING, OCTOBER 16, 1915

THE PLAYWRIGHT INTERVIEWS HIMSELF FOR THE PRESS AGENT

The Author of "Under Cover" Submits to an Auto-Interview, but Refuses to Discuss "The Decay of the Drama"

By ROI COOPER MEGRUE

Continued on Page Eight

WHY I WENT INTO MOTION PICTURES TO PUT "CARMEN" ON THE SCREEN

The Noted Prima Donna Tells How She Found a Phantom Audience to Act To and How She Felt the Thrill of a New Art

By GERALDINE FARRAR

GERALDINE FARRAR'S CARMEN

Shakespeare the First Scenario Writer

By JOHN EMERSON

FIGURE 29. "Amusement Section," *Philadelphia Evening Ledger*, October 16, 1915.

for Peace at the Metropolitan Opera House, and Geraldine Farrar in *Carmen* at the Garden.[277] With few exceptions, then, the *Ledger*'s photoplay editor initially seemed concerned with selecting industry news focused on stage actors who were turning to photoplays, as well as particular feature films.

NEWSPAPERS MAKE PICTURE-GOERS FROM COAST TO COAST (2)

On the opposite coast, Los Angeles may have been the emerging center of "movie land," at least in producing its fantasies,[278] but the city's newspapers were slow to show much interest in moviegoers. In 1914–15, to be sure, both the *Los Angeles Herald* and *Los Angeles Examiner* carried large ads for the Pathé serials *The Perils of Pauline* and *The Exploits of Elaine*, along with their fictional tie-ins.[279] A Hearst paper, the *Herald*, also printed story episodes of Eclectic releases such as *War* (Alfred Machin's *Cursed Be War*) and *Loyalty*.[280] Occasionally the *Herald* prominently displayed unsigned photo stories of movie actors, including girls in local juvenile productions.[281] In late August 1914, the *Examiner* began to augment Otheman Stevens's theater page each Sunday with short descriptions of the "film plays" or "moving pictures" at eight to twelve major theaters.[282] As in other papers, photos of current films and stars supplemented those descriptions, supported by the theaters' ads, especially the flagships of the Tally and Clune chains.[283] Not until early 1915 did the *Herald* introduce a "Motion Plays and Pictures" page in its Saturday edition.[284] That page seemed to imitate the *Examiner*'s half page with program descriptions of many of the same picture theaters, framed by a long column of their ads. Although no editor was named, the page did include a column written by Guy Price (apparently no relation to Gertrude Price), who previously had written about local legitimate theaters in a weekly "Facts and Fables of the Foyer."[285] Rather than adopt "Matinee Girl," the sobriquet for the stage-struck female of yore, Price flippantly dubbed any female fan who sent him a letter or query a "Movie Molly."[286]

Beginning in January 1915, the *Birmingham Age-Herald* may have been the second newspaper in the Deep South to establish a motion picture page in its Sunday edition.[287] Initially bannered "With the Local Photoplay Houses" and edited by Ellis C. Hollums, its focus and format were similar to that of the *Pittsburgh Leader* and *Buffalo Times*. Nearly all of the lengthy columns and the limited number of small photos featured the films and stars appearing that week in at least four theaters—the Trianon, Odeon,

Odeon Two, and Princess—that regularly placed relatively large ads on the page. In case readers wanted to cut out a crib sheet, another column listed in small type the daily film titles playing at those same theaters. Readers also could find local-interest stories: E.H. Colley now owned the Princess theater and was contracting with General Film; the new Majestic Theater opened with a program of Paramount features; and all the theaters screened special programs one Sunday and shared profits with the city's poor, in support of a petition to the city commission allowing them to operate regularly on Sunday afternoons.[288] Sometimes industry stories could fill out a page, from a star profile of Mary Pickford or Pearl White to news that VLSE would release "great feature pictures" to the Odeon Two.[289] Joining the latter stories were occasional ads for Reliance's serial *Runaway June,* or the booklet *Be a Movie Actor* by "master instructor" James Cruze.[290] Hollums's name vanished from the masthead in early April; in late October 1915 the Sunday page gained a new permanent editor, Richard F. Lussier, who also immediately introduced a daily column, "Footlights and Screen," largely filled with motion picture news and gossip and short reviews (see chapter 4).[291]

Two weeks after taking over, Lussier recast the Sunday page with a new boldface banner, "Film Love Casts," and four large, framed photos of movie actors, sometimes in production stills.[292] The rest of the page remained mostly the same in its focus on local programming despite fewer theater ads, but those migrated to the paper's Wednesday edition, bannered "At the Photoplay Houses."[293] In his daily "Footlights and Screen" column, Lussier inserted items of special interest to the city's moviegoers. He described the effect of American's adaptation of the French play *Damaged Goods* as analogous to "the fiendish agony" perpetrated by a dentist who keeps "digging at the nerve" of a tooth, but then urged everyone to see it: "It educates the weak and serves as a warning to the strong."[294] The Strand's first Triangle films, notably Douglas Fairbanks's *The Lamb,* elicited exceptional applause from large crowds.[295] Essanay's *The Raven* may have been a mediocre film, but moviegoers flocked to the Trianon to see Henry B. Walthall, who claimed Birmingham as his home.[296] In late December, *The Birth of a Nation* was a sellout at the Jefferson theater (at one dollar a ticket), and the *Age-Herald* sponsored a matinee for "Confederate veterans";[297] yet weeks later Lussier reported that audiences thought Vitagraph's *The Battle Cry of Peace* "slightly overshadowed" Griffith's epic "in dramatic thrills" and convinced him that all the "peace talk" about the European war "was nothing but pure and simple bunk."[298] Like other writers beholden to local interests, he celebrated the opening of a new theater, the Colonial, with its "interior decorations . . . of old rose, in contrast with gray" and "an artistic ladies' parlor on the second floor."[299] By contrast, he floated the idea that the *Age-Herald* should hand out "brickbats disguised as bouquets" so moviegoers could pummel automatic pianos and those who read captions aloud and added explanations.[300] Finally, exhorting exhibitors to "advertise—and then advertise some more," Lussier claimed that his column should convince them of "the virile fact that advertising in The Age-Herald pays."[301]

In early 1915, the *Augusta Chronicle* ended its syndicated subscription to the *Chicago Tribune*'s "In the Frame of Public Favor" and had an unnamed editor establish its own Sunday page, bannered "With the Photoplays and Players."[302] This page settled into a standardized format resembling that of the *Toledo Times* and was convenient for reading.[303] Large double-column ads for the Dreamland and Modjeska theaters' weekly programs occupied the top left and right, respectively, with another double-column ad for the Strand's weekly programs centered at the bottom. Lengthy descriptions of those programs, probably supplied by theater managers, filled much of the rest of the page, supplemented by publicity photos or poster images of stars and current films. As with other papers, brief news items often served as column "fillers." Some were of local interest: large crowds attended the last episode of *The Master Key* (despite heavy rain); patrons persuaded the Strand's manager to book a return showing of *Hypocrites;* the Strand and Modjeska held successful "children's day" screenings.[304] Others offered bits of industry news: *The Birth of a Nation* was a sensation in New York; Lois Weber and Phillips Smalley were drawing ideas from newspaper editorials for their films.[305] A short column, "Film Fancies," also enticed readers with tiny snippets of gossip about the stars. But the *Augusta Chronicle*'s interest remained local, further evidenced in a daily column of program synopses under the banner "In Movie Land," borrowed from the *Chicago Tribune* but with the name now given a newly local habitation.[306]

Farther west along the Gulf Coast, in April 1915, the *New Orleans Item* assigned an unnamed editor to assuage fans with a Sunday page promoting the movies.[307] This page was designed with a balance (both spatial and numerical) of local picture theater ads and industry production stills (half a dozen each) as well as columns of theater program synopses and "filler" industry news. Within a month, readers could consult a calendar of daily programs at a dozen theaters.[308] In July, new columns—"Facts About Future Releases," "Picture Players—Purely Personal," and "Little Stories Gathered from Local Theaters" (all actually rather generic)—began to reorient the page slightly, supported by ads from the regional offices of Universal (for its serial, *The Broken Coin*), World Film, and Metro.[309] That reorientation continued after the page acquired a consistent banner, "The Item's Movie Page," as local ads declined, the "Little Stories" column disappeared, and industry news and gossip about stars became more prominent (fig. 30).[310] In November, an *Item* editorial congratulated its own pioneering work (at least regionally) in "devoting a page of space weekly to the moving picture."[311] It also announced "a daily column, giving the news of the moving picture business," and, in early 1916, expanded its Sunday coverage to two full pages.[312] More theaters took out ads to support this expansion, particularly the new Triangle Theatre (presenting Triangle films) and the Crescent, an exclusive venue for "Paramount Features." And the newly named editor, R. E. Pritchard, contributed a column, "Says the Movie Editor," in which he defended the *Item*'s choice of "movies" for its banner—because that was the public's "name of affection"—and encouraged "fans" to read the "Daily Movies" column.[313] Because those fans were more and more interested in stars, in April the *Item* offered readers free "beautiful art portraits of motion picture stars," one each Sunday for the next sixteen weeks.[314] Pritchard also promoted the city and its environs as ideal for companies in need of "genuine" location scenery.[315]

In late 1915, even farther west, the *Salt Lake Tribune*'s Sunday edition carried on the insistent lure of alliteration with a "Fancies and Features of the Films" page.[316] The format resembled that of the *Pittsburgh Leader* and *Fort Worth Star-Telegram* in that columns of text dominated the page, with several large star photos and production stills (clustered or separated) at the top and smaller ones arranged near the bottom. Instead of placing ads, half a dozen picture theaters supplied synopses of their programs in short columns, expanding on what already was listed in a top corner box—sometimes offering a separate story for each of several specific films.[317] This local orientation remained typical, but the unnamed editor did include some broader industry news and gossip. That came initially in a column titled "About Players, Pictures and Everything," soon retitled "Melange of the Movies," and another, "Who's Who in the Movies," that first profiled not stars but filmmakers, namely Griffith and Ince.[318] The editor also reprinted stories such as a spirited rebuttal by John C. Flinn (of the Lasky Company) to Eaton's attack on the movies in *American Magazine*, a defense of higher admission prices for feature films by George E. Carpenter, and a claim by Cecil B. DeMille that the music accompanying a film's exhibition must not distract from the emotional impact of its lighting effects.[319]

The Item's Movie Page

BIG $1,000,000 PICTURE PLANT FOR N. Y. CITY

Famous Players' Company Makes Huge Investment and Shows Its Faith in Future of Movies.

PHOTOGRAPHS show scenes from the war pictures at Pearce's Trianon; Nat Goodwin, in "Business is Business," at Fichtenberg's Dreamworld, and Ernst Boehringer, manager of the beautiful new moving picture palace, the Columbia, at Canal and Burgundy streets. The war pictures are of actual warfare and are said to be the best ever brought here.

HERE'S MOVIE LEADING MAN HATING GIRLS

"They're No Good," Verdict of Georgie Stone, 6-Year-Old Star of "Kid" Plays. Child Takes Many Risks.

PEARCE SHOWS WAR PICTURES, TWO ORPHANS

Former Appears on Screen at Trianon and Latter at Tudor; Little Mary Pickford Will Be Seen at Bijou Dream.

'Tillie's Punctured Romance'—Columbia

GOODWIN IN 'BUSINESS' AT DREAMWORLD

Picture Players—Purely Personal

COLUMBIA THEATRE

"NEAL OF THE NAVY"

"Tillie's Punctured Romance"

PEARCE'S MOTION PICTURE THEATRES

Week Commencing Sunday, Sept. 12

TUDOR 610-612 CANAL ST.	TRIANON 814 CANAL ST.
SUNDAY Fox 5 Reels Drama "The Two Orphans" Featuring Theda Bara.	SUNDAY Special 5 Reels EUROPEAN WAR PICTURES Official German Films.
MONDAY, TUESDAY AND WEDNESDAY Vitagraph 4 Reels Drama "Island of Regeneration" Featuring Edith Story and Leo Delaney	MONDAY, TUESDAY AND WEDNESDAY. Lasky 5 Reels Drama "THE CASE OF BECKY" Featuring Blanche Sweet
THURSDAY, FRIDAY, SATURDAY AND SUNDAY Fox 5 Reels Drama "The Song of Hate" Featuring Dorothy Bernard and Betty Nansen	THURSDAY AND FRIDAY Metro 5 Reels Drama "THE SOUL OF A WOMAN" Featuring Emily Stevens. SATURDAY AND SUNDAY Comedy Special 4 Reels Comedy "AMBITION" Featuring Charles Chaplin

SPECIAL ANNOUNCEMENT

Popular Theatres That Will Show the Universal Film Manufacturing Company's Latest Serial Success.

THE BROKEN COIN

15 WEEKS 30 REELS

Alamo Theatre	1027 Canal—Monday
Picto	Canal and St. Charles—Sunday
Hippodrome	522 Baronne—Sunday
Washington	Washington and Magazine—Tuesday
Escorial	Banks and Salcedo—Saturday
Arcade	2519 St. Ann—Monday
Carrollton	Canal and Carrollton—Tuesday
Keystone	St. Andrew near Magazine—Wednesday
Royal	1005 Royal—Thursday
Colonial	1800 Cambronne—Friday
Market	Algiers—Wednesday
Sardonyx	St. Ferdinand and Marais—Thursday
Hip Airdome	Dauphine and Congress—Friday
Bell	Dorgenois and Bell—Saturday
Mars	St. Roch and Roman—Tuesday
Napoleon	Napoleon and Camp—Thursday
Magic	Josephine and Freret—Saturday
Ruby	2230 Dauphine—Tuesday
Thelma	5400 Magazine—Thursday
Bonita	Elysian Fields and Roman—Saturday
Iberville	Iberville and Rocheblave—Monday
Trymore	4104 Magnolia—Tuesday
Palace	Third Near Dryades—Wednesday
Elm	8212 Elm—Saturday
Rex	Magazine and Seventh—Friday

Yours for Universal Peace

Consolidated Film & Supply Company

PHONE MAIN 304. ASK FOR FEATURE CLERK. SHE WILL TELL YOU WHAT THE ABOVE THEATRES ARE PLAYING ANY DAY YOU REQUEST.

METRO PICTURES

PRESENTS THE BIGGEST 4

MME. PETROVA · MARY MILES MINTER · FRANCIS X. BUSHMAN · WILLIAM FAVERSHAM

Constituting the most formidable quartet of stars ever offered as permanent attractions on any program.

SOUTHERN METRO PICTURES CORPORATION

NAT C. GOODWIN

DISTINGUISHED AMERICAN ACTOR IN THE FILM EVENT OF THE YEAR

FICHTENBERG'S DREAMWORLD Canal and St. Charles Sts. 1 WEEK COM. TODAY

"BUSINESS IS BUSINESS" Octave Mirbeau's Famous French Tragedy.

"And My Own Child Called Me Judas" THE PICTURE THAT WILL HAVE EVERYONE TALKING.

COMING NEXT SUNDAY FOR ONE WEEK Elinor Glynn's Famous Novel of Supreme Passion "THREE WEEKS"

FIGURE 30. "Item's Movie Page," *New Orleans Sunday Item*, September 12, 1915.

Although the *Tribune* valued "Fancies and Features of the Films," in a Sunday edition ad, the page ranked far lower than "Right Off the Reel" in the *Chicago Sunday Tribune*.[320]

Just north of Salt Lake City, the *Ogden Standard*'s Saturday coverage of motion pictures underwent very different changes. In May 1915, a year after its contract with Leslie's Syndicate Film ended, the paper instituted a two-page spread, bannered "What's Doing in the World of Footlights, Spotlights, Photoplays" (no editor was named).[321] These pages generally included a balanced mix of articles on plays and photoplays (including a "Movie" jokes column), sponsored almost entirely by ads from the city's main picture theaters.[322] An equally balanced mix of feature films, serials, and stars typified the photoplay texts and photos.[323] Early that fall, "What's Doing Next Week at Playhouses" turned into "With the Movies," summarizing the weekly programs of the six or seven advertising theaters.[324] This increasing attention to motion pictures also meant longer articles on stars such as Anita Stewart, Francis Ford, and Dustin Farnum.[325] In early January 1916, the *Standard*'s coverage shifted to its "Saturday Magazine" in a full page bannered "The Photoplay Forum."[326] Most of this new weekly page now came syndicated from the *St. Louis Globe-Democrat*: prominent star photo profiles, A.H. Giebler's column "As to Photoplay Writing," and his syndicated series of satirical dialogues and short stories about the comic adventures he supposedly experienced while seeking to become a screen actor (see the next section of this chapter).[327]

In mid-November 1915, just as the *New Orleans Item* was boasting of its pioneering work, the *New Orleans Times-Picayune* got into the motion picture game with a daily column, "News of the Photoplays."[328] This unsigned column could be quite informal in its direct address to readers: "You don't have to have a burning ship, a railroad wreck or some other manifestation of human calamity to tear up the landscape in order to produce a very acceptable picture."[329] Within a week the newspaper added a Sunday page, whose simple banner soon turned into "News of the Photoplays and the Photoplayers,"[330] and whose tone was very different. An initial paragraph justified the page with extravagant claims for the "healing" power of what on thousands of screens "seems more real than reality itself."[331] For several months, the unnamed editor lined the top of the page with artfully framed star photos, filled the rest with industry news and gossip, mostly reprinted—for instance a long, chatty piece on Pauline Frederick; praise for Famous Players shooting a film on location in Savannah, Georgia; recognition that churches and schools were using motion pictures for educational purposes; a dubious claim that audiences were tiring of features and wanted more short films—except for a small box listing "Features for the Week."[332] As more local stories appeared—stars who came from the area (Mary Miles Minter, Irene Fenwick); New Orleans as a regional "motion picture center"—

picture theaters began to support the page with ads.[333] By late February 1916, much of the page now catered to local interests, as in the photo spread of "Popular New Orleans Film Exchange Managers" and a Fox Film official celebrating the taste and judgment of Southern audiences.[334]

THE MIDWEST MARKET FOR MOVIE MENUS CONTINUES TO BOOM

Just as the Midwest had been the region so favorably disposed to the initial crop of weekend movie pages, so was it again in 1915. Surprisingly, several small-town newspapers added weekly columns or pages, often for the benefit of local theater owners as much as readers.[335] One of these first appeared in the *La Crosse Tribune* (Wisconsin) in February 1915: "Week's Offerings in Movieland as Seen in La Crosse," edited by a young reporter, N.D. Tevis.[336] From early on, Tevis assured his readers that anyone in the town could be "a Reel Fan": "You do not have to go to New York to see a good moving picture" (or "movie," actually his preferred term).[337] He concisely differentiated theaters that showed features (the Bijou and Casino) from those that held onto a variety format (the Star and Dome),[338] and from the Lyric, whose films appealed "to the lover of the startling and the melodramatic." He also each week highlighted several "best pictures," pointing out for instance in early March that Mary Pickford's *Cinderella* attracted "the largest audience in three years" at the Bijou.[339] He even took the rare position of questioning *The Birth of a Nation*'s depiction of the "black man [as] even blacker than the blackness of his skin" and wondered whether the "negroes of La Crosse [would] revolt" against the film (as they had in St. Paul and Janesville), and yet admitted his own fascination with the "world's greatest film production."[340] In January 1916, his column became part of "The Tribune's Saturday Feature Page," and he named the first week's directory of programs "Menu Today at Local Film Houses."[341] Within a month, "Week's Offering in Movieland" was taking up two-thirds of that page, with added items such as a "Filmy Stuff" column and a row of six or seven cameo star photos.[342] Tevis himself now posted specially framed commentaries, whose titles drew on movie lingo: "Closeups," "Cutbacks," "The Movie Lens," "Reel-Offs."[343] After a year, he concluded this about his weekly page: "The best use to which this department can be put is when it serves the purpose of a weekly directory of the movie game," that is, as "a barometer" for readers of local theaters and programs.[344]

THE MINNEAPOLIS SUNDAY TRIBUNE: MAY 2 1915

THE SILENT DRAMA

PHOTO PLAY NEWS FOR THE MOTION PICTURE LOVER

HEADLINE MOVIES THIS WEEK.

LYRIC—Dustin Farnum in "Captain Courtesy."
STRAND—Theda Bara in "The Clemenceau Case."
NEW GARRICK—"The Christian."
ISIS—"Almost a King."
SEVILLE—J. Warren Kerrigan in "For Cash."
PRINCESS—Mary Fuller in "The Honor of the Ormsbys."
REGENT—"The Mysterious Airship."

Film Men Will Mix Business and Pleasure in Minneapolis Convention

New Grand Patrons Have a Chance to Win $10,000

ANSWERS TO MOVIE FANS

WAR'S EFFECT ON THE MOVIES.

Theda Bara in "The Clemenceau Case" at the Strand.

Blanche Sweet, to appear at the Lyric in "The Captive."

FIGURE 31. "The Silent Drama" page, *Minneapolis Sunday Tribune*, May 2, 1915.

No longer contracted with Leslie's Film Syndicate, in early 1915 the *Minneapolis Tribune* assigned an unnamed writer to edit a Sunday page under a banner that flagged motion pictures' legitimacy: "The Silent Drama" (fig. 31).[345] With ads from at least eight theaters, this page was a composite of local program synopses, bits of industry news and gossip, star photos and production stills, and an "Answers to Movie Fans" column.[346] Most weeks there was a lengthy featured story, whose subject occasionally was national, for example a New York minister who resigned his pulpit to write movie scenarios; the coming debut of opera star Geraldine Farrar in *Carmen;* or Vachel Lindsay's "Epitaph for John Bunny" (syndicated by the *Chicago Herald*).[347] Along with the story on Farrar were more photo profiles on stars such as Clara Kimball Young, Marguerite Clark, Mary Pickford, and Fannie Ward.[348] But the majority of stories addressed local interests: reports on the Motion Picture Exhibitors of the Northwest convention, local exhibitors' opposition to film censorship, a series of special film programs for children, the lifting of a ban on screening *Hypocrites,* the city's eye specialists concluding that motion pictures do not harm one's sight.[349] There also were frequent notices and ads for the *Northwest Weekly,* a regional newsreel that the *Tribune* itself produced and distributed (see the first entr'acte).[350] In late August, the paper changed the Sunday page banner to the more popular "Movies"—once even "Movie Menu"—and added new columns sometimes printed on a second page.[351] Among the latter were "Gossip of Film Favorites," "Bits of News for Movie Fans," and a graphic box of "What You Can See This Week" at six of the city's leading picture theaters, as well as a rare admission that "press agents" signed the weekly column of program synopses.[352]

The *Tribune*'s Sunday page underwent a number of changes during 1916. The banner title kept shifting, often between "Movies" and "At the Movie Houses," and once adopted the imaginary space of "Movieland."[353] In late June, it settled on "Cinemas," one of the earliest uses of a term that would later become common.[354] Besides the synopses of local program listings, the page now had little other than industry news and gossip, such as a photo profile of Louise Glaum's gowns in *The Wolf Woman,* a reprint of David Belasco's interview on "the movies," and an anonymous weekly column titled "Little Stories of the Stars."[355] Two of the more interesting were an unsigned article on one hundred women from the upper Midwest (all named) who planned to attend the Motion Picture Exhibitors Convention in the city[356] and a syndicated piece heralding the General Federation of Women's Clubs' "Better Movies" movement.[357] Another column of brief industry items that cropped up irregularly was "Screenings by Anna Mait"; the name may well have been a pseudonym for "animate," not unlike Mae Tinee's.[358] The most important column first appeared in late August, "Motion Pictures by Philip H. Welch," which soon became a daily feature.[359] Whether or not Welch edited the Sunday page remains uncertain, but his column offered moviegoers an unusual mix of astute commentary and reviews of individual films (see chapter 4).

If few substantive changes marked well-established newspaper pages from Buffalo and Pittsburgh to Toledo and Chicago, they were noteworthy in Cleveland. Relocated to the "Dramatic" section and still often supported by dozens of theater ads and a cluster of star photos, the *Cleveland Leader*'s Sunday page, in June 1915, introduced a series of industry news articles by Archie Bell, who may have taken over as editor from Stoddard: Wall Street investment in Aitken's new Triangle Film Corporation; state censorship of *The Devil's Daughter,* starring Theda Bara; the threat to the legitimate theater because its stars were abandoning the stage for the movies; and claims that more people now saw films than read best-selling fiction.[360] In October, a new daily page devoted to "Society," "Theaters," and "Clubs" had Bell signing the "Theaters" columns, half of which were devoted to motion pictures.[361] Surprisingly, the *Leader* now followed other papers in sponsoring a "Movie

Talent Contest" in which forty girls would compete for a potential acting career with Metro (see the second entr'acte).[362] That contest coincided with an increasing number of long articles on individual stars—George Beban, Theda Bara, Geraldine Farrar, Mary Pickford, and others—written mostly by Bell with a few signed by John D. Raridan.[363] At the same time, the *Leader* published a syndicated series by Anita Stewart on her "road to fame in the movies" as well as more photos of "favorite stars," including the "Rotogravure Supplement" on a full page opposite another of production photos exemplifying "Art and the Films."[364] In general, the *Leader* seemed to shift away from its initial interest in local matters to offer all kinds of "insider" information on the larger industry and its stars, perhaps in response to readers/fans and apparently with the tacit approval of picture theaters, which continued to support the Sunday page with a large number of ads.

The *Cleveland Plain Dealer*'s Sunday page, by contrast, saw an increase in matters of more local interest. In early January 1915, the unnamed photoplay editor asked exhibitors to send in comments on current problems and introduced a "Question Box" column that quickly flooded his office with hundreds of letters from movie fans.[365] During the spring, the newspaper printed a full page on the Liberty Theater's opening in the eastern suburbs, a photo profile of Marguerite Clark as a "full-fledged Ohioan," and a contest soliciting from readers the best letter explaining why they had a favorite movie actor or actress.[366] The most important changes occurred almost simultaneously with those at the *Sunday Leader*. Drawn perhaps too closely from Mae Tinee's innovation in the *Chicago Sunday Tribune*, the *Plain Dealer* featured a prominent star photo profile, "In the Frame of Public Favor" (the frame did differ), and asked readers to vote on which star best deserved that "public favor."[367] This "Frame" lasted only two months, but, like the *Leader*, the *Plain Dealer* correlated a cluster of star photos with its weekly program synopses, which closely matched a dozen or more picture theater ads.[368] In late August, the "photo play editor" was identified as E. Arthur Roberts, who not only continued the "Question Box" column but also began contributing a series of featured articles whose subjects ranged from Ohio censorship issues and Cleveland's importance as a "leading photo play city" to the strain put on Theda Bara in playing "vampire" roles and, echoing "Wid," the "flagrant disregard for correctness of detail" that marred even the finest films.[369] By early 1916, the *Plain Dealer* was challenging its rival with a daily half page, signed by Roberts and flaunting that familiar banner, "News of Photo Plays and Players."[370]

Much like other papers, the *St. Louis Globe-Democrat* had been reprinting the *Chicago Tribune*'s syndicated "Right Off the Reel" pages[371] until mid-

August 1915, when an unnamed editor substituted his or her own Sunday magazine page bannered "The Photoplay Forum: What's What and Who's Who in Movie Land."[372] This page still followed Mae Tinee's format, with a central star photo profile—these included Bessie Barricale, Myrtle Stedman, Mabel Normand, J. Warren Kerrigan, and Marguerite Clark[373]—and columns titled "Answers to Fans" and "Film Facts." Featured, however, were two columns written by A.H. Giebler: "As to Photoplay Writing," in which he gave tongue-in-cheek suggestions to letter writers, and another that focused on a different subject each week. One of the latter, "How Would You Like to Be a Movie Star," stitched together sarcastic observations that described a studio stage as "a sort of superlative crazy house" peopled by "the looniest lunatics of Looney Land."[374] His specialty was the satirical conversation between a movie player and a fan, as in "Her First Part: A Movie Dialogue" and "Movie Mail: A Dialogue."[375] This turned into "Letters from a Correspondence School Actor," Giebler's long-running serial fiction in which a supposedly successful actor regaled a fan with comic fantasies of his escapades in "movie land."[376] In late 1915, the Sunday page bannered unsigned featured stories for weeks, including "War on the Film Censors Is Begun by Producers" and "Motion Picture Kisses Measured by the Foot Rule" (defined by "kissing rules").[377] In early 1916, a series of banners linked to the week's star photo profile began to snag readers with catchy phrases: "Queen of the Cowboy Movies [Anna Little]," "Putting 'Pep' in Motion Pictures [Virginia Pearson]," "A Flash in Motion Pictures [Jackie Saunders]."[378] Because it rarely showed any interest in local matters,[379] the *Globe-Democrat* could and did syndicate its page, or at least Giebler's columns, in several other Midwest newspapers.

Despite being located in the country's eighth-largest metropolis (and within range of Cleveland, Toledo, and Chicago), newspapers in Detroit inexplicably were slow to show much interest in either movies or moviegoers. Perhaps provoked by the *Weekly Film News,* the opulent house organ of the J.F. Kunsky theater chain, the *Detroit Free Press* and *Detroit News-Tribune* finally, and at the same time, acceded to readers' demands for up-to-date motion picture information. In early September 1915, the *Free Press* introduced a Thursday column entitled "The Reel Players," with support coming in part from Paramount, whose weekly ads loomed large on the page.[380] This unsigned column usually featured the photo profile of a single star (almost exclusively women) and initially included synopses of current films at four or five downtown picture theaters. The column soon expanded to cover more theaters and added a sub-column, "Film Flashes," with brief news items and gossip about the industry, upcoming films, and stars.[381] In December, the paper began printing a full page under the simple title "The

Screen" (again, no editor was named) within a special Sunday section called "Stage Music Screen."[382] This page adopted the familiar format of surrounding short synopses of featured films at nine or more picture theaters with half a dozen star photos and production stills, several large theater ads, and a sub-column, now retitled "Flickers from Film Land" (poached from Kelly). The overall orientation, consequently, was very like those in the *Pittsburgh Leader, Buffalo Times,* and *Toledo Times*: decidedly local.

In late August 1915, the *Detroit News-Tribune* already had upstaged the *Free Press* by opening a Sunday page simply bannered "The Movies."[383] This page had a more balanced variety of menu items: half a dozen downtown theater ads, half a dozen star photos (with a special one of Geraldine Farrar), short columns about the films and stars appearing at those advertised theaters, several stories about stars, a couple of industry pieces, and a sub-column of "Close-Ups."[384] Within weeks, the banner was upgraded to "Photoplays," more and more picture theaters placed ads, and George W. Stark signed a "Motion Picture Comment" column that incorporated the previous synopses of theater programs.[385] Within a few more weeks, the *News Tribune* (with Stark perhaps as editor) expanded its Sunday coverage to two full pages that included far more industry news—the war's impact on Kleine's new studio in Italy, Henry Ford's visit to Universal City—and photo profiles of stars, all supported by up to sixteen theater ads.[386] Assuming an explicitly moral tone quite different from predecessors such as Mae Tinee, "Wid" Gunning, and Gardner Mack, Stark weighed in on a range of national and local issues: the Detroit women's campaign in support of censorship policies, praise for an actress who decided to reject any scenario she considered immoral, manufacturers' misguided efforts to turn stage performers into movie stars, the overblown language of motion picture press agents.[387] Moreover, ads from Universal, World Film, Metro, and Triangle ensured that figures such as Carl Laemmle, Clara Kimball Young, Mary Miles Minter, Mae Marsh, and William S. Hart received extra attention, especially in relation to screenings of their current films.[388] This balance of the national and the local also was evident in the *News Tribune*'s unusual interest in music, which included an article by the composer Carlyle Ellis on "photo music drama" and several reports on S.L. Rothapfel's Mutual-sponsored talk at a banquet for the city's movie men.[389]

In October and November 1915, weekly pages were launched in several papers located in the northern plains. The *Omaha World-Herald* borrowed its initial banner from the *Chicago Tribune:* "Right Off the Reel/Facts for Movie Fans."[390] Within weeks, editor Ross H. Chamberlen (perhaps a young sports writer) dropped that for the more prosaic "Latest Reels and What's at the Theaters This Week" and added a second Sunday page, "All the News About the

Moving Pictures."[391] As "Omaha's guide to the higher class screen productions," his stated aims were: avoid mentioning "improbable 'western' pictures, or those suggestive of crime, immorality and the like," and accept ads only from "theaters whose moral tone is above reproach."[392] The theater programs supposedly meeting that standard he listed in a "Photoplay Guide" and an "Advance Agent" column, "provided by their press representatives."[393] Each week he featured a prominent industry story, half a dozen "fillers," several star photo profiles, and a column of "Breezy Gossip About Photoplay Favorites." One story described Victor Freeburg's scenario writing class at Columbia University.[394] Companies soon supported these pages with ads: Laemmle's publicity for *The Broken Coin,* Triangle's celebration of its contract with the Strand, Metro's promotion of Minter in *Barbara Frietchie.*[395] The paper was unique in reprinting, with permission, *New York Morning Telegraph* editorials that praised motion pictures as "the greatest aid to the study of history and science," and it countered a Glass Workers union charge that the industry misrepresented American workingmen, still a significant segment of the audience.[396] While offering his readers a condensed version of trade press and fan magazine material, Chamberlen also addressed specific local interests. He introduced a "Query Box" column to answer fans' letters[397] and printed pieces relevant to the region (for instance an item on the value of motion picture exhibition to rural farm communities) and to local movie men (a piece about *The Movie Man's Friend,* a booklet of exhibition tips from a manager in Grinnell, Iowa).[398] His Sunday page quickly received praise from *Motion Picture News* as "intelligently edited, presenting a variety of news and comment touching nearly every angle of the motion picture industry."[399] The *News* also printed a dialogue written by Chamberlen to reveal why movie page editors so often had to reduce and rewrite the windy, irrelevant material that theater press agents sent to newspapers.[400] Chamberlen, in turn, drew on the *News* to write his own self-congratulatory editorial "booming" the *World-Herald*'s motion picture department.[401]

Farther north, also in mid-October 1915, the *Duluth News Tribune* renewed its interest in motion pictures with a full Sunday page of news, information, and gossip.[402] For several months this page assumed a regular format of four or five lengthy columns apparently syndicated from the *St. Louis Globe-Democrat*—"As to Photoplay Writing," "Film Facts," "Close Ups," "Answers to Fans"—a single photo profile (D.W. Griffith was the first), and a bit of doggerel. A.H. Giebler signed the column on "Photoplay Writing," but there was no specific source for any of the industry information. In early December, the *News Tribune* dropped the *Globe-Democrat*'s syndicated material, and an unnamed editor gave the page a catchy banner, "Reel Facts about Reel Folks."[403] At least three picture theater ads now supported the page, and short columns usually described the films featured on their programs. Industry news, however, comprised most of the space, along with a large star photo profile headlined "Close Ups of Film Favorites" (literalizing the term's double meaning)[404] or a current production still and several small star photos. Among the many non-sourced pieces were others from producers and stars—Samuel Goldfish and E.D. Horkheimer lamenting the high costs of film production; Mutual's John Freuler urging Americans to condemn censorship (a year after the U.S. Supreme Court upheld Ohio's censorship claims); Theda Bara warning "screen-struck girls" of the sacrifices required of movie actors—and even from the *Detroit News-Tribune*'s George Stark.[405] Surprisingly, excerpted on this page was Vachel Lindsay's praise of Henry B. Walthall's acting from his recently published *Art of the Moving Picture.*[406] Overall, the *Duluth News Tribune* seemed intent on whetting readers' appetite for more and more background information on the industry, its films, and stars with easily digested summaries and reprints of press material.

Closer to Omaha, the *Des Moines Evening Tribune* had been printing a daily, unsigned "News of the Movies" column since mid-August 1915. That column often had brief notes on films booked in picture theaters that advertised in the paper, along with bits of industry news: more and more "well known literary people" were "turning their hands at film plays"; the U.S. government provided locations and equipment for Balboa's serial *Neal of the Navy;* and, unlike Iowa, the Ohio censorship board continued to ban screenings of *Hypocrites.*[407] Some items came directly from publicity departments, noted in a Fox story about Annette Kellerman's next film, a press release on "Mme Petrova in 'The Vampire,'" and a Vitagraph story on the contraption its fat comic Hughie Mack invented to let him sleep standing up.[408] The column also included news of regional interest: A.H. Blank (who owned several downtown theaters) planned to renovate a large house in Omaha; his Garden theater orchestra expected to perform music to better "fit the pictures"; and an Iowa City woman had joined Essanay to write scenarios.[409] "News of the Movies" also suggested that serials were as popular in Des Moines as elsewhere: one week had stories on *Neal of the Navy,* Vitagraph's *The Goddess,* and new episodes added to Universal's *The Broken Coin.*[410]

In early November, while continuing its daily "News on the Movies" column, the *Tribune* expanded its coverage to a full Wednesday page with the alliterative banner "Flickerings and Flashes from Filmland."[411] Each week, columns described the programs at half a dozen theaters supporting the page with ads while others promoted the industry: a Motion Picture Board of Trade "pamphlet titled 'If Shakespeare Fell Among the Censors'"; a short history of Pathé's rise to prominence; and Fox's success in urging exhibitors to use its "vivid, shrewd advertising in the daily newspapers."[412] As in other papers, several illustrated profiles of stars in current films often topped the page, but the photos were smaller, similar in size to those displayed in occasional theater ads.[413] The *Tribune* also carried a company-approved article in which Theda Bara denied she was "the world's wickedest woman," a second in which Anita Stewart offered experienced advice to young women who wanted to become movie actresses, and a third that praised Mary Pickford for being the first to "exploit her hair with halo light effects" (backlighting).[414] Local news took up less space in this Wednesday page, but what appeared could be fascinating. Several stories described Triangle's decoration of the Majestic to prepare for its opening program on November 21, with "special music," and large ads supported this promotion for weeks.[415] The YMCA placed an ad to engage area college students in extension classes with a free screening of *The Making of an Automobile* and *The Making of an American Citizen,* and the *Tribune* made a rare reference to the organization of a "Film Club" by the city's "local motion picture fans," sponsored apparently by the Business Women's Clubs.[416]

In late January 1916, the *Tribune* dropped the "Flickerings and Flashes from Filmland" page and instead began adding sections to the daily "News of the Movies" (fig. 32). First to appear was a "Questions and Answers" column that, modeled on those of other papers, invited letters addressed to the "Photoplay Department." Another listed seven or eight theater programs, simply labeled "Today at the Movies."[417] Next came a banner, "Plays and Players," that separated all the industry news and gossip into a third section.[418] In late February, Dorothy Day (Dorothy Gottlieb)[419] was given a byline for these columns, as "Questions and Answers" became "What Do You Want to Know About the Movies?" (as if directly addressing each reader), and "Plays and Players" turned into a lengthy column with its own large boldface head that led into the first of half a dozen or more stories.[420] At the end of March, a line drawing of Day looking straight at the reader replaced her byline at the top of each lengthy column; two weeks later, she was identified—like Mae Tinee, Mary B. Leffler, and Louella Parsons before her—as the editor/writer of all the material beneath the banner "News of the Movies."[421] Also much like predecessors such as Kitty Kelly, Parsons, and "The Film Girl," she increasingly served up short reviews of specific films (see chapter 4).

NEWSPAPER PAGES KEEP MOVIE FANS IN THE PICTURE

In late 1915, Sam Spedon, Vitagraph's publicity manager, claimed "there were over 400 newspapers in the United States with established motion

NEWS OF THE MOVIES

LITTLE INTIMACIES OF MOVIE STARS AS TOLD BY DOROTHY DAY

Film Actor Gets Hurt in Accident Intended for Make-Believe.

KENTUCKY SCENES ARE MADE IN CALIFORNIA

Pete Prindle in "His Picture in the Paper," Scream at the Majestic.

BY DOROTHY DAY.

WORK on the final scenes of "The Pawn of Fate," in which Beban plays the lead at the Casino today, was interrupted by a painful accident to the star. During the enactment of the scene in which Beban engages in a fierce hand-to-hand battle, the star received a deep cut across the fingers of his right hand, temporarily disabling him.

TODAY AT THE PHOTOPLAY HOUSES

STRAND—Today—"The War God's Decree," and the comedy, "The Rural Rough Necks."

ELITE—Today—Tully Marshall and Thomas Jefferson in "The Sable Lorcha," and Ford Sterling in "Following His Father's Footsteps." A Triangle program.

UNIVERSITY—Today — Ruth Roland in "Who Pays," a Pathe comedy and the Pathe News.

GARDEN—Today — Florence Rockwell in the Pallas-Paramount production, "He Fell in Love With His Wife."

PALACE—Today—William Farnum and Dorothy Bernard in "Fighting Blood."

MAJESTIC—Today — Douglas Fairbanks in "His Picture in the Papers," and the all-star Keystone cast in "His Hereafter."

CASINO—Today—George Beban in "The Pawn of Fate."

UNIQUE—Today—"The Girl Telegrapher's Nerve," "Hamlet Made Over," and "Tubby Turns the Tables," two comedies and the drama, "The Uncut Diamonds."

ROYAL—Today — Winnifred Greenwood in "The Happy Masqueraders," and George Ovey in "Going Up."

BLANCHE SWEET, a popular Paramount star.

WHAT DO YOU WANT TO KNOW ABOUT MOVIES?

BY DOROTHY DAY.

6,000 GREEKS SEEK PAROLE FOR CHIRIKOS

ANOTHER FILES HERE FOR VICE PRESIDENT

MAXEY ASKS FOR REVIEW

MAJESTIC

"IN A CLASS BY ITSELF"

Triangle Picture Plays

CONTINUOUS SHOW DAILY FROM 12 m. TO 11 p. m.

Sunday - Monday - Tuesday - Wednesday

GALA PICTURE PLAY EVENT

Miss Billie Burke

In Thomas H. Ince's Master Picture Play De Luxe In 8 Parts

"PEGGY"

This is Miss Burke's First Appearance in Motion Pictures

NO ADVANCE IN PRICES—Quite Unusual Isn't It?

House Scale of Prices in effect for all attractions. Afternoon and Nights:

MAIN FLOOR All Seats 10c

BALCONY All Seats 5c

Children Always 5c

LAST TIMES TODAY DOUGLAS FAIRBANKS and LOUISE FAZENDA KEYSTONE COMEDY

Change of Show Every Sunday and Thursday

Coming Mar. 16-17-18, De Wolf Hopper in "Don Quixote"

Children are cordially invited to attend this Theatre "Always a Clean Show"

CASINO THEATRE

Today—Last Times

GEORGE BEBAN IN "The Pawn of Fate"

America's Foremost Character Actor in his Crowning Achievement.

ROYAL

For Sunday Only

"DOUBLE CROSSED"

"All Balled Up"

UNIQUE NOW 5¢

FIRST RUN PICTURES

NEW SHOW EVERY DAY

Helen Gibson & Fritzi Brunette

Are on Today's Program

Bed Time Tales

FIGURE 32. "News of the Movies," *Des Moines Tribune,* March 4, 1916.

picture departments," each of which likely was giving readers a variety of news and gossip about the movies in weekend pages and/or daily columns.[422] Spedon's claim may have been hyped, for he was still cajoling more papers into taking motion pictures seriously. But the scores of pages and columns surveyed here suggest that newspaper coverage across the country certainly was extensive. Moreover, many papers singled out in *Motion Picture News* (the *Decatur Herald, Milwaukee Leader, Milwaukee Sentinel, Kansas City Post, Waterloo Times-Tribune, Chattanooga News, Cincinnati Times-Star, Jacksonville Times-Union,* and *Buffalo Sunday News,* among others)[423] as well as surely more not mentioned, definitely demand further research. And there would be others in Canada to consider—the *Toronto Sunday World, Toronto Star Weekly, Montreal Herald-Telegraph, Montreal Gazette,* and *Winnipeg Tribune,* for example—if one expanded the scope of inquiry to examine the homogeneity or heterogeneity of a "North American" film culture.[424] To return to the bounds of this study, however, researchers can look ahead to the subject of the fourth entr'acte: the special weekly supplements that a few newspapers began to publish, with industry support, in 1916.

For now, the movie menus that fans found in their newspapers by 1915–16 were quite diverse, yet had much in common. The formats of the weekly pages could vary widely. Some newspapers followed the *Cleveland Sunday Leader* in offering a more or less equal amount of industry and local news items (which could shift over time), usually sponsored indirectly by local theater ads and sometimes by those of regional rental exchanges. Others followed the model established by Syndicate Film Publishing—or adapted variants of one kind or another—that focused largely on industry news and gossip, whether sponsored by local theater ads or not. Nearly as many adopted formats more local in orientation, whether theaters supported the pages with ads, supplied them with program descriptions and film synopses, or, rarely, neither. Whatever the case, certain menu items appeared with regularity. Depending on the format, readers could expect one or more columns on the films currently playing (or booked to play) in selected theaters, one or more columns of star profiles and related gossip, and articles or "filler" pieces focused on either industry or local issues. They could often find columns or boxes responding with brief answers to the increasingly numerous questions submitted by fans such as themselves, an interchange that directly solicited their engagement and participation in the network of an emerging fan culture. Perhaps the most regular items were photos of stars and/or production stills of films currently appearing in local theaters, which topped the page or were artfully arranged elsewhere to catch and direct a reader's attention. As a whole, these newspaper pages, especially those with a local or regional orientation, offer a cumulative wealth of material for specific case studies of distribution and exhibition, movie star popularity, and differing social and cultural interests in the movies.

What newspapers assumed most interested their readers, or what they thought *should* be of interest, was hardly uniform. A telling sign was the term chosen to designate the subject of a weekly page or daily column, often flagged in its banner.[425] Was it "motion pictures" or "moving pictures," generic forms derived from the trade press? Was it the neologism "photoplays," which usually signaled an intent to elevate the industry's "product" and proselytize a new "dramatic art" for a more cultured adult audience? Was it "movies," allegedly the "street slang" of youthful fans and a sign that a paper wanted to appear "up-to-date" and aligned with a young mass audience? Or was it "film," a one-syllable variant linked more closely with the materiality of production and exhibition, and susceptible to alliteration?

Across the board, however, newspapers made at least two assumptions about what attracted or should attract fans. One was the "picture personality" or star, which the *Chicago Tribune* was the first to display in a close-up "frame of public favor" that fans could cut out and collect. Stars also figured prominently in the columns of gossip and "answers to fans," and even in the heads of theater program descriptions, whether they were highlighting serials/series or feature-length films. The other assumed attraction was the feature film, which the industry—from manufacturers and distributors to exhibitors—increasingly promoted in ads and press material. Some newspapers also exploited their readers' desire to be more than movie fans and imagine themselves as participants in the industry (see the second entr'acte). Finally, newspapers that identified the editors/writers of their motion picture pages and columns—from Mae Tinee and "Wid" Gunning to Mary Anne Smith and Gardner Mack—encouraged them, in line with the industry's own interests, to develop distinctive, conversational voices, all the better to engage their readers as movie fans themselves, sharing while also shaping their tastes.

DOCUMENT

"RIGHT OFF THE REEL!" *CHICAGO TRIBUNE*, FEBRUARY 22, 1914

Right Off the Reel!

The Tribune next Sunday will begin a department devoted to the silent drama and the silent players. It will be conducted for the patrons of this popular amusement. It will be different. It will be dignified. It will abound in color and pictures, humor and romance. It will give you local, national and international news of your favorite players. It will give you intimate and personal gossip of your favorite players. It will show you the latest pictures and poses of your favorite players. It will print the principal scenes in which your favorite players are playing.

This department will be entitled
Film and Screen

It will take you into its confidence, ask your wishes about what you want to read and see in it, and give you any and all information you desire concerning moving pictures and their people. It will take you into the home and depict the comedies and tragedies therein. It will flash leading events in the United States. And it will lead you into the far reaches. In a word, it will bring you, every Sunday,

FACE to FACE with the WORLD!
Turn, *THE FIRST THING,* next *SUNDAY, MARCH 1,* to
THE COLOR SECTION OF THE SUNDAY TRIBUNE,
where you will find the latest Tribune feature,
Film and Screen

ENTR'ACTE Newspaper Movie Contests

A Word in Your Ear About Our Two (2) Scenario Contests!
Chicago Sunday Tribune, December 13, 1914

Columns of queries and answers satisfied hungry appetites only so far. Newspapers could further entice readers by stoking their desire to be more than just movie fans and imagine themselves as participants, whether explicitly or implicitly, in the industry. Such enticements usually took the form of writing contests or competitions, sometimes in collaboration with one or another film company. Although these contests had parallels in fan magazines, the latter tended to sponsor popularity contests focused on picture personalities or stars and their growing importance in promoting the industry as a whole. These initial contests, in late 1911 and early 1912, offered rewards to the winning picture personalities themselves: Florence Lawrence in the *New York Morning Telegraph* and Maurice Costello in the *Motion Picture Story Magazine*, both Vitagraph stars.[1] If that seems puzzling, the contests' real aim apparently was to solicit not only votes but also letters that would give producers ideas for exploiting and promoting their players' perceived talents.[2] Both publications sponsored a second contest in the fall of 1912, but the fan magazine awarded its prizes to the winners of a "Prize Puzzle Contest" that required readers to test their knowledge by filling fifty-seven spaces left blank in a brief history story, each one with the different "name of a Photoplayer."[3] *Ladies' World* staged a monthly essay contest at the same time, asking its million or more readers to guess the outcome of *What Happened to Mary?*'s next episode.[4] During the first half of 1913, *Photoplay* and *Motion Picture Story* simultaneously ran simpler contests, in which readers cast J. Warren Kerrigan as the most popular picture player in one, and an alleged half a million subscribers (most of them women) voted for Romaine Fielding in the other.[5] Finally, a year later, *Ladies' World* launched a variation with its "Hero Contest," inviting readers to vote on which of seven actors was best suited to play the lead character in a serialized Louis Tracy story.[6] After an extensive promotional campaign—lantern slides projected in thousands of theaters, "three-colored cards telling the story" and containing all seven actors circulated on New York subway cars—the role went to Francis X. Bushman.[7]

Newspaper contests, by contrast, were wide-ranging, involved different kinds of participation, and almost always awarded their prizes to the winning contestants. In early 1911, the *Toledo Blade* sponsored perhaps the first contest that asked readers to submit short pieces of moving picture criticism for weekly cash prizes.[8] Each Saturday for four weeks, the *Blade* printed the winning entries and seemed surprised when girls and young women won the majority of prizes, writing about the films they saw (three even chose westerns at neighborhood as well as downtown picture theaters).[9] Although short-lived, this contest preceded by a year a similar one mounted biweekly over five months by the *New York Dramatic Mirror* in an effort to stimulate serious film reviewing in the public press.[10] Despite this trade paper's very different readership, women submitted nearly half of the winning reviews.[11] About the same time, in May 1912, Epes Winthrop Sargent advanced an educational variant on such contests that the Selig company floated as a scheme to promote its three-reel *The Coming of Columbus*: "To interest the school teachers and pupils, have a prize contest for the best essay on Columbus, offering one prize of tickets for each grade and letting the various schools compete for the same prize . . . [and] give a special matinee for the schools."[12] Among an unknown number of exhibitors that picked up on the scheme, the manager of the Orpheum in Canton (Ohio) arranged a special children's morning matinee two weeks before the film's scheduled weekend run.[13] This kind of contest in which readers competed for cash prizes at least initially did not lead to what the industry expected of the public press. For more than a year, newspapers seemed to abandon the demands for written compositions. In fact, the three-month contest that the *Cleveland Leader* ran, from December 1912 through February 1913, asked little more of its readers than to name the titles of the four to eight film production stills printed across the top of its Sunday photoplay page, a contest that did distribute each week, however, up to twelve hundred free tickets to lots of movie fans.[14] A couple of months later, an even simpler contest ran for a few days in the *Washington Herald*: The twenty-five readers who named the actor in a printed photo would each receive "four tickets to a leading motion picture theater."[15]

By late 1913, some newspapers returned to the idea of competitive essays or reviews. The *Cleveland Plain Dealer* launched a contest asking readers to send a one-page letter to its "Moving Picture editor" "telling what movie you liked best last week," with a stipulation that favored its advertisers: They could only select movies mentioned in the paper (fig. 33).[16] This contest ran from late November through mid-January 1914, and all but two of the winning letters prominently featured were from girls or young women. Their favorites ranged from Lubin's *The Rattlesnake* (with Romaine Fielding) and Vitagraph's *The Frozen Trail* to Edison's *Janet of the Dunes* (with Mabel Trunnelle).[17] The latter had "three things necessary for a successful picture," one winner, Julia Bates, wrote: "drama, action, strength of plot and beautiful scenery."[18] In late January 1914, the *Toledo Blade* held a single "Movie Contest" that offered a "$3 cash prize . . . for the best worded and most definitely critical letter about 'The Movie I Liked Best This Week.'"[19] Three weeks later the *Blade*'s newly expanded motion picture page included Nan Hart's winning entry along with "Rorke's Drift," the first in the "Best Moving Picture Story" series.[20] Within a year, even the *Chicago Tribune* found the idea tempting. Assuming that her readers shared a greater interest in stars than in stories, in May 1915, Mae Tinee announced a contest that set them the task not only of voting for their favorite picture player from among the star photos reproduced in each Sunday's rotogravure section but also, for the lucrative prize of $50 (a month's salary for a shop girl), of "writing an essay of 200 words or less telling just why your favorite is your favorite."[21] Weeks later the *Cleveland Plain Dealer* sponsored a similar contest that solicited the best letter explaining a contestant's choice of a favorite movie actor or actress.[22] At the same time, Selig introduced its own contest to award three people a special train tour of the West for writing "the most interesting letters about any Motion Picture Play advertised by any theater" in the *Tribune,* and the Ziegfeld challenged Chicago's censors by offering a "$25 cash prize" for the best letter "stating frankly and briefly your candid opinion as to whether or not that stirring photoplay," *The New Governor,* should be allowed to continue its run at that downtown theater.[23] The *Birmingham Age-Herald* later offered a $10 gold piece for the best hundred-word letter answering this question about *The Outcast:* Should the heroine have married the hero?[24]

As serials turned into an astonishingly popular attraction for movie fans in 1914, several manufacturers quickly came up with novel contests to stimulate their cravings and keep them hooked until the final episode. Partnering with scores of newspapers through Syndicate Film Publishing, Thanhouser developed such a promotional scheme with its release of *The Million Dollar Mystery* in late June 1914.[25] From reading each story installment and picking out its "clew," contestants were asked to "write your solution to the mystery" with "the best 100 word solution" and were

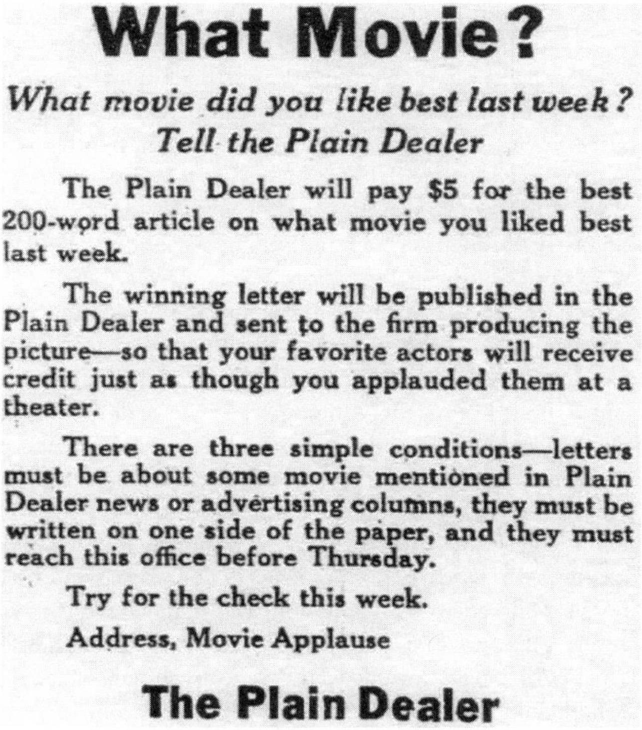

What Movie?

What movie did you like best last week? Tell the Plain Dealer

The Plain Dealer will pay $5 for the best 200-word article on what movie you liked best last week.

The winning letter will be published in the Plain Dealer and sent to the firm producing the picture—so that your favorite actors will receive credit just as though you applauded them at a theater.

There are three simple conditions—letters must be about some movie mentioned in Plain Dealer news or advertising columns, they must be written on one side of the paper, and they must reach this office before Thursday.

Try for the check this week.

Address, Movie Applause

The Plain Dealer

FIGURE 33. *Cleveland Plain Dealer* essay contest, November 30, 1915.

vaguely promised a reward of "$10,000 in cash." More specific guidelines and deadlines, the company's ads teased, might be found at picture theaters screening the serial. A young stenographer in St. Louis, Miss Ida Damon, did actually win that astronomical prize; in the *Chicago Tribune*, she wrote of being "first attracted" to the serial on a summer visit to the city and came up with her winning solution by analyzing other serials and their characteristic narrative form.[26] Later that year, Universal tantalized fans with a variation on Thanhouser's puzzle contest, asking moviegoers to identify those situations in *Trey O' Hearts* that "the producer . . . claimed could not be portrayed in pictures. . . . See if you can find these situations in the story and pictures."[27] This "contest" came without cash prizes, the assumption apparently being that viewing the episodes and closely reading the installments were rewards enough. And that assumption seems to have held true for another year or two, as more serials streamed steadily and profitably through newspapers and picture theaters throughout the country.

Another kind of writing competition for movie fans, however, proved much more engaging and enduring. This probably appealed to newspapers because it counteracted the many ads promising dubious fortunes in the movies, and also garnered joint ventures with the industry. Most important, it tapped into the desires and dreams of so many readers (again, mostly young women) to enter the industry through writing and selling scenarios. Louella Parsons's column on scriptwriting in the *Chicago Sunday Herald,* beginning in December 1914, boosted such competitions, and she herself may have been spurred by earlier contests in several papers. In July 1914, the *Fort Worth Star-Telegram* ran an unusual $25 scenario contest with columnist Mary B. Leffler as judge and a promise that the winning scenario would be produced and exhibited in Fort Worth.[28] In a series of short articles, one of the proposed actors, Bettie Braun, even offered tips for contestants.[29] In early November, together with Essanay, the *Chicago Tribune* sponsored a contest to select from readers' submissions "the three best two-reel dramatic or melodramatic scenarios" for cash prizes worth $250, $150, and $100, respectively.[30] The deadline for the five-hundred-word submissions was January 16, 1915. The only guidelines were "IDEAS" and "ORIGINALITY," but "not technical perfection." The panel of judges included Francis X. Bushman of Essanay, Mrs. Hobart C. Chatfield-Taylor, and the *Tribune*'s Kitty Kelly, who for months had been writing daily reviews for the newspaper (see chapter 4). A month later, Thanhouser and American Film teamed up with the *Tribune* and other papers to sponsor a scenario contest "for a SERIAL photoplay—like 'The Million Dollar Mystery.'"[31] The submission deadline was similar (January 17, 1915), and scenarios were recommended to be "at least 1,000 words long," the stories "sufficiently NOVEL, DRAMATIC, EMOTIONAL, or MYSTERIOUS," and the ideas packing "punch." The $10,000 prize-winning scenario turned into American Film's *The Diamond in the Sky,* released in early May, and the company immediately announced a second contest in search of a sequel, for the same extravagant figure.[32]

By then, however, would-be scriptwriters were overwhelming manufacturers with scenarios and scenario ideas, which greatly lessened the need for newspapers to sponsor contests. Besides reading Parsons's column in the *Chicago Sunday Herald,* movie fans could consult a number of manuals beginning to be published by industry insiders. In May, the *Philadelphia Evening Ledger* printed a small ad for one of those, Epes Winthrop Sargent's *Technique of the Photoplay,* based on his own experience with several companies. Nine months later, it promoted William Lord Wright's *The Motion*

Picture Story.[33] In February 1916, however, the *Omaha World-Herald* went ahead with a "live-wire scenario" writing contest for its readers in Nebraska and western Iowa, with certain conditions. The most important required that any submitted story not only "must be laid in Omaha" but also "must include an incident at the state university in Lincoln."[34] In less than a month, the newspaper found itself inundated with a hundred scripts.[35] As late as July 1916, after offering Harry O. Hoyt's column, "Lessons in Scenario Writing," over a four-week period,[36] the *Evening Ledger* in conjunction with Metro Pictures[37] even mounted its own "Prize Scenario Contest," prefaced by a two-reel model script for Max Figman's comedy *The Mis-Fire Microbes.*[38]

As might be expected, some newspapers also began to exploit another desire of readers, especially girls and young women: to be swept into "the land of dreams" and become a successful movie actor or even a star. This produced contests in which readers competed for the lead role in a potential film production. The *Chicago Herald* sponsored one of the first of these in 1914, following the *Tribune*'s serial story of Peggy, the young woman who becomes a movie actor (see chapter 2), and its own series of late-summer stunts in which Madeleine Bode, the "Herald Movie Girl," led a staff photographer on a fictional tour of the city.[39] In late November, this contest invited readers to vie to be chosen as "Chicago's prettiest girl to take the leading role of 'Sue' in a scenario" written by Victor Eubank and produced locally by Essanay (fig. 34).[40] Within a month, a panel of five judges selected forty candidates, and the newspaper solicited votes from readers based on the photographs it reproduced.[41] The winner was Dorothy Warshauer, and she and several runners-up soon were engaged in Essanay's single-reel production.[42] Warshauer may not have taken up a career in acting, but the number of contestants and readers involved (the winner and first runner-up together received three million votes) certainly energized movie fans and proved a successful scheme for both the *Herald* and Essanay. A few months later, the *Cleveland Sunday Leader* advertised a similar "Movie Talent Contest" in which "movie audiences will pick one [of] forty girls" who could become "a real star in a real film production."[43] This time not one but six winners would be invited to the Metro Pictures studio in New York to perform in a planned feature film.[44]

Perhaps because many female stars were starting to warn young girls that acting in the movies was no piece of cake and involved hard work (see chapter 3), an intriguing variation on this kind of contest cropped up. This was the look-alike contest, more locally focused and more limited in its appeal, yet confirming the popularity of certain stars (recent manifestations, of course, have led to careers for all kinds of impersonators). Just prior to its "Movie Talent Contest,"

CHICAGO SUNDAY HERALD, DECEMBER 6, 1914.

WHO Will be SUE? *Is she here?*

Illinois Up to Date.

MISS GENEVIEVE BROWN.

MISS MARIE McDONALD

MISS HELEN McDONALD

BY ALLEN C. RANKIN.

WHO will be Sue?

Today we are reproducing photographs of several of the candidates entered in the contest to find Chicago's prettiest girl to take the leading role as "Sue" in the scenario to be sent over the entire world by the Essanay Film Manufacturing Company. It is impossible to reproduce all of the photographs received, but during the next week as many as possible will be shown to the Herald family and the patrons of the Herald Movies. One week from today the girls selected by the judges as the forty prettiest girls in Chicago and the ones who will be voted for will be shown on the "Who Will Be Sue?" page.

The contest has, during the last week, met with favor among Chicagoans and the many pictures submitted have made the judges' task no easy one, and when the last photographs are received Friday noon and the work of the board completed that night the photographs of the girls chosen will be turned over to the Herald artists for the "Who Will Be Sue?" page.

Many requests have been received during the week, both by telephone and by letter, as to the rules of the contest. The only requirement is that the photographs of the candidates be in the Herald office by noon Friday. The name and address must accompany the picture. No addresses will be published. The pictures will be judged by a board of five headed by Lorado Taft, the world's famous sculptor. Mr. Taft will not only assist in the selection of the forty girls to be entered in the final contest, but he will supervise and advise the board in its work.

* * *

All during the week the staff of the Herald Movies, the Photoplay Editor of the Herald and the scenario staff of the Essanay Company have been busy answering questions from girls who desire to enter the contest or from friends who are positive that they know "Sue." "Sue" is becoming harder to find each day, as every mail brings many photographs of beautiful Chicago girls who wish to play the leading role in the scenario. It is going to be difficult to select the forty prettiest and the judges each day grow more enthused, but at the same time more weary of their task.

The Herald Movies staff has completed its preliminary work and now awaits the time when the forty survivors are named. The camera men of the Herald Movies will then take pictures of the forty girls and they will be flashed on the screen in hundreds of theaters in Chicago and vicinity.

* * *

"Sue," besides winning the chance to become a great actress in the film world, will be awarded with a $200 diamond. This ring has been on exhibition in the Adams street window of C. G. Peacock's store at Adams and State street since last Monday. The ring, which is a beauty, has attracted a great deal of attention and will be exhibited throughout the contest.

Prizes will also be given to the three other leading candidates. The selection of the other awards will be made within a few days and announced during the week. Remember the last day for submitting pictures and entering candidates is next Friday. The preliminary search for "Sue" will end Friday night and then the battle of votes to determine "WHO WILL BE SUE?" will be started. Send photographs to the Photoplay Editor of the Herald.

Here Are a Few of the Candidates Entered in the Motion Picture-Beauty Contest. Watch for the Judges' Selections to Be Published Next Sunday. Vote for Your Favorite.

FIGURE 34. "Who Will Be Sue?" contest, *Chicago Sunday Herald,* December 6, 1914.

the *Cleveland Leader* highlighted an early one in which a young woman gained first prize in a Charley Chaplin imitation contest at a local amusement park.[45] In late 1915, the *Leader* announced its own contest, asking readers "what photoplay actresses . . . you resemble" and inviting submissions of photographs to be judged. The fantasy pitch: if a "first-magnitude star suddenly became unable to complete a motion picture," would "you look like her enough to fill the vacancy," no matter the talent or training?[46] The named stars: Beverly Bayne,

Mary Pickford, Marguerite Clark, Theda Bara, Ruth Roland, and Mabel Normand. Not long after, the *Des Moines Tribune* announced a similar contest for that city's girl who most looked like Pickford, and Pickford herself agreed to write a personal letter to the winner.[47] At the same time, despite the warnings, several newspapers kept sponsoring movie contests whose winners would be cast in local film productions. In February 1916, the *New Orleans Times-Picayune* offered an unusually inclusive "photoplay opportunity" to one "girl or woman reader" from each of the city's districts and fifteen others in the region, all of whom would be chosen to make up an entire cast of female characters (fig. 35).[48] The film, *Cupid and Contraband,* eventually played at a local theater for three days in early December 1916 and was booked for the region through the Southern Metro Film Exchange.[49] That summer, the *Pittsburg Press* joined with the city's Rowland & Clark theaters to hold another contest to choose eleven cast members for a "great photo drama" and award small cash prizes.[50] That fall, even the *Chicago Herald* rejoined the bandwagon with a "People's Movie Star Contest," in which contestants could "win one of 89 parts in a great photoplay feature" to be written by Louella Parsons and produced by Essanay.[51]

At least two other enticements bear mentioning in this admittedly brief survey. In May 1915, the *Chicago Sunday Herald* introduced a unique contest awarding avid movie fans a whole dollar for "bright bits of information" or "a bit of conversation heard in a filmhouse" that would be published in the newspaper.[52] This contest elicited lots of "brief and breezy" entries for the next several months from what the newspaper called its "associate editors."[53] And what "bright bits" rated that dollar?

> A young boy enjoyed *Uncle Tom's Cabin* so much that his mother took him to another show. "A picture of ballet girls dancing a cabaret scene came on, when he exclaimed in a loud voice: 'Oh, mamma, look! All the Little Evas has got union suits on.'"[54]
>
> At the sight of an old stove in a feature film, "the voice of a little girl piped up. 'Oh, look, mamma,' she said. 'They've got a stove just like ours.' 'Hush, you mustn't talk now,' said the embarrassed mother. 'All right, but it is just like ours,' answered the same shrill voice."[55]
>
> "A little girl sitting in front of me in a Madison street moving picture theater became much excited as a storm was being portrayed on the screen. Jumping up in her seat, she exclaimed: 'Stop playing the piano, man, I want to hear the thunder.'"[56]

If an "out of the mouths of babes" cliché governed the *Herald*'s choices, the winning entries also served to portray, even if ironically, that highly

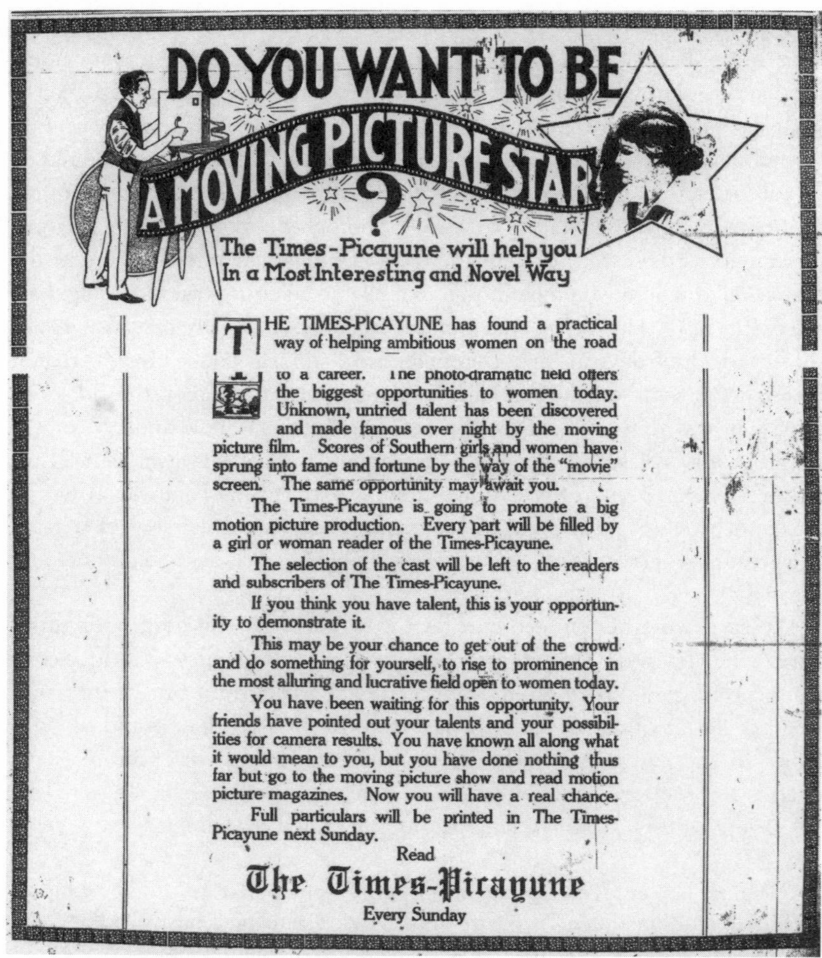

FIGURE 35. *New Orleans Times-Picayune* actress contest, February 13, 1916.

desirable group of movie fans—women and children—and further legitimize, of course, the whole industry. Nearly a year later, the *Des Moines Tribune*, together with eighteen other local businesses (only four of them picture theaters), invited readers to name the movie stars inserted into a two-page spread of ads for the Emporium, Graber Cavender women's clothing, Kirkwood & Richard men's clothing, Family Shoe Stores, Kimball Hat, Haddorff Music House, Griggs Music House, dentist G.R. Miller, Fulton

Fish Market, Munger's Laundry, Des Moines Water Company, O.C. King Hardware, and Jewett Lumber.[57] Although winners received prizes of merchandise or services from the sponsors, the overall effect of the contest was to afford the movies the same status as all kinds of other family-oriented businesses in the city.

3. "In Movie Land, with the Film Stars"

> We had faces then.
>
> GLORIA SWANSON, *Sunset Boulevard* (1950)

> It's not a movie unless the people on the screen are larger than those who watch it.
>
> attributed to CHRIS MARKER

Where could one of the many, many fans flocking to the movies in the early 1910s find and feast on information and gossip about their favorite players or stars? One source might have been the new monthlies *Motion Picture Story Magazine* and *Photoplay Magazine,* as long as a fan had enough money to subscribe or buy copies at a newsstand or picture theater—or had a friend who would share. Throughout 1911, for instance, *Motion Picture Story Magazine* displayed a "Gallery of Picture Players" in each issue's opening pages; these were large publicity photos that readers could cut out and collect.[1] Within a year that "Gallery" was taking up sixteen pages.[2] In August 1911, the magazine started the column "Answers to Inquiries," which was originally intended to address readers' letters asking about manufacturers and their studios, but the "picture players" were asked about far more frequently.[3] At least initially, the tone of the "answers" was surprisingly condescending. Several letter writers were told bluntly that their "questions are not of general interest." Others were slapped and corrected: "Your suggestions are ingenious, but not in accordance with the facts"; "The clipping you send conveys an erroneous impression"; "You are confusing two names"; "You are mistaken in your belief that photoplayers are underpaid." By early 1912, however, the magazine was taking more notice of readers' interest in the "picture players." "Answers to Inquiries" was twice as long, due to the "increasing pressure" of letters, but also more restrictive: "Involved technical questions will not be answered. Information as to the matrimonial alliances of the players and other personal matters will not be answered. *Questions concerning the marriages of players will be completely ignored.*"[4] Another column, "Chats with the Players," was of purported interviews with three or four actors each month, written up by an unnamed young man (at least according to a glancing remark by Francis

X. Bushman).[5] But when and where could fans turn to their local newspaper as another important source?

By fall 1911, that would have been Cleveland, where movie fans found scraps of gossip and information in the *Cleveland Sunday Leader.* Along with ticket coupons and brief "Calcium Flashes," the newspaper's initial "Moving Picture World" pages printed small photos of "popular photo play" actors such as Bushman and Edith Storey.[6] In late October, a relatively large photo profile of Mary Pickford seemed to signal a greater attention to movie stars, but the next month saw only a few small photos of John Bunny and the Solax Kid.[7] In late November, a short column promised to address picture fans' questions—with the warning to "leave matrimonial and love affair questions out of the letters"—but only one other column ever appeared.[8] In late December, following the introduction of the "Photo-Plays and Players" page, the *Sunday Leader* did play Santa Claus for its readers and mount a display of "stationary portraits of [ten] moving picture stars,"[9] which led to a series of photo profiles apparently imitating the photo spreads in *Motion Picture Story* and *Photoplay.* From January through late April 1912, editor Ralph Stoddard singled out one star each week for the "Leader's Gallery of Popular Photo Players," but only one, Lillian Walker, rated more than a narrow column in width.[10] As the *Leader*'s Sunday page shrank in size for the next six months, that "Gallery" disappeared. A few star photo profiles reappeared when Stoddard reclaimed a full Sunday page in early November 1912, but the greater interest he always had exhibited in current film productions persisted.[11] An immediate consequence was a contest that asked readers to identify the films, not the stars, of a weekly series of four to eight production stills.[12]

THE "MOVIE EXPERT" OF THE SCRIPPS-McRAE NEWSPAPERS

It was in October 1912 that Mabel Condon began interviewing movie actors for a regular column in *Motography,* a monthly trade journal published in Chicago.[13] With a title borrowed from the theater, "Sans Grease Paint and Wig," Condon's column, along with those in *Motion Picture Story* and *Photoplay,* may have induced the Scripps-McRae newspaper chain to initiate the first important newspaper column of information and gossip on movie stars. Appearing in daily rather than Sunday newspapers, beginning in November 1912, "The Movies" featured frequent syndicated stories or "personality sketches" written by Gertrude Price, identified as Scripps-McRae's "moving picture expert" (fig. 36). These circulated not only in

Movie Beauty Risks Life to Put Thrill in the Pictures

By Gertrude M. Price,
The Daily News Moving Picture Expert.

There are plenty of M. D.'s and Ph.D.'s and A.B.'s in the world. But the moving picture business has created a new alphabetical suffix or appendix or whatever the right name may be.

It is B.B. and it stands for beauty and bravery.

Anna Quirentia Nilsson is a real B.B., having demonstrated her right to both titles on the Kalem screen every day for several months. She is one of the best looking girls in the business. Her accomplishments include park and cowboy riding, clever boy impersonations, the southern girl sweetheart roles and all sorts of fights against time and circumstance.

Miss Nilsson was the heroine in "His Mother's Picture," a reel of the Kalem company taken down south at Jacksonville, Fla.

To carry out the story of the picture she was obliged to stick her foot into a switchrail and have it bent over until she cried out with the pain, while a great lumbering engine, with numbers of freight cars attached, rushed past too close for comfort or safety.

In speaking of it afterwards she said she had to shut her eyes and grit her teeth to force herself to keep the position, although she couldn't possibly have removed her foot without running the risk of getting it cut off by the wheels of the hurrying train.

This sort of incident sounds all right on paper. But it's another thing when you actually have to experience it—just to make a thrill in a picture.

Miss Nilsson's special suitability to the soft, southern girl part is excellently illustrated in "Under a Flag of Truce." She showed her versatility well in the picture called "The Darling of the C. S. A.," in which she played the difficult role of a spy appearing a part of the time as a boy.

Anna Quirentia Nilsson, B.B.

FIGURE 36. Gertrude M. Price column, *Des Moines News*, February 7, 1913.

daily papers that were part of the Scripps-McRae chain, but also in others subscribing to the United Press service. Consequently, Price's stories may have reached as many movie fans as whatever material exhibitors passed on from the manufacturers or trade press as well as the photos and interviews that the monthly magazines were offering.[14]

The general readership of Scripps-McRae newspapers, according to Gerald Baldasty's research,[15] suggests that Price's syndicated stories may well have assumed a particular, targeted audience. In a 1906 letter to Robert Paine, the nationwide editor of his chains, E.W. Scripps (sounding a bit like Charles Foster Kane) described his "string of small, cheap, working-class newspapers" as "friends, advisors, and even special pleaders of the ninety-five percent of the population that were not rich or powerful."[16] Indeed, most of the papers that Scripps bought or started up after 1900 pledged allegiance to the "common people," promising to act as the "organ, the mouthpiece, the apologist, the defender and the advocate of the wage earning class."[17] This pledge extended to giving substantial coverage to labor issues and strongly supporting organized labor.[18] Scripps's papers also paid special attention to women readers. As Paine once wrote, "The woman in a house who swears by a paper is worth five men who buy it on the street."[19] But the Scripps-McRae papers were different, as Baldasty argues, in "making a particular effort at providing content of interest to working-class women."[20] The *Des Moines News*, where Price's stories were frequent, had a "large clientele among . . . workingmen," and was "a vigorous supporter of labor interests."[21] The *News* also showed an interest in women with blue-collar, white-collar, and even professional jobs in the city.[22] Unlike the *Des Moines Register and Leader*, which followed the trade press, writing manuals, and other papers such as the *Cleveland Leader* in favoring the term "photoplays,"[23] the *News*—and Price herself—opted for "movies," a term often linked alliteratively with "menace"[24] but familiar as the popular slang spoken by most moviegoers.

Given that context, what were the personalities that Price tended to profile? Not unexpectedly, they were exclusively American and initially associated with the licensed manufacturers—early examples ranged from Maurice Costello and John Bunny to Mary Fuller and Dorothy Cassinelli—but gradually she added those working for Independent companies, from King Baggot to Mabel Normand.[25] There were several striking patterns in her choice of stars. One is the frequency of child actors, from Helen Armstrong, the tiny "starlet of the 'Flying A,'" or Baby Lillian Wade of Selig's "wild animal pictures" to Judson Melford, a "natural . . . clever picture-player" and son of a Kalem filmmaker.[26] In fact, not only did Price write more than a dozen stories on child actors, but she also likely signed several pieces as "Aunt Gertie," notably a story about Thomas Edison, "who invented the phonograph, and the electric light, and the moving picture, too."[27] Using that nom de plume, from May through July 1913, she composed a series of condensed fairy tales, from "Snow White" to "The Little

Mermaid."[28] In another she asked children to imagine the five-year-old Princess Ileana of Roumania sitting beside them in a movie theater.[29]

Another pattern was even more prominent. At least one out of four or five stars was described as acting in westerns, and the accompanying illustrations show men and women such as Edwin August (Powers), J. Warren Kerrigan (American), or Jack Richardson and Pauline Garfield Bush (also American) decked out in cowboy hats; others, such as Red Wing (Pathé American) or Mona Darkfeather (Universal), are in Indian costume.[30] Price's "colorful, readable copy" also underscores that emphasis, as in her description of Kalem's Ruth Roland as "an athletic girl" who "runs, rides, and rows with all the freedom and agility of a boy" in one of her "riding pictures," *The Girl Deputy.*[31] These columns, coming after several "Flying A" stories were published in Scripps-McRae newspapers in early 1912,[32] suggest that Price's fascination with cowboy, cowboy girl, and Indian figures was hardly unique. Moreover, the picture theater ads in those newspapers often promoted westerns, from Essanay's *Broncho Billy* series or Vitagraph's cowboy girl films to the multiple-reel Indian pictures of Kay-Bee, Broncho, and Bison-101. In late 1913, Price even wrote an exclusive series of nine stories on location about Buffalo Bill Cody's epic reenactment of several battles in the Indian wars of 1876 to 1891, produced by Essanay with U.S. government support.[33] These stories offer a rare record of *Indian Wars Pictures,* shown privately to government officials and clubs beginning in January 1914; its several versions received little mainstream distribution (for instance a one-day showing in May after the Des Moines Orpheum closed its vaudeville season).[34]

Most striking are the stories, at least two thirds of the total, devoted to women. As might be expected, familiar stars turn up—from Mary Pickford and Kathlyn Williams to Alice Joyce and Pearl White—but most now are forgotten, and several of those, such as Pauline Bush, appear more than once.[35] Among them one can count the "regal-looking Miriam Nesbitt" who, "bored by the world," turned to the movies and "likes rough and ready parts."[36] Or Jesslyn Von Trump, "a capital rider" at American, who "likes herself in a cowgirl costume very much, indeed."[37] Or that "tall woman of the picture players," Anne Schaefer, who enjoyed playing lead roles and character parts for Vitagraph's western unit.[38] Or "dainty, daring" Clara Williams, Lubin's "leading lady," "who can beat the boys at anything on a horse."[39] For the most part, these women were young, active, and independent—celebrated as skilled horsewomen and fearless "daredevils," often seen in westerns and adventure films. In fact, they resembled the champion cowgirl riders and sharpshooters, such as Bessie Herberg and Lucile Parr, promoted in performances of the 101 Ranch Wild West then touring the country to great acclaim.[40] Complementing these women were others who had become successful filmmakers and/or scenario writers: Nell Shipman; Lois Weber, who recently had joined Universal (fig. 37); and the earliest female filmmaker, Alice Guy Blaché, who had made most of Gaumont's films in Paris through 1906 and now headed her own production company, Solax.[41]

And who were the fans that may have doted on Price's syndicated stories? Certainly the texts, their elaborated, punchy titles, and the images of female stars could have appealed to men. One cannot ignore that. And those devoted to child stars could have targeted "*Daily News* youngsters," urging them to see the latest movie starring "The Thanhouser Kid."[42] They also invited the approval of mothers by describing moviemaking as a "family affair" and moviegoing as a safe, acceptable, enjoyable experience, not unlike the late 1913 Mutual ad that explicitly elicited such maternal consent. Only one story about Adrienne Kroell toyed with the conventions of romance, asking, "Girls . . . how'd you like to have the reputation of being the 'most engaged girl' living?"[43] But overall, Price's stories targeted other kinds of women. Most stars she described as athletic young women, carefree but committed to their work, frank and fearless in the face of physical risk. Strikingly, nearly all were unattached, without children. How desirable all this must have been for the young unmarried working women who formed an important core readership of Scripps-McRae newspapers, perhaps especially those in white-collar or even professional jobs in many cities' growing service industries?[44] For them, the desire to "go to the movies" would have been double. Certainly the film roles that women played could function as projective sites of fantasy adventure for spectators, lashing together reading, viewing, and consuming as pleasurable activities. But also the stars, as a new kind of active, attractive worker or professional—even Price herself, whose newspaper work uncannily paralleled that of Mary Fuller in *Dollie of the Dailies*[45]—could serve as role models to emulate.

Price's own political stance provides a further perspective on the continual parade of all these "picture personalities." An advocate of women's suffrage, also characteristic of Scripps-McRae papers, the *Des Moines News* printed stories in June 1912 about screenings of suffragette films such as *Votes for Women.*[46] Furthermore, not only did that paper cover the famous suffragette march on Washington in early 1913, but Price apparently joined the march to interview one of its leaders.[47] In writing about actors such as Pauline Bush, then, the following admiring remark was hardly surprising: that, much like herself, Bush was "an ardent suffraget."[48] Indeed, Price acknowledged women in the industry as political figures, highlighting the

Sad Endings Are All Right Says This Woman Director

Lois Weber.

BY GERTRUDE M. PRICE.

There should be a happy ending to every play which the public is invited to see!

The ending should not interfere with the artistic features of the play. If it is necessary to bring tears to the eyes of the public, in the last act and the last scene, in order to carry the artistic idea and the dramatic force of the production, do it by all means!

These are the two opposing theories which are "up" to Lois Weber to choose between.

The first, she claims, is the theory upon which the average moving picture manager goes. The second is, she says, her own idea of the matter.

Fortunately or unfortunately, Lois Weber is a producer of moving picture plays. She is one of the very few women in the business, and she finds there's a snag, here and there, along the road. This "happy ending" question is one of them.

"I write most of the plays I produce," she told me as I talked with her in her little California dressing room at Hollywood some time ago.

"I always have to consider the finale, though. And too often I am obliged to sacrifice some effect, artistic or dramatic, to make the picture end happily.

"The average manager seems to think that's the essential. I don't think so: at any rate, not always."

Miss Weber is the director of the Rex company; one of the Universal film brands. She has been writing scenarios for several years. She wrote and directed "Eyes That See Not," "Far Away Fields" and "A Prophet Without Honor."

Is Miss Weber right or are the managers right about the "happy ending" idea?

She would like to know.

FIGURE 37. Gertrude M. Price column, *Des Moines News,* September 27, 1913.

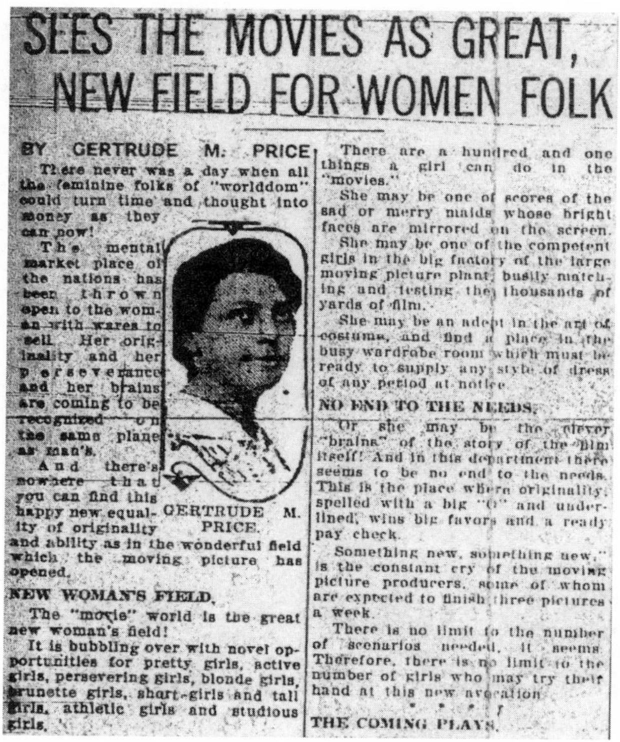

SEES THE MOVIES AS GREAT, NEW FIELD FOR WOMEN FOLK

BY GERTRUDE M. PRICE

There never was a day when all the feminine folks of "worlddom" could turn time and thought into money as they can now!

The mental market place of the nations has been thrown open to the woman with wares to sell. Her originality and her perseverance and her brains are coming to be recognized on the same plane as man's.

And there's nowhere that you can find this happy new equality of originality and ability as in the wonderful field which the moving picture has opened.

GERTRUDE M. PRICE.

NEW WOMAN'S FIELD.

The "movie" world is the great new woman's field!

It is bubbling over with novel opportunities for pretty girls, active girls, persevering girls, blonde girls, brunette girls, short girls and tall girls, athletic girls and studious girls.

There are a hundred and one things a girl can do in the "movies."

She may be one of scores of the sad or merry maids whose bright faces are mirrored on the screen.

She may be one of the competent girls in the big factory of the large moving picture plant, busily matching and testing the thousands of yards of film.

She may be an adept in the art of costume, and find a place in the busy wardrobe room which must be ready to supply any style of dress of any period at notice.

NO END TO THE NEEDS.

Or she may be the clever "brains" of the story of the film itself! And in this department there seems to be no end to the needs. This is the place where originality, spelled with a big "O" and underlined, wins big favors and a ready pay check.

"Something new, something new," is the constant cry of the moving picture producers, some of whom are expected to finish three pictures a week.

There is no limit to the number of scenarios needed, it seems. Therefore, there is no limit to the number of girls who may try their hand at this new avocation.

* * * *

THE COMING PLAYS.

FIGURE 38. Gertrude M. Price column, *Toledo News-Bee*, March 30, 1914.

1913–14 elections of several to public office in the newly incorporated Universal City.[49] Moreover, in a later signed story, she explicitly described the "wonderful field which the moving picture has opened" as a "great new field for women folk"[50]—from stars and lesser actors to writers and filmmakers—where a woman's "originality . . . her perseverance and her brains are coming to be recognized on the same plane as [a] man's" (fig. 38). And entering that field meant exploring what "the *new woman* means," as the feminist anthropologist Elsie Clews Parsons put it in 1916: "the woman not yet classified, perhaps not classifiable, the woman *new* not only to men, but to herself."[51] In that Price's syndicated stories of influential "new women" circulated so widely for more than a year to female fans of the movies—especially the "photoplay matinee girls"—they assumed a special significance for the ways they interconnected movies, working women of different classes, and the suffragette movement.

The other stories and interviews that movie fans could read in newspapers throughout 1913 and into early 1914 tended to contrast, sometimes sharply, with those of Price. Most followed the precedents of *Motion Picture Story* and *Photoplay*. The former magazine's "Chats with the Players" described the interview situation and process as often as the individual actor being interviewed.[52] Personal and "behind the scenes" gossip was of particular interest: an actor's physical attributes, likes and dislikes, and sometimes career details. Francis X. Bushman (Essanay) was "five feet ten inches tall, weigh[s] 176 pounds and like[s] all kinds of outdoor work or play"; he also "miss[es] the regular theater in some things."[53] "Small, cute, intellectual, versatile and industrious," Gene or "Genie" Gauntier (Kalem) was not only "a player" but also a writer of "a great number of successful scenarios."[54] Later columns by Mabel Condon, *Motography*'s "dopester," also adhered to this formula.[55] In February 1913, in an interview with Louise Lester of American's comic *Calamity Anne* series, Condon noted that she "cares not even the tiniest bit for athletics of any kind" and that, although "philosophy interests" her, "woman suffrage gets no portion of her attention."[56] The page or half page that Leslie's Syndicate Film shipped weekly to scores of newspapers included similar interviews, production notes, gossip, and brief news items, much of it concerning stars. In the *Ogden Standard*, King Baggot (IMP) sketched various stages of his career (from real estate promoter to movie actor) and opined on the difference between "good and bad acting."[57] Unsigned articles in this and other papers either hyped, with evident relish, the thrills and dangers that Price took more seriously or else wore pretentious heads such as "A New Constellation of Stars Twinkling in Amusement Firmament."[58] Another syndicated article lampooned the "love-sick swains" who sent "novel proposals" to their "screen favorites" or gifts of "pumpkin pies and eggs by parcel post."[59] This always personal, often professional, and generally apolitical gossip would more and more characterize newspaper columns from 1914 on.

"IN THE FRAME OF PUBLIC FAVOR"

The appetite for news and gossip of movie fans' "screen favorites" received a huge boost, shortly before Price's column became merely occasional, with the "In the Frame of Public Favor" photo profiles that Mae Tinee so prominently featured on the "Right Off the Reel" page of the *Chicago Sunday Tribune*. Because they were usually larger than any other images of faces in the newspaper, these "close ups," much like the "gigantic" images on a movie screen, likely held a unique fascination for readers. In the initial captioned profile descriptions, Mae Tinee offered a mix of information and gossip. Kathlyn Williams was "of the Anglo-Saxon strain—fair-haired and blue eyed," with "the classic cast of heroic face," and she had had a relatively successful stage career before being hired by Selig, where she "courted a dangerous situation for the sheer spice of novelty" and described it as "all in the day's work."[60] Francis X. Bushman supposedly was "an expert swimmer, boxer, horseman, swordsman, and wrestler"; he also had had a touring stage career before signing with Essanay and being selected by a number of artists to pose as "the typical American . . . for paintings and for statues."[61] There were implicit signs of fans' interests in their voting choices of several stars: both Maurice Costello and Mary Pickford were "married"; "Kerrigan lives in Hollywood, Cal., with his mother"; and Alice Joyce, "an expert horsewoman and swimmer" with "light brown hair and black eyebrows," was named "a particular favorite of feminine movie patrons."[62] There also were increasing signs of Mae Tinee's own interest in stars' work on- and off-screen: Costello allegedly "evolved the 'slow motion' style of acting" that had become typical of motion pictures; Florence LaBadie was known for her "pet fad [of] sketching her friends"; King Baggot was the "author of sixty or seventy scenarios"; and Pearl White, who had spent two years of her girlhood in a touring circus and then five years on stage before "becoming a 'movie' actress," was especially happy that the "moving picture field" gave her "so much time to be out of doors."[63]

Complementing these "close ups" were several regular columns on the *Tribune*'s Sunday page that solicited readers' questions about the "inside facts" that they wanted "to know about the motion picture field." The "Gossip of the Silent Players" column was invested in "the life of your favorite actor and actress outside the films": "A Brazilian sculptor is said to be making a plaster cast of John Bunny"; "Mary Pickford, Vivian Prescott, and Lillian Gish all worked together once as stage children"; and "Ethel Clayton (Lubin) is a fiend for motoring and owns a car which she bought with her own savings."[64] Mae Tinee's signed column "Answers to Movie Fans" also offered "inside facts" about fans' favorites and supplemented those with details about motion picture production: "It is true that [Kathlyn Williams] has a scar on her forehead caused by a leopard"; "Miss Mignon Anderson of the Thanhouser company is not Swedish [and] not married"; "Some of the scenes for 'The Adventures of Kathlyn' were taken in India, but most of them were taken in Los Angeles at the Selig zoo"; and "The 'Mutual Girl' series are taken in New York City[,] . . . show actual scenes and the prominent people are real."[65] For fans wishing to submit scenarios to film manufacturing companies, one of her first columns listed their mailing addresses, but Mae Tinee refused to recommend any "schools for scenario writing" or give advice on "how to become a photo player."[66] By early June 1914, the newspaper was inundated with so many queries that she had to warn fans "to read the column . . . each Sunday before sending in your inquiries, so that you will not duplicate inquiries that have already been made and answered."[67] Within weeks, she was forced to adopt a policy close to that of *Motion Picture Story*: "Questions considered as ridiculous will not be answered. Questions regarding relationships will be answered to the best of our ability, but we are not responsible if mistakes are made."[68] In a rare story on a non-American actor, Mae Tinee readily accepted the class prejudices of the period, repeating Gabriel D'Annunzio's remarks about how long it took Maciste to learn to act in *Cabiria* (1913), but she just as easily could sound a bit like Gertrude Price with her story about how "the march of suffrage continues" because one day, during the production of a Vitagraph film, Norma Talmadge quickly "added the operation of a motion picture camera to her accomplishments."[69]

Between August and September 1914, Mae Tinee introduced two more Sunday columns that solicited comments rather than questions from movie fans. One was a survey that asked, "Will You Take Your Star Married or Single?" Coming from Chicago and elsewhere (from Elgin, Illinois, to perhaps Augusta, Georgia), most responses said "either way," "it doesn't make any difference," or "I would not care less."[70] Only a few admitted that a star's marital status mattered. How representative these fans' letters were is difficult to determine, and that uncertainty may have led to the column's disappearance in mid-September. Soon replacing it was another, "The Voice of the Movie Fans," which largely focused on issues and concerns other than those involving movie stars.[71] Instead, "In the Frame of Public Favor" and "Answers to Movie Fans" continued to serve up a steady diet of information and gossip about readers' "favorite players." Sometimes in longer stories of humorous deception, more news crept into "In MovieLand," formerly "Gossip of the Movie Plays and Players" (fig. 39). In one story, a thief broke into the apartment of Wallace Beery, the star of Essanay's "Sweedie" comedies, and stole the character's huge diamond ring (a fake costing ten cents); in another, Norma Talmadge, one day, "in a spirit of adventure," left the set of Vitagraph's *A Question of Clothes* still cross-dressed as her character "Bob" Courtney. First she flirted with a woman on the street (and nearly got trounced by her male escort); nonplussed, she then "treated" two other young women "in the regulation boyish manner."[72]

By early 1915, the *Sunday Tribune* was expanding its coverage of movie fans' fascination with stars. Beginning with Mary Pickford's photograph,

Dorothy Gish will recover! Isn't that good news? Recently the little Griffith-Mutual star, in full view of the studio crowd at Hollywood, was struck by a racing automobile and dragged over forty feet before the big machine could be stopped. Her horrified friends rushed down the road to her, found her unconscious, and among those who helped lift her into the ambulance when it came was D. W. Griffith, who has done so much to make the younger Gish sister a star on the Mutual program. The director rode to Los Angeles with her, and her many other friends followed her there as best they could, by trolley, motor, or carriage. At the hospital surgeons discovered that the little Mutual star had had her left side very badly torn and one toe cut off. It looked like a bad case, but after several hours she began to rest more easily, and Mr. Griffith finally came out and announced that she would live, but that it might be several weeks before she would be able to work again.

In "Hounded" Ben Wilson risks his life in an escape from prison by climbing to a steeply sloping roof and again in scaling a prison wall. This picture is a portrayal of what a prison stain on a man's life can do.

The million admirers Florence La Badie gained for herself while playing in the "Million Dollar Mystery" will be delighted to learn of an opportunity to renew their screen acquaintance with the actress. She soon is to appear on the Mutual program in a two-reel Thanhouser feature called "Under False Colors." This is to be the first of a series of strong dramatic pictures in which Miss La Badie is to play the leads. Her work in the "Million Dollar Mystery," while it served to emphasize that girlish grace and charm which always have been hers, proved also that the little actress has a forceful dramatic instinct all her own. She has nerve, too, and there has yet to appear a risk she will not take on sight for the sake of making a picture good. No wonder her followers are a loyal lot.

Ford Sterling, who has been battling for some time with typhoid-pneumonia, has won out and will be at work again in a short time.

George Larkin has joined the Balboa Feature Film company. Also Ruth Roland and Henry King are being featured in a serial.

Irene Warfield will appear in an Alco release in the near future.

"It Is No Laughing Matter" is the title of a new film from Bosworth, Inc. Myrtle Stedman and Maclyn Arbuckle are the lead ng lights in the play.

Selig's has purchased about four miles of film from E. Swift Train, grandson of George Francis Train, who has also just come back from a trip to the Alaska-Siberian coast. He was gone eight months, and went as far north as Wrangel island, where they assisted in the rescue of eleven survivors from the Karluck, an arctic exploration vessel which was stuck in the ice for twenty-four days. Train secured some great pictures of native life.

That popular man to whom Mary Pickford is married, Owen Moore, has joined the Bosworth company. So, for a time—or a picture—has Elsie Janis. Some combination, isn't it? Mr. Moore will play opposite Miss Janis in her new comedy drama, "Betty in Search of a Thrill." As the title suggests, Betty's hair raising experiences will keep one on the ragged edge of mental precipices; she, pursued by the hero, does everything to give one shivery quivers, from scaling the side of a house, jumping off a bridge into the water, disguising herself as a boy to—but watch for the picture! It will be released by Bosworth, Inc., on the Paramount program, to follow Miss Janis' first picture, "The Caprices of Kitty."

Presented by an inspired contributor with his compliments to the readers of the "Right off the Reel" page:

THE PEOPLE AT THE MOVIES.

It always seems funny to me,
And I'm sure it does to you,
Just how the movies affect the crowds—
The fans—regular and occasional, too.

See that fellow ahead of us,
Over there beside the aisle;
He with the dark blue suit
And the ever broadening smile?

When J. Warren comes to view
And plays his hero part,
See how he intently watches,
And whispers to his friend apart.

Behind us I hear the giggles and the titters
Of a couple of painted lasses, I'll bet;
Who, nothing loath, are surely doting
On our famous hero pet.

Listen to our neighbors on the right,
Those two women near the fan;
I can hear the one remark, quiet like of course,
"Ain't he just a dandy man?"

It makes no difference where we look,
We may always be amused;
And if, perhaps, we stare too long,
We can surely be excused.

VICTOR E. CARPENTER.

Following is a letter received by Mary Fuller of the Universal company, which must have made her proud, sad—and happy:

SALISBURY PLAINS, England, Dec. 8, 1914.—Dear Miss Fuller: I was awfully glad to receive your picture which you so kindly sent me to Glacier, and which was forwarded to me here. As you can see, I have joined the Canadian troops to fight against Germany and Austria, as I considered it my duty to assist the mother country with my life, if necessary. So I have been unable to see you in another picture, but I hope it is only a pleasure deferred if I am spared. We are quartered on Salisbury Plains, sixteen miles from a town, and as it has been raining incessantly for the last two weeks, everything and everybody feels wet and miserable.

We will be glad when our turn comes to go to the front. We can be in France within thirty-six hours. But I think they intend to keep us here till later, as Britain has enough men on the continent at present. Without wishing to appear too romantic, I must tell you that your photo goes with me into the firing line. I have always got great pleasure from seeing you on the screen, and ever since I started writing to you I have taken a greater interest in your doings. A little word would be a great encouragement to me, but I suppose I have tried your patience quite enough and you have been very good to me. If I may, I would like to drop you a line occasionally, and if I don't write again you will know what has happened to me, and where one of your photos has found a last resting place with me. The above is my permanent address, if you should feel like sending me a card.

With best wishes for your future success, and may fortune always smile on you, I am, Sincerely yours, ROBERT WEBB, Canadian contingent, Salisbury Plains, England.

Vote for the Picture of Your Favorite Player

James Cruze received the highest number of votes for the last two weeks. His picture, therefore, will appear in The Frame of Public Favor next Sunday. Of the other players voted upon the following six are the leaders:

Lila Chester, Arthur Johnson, Richard Tucker, Henry King, Dorothy Kelly, and Norma Talmadge.

THE BALLOT

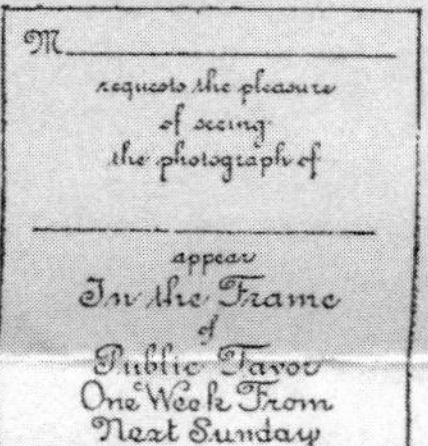
M____________________

requests the pleasure of seeing the photograph of

____

appear In the Frame of Public Favor One Week From Next Sunday

FIGURE 39. "In Movie Land" column, *Chicago Sunday Tribune,* January 3, 1915.

each week's edition included a "handsome insert, on special paper, all ready for framing FREE."[73] Mae Tinee herself was responsible for most of that expansion. In January, she visited the Essanay studios in Chicago to interview Charlie Chaplin, the company's new acquisition from Keystone. The comic confessed to not liking to be interviewed, she reported, because audiences can find "celebrities that are already made" overrated; and they laughed over the story of his first fan letter in which a "little chap" wrote: "You was certainly grand, Mr. Chaplin, all threw the pixter, but the way you squirted water out of your mouth was classic."[74] Within a month, she was supplementing "The Frame of Public Favor" with a new weekly column that titillated readers with stories about familiar favorites such as Mary Pickford, Francis X. Bushman, and Alice Joyce.[75] That soon gave way to the reproduction of an "old fashioned album" in which first Maurice Costello and then Florence LaBadie penned brief answers to two pages of questions about their own favorite things and what they considered "the ideal proportions of a member of the opposite sex."[76] By February, the "Right Off the Reel" page was so full that she added a further "Latest News from Movie Land" column in the Dramatic section of the Sunday edition. There too the "news" was all about the stars: Leah Baird "received from an unknown girl admirer in Marion, Ind., a book illustrating the story of her life in pictures clipped from numerous publications"; and Kathlyn Williams's name was being attached to everything from babies, a waltz, and a song to a perfume, a cocktail, and a "watch charm for single men."[77] Even when the column began to include a selected list of "Feature Films of the Week" and reports on Selig and Essanay scenario contests, stars remained the main attraction, even if only to report that "a $800,000 insurance policy has been written to cover the cast of 'The Diamond in the Sky.'"[78]

In summer 1914, at least one other gossip column appeared in Mary Leffler's "Flashes from Filmland" column, written several times a week for the *Fort Worth Star-Telegram*.[79] Headed "Gossip of the Film World," this was usually the smallest section of the column and included an idiosyncratic mix of bits and pieces. There were production notes, especially on various companies' western units: for *The Strike at Coaldale*, Éclair had the loan of a special train from the El Paso & Southern railway.[80] And announcements about serials: Bobbs-Merrill was publishing *The Adventures of Kathlyn* in book form, and Thanhouser was spending big on *The Million Dollar Mystery* (serialized in the *Star-Telegram*), which involved much shooting on locations such as the freight yards and docks lining the New Jersey side of the Hudson River.[81] Also, local news: the city's Airdome admitted children free for a special screening of *Quo Vadis?*, and each

Saturday engaged boys and girls in a singing and dancing contest.[82] But stars were favored. While Leffler assumed that her readers wanted to know about the daring stunts of such serial stars as Florence LaBadie and Cleo Madison, she also shared the news that Vitagraph's Anne Schaefer had won a St. Louis newspaper contest and Marguerite Snow had been a special guest of Washington politicians.[83] She even told the story of Norma Talmadge's playful cross-dressed flirtations—ten days before it appeared in the *Chicago Sunday Tribune.*[84] That fall, as Leffler enlarged "Flashes from Filmland" to a half page on Sundays, she also followed the *Tribune* in adding a "Questions of 'Movie' Fans" column that, not unexpectedly, solicited queries about "your favorite screen actor."[85] Soon that half page was giving extra attention to young actresses such as Marguerite Courtot, Anna Little (and "her rapid rise"), Mary Pickford, and a host of others "in private life."[86] Leffler even made a point of highlighting the exploits of "Grace Darling, the fearless little reporter of the Hearst-Selig news pictorial" (perhaps one of her own role models?), who was filming her cross-country trip to the San Francisco Exposition.[87]

"BEHIND THE SCREENS" IN EARLY 1915

Paralleling the gossip columns compiled by Mae Tinee and Mary Leffler were an increasing number of articles devoted to movie stars in what was now simply titled *Motion Picture Magazine.* In July 1914, that monthly fan magazine began supplementing its "Chats with the Players" and "Answer Department" columns with regular articles written by individual stars: "Extracts from the Diary of Mary Fuller," "Autobiography of J. Warren Kerrigan," "Extracts from the Diary of Crane Wilbur."[88] In August came Jean Darnell's "Ruth Roland, the 'Kalem Girl'" and Russell E. Smith's "Lillian Gish: 'The Most Beautiful Blonde in the World."[89] Soon joining such interviews each month were a handy reference guide ("Brief Biographies of Popular Players") and statements from half a dozen stars, apparently in response to the magazine's query "How I Became a Photoplayer."[90] Together with Mae Tinee's widely circulating weekly columns, *Motion Picture Magazine*'s discourse, along with those in *Photoplay* and *Motography,* may well have induced other newspapers to satisfy the appetites of their readers for more and more gossip about movie stars.

In July 1914, the Scripps-McRae newspapers hired Esther Hoffman as a syndicated movie columnist to replace Gertrude Price. Labeled a "picture play reporter," Hoffman initially followed Price with articles on Ruth Stonehouse's nonchalance in taking acting risks and Francis X. Bushman's shyness off-screen.[91] But she soon was in sync with the newspaper chain's shift, along with the United Press service's, to target a readership of women more aligned with consumption and domestic life. That had been signaled weeks earlier in Idah M'Glone Gibson's series on beauty and etiquette tips from Beverly Bayne,[92] and Hoffman fell in line with columns on Lillian Gish and Marguerite Courtot (both based on articles in *Motion Picture Magazine*) and Mary Pickford, "The Girl With the Curl."[93] From October through January, some of her columns acquired the banner "Who's Who on the Films": Grace Cunard, Norma Phillips, Marguerite Snow, and Helen Badgley, to name a few.[94] Another in the *Des Moines News* on John Bunny made the front page, and a rare column, in the *Reno Gazette*, reported that Ruth Stonehouse was donating dolls to war orphans in Europe.[95] Much like Mae Tinee, Hoffman served as a judge, along with "beauty expert" Gibson, in a heavily advertised contest to find "The Most Beautiful Telephone Girl in All America!" to star in Essanay's *The Woman's Way*.[96] Tellingly, Hoffman remained committed to consumer interests in related columns on Ella Hall (who designed her own clothes), Margarita Fischer ("Harrison Fisher's ideal beauty for 1915"), Clara Kimball Young (who loved "sheer, filmy fabrics"), and even daredevil Helen Holmes ("a true critic of make up").[97] And that carried over into the summer of 1915 in a syndicated series on Gish, "How to Be Beautiful."[98] Even Price occasionally returned to writing about the movies from her new base in Los Angeles. She spent one day in January 1915 as an "extra girl" on the set of a Universal film starring J. Warren Kerrigan, and later offered tips from comediennes Fay Tincher and Pauline Moran on "how to be funny" in the movies.[99]

By early 1915, movie fans could find a few more newspaper columns of gossip about their favorite stars, still mainly in Sunday editions. In Chicago the *Sunday Herald* followed the *Sunday Tribune*'s lead with not one but three columns consistently or at least partly devoted to movie stars. After his first column on Chaplin in January, Gene Morgan went to the local Selig studios to interview Tyrone Power, Bessie Eyton, and Kathlyn Williams.[100] Soon he turned to writing stories about fictional characters and their experiences with the movies—his "old friend Jimmy" who spent off hours in the municipal censors' projection room, and others who argued that the term "movies had come to stay"—but not before letting Mrs. Carter H. Harrison, the city mayor's wife and its "best movie fan," promote "motion pictures [as] a great library for the poor and those whom circumstances have denied education."[101] Jitney Jim would share many "movieland" adventures in Morgan's later columns.[102] At the same time each week, Rosemary Grey contributed short star profiles called "His Hobby" or

"Her Hobby" accompanied by a silly graphic that initially literalized the title: each actor's head sat atop a cartoon figure mounted on a rocking horse.[103] In April, Caroline Carr began composing a weekly star profile—with a large image prominently centered, as created by Mae Tinee—and headlined by catchy phrases reminiscent of Gertrude Price: "Ruth Roland Breezily Mixes Tea and Business"; "Pretty Grace Darmond, Who Rides, Swims, Acts"; "Hard Work and Luck Aid Miss Bayne."[104] Somewhat belatedly, the *Herald* devoted one page in its Rotogravure Section to selected photos of Charlie Chaplin and later published an exclusive series of articles allegedly written by the comic, "My Adventures in Movieland."[105] Also beginning in April came an unsigned column, "What Fans Want to Know," sometimes seconded by a shorter column addressing fans' queries or correspondence.[106] In May, the *Herald* introduced a unique contest awarding avid movie fans a dollar for "bright bits of information" or "a bit of conversation heard in a filmhouse" that would be printed in the newspaper.[107]

Again following the *Tribune,* in mid-March 1915, the *Herald* introduced a daily film review column, "Seen on the Screen," which Louella Parsons quickly took over from Caroline Carr (see chapter 4).[108] Parsons nearly always saved space for a section of "Answers to Questions," and, as expected, stars were the subjects of most fans' queries. From the beginning, Parsons was unusually courteous and often personal in her responses. "It is a great pleasure to greet old friends in this department; and I want to thank you for your nice letter"; "I am sorry that your question remained unanswered for so long"; "I agree with you that Edith Storey is an accomplished actress. You have excellent taste."[109] Occasionally, she herself conducted short interviews—with Lew Fields and Ethel Barrymore—fashioning a dialogue framed by her questions.[110] Prodded by countless readers' questions, she asked Kathlyn Williams and Francis X. Bushman exactly how many fan letters they actually received—five hundred to fifteen hundred a week, they revealed.[111] She advised one fan to convey her admiration for Caroline Carr's longer star photo profiles directly: "She will be delighted to hear that you are enjoying her interviews."[112] Much like other columnists, she expressed a concern for the many young girls hoping to make it in the industry. One she counseled to "obey your mother by all means" and don't "threaten to leave such a good home." Another, then acting as an extra, she warned not to "complain because someone in the studio spoke sharply to you," especially when one of the largest film companies, advertising for "thousands of pretty girls" to appear in "a spectacular production," received letters that "reached the ten thousands."[113] Instead, she congratulated one fan for her "splendid idea [of] saving all the pictures from the *Herald* rotogravure section for a scrapbook,"[114] as Edna Vercoe already had done (see chapter 5).

In June 1915, Parsons committed herself to giving readers even more information about industry figures, especially movie stars (fig. 40). For one thing, she conducted more frequent interviews in Chicago: with Geraldine Farrar, nibbling roses for breakfast, as she stopped in the city on her way to California; with Henry Walthall, who had just joined the Essanay company; with Valli Valli, who made a personal appearance for a screening of Metro's *The High Road* at the downtown Colonial Theater; and with Lois Weber ("Mrs. Smalley . . . in private life") as she was filming Anna Pavlova in an open-air studio at Sans Souci amusement park for Universal's *The Dumb Girl of Portici*.[115] Perhaps Parsons's crucial coup was to get the *Herald* to publish a weekly Sunday series in which major stars agreed to tell "The Story of My Life," with the assistance of either a press agent or Parsons herself. The series began appropriately with Kathlyn Williams and continued with Edna Mayo, Marguerite Clark, Lillian Gish, and Clara Kimball Young.[116] A large studio photo graced each story, and in its Rotogravure section the *Sunday Herald* also began adding more "pictures of movie stars that are worth saving."[117] Of these, the most important undoubtedly was "The Story of My Life by Charley Chaplin," which ran from July 4 through August 8.[118] Together with the *Herald*'s comic strip *Charley Chaplin's Comic Capers* (see the third entr'acte) and the comic's eagerly anticipated work at Essanay's Chicago studio, the six installments of this story made Chaplin the most publicized movie star in the city. After a one-month hiatus, Parsons resumed her star stories—beginning with Anita Stewart, Mae Marsh, Crane Wilbur, and Ruth Stonehouse—but now, as "the intimate friend of practically all the great stars," she made them successful examples in a new series, "How to Become a Movie Actress."[119] Tellingly, all but one of these stories of "How I Broke Into the Movies," featured young women, and Parsons seemed far less concerned about disabusing aspiring fans of their dreams than she had earlier that spring.

In February 1915, when the *Atlanta Constitution* introduced its "Moving Picture Page," one of its chief features was the column "Behind the Screens with Britt Craig" (fig. 41).[120] According to an ad for the "Best Sunday Newspaper the South Ever Saw," this column offered fans "the brightest, breeziest gossip" about "what the heroes and heroines are doing, how they got into the silent drama, who are married, and to whom [along with] plenty of pictures of your favorites."[121] A well-known police reporter and drama critic for the paper,[122] Craig used his weekly column to compile a miscellany of star photos and sketches, bits of information and gossip,

Here's Ideal Film Personality—Clara Kimball Young Is Playful Child and Brainy Woman

Also, She Is Described as Possessing Beauty, Brains, an Engaging Personality and Hereditary Ability as an Actress—Could Anybody Ask for a Better Foundation for a Successful Career Before the Screen?

I MUST admit that I had very early stage training. I have acted ever since I was 3 months old. I also admit that I have a husband who is one of the most capable motion picture directors in the world. Don't you honestly think, in spite of that, I deserve a little credit for what Clara Kimball Young has done? It is rather trying to have some one say: "No wonder Miss Young is a film star; look at her parents, look at her husband."

—*Clara Kimball Young.*

Miss Young's Dark Eyes Truly Are the Windows of Her Soul—Laughing and Joyous, They Hint of the Sensitive Feminine Personality. She Is the Fortunate Possessor of Beauty and Brains.

By LOUELLA O. PARSONS. asked. A dim remembrance of some there was consternation, and later; I told her that I did

FIGURE 40. Louella Parsons column, *Chicago Sunday Herald*, July 18, 1915.

Behind the Screens

With Britt Craig

The Only Vampires

What They Say

PATHE FILMS CONAN DOYLE'S FAMOUS NOVEL

Thomas Santschi Says.

"WINNING BACK"

One of the greatest society dramas ever shown on any screen will be repeated at The Strand

MONDAY

This picture made such an impression on those who saw it that hundreds requested that it be repeated

KEYSTONE COMEDY

An arrangement has been made whereby FOUR KEYSTONE COMEDIES will be shown each week—Monday, Wednesday (or Tuesday), Thursday and Saturday

THE STRAND

"The House of Quality"

Home of Mutual Movies

FIGURE 41. "Behind the Scenes with Britt Craig," *Atlanta Sunday Constitution*, March 7, 1915.

"borrowed biographies," industry news (acknowledging sources in the trade press), very brief reviews, doggerel, and, quite unlike others, pithy, often sarcastic quotes: "Elsie Ford, now suing Francis Ford, asks: 'Why is matrimony, anyhow?' Why is eczema?"[123] The column assumed that readers would be attuned to his snappy, colloquial chats that rarely were linked to films currently playing in the city. Early on he openly admitted that "Of all the words / So sad and solemn / The worst are these, / 'Go write your column!'" Weeks later he was still wondering, "What shall we write about?"[124] While sometimes flippant in describing fan favorites—"The Helen of Kalem gets paid a salary for taking more risks in a day than the Helen of Troy would take for the love of her country in a month"—he could also sound serious: "Mary Pickford has been added by a noted eastern professor of history to a collection of history's most illustrious characters," or, "Grace Cunard is one of the few women who can write, direct and play leads in a photo-play then write the titles, assemble the parts and even operate the machine."[125] In "jottings" that took note of readers' queries, he sometimes gave them voice: describing a publicity agent's "feverish" hype about *The Master Key*'s twelfth episode, he added: "A fair fan wrote to us to know if they supplied smelling salts at the door."[126] A year later Craig's snappy put-downs were undiminished: "Oh, no, Marg, it does not always require marvelous intelligence to star in the movies. The story comes to us of an artist of recent renown who, when told that her scenes needed more atmosphere, went over and raised the nearest window."[127]

In fall 1915, George F. Worts took over "Wid" Gunning's film column in the *New York Evening Mail* and began to intersperse industry news, especially about stars, with his synopses and reviews of motion pictures currently playing in the city. Occasionally, he simply compiled a series of brief comic items on what a whole bevy of stars experienced around Christmastime: Hazel Dawn's "Santa Claus" of a father gave her a "Pierce limousine"; an admirer gave Nell Shipman "a swagger stick cut from a manzanitta [*sic*] bush in which was carved the names of all the members of her company."[128] More often, Worts regaled his readers with stories about the most popular stars.[129] He admired Charlie Chaplin's "never seen" press agent who deceived "unsuspecting editors" with stunt after stunt that kept the comic in the "public gaze," such as dropping false leads as to his whereabouts during the fight over where he would work after the year at Essanay.[130] He was happy to write fictional dialogues in which Mary Pickford chided her mother for worrying about "a pin-point bruise" from a dog bite and "busted" the *Mail*'s "adding machine" for incorrectly contrasting her current salary and "the good old days" of "$50 a week" at Biograph.[131] In anticipation of "the

Motion Picture at Madison Garden," he also hyped the mystery as to who would escort Clara Kimball Young, now that she had won the privilege of leading the grand march in the huge ballroom.[132]

"NEWSY NOTES FROM MOVIELAND," IN THE VOICES OF THE STARS

Until 1915, most of the newspaper information and gossip about movie stars had come to fans through interviews, profiles, and brief stories or quips of one sort or another. In 1913–14, the Leslie Film Syndicate, as already mentioned, followed *Motion Picture Story* and *Motography* in supplying such menu items weekly to its hundreds of newspaper subscribers. Even earlier, theatrical stars such as Sarah Bernhardt (briefly) and Billie Burke had signed weekly syndicated columns that offered their opinions on a variety of subjects, from beauty tips and fashion notes to jealousy and "the stage as a vocation."[133] In 1914, *Motion Picture Magazine* began publishing pages from the purported diaries of fan favorites such as Mary Fuller, J. Warren Kerrigan, and Crane Wilbur, and then replaced those with a column in which several stars, or their press agents, wrote about "How I Became a Photoplayer." At the same time, one-off newspaper columns appeared, signed by Fuller and Blanche Sweet, along with a widely circulating series from Beverly Bayne (written with Idah M'Glone Gibson) on feminine appearance and behavior.[134] In early 1915, certain papers began running the syndicated weekly column "Talks with Screen-Struck Girls" by the stage star turned screen actor Beatriz Michelena, who one year later contracted for a second series with even wider distribution, if chiefly in small cities and towns.[135] By the summer of 1915, Fuller was authoring a weekly column that for at least a month gave her fans further inside information on the long, hard work of a motion picture actor.[136] One-off newspaper columns kept cropping up on Sunday pages in late 1915 and early 1916, from such old and new favorites (or their agents) as Anita Stewart, Helen Holmes, J. Warren Kerrigan, Blanche Sweet, and Theda Bara.[137] A weekly column, "Grace Darling Talks to Girls," also appeared in papers such as the *Minneapolis Sunday Tribune*.[138] Provoking these latter columns was a unique, long-running series from the movies' most popular star.

This was "Daily Talks by Mary Pickford,"[139] distributed to dozens of metropolitan and small-town newspapers by the McClure Newspaper Syndicate, which had been selling weekly features, stories, and games for more than twenty years, especially aimed at women and children (fig. 42).[140] Pickford's column first appeared on November 8, 1915, and, in offering "A Word About

THE WASHINGTON HERALD, SUNDAY, NOVEMBER 7, 1915.

The Most Popular Girl in the World

—AND—

The Highest Paid Artist Who Ever Lived,

MARY PICKFORD

will talk every day on the Woman's Page of THE WASHINGTON HERALD, beginning tomorrow

She will write on all sorts of vital and absorbing subjects in which her remarkable career since the age of five, and her phenomenal success on the moving picture stage, have made her experienced beyond her years, while she still retains the understanding and heart of a child.

Her articles will be full of anecdotes and the personal experiences of a young girl who has made herself famous.

This girl, who is loved throughout the world on account of the sweetness, grace, love and sympathy she can

silently express in her face and figure, is going to talk through THE WASHINGTON HERALD every day, and is going to say things worth reading.

You are invited to write Miss Pickford, through THE WASHINGTON HERALD, on any subject on which you would like her opinion or advice. She will reply either direct to you or in the correspondence department at the end of each daily talk.

Mary Pickford is only 22 years old, but it must be remembered that she has been an actress for seventeen years.

In that time, by her own efforts and without any "pull," she has become the most popular girl in the world. Her weekly guarantee, which continues irrespective of the number of plays she appears in, makes her the highest paid artist in the world, not excepting Caruso.

She receives over 200 letters a day from practically all over the world. With the aid of a secretary and stenographer she answers every letter.

Mary Pickford's experiences have been more varied, her work has been more continuous and severe and her opportunities of studying human character have been more extensive than the average person can boast in a lifetime. She is therefore fully fitted to write a daily letter for publication in a manner that will inform, entertain and help.

FIGURE 42. "Daily Talks by Mary Pickford" ad, *Washington Herald*, November 7, 1915.

Myself and My Little Plan," she was quite explicit about her motivation.[141] Missing the "direct communication with the public" that she supposedly had experienced on stage, Pickford saw "the press as a medium" for creating a kind of communal fan culture with her countless letter writers. Acutely aware of how newspapers could bind distant peoples together as one, she had a vision of fandom's interchange that was strikingly nostalgic: "The fact that we are reading the same newspaper every day with our letters to each other in it will give our association that little, intimate homelike touch it needs to enable us to be of much help [to one another]. It will be just as if we were gathered around the same table." Pickford followed other writers by including an "Answers to Correspondents" at the end of most columns. Early full-page ads in several newspapers confided that she would "write as a young girl to other girls and women" (she acknowledged receiving few letters from boys),[142] so it was telling that her "Daily Talks"—along with others from "Beauty Chats" and "Table Talks" to a syndicated column by the popular novelist Laura Jean Libbey—primarily found a place on most newspapers' Women's or Society pages that, unlike Gertrude Price's earlier columns, assumed a middle-class readership.[143] Although the series was written by, or dictated to, her friend, the scriptwriter Frances Marion, Pickford was quite invested in this enterprise, which ensured that, in both image and word, "the most popular girl in the world" (according to several large ads)[144] was a frequent and "welcome visitor" in millions of households. For its part, the McClure Newspaper Syndicate distributed "Daily Talks" so that, while columns could appear simultaneously in numerous papers, they also were available at different times for different papers. A few new columns were still circulating nearly a year after the series' initial appearance.[145]

In that first column, Pickford told her "friends" (as if anticipating Facebook) that to "make us feel more at home," she would share "something about myself" (fig. 43).[146] This autobiographical angle characterized the column for several weeks, with stories about her early childhood—her father's death when she was four (the oldest of three children), which meant that she would have to act as "the Daddy of the Family"; and "her abhorrence of debt," which led to her continuing habit of "get[ing] along with very few clothes"—and her early dramatic training, from playacting in "the parlors of my old home in Canada" (a rare reference) to stage acting in New York and on tour, which often kept her away from her mother, sister Lottie, and brother Jack.[147] Not long after, individual columns picked up the thread of her career, in moving from stage melodrama to her first days working at Biograph with D.W. Griffith, which she later claimed were "the happiest days of my life."[148] Very soon, she was describing her experiences making current films—taking care to get expressions and behavior right in *Madame Butterfly,* washing her hair on a "bitter cold day" for a scene in *Tess of Storm Country,* making a poignant visit to an orphanage in preparation for *The Foundling*—and observing the extras around her, for instance the delightful little girls who acted with her as orphans in *The Foundling,* and the "many old and broken-down character actors and actresses" for whom the movie studio was "a veritable refuge."[149] Only once did she take on critics to complain that negative reviews could have devastating effects and to stage a mock dialogue between

A Word About Myself And My Little Plan

(Copyright, 1915, by the McClure Newspaper Syndicate)

IT would be useless for one whose acting is confined solely to the screen to say that we do not miss the magnetic presence and enthusiastic applause of an audience. We do miss both very much, and while the realism and charm of nature in scenario work compensate for many things, nevertheless we miss that personal touch with the public that restrains, suggests, encourages and inspires.

One whose audiences consist day by day solely of a director and property men has no direct communication with the public except through its letters to him, and it has occured to me that in my case I might strengthen and facilitate this method of communication by using the press as a medium.

It will not only be simpler, then, for my letter friends to reach me, but the fact that we are reading the same newspaper every day, with our letters to each other in it, will give our association that little intimate, homelike touch it needs to enable us to be of mutual help. It will be just as if we were gathered around the same table to make our little plans for the future, to laugh at the plans that went awry, to cheer each other, a little bit, for I contend that we tease always when we love.

A Welcome Visitor.

What great times we will have! The newspaper, which has always meant something to which father has the prior right, gets cross about if it is late and grumblingly hides behind, will then have a more personal, a more intimate, meaning to each of us. Always the one visitor every member of the family welcomes, think how much warmer that welcome will be when it becomes the medium of our daily little friendly talks! In a very pleasing way the scenario artist has an advantage over what some please to call the "legitimate" actor. We do not have the exquisite joy of seeing the smiles and tears in the faces before us; we miss the supreme bliss of the curtain call, but—and think what this means!—our friends, our admirers, our critics are not confined to the few cities where we have appeared.

They are broadcast, and as letters from every point in the globe, from South Africa to Alaska, pass through our hands, we can afford to smile a little triumphantly at our bowing and scraping rival. True, we have not the joy of the curtain call, but neither are ours the narrow limitations of one little stage. He has a season in Chicago, for instance, and only those who are fortunate enough to be in Chicago, see him. We have a few busy days in studio, in the country, on the hills or in the valley, wherever realism takes us, and appear in the next month almost all over the world.

And those to whom we appear, realizing that we are blind to tears and smiles and deaf to applause and feeling that they must find an outlet for their admiration, find it through the ink-bottle. Bless its inky face! I say, for it has done more through those who hover around it to encourage and help me than anything else in the world. What a greater medium of help the newspaper will now become!

An Early Awakening.

Would it make us feel more at home, I wonder, if I tell my friends right at the beginning something about myself?

I was a tiny girl of four when my aunt carried me downstairs one morning, and I knew by the manner in which she held me tight to her breast when we passed a certain door that my father lay dead behind it. I knew, too (the tragic precocity of it!) that I was my mother's oldest child, and now must help her.

We had no means. I was four, Lottie was three, Jack was a baby in arms, and our grandmother, a helpless paralytic, was a more hopeless burden than we. In looking backward now, I can see that the seriousness of our situation was magnified in my childish imagination. I seem, in my mind's eye now, never to have known the care-free, happy-hearted childhood which is every child's due. I always clung closely to my mother, as if I instinctively knew that she must not be left alone to grieve and work, and one of the first questions I remember asking her was how many years it would be till I would be old enough to work and help her, and of counting off the years on my fingers when she replied that I could not earn money before I was fourteen.

But God was good to me, and I did not have to wait that long.

ANSWERS TO CORRESPONDENTS.

Phyllis, sixteen, writes from Seattle to ask which I think is greater—a home life or a career. A home life, beyond doubt. We who were foolish enough to have chosen a career have nothing but empty hands and arms when we are old. And empty hearts, too.

Mrs. R. M. concludes a long letter with the question: "I have begged and threatened and told her of his worthlessness, but she refuses to give him up. What shall I do now?" If girls in Dallas are like all other girls, this mother has fairly driven the girl into the man's arms. Of course she won't give him up under such encouraging treatment. Try praising him for such traits as even she will see he does not possess.

Alice, a little Indian girl, who encloses a picture showing the straightest of hair, wishes to know if use of the curling iron works injury. I do not know from experience: I have never used it, but am quite sure that it does the hair no good to cook the life out of it. Straight hair is as pretty as curly if kept well groomed.

Mary Pickford.

MUST STAMP ALL COLD STORAGE EGGS

New York, Nov. 8.—(A. P.)—All cold storage eggs sold in this city after November 15, must be stamped as such and all dealers in them must display signs stating that cold storage eggs are on sale, says John J. Dillon, state commissioner of foods and markets, in a warning bulletin received by egg merchants today.

FIGURE 43. "Daily Talks by Mary Pickford," *Canton Repository,* November 8, 1915.

a know-it-all movie spectator "knocking" *Tess* to his adoring companion.[150] Pickford's consistent interest in children led her to share more childhood stories, without specifically referencing Canada: the street musicians and "hurdy-gurdy man" who played in her neighborhood, an early-morning climb into an old, gnarled apple tree, the games she and Lottie concocted to make housework bearable.[151] That interest often turned into a strong concern for her readers' welfare as she joined others in warning girls that the "merciless camera" could be unkind to beautiful faces, that film work required acting experience, dedication, and patience, and that a "flashy girl" usually had to accept work merely as an extra.[152]

The moral, even sanctimonious tone evidenced in these columns suggests that Pickford was well aware that, as a young woman herself, she had to perform as a role model for her fans. Several strategies probably made her advice more palatable. Quite often it came in stories that showed how adept she (or Marion) could be at writing scenarios or working variations on her earlier Biograph films. There were stories of disappointment, loss, and grief: the tall, handsome cowboy who served as a guide on a Biograph film shot in a Southern California desert took an interest in Pickford, and showed up in Los Angeles in the unfortunate guise of what he thought one should look like in the city.[153] The ship's captain who, after spending months at sea away from his new bride, returned in the spring to find her and her baby dead and tearfully wondered how the robins' "gay springtime melody" could "still ripple on."[154] Others underscored the value of patience, curiosity, and new experiences. The homely girl in the "Leopard's Spots" story who, "in the chrysalis of time," turned into a "beautiful and distinguished" woman.[155] The boy who disobeyed his father one day, slipped away and under a touring circus tent, only to find the "stern, old, cross disciplinarian" enjoying the clowns and trapeze artists more than anyone else.[156] The day that she, like Norma Talmadge earlier, went sledding in her orphan costume from *The Foundling,* got into a fight with several boys, and fled back to the studio.[157] The night she and Clara Kimball Young went "slumming" to "the largest of the East Side motion picture theaters" and found themselves asked to speak to an admiring audience "packed with Russians, Poles, and Jews."[158] Finally, there was the spaghetti dinner invitation from a character actor in *Poor Little Peppina,* which led her on a walk through the "crooked, crowded streets" of Little Italy to an unexpectedly clean "cubbyhole" apartment and later to "little Russian brass shops" where she bought some gifts for the actor's family.[159]

So committed, apparently, was Pickford to giving advice that she could use a whole column, rather than simply "Answers to Correspondents," to address the more egregious of her letter writers directly. To those convinced they were long-lost relatives, she tartly reminded them that she had "only one brother and one sister."[160] To those pleading for money, she wrote that she could not fulfill such requests, explaining that she received too many letters that turned out to be deceptive.[161] Other letters she found quite poignant, whether from "the lovelorn" desperate to know "what had I better do," or, in a gesture of feigned neutrality, from the British girls whose fathers or brothers perhaps were lost in the war, "a boy from the French frontier," and even a German mother who sent "a little knitted sack and a pair of bedroom slippers . . . in memory of her daughter."[162] Occasionally a column would reveal how conventional or unconventional Pickford's thinking was for the time. Whereas the experience of a widowed studio charwoman provoked her publicly to promote the great benefits of nursery day care, the illness of one of her family's "colored maids" only prompted her to declare her "love [for] little pickaninnies" and wonder what would happen to them "without their mother's sheltering care."[163] By the summer of 1916, Pickford had become more deeply involved in her own production company (partnered with Adolph Zukor), and, for its last months, especially after Marion fell ill, the column turned into a series entitled "Personalities I Have Met," beginning with former stage celebrities and then turning to movie personnel.[164] In the end, what had been a unique and popular column reverted to the well-established format of the personality sketch, even if drawn from Pickford's working relations with her subjects.

Before then, however, the Pickford of "Daily Talks" exhibited certain relatively consistent characteristics in a possible effort to center and control the reception of her star image. She was usually an adolescent girl speaking to other girls, much like a single older sister. Implicitly, she was "white," with the unspoken privilege of being able to blend in with ethnic communities or even "pass," as if playing one of her frequent poor and sometime orphaned screen characters, whose social rise must have had a special appeal to both her working-class and middle-class fans.[165] Moreover, she always was part of a family, whether with her mother, brother, and younger sister or with her fans "gathered around the same table" in a fictional kitchen or dining room—contradictorily existing both outside and inside a seemingly invisible patriarchal system of social relations. And never, ever was she a sexualized figure, a married woman, or a savvy businesswoman. Even her advice came couched in stories about the joys and sufferings involving family members of one kind or another. For Pickford, as a frequent and welcome visitor in millions of households, family trumped any other social category of identity, subsuming most, if not all, social differences—at least in fans' imaginations.

NEWS NOTES from MOVIELAND

by DAISY DEAN

"The girl with the saddest face in films"—that is what they say of pretty Mae Marsh of Griffith Triangle fame, and it certainly is a face capable of wonderful expressions. But while sad in many of the pictures, it is a winsomely merry little countenance, when Miss Marsh is not at work. Miss Marsh, when she appeared at the Biograph studio some years ago, was, however, not the attractive person she is at the present day. Her best friends say that she was ungainly and awkward, wore her hair plastered tight to her head and tied in two pigtails down her back. She was sunburned and freckle faced and altogether not what any director would have been apt to choose for his star of stars. Mr. Griffith is the possessor of a miraculous intuition and he saw what lay behind. She was installed as a member of the Biograph company and under Mr. Griffith's instruction she improved rapidly and before many months had elapsed she was acknowledged by every one engaged at the studio to be one of the best actresses there. While she appears principally in tragic roles, she has been featured in comedies more than once, she can be just as funny as she can be sad. Miss Marsh weighs 106 pounds, is slight, has large gray eyes and brown hair.

Mae Marsh.

Pavlowa Plans Oriental Play.

Now that Anna Pavlowa, the great Russian dancer, has had her first experience in cinematography, and has personally witnessed her debut in the silent drama with considerable satisfaction over her first effort, she has become so enthused that she is personally working on a Nippon love story in which her dancing will again be featured, which she proposes to complete before the end of the present theatrical season. Then she will go over the scenario with Lois Weber, her personal director of photoplays and they will then put on an original production for the Universal far exceeding even the massive production of "The Dumb Girl of Portici."

Florence La Badie is learning how to run a typewriter. "Everyone should know how to do two or three things, so that if one should fail, one would have something to fall back upon," says the charming star of Thanhouser (Mutual) pictures.

"The Conqueror," a coming Kay-Bee-Triangle, with Willard Mack and Enid Markey, is an arraignment against snobbishness.

CHAUFFEUR MARRIES HEIRESS TO $500,000

New York, Jan. 26.—Priscilla K. von B. Ebling, heiress to $500,000, and Fritz Wolfort, formerly her mother's chauffeur, were secretly married in Gloucester, Mass., November 9.

It was the intention of the young couple to keep their secret until the bride reaches her 21st birthday next month. An alert reporter upset their plans.

Mrs. Wolfort's mother, Mrs. Amanda Ebling, widow of Philip Ebling, the brewer, has forgiven the couple. Wolfort came to this country five years ago from Germany to make his fortune. He is of good family. His employment was as chauffeur in the Ebling family, where he met pretty, demure Priscilla. Wolfort later left the employ of the Ebling family and prospered.

Camille.
Final showing at the Grand today.
—Advertisement. 1t

FIGURE 44. "News Notes from Movieland by Daisy Dean," *Canton Repository,* January 28, 1916.

As Pickford's "Daily Talks" became an increasingly familiar menu item across the country, another daily column with a more limited range was whetting movie fans' appetites for gossip about their favorite stars. This was Daisy Dean's "News Notes from Movieland" that the Central Press Association distributed as a daily column, chiefly to Midwest newspapers, beginning in January 1916 (fig. 44).[166] Although billed as a "celebrated movie writer," Daisy Dean seems to have been the pseudonym of a yet-unknown young woman, who may have derived the name from the main character in Lois Weber's *Scandal,* a five-part Broadway-Universal feature released in the summer of 1915.[167] Papers such as the *La Crosse Tribune*

(Wisconsin), *Canton Repository* (Ohio), *Hutchinson News* (Kansas), *Janesville Gazette* (Wisconsin), and *Lima Times-Democrat* (Ohio) initially carried the same syndicated column on the same day of the week, but by late 1916 any one column could appear several days apart in those and others such as the *Eau Claire Leader* (Wisconsin) and *Sandusky Star-Journal* (Ohio). The *La Crosse Tribune* allegedly began running Dean's column because movie fans were growing impatient waiting for its Saturday evening column from Dean Tevis (see chapter 2), and it identified those fans, much like those of Gertrude Price and Mary Pickford, specifically as women and girls.[168] "News Notes" bore similarities to Price's earlier column not only for the frequency of its circulation but also for its chief feature, the small photo profile of a single movie star, usually in close-up; the column also did not always appear on the same page nor in the same position on a page from one day to the next. Although Dean eschewed the punchy, slangy heads that characterized Price's pieces, she sometimes worked in quips that rivaled those of Britt Craig. In February, she reprinted *New York Tribune* drama critic Alan Dale's snarky comment: "When 'Romeo and Juliet' is screened, the story probably will start at the beginning, and 'we shall be shown Mother Capulet giving little Julie a bath.'"[169] In April, she shared a bit of studio slang: A "lens louse" was a new picture player who "insisted on stealing the foreground" of a shot.[170] In June came this: "House Peters always wanted to be an outlaw until he grew up—then he became an actor."[171]

The brief items that Dean sifted out for her readers ranged far and wide. Most were informative in one way or another. She reported one day that "Pittsburgh censors barred a scene from the 'Battle Cry of Peace'" and later quoted George Bernard Shaw: "The danger of the cinema . . . is not immorality but of morality."[172] In April she noted that Thanhouser was honoring the "Shakespeare centennial celebration" by releasing *Master Shakespeare, Strolling Player,* which starred Florence LaBadie "as a girl of today" taking on the "Baconian controversy"; in August, she claimed that "seventeen hundred churches have taken out movie licenses and charge admission."[173] And she could be whimsical: Henry Walthall frequently strolled through Chicago's loop and "invariably returns home with an odd assortment of lead pencils, shoe strings and such."[174] Her choice of photo profiles clearly followed Price's precedent. The great majority of featured stars were women, and they tended to be associated with particular companies: Mutual, Fox, Metro, and Triangle more than Paramount; Vitagraph, and Pathé, and Gaumont (at its Jacksonville studio) more than Essanay, Edison, and Selig. Much like Price, Dean highlighted stars who were not only beautiful (Norma Talmadge, Marguerite Clark, Mary Pickford)[175] but also unusually versatile.

She loved "dare-devil" roles. Lucille Taft and Louise Glaum learned to fly airplanes; Juanita Hansen took on dangerous stunts in *The Secret of the Submarine;* and Cleo Madison had in various films "fought on the edge of cliffs, leaped from speeding express trains, plunged from burning buildings into nets, [and] leaped from a fast-going automobile onto the rear platform of the California Limited."[176] Dean also called attention to the work that Lois Weber, Ruth Stonehouse, and Lule Warrenton did as writers and directors as well as actors at Universal, each of the latter two for her own series of children's films.[177] And she joined her fellow columnists in warning young girls that movie acting was more arduous than it might seem by posting Clara Kimball Young's daily routine, from arising at 7 a.m., working from 9 a.m. to 5 p.m. at World Film's New York studio, and often "visiting various theaters" where one of her films was being screened to "delight her audience by appearing in person."[178]

Another set of columns appeared in the Midwest almost simultaneously with Daisy Dean's "News Notes from Movieland." These were signed by Dorothy Day (Dorothy Gottlieb) and together made up "News of the Movies," which she edited in the *Des Moines Evening Tribune* beginning in February 1916. As suggested in chapter 2, Day likely had been writing a daily column with that title since August 1915 and also editing a weekly "Flickerings and Flashes from Filmland" page since November that year. Once her byline appeared in February, in her expanded daily column, she not only was writing short film reviews (see chapter 4) but also was dealing with fans' letters in "Questions and Answers" and "What Do You Want to Know About Movies?"[179] Although she may have addressed fans directly and colloquially, she at first betrayed a condescending tone not unlike that of *Motion Picture Story*'s first issues: "You surely do not peruse the daily programs closely"; "Why ask me such foolish questions?"; and "My dear young lady . . . go to the Royal tomorrow and gaze [on Harold Lockwood] to your heart's content."[180] Perhaps pressured by the *Tribune*'s editor, Day quickly abandoned such responses, accepted a heading that claimed she took "great pleasure in answering all questions related to the movies," and stuck to dispensing information: "The last syllable of Farrar is accented"; "Miss Farrar's family is plain American."[181] In separate one-off columns, she also collected brief biographical sketches of stars, among them Roscoe Arbuckle.[182] At least once, the *Tribune* even printed a nearly full-page article about Anita King, "the Paramount Girl," whose coast-to-coast trip in an eight-cylinder King motorcar promoted her "thrilling automobile picture," *The Race,* apparently sponsored by A.H. Blank's Garden Theatre and Holsman Stevens Auto, King's dealership in the city.[183]

Newspaper readers in the New York City area could chance on a different sort of column profiling a single actor or actress in late 1916. This was a series of lengthy interviews in the *New York Sunday Tribune* written each week by Harriette Underhill, who early on had toured as a stage performer and then, on her father's death, taken over writing his sports column for the *Tribune*. With "flaming orange" hair often framed by "a large black picture hat," in the words of Ishbel Ross, "she was cynical to the core, scorned sentiment, had a sophisticated wit, [and] was generous and courageous."[184] Drawing on her theatrical connections, Underhill spoke with stage actors who had turned to motion pictures in New York studios. A fluid, articulate writer, she took a distinctive attitude in her interviews, calling herself "a visitor" and rarely uttering a word, letting her subjects respond to unstated questions. Her profile of Olga Petrova concentrated on her face, "alabaster skin," red hair, "sad, almost tragic eyes," and "the wonderful piquancy" of her voice.[185] No less unequivocally than others, Petrova stated that, in screen acting, "repression is the keynote to success." Underhill let Nance O'Neil burble on happily about her philanthropic project, a Bide-a-Wee home for friendless animals, until she realized she had to say how much she loved working in "the silent drama."[186] Interviewing young Marjorie Rambeau, Underhill staged a dialogue in which her mother's constant harping on her daughter's poor profile led the latter to try always at first to face the camera.[187] She found Frank Keenan especially interesting for his easy storytelling, and noted his astute comment that both scriptwriting and editing were equally important for the success of a motion picture.[188]

What did these early newspaper columns feeding movie fans information and gossip about their favorite stars share with one another, and what not? With few exceptions, the writers were women, who already had experience as journalists of one sort or another. And, through syndication, most reached far more readers than they would have if limited to a single newspaper. From Gertrude Price and Mae Tinee to Mary Pickford and Daisy Dean, moreover, they tended to favor women in the industry for their profiles, interviews, and brief stories of featured stars or personalities. Those choices were in sync with their presumed readership, either explicitly in the case of Pickford and Dean or implicitly in that of Price and Mae Tinee. Whatever differences appeared among the women or their columns seemed partly due to changes in historical conditions between 1912–13 and 1915–16. Within the framework of Scripps-McRae newspapers, through 1913, Price's columns seemed chiefly aimed at working-class and white-collar women and promoted the new industry as an unusually open field for working women. The columns of her colleagues that followed, however, seemed to target a broader range of women, including a growing middle class of "new women" and those with such aspirations. Finally, each of these columnists developed a relatively distinctive voice to attract and hold their readers/fans. Whereas Price, Dean, and Mae Tinee adopted slightly different forms of "colorful readable copy" and Britt Craig relied on the snappy quips of a sportswriter, Louella Parsons was almost unctuously courteous and deferential, and Pickford doled out wholesome advice in a fictive environment of homey intimacy. All in all, they staged performances in print in parallel with star performances on- or off-screen.

From our perspective one hundred years later, this weekly and daily gossip about movie stars might look like a smorgasbord full of "empty calories" with dubious side effects. All of those close-up faces and personality sketches certainly served as beguiling objects of desire that, to the industry's benefit, lured "star-struck" fans repeatedly back into picture theaters. Viewed as mirrors of projection, moreover, they may well have encouraged girls to seek fame and fortune in the movies, particularly as actors. Yet the columns also did much to create and sustain a nationwide community of like-minded fans—an imaginary community chiefly of other girls and young women, perhaps largely middle class and white by the mid-1910s, that extended beyond their neighborhood, town, or city, and through which they could share, sometimes quite frankly, their good and bad experiences, their loves and fears, their problems and questions. Without insisting too much on the point, this popular fan culture of an older "virtual" community could be said to rival in its effects the more established institutional communities within which they had to live—family, school, church, workplace—because, as a modern agent of self-fashioning, it seemed at least partly of their own making. And within this community, fans could accept more readily the advice offered by their columnist "friends" or even the stars themselves, especially when, fearing that too many girls were seeking fame and fortune in the movies, and far too unreasonably, the latter could counter such temptations by recommending that fans covet their favorites securely and safely by mounting them in scrapbooks.

DOCUMENT

"THE MOVIES," *CHICAGO DAY BOOK*, NOVEMBER 11, 1912

Here You are Folks! All about "The Movies"

Right here in the pages of The Day Book the editor is going to introduce you to that Golden-Haired Girl, and that Beautiful Child and that Athletic

Young Hero, and that Gun-Toting Cowboy—and scores more—all old friends of yours!

Why, of course, we mean the Moving Picture Folks you see each week in your favorite theater, the people you recognize again and again as the picture machine makes them act nightly before your eyes.

We're going to tell you about them—what they are like personally, how they live, and what they do between times. With us you will visit them in their native haunts, interview them, sketch them.

Some bright youngster gave moving pictures an apt, vivid name, and it has spread all over the United States. He called them

"The Movies"

So The Day Book, recognizing "the movies" as the biggest, most popular amusement in the world, will tell you all about it from every angle. A member of our staff has been at work on the subject for weeks, traveling, investigating, interviewing—getting facts and pictures about this rival (in size) of the automobile industry, which nightly entertains 5,000,000 American people, gathered in 20,000 theaters. This writer, Miss Gertrude M. Price, has worked on the subject till she has become an expert—your "Movie" expert. She will keep at it, entertaining and posting you on this theater we all enjoy.

ENTR'ACTE Cartoons and Comic Strips

Here's Haphazard Helen, most piquant of girls;
Through maddening adventures she daringly whirls.

Chicago Herald, January 2, 1915

Newspaper readers could find cartoons of one kind or another, as well as syndicated comic strips, as savory side dishes either appended to movie page menus or scattered in other sections. Comic strips, of course, had offered a rich source of ingredients for early filmmakers, from Lumière's *Arroseur et arrosé* (1896) to "bad boy" films.[1] Particularly in popular science and satirical magazines, cartoons reciprocated, catching in a concise visual form, much of the amazement, menace, and behind-the-scenes "magic" of motion pictures. Stephen Bottomore's *I Want to See This Annie Mattygraph* (1995) collects a broad spectrum of cartoons portraying everything from making and going to the movies to regulating them.[2] Occasionally similar cartoons cropped up in newspapers, but they became more noticeable in the early and mid-1910s as motion pictures turned into a popular form of mass amusement. What follows is a sample of "bits and pieces."

Singular cartoons could cover a wide range of subjects, whether acting as editorial commentary or, more often, serving to illustrate short articles or even as filler. In September 1913, the *Des Moines Tribune* editorialized on the clichéd difference between movie fantasy and real life, contrasting the image of a fierce, triple-threat pirate with one of a sideshow impersonator selling photos to a few puzzled customers.[3] About the same time, the rival *Des Moines News* carried a rather disingenuous story on making a home movie camera that showed a young boy filming his mother and baby sister. Others slightly later in the *News* picture a small audience learning tango steps from a film of the Castles, "New York's most famous tango dancers," and a man buying a ticket to see what will be a series of bloody moving picture murders—and blithely thinking of his after-dinner dessert.[4] Sometimes small graphics humorously highlight an item in the columns of Mae Tinee and Kitty Kelly. One shows a woman operating a movie camera to illustrate several lines of gossip about Norma Talmadge taking over the filming of a scene in one of her Vitagraph films.[5] Along with other papers, the *Tribune* even adopted the look of celluloid film stock to illustrate news stories, framing each in a quasi-narrative series of photos with imitation sprocket holes.[6]

It was not uncommon to come across stories told at least partly in motion picture frames. In early January 1913, the *Cleveland Leader* published "The Triumph of the Movieman," a fictional scenario that celebrated Sam Morris, one of the city's exhibitors.[7] The scenario itself included a cast of a dozen characters and a synopsis of twelve scenes in which Mr. Movieman convinces the city's young mayor to appoint a new "large-minded film-censor" who will allow his theaters to prosper. Illustrating this scenario is a large panel in which Morris operates a projector showing the Thanhouser Kid and a warbling Ella Reichert on a screen, with Francis X. Bushman and two older women (city reformers?) "waiting" in smaller adjacent panels. Some of these stories comprised graphic panels separated by imitation intertitles. In July 1914, the *Des Moines News* printed one "in three reels" about a family celebrating the Fourth of July in which three stick figures plan a day at a park, endure several adventures, enjoy the evening fireworks, and return home to fall into bed exhausted.[8] Later that year, another in the *News* summarized, in brief scene synopses and tiny celluloid frames, the story of a college hero, Johnny Poe, who engages in many pulp fiction adventures—all supposedly "in thirteen reels."[9] The final one, however, turns unexpectedly serious when Poe joins the French army as "a gun captain" and serves honorably during the Battle of Ypres.

Initially, comic strips seem to have come in weekly or even daily series with little direct connection to other newspaper discourse on the motion pictures. One of the first was Harry Hershfield's *Desperate Desmond*, a cliff-hanger serial that ran three or four times a week in Hearst's *New York Evening Journal* from mid-March 1910 through mid-June 1912.[10] To depict Desmond and his harassment of the hero and heroine, Claude and Rosamond, Hershfield "drew primarily upon the conventions of serialized fiction" and sensational melodrama, Jonathan Lambert writes, and, in blatant parody, "squeezed as many sensations as he could into his panels."[11] "Hershfield was obviously fascinated by cinema," adds Lambert, and occasionally he concocted "movie-themed strips" or "movie-related riffs": for instance "a joke about annoying prescreening advertisements" or Desmond's attempt "to sneak up from behind on the hero . . . caught in the cameraman's 'finder.'"[12] Relatively early in the strip's run, Claude stops to view a film in an old-fashioned Kinetoscope, remarks that the heroine's predicament is very like that of Rosamond, and easily is handcuffed by Desmond, who laughs: "I knew Claude would fall for that Laura J. Libbey stuff."[13] In late 1911 and early 1912, Nestor negotiated with Hershfield to produce a biweekly series of comic films largely derived from his comic strip.[14] This short-lived series of one-reel *Desperate Desmond* films involved Hershfield's characters in singular live-action episodes that adapt some of the strip's plots and sensation scenes but not the cliff-hanger formula.

Other comic strips parodied the movies and their effect on audiences more directly. From October 1912 to at least May 1913, the major Yiddish newspaper, *Varheit*, "warned" its readers in a tongue-in-cheek daily strip against going to the movies by repeatedly having two "bad boys" see some kind of movie action or behavior, imitate it (with dire results), and suffer a spanking or tongue-lashing from their mother.[15] In one (November 13, 1912), the boys play detective and follow a trail of spills to a pantry, only to have their mother discover them with jam all over their lips. In another (April 22, 1913), the mother orders the boys away from a pot of potatoes she is serving her boarders, and they get the idea from a filmed baseball game to lob a few snatched potatoes into the dining room. In a third (April 30, 1913), after watching a hunter shooting ducks, they release the mother's pet parrot and attack it with broomsticks (fig. 45).

At the same time, another strip in the Scripps-McRae newspapers, *Osgar and Adolf* (a kind of vaudeville sketch), sent up its "heroes" as amateur filmmakers and parodied the conventions of, first, historical films, then, westerns, as well as Sarah Bernhardt's famous death scene in Famous Players's *Queen Elizabeth*—which assumed that some audiences must have laughed at that scene in the theater.[16] Later renamed *Oscar and Adolph*, this strip sometimes returned to the movies, as in the Pretzelgraph company's "Stung by the Black Hand!," in which Oscar ironically cons Adolph (a "prosperous cheesemonger") into putting enough "jitney in his jeans" for a beer at the local saloon.[17] For a short time in early 1914, the Scripps-McRae papers also ran a second strip with the mocking title *Diana Dillpickles in a 4-Reel "Screecher" Film*. In one set of panels, Diana orders her parents to keep quiet as she entertains an "orful refined . . . young man," until her mother yells from off frame: "Yuh big stew—Take ya foot offa th' stove! Ya maks th' kitchen smell lika joss house!"[18] In another set, after complaining about being served cabbage for dinner all week, Diana's "papa" claims a winning theater ticket—and is rewarded, of course, with a "beautiful cabbage."[19]

Several later comic strips exploited "movie madness" even more explicitly. In December 1914, the *Chicago Sunday Tribune* began running *Adventures of the Silly Gallillies in Movie Land* in the bottom corner of its

FIGURE 45. "Bad Boy" comic strip, *Varheit*, April 30, 1913.

"Right Off the Reel" page.[20] This weekly six-panel strip that Quinn Hall conceived as a serial made fun of two young women, Nora and Jennie, who imagined, against all odds, that they could become successful actors in the movies. Early on, when trying to get close to Jack Coran, their favorite player, Jennie faints and is horrified to find the "villain" coming to her aid.[21] Coran, of course, avoids them as much as possible but does pass them off to a friend at the Frazzle Film Company for work as "extra girls."[22] They promptly ruin shots—dropping a paper, looking the wrong way, scratching an itching ankle, sneezing, running unbidden past the camera—or, hailed by a movie tough, get lost in a mob scene.[23] In their persistent pursuit of Coran, the two find themselves doing more and more dangerous stunts. Once, after they are ordered to jump into the sea, Coran refuses to rescue them, and the director worries: "Do extras ever drown?" (fig. 46).[24] Later, in order to make a quickie educational film during a voyage to Hawaii, they

FIGURE 46. "Adventures of the Silly Gallillies in Movie Land," *Chicago Sunday Tribune,* May 16, 1915.

are thrown into the ocean as "bait" and several whales appear as if on cue, fascinated by these strange creatures.[25] Perhaps acknowledging the career paths of several current stars, along with that of pulp fiction heroines such as the "Motion Picture Girls" and especially Ruth Fielding,[26] Quinn's strip eventually did succumb to "every girl's dream" and gradually allowed the pair to overcome all obstacles. At the end of a year-long run, *Adventures of the Silly Gallillies in Movie Land* posted this "secret revealed": Nora and Jennie have "adopted" Coran and started their own film company.[27]

Perhaps no other newspaper was as heavily involved in movie-themed strips as the *Chicago Herald.* In early January 1915, the *Sunday Herald* announced that *Haphazard Helen* was joining its staff as that "most piquant of girls," who "tangoes and swims, goes shooting and rides—Yes, she's always on hand whatever betides."[28] Drawn from Kalem's newly popular *Hazards of Helen* series by the "Carothers Film Company," perhaps with the film company's permission, *Haphazard Helen* was a comic strip tie-in that ran in the Sunday comic section for nearly a year and on occasion resorted to the serial continuity of cliff-hanger endings.[29] Helen was not unlike the active, adventurous series and serial queens of the time: she could replace an injured jockey at the last minute (and win the race), punch out a Mexican bandit, and cycle after a fleeing robber to shoot out one of his stolen car's tires (fig. 47).[30] But she also got into tight spots where she needed rescuing, whether tossed into a dangerous river or tumbling out of a railcar crossing a high bridge. Although most of these strips stressed the character's athleticism and agency, some differed from the movie series that starred Helen Holmes by resolving their brief stories in the last of twelve panels where the cartoon Helen ends up in a romantic embrace with an equally heroic male figure—joined in one case by that grinning, winning horse.[31] At the same time, the *Cleveland Leader* ran a more elaborate, if short-lived, *Movie Story, Complete Each Sunday* in its Dramatic section.[32] Written by a different author each week, but always illustrated by Fred G. Long, these comic strip stories followed a strict format of five parts of five panels each. They also were much more conventional in their melodramatic plots and character types; even in the one where a young woman is the main character, she has to be rescued not once but twice.[33]

For more than three months in early 1915, the *Chicago Sunday Herald* also carried a comic strip offering advice that parodied "how to" manuals and columns. Initially, these focused on acting: "would-be comedians" getting hit in the face with pies or spraying hoses; would-be stars role-playing, practicing "facial and bodily expressions," and running through the gamut of emotions.[34] But they soon took up other work. A cameraman

FIGURE 47. "Haphazard Helen" comic strip, *Chicago Sunday Herald,* April 4, 1915.

filmed all kinds of mayhem and, when his footage was rejected, could barely refrain from taking "a smoke on a stack of film."[35] A director had to be wary of his casting and realize, for instance, that "cowboys are working men, and not highly decorated arsenals."[36] A male scenario writer—as different as possible from Louella Parsons—had to "assume a literary appearance," "drink a pint of red ink to insure a fund of local color," and, after "hammering out 39 or 50 pages," keep running up his grocery tab.[37] This series wrapped with tips for young ladies wanting to "become a film star without leaving the flat"—accusing a boyfriend, strangling the parlor rug—and waiting for managers to "call with SEALED BIDS" (fig. 48).[38] For a short while, the *Herald* even ran a strip across the top of its daily sports page titled *Our Sport Movies (A Thrill an Inch). . . . Passed by the National Board of Nonsenseship*.[39] At least one other singular cartoon in the *Chicago Sunday Tribune* lampooned historical figures and events, as if they had been recorded by a movie camera: Jonah would have sought "movie rights"; Washington would have raced across the Delaware; Paul Revere would have postponed his ride until morning; "'See America First' films would have saved Chris Columbus a lot of trouble"; and "Shakespeare might have developed into a first class scenario writer."[40]

Within two months of Chaplin's hiring at Essanay, the *Chicago Herald* also arranged rights with the film company to publish one more comic strip. *Charley Chaplin's Comic Capers* was a daily strip of six or seven panels "drawn by an artist who has made a study of Chaplin," according to large ads, and "fans will be amazed at the accuracy with which his infectious humor has been transferred to paper."[41] The initial strip introduced the cartoon figure in various guises allegedly derived from several of his popular films: an unrecognizable man on the street, a tramp, a boxer, a flirt, an "officer and a gentleman."[42] From then on, the strip sometimes served as a tie-in to promote a current Chaplin film. One paralleled *The Boxer*, where Charley displays surprising luck as a sparring partner because he's hidden a horseshoe in one of his boxing gloves.[43] Another linked more loosely to *The Tramp*: A tired Charley falls asleep on a log, drops a cigarette into a pile of dry leaves that flare up and catch his pants on fire, and races off to douse himself in water flowing from a large drainpipe.[44] The strip also showed off Charley's skill as a thief, deftly filching a string of hot dogs from a vendor and, after his hunger is satisfied, letting a pickpocket steal the remaining weenies while he nonchalantly lifts a stolen purse from the latter's coat pocket (fig. 49).[45] But he too could be deceived: in a later strip set on a beach, he seems to proposition a woman (costumed in the latest Keystone fashion), who nonchalantly reveals her police badge and drags him off toward a police station.[46] The *Herald*

FIGURE 48. "How to Become a Movie Star Without Leaving the Flat," *Chicago Sunday Herald,* April 4, 1915.

offered the strip to other newspapers through its syndicated service,[47] and a longer version also appeared for a while on the first full page of the *Sunday Herald*'s Comic section.[48] For well over a year, and long after Chaplin had signed a new contract with Mutual, the *Herald* continued to run *Charlie Chaplin's Comic Capers* as a daily feature, now copyrighted by J. Keeley and yet, intriguingly, still by "arrangement with Essanay."[49]

By 1915, the industry's investment in film series, serials, and features had redefined the intermedial relations between cartoons or comic strips

FIGURE 49. "Charley Chaplin's Comic Capers," *Chicago Herald,* April 1, 1915.

and the movies. Some strips were tied closely to the stars or characters now so popular with fans. *Charley Chaplin's Comic Capers,* for instance, sent the cartoon figure of the newly famous comic through one skit after another, repeatedly stressing what captivated moviegoers: his nonchalant attitude, quick thinking, sly behavior, and resilience. Although the heroine of *Haphazard Helen* did not look like Helen Holmes, she was no less fearless and daring in little stories that sometimes bore parallels to those of Kalem's long-running film series and occasionally carried over through a pair of strips. *The Adventures of the Silly Gallillies,* by contrast, engaged ever so lightly with a real-life phenomenon that concerned many reformers as well as the stars themselves—all those girls heading for Los Angeles in hopes of making it big in the movies—by depicting the blindly delusional bumblings of two caricatured wannabe stars in a year-long miniseries that resembled an overly extended feature film.

4. "Film Girls" and Their Fans in Front of the Screen

Even a soured and saddened cynic who never visits picture shows can enjoy the clever writings of Kitty Kelly, and if you're a motion picture fan they're almost indispensable.

Advertisement, *Chicago Tribune*, April 30, 1916

In the early 1910s, movie fans may have eagerly read a variety of newspaper menus to gather the latest publicity from industry sources, as well as information or gossip, about their favorite players. But what they would *not* find was anything like reviews of individual films. Trade journals such as the *New York Dramatic Mirror, Moving Picture World, Motion Picture News,* and the *New York Morning Telegraph* featured weekly or biweekly film reviews, but their readers were chiefly involved in distribution and exhibition. At the same time, reviewers such as Frank Woods at the *Mirror* also presumed that their "criticism" might correct what they saw as production errors and thus guide producers in their future work.[1] For decades, newspapers had offered readers—quite regularly, usually in weekend editions—reviews of current books, stage plays, operas, and art exhibitions, presumed to be forms of high culture. Whereas the weekly reviews of stage performances tended to be written by men, those dealing with books, especially fiction, often were accepted as "women's work."[2] In the *Chicago Tribune,* those women working for Sunday editor Mary King[3] included Fanny Butcher, Elia W. Peattie, Jeannette L. Gilder, and Audrey Alspaugh.[4] A primary aim of such reviewers seems to have aligned with Progressive principles of social and cultural uplift. That is, their efforts involved "training" readers, in the words of Charles Johanningsmeier, to accept their standards of appreciation or systems of value and thus learn how best to read and understand artistic texts, works, and performances.[5]

By 1914, a few papers were starting to add regular reviews to their movie menus, and the different "reading fields" within which fans encountered them raise important questions that shape this chapter's analysis. Who were these reviewers? Were they mostly men or women? Were they established journalists (with what kind of experience?) or young writers just entering the profession? What was the basis of their authority, and what made their voices authoritative? What explicit or implicit principles did they rely on—perhaps drawn from other cultural practices—to compose their commentaries and criticisms? What kinds of films did they tend to choose as the subjects of their columns: features, series and serials, short films, or certain genres? How much did they attend to "favorite players" or stars? In which section of the newspaper was their column located, and how often did that column appear? What was their presumed audience of readers, and how did they address them? What rhetorical strategies did they deploy to attract readers and keep them wanting to read more? Can one gauge the possible significance these reviewers had, whether (as "cultural superiors") in "training" fans to become discriminating spectators or (as fans themselves), performing a kind of authenticity in which they shared their likes and dislikes, their sense of taste, all the while promoting the moviegoing experience?[6] In short, what kinds of "interpretive communities" were they engaged in creating for fervent moviegoers, what tastes did they share or not share across cities and regions, and how might those tastes have differed from that of the industry's "interpretive community" as expressed in the commercial trade press?

SETTING THE TABLE FOR TASTING

At least one photoplay page editor did write film reviews on a trial basis in 1911–12: Ralph P. Stoddard in the *Cleveland Sunday Leader*. For three weeks in October, the *Sunday Leader* highlighted "the films most popular during the past week" in the city by reprinting half a dozen reviews of licensed and unlicensed films from the *New York Morning Telegraph*.[7] Perhaps because these reviewed films were not yet playing in first-run Cleveland theaters, in November Stoddard himself began signing a column titled "Films All Should See," in which he selected half a dozen films—"the best of the current offerings"—for brief praise. Some snapshot reviews seemed aimed at exhibitors, while others addressed moviegoers. On the one hand, he called IMP's *The Waif* "one of the most artistic and consistent photo-plays of the year" and suggested "managers will be begging for it for many months to come."[8] On the other, he urged readers who had not seen Selig's *Lost in the Jungle,* "one of the most wonderful and exciting films ever made," not to "miss their first opportunity when they see it billed at any picture theater."[9] Stoddard's column, sometimes under a new title, continued for several months into early 1912, whether exhorting readers to "See Cinderella," urging young men to study Edison's *Life in the U. S. Army,* warning women not to miss "the latest

Paris models so effectively displayed in Pathé's Weekly," or trying to cover as many as fourteen new films.[10] From late March through mid-April 1912, "Reviews of Films by Reo Stadt" replaced Stoddard's column, and some comments now seemed to come from an observer of audience reactions.[11] "The audience sits on the edge of the opera seats" to see "the most exciting railroad race ever filmed" in Biograph's *The Girl and Her Trust*; "at the Mall Monday the crowds were waiting for seats" to see Bison-101's "thrilling" *War on the Plains*, so "remarkable" was its photography.[12] But by then, with rare exceptions,[13] Stoddard's concern as "Photo-Play and Player" page editor was industry news of interest to the city's exhibitors and rental exchanges as well as to movie fans (see chapter 2).

During the first half of 1914, regular menus of movie reviews finally appeared in tandem with the new weekend motion picture pages in several newspapers. The *Chicago Tribune* was responsible for the first, printed several weeks before Mae Tinee began editing its Sunday page. This column developed out of "Today's Best Moving Picture Story," the fictional tie-in strategy in which the industry supplied metropolitan newspapers with the synopsis of a "daily short story" that promoted specific films in advance of their release.[14] The *Tribune* briefly complied with this strategy and then began printing, just twice a week, its own column of synopses (drawn from industry sources) of four to five films on average, usually placed atop its block ads of "High-Class Moving Picture Theaters" programs. Initially unsigned, some synopses soon evidenced signs of something beyond a plot summary. On February 11, the column introduced Hobart Bosworth's adaptation of Jack London's *The Sea Wolf* (playing at the 677-seat Ziegfeld)[15] with "Nothing, apparently, has been spared to give the motion picture story the action and 'punch' which made the book a success. In vividness and realism the pictures are remarkable."[16] Although "the whole interest of the story is centered in [Wolf] Larsen," the synopsis focused first on how "the audience is made acquainted" with the other principal character, "a young literary critic," a passenger on board a sinking ferry boat—the film's "first real thrill." Three days later, the *Tribune* exhorted readers to collect its re-bannered "photo play" stories as "the easiest way to follow your favorites and avoid bad films."[17] The synopses that day were fitting: *Bunny's Birthday* (Vitagraph) "is another one of the popular Bunny films, funny in its irresistible 'Bunny' manner"; aptly timed for the season, *The Skating Master* (Thanhouser) "furnishes excellent illustrations of fancy skating"; *The Reward* (Lubin) "bristles with bandits and reeks of what would be blood were it not for the censorship." Unlike the reviews in the *Leader*, these clearly were intended to benefit the area's movie fans.

During the next few months, this column of "photo play stories" continued to take up more short films than features. Although each column included a small star photo (sometimes with a brief profile) linked to one film story, only a few synopses highlighted "favorites," for instance Sidney Drew and Florence Lawrence, respectively, in the comedies *Never Again* (Vitagraph) and *Diplomatic Flo* (Victor).[18] Well-crafted plotting, however, increasingly became a criterion of criticism. The "complicated plot and well sustained suspense" of *The Double Knot* (Majestic) gave to the motion picture "real rank as a narrative type," such that "it equals in interest many magazine stories."[19] This was the case in *A Terror of the Night,* "one of the most interestingly compact and thrilling" of *The Adventures of Dolly* series (Edison) and *The Forbidden Room* (Bison-Universal), which, although "a most uncomfortable film to observe . . . must be credited with an unusually skillful plot" that (adding a woman's touch) contributes "as essentially to the perfect knitting of the whole as does a single stitch in a silk stocking."[20] Another point of criticism was the quality of a film print. Whereas a "Napoleon film" "would be more interesting if less marred by blemishes and more stable to the eye," *A Marriage for Money* (Éclair) was "attractively tinted . . . with the colors soft toned and unflickering." So absorbing was the excellent photography in *A Tragedy of the Orient* (Broncho) that one "forgets it is only a celluloid presentment."[21] The writer's take on some films even grew playfully exuberant. In *Lost by a Hair* (Rex), "a bright, fluttering bit of shimmering sunshine," "the courses of true love are running along into a tremendously strong current until suddenly, splash, splosh, they run against an impenetrable barrier."[22] As a "rollicking, dashing farce-comedy," *Mabel at the Wheel* (Keystone) "involves a vast amount of chasing, retreating, falling down, and being run over, bomb throwing, weeping, laughing, and other emotional expressions . . . while the properties of the play are automobiles, motorcycles, mud puddles, hose and water, false mustaches, ropes and bombs, and any other thing necessary at the moment."[23] By contrast, *Lost in Mid-Ocean* (Vitagraph) "heaps up more horrors on a lone woman's head than one would expect twenty of even the strongest feminine examples to endure."[24]

Beginning in June, the *Tribune*'s column occasionally included something with a local flavor. Drawing repeated attention were Essanay comedies such as *The Brash Drummer and the Nectarine,* based on the Chicago writer George Ade's stories and fables.[25] A short section on "cinema chatter" or "cinema loop locals" either raised the level of gossip that Mae Tinee already was dishing out or promoted benefit screenings such as Vitagraph's *The Christian* to aid a charity "caring for widowed mothers and dependent children."[26] Most intriguingly, the column began concluding with a section on specific "cutouts" or outright rejections ordered by Chicago's "municipal censorship bureau."[27] Sometimes these "cutouts" were extensive, and they targeted a surprising range of films. Popular serials were hardly immune. Excised from the tenth episode of *The Adventures of Kathlyn* (Selig) was a scene of "setting fire to a house" and a "subtitle: 'String him in the murderer's pit and feed him to the lions.'"[28] An early episode of *The Perils of Pauline* (Pathé) lost "five scenes of gagging and binding [the] girl"—which makes one wonder what "sensation scenes" remained.[29] Keystone comedies also could fail to pass scrutiny. "All holdup scenes" were cropped from *Mabel's Heroes*, and an "entire bedroom scene" vanished from *Across the Hall*.[30] Rejections were less frequent, but one of the more interesting involved Éclair's *The Renunciation*, which, it was feared, would "'disturb the public peace' of the Catholic citizens by showing that a monk keeps the photograph of the sweetheart of his youth and at the end tears it up and throws it at the image of the Virgin Mary."[31] According to a column in late April, even the municipal court chief justice endorsed the city's censorship with this startling claim: "Uncensored motion pictures would double Chicago's crime in a short time."[32] However transcribed in summary snip-its, this "archive" of Chicago's censorship records, which ran for more than a year, deserves a separate and thorough analysis of its own.

Finally, on July 1, the writer of this twice-weekly column was identified as Kitty Kelly, who also (as Audrey Alspaugh) dabbled in book reviewing for the *Tribune*.[33] Almost immediately, the column found a regular space on the Society or Women's page, retitled "Photoplay Stories and News," and the reviews now focused on a single film.[34] Kelly's exuberant style, spinning out tongue-in-cheek metaphors, must have snagged and held readers' attention. *The Living Fear* (Edison) was "all about a nice young man whose moral nature got badly singed in the dazzling rays that emanate from diamonds."[35] *The Horse Thief* was one of those "western Vitagraphers [that] dash across miles and miles of low rounded hills, flashing past the camera eye so swiftly that it is hard to believe one sees only the registration of the ponies' shining flanks instead of the original."[36] In *Out of the Depths* (Rex), "Thrills are turned loose from the standby reservoirs of love and vengeance, the two streams being nicely mixed together in order to sustain interest and develop a complicated situation."[37] This love of language, sometimes verging on "showboating," also led her to chastise manufacturers for "releasing pictures under names about as attractive and suitable as a fur coat in August."[38] But Kelly could be relatively straightforward in praising a film (fig. 50). Her review of *The Rival Railroad's Plot* highlighted Kalem's series of "stirringly interesting pictures" that assumed "the romance of the railroad [was] as genuinely American . . . as that of the Indian" as well as its star, the "dark-eyed and daring" Helen

Photoplay Stories and News

By Kitty Kelly

"THE RIVAL RAILROAD'S PLOT."
Kalem.

Myrtle....................Helen Holmes
Jerry....................William Brunton
Manton....................N. Z. Wood
Henley....................Leo D. Maloney
Tim Downs....................Charles Wells

THE romance of the railroad is as genuinely American romance as that of the Indian, and the Kalem company, recognizing this, have been making a number of stirringly interesting pictures, both in comedy and straight drama, featuring the iron moguls and their masters that cut our multitudinous miles into mere fragments of space.

Today's picture pulses with the vibrant theme of the rivalry between two railroads for the privilege of carrying Uncle Sam's mail across the country. The rival railroad, in seeking to undermine the running record already established by road No. 1, stoops to villainy as interestingly adaptable to pictures as any villainy [illegible]viewed. And this villainy would have changed the award of the governmental contract had the road not then been under the protective guardianship of Cupid at this particular crisis in its career. He was not an aristocratic or a general manager cupid, merely a humble fireman one, but he served the purpose beautifully in dislocating the plans of the arch conspirators.

Jerry, fireman on the great engine of the mail train, was in love with Myrtle, the little telegrapher at Barnum's Junction, and had to do most of his wooing as he passed through on a high speed schedule, which made it rather sketchy to say the least. To Myrtle, however, the few seconds of his going by made the whole day bright. Before the day of the race for the record Jerry had been approached by a gentleman from the rival railroad affably offering him a handful of greenbacks in return for a slight favor. Jerry's ready response had been to knock the gentleman to the ground, in the process scattering the bills all over [illegible] filmscape.

The rival railroad has other steps to take besides mere bribery, however. The company's agents became even more direct in their methods by going to Jerry's room in the morning as he was dressing to make his big run, reducing his personality of arms and legs into a solid section of trussed up firemanship, and plugging up his vocal apparatus with a gag.

Then, Henley, the assailant, substituted for him on the engine, supplying himself on the sly with some lime and cottonseed oil, recommended by the road's chemist as having disastrous effects on the contents of an engine's boiler. As the wheels went speeding round, making a great hole

MISS HELEN HOLMES
KALEM

MISS HELEN HOLMES, dark eyed and daring, has been for some time circling the globe with her charms in the series of railroad pictures the Kalem company has been producing. She has been about the railroad yards so much that she has become quite a pet of the employés, who recently presented her with a little horseshoe stickpin of diamonds as a tangible token of their affection for her.

in the allotted schedule, the efficient subfireman mounted to the engine's top and at a watering station, dumped his special speed killing dope into the interior works of the engine, soon stopping it, to the engineer's alarm and chagrin.

While Manton fussed over his engine, Myrtle, anxiously waiting at Barnum's Junction to flutter Jerry a good luck wave as he smiled at her from the cab of the thundering mail train, fussed over the nonappearance of the train, and Jerry helplessly tied into a ball into his room, fussed over his situation. In the dispatcher's office, too, there was fussing, for they had lost trace of the mail train, due to a fallen tree branch which had choked off telegraphic communication.

Then all at once, like the Mother Goose jingle, they all began to do something all but the engineer, who couldn't stir his balky steed. Myrtle commandeered an engine from her side track to go out and look for the mail train. The linemen set out hunting for the broken wires, and Jerry wiggled himself over to the window, the sharp edges of whose smashed panes he utilized as knives to cut his bonds. When the engine found the train, it hitched on and started in once more on the record making run, but was again delayed by the fireman extraordinary, who, pistol in hand, highway manned the new crew, bringing the train to another standstill.

By this time, however, the wires were fixed and Jerry had reached the dispatcher's office with the news of his attack. Help went out at once and reaching the train soon after Henley's last bit of desperateness, proceeded to take it on its much disputed way once more. It swung into its destination after all that, one minute ahead of its own record.

The railroad officials had a lot of reasons and explanations, but they all mi[illegible] the real secret of the success. However, Cupid, being a modest fireman, one didn't mind, since the result led indirectly anyhow to his promotion to an engineership, well engineered by the former telegrapher of Barnum's Junction.

The picture is thoroughly creditable on the score of theme and handling. The action is on a large scale, and the players are subordinated somewhat to the engines, but this doesn't lessen the quality of their performance, while emphasizing the railroad atmosphere.

* *

As to Titles.

Every once in a while some editorially minded person raises his voice via his typewriter in regard to the sensationalism and inappropriateness of many of the titles bestowed upon motion pictures to their public discredit.

But in all the din of the "biggest thing yet" put on and the train wrecks and automobile smashups and airship ascents and deep sea dives for the sake of instilling thrills into the celluloid, these modest protests have been quite overlooked, and companies go on releasing pictures under names about as attractive and suitable as a fur coat in August.

The editorially minded folks aren't the only ones who notice this, however. Exhibitors, with their fingers catching every beat of the public pulse, have the matter of names down in their diagnosis of public taste.

Two of them were consulting their lists of films the other day. Mr. A., skimming through the names with exhibitorial comment, as to the worth of the pictures, stumbled and stopped.

The Lure of the Car Wheel, he exclaimed. "Now, say, can you imagine a car wheel with a lure?"

No, but the Reliance got out one last week called 'Blue Pete's Escape.' Can you think of anything much worse than that?" replied Mr. B.

"In that 'Hand of Horror' Edison put out about as rotten a title for a good picture as anything I ever saw," commented Mr. A.

There might have been more titular criticism if an interruption hadn't happened just then. But in that much there is the straight stuff of honest, off-hand opinion, not biased by any editorial finickism. It will be a happy day for every one when there is just as much care applied to supplying a photoplay with a creditable title as to killing the villain dead in a hard struggle without incapacitating him for future villainies.

* *

Cinema Flashes.

There are by-products, profitable ones, even in the picture business. Recently at the animal farm of University city, the camels were sheared and the hair crop brought in the neat little sum of $350.

"Cabiria," beginning its fifth week at the Illinois, is so satisfactorily successful to the box office that the opinion is expressed that it is quite certain to run through the summer season.

* *

Film Cutouts.

The following cutouts in moving picture films were ordered by the municipal censorship board at the city hall yesterday:

CUTOUTS.

"The Mirror" [Imp-Universal]. Bribing police officer.

"The Mystery of the Hindoo Image" [Majestic-Mutual]. Shorten three dead body scenes to flashes; binding and gagging man; scene showing snake crawling around man; vision scene of killing man.

"The Broken Barrier" [American-Mutual]. Scene in which man attempts to assault woman in café.

"Gwendolin, the Sewing Machine Girl" [Biograph]. Police officer playing marbles; binding girl and placing her on table where she is dragged to machine by her hair; subtitle: "Counterfeiting machine."

"A Matter of Record" Lubin]. Entire second café scene in which intoxicated man dances.

"A Matter of Record" [Lubin]. Entire sec- "He substituted the blood of a diseased patient, etc.," "The sins of the father. You are not in a condition to marry," and "The sins of my father are upon me, tell Grace to forget me."

"Who Seeks Revenge" [Lubin]. Indian stabbing army officer and sick woman in bed: subtitles: "A pretty girl like you can have all the fine things you like," "Your son is getting tangled up with a piece of factory trash. She is a bad one." "You are being entrapped by an evil thing, you must sever your shameful relations," and "Your daughter is now the mistress of the man you raised as your son"; scene showing vision of soldier exchanging infants.

"A Traitor to His Country" [Lubin]. Close to camera scene showing tatooing of man.

FIGURE 50. "Photoplay Stories and News by Kitty Kelly," *Chicago Tribune*, July 22, 1914.

Holmes—strongly suggesting why the company soon invested in the long-running railroad series *The Hazards of Helen.*[39] Delayed in reaching Chicago, *Traffic in Souls* (Universal) she described not only as "the 'Uncle Tom's Cabin' and the 'Ten Nights in a Barroom' of the white slave trade" and "perfectly 'nice' in view of all the publicity on the theme" but also appealing as "a sort of animated dictionary teaching the meaning of slang terms such as 'go-between,' 'man higher up,' and such like."[40] Moreover, Kelly enlisted *Tribune* readers in support of her playful put-downs and appreciative nudges, insisting, with dubious sincerity, that "the improvement of the movies . . . lies directly in the hands of movie fans."[41]

Throughout the late summer and fall, several new interests emerged in Kelly's reviews. She began giving special attention to the sources from which some films were adapted. Those included magazine stories, which she agreed were the most common form of "filmization," for instance Francis Lynne's "In Christmas Cañon" for *Across the Burning Trestle* (Edison), a *Ladies' World* story for *The Plum Tree* (Essanay), and a Robert Burr story from the *Saturday Evening Post* for *The Premature Compromise* (Edison).[42] Also stage plays: Eugene Walter's drama for *The Wolf* (Lubin), or Paul Armstrong's dramatization of a Bret Harte story for *Salomy Jane* (California).[43] Even a Marie Corelli novel for *Vendetta* (Kleine's Italian import), "a double header coup, corralling Corelli fans to the film and rallying picture enthusiasts about Corelli for book and picture supplement."[44] Kelly singled out for praise scenario writer Mabel Heikes Justice for *The Horse Thief* (Vitagraph) and *The Other Man* (Essanay), and took note of a Northwestern University student who had written scenarios for several companies.[45] Soon after the Studebaker became an exclusive downtown venue for Paramount Pictures in early September, she gravitated more and more to feature films.[46] One of the first, besides those already mentioned, was *Such a Little Queen* (Famous Players), which she and the audience found "exquisite in its shimmering humor and its intrinsic humanness," partly because "little Mary Pickford in charm and all around winsomeness is excelled by no one."[47] Later, as if to legitimate such features, she reported that playwright Channing Pollack was "beautifully satisfied with the celluloid version . . . of my little comedy."[48] Only occasionally did Kelly give an actor the star treatment. Although Tom Mix could be celebrated as "characteristically a cowboy hero" in *The Real Thing in Cowboys* (Selig), she whipped up the following recipe for the film itself: "a pudding full of the conventional plums of love and effort and accomplishment, tinctured with a dash of slapstick fun that lightens its sentiment pleasantly."[49] And she kept on making savory put-downs: *Jailbirds* (American) was simply mediocre, its "links of logic . . . sprung in spots"; as for another Mix vehicle, *In the Days of the Thundering Herd* (Selig), she "could be happy with just a typical cross section rather than the whole trip."[50]

In September 1914, the column underwent another, more important title change, first to "In Celluloid Land with Kitty Kelly" and then more permanently (as well as alliteratively) to "Flickerings from Film Land by Kitty Kelly."[51] That was the moment when Mae Tinee's Sunday gossip column also adopted its simpler but no less prescient moniker "In Movie Land."[52] By November, readers checking the Society or Women's page now could find "Flickerings from Film Land" three or four times a week. These changes seemed to mark the *Tribune*'s dawning recognition that the movies, in more ways than one, were creating an American fantasy space of desire—and of imaginary participation. In early January 1915, a full-page ad confirmed this recognition by displaying photos of many of the *Tribune*'s writers and artists—"the greatest array and greatest variety of stars ever employed by any newspaper"—with both Kelly and Mae Tinee among them, described as "experts" in writing about moving pictures.[53] Soon Kelly's column was featuring one film review each weekday, along with the customary censors' cutouts and rejections and occasional local "chatter."

Almost simultaneously with the *Tribune*'s initial film reviews, in mid-February 1914 the *Cleveland Plain Dealer*, with no advance notice, introduced a review column on its weekly Sunday page. This unsigned column singled out one title, and only sometimes a feature, as "The Film of the Week"—as if for readers who may have missed the film's first-run exhibition. The review of *Jane Eyre* (IMP) laid out several principles of criticism—the quality of the adaptation, plotting, acting, and photography—to which others soon added scenery and costumes.[54] This reviewer had clear personal preferences, which suggested her or his class position vis-à-vis audiences: *When Men Would Kill* (Warner) was "a thrilling feud story which will please a certain clientele"; *Eugenics Versus Love* (Beauty) was "a pleasant little rural comedy . . . in these days of slap-stick, rough-and-tumble 'movie' comedies"; and *The Trap* (American) was "a moonshiner story with no unusual merit of plot."[55] Despite a distaste for "Wild West" films, she or he could praise *The Legend of the Phantom Tribe* as "an Indian picture of actual worthiness" and *The Hills of Silence* (both Bison-Universal) for "an artistic excellence . . . so high that the spectator readily forgives its dramatic commonplaceness."[56] Noteworthy was the column's consistent interest in female stars. The reviewer complimented Margarita Fischer for working for a company "created to exploit her personality," as in *Bess the Outcast* (Beauty).[57] A lengthy accolade followed for "Little Mary" Pickford's "remarkably charming personality and beauty," so evident in *Hearts Adrift* (Famous Players).[58] Though much diminished as a star, Florence Lawrence, with her "euphonious name and super-abundant vivacity," was "worth watching in whatever she attempts," from *Her Ragged Knight* to *The Madman's Ward* (both Victor).[59] "Good in every scene in which she appears," Cleo Madison was another distinct asset in *The Hills of Silence,* partly for "some daring riding."[60] Finally, in a relatively rare note, this reviewer called attention to Kathlyn Williams as the writer and director of an original and plausible story in *The Leopard's Foundling* (Selig).[61]

In July, just weeks after Kitty Kelly was named, the *Plain Dealer* added another review column purportedly written from "the perspective of the 'movie fan,'" in which summaries of "merits and failings . . . should be of convenient avail as a guide to 'what to see.'"[62] This was "Minutes 'Mong the Movies" signed by a Miss Ruth Vinson. Her task was daunting because she was asked to review as many pictures as she could "personally see," and with few exceptions that ranged each week from fifteen to twenty titles, necessarily short films. The general result was just enough space for a brief plot summary, the names of the producing company and one or more actors, and little more than a sentence of criticism. Given these limitations, Vinson gamely offered snapshot judgments in which she usually highlighted the best and worst of the week. In late July, she agreed with Kitty Kelly on the merits of *The Rival Railroad's Plot,* and found "little to commend" in *The Gateway of Regret* (IMP) and "nothing" in *Harry's Waterloo* (Thanhouser) "except the extremely clever work of Harry Benham."[63] Two weeks later, she highlighted two good detective films from Essanay, *The Seventh Prelude* and *Trinkets of Tragedy,* faulted the "defective photography" in *The Coast Guard's Bride* and *A Man and His Brother* (both Victor), and found the comedy in *Back to the Simple Life* (Edison) "simply dull."[64] Repeatedly, she also complained about Biograph's reissues of films from several years before—especially Pickford's, on which the company was trying to capitalize—which only made her realize that "times have changed."[65] Occasionally Vinson urged her readers explicitly to "see it" after reviewing a film such as *Detective Dan Cupid* (Nestor), and she shared fans' pleasure with John Bunny and Flora Finch in *Polishing Up* (Vitagraph): "The audience with me rocked with laughter all of the time the film was being run, which says more than any criticism."[66] She once admitted that in *The Sheriff's Choice* (Reliance), "the opening scenes [were] so obscure" that "it took me quite some time to 'get' the plot."[67] Just as abruptly as they began, however, and without explanation, both Vinson's column and "The Film of the Week" (still unsigned) ended in early October,[68] and film reviews did not return when Arthur Roberts began editing the *Plain Dealer*'s Sunday photoplay page in late August 1915.

Elsewhere, shortly before Vinson began compiling "Minutes 'Mong the Movies," Mary Leffler already was adding a "Comment and Criticism" section to her "Flashes from Filmdom" column in the *Fort Worth Star-Telegram.*[69] For several months, two or three times a week, Leffler selected three films for comment; although separate from the column's film synopses, all were currently playing at local theaters. Her choices ranged widely, from features to serials or series and one-reelers. In late June, she described *The Inside of the White Slave Trade* (Moral Feature Film) as "showing better than anything ever shown the actual conditions existing because of this evil trade" and admitted, despite her dislike of the genre, that *Broncho Billy's Jealousy* (Essanay) had "unusually interesting Western scenes reproduced with photography which is extremely good and a wealth of action that is sensational in the extreme."[70] In early July, it was the turn of *The Million Dollar Mystery* (Thanhouser), whose mystery "grow[s] deeper with each foot of the film," and *The Perils of Pauline*, so "very enjoyable for the fact that the pictures get more interesting with every release."[71] Leffler could criticize a film like *The Test of Courage* (Lubin) for its rather slow action and poor photography or *This Is Life* (Essanay) for several plot points that made it much less funny than it could have been.[72] Yet for the most part, she touted films that her readers should see. She was especially taken with *Judith of Bethulia* (Biograph)—the "acting, photography, settings, and backgrounds are all that could be required to make an up-to-date offering"—and Famous Players's features such as *One of Our Girls*, with "the famous legitimate star, Hazel Dawn," doing "exceptionally good work throughout," and *The Eagle's Mate*, "full of exciting and interesting novelties from start to finish."[73] Days later, the latter film led to an admiring profile of Mary Pickford, with an early claim that "a San Francisco motion picture exhibitor always announces her as 'America's Sweetheart,' and indeed she is."[74] With few exceptions, Leffler dropped these "comments" from her column from August until early 1915.

During the last months of 1914, the *New York Evening Mail* also began offering a weekly column of film reviews, but this one was quite different.[75] First, the column focused exclusively on "photo-play features," half a dozen on average. Second, it included not only a paragraph of criticism for each but also a graph of brief comments on several categories of information (title, kind of story, stars, length) and evaluation (acting, settings, photography). Third, initially attributed to "THE CENSOR," the reviews soon came "recommended by 'Wid'" Gunning (fig. 51).[76] Nearly all of the films selected came from rental exchanges that advertised in the newspaper (the major exception was Paramount). For the first week, "THE CENSOR" praised most of the films—*The Spoilers* (Selig) for a return engagement and *Tillie's Punctured Romance* (Keystone) especially for Charlie Chaplin, "no funnier man in pictures"—but condemned *A Woman Who Did*, apparently a foreign import whose "most horribly assembled mélange" evoked

WORTH-WHILE FEATURE FILMS

Recommended by "WID."

Mabel Taliaferro, in "THE THREE OF US"
Rolfe-Alco Release.

As a Whole..........Fine
Story (from play)..........Good
Photography..........Great
Settings..........Very Good
Detail..........Good
Star..........Fine
Support..........Fine
Direction..........Excellent
Length..........Five Parts

This first production by the B. A. Rolfe company sends them away to a flying start. Director John Noble deserves a lot of credit for his work, and the star, Miss Taliaferro, and her chief support, Irving Cummings and Ed Carewe, are to be congratulated upon the manner in which they bring out their characters. The youngster playing the part of the little brother also registered many bits of business very effectively. In a way the story was a hard one to put over in pictures, because it all centered about one incident, but Mr. Noble worked up to this incident with fine lighting effects and clever little human touches which win you and keep you interested. Then comes the big scene, which he put over with a real punch. It is a very good feature and remarkably good as a first production, on which some of the work had to be hurried. The haste is not evident in the finished product. B. A. Rolfe has registered.

Alice Brady in "As Ye Sow"
World Film Corp.

As a Whole..........Very Good
Story (from the play)..........Well known
Photography..........Splendid
Settings..........Excellent
Detail..........Perfect
Star..........Charming
Support..........Very Good
Direction..........Excellent
Length..........Five Parts

Taking a story which is not new, and in fact has, in one form or another been done before many times in pictures, Frank Crane has given us here a feature picture which, while we know, or at least guess, and guess rightly, how things are going to turn out, even though we didn't see the play—still by little touches that appeal to the heart and not the head, he holds you fascinated and gradually wins you. It is a film you will like and your wife will like. The young folks will like it and the old folks will like it. It has the heartstring pull that counts. Miss Brady does splendid work and holds the eye whenever she is on the screen. She photographs beautifully and wins you early. John Hines got many good laughs by his clever light comedy—the lad is certainly able to put over screen comedy. "As Ye Sow" is very much "worth while."

Marie Dressler in "Tillie's Punctured Romance"
Keystone-Alco Release.

As a Whole....One Hearty Laugh
Story....You Don't Care Much
Photography..........Good
Settings..........Some Very Good
Detail..........No Such Animal
Star..........A Scream
Support..........Two Screams
Direction..........Wonderful
Length..........Six Parts

The wise ones, and many who have not even claimed wisdom, have said often and sadly that it "can't be did"—but Mack Sennett, the director, and Marie Dressler, Charlie Chaplin and our pretty friendly "Keystone Mabel" did it. What? Well, they made a funny, six-part, horse-play comedy. It is Keystone from start to finish, but it is good Keystone—and what more could one ask. This should be one of the most successful films ever produced financially and from an entertainment viewpoint—because it is certainly good for many, many laughs, chuckles, grins and a few little two for a nickel snickers. They try to follow a plot—but who cares about a plot when Charlie and Mabel are working, and when you have Marie Dressler with them? "Oh, boy"—you, Charlie—it is quite "worth while."

Florence Nash in "SPRINGTIME"
Life Photo—Alco Release.

As a Whole..........Good
Story..........Sweet
Photography..........Fine
Settings..........Fair
Exterior Locations..........Beautiful
Detail..........Good
Star..........Very Good
Support..........Good
Direction..........Fair
Length..........Five Parts

A sweet story, some very, very pretty locations, perfect photography and Florence Nash make "Springtime" worth while. It is a film you will like. It leaves you pleased. The work of William H. Tooker, Frank Holland and Warner Richmond stands out strong in support of Miss Nash, who was splendid at all times, fitting beautifully into the character. Charles Travis, as the hero, was quite weak, but he was unable to injure the film to any appreciable extent. The story is one that requires simple telling, and it has been well presented, considering what there was to work with. The fact that the locations were so well chosen and the technical work so good helped the feature decidedly.

Dorothy Donnelly in "THE THIEF"
Box Office Attractions Co.

As a Whole..........Very Good
Story..........Dramatic
Photography..........Good
Settings..........Fair
Locations..........Good
Detail..........Good
Star..........Splendid
Support..........Good
Direction..........Good
Length..........Five Parts

Dorothy Donnelly has gone over as a "screen success." Her first appearance before the camera in this feature demonstrates the fact that she has the power to hold a "screen audience." Her eyes seem to be particularly expressive on the screen, and since the eyes are most important in film work, Miss Donnelly can count herself quite a success. The story of "The Thief" is, of course, well known. In the film the action moves a bit slowly at the first, while the characters are being established. The final "punch" is well approached and nicely put over, although the print I saw was not trimmed quite as carefully as it should have been in flashing back and forth on some very important scenes. I want to take objection to one big setting, showing two rooms and a hallway in between (sectional view). This was unnecessary—their relative location could have easily been established in another way—and the setting, prepared as it was, takes away much from the realism of the film at that point. It completely spoils the illusion. As a whole, however, "The Thief" is a success.

FIGURE 51. "Wid" Gunning, "Worth-While Feature Films," *New York Evening Mail,* December 19, 1914.

"indescribable anguish," and *The Wishing Ring* (World Film), which "had no momentum of any notice" and whose "significance was buried beneath the debris of good detail in the story."[77] Two weeks later, "Wid" wrote the opposite about *The Man of the Hour* (World Film), a "wonderful success" also directed by Maurice Tourneur, and could do little more than call *Behind the Scenes* (Famous Players) "a gem," with Mary Pickford "at her best."[78] While recommending several films, "Wid" also could be critical of a director who did not handle crowd scenes well, as in *The Ghost Breaker* (Paramount), or an editor who did not trim scenes where needed, as in *The Tigress* (Alco) and *The Thief* (Box Office Attractions).[79] In a change of pace, he drew attention to the popular song "taken up by the Allies in the present war" in complimenting the British import *It's a Long, Long Way to Tipperary* (Eclectic), and was enchanted by the "beautiful locations, perfect photography, and wonderful light and color effects" of Edward S. Curtis's *In the Land of the Head Hunters* (World Film), even though he "lost the thread of the story."[80] The review of *As Ye Sow* (World Film), with Alice Brady, revealed that his presumed readers were clearly other men: "It is a film you will like and your wife will like" too.[81]

DAILY DIETS AT THE TASTING TABLE

Throughout much of 1915, Kelly and Gunning, respectively, kept up a steady output of daily or weekly film review columns. In Fort Worth, however, Mary Leffler revised her column to tie her film synopses and "comments" to the city's half a dozen downtown theaters. Although the number of comments decreased, they continued to take up short films, serials, and feature films and included a wide variety of observations of apparent interest to her readers. One week she praised *Across the Pacific* (World Film), whose "story has a powerful grip and [is] so well constructed that the interest never wanders from the first to the final fade-out."[82] The next week it was the turn of *His New Job* (Essanay), based on Chaplin's move from Keystone to Essanay, but allegedly "produced without any scenario whatsoever, Chaplin himself directing it offhand."[83] Occasionally she remarked on the skillful acting of stars: in *Kreutzer Sonata* (Box Office), Theda Bara "does exceptionally fine work" in a vampire role similar to that in *A Fool There Was* (World Film); in *The Man From Mexico* (Famous Players), "all the delicious humor of [John] Barrymore's delightful personality is at its best."[84] She also began taking note of those working "behind the scenes": Lois Weber's direction of *Hypocrites* (Bosworth), Owen Davis's adaptation of a John Oxenham novel for *Hearts in Exile* (World Film), and D.W. Griffith's exceptional "screen work" in *The Avenging Conscience* (Mutual).[85] There were what she considered unusual techniques to highlight as well. In *Old Dutch* (World Film), "the characters are all introduced in a novel way," but exactly how, she failed to specify.[86] In *The Quest* (Mutual Masterpicture), she urged viewers to look out for the "double and triple exposures of great beauty."[87] Perhaps recognizing her readers' tastes, she closely followed serial episodes of *The Black Box* (Universal) and *The Exploits of Elaine* (Pathé), which, drawing on a case in Los Angeles months before, made dramatic "use of Professor Leduc's method of electrical resuscitation."[88] By mid-May 1915, she had become too busy editing the newspaper's Sunday page, "In the Photoplay World," to keep on writing reviews.[89]

In New York, "Wid" Gunning maintained his own demanding schedule of editing the *Evening Mail*'s Saturday page and reviewing on average four feature films a week. His reviews very explicitly did double duty. On the one hand, he usually urged readers to see the film he chose to review; repeatedly, he would conclude that, despite any reservations he might have, it was "very worth while" or "you will enjoy it." On the other, his critical comments, like Frank Woods's earlier, often seemed aimed at industry personnel, either to encourage better work in the future or else to assist in fine-tuning release prints. To that end, he constructed a graph of eight criteria to use when evaluating a film—Story, Photography, Settings, Locations, Detail, Star, and Direction—and judged each in a word or two.[90] Representative of the good work he sought was *From Headquarters* (Vitagraph)—"a really great film"—and he offered three reasons:[91] It had "a big story, perfectly portrayed and directed," in which Ralph Ince's "handling of the tempo of the emotional scenes is just right." It included "several surprises in the course of the story that help give it the power which compels your sympathy." And in "the close up bits of business when every turn of the eye has significance," Anita Stewart was "especially strong." Equally exemplary was *Hearts in Exile*: "The story is strong, the action splendidly timed, there is the proper tempo in developing the big situations, and then again there is Clara Kimball Young."[92] This blend of elements especially marked a "successful feature film," and, earlier than either Kitty Kelly or Mary Leffler, "Wid" attributed that blending to figures "behind the scenes." After seeing *It's No Laughing Matter* (Bosworth) and *Hypocrites*, he saluted Lois Weber as their writer and director.[93] Similarly, *The Clemenceau Case* (Fox) stamped Herbert Brenon as "a master of screen drama": "The tempo of the action is perfect, the assembling of the scenes . . . remarkably well handled."[94] Emile Chautard's direction of *The Boss* (World Film), the former French filmmaker's "second film in America," was so successful that "Wid" ranked it on a par with *Alias Jimmy Valentine* (World Film), directed by his fellow countryman, Maurice Tourneur.[95] And credit for the excellence of *The Kindling* (Lasky) was due to Cecil B. DeMille and Wilfred Buckland, especially for its "splendid lightings and those carefully worked-out sets and exteriors.[96]

Several of his reviews suggest that "Wid" was knowledgeable about the process of filmmaking, for he frequently singled out specific techniques he considered necessary—besides a sustained, strong story—to film's overall development. Well before Kelly or Hugo Münsterberg, he argued that, more than any other technique, the close-up revealed the distinctive artistic possibilities of film, as in *Hypocrites* or *The Caprices of Kitty* (both Bosworth). Actors could, "through bringing the characters so close to every one in the audience . . . 'put over' the little bits of expression that could not be done in the theatre effectively."[97] This led him to complain that, in *The White Sister* (Essanay), "moving the camera forward and back" was far less effective than "properly inserted" close-ups, or that, in *The Devil's Daughter* (World Film), Theda Bara failed "to show to as good advantage" as before "due to the absence of timely close-ups of that wonderful face."[98] He highlighted the different effect, in *Their Only Love* (Thanhouser), of the "wonderful night photography, depicting battle scenes that carry you with them, due to the well-directed action."[99] Or the unusual camera position in *Alias Jimmy Valentine* (now often remarked on) when, "on a scaffolding high up near the roof of the studio" over the constructed set of a bank interior, Tourneur "filmed the action . . . showing a very exciting chase and fight in the various rooms."[100] "Wid" seemed acutely attuned not only to the choice and placement of shots but also to the pace and rhythm of editing. Like most Bosworth films, *Buckshot John* was "well cut and edited . . . full of bang-up action that keeps moving."[101] In *The Juggernaut* (Vitagraph), he found "the master hand of Ralph Ince" especially evident in the "properly timed and effective" dramatic scenes.[102] This near obsession with editing led him to admit that, by May 1915, often he was watching previews in a screening room and noting that further cutting or editing would make films such as *The Plunderer* (Fox), *The Alien* (New York Motion Picture), and *The Earl of Pawtucket* (Universal) much more enjoyable.[103] In one of his last columns, "Wid" even took some credit, if only implicitly, for film "becoming an 'art' instead of a commercial proposition to the extent that the manufacturers have realized they must make better films to hold the patronage."[104]

Apparently "Wid" did not spend all his time in screening rooms and sometimes either took note of picture theater audience reactions or made assumptions about them. He was not above calling *The Goddess* (Vitagraph) "the greatest serial yet presented," corrected a few exhibitors who thought "there was not enough action," and dropped in on various theaters to "catch up" on half a dozen of the serial's episodes and confirm that "the story is building bigger all the time."[105] A screening of *The Champion* (Essanay) in a "big New York theatre" proved to him Chaplin's popularity: "Not often do you find a film audience applauding any star as they appear."[106] A rare comment followed his fourth viewing of *The Birth of a Nation*, when "some views of the Hampton Institute, a negro industrial school," were tacked on at the end. To "Wid" and others he talked to, this was "a direct slap artistically," turning the "tremendous drama" he admired into "a treatise on the race problem."[107] Although he very much liked Majestic's adaptation of Henrik Ibsen's *Ghosts* because he "love[d] to watch Henry Walthall in big emotion parts," he realized that it was not "going to be popular 'entertainment.'"[108] Perhaps recalling his boyhood in a "little Ohio burg," where, as an usher, he had handed out theater programs, "Wid" claimed that the "many very clever titles" in *Just Out of College* (Frohman Amusement's adaptation of a George Ade story) would please the "better houses" more than the "cheaper houses."[109] Although his column did not hang out a "men only" sign, he did continue assuming that his readers were mostly male: whether or not *Bootle's Baby* (London Film) was "worth while" was to be "answered by the ladies to whom this will particularly appeal."[110] Might that blithe gender distinction partly explain his overwhelming appreciation for *A Fool There Was* (Fox)? "Theda Bara is an attractive, alluring vampire and handles her part splendidly. She is a true type and a finished actress."[111]

In Chicago, Kitty Kelly became more incisive without losing any of her skill as a wordsmith. *The Girl of the Golden West* (Lasky) gave her another chance to enumerate "the essentials of successful entertainment": "excitement and suspense of a logical sort," "heroism and humor and love," star personalities, and "attractive atmosphere" (fig. 52).[112] Further evidence came in *The Goose Girl,* a Lasky fairy tale with Marguerite Clark that was "as fresh as the dew drenched grass, as sweet as a field of clover."[113] No less complimentary was her review of *Mistress Nell* (Famous Players), primarily for making Mary Pickford, a "bubbling artesian well sort of personality," "the live center of the picture" in disguises that showcased "her tricks of mannerisms, her swaggers, and her mischievous asides . . . as pleasant to watch as a kitten's frolics."[114] Kelly could also recommend shorter films such as *Minerva's Mission* (Majestic), a "real comedy" that, unlike slapstick, leaves the viewer with "a pleasant mental taste," especially because Dorothy Gish hesitates "never a bit to screw her hair back into uncompromising funniness."[115] And, despite her aversion to slapstick, she had to admit that *Tillie's Punctured Romance* (Keystone) gave her a "good opportunity to study" why audiences erupted in continual "shouts of laughter."[116] Increasingly, Kelly began to pick out specific details to highlight in a film. In *The Morals of Marcus* (Famous Players), "the subtitles contribute much to the humor of the whole, their crisp pointedness assisting the action every time."[117] In *Alias Jimmy Valentine,* like Gunning she noted the unique perspective of the crime scene, "in which the camera mounted high overlooked the tops of all the small partitions subdividing the robbed

FLICKERINGS from FILM LAND

by KITTY KELLY

"THE GIRL OF THE GOLDEN WEST."

Lasky.

The Girl ....Mabel Van Buren
Jack Rance..............Theodore Roberts
Ramerrez ....House Peters

THE Lasky company is a year old. In that time it has made seventeen pictures and raised its reputation from mediocrity to excellence, even in the face of the rising standard of photoplay requirements.

This picture, "The Girl of the Golden West," is the last production in that period and is evidence of the Lasky standing in the realm of picture makers. That David Belasco by his affiliation with the company had an important effect on the rise in its artistic temperature, is a safe thought to cherish. The pictures with which he has been connected, as this one, show the value of the Belascoan method in celluloid land and spoil observers for watching carelessly lumped claptrap.

Belasco and Lasky are carrying the banner of artistic pictures to the van and it is to be hoped that they will be generously rallied about before the year's end by other makers. Some are with them now, but there is room for more.

This picture contains all of the essentials of successful entertainment presented in most mentally appetizing form. There is excitement and suspense of a logical sort, there is heroism and humor and love, and there are stars, three in number, each one of them independently good, and there is attractive atmosphere creating setting throughout.

Mabel Van Buren has the skill to win even the prejudiced observer's liking and she does it thoroughly in her rôle of pretty, flirtatious, independent owner of "The Polka," the saloon mecca of all the miners of the mountains. Theodore Roberts as the gambler is a delight in his impersonation, and he gets more effect out of his judiciously flapped coattails than would many a person out of his whole cosmos. House Peters, as Ramerrez, the mysterious bandit, is muscularly heroic, an obvious reason for the girl's love.

When the jilted Mexican girl sets the tribe of law upon Ramerrez's trail, the girl is likewise heroic and she puts up a fight that is, with the gambler for her sweetheart's life. Playing square doesn't worry her a bit, in the stakes she is after, so when they play poker for his life, she arranges to win by the safe method of ensuring the cards she will need in her stocking, while denying her opponent the privilege of using his well disciplined deck. And then later, when Ramerrez is caught again and falls lawfully into the hands of the gambler, she doesn't hesitate to brand him a cheat and insist that he stick to his bargain. Miss Van Buren demonstrates that she is the right kind of a girl all right.

Besides all this there is the "atmosphere," that mysterious thing which takes one out of the murk of Chicago and plants one, in this instance, in the days of '49 looking out over the prairie schoonered trails that led as many to disaster as to fortune. The first few feet presenting a wide and wonderful glimpse of this, are worthy of preservation as a historical contribution.

Sparks from the Reel.

Thomas H. Ince, the director of the Inceville enterprises in the shape of Domino, Broncho, and Key Bee releases, sleeps only four or five hours a day and thrives on it.

Thelma and Beulah Burns are the two little folks who help in putting "heart interest" into Griffith Mutual pictures.

The Favorite Players are going to produce Jacques Futrelle's "The High Hand," with Carlyle Blackwell in the lead.

FIGURE 52. "Flickerings from Film Land by Kitty Kelly," *Chicago Tribune,* January 6, 1915.

office."[118] Still, she could not ignore what she called "the dark side" of criticism, lamenting the absurd plot in the otherwise charming *Her Supreme Sacrifice* (Kalem) or the "plot deficiencies" in *The Glory of Clementina* (Edison), and counting off the reasons she disliked *A Gentleman of Leisure* (Lasky): the hero's "sophomoric" appearance, his "painfully trite plan" of burgling a house, and "other spots [where] the picture slips up on the banana peel of logic."[119]

At the same time, Kelly included within or appended to her reviews notes on local matters or the conditions of her own viewing. She apologized for errors in identifying the players in *The Three Brothers* (Majestic) because she had "no synopsis at hand," a usual resource for newspaper writers.[120] In describing Universal's new quarters in the city, she admired the "commodious" exhibition room, adding that its comforts seemed intended to induce "more amiable judgements than arise from a mind prisoned in a cramped, smothered, walked over, stepped on, neck obscured, breathless body."[121] She reported on a special screening organized by the Women's City Club to demonstrate "the educational value of moving pictures," followed by a reception for two social reformers, Miss Jane Addams and Mrs. Ella Flagg Young.[122] She promoted a public lecture on Motion Study, illustrated by several films, before a class in factory management at Northwestern University.[123] By contrast, a commercial screening of Henry W. Savage's nine-reel *Uncle Sam at Work* at the Auditorium was marred by a lecturer speaking "a bit too rapid to be comfortably clear to those not near at hand" and by the "tin-panny bombardments" of the sound-effects men that stopped "at no sound except that of people eating soup."[124] Walking past the many theaters on busy Madison Street led her to offer graphic design advice to the industry's poster makers, wishing they would "realize that thick, fat letters stretching clear across the sheet of 'paper' are far less easy to read . . . than thin, slim letters that the eye can get in a single glance."[125] On another occasion she quite reasonably urged exhibitors to announce the starting times of their shows, which would "enable people to calculate their arrival" and also preserve "the dramatic force of the picture, by not obliging the drifters-in to watch the heroine or hero die before their story is begun."[126] In early March, she even invited female readers to share her tongue-in-cheek delight with a press release puffing Francis X. Bushman's addition of "an amethyst colored automobile to his collection of 'jewels'": "My Goodness Gracious, Girls! Isn't He Lovely?"[127]

During much of March and April, Kelly took a break from serving up daily film reviews and traveled West to report on the opening of Universal City (see chapter 1) and interview actors, directors, producers, and scriptwriters in "film land."[128] Once back in Chicago, she resumed her role as "a professional picture see-er" of "dozens . . . each week," very few of which persisted in her memory.[129] One of those was *The Women* (Lasky), which allowed her not only to begin calling attention to an excellent director—George Melford—but also to summarize her critical principles. His adaptation of William DeMille's play "gives opportunity for development of both character and atmosphere, and the observer follows the moods and emotions of the players [because] the situations all have point, and they are crisp—cut off just before one begins to feel there is a touch too much."[130] Another was *Stolen Goods* (Lasky), and she named more of those responsible for its success: "Blanche Sweet, alluring, heart winning . . . ; Margaret Turnbull, interest impelling author; George Melford, shrewd director; and the artist behind the camera and in the darkroom."[131] Moreover, the film was exemplary in giving her a newly desired experience of absorption and identification. There was "such careful manipulation of the suspense threads, such skillful selection of the high lights of interest, such compactness and yet such completeness that . . . the observer comes as near to sharing the vital experience of any third person as he can come in life." Yet Kelly just as frequently dissed "less digestible productions." "A pleasant bit of mediocrity," *Niobe* (Famous Players) "was greatly redeemed by the individual performance of [Hazel Dawn], forgivable for its commonness through its absolute cleanliness."[132] *Graustark* (Essanay) she found concocted as "a nice, sweet, perfectly polite, sugar plum picture, containing no harmful effects for 'nobody.'"[133] By contrast (especially to "Wid" Gunning), *A Fool There Was* definitely gave her indigestion: "a dime novel theme . . . arousing no particular storms of protest, scenarioized in terms of mediocrity and produced and acted with super mediocrity [with] little shock."[134] She did not even deign to name Theda Bara and instead noted how the censors merely helped to publicize the film.

Along with her reviews, Kelly continued to inform readers of the city censors' outright rejections and ordered "cut outs." Based on her own viewing of *The Birth of a Nation* in Los Angeles, she argued for the film's screening in Chicago, especially after censors permitted a "display of 'The New Governor,' adapted from the notorious 'The Nigger.'"[135] Insisting that *Birth* "far exceeds *Cabiria*," she praised D.W. Griffith for weaving "all of the threads of life" into "his wonderful fabric." She acknowledged its Southern bias, which stirred "in some the chord of controversy," but she claimed that "free minded American folk" would see that, if it showed "the negroes . . . falling into the hands of false leaders," those leaders were "white ones."[136] Still, at the film's return engagement in October, Kelly revealed her own bias, as she briefly extolled the climactic rescue by "the poetically imaginative Ku Klux Klan riders."[137] As for "cut outs," the imported war picture *With Serb and Austrian* lost its "cast of characters and three-part forward" and two dozen intertitles, all of which rendered the film incomprehensible and its position on the European war quite ambiguous.[138] Popular serials and series still could not escape censure: A "long scene in a house of ill fame" disappeared from *The Black Box #9* (Universal), and two crucial plot points were cut in an episode of *The Hazards of Helen* (Kalem).[139] She listed in boldface the many scenes and shots "expurgated" from *The Woman* (Essanay), arguing that "the much maligned Chicago board of censorship" saved Chaplin's "reputation among decent folk."[140] She herself came close to condemning the film, reprinting letters that supported her position and pointedly quoting the remarks of offended men in an audience.[141] One month later, however, *The Bank* (Essanay) seemed to redeem Chaplin in her eyes—"This picture is so absolutely clean that an investigative finger couldn't scrape up even a suggestion of dust"—but she also had to admit that, in the *Incorrigible Dukane* (Famous Players), John Barrymore was "as funny" in his own way as Chaplin.[142] Likewise, she pointed out how Mary Pickford's performance in *Rags* (Famous Players) transformed a simple story into "quite a little confection," or how Marguerite Clark's "poignant helplessness" in *Helene of the North* (Famous Players) was heightened for an overflow audience by a story with such "popular punch," whereas Elsie Janis in *Nearly a Lady* (Famous Players) kept "insisting on being every large bead on the chain" rather than making herself an integral "part of a story."[143] Although the casting was acceptable in *Puppet Crown* (Lasky), Kelly could not resist whipping up a description of its story as "macroony, or maybe divinely fudgey," while confiding to her readers, "We like those things on our physical diet, so why not have some as mental dessert."[144]

That summer Kelly began to offer readers an informative credit box at the top of her daily film reviews.[145] Each of these included not only the cast list of major players but also the company responsible for the film and the downtown theater where it was currently playing. In pinpointing what contributed so much to an audience's experience of a good film, Kelly also drew attention to the personnel behind the scenes. In *Chimmie Fadden* (Lasky), a perfect example of a "good legitimate comedy," she singled out director Cecil B. DeMille, photographer Alvin Wyckoff, and technical director Wilfred Buckland.[146] And she noted how important it was, in *The Marriage of Kitty* (Lasky), that "the bits are looked after as carefully as the big parts"—that is, neither the minor players or extras nor the star Fannie Ward make any effort "to wring a laugh, yet from every movement of almost everybody little chuckles spring out irresistibly."[147] Intriguingly, her advice to readers was that the best seat in a picture theater was not the best in a legitimate theater: "To see a picture enjoyingly one must be far back in the center of the house."[148] So it is surprising that, in contrast to "Wid" Gunning, it was not until July 1915 that she acknowledged the significance of actors' faces in close-ups.[149] When she did, however, she quickly recognized the impact of "effective close up after effective close up" in a film such as *The Clue* (Lasky), where Sessue Hayakawa so distracted her with his "marvelous face, with its slow narrowing of narrow eyes, its flicker of flexible lip."[150] And it was the specific power of such close-ups, along with other camera perspectives and editing practices, that led Kelly to the prescient conclusion that "pictures nowadays have their special styles of diction, just as does fiction."[151]

A SMORGASBORD OF TASTING

Joining these pioneers in 1915 were at least five others: Louella Parsons in the *Chicago Herald,* James Warren Currie in Hearst's *Chicago Examiner,* George Worts in the *New York Evening Mail,* Richard F. Lussier in the *Birmingham Age-Herald,* and "The Film Girl" in the *Syracuse Herald.* In mid-March 1915, before she began writing star profiles, Caroline Carr (another young scriptwriter)[152] signed several *Herald* columns entitled "Seen on the Screen," one of which reviewed *The Governor's Lady* (Famous Players) as if for readers unfamiliar with the stage production.[153] Soon Parsons took over this daily column, starting with a review of *In the Park* (Essanay), in which she concisely caught Chaplin's "ridiculous goose-walk stunts, kicking right and left with his No. 12 shoes, in the most matter of fact fashion."[154] Much like Kitty Kelly, she chose just one film to review—the "most entertaining" or "unique" of the day's releases—and, from the start, included a cast list along with brief local items, industry news, and an "Answers to Questions" section (as opposed to Kelly's censorship "cutouts").[155] Her initial reviews revealed a range of interests, and several became characteristic: a preference for feature films, especially stage play adaptations, an attention to actors' skills, an appreciation of local audiences, and a sense of moral approbation. *Are You a Mason?* (Famous Players) not only was "a most acceptable screen offering of Leo Ditrichstein's comedy," but John Barrymore also brought "a laugh from the first peep we have of him as the dutiful husband until the last bit of film fades from our sight" (fig. 53).[156] Keenly interested in local events, she praised the Studebaker for inviting a group of "Italian" children to a special screening of Salisbury's *Wild Animal Life,* and later reported on the audience applause for "the scenic portions" of *The Eternal City* (Famous Players) at the same theater, quoting a young woman seated next to her who had lived in Rome: "They are by far the best pictures I have ever seen of the Italian city."[157] Yet her moral sense was much offended by *The Fight* (World Film), largely because "the story [was] sordid and unwholesome and not the sort of material the censor board has educated us to expect on the screen."[158]

Within weeks, the *Herald* located Parsons's column on the Society or Women's page, again following the *Tribune*'s practice with Kelly's. She

SEEN on the SCREEN by Luella O. Parsons

Jack Barrymore Furnishes Whole Screenful of Laughs

"ARE YOU A MASON?"

Frank Perry	John Barrymore
Helen Perry	Helen Freeman
Father	Charles Dickson
Mother	Ida Waterman

JOHN BARRYMORE brings a laugh from the first peep we have of him as the dutiful husband until the last bit of film fades from our sight. The Famous Players have made a most acceptable screen offering of Leo Ditrichstein's comedy, "Are You a Mason?"

Poor Jack Barrymore must have worked harder in this complicated movie than in any stage production he ever took part. Life is one strenuous bit of action, mixed up with all sorts of hardships, from taking nasty looking concoctions to scaling high walls, being wrecked in an automobile and lying prone in the street.

Barrymore as Perry is brought first to our vision as a loving husband saying good-by to friend wife, who is leaving to visit mother. Perry has a severe cold and is left to the tender mercies of Nora, a good maid but a better spy. All goes well until a friend suggests the club with "rock and rye" as a cure. Perry falls. When he returns home at 5 a. m. after an all-night session Nora wires his mother-in-law of the downfall. His celebration has taken the form of entering a strange house, where he sheds his coat and gets chased out as a burglar, of decorating the statue of Venus de Milo and of reaching home with only a few remnants of his former plentiful wardrobe.

Wifie plans to return home at once with all the loving family, father, mother and the two girls. Mother thinks if only Perry could be induced to join the Masons he might be saved. Father has represented himself as being grand master of one lodge.

Perry's only salvation seems to be to declare he joined the lodge the night before and that his celebration was an initiation. He is forgiven by his wife, but he and his father-in-law have a hard time "stalling at the high signs," each hoping to deceive the other.

The detective arrives with Perry's coat and a warrant for his arrest. Perry buys him off with a worthless check. The best friend, who is a suitor for one of his sisters, makes Perry tell he also is a Mason. The plot grows with the discovery of the fraud by the sweetheart of the other sister.

The detective soon returns with Perry's worthless check and is taken riding in an automobile. A smashup follows and the two men are brought to Perry's home, where the latter finds a check for $2,000 from father on the strength of his Masonic make-believe to pay off the troublesome detectives.

All the tangles are smoothed out and the last reel ends with a terrible nightmare, with Perry as the victim. He dreams he is being initiated into the Masonic order.

Ida Waterman as the bossy mother-in-law is excellent and Charles Dickson is good as the guilty father-in-law. The rest of the cast make a capable support for the star.

+ + +

If you like fairy tales, interesting stories of wicked witches and beautiful princesses with a dear little boy and girl, you will enjoy the "New Wizard of Oz," released on the Alliance program.

The photographical effects in this adapted musical comedy add much to the picture. The children will revel in the part where Mombi, the witch, is dissolved into a can of sandwiches. Perhaps you will too, that is, if you are still a child at heart.

+ + +

Information reaches us that we are soon to have a treat. The Italia Film Company has ready for shipment "The Serpent," written by Dante Testa, Italian author and dramatist. Best of all, we are to see many of the Cabiria stars in this new production.

+ + +

George Kleine's next big offering will be the photodramatization of "The Commuters," by James Forbes. It will be told on the screen in five reels, and we are promised a "reel" comedy that contains a laugh in every scene.

+ + +

Harry Walthall's sister, Anna May, has joined the Balboa Company. She has the ingenue lead in "The Light o' Love."

+ + +

Harry Mestayer of the "On Trial" Company is holding down two jobs at the same time. When he is not starring in "On Trial" he is out at the Selig studios, where he is acting in Anna Katherine Green's "Millionaire Baby." Mr. Mestayer will be remembered in Kleine's "Stop Thief."

Answers to Questions

OLD ADMIRERS—It is a great pleasure to greet old friends in this department, and I want to thank you for your nice letter. Florence Turner is with her own company in England, but somehow the films seldom get to America.

+ + +

M. E. K.—Ruth Stonehouse is married to Joseph Roach, a scenario writer. Francis X. Bushman says he is not married. He played in stock for seven years before he came to Essanay, and also played in a number of successful Broadway productions. Mary Pickford is still with the Famous Players Company. Yes, I thought she was adorable in "A Good Little Devil."

+ + +

DICK—Both "The Champion" and "In the Park" were produced in Niles, Cal., where the western Essanay studios are located. Chaplin wil return to Chicago later in the season.

+ + +

QUESTION MARK—If you could give me the name of the play that the dark-eyed leading woman played in I could help you to locate her. Your description is rather vague. There are so many handsome, dark-eyed leading women.

Where They Show Today.

Hamlin—"The Girl of the Music Hall," in three parts.

Crawford—Wilton Lackaye in "Children of the Ghetto."

Shakespeare—"Jack's Charity."

Gold—"Clothes."

Parkway—"David Harum."

World—Charles Chaplin in "In the Park."

E. A. R. (Sixty-ninth and Wentworth)—"The Champion."

FIGURE 53. "Seen on the Screen by Luella O. Parsons," *Chicago Herald*, March 22, 1915.

found more pictures to condemn, although crowds flocked to them: *Three Weeks,* based on "Elinor Glynn's salacious book," was an inexcusably "immoral tale" that caught "the Pennsylvania board of censorship . . . asleep on the job." And not only was *A Fool There Was* "appalling in its grewsome unreality," but Theda Bara "gave almost too harsh an impersonation of her unpleasant character."[159] Despite her distaste for melodrama, she could appreciate Helen Holmes's skillful stunts in the *Hazards of Helen* railroad series and the "thrill a minute" action in *The Eagle's Nest* (Lubin), starring Romaine Fielding.[160] Critical of the industry practice of adapting "unsuitable" magazine stories, as in a "hopelessly dull" *The Opal Ring* (Essanay),[161] Parsons played the constant advocate for adaptations. Especially favored were: *Graustark* (Essanay) with Beverly Bayne, "every inch a queen"; *Fanon the Cricket* (Famous Players), with "Pickford, sweet and winsome in all her rags," charming a "large and enthusiastic audience"; and *The Carpet from Bagdad* (Selig), "a fanciful story, but told in a clear, concise way that makes one realize the day of big features is at hand."[162] Features such as these provoked her to confess that each week she was "more and more impressed with the wonder of it all."[163] As further evidence she viewed *The Avenging Conscience* not once but three times, having first deftly described "the delicate touches, the beautiful scenic effects and the stirring suspense" that so characterized D.W. Griffith's direction.[164] As for *The Birth of a Nation,* at the end of its long run she marked it as unique—"We are going to recall when we saw it, where we saw it and how we wept and were overcome at the Little Colonel's daring"—and hoped city censors would permit people under twenty-one to see "the facsimile of these greatest American events."[165] Her interest in local matters continued unabated. She reported that audiences thronged *The Lady of the Snows* (Vitagraph) because the mayor's wife had written the scenario; praised the Strand for organizing a premiere of *The Women* (Lasky) for specially invited guests at the Orchestra Hall; complimented the Fair Hope League for selecting films suitable for "the 'kiddies' of Oak Park"; and shared a letter that wished for an "open season" on the "pests" that, in their "boob-osity," read intertitles out loud during a film screening.[166]

Perhaps as expected, given her long-running column "How to Write Photoplays," Parsons paid particular attention to a film's story construction, whether or not it was an adaptation. She was quick to fault *Fine Feathers* (World Film) for its "execrable taste in furnishings" and for Jane Beecher, "who had better remain on the stage," but mainly for its "poorly constructed" scenario that turned a "strong play [into] an intensely weak picture."[167] She grew tired of all the densely forested outdoor scenes in *The*

Sealed Valley (Metro) but objected most to the story's lack of continuity: "The space between scenes is of too great duration," and "characters . . . do not appear for so long a time that one is apt to forget their existence."[168] *Nearly a Lady* (Bosworth) she found "so obviously written [to give] Elsie Janis the opportunity to wear every sort of costume designed for the fair feminine . . . that it seems absurd to take the photoplay seriously."[169] By contrast, noting that adaptations always carried the risk of becoming lambs or goats, Parsons complemented the scenario department at American Film for turning the novel of *The Girl from Our Town* into such "a clear, concise . . . lamb-like" film.[170] Likewise, she claimed that *The Kindling* (Lasky) would be as "popular in the pictorial version" as it was "a success on the stage" because "there are no loose ends, and each scene fits into the succeeding one with admirable smoothness."[171] Finally, she summed up the advantages that the "movies" had over stage dramas: "quick action," "more latitude," "the excitement of having our emotions visited by a transition from grief to laughter and back again in less time than it takes to write."[172] That latitude was evident in William de Mille's scenario for Lasky's *Carmen,* but she agreed that the film's real revelation was the "radiant personality" of Geraldine Farrar: "an irresistible Carmen, charming but cruel and wanton, full of whims, preferring always to be loved without giving of her love" (fig. 54).[173] As it was too in *Madame Butterfly* (Famous Players), with its changed death at the end. Moreover, in taking "the opportunity to show her versatility," Mary Pickford was only one of the treats in this "dainty screen gem," a "masterpiece . . . of exquisite workmanship."[174]

Beginning in May 1915, James Warren Currie's column "The Turn of the Reel" in the *Chicago Examiner* chiefly served up star interviews and profiles, industry news, and occasional local pieces, but he could offer infrequent film reviews.[175] Like Kitty Kelly and Louella Parsons, Currie usually restricted his viewings to the city's major downtown picture theaters, but his comments were brief and often paled in comparison to theirs. The photoplay version of *The Arab* (Lasky) he praised for its "realism," the acting of Edgar Selwyn (who was the author and playwright as well), and the "quaint and mystic" music performed by the Strand Theater orchestra.[176] Olga Petrova made *The Vampire* (Metro) quite "seeable" despite its "naughty name" and lack of "naughty situations"; in fact, "no one but a fraud would hang out the sign 'No Children Allowed.'"[177] The scenario "from the facile pen of Sir Henry Arthur Jones," the choice of interiors, and the acting of Hazel Dawn perhaps accounted for his swooning over a "vigorously British" *The Masqueraders* (Famous Players), "redolent in every scene of rosy-cheeked English girlhood, roast beef, the fragrance of well-kept downs, ale, and porter."[178] He urged

Seen on the Screen

"CARMEN."

Carmen (the gypsy)..Geraldine Farrar
Don Jose (young officer)..........Wallace Reid
Escamillo (a toreador)..........Pedro de Cordoba
Morales (an officer)... William Elmer
Pastia (tavern-keeper and smuggler)..............Horace Carpenter
Frasquita (cigaret girl)..........Jeanie MacPherson
Mercedes (a gypsy)......Anita King
Garcia..................Milton Brown

By LOUELLA O. PARSONS.

THE Strand standard prevailed last night in the opening of the Strand Theater. The 1,600 guests were greeted by E. C. 'Divine, president of the Strand Theater Company; E. Q. Cordner, managing director, and A. J. Partridge and Joseph Interrieden, the other officers of the organization, ir their beautiful new home, Wabash avenue and Seventh street.

Standing out in harmony of color and beauty of decoration, the interior of the old panorama building, more recently known as the Globe Theater, presents a surprise for those who remember the former barnlike structure.

It was as if fairy hands had transformed dullness to magnificence. Japanese blue rugs cover the floor and upholster the Circassian walnut chairs. Scarlet hangings fall softly from the stage, with artistic lights shedding a subdued radiance here and there. The Strand company has lived up to its reputation and given the public a theater in keeping with its program.

"Carmen" in opera is so popular that the thought of "Carmen" in motion pictures seems to many lovers of this tuneful opera a sacrilege. But when Geraldine Farrar, as the beautiful, bewitching Spanish girl, pulsating with life and expressing every emotion known to Prosper Merimée's heroine, smiled at the audience, all doubts were stilled.

William De Mille, who prepared the scenario, describes the Carmen of the novel rather than the opera. There is more latitude naturally in the film, and this Mr. De Mille uses to good advantage.

+ + +

Geraldine Farrar is a revelation. Had she been a little extra girl chosen to enact this role she would have been just as remarkable. It is not the magic name of Farrar that compels one to admire the work of this artist. I: is her portrayal, so real and so expressive. Miss Farrar looks like a slip of a girl of 18. Her vivacious and carefree air strengthen the youthful illusion, and we take Geraldine Farrar's Carmen straight to our hearts.

The story opens in the camp of the smuggels. We are introduced to Carmen's people—a band of desperate men who live and thrive on their illegitimate plunder. It is Carmen's duty to fascinate Don Jose, the handsome commander of the customs officers. This she does by every wile and art known to the feminine charmer. Jose steals and kills for her, and even then she spurns him.

Escamillo, the bold and fearless toreador, wins her attention through the clothes and luxuries he bestows upon her. She accompanies him to Seville and there watches him enter the arena to participate in a bull fight. There is a real bull, panting and snorting while he angrily paws the dust. He is ready to trample Escamillo beneath his hoofs, though, of course, the toreador vanquishes the bull, but for humane reasons we are unable to see the actual finish of this maddened animal.

GERALDINE FARRAR.

Then Don Jose follows her to Seville and plunges a knife into her breast. She dies in his arms, game to the last.

It is Geraldine Farrar who makes the picture. She is the irresistible Carmen, charming but cruel and wanton, full of whims, preferring always to be loved without giving of her love. Without Miss Farrar's radiant personality the picture would attract no unusual attention. From the standpoint of pictorial perfection Lasky has done even better things, but they have never brought to the screen a more delightful picture star than Geraldine Farrar.

Wallace Reid's Don Jose and Pedro de Cordoba's Escamillo are convincingly portrayed. There are some good scenic effects and frequent artistic touches that show the guiding hand of Cecil De Mille, Lasky's director in chief.

The music from "Carmen," with the Toreador song and other bits from the opera, accompany the picture, and are for those who know and love its score a necessary part of the entertainment.

New Loop Attractions

The Olympic throws open its doors Sunday evening for the first time to pictures. J. Stuart Blackston's photo-spectacle, "The Battle Cry of Peace," will be offered to the public. The program at the Studebaker changes and on Sunday afternoon "The Disciple," "The Martyrs of the Alamo" and "A Game Old Knight" will succeed the present entertainment. The new Strand Theater will present Geraldine Farrar in a pictorial version of "Carmen," also an accompanying musical program. The Ziegfeld bill changes this afternoon and Ethel Barrymore will be seen in "The Final Judgment," with Marie Doro in "The White Pearl" as an added attraction. The entertainment at the Fine Arts starting this afternoon will consist of Carter and Flora De Haven in "The College Orphan" and Kathryn Osterman in "The Bludgeon," the latter a screen version of Paul Armstrong's celebrated play. "The Birth of a Nation" continues at the Colonial.

FIGURE 54. "Seen on the Screen by Louella O. Parsons," *Chicago Herald*, October 16, 1916.

spectators to see both the Lasky and Fox versions of *Carmen*, but Currie preferred the latter: Theda Bara was "a wonderfully alluring Carmen," no detail was neglected in contributing to its "realism," and "thrill follows thrill in endless procession," culminating when "Carmen's slayer, fleeing from the gendarmerie, plunges with his horse over the edge of a chasm into a pool of water 150 feet below [making no less than] three complete somersaults."[179] His position, by contrast, was undivided on American Correspondent Film's "documentary" feature *The Warring Millions* and Vitagraph's *The Battle Cry of Peace:* Both countered "that bugaboo of the cracker box politician, 'militarism,'" and, despite the pacifist stance of the latter, made a convincing "argument for national preparedness."[180]

Once he took over editing the *New York Evening Mail*'s column, George Worts generally accepted "Wid" Gunning's principles of taste, but he wasn't as thorough. His review of *Esmeralda* (Famous Players) is representative: "In every detail the play is completely satisfactory": "an ingenious plot," faultless photography, excellent direction, and an "exceptionally well chosen" cast led by Mary Pickford's "naturalness and ingenuousness."[181] Those details also came together in two Lasky productions, *The Case of Becky* and *Out of Darkness*, leading him to claim that "psychology has entered motion pictures" and "can be understood just as well on the screen as on the stage—perhaps better."[182] Much like Gunning, Worts singled out directors as most responsible for the quality of any one film. He may have wrongly attributed direction of *The Conqueror* (Triangle) to Thomas Ince—evidence that Ince's productions were "now cutting circles around the productions that come from the Griffith studio"[183]—but he was on firmer ground praising Cecil B. DeMille's work for Lasky. If *The Golden Chance* was striking for its "unique and pleasing lighting effects," notably in the night scenes, *The Ragamuffin* demonstrated "what good direction can do for a film" in skillfully handling the transitions in the main character's transformation within an assuredly logical narrative—aided, of course, by the acting of Blanche Sweet.[184] And, like Gunning and Currie, he was enamored of Theda Bara in Fox's "wild, untrammeled version" of *Carmen*, despite poor projection in an unnamed picture theater.[185] Worts also could admire both male and female actors, especially "the nimble-footed" Douglas Fairbanks in *The Lamb* and *His Picture in the Papers* (both Triangle) "as an all 'round rubber-spined jumping jack he is entirely in a class by himself."[186] Surprisingly, he lambasted one Ince production, *Hell's Hinges* (Triangle), as a "bellowing, mawkish melodrama . . . a disordered sequence of shooting scrapes, hold-ups, drunken orgies and license," so shameful as to give cause for censorship.[187] Worts continued editing the *Mail*'s column until June

1916, but the reviews grew less frequent and were signed by others—Stanley Olmsted, T.E. Oliphant, Frederick James Smith, and Sara Moore, among them—with the dramatic editor, Burns Mantle, even writing those on *Marvelous Maciste* and *Ramona*.[188]

At the same time, in the *Birmingham Age-Herald*, Richard F. Lussier's "Footlights and Screens" column occasionally offered his take on a current film. Unlike Worts, Lussier found Fox's *Carmen* "not a picture of the same artistic calibre" as Lasky's, and Theda Bara "at a disadvantage when compared with the artistry of Farrar."[189] Yet he followed others in defining a good film according to a shared set of principles. *The Gentleman from Indiana* (Paramount) was "an admirably balanced production, logical in its plot development, true in characterization, dramatic when the big moments in the story are reached and spectacular in the presentation of scenes requiring a large company of supers."[190] As an adaptation, moreover, it was "faithful to the phase of American life" depicted in Booth Tarkington's source novel. Intriguingly, to prepare for *The Birth of a Nation*'s appearance at the Jefferson Theater in late December, Lussier compiled a profile of D.W. Griffith illustrating the well-worn cliché, "Behind every great work stands a great man." Claiming "there is something compelling, sweeping, irresistible about the pictures that come from Griffith's hand of command and the Griffith master brain," Lussier took the position, perhaps expected of a Southerner, of channeling the promotional discourse circulated for years by Griffith himself.[191] He also praised his newspaper for inviting "surviving Confederate veterans" to march "in a body" to attend an early screening and reported days later on the theater's record-breaking attendance.[192] In January 1916, his column began to fill up with brief notes (often just a few lines) on five to ten films then playing at the city's theaters. Rarely now sharing his opinions, Lussier kept on reporting audience responses—as in Pickford's "peculiar appeal" that packed screenings of *The Foundling* (Famous Players) at the Strand and "turned crowds away"[193]—and increasingly summarized the industry's publicity notices as well as information supplied by local exhibitors.

Much more interesting was the daily column that the *Syracuse Herald* began running in June 1915. Also titled "Seen on the Screen," it was signed by "The Film Girl," a young woman whose name, Marjorie Dunmore Tooke, was not revealed until late 1918.[194] Much like Kitty Kelly and Louella Parsons, The Film Girl opened her column with a review (usually of just one film), followed by some industry news and gossip (often about stars), and eventually one or more readers' letters and her brief responses. One admiring reader later called the column "the best edited in the State," but his description of its tone as "breezy and snappy" seemed to better fit that of "Wid" or Mae Tinee.[195] Instead, The Film Girl addressed readers in a colloquial, chatty, personalized style that, unlike Kelly's, rarely called attention to itself. She was writing a "coly'um" simply as a "maid of the movies" or a fan much like her readers. While the column shifted around among several pages, sometimes paired with a piece of serialized fiction, on Saturdays it often nestled near a schedule of church events, and in November it frequently occupied the same page as "Daily Talks by Mary Pickford."[196] From very early on, The Film Girl confessed a preference for a local variety program of short films: "After I have seen a really good old fashioned kind of a movie show consisting of a two reel feature and about three good one reel photo plays, I am inclined to think that I'd just about as soon go in the 5-cent theater as in the 15-cent one" (fig. 55).[197] This led to reviews of programs at neighborhood theaters—the Happy Hour, Novelty, Hippodrome, Crescent, and Regent (near Syracuse University)[198]—almost as often as features at the downtown theaters—the Strand, Eckel, and Savoy. Included in those programs at the Happy Hour and Novelty was *The Goddess,* the only serial that she found of "sustained interest" and recommended "for sheer originality of plot."[199] Moreover, she aligned herself closely with movie fans by lauding the Crescent for its "good scheme . . . of showing feature pictures which are not altogether new" because "not all those who would have liked to were able to see them" when first screened in the city.[200] The Savoy's policy of showing features for "one-day engagements only except on rare occasions," however, might have compromised her advice about whether or not to see a particular film.[201]

Feature films, however, usually received The Film Girl's more sustained reviews. Compared to Kitty Kelly, Louella Parsons, and "Wid" Gunning, she was not as concerned with films as art, nor did she "claim that they are instructive or that they benefit one mentally. . . . Their mission is as a diversion—a relaxation. Therefore, we need them in our lives."[202] Accordingly, her appreciation of a really good feature was impressionistic. "I laughed aloud during the greater part of 'Chimmie Fadden,' which is my method of conveying the impression of what an excellent production I think it is."[203] *The Kindling* "beggars comparison with anything I have yet seen," with Charlotte Walker making "her screen debut under the happiest of auspices."[204] One of the few current Famous Players features starring Mary Pickford that she considered up to the standard set by the earlier *Tess of Storm Country, Such a Little Queen,* or *Hearts Adrift* was *A Girl of Yesterday,* which she described in rare mixed metaphors: "a pleasant vehicle built just her size—a rambling vehicle—sweet and without plan as were

By THE FILM GIRL.

After I have seen a really good old fashioned kind of a movie show consisting of a two reel feature and about three good one reel photo plays, I am inclined to think that I'd just about as soon go to the 5-cent theater as to the 15-cent one. And there are times which happen not infrequently when the many reeled feature does not appeal at all. I never remember seeing a better all around show than yesterday at the Crescent. To begin with there was Blanche Sweet, pretty and blonde, attempting to disguise herself in a black wig in "Judith of Bethulia," an Apocrypha story. Well, I remember the "Judith" of my school days, for she and her sisters of an ancient line helped to make the study of the Bible and of Bible times interesting. There on the screen, beautifully done, was "Judith's" story. Then there was Marian Sais in a detective story, not at all bad, and Lillian Walker in a pretty piece entitled "The Little Doll's Dressmaker," and something else for which I, unfortunately, didn't have time to stay.

The readers of Mary Roberts Rinehart's famous "Tish" stories which have been run from time to time in the Saturday Evening Post will have the further pleasure of seeing their heroine filmized, for the Essanay is making pictures of the series in the mountains and valleys of Tennessee.

"Your funny face is your fortune, Harry," said one of the Universal directors the other day, and who do you suppose he was talking to? The answer is that it was none other than our old friend Harry Gribbon, comedian at the Valley last summer. It would seem that Mr. Gribbon is even more popular in the movies than on the musical comedy stage, for he is being featured in a number of coming releases. One of these is "A Dismantled Beauty," soon to be seen on local screens.

It will be of interest to some of the fans to know that Mr. Manly, who plays the role of "Daddy" in so many Universal offerings, is scarcely made up at all for his roles. He is 80 years of age.

An echo of the days when Baltimore was the social center of the South—when men wore swallow tail coats with brass buttons, tight fitting trousers, lace bosoms to their shirts, low cut fancy vests and high beaver hats, and the women wore crinolines was staged in "Kennedy Square," F. Hopkinson Smith's charming story by the Vitagraph.

The transcontinental trip of Geraldine Farrar in her private car from New York to the Lasky studios in Hollywood, Cal., was a triumphal progress and when she arrived the mayor of Los Angeles, Mr. Lasky, Cecil B. De Mille, Samuel Goldfish and other officials of the Lasky company, together with 5,000 school children gave her a flower shower. But that was not all—that night there was a dinner in honor of the famous prima donna, now a movie donna as well, and all the officials of the city and all of the prominent artists in the vicinity were invited.

To-morrow Edgar Selwyn in "The Arab" will be seen at the Strand theater. As this is one of the biggest releases for the summer, considerable importance attaches to its presentation. The settings are said to be marvelous in their splendor and the story thrilling and unusual. It deals with an American girl, the daughter of a missionary

FIGURE 55. "Seen on the Screen by The Film Girl," *Syracuse Herald,* June 22, 1915.

our grandmothers' gardens," leaving "a fragrant memory."[205] That appreciation also could be measured by audience response. She praised *The Sins of the Mothers* (Vitagraph)—"Its story is gripping and interesting, the photography is excellent throughout [and] Anita Stewart . . . is singularly charming"—but what she noticed at an afternoon screening were the "many women who obviously had come because the name of the piece suggested something which they should see—and how greatly they enjoyed themselves once they were there."[206] Joining her in enjoying the "rollicking, romancing, imaginative" *Peer Gynt* (Oliver-Morosco) were all the "fillum girls" who made it a "standing room only" attraction at the Strand, and, unlike "Wid," she had no qualms that *Ghosts*, another adaptation of an Ibsen play, would be suitable for the picture theater audiences in Syracuse.[207] If *Seven Sisters* (Lasky) allegedly would "refresh the weary worker at the fag end of a midsummer day," she added, "any good movie fan" could enjoy *The Regeneration* (Fox), with its sustained blend of "tense, dramatic moments . . . spectacular scenes . . . and moments of gentle pathos."[208]

The Film Girl's reviews sometimes did get more specific, calling attention to filmic details and admitting her own fascination with certain stars. She deplored the rerelease of older Biograph, Kalem, and Keystone films (especially in poor prints), except for their evidence of how much films had advanced in just a few years.[209] She confessed to disliking camera movement as "fatiguing to the eyes" as deployed "at frequent intervals" in *The Second in Command* (Metro), but, unlike Gunning and Kelly, did not highlight the benefit of close-ups.[210] By contrast, she was more attuned to the differing attractions of scenic effects and film titles. There was the "enormous bed" mounted by means of a stepladder in *Seven Sisters,* the remarkable night scenes of a pleasure party floating on a river raft engulfed by flames in *Craters of Fire* (Universal), and the "Italian cavalry charge down a 300-foot incline" in *Armstrong's Wife* (Lasky).[211] If she thought the title of *The Scarlet Sin* (Universal) deterred "several hundred of the better class of cinema patrons" from attending the Savoy one summer day, she had to acknowledge Fox's advertising genius for titling the Theda Bara vehicles *Sin* and *The Galley Slave.*[212] Geraldine Farrar may have enthralled her and others in *Carmen* (Lasky), but The Film Girl most admired the "wickedly beautiful" Theda Bara in Fox films, from *The Devil's Daughter* in June, for which people had to wait "three quarters of an hour to get inside the lobby and a half hour more to find a seat," to *Destruction* in December, in which "Mephistophelian glee sends strange, distorted smiles" across her face "as victim after victim is subdued" (fig. 56).[213] Yet she personally preferred Bara in roles other than vampires, for instance *The Galley Slave,* which was

BY THE FILM GIRL.

Should one search the country far and wide for authors who issue a positive money-back guarantee unless they put a thrill in every chapter—should one dig down among the musty melodramatic tomes of fiction of an elder day—even then one could scarcely find a more Fox like production than "Destruction," in which Theda Bara may be seen for the last time to-day at the Eckel. There is always an appreciable difference in the size of an audience when Theda Bara is featured. How these audiences of yesterday must have enjoyed a production even more Bara-like than usual.

Truly Theda has never been so Bara as in "Destruction." Mephistophelian glee sends strange, distorted smiles across that cruelly beautiful face of hers as victim after victim is subdued. An extensive acquaintance with vampires of the movie variety convinces me beyond doubt that it is always necessary to look the part. Here Miss Bara makes it impossible for other vampires to achieve the fame which is hers. Her success lies not greatly in her ability, in which there is, apparently, no real depth, but in her beautiful face and body, which she can twist and contort into the most fiendish of postures.

The scenes of "Destruction" are, for the most part, managed with rare good taste, particularly those in a foundry where curious red-black shadows glance over the figues of the players. Extreme luxury characterizes the interior scenes. Did I not say Fox made the picture?

As refreshing as a cool dash of air in an overheated room is "Double Trouble," in which Douglas Fairbanks was seen yesterday and Sunday at the Strand. Here is a story, improbable beyond all improbability, but offering so many delightful opportunities to its talented star that no one thinks of minding. The play is wholly enjoyable and it provides opportunities for endless fun on the part of Mr. Fairbanks, who plays his dual character with equal ease.

In a dazzling manner he is changed from the president of the Sabbath Day society to "Eugene Brassfield," a young whirlwind of energy, who swoops down upon a hustling Western town, wrests a fortune from it, becomes its lion, buys its votes and becomes its mayor, all things which shock beyond measure the president of the Sabbath Day society to which identity he is returned at intervals by an extremely pretty sorceress. The reason for the two identities is that the young man was hit on the head by a thug and that when he awoke, he awoke a new man, totally foreign to his previous quiet existence. In Mr. Fairbanks we have a real comedian, one who is [illegible] scenes. To-day the Strand offers Valeska Suratt, who was somewhat of a surprise in ability as a screen actress when she appeared some months ago in "The Soul of Broadway." Miss Suratt will be seen in "The Immigrant," in which she is supported by a stellar Lasky cast, including Theodore Roberts and Thomas Meighan.

FIGURE 56. "Seen on the Screen by The Film Girl," *Syracuse Herald*, December 28, 1915.

"infinitely superior in showing real ability on the part of the famous player."[214] And she was partial to certain male stars: Sessue Hayakawa in *The Clue* (Lasky), John Barrymore in *The Incorrigible Dukane*, and even William S. Hart in *The Disciple* (Triangle).[215] Moreover, she was quick to see Douglas Fairbanks as a "new star . . . the most refreshing of comedians" in *The Lamb*, a "brilliant" production with so much "dash and ginger" and "the best sub-titles" she'd ever seen.[216]

Within her reviews, The Film Girl offered readers perceptive and/or acerbic comments on the movie industry. In fall 1915 she noticed an appealing trend in having actors play dual, sometimes opposite, roles, for instance William Farnum in *The Wonderful Adventure* (Fox), Blanche Sweet in *The Secret Sin* (Lasky), or Cleo Madison in *A Mother's Atonement* (Universal).[217] Far less appealing was the industry's only partially successful effort to turn well-known stage actors into movie stars, from Ethel Barrymore in *The Final Judgment* (Metro) to Blanche Ring in *The Yankee Girl* (Oliver-Morosco).[218] One of her more intriguing observations was to note how seldom films actually showed men or women working: "Professional men are not often to be found at work unless the stenographer is mixed up in the tale."[219] Perhaps she sought to counteract that lack by taking the unusual step of promoting the work of a number of prominent women in the industry. In celebrating *Scandal* (Universal), and its shocking last scene, she credited Lois Weber, along with Phillips Smalley, as writers, directors, and stars.[220] Grace Cunard she singled out as "the author of 400 scenarios," among them the Universal serials *Lucille Love* and *The Broken Coin*.[221] Another scenario writer, specifically for *The Secretary of Frivolous Affairs* (Mutual Master-Picture), was May Futrelle, the widow of Jacques Futrelle, who had drowned on the *Titanic*.[222] Other women included Alice Guy Blaché, who directed Olga Pavlova in *My Madonna* (Metro), and Cleo Madison directing herself in *A Mother's Atonement*.[223] The Film Girl also sometimes reviewed films according to the gendered segment of the audience they seemed to address. *The Man Trail* (Essanay) was clearly "a man's photo drama" that contradicted the assumption that "producers make pictures which are bound to delight women and girls."[224] Similarly, Ince's *The Coward* was "a man's play," which she contrasted with another Civil War film, *Barbara Frietchie* (Metro), starring Mary Miles Minter in all her "winsome beauty and charm."[225]

The Film Girl was unusually forthright and generous in sharing her own practices as a reviewer and her observations on moviegoing. She could be deferential to readers. Early on, she apologized for taking a day off on Sunday and regretted not viewing as many films as she wished on Saturday;

once she simply turned the column over to certain managers who described their current or forthcoming programs.[226] When a storm kept her from a return screening of D.W. Griffith's *Home Sweet Home,* she was sorry not to offer her thoughts for her "regulars."[227] Advance notices and starting times concerned some readers. "A country woman, the mother of a growing family, and an ardent devotee of the movies" wrote the Happy Hour manager asking that he advertise "a day ahead in the newspapers" so she could plan her trips into the city.[228] She herself lauded the Savoy for advertising the starting times of its programs and warned fans that, to follow a fine film's complicated story at the Crescent, one had to arrive at the beginning.[229] Alerted by her regulars, she began to comment on the "musical programmes" accompanying the films.[230] The week of the annual state fair, the Strand hired a prominent pianist from Boston to conduct its orchestra; later she noted that even the Regent, a neighborhood theater, now had an orchestra.[231] However, she could also pose as an "instructor" or "social reformer" of proper behavior. Perhaps prompted by the conditions one rainy day—"aisles littered with protruding ends of wet umbrellas and paved with small rain water puddles through which run a succession of foot tracks both large and small, and a damp rubbery atmosphere"—she gently prodded inconsiderate moviegoers with a "training" session "on how to enter a motion picture show and sit down, and how to arise and leave without bumping against the heads of the people in the row in front."[232] Later, in response to a letter's complaint, she spoke more specifically as a considerate, well-behaved moviegoer: "The first requisite is to enter the theater quietly; next remove your hat as quickly as possible; never, never read the sub-titles from the screen; never say anything which you may happen to know about the play or the players; never talk at all until you leave the theater; [and] do not keep time to the music with your feet."[233]

THE SMORGASBORD TURNS INTO A BANQUET

By 1916, newspaper readers could find daily reviews of individual films in even more cities, and Kitty Kelly, Louella Parsons, and Mae Tinee had become well-known and respected arbiters of taste far beyond Chicago. Two of those cities, once again, were located in the upper Midwest, and their newspapers already had flourishing pages and/or columns devoted to motion pictures. One was the *Des Moines Evening Tribune,* in which Dorothy Day's "News of the Movies" column was becoming a prominent daily feature. Although Day did not sign the column until January 1916 (see chapter 2), months earlier, as the probable author, she gave hints of a personal take on several films. The description of *A Royal Family* (Metro) is replete with tongue-in-cheek barbs.[234] The story is set in "Arcadia, you know, a little central Europe country bordering Kurtland." Because "he evidently recognizes the usual duty of a movie heir-apparent's uncle," the villain kidnaps the little prince, raises him as a bartender, and later "as a minister of war or something like that" engineers a conflict with Kurtland. After the prince, now grown, is "rescued from his grogshop identity," he kills the uncle, but not before all eight soldiers in the Kurtland army "show they know how to fight." A similar flippancy marks the review of *When a Woman Loves* (Metro), in which "a pretty, poor, but virtuous country maiden" turns into the "p.p. but v.c.m.," and the scenario has her mother fall ill and not have enough money to eat even though "the family owns a chicken farm."[235] According to the actor Wilton Lackaye, "The movement of the eye is often all that is necessary on the screen" for the "bigger emotional work in the climaxes," so Day thanked *La Tosca*'s director for "casting aside the 'heaving bosom' stuff" and showing "the mental anguish in [close-up] facial expressions."[236]

Much like Kitty Kelly and The Film Girl, Day cajoled her readers with a writing style that was chatty and colloquial. Here is how she described the comic action in *Ham Takes a Chance* (Kalem): "As usual, the big fellow knocks the other [Bud] about, throws him down and walks on him, but the little fellow bobs up serenely for the next onslaught."[237] Her endorsement of Douglas Fairbanks in *His Picture in the Papers* ended with this claim: "I would be willing to stake my job against the president's that the public will be more than pleased."[238] Day also shared with The Film Girl a liking for direct address. "I am glad," she wrote one day, "that there is another chance for all you who have missed 'Blue Blood and Red' . . . to see that thoroughly pleasing Fox production again"—"a picture that I like whether any one else did or not."[239] Describing a newsreel item on another occasion, she sounded like Kelly: "Ladies, ladies, you are to be enabled to see just how the president's wedding cake was made and decorated. Think of it. A recipe of the cake and how to decorate it."[240] She also joked with readers: "Do you believe in fairies? You don't? Well, for mercy sakes, you'd better hie yourself to the Garden and see them [in Famous Players's *Little Lady Eileen*]. . . . Yep, right on the screen you can see them, and you know the camera never lies."[241] Similarly, Day could chat about her moviegoing experiences as if conversing with friends. One night "she missed [her] dinner to see the finish of a wonderful picture," *God's Country and the Woman* (Vitagraph), and added "it is too bad if any one, as I did, gets in on the fifth or sixth reel, for . . . to see the last part first is indeed unfortunate."[242] Another time she confessed that tonsillitis kept her from the movies for several days, "so instead of reviews today you are going to have a very few items—for my head is fairly 'busting.'"[243] Responding to one of "many delightful letters from many delightful girls," Day wondered, when going to the movies, "if my neighbor is by chance one of my 'unknown friends,'" and then admitted that, in contrast to her column's picture, she actually looked "nothing at all like Dorothy Day."[244] Among the "sensations seekers" expecting to be shocked by Lois Weber's *Where Are My Children?,* she found "a wonderfully enacted, splendidly and carefully produced" film that asked the public to consider "two great questions": Can a "good, conscientious physician" be justified in giving poor women "the secrets of birth control," and, by contrast, can "women, blessed with health and good homes" be justified in seeking an abortion because it would inconvenience their "pleasure loving"?[245]

Day repeatedly called her readers' attention to the essential elements she looked for in judging a motion picture. In praising *The Golden Chance* she focused particularly on the "uncommonly strong" story—with its "well constructed introduction" and "unexpected" twists—and, sounding like Kelly, pulled out the three "threads" woven into the film's "exquisite texture."[246] Later, in reviewing *God's Country and the Woman* and Nell Shipman's screen debut, she followed her predecessors by ticking off those elements with concision: "a strong, gripping story, with magnificent scenery, excellent acting and capable directing."[247] More specifically, she advised readers "to pay quite a little attention [to] the backgrounds [that] are getting to be a very important part of the entertainment," as in "the pleasing New York views" in *His Picture in the Papers.*[248] At the same time, she exposed specific flaws in films such as *The Unwelcome Mother* (Fox), which was "peculiarly developed and strangely put together, and to cap the climax the end [came] unexpectedly and rather forced," or *The Kiss* (Famous Players), whose star, Owen Moore, was "a wiggly fellow" she disliked, making the picture ordinary in her eyes but not for "the young ladies" who flocked to the screening.[249] Day rarely named a film's director, but she did single out "C. Gardner Sullivan, one of Ince's best scenario writers," for dealing with "the amazing social revolt of the modern woman" in *The Stepping Stone* (Triangle).[250] And she could admire other Ince productions if they starred William S. Hart, whose "wonderful physique and powerful countenance" lifted *The Apostle of Vengeance* and *The Patriot* (both Kay-Bee) above the ordinary—even when, in the latter, there were "no women in the cast."[251] When *The Birth of a Nation* reached the city in May 1916, she described it as "a wonderful moving picture . . . whether historically correct or a finely constructed tissue of falsehood."[252] Despite this reservation, she shared the audience's enthusiasm for the film's second half, focusing on the trauma of Flora's death and how, enhanced by the orchestra, "the house went crazy over the wonderful scenes of the clansmen." Finally, Day used Famous Players's rerelease of *Tess of the Storm Country* to summarize those elements that, if the same company remade the film, defined "the progress of the silent drama": "smoothly running, better subtitles, more close-ups, players far better prepared, and more adequate studio settings" (fig. 57).[253]

A second newspaper in the upper Midwest to introduce a daily column of film reviews was the *Minneapolis Tribune*. First appearing in late August 1916, this column was written by Philip H. Welch, whose knowledge, interests, and style were distinctive. Apparently well educated, Welch often drew on his sophistication either lightly or tartly. He was as familiar with Greek mythology as with Shakespeare, as knowledgeable about art museums as of theatrical history, and attentive to motion picture developments and motion picture audiences. "The analogy between the Shakespearean stage and the modern motion picture business," he argued, "is far more real than one would suppose off hand."[254] The "slow art" of the museum supposedly made him appreciate the fast-paced movies even more: "Give me the picture [painting] which expresses a mood or catches the spirit of the 'eternal quiet'; if the [motion] picture is going to tell a story, let it move rapidly and tell much."[255] Yet Welch clearly followed the trade press and frankly admired the facetious ingenuity of the industry's press agents "who send to newspapers all over the country advance material concerning the photoplays . . . in the process of preparation."[256] He had read Münsterberg's work on the psychology of motion pictures and quoted Victor Freeberg, probably from interviews about his course on "Photoplay Composition" at Columbia University: "For Heavens sake, leave something to the imagination. The photoplay, the audience, and the producer will benefit."[257] Occasionally Welch would address his readers directly, but he was more prone to comment, sometimes ironically, on his moviegoing experience. For a quiet afternoon chat, he recommended no better place than a picture theater running a serial, especially in the balcony, where there were always empty seats.[258] Collecting quotes from moviegoers, he contrasted those so "phlegmatic or self-centered" that they were bored by the movies with the "working girls and boys" who had good reasons to like them.[259] After one night "movie-slumming" among "a slouchy-looking bunch" at a neighborhood theater, he had to admit that the house was neat and cozy and the "melodramatic detective story" was at least worth the five-cent admission.[260]

Given his artistic education, Welch advocated "taking a critical attitude" in judging a film "by analyzing the structure . . ., observing the beauty of the

NEWS OF THE MOVIES

by Dorothy Day

Tess of the Storm Country.

The styles of two years ago invariably make the ladies of today smile. The precise copybooks of our school days look very stiff and queer to us now. So does a masterpiece of more than two years ago look crude and very, very bad to we more modern movie fans. "Tess of the Storm Country" seemed anything but a pleasing photoplay last night at the Garden. I have nothing but praise for Mary Pickford's portrayal of Tessibel. The role is one that Mary can excel in and even with her poor surroundings the work of that little star stands out cameo-like. But such a supporting cast and for the most part such settings. I do not speak of the exteriors for they were good, but the studio sets, the snow scenes, the courtroom and the church scene looked made to order.

DOROTHY DAY

I know that every time Harold Lockwood looks at his characterization of Frederick Graves he wishes he had committed suicide before he did the work. For now, honestly, wasn't he awkward and positively "jakey" looking? Poor Olive Fuller Golden as she appears with Harry Carey in the Bluebirds now surely must crawl under the seat when she sees herself as the misguided daughter of the deacon. And I didn't recognize anyone else. But Mary, bless her little heart, she had a role that exactly suited her and her curls and the elaborate dress she wore will never go out of style.

And such a jumpiness of the pictures. Interested in one scene, with no hint of a change, you are introduced to another situation on another day with perhaps the same character. No interesting close-ups and how I missed them. If nothing else "Tess of the Storm Country" shows the progress of the silent drama. What a different production the Famous-Players-Paramount could bring about, using the same story and the same cast. Smooth running, better subtitles, more close-ups, players far better prepared, and more adequate studio settings—these and many more elements would go to make up a production that could not be surpassed.

Time has been lenient with Mary Pickford and she is if anything prettier than two to three years ago, so her work in a new version would be about the same. But imagine the way Harold, the favorite of so many, could play the part of Frederick now. Olive Fuller Golden could put just the right shading in the role of the daughter. But I suppose they never will make another "Tess of the Storm Country."

÷ ÷ ÷

The Picture Play Magazine for September says that Charles F. Eyeton, the new husband of Kathlyn Williams, is the recently divorced husband of fair Bessie Eyeton. But I don't know how true it is, for I have read things in these monthly photoplay magazines that proved to be somewhat farfetched. Take for instance my "discovery" in the Photoplay that Lockwood and Allison were married.

÷ ÷ ÷

The report has come to me that Gordon Johnson, the daughter of the late Arthur Johnson, favorite screen star, is to join the movies soon. Under what banner she has not decided. Miss Johnson, if she has the talent of her father, should make an enviable screen success. She says that her father encouraged her to go to the screen instead of the legitimate.

÷ ÷ ÷

TODAY AND FRIDAY AT THE MOVIES.

CASINO—Dorothy Gish in "The Little School Ma'am" and a Keystone comedy.

PALACE—Edna May in "Salvation Joan."

GARDEN—Mary Pickford in "Tess of the Storm Country." Tomorrow—Hazel Dawn and Owen Moore in "Under Cover."

ROYAL—Blanche Sweet and Dorothy Gish in "The House of Discord," "The Heroes," and the Selig Tribune. Tomorrow—"Otto the Gardner," "The Blue or the Grey," and Ham and Budd in "The Heart Menders."

UNIQUE—Crane Wilbur in "The Haunting Symphony," and "A Squaw's Loyalty." Tomorrow—"The Masque Ball," "A Circumstantial Hero," "The Live Wire," and "Seeing America First."

FAMILY—Hobart Henley in "My Lady's Millions," and "Where Is My Husband?" and a L-KO. Tomorrow—Hobart Henley in "Temptation and the Man."

UNIVERSITY—Blanche Sweet in "The Ragamuffin." Tomorrow—Florence Reed in "The Woman's Law."

ELITE—A masterpicture and a Vogue. Tomorrow—William H. Tooker in "The Avalanche," and a Keystone.

WHAT DO YOU WANT TO KNOW ABOUT MOVIES?

Miss Day takes great pleasure in answering all questions relating to the movies. If you want to know about a star, film making or anything of that sort, write Miss Day, care of The Evening Tribune.

BY DOROTHY DAY.

Age 12—I like Grace Cunard for truly she is not an imitation. She is simply Grace Cunard. She is still with the Universal just finishing "Peg O' the Ring." And now she is going to begin work on another serial, "The Adventures of My Lady Raffles." If you have ever seen any of the mystery pictures that she and her co-star, Ford, have done you will have some idea of the treat to come. Grace is not married. Thank you for the pleasant things you have to say about my movie news.

Esther R.—Address Billie Burke, care of George Kliene, 807 East 175th street, New York City. Harold Lockwood and May Allison, care of the Yorke-Metro studio, Hallywood, Cal.; Helen Holmes, care of the Signal-Mutual studio at Santa Barbara, Cal. Victor Moore, and Blanche Sweet at the Lasky studio, 5284 Selma avenue, Los Angeles. Ann Pennington, Zeigfield Follies, New York City. Francis Bushman and Beverly Bayne at the Quality studios, 8 West Sixty-first street, New York City. Warren Kerrigan at Universal City, Cal. Jack Richardson and William Russell at the American studios at Santa Barbara, Cal. William H. Thompson, Charles Ray at Inceville, Cal. Crane Wilbur at the Guamont, Jacksonville, Fla. William Farnum and Vivian Martin at Morosco studio, 201 North Occidental boulevard in Los Angeles. Chester Conklin at the Keystone studios at 1702 Allesandro street, Los Angeles.

Girlie—Robert Harron was born in New York City April 12, 1894. He is not married, is playing under his own name, has black hair and brown eyes and did used to be the office boy at the old Biograph studios. In some plays, he is splendid. Yes, Ralph Ince, Tom and John, are brothers. Tom is with the Triangle, Ralph, the Vitagraph and John the World-Equitable.

Amusements.

EMPRESS—Continuous advanced vaudeville. Four shows daily. Complete change of program Sundays and Thursdays. Every afternoon at 1:30 and 3:15; all seats 10c. Every night at 7:30 and 9:15; balcony 10c, entire main floor 20c. Bill now playing headed by Col. Jack George, humorous blackface stump speaker.

RIVERVIEW—Bathing beach, boating, Henry and has band, bowling, cafe and other features. Extra added feature this week (nightly) Zemater and Smith, horizontal bar comiques.

SOCIETY.

CONTINUED FROM PAGE FIVE.

Hohl will compliment her at an afternoon kensington at her home, 609 Ovid avenue.

Mr. and Mrs. M. P. Wickersham will be hosts to the members of the bridal party at a dinner party Wednesday evening at their home in Urbandale. Covers will be laid for twelve.

WITH THE TRAVELERS.

Miss Cecil Bradshaw of St. Louis, Mo., will arrive in the city Saturday for a visit with Miss Marion Moore, daughter of Mr. and Mrs. T. H. Moore. Miss Bradshaw and Miss Moore were classmates last year at Vassar.

points in Colorado and California, she will return to her home in Dallas.

Miss Louise Stevenson of Lowell, Mass., and a member of the faculty of the Mount Holyoke college in South Hadley, Mass., is visiting friends in and near Des Moines for two weeks.

Mrs. M. Gregg, juvenile court officer, is spending her vacation at Colorado Springs.

Miss Myrtle Hardenbergh, deputy in the office of the county superintendent of schools, Tuesday attended at Harlan the wedding of Miss Helen Pierce and Mr. Donald Streat.

Mrs. Arthur Meredith is seriously ill at Methodist hospital.

M. C. Huttenlocker, trustee of the Hubbell estate, will leave Staurday for Spirit Lake to spend two days vacationing.

FIGURE 57. "News of the Movies by Dorothy Day," *Des Moines Tribune,* August 3, 1916.

photography, including the composition and 'color' values, studying the truthfulness of the treatment, etc."[261] He also could indulge in comparing the filmmaker's task to that of someone choosing items from the "bewildering display of dishes" in a "cafeteria": "The artist is the person who selects a well-rounded, palatable meal at a reasonable price."[262] Specifically, he focused on menu items or "details" that a spectator with the "power of observation" should notice in good as well as bad motion pictures. One was the crafting of highlights drawn from painting and sculpture, as in "the children coming through the twilight in the prologue to 'The House with the Golden Shutters' or in Charlotte Burton's 'animated bronze' figure in 'Soul Mates' [American Film]."[263] Another was double exposures, "all the rage now," which he found ineffective, partly because of film's own doubleness: "The picture itself is a sort of a ghost of a real person."[264] A third was the unexpectedly apt intertitle, as in the "final line" of *The Thoroughbred* (Mutual Master-Picture), which Keenen coos to his winning horse after a climactic race: "Miss Minta, you're a vampire."[265] A fourth was the "cut-back"—or the flashback "identifying the past actions of a character or the past development of an idea with the present moment"—which reminded him of the leitmotif in the music of Richard Wagner.[266] A fifth, following "Wid" Gunning and Kitty Kelly, was "the artistry of facial expression" in close-ups, as in the "five big emotional scenes" in Fox's *The Sins of Her Parents,* where Gladys Brockwell "is able to sharply distinguish" her double role as mother and daughter.[267] Finally, Welch was fascinated with how a film could symbolize ideas through "concrete objects," also in close shots, and his prime example was *Shoes*: "A dish of cabbage, a wrist-watch, a trashy paper-covered novel, a heavy carpet, a cat in an ashbarrel, a can of condensed milk, the cover of a card board box and a pair of old shoes, these things were the symbols of the desolate tragedy which overtook a poverty-stricken 18-year-old girl" (fig. 58).[268] And he praised "the maker" without naming Lois Weber.

Welch's most sustained critical effort came in evaluating the Metro and Fox productions of Shakespeare's *Romeo and Juliet,* which screened almost simultaneously in the city. He expressed misgivings about "filming Shakespeare" and believed that the industry required "the development of a technic which does not yet exist,"[269] but he had to admit that the two films did offer much more than the "filmization of ... Lamb's Tales from Shakespeare." Running eight reels, the Metro version allowed the makers "to have every detail correct," which Welch claimed "actually adds to and illumines Shakespeare's play."[270] Most of the review, however, he used to point out general problems in adapting such plays: the settings and costumes, even if beautiful, were anachronistic, as were the intertitles stuffed

Motion Pictures

By Philip H. Welch

Poverty is a sad thing. True, you say, but what of it?

"I am poverty stricken, lend me $25." How much more effective that is. It is concrete, it gets closer to real life; your particular case and the exact amount you need.

If one would make an appeal in art or financial circles one must be concrete. The human brain is accustomed to deal with facts. When it tries to handle ideas it becomes surely intellectual unless those ideas are symbolized by some concrete objects. The greatest definition of poetry ever penned contains the line, "and give to airy nothing a local habitation and a name."

* * *

A motion picture was shown here yesterday, and also two months ago, which was concrete from start to finish. A dish of cabbage, a wrist-watch, a trashy paper-covered novel, a heavy carpet, a cat in an ashbarrel, a can of condensed milk, the cover of a card board box and a pair of old shoes, these things were the symbols of the desolate tragedy which overtook a poverty-stricken 18-year-old girl.

It was the story of a girl who struggled in vain against poverty and finally sold herself for a pair of shoes.

The cat in the ashbarrel on the landing outside her flat was a symbol of the sort of flat it was; the cabbage and the makeshift milk, manufactured from condensed milk, was a symbol of the cheapness of the food the family ate; the wrist watch was the symbol of the morality of another girl who had sold herself, not for a necessity but for a trinket; the cover of the cardboard box was a symbol of the universal experience of people up against it who have tried to protect the bottoms of their feet against the wet cold pavements of this world, and the trashy novel was the symbol of her father's lack of moral fiber, which could allow him to try to forget his surroundings in the unreal world of the novel rather than better them by seeking a job.

* * *

I have not by any means exhausted the concrete symbolism of this remarkable film, "Shoes." The title itself is a symbol which could scarcely be surpassed. It was taken from Jane Addams book, "A New Conscience and An Ancient Evil." Mary MacLaren plays the leading role with intelligent restraint and the supporting company does excellent work, but the best work was done by the maker of the story. Unfortunately, like so many good pictures, it goes to pieces and becomes mawkish and sentimental at the end, but that's a mere detail.

Classes in drama should study "Shoes." It might have been written by Ibsen.

RIVERMEN TO MEET IN WINONA IN 1917

Wilkinson Is Re-elected President—to Serve Fifteenth Term.

La Crosse, Wis., Oct. 27.—Thomas Wilkinson, La Crosse, was re-elected to serve his fifteenth term as president of the Upper Mississippi River Improvement association, and Winona selected as the 1917 meeting place at the convention of the association here yesterday. J. B. Ekert, Guttenburg, Iowa, was chosen secretary to succeed L. B. Boswell.

The following vice presidents were elected:—B. J. Mosier, Stillwater, Minn.; William Torrance, La Crosse, Wis.; C. F. Berry, Quincy, Ill.; P. M. Hanson, St. Louis, Mo., and John Paul, Burlington, Iowa.

FIGURE 58. "Motion Pictures by Philip H. Welch," *Minneapolis Tribune,* October 27, 1916.

with the playwright's poetic language. The latter made the balcony scene "decidedly too talky." If Beverly Bayne's performance as Juliet was excellent overall, and especially fine in scenes with the nurse,[271] Francis X. Bushman's as Romeo was merely "acceptable." The Fox version, by contrast, ran five reels and "move[d] rapidly and surely as a good story should."[272] It also cleverly handled several moments—when Juliet "deceives her father, saying she will marry Paris" and "the climax scene in the tomb"—and added details such as "two sassy little children" in a "thumb-biting episode." Despite his reservations about Theda Bara as Juliet, he confessed that "she carries the part through," although not as well as Bayne. Harry Hilliard, however, admirably "catches the boyishness" of Romeo and "far surpasses" the "stilted, stagey" Bushman.[273] In two later columns, then, it is surprising to find Welch choosing the Metro film as "decidedly the better of the two." The reasons seem elusive, unless he objected to the Fox film's changed ending "in the interest of melodrama" and thought a "fuller text" made the Metro film "a truly educational picture for child or adult," provoking "one to renew one's acquaintance with the text." In the end, Shakespeare trumped the movies.

And what were the young women in Chicago and Syracuse serving up daily for their readers? The Film Girl, as if conversing with friends, continued to comment on her moviegoing experiences. Reviewing *Barbara Frietchie*, she noted the Eckel's clever stunt of having its ushers "wear the most bewitching of red, white, and blue [Union] soldier hats and sashes. . . . in keeping with the patriotic spirit" of that Civil War film.[274] Once when another woman seated behind her repeatedly kept asking aloud why Vivian Reed's face was so familiar, she answered—but only in print, so as not to disturb others in the theater—that formerly Reed had posed for many poster calendars.[275] Reviewing *Temptation* (Lasky), which starred Geraldine Farrar, she warned readers that the night before, "a line of people eager to see it waited in the cold on the curb [and] many must have stood for a long time."[276] When a young "constant reader" confessed that J. Warren Kerrigan, at her bold request, agreed to display a Syracuse pennant in an upcoming film, The Film Girl risked sharing her secret with other Kerrigan fans.[277] She herself made a different confession: one day the "atrocious" ventilation and "fetid atmosphere" of an unnamed theater kept her from reviewing a particular film, and she knew readers "wouldn't have your film girl endanger her health and reason."[278] But she retained her fondness for the "very ordinary sort" of theater and devoted two whole columns to her best example, the Novelty, one prompted by a little girl who told her "in awe-struck tones that nothing is too remarkable to happen there" and the other by "the pleasure which the regular patrons of this theater take in the pictures in which old favorites appear," especially in the "short reel films" supplied by General Film and Universal.[279] Although that little girl confirmed her belief, in early 1916, that "the movies are our modern Arabian Nights," even she had to admit that, by year's end, "the short length programme . . . had so degenerated as to be a positive bore in most instances, when contrasted with the fresh and elaborate features."[280]

Perhaps in response to her readers' interests, The Film Girl increasingly paid more attention to new as well as "old favorites," especially in feature films. If Theda Bara always attracted large audiences, she appealed to The Film Girl less for her acting ability than for "her beautiful face and body, which she can twist and contort into the most fiendish of postures."[281] Others she admired more for their acting included Farrar in *Temptation*, the "tender and passionate" Clara Kimball Young and Paul Capellani in *Camille* (Selznick), and the "never disappointing" Douglas Fairbanks, "a kind hearted and lovable desperado" in *The Good Bad Man* (Triangle).[282] By contrast, she found the lack of "depth" in acting ability a detriment to her enjoyment of Hazel Dawn and Mary Miles Minter in *The Saleslady* (Famous Players) and *Lovely Mary* (Metro), respectively, despite their lovely youth, winsomeness, and appeal in wearing "clothes wonderously well."[283] Older stars from the legitimate stage came in for even harsher criticism; for instance, Valli Valli was not pretty enough to play a "leading lady" in *The Turmoil* (Metro) and exemplified "the English type of actress much addicted to trailing scarfs and floppy hats."[284] This aversion to actresses serving as models for expensive clothes led her to share a gossipy story about Edna Mayo caught between obeying a dress designer or her film director: instead of showing up one day for work on J. Charles Hayden's production at Essanay's Chicago studio, Mayo took the train to New York, at Lady Duff Gordon's request, to try on several new gowns she was having made for the film.[285]

Although The Film Girl's reviewing remained impressionistic, she increasingly stressed the importance of story. One sign was her reprinting of Carl Laemmle's alleged letter to "Old Bill" Shakespeare.[286] Sketching a history of filmmaking in several paragraphs, Laemmle claimed the industry now had it right: "When you said 'The play's the thing,' you said a large mouthful, Bill." Barnum-like, he added: "We don't care a tinker's dam who wrote it. We don't carry a bouquet in hades whether we have a leading stage actor or not. If it's a good play, nothing can put a kibosh on it." The Film Girl took those words as gospel in criticizing Metro's otherwise excellent *What Will People Say?* The liberties it took with Rupert Hughes's novel confirmed the dictum "A poor story is to a picture production just what a weak foundation is to a large building."[287] This too was one of the criticisms she leveled at Fine Arts's *The Lily and The Rose,* and much later at Thomas Dixon's *The Fall of a Nation,* "a fanciful, wholly improbable tale" unworthy "of serious consideration."[288] By contrast, a strong foundation was what she admired about Lasky's *The Golden Chance:* "The story to begin with has a real punch, and though nothing remarkable as to inscrutable plot, lends itself admirably to the screen."[289] There were other things The Film Girl looked for in a really good film. In Vitagraph's *The Battle Cry of Peace,* it was the "tremendous . . . theme," "a vigorous attempt to make Americans realize the unpreparedness of America" during the Great War.[290] After a second-run screening of *A Soul Enslaved* (Universal) at an "ordinary" theater—with Cleo Madison directing and playing the leading role—she wrote "frankly that of all the melodramas which I've seen on the screen in some weeks this was done most cleverly and was the most interesting."[291] Finally, in the repeat screening of *Madame Butterfly* (Famous Players) at the same theater, it was Mary Pickford's performance that led her to rank it, along with *Tess of the Storm Country* and *Dawn of a Tomorrow,* as one of the star's "best pictures."[292]

In Chicago, Louella Parsons kept up a demanding pace, editing the *Chicago Herald*'s Sunday motion picture page and writing a daily "Seen on the Screen" column. In parallel with the Sunday page's prominent interviews and stories, Parsons's column now paid increasing attention to stars. Theda Bara remained one of her favorites, whose acting skills she promoted in "non-vampire" roles from Fox's *The Galley Slave* to *Under Two Flags.*[293] Beverly Bayne gained similar praise for "the strong individual work" in her Metro films, where she was unaffected "by any of the monopolizing mannerisms" of her partner, Francis X. Bushman, and had "a little coterie of admirers all her own."[294] She admired William S. Hart (unlike Bushman), whose "rugged, open countenance," in Ince's *Between Men* "fits nicely in with the popular idea of the western hero."[295] For other stars, Parsons invoked the "dependable" concept of "personality," even if too often "overworked," especially for Geraldine Farrar, who "radiates life and beauty" in Lasky's *Maria Rosa,* and the "effervescent Douglas Fairbanks," who makes the scenario so much more funny in his suicide comedy *Flirting with Fate.*[296] She even had to admit that Chaplin was outgrowing the vulgar comedies she so disliked, particularly in *The Vagabond* (Mutual), "with its delicate touches of pathos."[297] At the same time, Parsons took several famous stage actors to task for their less than stellar acting in motion pictures—from Billie Burke in *Peggy* (Triangle) to Constance Collier in *The Code of Marcia Gray* (Morosco)—or the disdain they had for the movies—most notably Blanche Ring.[298] And she shared with readers the fears and misgivings of other actors: Anna Held, who thought her eyes seemed "so old and tired" in close-ups, and Elsie Janis, who looked at "all those fluffy darlings" in the movies and said to herself, "better stay on the stage."[299] In several columns prior to the Motion Picture Exhibitors League's national convention in Chicago in July 1916, Parsons enticed fans with the dozens of stars who would be attending.[300] As part of the *Herald*'s coverage of the convention (much of it open to the public),[301] she wrote separate stories devoted to popular female stars: Alice Brady, Clara Kimball Young, Edith Storey, Lillian Walker, and Pearl White.[302] After describing the "great crowd of girls" who came to see Brady, she noted how "very wisely reserved" the star was in answering their many questions.[303]

In line with her column "How to Write Photoplays," Parsons still attributed the success of a motion picture largely to its scenario. *The Misleading Lady* (Essanay) offered an example of the well-constructed scenario: It "runs smoothly with no apparent forcing of situations [and] has a solid little punch with a running vein of humor that is natural enough to be clever."[304] In reviewing *What Happened at 22* (World Film), she made the concept of construction literal, stressing "the carpentry of the scenario": "I say carpentry, for I feel the tucking in of odd corners, and the sequence in plot is due to the mathematical working out of the photoplay."[305] Likewise, she praised Gaumont's two-reel *Paying the Price* because it had "a foundation to work on . . . a plot with human interest and that precious thing in pictures, a 'punch.'"[306] Parsons also consistently remarked on the quality of adaptations, whether from novels, as in *D'Artgnan* (Triangle), or from stage plays, as in *David Garrick* (Pallas).[307] Moreover, she lauded certain scriptwriters such as Marguerite Bertsche ("Vitagraph's scenario editor"), Caroline Lockwood, Anita Loos, and C. Gardner Sullivan, who "has done much to bring the cinema to the present ability to tell a pictorial story as thoroughly and nicely as if it were being unfolded in fiction."[308] A noteworthy example of the latter's work was "the Ince production" *Honor Thy Name*: "The story is somewhat new as to construction and angle . . . [and] runs smoothly to the end," with "all complexities soldered . . . artfully."[309] Special accolades also went to Lois Weber, "the director and photoplaywright," who, in *The Dumb Girl of Portici*, "took the original opera and by consistent treatment and some elaboration put it into a motion picture scenario" that starred "the graceful figure" of Anna Pavlova (fig. 59).[310] Similarly, if "the name DeMille" guaranteed "an artistic film triumph," *The Ragamuffin* was doubly blessed, with Cecil B. as director and William C. as scriptwriter.[311]

Parsons tended to fault films for one problem or another in story construction. Quite often this had to do with either pacing the action or leaving

Seen on the Screen

"THE DUMB GIRL OF PORTICI."

Fenella .... Anna Pavlowa
Mansanlello, brother of Fenella. .... Rupert Julian
Duke d'Arcos, the spanish viceroy .... Wadsworth Harris
Alphonse, elder son of the duke. .... Douglas Gerrard
Conde, younger son of the duke. .... John Holt
Isabella, daughter of the duke.. .... Betty Schade
Elvira, Spanish princess, betrothed to Alphonse. Edna Maison
Perrone, captain of the guards.. .... Hart Hoxie
Pietro, friend of Alphonse...... .... William Wolbert
Rilla, the widowed sister of Pietro .... Laura Oakley
Father Francisco.... N. de Brouillet

By LOUELLA O. PARSONS.

"THE Dumb Girl of Portici," much heralded and widely discussed, took possession of the Colonial Theater last evening, with Mme. Pavlowa, the star, and Carl Laemmle, president of the Universal Company, present at the initial performance. Ever since Lois Weber and Phillips Smalley, with a selected company, arrived in Chicago last summer to produce this biggest of any Universal feature, interest has centered around "The Dumb Girl of Portici."

Sans Souci Park, with its quaint style of architecture, was used for many of the scenes, and while Pavlowa danced before the camera and created the role of Fenella, all Chicago looked on expectantly awaiting to see how all these preparations would look on the screen. The day has arrived for Chicago to see, and judging from last evening's entertainment, Pavlowa in the celluloid will be a rival of Pavlowa in the flesh.

+ + +

"The Dumb Girl of Portici" came into existence many years ago. It is from the opera of Francois Auber and probably the best known of his works. In those days opera was not the art it is today, but the grim tale of the revolution of Italy in the seventeenth century has lived in the minds of some few music lovers. Auber's opera has been resurrected not alone for its music, but for the great mass who compose the motion picture public.

It was Lois Weber, the director and photoplaywright, who first saw in "The Dumb Girl of Portici" the possibilities for screen adaptation. She took the original opera and by consistent treatment and some elaboration put it into a motion picture scenario. Miss Weber had the assistance of her husband, Phillips Smalley, in directing this big photo-dramatic spectacle, but most of the scenic effects, costuming and colorful arrangement were personally planned by her alone.

+ + +

A tremendous thing is this operatic picture. There are those who may feel the picture is overlong and that the scenes of strife and revolt are too many, but the grace of Mme. Pavlowa and the pictorial splendor of the settings mark a new period in film art.

The cruel tyranny of the nobility, the licentious viceroy who puts an unjust tax upon the simple fisher folk, the leadership of Masaniello and the appealing helplessness of Fenella, his dumb sister, are all important parts of this unhappy tale.

Conde and Alphonse, sons of the viceroy, go to the fishing village dressed as peasants to learn the people's real feelings. Fenella falls in love with Alphonse and he cruelly deserts her. The girl is cast into prison by the viceroy, who fears trouble, and is subjected to unspeakable torture. While all this is transpiring Alphonse is preparing for his marriage to Elvira, a Spanish princess. Spain is in power, and is driving the kingdom of Naples to desperation.

+ + +

The final revolt of the peasants, the destroying of the castle under the leadership of Masaniello, the freeing of Fenella, who warns her sweetheart of the rioters; the sacrifice of Fenella life, the insanity of Masaniello, are all the creation of a mind who wrote of the crude passions and seemingly impossible situations of the seventeenth century. One evil thing after another follows in rapid succession until death to Masaniello and Fenella is a happy solution. More of a grand photo-spectacle is "The Dumb Girl of Portici" than a strong story, but it is a picture that every one will want to see. It will be one of the talked-of pictures of the year, and as one of the first big film features will take its place in motion picture history.

Mme. Pavlowa as Fenella is the poetry of motion. She is one of the most graceful figures ever seen on the screen. We are sorry not to see more of her dancing. The Ballet Russe also does some pleasing work, but it was Pavlowa as an exponent of dancing who has registered a supreme effort in this picture.

Edna Maison as Elvira, Rupert Julian as Masaniello, Wadsworth Harris as the viceroy and Douglas Gerrard as Alphonse are also important members of the cast.

Bits of Auber's opera, with a score especially adapted to the picture, are given with pleasing effect. The music is written to accompany Pavlowa's graceful movements.

FIGURE 59. "Seen on the Screen by Louella O. Parsons," *Chicago Herald*, January 31, 1916.

out transitions. So "padded" was *Bullets and Brown Eyes* (Triangle) with "scenes that should move with acceleration and situations that require only one appearance come back again and again" that an audience she observed "acted bored to death."[312] Other films were more egregious: Mutual's *The White Bowtie* was the perfect example of a one-reel picture padded out to five reels.[313] Although she admired his productions, she had to admit that Thomas Ince liked "to take his own time in telling a story" and tended to "drag out his features," even in an otherwise fine film like *The Deserter.*[314] She was far less charitable with Chaplin, who "violate[d] two rigid laws of photoplay-taking" in *One A.M.* (Mutual): "Scenes run interminably long, and Chaplin is the only character to sustain the action."[315] A different problem compromised films such as *Diplomacy* (Famous Players), which sometimes left "the reviewer in total darkness as to subsequent events," *The Code of Marcia Gray,* which also exhibited "frequent spots of unexplained action," and *The Stronger Love* (Oliver-Morosco), which failed to get the multiple "threads of plot all tied up at the end."[316] If American films—*Susie Snowflake, The Crucial Test,* and *The Beast*—too often staged overly familiar, conventional, even improbable stories,[317] *The Shadow of the Past,* an Italian import starring Lina Cavalieri, could not escape the stereotype of the "nearly chronic sordid" foreign film, which—in an atypical diatribe—"would have been a rip-snorting name for a two-reel 'mellerdrammer' of the 'go-and-never-return' variety back in 1908."[318] As for *The Weakness of Man* (World Film), badly adapted from a Tolstoy play and badly chosen to screen at the Studebaker on Independence Day, she excoriated it as "sentimental drivel," "maudlin trash," and "one of those sweetly sickening dramas in which kisses and embraces win the day."[319]

And who did Parsons presume to be her readers? Most seemed to be moviegoers simply wishing to be entertained without being offended, which led to a deeply conflicted review of *The Little Girl Next Door,* a white slave film approved by the Illinois State Vice Commission.[320] In the Christmas shopping rush, she urged moviegoers to take "a few hours rest in some quiet corner of a motion picture theater" and suggested *The Reform Candidate* (Pallas) as just the "comfortable, wholesome sort of picture with enough snap and vim to keep it from being wearisome."[321] She frequently also advised them about movies that might appeal to children. Famous Players's *Molly Make-Believe,* a "thistle-down adventure" starring Marguerite Clark, was one: "Delightful in its simplicity, amusing in its improbability, it is a refreshing plunge into the land of pretty romance and something the kiddies can enjoy."[322] Such advice was especially pertinent in the summer, and she offered two titles days before the national convention in the city. One was *Caprice of the Mountains,* which she saw in Fox's projection room and thought "the kiddies will love," lamenting that "there are so few motion pictures the little people can understand."[323] Another was *The Little School Ma'am* (Fine Arts), "a simple, wholesome pictorial offering, entirely suitable for the children." Dorothy Gish starred, but Parsons was most taken with the studio children who played "the pupils in the little rural school": "They bubble with youthful spirits and weep with the natural tears of childhood."[324] Even her description of Metro's *The River of Romance,* shortly after the convention, made it a "well balanced . . . composite ideal" for the whole family: "exquisitely charming in scenery and setting, winsome in its naïve yet virile romance, heat-obliterating in its novelty."[325] She blithely predicted that long after "Chaplin comedies are filed in a neglected corner of our minds," *The River of Romance* would be her answer to "What was the most wholly pleasing picture I have ever seen." In sharp contrast, Parsons again was conflicted by *Where Are My Children?* Although "a wonderfully effective picture . . . from a photographic standpoint," Lois Weber's film so offended her morally that she wondered if it should "be seen by a mixed audience" and then confessed that, had she a daughter, she would hesitate to let her "see vital questions of life on a moving picture screen."[326]

When she was not viewing movies in studio projection rooms,[327] Parsons tended to patronize theaters in the Loop, but she did note some of the fine "outlying theaters": the West Side Hamlin (twelve hundred seats) with its special room for "kiddies," the South Side Harper (fourteen hundred seats) with its "screen set in an Italian garden," and the West Side Crawford (twelve hundred seats) with its new ventilating system.[328] Overall, however, she came close to promoting the Studebaker, the Strand, and the Castle, this last "a small picture house . . . artistic in arrangement."[329] The Strand offered what she considered a program of "just the right length," in contrast to the Ziegfeld, with its "double-feature program" that she thought "a bit too long for the average spectator."[330] The Studebaker's new interior prompted her to write a rare description of its stage setting: "A moon throws its rays upon rippling waters, roses placed here and there on a trellis and in huge bouquets stand between the graceful columns which form a sentinel for the screen. Best of all and most welcome is the orchestra music that really synchronizes with the films."[331] In December, she had praised the Studebaker's shorter programs, now supplied by Triangle, and claimed that they suited "most people [who] like to wander in and out of a moving picture theater."[332] But seven months later, she confessed that coming into the middle of a film convinced her that continuous shows had to change, for "many a good picture goes wrong through being seen in sections."[333] The practice of re-editing a film, which she also praised, raises the legal question of how common that was: "Every piece of unnecessary film, all the poor bits of photography, undesirable close ups and superfluous subtitles are cut out of the print exhibited on the Strand screen."[334] At times she shared the experience of moviegoers such as those "swept with emotion" one afternoon at the Studebaker (despite the "giggling theater party" that nearly ruined the show), those "aroused [to] the wildest enthusiasm" by *How Britain Prepared* at the Colonial, and the crowds that thronged the Castle to see Pickford rereleases such as *In the Bishop's Carriage* and *Hearts Adrift*.[335] And all those moviegoers, beginning in mid-June 1916, found Parsons's column featured as part of the *Herald*'s "News of the Movie Theaters" page, with its directory of scores of Chicago-area movie theaters.[336]

At the *Tribune*, where "Flickerings from Film Land" also was coupled with that paper's "Motion Picture Directory" in early July,[337] Kitty Kelly offered her readers a movie diet somewhat different from and, arguably, even richer than that served up by Parsons. In contrast to Parsons or The Film Girl, that diet did not include large helpings of stories about the stars. Instead, Kelly restricted her remarks usually to their performances within films. There were a few exceptions, when she interviewed a star passing through the city or making a publicity tour. One was Mae Marsh, who, supposed to speak at the Colonial during an intermission for *The Birth of a Nation* in October 1915, feared she might blurt out "How do you do? I'm here. Good-by!"[338] An appended "bulletin" then reported that a "gold laced ticket collector" refused to let her enter the theater: "The city won't let no kids see this here fillum. Get me?" Months later, others included Mary Miles Minter, making appearances at the Ziegfeld and other Alfred Hamburger houses, and Charlie Chaplin traveling west with his brother Syd and defensively justifying his rising salary.[339] More months went by before Kelly caught up with Douglas Fairbanks at the Blackstone Hotel, where he talked expansively about the industry, its amazingly high salaries, and its equally amazing lack of imagination.[340] "If I had a studio and Anita Loos, who writes the funny captions, and John Emerson to direct me," he added, "That's all I ask for." During the national convention so prominently covered in the *Herald*, Kelly offered only one interview, and that was with J.A. Berst, Pathé's vice president and general manager, rather than the two Gold Rooster stars accompanying him, Pearl White and Tom Moore.[341]

Like Parsons, Kelly reported on the physical spaces and show practices of the downtown picture theaters. For *The Battle Cry of Peace*'s premiere at the Olympic, she gave a lengthy report on the "flag decked and cannon mounted" theater front and the speeches by the G.A.R.'s Capt. Jack Crawford and Commander J. Stuart Blackton.[342] After the Studebaker had failed to draw audiences over a scant five months for its expensive Triangle programs,[343] she too described the theater's new stage frame, yet thought it merely a "pleasant though not riotously artistic development."[344] A week earlier, she had criticized the Colonial—where Triangle films now began showing at more normal prices—for ruining its "Italian garden stage setting" with a "festive light machine [that] reveals it as an ordinary landscape backdrop" with pasteboard shrubbery, artificial balusters, and "trellis twined over with vivid artificial flowers."[345] Although she welcomed the Colonial's orchestra music, arranged by Rothapfel, she was startled one day to find a "rapid fire Keystone saddened by organ music evidently intended for funeral or church use."[346] In response to a letter writer asking theater managers to advertise their programs' starting times throughout the day and evening, Kelly offered an example from *Moving Picture World* of an exhibitor's schedule card distributed to audiences; soon she found the Colonial worth praising for adopting the practice.[347] The Colonial's publicity man she also singled out for using the telephone, rather than relying on typewritten copy, to transmit daily program information to the *Tribune*.[348] If she too accepted the Strand's practice of cutting a film to fit its "customary program length" (Thanhouser's *Silas Marner* was reduced by six hundred feet), she did get the manager to reveal that Geraldine Farrar's *Carmen* netted "19,907 paid admissions" for the first few days of its run.[349] At the Ziegfeld, by contrast, she worried that poor projection—specifically running films off too rapidly—was compromising its reputation.[350] Unlike Parsons, Kelly did not confine herself to the downtown theaters. She promoted the newly constructed Oakland Square (Oakwood and Drexel boulevards), the renovated Crawford (Garfield Park), and the Covent Garden auditorium (upper North Clark), among others.[351] And she was not afraid to report on a local labor dispute, the "war between rival motion picture operators' unions" that led in March 1916 to early-morning bombings that wrecked the fronts of two small neighborhood theaters.[352]

Kelly's presumed readers seem rather unlike Parsons's. Apparently in sympathy with the suffragette movement, she heralded a special morning performance of *The Battle Cry of Peace* honoring two suffragists motoring across the country with a huge petition for President Wilson.[353] Like Dorothy Day and The Film Girl, she chatted with readers, apologized for leaving Cohen's Grand Theater one night while Ince's *Civilization* "was still unreeling," and encouraged youngsters to see Kay Bee's *Honor Thy Name* and learn the good that comes from a father's trust in his son.[354] When the city banned *Hypocrites*, she urged readers to take the L train to the western suburbs, where it was showing at the Oak Park Theater.[355] Unlike Parsons, Kelly had no qualms about anyone viewing *Where Are My Children?,* "a serious film . . . characterized equally by its strong purpose and its good dramatic and pictorial construction" (fig. 60).[356] Lois Weber convinced her "how much may be accomplished by mere suggestion, how little need there is for [imprudent] suggestiveness in the relating of a powerful story on a delicate subject." The ending especially impressed her "with the lonely couple sitting before the fire while a fade-in brings visionary children playing about them." Time passes, the couple ages, and the imaginary children grow into adulthood. Weeks earlier, however, she did print a letter from a father (with a fifteen-year-old daughter) who hoped that producers would make more films like Mary Pickford's *Hulda from Holland* for "family audiences [at] neighborhood houses."[357] In a contrasting letter, an out-of-town woman sniffed like a startled social reformer that, in the theaters she attended (full of "young people and born, many of them, in foreign lands"), audiences "show[ed] so little patriotic enthusiasm" that she asked managers to have them "at least salute the flag and rise for the 'Star Spangled Banner.'"[358] Yet often Kelly simply listened to audiences, reprised their responses, and saluted their intelligence. During a screening of the otherwise "brisk, coherent mystery yarn" *What Happened at 22,* she found herself at one with an audience that "laugh[ed] at those things producers had not meant them to."[359] As for *The House of Lies* (Oliver-Morosco), she let women seated behind her speak in her stead: "absurd," "ridiculous," "that's the pifflingest picture I've ever seen."[360]

As expected, Kelly's own judgment and sense of taste usually dominated her column, and what she "trained" fans to look for in motion pictures now seemed more encompassing and sophisticated. She was as alert to story construction and pacing as Parsons, but hardly gave that her nearly exclusive attention. Edison's *The Catspaw* was a "thrillful detective story [because] it proceeds logically, punchfully, and mystifyingly, possessing in addition a strong human interest love theme."[361] Adapting Alexandre Dumas's *The Three Musketeers* for *D'Artagnan,* an "inspired scenarist" stuck closely to the old story, and, along with the film's "luminous photography," she praised "the coherence with which it moves in its swiftness, leaving no points in haziness."[362] Several scriptwriters at Triangle impressed Kelly enough to be named: Anita Loos for *The Little Liar* (with Mae Marsh) and C. Gardner Sullivan for *The Moral Fabric* and *The Return of Draw Egan* (with William S. Hart)—the latter for those "who like a brisk action story briskly told, with some delicately tender episodes included."[363] She also urged fans to catch the performances of stars such as Douglas Fairbanks

FLICKERINGS from FILM LAND

A Clean Photoplay Despite the Ads

"WHERE ARE MY CHILDREN?"

Produced and released by Universal.
Directed by Lois Weber.
Presented at the La Salle.

Richard Walton	Tyrone Power
Mrs. Walton	Helen Riaume
Mrs. Brandt	Marie Walcamp
Walton's housekeeper	Cora Drew
Lillian	Rene Rogers
Roger	A. D. Blake
Dr. Malfit	Juan de la Cruz

BY KITTY KELLY.

IN the wake of the lurid "Little Girl Next Door," and on the wings of hectic advertising hinting at more sensationalism, out of the shadow of metropolitan amazement and national board of review disapproval, comes to the La Salle theater one of the most finely mannered photoplays yet produced.

Those who pay their quarters seeking satisfaction for prudent tastes will find their measurement one of disappointment, unless the distinction of the picture can pierce their sordidness, for there is nothing more suggestive about it than the title itself, "Where Are My Children?"

It is a serious film, purposefully produced, but it bears no propaganda earmarks, nor is it pictured with the crude strokes usually employed when some one aims to make a celluloid preachment.

An artist worked skillfully with the materials of her expression and wrought a photoplay characterized equally by its strong purpose and its good dramatic and pictorial construction. If one is not interested in the theme, the story in itself, with its dramatic complications and its attractive directorial handling, is satisfying entertainment. It is, in fact, one of the few cinematic displays in which one loses thought of the time.

The theme is that the wages of sin is death to happiness, the particular sin being the selfishness that abjures motherhood. In this it is an echo of an earlier production, American's "The Miracle of Life," but a much more finely and artistically done thing.

The district attorney, played most compellingly with a quiet, commanding dignity by Tyrone Power, longed for children in his beautiful home. His wife, played with equal distinction and sureness by Helen Riaume, along with others of her set, frivolous fashionables, takes care to have no social engagements upset by interventions of nature.

Things go very merrily, except for the attorney's father hunger, until a crisis is precipitated when the young brother of the attorney's wife seeks aid from her for the housekeeper's young daughter, whom he has wronged.

Outraged at the occurrence—for she is a very nice woman, except for her selfishness—she gives the youth her doctor's name. The result is the girl's death, the doctor's haling into court, and a flurry of consternation amongst the local birds of paradise. From the doctor's ledger the attorney gleans much knowledge.

His wife, before this realizing his desire for children, and determining to bring him the happiness he sought, finds, as the subtitle puts it, that "she is no longer physically able to wear the diadem of motherhood," and all their lives together she must face that mute question, "Where Are My Children?"

The conclusion is impressively beautiful, with the lonely couple sitting before the fire while a fade-in brings visionary children playing around them. The years pass, and still they sit while the ghosts of children grown up come about them.

Everywhere the most exquisite delicacy rules every situation. How much may be accomplished by mere suggestion, how little need there is for suggestiveness in the relating of a powerful story on a delicate subject, is here convincingly demonstrated. This compares to a straight, clear-cut, well written newspaper story, containing facts and characterization and significance, in contrast with a murky Elinor Glynn novel. It takes a problem of the day and looks at it honestly and cleanly instead of with the vice venfering moral hypocrisy that produced "The Little Girl Next Door," playing up salaciousness for box office benefits.

Of course, here there may be no box office benefits, for the picture doesn't bear out some of the insidious announcements about it. It may be too fine a thing for the theater's clientèle established through the past months. But for people who wish to see uniformly good acting, with never a bit of overdoing, a forceful story, forcefully, delicately, and humanly told, here is a rare opportunity. With the production of this picture Lois Weber has given power to her name.

* *

Gaumont to Import Films.

Gaumont is bringing such films from France as the American taste will approve of, for release on the Mutual program to supplement its present offerings. Two of the productions are "The Fall of Constantinople" and the "Fantomas" series.

FIGURE 60. "Flickerings from Film Land by Kitty Kelly," *Chicago Tribune*, July 31, 1916.

in *His Picture in the Papers,* a "deft and sparkling playlet through which [he] frolics"; Fannie Ward, whose "delicate precision of manner, a daintiness of movement, aureole hair, and a cameo face" elevated the Bret Harte story *Tennessee's Pardner* (Lasky); Lillian Gish, whose role of "restrained characterization" in *An Innocent Magdalene* (Fine Arts) was handled "with a delicate subtlety"; and Mary Pickford, of course, who proved such "a gifted purveyor of charming personalities" not only in *The Foundling* but even in revivals of *In the Bishop's Carriage* and *Caprice.*[364] And she repeatedly drew attention to directors: Cecil B. DeMille, the Lasky company's top talent; Allan Dwan, who "put vitality into the most futile sort of tale"; and Albert Capellani, the "wizard of the celluloid, whose touch invariably transplants one to Paris" in World Film's *La Vie de Boheme* (starring Alice Brady), most memorably in "quiet settings" such as "the scene of the street with the snow falling."[365]

Several titles released between October 1915 and March 1916 gave Kelly the opportunity to enumerate certain qualities of a superior film. One was Lasky's *Carmen,* in which "cleancut, directness of incident and action carries the tale through its course of hectic emotionalism to its pathetically beautiful tragedy" (fig. 61).[366] Moreover, Farrar was "a tremendous creature": "Every movement, every flicker of expression is instinct with vitality and the slightest shades of change are caught by the camera." Another was Lasky's "drama of undress," *The Cheat,* "a snappy bit of deceitful procedure . . . put across with so much pop and intensity."[367] Among its striking features were the vivid acting of Fannie Ward and Sessue Hayakawa, the sophisticated intrigue of "domestic dissatisfaction" that "plunges into melodrama," a court scene that forces spectators to sympathize with a mob, and "half lights and almost no lights," along with close-ups, that emphasize key moments in "the house of sliding doors." A third was *The Dumb Girl of Portici,* starring the "lithe, spirited" Anna Pavlova "under the tutelage of Lois Weber," which she ranked with *Cabiria, The Birth of a Nation,* and Lasky's *Carmen,* notably for its skillful adaptation of the opera and its "exquisiteness in details" (fig. 62).[368] Among the latter were the "fisherfolk" extras; the "elaborate and beautiful" interiors; "the scenes outdoors, with their grouped and moving people"; "mobs, in their massed effect" that "approximate, in feeling, paintings"; and "the animated vignettes illustrating the spirit of the subtitles." A fourth was *Betty of Greystone* (Fine Arts), a "charming comedy of character" starring Dorothy Gish, and "told with a distinct pictorial style."[369] Allan Dwan, the director, she likewise singled out for having "an eye for bits emotionally as well as scenically" that "in picturedom . . . count as in nowhere else." In reviewing *The Moral Fabric* (Kay-Bee), an austere film "of refined brutality,"

FLICKERINGS *from* FILM LAND

Farrar's Carmen Opens New Strand

"CARMEN."
Produced by Lasky.
Released by Paramount.

Carmen	Geraldine Farrar
Don José	Wallace Reid
Escamillo	Pedro de Cordoba
Pastia	Horace B. Carpenter
Cigaret Girl	Jeanie MacPherson

At the Strand.

BY KITTY KELLY.

THE Strand is in its new home and "Carmen," which has been so long coming, has come and conquered. These two breath taking events in picturedom were consummated last night amidst a glow of color and a warmth of music that, plus a capacity house, filled the walls of the old Globe with enthusiasm.

The performance last night was differentiated a bit from all successive ones by the Pagliacci prologue sung from the darkness by Burton Thatcher, symbolizing in Manager Cordner's intent the prologue of many things.

Thereafter followed the first edition of the regular Strand program, which is to continue day by day, a lovely Pathé scenic, "Geithorn, a Rustic Venice," taking the place of the South American travel series, the regular Strand topics of the day, the conclusive comedy, soloing by Burton Thatcher and Naomi Nazor—and "Carmen."

And now to "Carmen," the vehicle with which the Lasky company captured grand opera for the celluloid, and Geraldine Farrar, the star they used to light up picture possibilities for the skeptical many.

GERALDINE FARRAR in "CARMEN"

The result of their weeks of work and mountains of money is a high powered illuminator. "Carmen" is so good a picture that it scarcely seems a picture. It tells the Carmen story more coherently than does the opera for the common consumer, and the musical impression in large part is carried by the orchestral accompaniment gleaned from the Bizet score, for the Strand presentation.

Clean cut directness of incident and action carries the tale through its course of hectic emotionalism to its pathetically beautiful tragedy. Most film deaths are bitter things to view. Farrar never looked lovelier, even at the climax of her hot-breathed enthralling, than when she lay limp in her blighted officer's arms.

But that is getting rather ahead of the story. One would say kind things of the settings, the supporting cast, the direction, the photography, but the "Carmen" of it, with all of Farrar's vigor and dominating personality, swings in, and the whole impression crystallizes into—"Carmen."

She is a tremendous creature, this Carmen of the films. Except on the indisputable evidence of seeing, the existence of such vitality as Farrar embodies and its registration by the celluloid would be unbelievable. She is the livest collection of atoms imaginable. Every movement, every flicker of expression is instinct with vitality, and the slightest shades of change are caught by the camera.

In her love making, her shifting between toreador and officer, one reads her purposes without the need of subtitles. In her glowing, changing face are written the lines of the drama which the silent play does not permit.

And Miss Farrar has adequate support in her matador and officer. Pedro de Cordoba is a fine type of the bull fighter, while Wallace Reid as José is slim and good looking—thereby putting it over most of his operatic predecessors—and a lover to match Carmen's own vintage of emotion.

It is no Sunday school play, this picture version of the classic heart bandit. There's a plentiful showing of emotions as they are, not as they are refined by civilization and the "what will people say" idea, but it is all done with a swift deftness that makes the point without the wearisome tediousness of other directors less artistic than Cecil de Mille.

His long scene theory is in satisfying evidence, too, giving the story stretches of pictorial narration that hold the interest and avoid the mental jerkings of frequent flashbacks.

Besides the lady of the picture there's the bull fight, in itself quite worth seeing. One needn't jog into dangerous Tia Juana for this amusement, for there it is in all its glory and energy, minus its gore and tragedy, thrillingly reproduced by such clear photography that it scarcely seems a second hand medium, except for the lack of noise and smells.

One cannot do justice to "Carmen." It is a picture of fineness, encompassing the sincere efforts of a great player—even to the point of very rough treatment accorded the expensive person of a prima donna—of a great director and of a loyal studio support. It satisfies anticipations and it will go down on the records as a classic technically and histrionically.

Another Great Film Combine?

Last night the Los Angeles correspondent of THE TRIBUNE wired in the following story:

Los Angeles, Cal., Oct. 15.—[Special.]—With financial backing aggregating more than two and one-half million dollars, negotiations are under way for the launching of a giant motion picture corporation to co-star Mary Pickford, $75,000 a year "queen of the film," and Charley Chaplin, whose net yearly salary exceeds $65,000.

This is the biggest deal concerning the photo drama industry since the consolidation of the "Triple Alliance" of D. W. Griffith, Thomas H. Ince, and Mack Sennett into the Triangle Film corporation.

The negotiations have been under way for several weeks, but have just reached a tangible form.

As in the case of the Triangle, it is proposed to consolidate three or four leading film concerns and concentrate their artistic efforts to produce pictures of a caliber worthy of $2 patronage.

The firms which are said to be promoting the plan are Famous Players, the Jesse L. Lasky Feature Film company, the Essanay, and perhaps two others.

A telegram was at once sent THE TRIBUNE'S New York correspondent to interview Daniel Frohman, managing director, and Adolph Zukor, president of the Famous Players, and other officials of the Lasky and Paramount companies. Here are his replies:

New York.—Had Daniel Frohman on telephone, and he was surprised into admitting that there was something doing in film combination, but later said he knew nothing about it and refused to be quoted in any way. We are trying to get some of the others.

New York.—Adolph Zukor, president of Famous Players, says there is no truth whatever in the story of combination of film companies.

George K. Spoor, president of the Essanay, could not be reached at his Chicago residence at night. E. Q. Cordner, manager of the Strand theater, said: "We are in close touch with the Paramount and its releasing companies and we haven't heard a hint of any combine."

Bulletin—1 a. m.—"Vic" Eubank of Essanay phones in: "Nothing to it. Essanay are satisfied with their releases through V. L. S. E. and General. Why should they change?"

Now go ahead and dope it out any way you want to.

Censors O. K. 'Battle Cry of Peace.'

"The Battle Cry of Peace" tomorrow night turns the Olympic theater into a home for pictures. This big Vitagraph production is a matter of a message through a story, weaving in the meshes of human hearts the cost and waste of war defenselessness. Hudson Maxim's book, "Defenseless America," inspired J. Stuart Blackton to the making of his picture by which he hopes to waken people to what he regards as the dangerously defenseless state of the country.

Charles Richman has the lead part, with favorite Vitagraphers filling the supporting rôles. A special orchestral accompaniment was arranged for the picture by S. L. Rothapfel.

The municipal censors yesterday granted a permit for the film, following a few minor cutouts.

Round the Loop.

Colonial—"Birth of a Nation."

Fine Arts—"The Bludgeon," with Kathryn Osterman, and "The College Orphan," with Carter and Flora Parker de Haven, beginning today at 10 o'clock.

Olympic—"The Battle Cry of Peace," opening tomorrow night.

Strand—"Carmen," from noon till night daily. Children's hour at 10:30 today, with Mary Pickford in "Sweet Memories," "The Pied Piper of Hamelin," and other attractions.

Studebaker—"Old Heidelberg," "The Coward," "Stolen Magic," and "Favorite Fool" until Monday. Then "The Martyrs of the Alamo," "The Disciple," and "A Game Old Knight."

Ziegfeld—"The Final Judgment," with Ethel Barrymore, and "The White Pearl," with Marie Dore, beginning today at 1 o'clock.

FIGURE 61. "Flickerings from Film Land by Kitty Kelly," *Chicago Tribune*, October 16, 1915.

FLICKERINGS from FILM LAND

Another Step in Photoplay Progress.

'THE DUMB GIRL OF PORTICI'

Produced and Released by Universal.
Directed by Lois Weber, assisted by Phillips Smalley.
Presented at the Colonial, Jan. 30, 1916.

Fenella .... Anna Pavlowa
Masaniello .... Rupert Julian
Duke d'Arcos .... Wadsworth Harris
Alphonso .... Douglas Gerrard
Conde .... John Holt
Isabella .... Betty Schade
Elvira .... Edna Maison
Perrone .... Hart Hoxie
Pietro .... William Wolbert
Rilla .... Laura Oakley
Father Francisco .... N. De Brouillet

BY KITTY KELLY.

AGAIN the celluloid has demonstrated that one supreme in an associated art is likewise great as a dramatic artiste. Pavlowa, who came out of Russia not so long ago, traveling on a reputation builded on dancing, now, under the skillful tutelage of Lois Weber, merits consideration as a player of flame and fancy.

"The Dumb Girl of Portici," made out of the old opera well known as "Masaniello," opening last night in picture form at the Colonial, proves this, besides doing some other things to the regular photoplay situation.

This skillful picture rendition of the opera tale marks another step along the path of picture progress. It is a sentinel that will stand out in the mind along with the few, witnessing to the particular phase of development it represents.

"Cabiria" stood for spectacle, "The Birth of a Nation" for emotional thrill, "Carmen" for individual force, "The Dumb Girl of Portici" for artistry.

While it possesses some of these other attributes, as they possess some of this, it excels for its exquisiteness in details. It is beautiful in all of the little things, and the little things are legion.

—◆—

The story, though based on opera and history, is that one told many times: oppressing nobles, a handsome youth, a peasant girl, a brief bit of floodtide love, and then remorse, which, engineered by a hot blood brother of the maiden, precipitated crown tumbling revolution.

It is not the matter so much as the manner. Fenella is interesting, but one's heart does not thrill for her nor for the duchess with whom she shares Alphonso, though strong dramatic incidents there arise. But the manner is beauty.

The scenes, outdoors, with their grouped and moving people, approximate, in feeling, paintings. The fisherfolk are types as if they had stepped out from canvases. Interiors are elaborate and beautiful, some of them larger than any I have felt conscious of, furnished with taste and regard for the time. The mobs, in their massed effect—some of the most wonderful photoplay mobs yet seen—are sheer picture.

—◆—

Pavlowa's Fenella is chief of the cast, a lithe, spirited creature, dancing from delight into grim death, sometimes, in the little rooms, with her features made too hard; sometimes elfishly beautiful, always the sincere player, not taking her film work with lackadaisical lightness. She wins our interest rather more than our heart. She, too, makes pictures everywhere, on the beach, in the dells, in the palace and the prison. The cast ably supports her.

One of the most pleasing of the little things are the animated vignettes illustrating the spirit of the subtitles, so delicate that sometimes their fleeting meaning comes only after the picture has flashed back, but always hauntingly delightful.

All of this fine workmanship, this beauty, delicacy, detail, was woman made. Lois Weber [Mrs. Phillips Smalley] adapted the opera and directed the photoplay. The results are to her credit.

—◆—

About nine reels are given to the production, which has an introduction and an exquisite finale of Pavlowa the dancer bounding the opera story, in which she is the peasant maid, whose dancing is only incidental to her living, loving, and dying. With the picture is a musical score, arranged from the opera by Adolph Schmid, Pavlowa's personal director, who conducted last night.

Pavlowa from her post of attentive observing of her shadow self upon the screen in the box occupied by Carl Laemmle, president of Universal, and other officials of the company, during the intermission answered the calls of the audience by bowing response.

FIGURE 62. "Flickerings from Film Land by Kitty Kelly," *Chicago Tribune*, January 31, 1916.

Kelly stressed its "unusually fine workmanship": "Stereoscopic photography rules, the sets are beautiful in their artistic simplicity, the subtitles, inset on interesting fabric background, emphasize the theme."[370] She also cited the weaknesses of a British import, *Liberty Hall*, to highlight the "quality of our American made photoplays."[371] Later she would align herself with people who were "looking for realism and probability in their picture entertainment" and offer *Pasquale* (Morosco), starring George Beban, as a "gem of a photoplay"—a story of "romance and real life and sacrifice and pathos and humor and final happiness," the kind of film that even neighborhood theaters could enjoy.[372]

As the above comments suggest, Kelly increasingly drew her readers' attention to certain elements of "pictorial style" unique to motion pictures. Perhaps the most unusual were intertitles. Ince's *The No Good Guy* led her to pronounce on how important they had become in provoking audience laughter: "Clever captions, illustrated by slangy little cartoons that set off the situations and cast shadows of coming action, are a new step . . . in the photoplay world."[373] And interspersed throughout her film review were half a dozen little captioned illustrations—such as "When he's saturated he falls for sob songs like a squirrel for a nut"—in a mild kind of mimicry (fig. 63). In a very unusual move, moreover, Kelly devoted an entire column to a brief history of intertitle advances, highlighting those of the Ince studios but also noting the slang introduced in Essanay's "George Ade fables" and the "tiny ornamental moving vignettes" gracing the captions in *The Dumb Girl of Portici*: a "butterfly poising on the rose slowly fluttered his wings"; a "knight's plume stirred slightly in the breeze."[374] In Chicago, the *Tribune*'s own "second series of war pictures," *The German Side of the War*, boasted "artistic illuminations" designed locally by an ad man.[375] Kelly also was struck by how "lighting can be made to accomplish" so much in a motion picture. In *Tennessee's Pardner*, she specifically noticed the scene in which "Miss Ward, candle led, slips down the stairs to release the outlaw."[376] In the otherwise ordinary *The Heart of Paula* (Pallas), she pointed to the "beautiful effect . . . toward the end, when Paula, in shimmering white, goes from the moonlit night into the dark room in which a shaft of moonshine shoots through a single window."[377] And then there were close-ups. The Fine Arts production of *Going Straight*, starring Norma Talmadge, Kelly considered especially unusual: "Half of its points are made by close ups so satisfying that they do not grow monotonous."[378] Similarly, in Lasky's *A Gutter Magdalene*, she picked out how nicely Fannie Ward's "bits of characterization, given close up treatment, accomplish[ed] vivid cinematic effects."[379] And she recalled such effects in reviewing *Phantom*

FLICKERINGS from FILM LAND

Subtitles Funnier Than Mr. Collier.

"THE NO GOOD GUY."
Produced by Kay Bee.
Released by Triangle.
Presented at The Strand.

Jimmy Coghlan	William Collier
Lucia Andrada	Enid Markey
"Big Malone"	Charles K. French
"Hair Trigger" Joe	Robert Kortman
Francisco Andrada	J. Frank Burke
Hawkins, Jimmy's valet	Walter Edwards

BY KITTY KELLY.

MR. WILLIE COLLIER, who didn't do well with Mack Sennett's pie throwing plays, has moved over into the Ince ranks and participated in his first Kay Bee comedy.

Mr. Collier is more successfully funny than he was in his previous experiences, but still I don't think our established

ON

Douglas Fairbanks and Victor Moore need go about trembling in their boots. For Mr. Collier doesn't sparkle so much with originality, nor does he have that bubbling youthfulness which gives good comedy its mischievous turn. He is a bit in the sere and faded, and the camera acknowledges it. Like so many stage folk, too, he still thinks he is playing to the scalpers' rows, forgetting that his

OFF!

fun reaches just as easily to the back row of the gallery, and doesn't need so much effort to be pushed over.

Mr. C. Gardner Sullivan, that unfailing fount of scenario production, is said to have done this script in one day or two days, or some such bit of time. And so he did, it is quite easy to believe, but the practice of dashing off is not to be recommended.

The excellent title, "The No Good Guy,"

"YOU BE IN POLICE COURT TOMORROW AT NINE O'CLOCK OR THERE'LL BE TROUBLE."

covers the slim story of a ne'er do well who gets the goods on his ne'er do well—in a different way—uncle, and by the magic chemistry of the celluloid falls in love with the girl, whom he has known for about two reels, and not intimately at that.

The picture has a lot of intoxication in it, the kind we see so frequently on the

NINE O'CLOCK THE NEXT MORNING

stage, and in this phase the trick photography resorted to is far funnier than the hero himself, though he does react cleverly to some of the unaccountable conditions.

Trick photography is a resource not to be ignored, it is so wholesomely amusing. Though it may have been done to death in the old days, it has a new lease on life in clever manipulation in the newer, better type of film fun, which the better type of people are coming to appreciate.

A rare part of the photoplay, contributing, I believe, the greatest per cent of laughter to the whole, is in the subtitling. Clever captions, illustrated by slangy

"DETECTIVE? WHY, HE COULD N'T UNRAVEL A BALL OF TWINE!"

little cartoons that set off the situations and cast shadows of coming action, are a new step and a thoroughly satisfactory one, in the photoplay world. This experiment is most successful, planting a taste for more of the same kind of treatment.

The accompanying reproductions give an idea of what the Ince studios have done in subtitular originality.

Excellent photographic effects, especially some night scenes, stamp the film still further as unique.

The musical accompaniment merits

"WHEN HE'S SATURATED HE FALLS FOR SOB SONGS LIKE A SQUIRREL FOR A NUT."

comment. With the gradual supplanting of piano and drum with "$10,000 pipe organs" and "symphony orchestras," the ability properly to accompany comedies seems to have disappeared from our feature houses. Recently at the Colonial an exceptionally rapid fire Keystone was saddened by organ music evidently intended for funeral or church use. Not a syncopated note. Yesterday at the Strand the big orchestra played some of the best ragtime heard recently in movieland, and it added much to "The No Good Guy."

* *

FIGURE 63. "Flickerings from Film Land by Kitty Kelly," *Chicago Tribune*, April 20, 1916.

Fortune (Vitagraph)—a story "Jewish in every thread of the fabric and genial as sunshine in September"—where "effective uses of close ups clinch points of emphasis, characterization."[380]

Kelly's taste for wit and wordplay seems to have lost none of its allure, especially when provoked by Douglas Fairbanks's films. "If you're contemplating suicide and you haven't quite rounded out the details in your mind," she chirped in one column, "make a trip to the Strand and—if you still feel in the mood, you at least won't botch things the way Douglas Fairbanks did in 'Flirting with Fate.' And very likely you'll gain a viewpoint which will get 'kicking off' altogether out of mind."[381] Whipping up metaphors and alliterative phrases for verbal spins and twists, however, usually was reserved for the films she considered not up to snuff. Metro's *The Upstart* was one of those that, "like the scutter of snowflakes, leave no impression on one's gray matter," for too many things were "rumpled and jumbled, with no finesse of treatment, no deftness of development."[382] *Ben Blair* (Pallas) was another whose story, "while well woven in its central fabric, has a lot of loose threads flying."[383] As for *The Feast of Life* (World Film), "If you're looking for the vale of tears, here's the gateway hither" for "it drags one down to the depths, and does it with unconscionable slowness too."[384] For stories like that of *Perils of Divorce* (also World Film), she recommended "beautiful heroines keep on hand chaperones of the ax-bearing sort—thus we would be saved many garment tearing, hair tumbling struggles, and many feet of film weariness."[385] Using a phrase Kurt Vonnegut later made famous—"So it goes"—Kelly even had her own reservations about the allegorical figure of Truth in *Hypocrites*: in her initial appearances, "there was no need for her scampering about coquettishly like a wood nymph instead of a great moral force."[386] With tongue firmly in cheek, she praised *Jaffrey* (Golden Eagle) as "a real treat" for those, unlike her, "who like respectable folk before them on the screen as well as beside them in the theater."[387] But she could also lambast all those films in which "young ladies . . . hop, skip and jump through their scenes, like automatic jumping jacks [as if] supplied with springs that work in the same fashion regardless of the stimulus," along with those that revel in "a lot of sugared sentiment—it must be very toothsome to a multitude of appetites."[388]

At least one more thing made Kitty Kelly unique among newspaper film reviewers. She read widely in the trade press and other sources and often shared what she found important with her readers. The March and April 1916 issues of *Photoplay* "were not to be missed": one for Channing Pollock's argument against censorship, the other for an article on the *Selig-Tribune*'s "film newspaper."[389] A *New York Morning Telegraph* article was knocked for seeming so wishy-washy about the possible results of any film company mergers, when fans, Kelly thought, simply wanted fewer and better features released each day.[390] To bolster her argument that "the poster is the exhibitor's show window," especially in smaller theaters, she quoted W. Stephen Bush in that week's *Moving Picture World,* urging exhibitors to insist on "attractive posters . . . that will invite business and not frighten it away.[391] In the same column, she recommended Mabel Condon's compilation of articles in the *New York Dramatic Mirror* as "full of information and personal interest" about the Fine Arts studio in Los Angeles. For those seeking further information on current studio personnel, she promoted the *Motion Picture News Studio Directory,* "a well arranged and comprehensive reference volume," which, for only fifty cents, included two hundred biographies in 158 pages.[392] Perhaps most intriguing was a full column in which Kelly derided all those "highbrows" who rarely went to the movies but spread so much misinformation and attacked them with "a submarine flotilla under the commandership of Hugo Munsterberg."[393] At once a glowing review of *The Art of the Photoplay,* the column also deployed quotes from Münsterberg to define "the aesthetic feeling" induced by the movies' "psychological conditions": "The massive outer world has lost its weight. It has been freed from space, time and causality, and it has been clothed in forms of our own consciousness. The mind has triumphed over matter and the pictures roll on with the ease of musical tones." Another boldface quote signaled Kelly's assent: "Everybody ought . . . to make the art of the film a medium for an original creative expression of our time, and to mold by it the esthetic instincts of the millions."

In mid-October 1916, Kitty Kelly's film reviews disappeared from the *Chicago Tribune,* apparently "owing to the merging of the Sunday and daily departments devoted to moving pictures.[394] Perhaps dissatisfied with her reassignment to another department, months later she began writing the same column for the *Chicago Examiner.*[395] Without missing a beat, Mae Tinee took over Kelly's column and within days retitled it "Right Off the Reel," in line with her edited Sunday page.[396] In mid-November, the column returned to the *Tribune*'s daily Women's page; three weeks later Mae Tinee dropped the brand name and titled each column with a boxed headline linked to the feature film under review.[397] Initially her column showed some local interest: "the purple drapings over the doorway of the downtown Bandbox theater" whose funeral trappings the manager mistakenly thought fitting for the anti-abortion film *The Unborn*; the letter from a neighborhood woman protesting theater signs such as "For Adults Only" or "No Children Admitted," which served to "pack the houses to the doors"; and the Chicago Planning Commission's film *A Tale of One City,* showing each evening at Bismarck Garden.[398] Increasingly, however, she turned to reporting on industry matters and introduced a section answering readers' questions under the subhead "Ask Me! Ask Me!"[399] Intriguingly, sometimes Mae Tinee seemed to be ventriloquizing Kelly. Francis X. Bushman was the same "lavender lined hero" in *The Diplomatic Service* (Metro), where "the Bushman amethyst, the Bushman wardrobe, and the Bushman valet are liberally displayed."[400] Fascinated by Montagu Love in *Bought and Paid For* (World Film), she exclaimed: "Girls, here's a good looking man who can act."[401] She also shared a smidgen of interest in intertitles. *The Common Law* (Selznick) supposedly "set a record for the lowest number of titles ever used in a seven reel picture," fulfilling its star Clara Kimball Young's wishes, and a brief photo profile featured Anita Loos for writing all the intertitles "that make you laugh" in Fairbanks's films—at his request.[402] She may have tried to one-up Kelly by writing a review in what she called "vers libre" to say that Chaplin's *Behind the Screen* (Mutual) "is quite as funny as ever"—and then oddly judged the effort "quite punk."[403]

Perhaps because her work at the *Tribune* was as demanding as Louella Parsons's, Mae Tinee often filled her columns, more than Kitty Kelly did, with synopses of the day's chosen film. Although her recommendations to readers, consequently, tended to be terse, she too had a taste, sometime literally, for wordplay. "Cometh now this critic, purring, as it were, to announce that she hath found, figuratively speaking, cream. The delectability in question is *The Storm* (Lasky), a deftly blended combination of good story, good acting, and admirable direction."[404] "Scenically, photographically, technically, humanly, Triangle's *A Corner in Colleens* is a delight"—"a pictorial panful of pure, delicious, home-made fun."[405] Famous Players's *Miss George Washington*, starring Marguerite Clark, was "a crisp, clean, clever comedy from start to finish," and Bluebird's suspenseful *The Sign of the Poppy* was "terse and snappy," its five reels running "along at a lively tempo, keeping you pleasantly interested and wrought up."[406] In the latter film, Mae Tinee invoked the racism of the time to describe the villain as "a Chinaman in the woodpile"; by contrast, again characteristic of the war period, she had only praise for the Japanese actors Sessue Hayakawa and Tsuru Aoki in their latest release: "If what is best in acting, plot, production, and scenery appeal to you, *The Soul of Kura-San* (Lasky) is a production you cannot afford to miss."[407] Like her colleagues, she could not resist Mary Pickford in her first Artcraft production: "Like a brisk, fresh breeze, Mary Pickford in *Less Than Dust* has blown into the La Salle . . . making the little playhouse once more a pleasant place to visit."[408] She agreed with Philip H. Welch that Metro's version of *Romeo and Juliet* was superior to Fox's, but cast even more derision on Francis X. Bushman's Romeo and Theda Bara's

Juliet: "Certainly no funnier pair ever unwittingly made burlesque of tragedy. Metro's Romeo with his set sweet smile and biceps! Fox's Juliet with the experience of a hundred vampire roles writ large across her face."[409]

Other films Mae Tinee faulted for their unfortunate casting of stars, or misuse of them. Horrified at watching the famous Shakespearean, E.H. Southern, in *The Chattel* (Vitagraph), she worried that his debut might also "be his swan song": "He makes his entrance with the oily perfunctoriness of an undertaker coming into a house of death."[410] Two things were wrong with *The Return of Eve* (Essanay): "the story and the despicable system which allows one person to 'hog' an entire production" (in this case, Edna Mayo).[411] And there were other flaws Mae Tinee was not afraid to condemn. "A waste of time," *The Price of Fame* (Vitagraph) needed at least a competent director to rein in Bryant Washington's overacting.[412] Despite its alleged cost, "something was radically wrong" with *The Prince of Graustark* (Essanay), which she labeled "palpably false as a mountain of tinfoil."[413] After confessing "to a sneaking fondness for William S. Hart," she tarred *The Discipline* (Kay-Bee) as seemingly "played much as a bunch of youngsters might play it if left to their own devices."[414] Lois Weber's *Idle Wives* she failed to understand at all, describing it scathingly as "a pictorial goulash."[415] Sounding like Louella Parsons, she devoted a whole column to decry "the wave of sensationalism" engulfing the industry, but without naming a single film.[416] Was she thinking of *The Unborn,* still playing at the Bandbox for four weeks, which she found completely unconvincing as an argument against abortion, although women were flocking to see it?[417] And she was equally puzzled by D.W. Griffith's three-and-a-half-hour *Intolerance,* "a spectacle that dazes and dazzles by its stupendousness," but at the end "your brain is all of a heap, and you say to your neighbor, as your neighbor says to you: 'Wasn't it wonderful—wonderful? But just what was it all about?'"[418]

AFTER ONE HUNDRED YEARS, SEVERAL TOASTS

First, a toast to what these newspaper reviewers "trained" moviegoers, however differently, to see and appreciate when they went to a picture theater in 1915–16.[419] There were principles of judgment and taste: well-constructed stories (from scriptwriting to editing), attractive stars or personalities and their acting skills, effective and/or striking camera work (from framing to lighting, in studios and on location), and subjects that could be timely and provoke debate. There were stars that drew almost unanimous acclaim—Mary Pickford, Blanche Sweet, Clara Kimball Young, Geraldine Farrar, John Barrymore, Douglas Fairbanks—and others that either deeply divided reviewers or were objects of scorn, for instance Theda Bara, Francis X. Bushman, William S. Hart, even Charlie Chaplin. There were artists and craftspeople behind the scenes that reviewers praised for consistently producing excellent work, and not only directors—D.W. Griffith, Cecil B. DeMille, Lois Weber, Allan Dwan—but also scriptwriters, set designers, cameramen, and editors. Moreover, there were individual films that either set high standards of artistry or else elicited controversy—Griffith's *The Avenging Conscience* and *The Birth of a Nation*; *The Battle Cry of Peace*; the two versions of *Carmen*; and Weber's *Hypocrites, Where Are My Children?*, and *Shoes*. If reviewers tended to promote the atmosphere and convenience of certain venues, from palace cinemas to neighborhood houses, and to highlight special local screenings, some also, taking the role of social reformer, presumed to "educate" audiences in proper public behavior. And their largely informal, colloquial, even chatty voices—unusually playful in the case of Kitty Kelly—lured moviegoers into participating in movie fandom's new "interpretive communities," which (with exceptions, of course) increasingly were being modeled as white and middle class.

Although none of these reviewers could be mistaken for early film theorists, might we accept "Wid" Gunning and Kitty Kelly in particular as precursors in their promotion of certain concepts that other well-known writers developed over the course of the next few years? And in Kelly and Mae Tinee's language, might we sense the inklings of a vaguely phenomenological concept of the spectator and her physical, psychological experience of cinema? In late December 1915, an editorial in *Moving Picture World* asked: "Are we making a little too much of close ups?" But the trade journal saw close-ups mainly as "the italics and the 'caps' of the screen," as graphic signs of emphasis.[420] Writing at about the same time, Vachel Lindsay hewed closer to Gunning and Kelly in one brief passage that deployed an apt metaphor to praise "Griffith's pupils" Henry Walthall, Blanche Sweet, and Lillian Gish: "Their faces are as sensitive to changing emotion as the surfaces of fair lakes in the wind."[421] The following year, more in line with Kelly and Mae Tinee, Hugo Münsterberg sketched out an explicitly psychological basis for the importance of close-ups: "The close up has objectified in our world of perception our mental act of attention and by it has furnished art with a means which far transcends the power of any theater stage. . . . Any subtle detail, any significant gesture which heightens the meaning of an action may enter into the center of our consciousness by monopolizing the stage [screen] for a few seconds."[422] Within another year, in France, Louis Delluc made even more of Sessue Hayakawa's face, which had so distracted Kitty Kelly: "His eyes are so cold in the face of suffering that, when open, they seem as if they had been closed forever. And especially his strangely drawn smile of child-like ferocity."[423] In the famous essay that opens *Bonjour Cinéma* (1921), Jean Epstein turned one of the American close-ups he so loved into an amazingly original metaphorical landscape:

> Point blank. A head suddenly appears on screen and drama, now face to face, seems to address me personally and swells with an extraordinary intensity. I am hypnotized. . . . Muscular preambles ripple beneath the skin. Shadows shift, tremble, hesitate. Something is being decided. A breeze of emotion underlines the mouth with clouds. . . . Seismic shocks begin. Capillary wrinkles try to split the fault. A wave carries them away. Crescendo. A muscle bridles. The lip is laced with tics like a theater curtain. Everything is movement, imbalance, crisis. Crack. The mouth gives way, like a ripe fruit splitting open.[424]

Among all that Gunning and Kelly found so alluring and unique, perhaps the most intriguing were such close-ups of star's faces.[425] And they continue to mesmerize us.[426]

Second, a toast to the Chicago "film girls" and the visibility they had achieved by 1915–16. For evidence, one only has to look in other newspapers farther afield. Exhibitors increasingly used their names and quoted phrases or lines from their reviews in local ads promoting specific films. We might expect to find Parsons cited as an authority, and she was. In late August 1915, the Orpheum (Rockford, Illinois) quoted her to assure readers that *The White Sister* was safe to see: It "grips our feelings but leaves no scar or sordid uncleanliness."[427] By October, the Palace (Waterloo, Iowa) called Parsons "the celebrated critic" and reprinted her wickedly vivid portrait of Theda Bara in *The Supreme Sin* (Fox).[428] A week later, a promotional piece repeated the honorific and her portrait for the Queen Theater in Galveston, Texas.[429] In February 1916, the Magnet ("The Home of Paramount" in Lincoln, Nebraska) quoted her description of a Chicago audience to hype Mary Pickford's *Poor Little Peppina* (Famous Players).[430] In June the Majestic Theater (Fort Wayne, Indiana) used her name to give a stamp of approval to the white slave film *The Little Girl Next Door*, seen by "200,000 people . . . in six weeks at the LaSalle Opera House, Chicago": "a vivid picturization of vice with all the trimmings."[431] In August, even Kitty Kelly had the grace to mention Parsons's lecture tour "in the interests of the photoplay."[432] Mae Tinee, of course, had become familiar to readers as early as 1914 through the *Chicago Tribune*'s syndication of "Right Off the Reel" and then through "The Diamond from the Sky" contest, where she was identified as "editor" of the "Right Off the Reel" page. [433] Just as she was taking over the *Tribune*'s film review column in late 1916, the

Bijou Theater (Racine, Wisconsin) used her name to guarantee that *How Molly Made Good* (Photo Drama) would be "a HIT!"[434] In early 1917, a Happy Hour ad in the *Syracuse Herald* sidelined The Film Girl and printed a lengthy quote from Mae Tinee's review of Essanay's *The Truant Soul,* with Henry Walthall: "As the reels unfold you find yourself shaken by pity, horror, repulsion and finally joy. . . . There is not one moment during the entire picture when the suspense slackens."[435]

But neither came close to matching the extent of Kitty Kelly's influence. As early as spring 1915, a few exhibitors were puffing their ads with her take on either a short film or feature: the Pastime (Sheboygan, Wisconsin) for the comedy *Paying His Board Bill,* and the Garden (Muskegon, Michigan) for *The Blue Mouse* (Photoplay Productions).[436] In August, the Orpheum (Rockford) paired Parsons's moral approval of *The White Sister* with Kelly's more neutral comment: "a standing testimonial that results warrant the expenditure of time, money and consideration."[437] That fall her quoted blurbs became more frequent. The Bijou (Racine) promoted Chaplin's *Shanghaied* (Mutual) with her "best" recommendation, which urged "mothers to send their children as it is filled with good, clean, wholesome comedy."[438] The Jefferson (Fort Wayne) quoted her praise of Lasky's *Carmen* as "a picture of finesse," and the Palm (Rockford) reported her pronouncement that *The Alien,* with George Beban, was "the greatest photo-play ever produced."[439] The manager of the Plaza (Waterloo) even boasted that he ordered five thousand copies of her column comparing the two versions of *Carmen* to be given to his theater's patrons.[440] By December, an exhibitor such as the Palm (Rockford) could ask his local newspaper to reprint all or most of a column, apparently through the *Tribune*'s syndication service.[441] The most intriguing references to Kelly involved a startling *Tribune* editorial in October objecting to her alleged denunciation of vulgar Keystone comedies.[442] The Rex (Duluth) used that denunciation to promote its screening of *Fickle Fatty's Fall,* and the *Iowa City Citizen* reprinted the *Tribune*'s entire editorial, accusing its own critic of being too "ladylike."[443] It's true that Kelly did criticize films like *Fickle Fatty's Fall* as "vulgar and pointless" that month, citing the words of a fellow spectator and faulting the city's censors for "unbelievable leniency."[444] But at the same time, she thought the four-reel *My Valet* "demonstrated beyond cavil . . . what fun Keystones could be," and by early 1916 she was singing the praises of multiple-reel, cross-class comedies such as *Dizzy Heights and Daring Hearts, Perils of the Park,* and *His Hereafter.*[445]

Throughout 1916, Kelly remained a favorite source of knowledgeable taste for exhibitors to lure moviegoers into their theaters. The manager of the Magnet (Lincoln) highlighted her appraisal of *The Cheat*: "a compelling picture, weird in setting, but underlyingly human" and "a tense example of modern photoplay art from all angles."[446] While some seized on her enthusiasm for Chaplin's *Police* and *The Count* (both Mutual), which had "story, speed, and spontaneity," the manager of the Victoria (Harrisburg, Pennsylvania) took an opposite tack, repeating her liking for Harry Watson in *Mishaps of Musty Suffer* (George Kleine), "an original comedian" whose "genuine funniness . . . doesn't show a trace of Chaplinitis."[447] Several small-town newspapers followed the *Rockford Republic*'s example and reprinted an entire column—from her article on studio mergers to her reviews of *Misleading Lady* and *The Bugle Call* (Kay-Bee)[448]—and an *Idaho Statesman* (Boise) writer tried to imitate her wordplay, describing a reprint of her review of *Fate's Boomerang* (World Film) as a "roast" and "a whack" at producer William Brady, full of "acidulous amenities."[449] Snippets from her review of *Gloria's Romance* (George Kleine), starring Billie Burke, appeared in picture theater ads from Fort Wayne and Muskegon to Cedar Rapids and Aberdeen, North Dakota—that last also included a rare blurb from Dorothy Day of the *Des Moines Tribune.*[450] Cropping up in even more theater ads for the white slave film *The Little Girl Next Door,* Kelly's cryptic comments—"giving the public what it wants"—often again came paired with Parsons's sensational "visualization of vice."[451] The appeal of Kelly's column also extended to an unattributed weekly column, "Flickerings from Filmland," that ran for six months in the *Marble Rock Journal* (Iowa).[452] Most striking of all was the *Sunday Tribune*'s own huge ad in late April 1916 extolling "the clever writings of Kitty Kelly" and graced with a "star" photo to match Mae Tinee's: "If you're a motion picture fan they're almost indispensable."[453]

DOCUMENT

"WID" GUNNING, "'CLOSE-UPS' ARE VERY IMPORTANT," *NEW YORK EVENING MAIL*, JANUARY 9, 1915

If you will think over the best films you have ever seen—that is, the ones you enjoyed the most—you will surely remember that there were many "close-ups" in them. That is, in many places where there was a bit of emotion to be expressed by one of the principals, the camera was moved up close so that the face became very large on the screen, making it very easy for you to see just what those features you were watching so closely were doing. In other words, you were handed a pair of opera glasses without your noticing that you had received them—they were all focused to the eye, you didn't have to hold them until your arm became strained—and yet you got the same effect, only with more powerful lenses.

There are some producers who still seem afraid of the use of the close-up, or else they do not thoroughly understand where it should be used or how to use it. It is truly one of the hardest bits to do technically, to do it well—and the principals who are to do the close-up must be very carefully directed, and also capable of really feeling and "getting over" emotion. The fact remains, however, despite the contention of a few of the old-time producers, that figures should be full size and walk about—with their feet showing, etc.—that the public wants pictures with the faces of the principals close enough at all times so that they can distinguish what emotion is being expressed without "straining" to reach for it.

I have felt this for some time, and I consider myself, when looking at a film, as just one of the public, who, let it be sorrowfully said, are not considered to know much by many producers. For the past few years I have discussed this matter pro and con with many persons directly interested and with many who were only film fans, and now feel certain that "close-ups" do help a film, if properly handled. In fact, a good producer with capable principals can make a splendid, interesting film from a very poor story if he uses good lighting effects, beautiful outdoor locations, impressive sets and many "close-ups." Of course, this is no argument against a good story. I always consider the story the first essential of any film, but I know of many cases where poor stories have been made into good films because of bringing the faces of expressive artists up where every one can follow the drooping of an eyelid.

All of which is to say, that I believe one of the most important reasons for the popularity of films is that it allows the artists, through bringing the characters so close to every one in the audience, whether they be in the orchestra or gallery, to "put over" fine little bits of expression that could not be done in a theatre effectively. You like "close-ups," don't you? Yes, of course: well, it is to the "close-up" that we can attribute the popularity of some of our most successful screen stars. And for that reason, if it were for no other, I would be in favor of the "close-up." More power to the directors who use them well.

DOCUMENT

KITTY KELLY AD, *CHICAGO TRIBUNE*, APRIL 30, 1916

[. . .] Because the motion picture art has grown so great, because it fills so high a place in modern life, you find high up within the galaxy of famous Tribune writers the motion picture critic, *Kitty Kelly.*

MISS KITTY KELLY
The Tribune's Motion Picture Critic

FIGURE 64. Miss Kitty Kelly, *Chicago Tribune*, April 30, 1916. David M. Rubenstein Rare Book & Manuscript Library, Duke University.

Every day throughout the week, excepting Sunday, Kitty Kelly's "Flickerings from Filmland" attract, inform and entertain Tribune readers by the scores of thousands.

She tells you all about the newest plays and how they're played.

She gives an added zest to every film you see because you know beforehand what it's all about, wherein its special virtue lies and how your favorite star fits in the part that he or she is playing.

Even a soured and saddened cynic who never visits picture shows can enjoy the clever writings of Kitty Kelly, and if you're a motion picture fan they're almost indispensable.

She doesn't use as many ponderous polysyllabic parts of speech as Percy Hammond nor is she as cuttingly sarcastic as "B. L. T.," but every paragraph beams forth a cheerful brightness all its own, reflects the radiance of a brilliant mind that knows all filmdom and all filmdom's stars from A to Z.

READ KITTY KELLY
In The Tribune
EVERY MORNING

ENTR'ACTE Motion Picture Weeklies

> This magazine is being issued for your direct benefit, your benefit as a moving picture patron.
>
> *New Orleans Item*, November 5, 1916

By 1916, moviegoers in more than half a dozen cities had the good fortune to read at least one newspaper publishing a weekly supplement devoted largely or even entirely to the movies. Most circulated as a section within the weekend edition, one that either included a variety of amusements or could be purchased as a separate magazine. The earliest may have appeared on the East Coast, but the majority emerged to whet the appetites of movie fans in the Midwest and elsewhere. Although they differed in format and design and in what they chose to offer readers, generally they depended heavily on industry sources, from manufacturers to exhibitors, and tended to downplay issues of local interest. They offer further evidence of the industry's increasingly diverse efforts to orchestrate national coverage of the movies and create a homogeneous film culture.

In early September 1915, shortly after "Wid" Gunning began to turn "Films and Film Folk" into a separate trade paper, the *New York Evening Mail* announced, without naming an editor, that it would be inserting a supplement, the "Motion Picture Mail," into each Saturday edition (fig. 65).[1] Apparently the only extant copies run from the beginning to the end of 1916,[2] and the weekly issues overall remained relatively standardized in format, design, and contents. Each issue took up sixteen pages, with large star photos gracing the covers and others scattered throughout, usually linked to articles. The January 1, 1916, issue was called the "Mary Pickford Number" and included a score of publicity photos, from older Biograph and IMP to more recent Famous Players production stills, the one on the back cover posing her as the main character in *Poor Little Peppina.* Scattered throughout were eight articles: a survey of her career, a story synopsis of *The Foundling* ("written from the screen by Robert Burns"), "When Mary Fell in Love with Owen Moore," "Letters They Write to Mary," "Being a Movie Queen Is No Easy Task," "Her Advice to

FIGURE 65. "Motion Picture Mail" cover, *New York Evening Mail,* January 15, 1916.

Movie-Stricken Girls—An Interview," and "How Do I Register Emotion? Why Just Like This," accompanied by half a dozen facial expression photos.[3] Other issues were more representative in covering many different stars and current films. The January 22 issue had publicity photos on the front and back covers of Mary Fuller and Blanche Sweet, respectively, framing stills from the Bray studio's silhouette animation *Inbad the Sailor,* Hearst-Vitagraph and Pathé News photos, a story synopsis of *Hell's Hinges,* a telephone interview with Mary Fuller, and photos of Theda Bara depicting "How Do I Register Emotion?" The January 29 issue also included H.H. Van Loan's "Are the Movies Safe for Respectable Girls?" which answered the objections of a Los Angeles minister.[4] By June, there was another addition: short "Candid Reviews of Current Features," written by the newspaper's male staff.[5] The "Motion Picture Mail," consequently, resembled a fan magazine for both men and women, if smaller, more frequently distributed, and locally produced.

In Philadelphia, the "Amusement Section" of the *Evening Ledger*'s Saturday edition continued to cover photoplays, theater, dancing, and music through much of 1916. Nearly half of the section's four pages was given over to articles and photos devoted to motion pictures.[6] A persistent subject was the relationship between stage and screen: for instance an editorial on whether or not picture producers should hire stage stars, an article in which stage actors assessed "the art of the photoplay," others entitled "Do Stage or Films Inspire Actors Most?," and another asking "if Shakespeare would now write scenarios."[7] Given its overall high-culture assumptions, the *Ledger* even printed an article on Hugo Münsterberg's "ideograph" experiments at Harvard University, included as one story in a weekly issue of *Paramount Pictographs.*[8] As expected, many articles and photos promoted stars such as Mary Pickford, Charlie Chaplin, Blanche Sweet, and Frank Keenan, but just as many depicted studio spaces, acclaimed directors such as D.W. Griffith, Cecil B. DeMille, Herbert Brenon, and Hugh Ford, or turned for advice to producers such as Jesse L. Lasky, John Freuler, and William A. Brady.[9] Intriguingly, DeMille contributed two articles on the importance of lighting, referencing the Rembrandt effect in *Carmen,* but he also argued that the real success of a photoplay depended on proper exhibition.[10] In terms of exhibition, one of the few issues of local interest was an alleged need for children's movies, and Edward Bok singled out the Merion Civic Association's model school for its Saturday morning programs, mostly of short films.[11] The *Ledger* itself invited boys and girls to submit their choices of "the six greatest photoplays" they had seen and, in exchange, receive free theater tickets.[12] The main sponsor of these pages was the Stanley Booking Company, with its quarter-page ad for some fifty picture theaters in the area, but others included Lubin, Pathé Exchange,

Triangle, Metro, and Bluebird, plus ads from the Chestnut Opera House for a four-week run of *In the Line of Fire with the Germans,* the Victoria for Triangle and then Chaplin films, and the flagship Strand for Chaplin's *Police.* In contrast to the "Motion Picture Mail," then, the *Ledger*'s supplement read like a miniature trade journal with an overall aim of boosting motion pictures as a photoplay art as well as an educational force.

Beginning in early February 1916, perhaps the largest supplement other than the *Evening Mail*'s appeared in the *Cleveland Sunday Leader.*[13] Presumably the editor was Archie Bell, who signed some of the paper's daily "Photoplay and Players" columns, and a large ad proclaimed that "This Magazine" would be "devoted exclusively to the 'movies'—and the big new films, the film stars, and the people who are making them."[14] The first of its twelve pages (like the "Motion Picture Mail") displayed a prominent photo of a current star, often accompanied by a profile, sometimes signed by Bell; the exception, in mid-March, had a drawing of "The Movie Fan" as an entranced, stylish young woman seated alone in a theater (fig. 66).[15] The last page posted a single ad for picture theaters such as the Standard, Duchess, Strand, or Orpheum; scattered through the other pages were large and small ads for a dozen theaters, also listed in "Daily Programs at Film Shows This Week," along with those for a few manufacturers, distributors, and local companies.[16] In the initial issue there was even a full-page ad for "Mary Pickford's Daily Talks," followed in later issues by smaller ad reminders.[17] Four or five pages of each issue had relatively full plot synopses for up to a dozen feature films then playing or about to play in the city.[18] Bell himself signed articles on Pauline Frederick and Mary Pickford as well as films such as *The Bondman* and *The Ne'er-Do-Well;* Louise Graham (the "Clubs" column editor) contributed pieces on Olga Petrova and Marguerite Clark.[19] There were plenty of unsigned articles on both stars and new films, probably supplied by industry press agents, but also some signed by Pearl White, Anita Stewart, and Bertha Kalich (a stage star converted to the movies).[20] Overall, then, the "Motion Picture Leader" struck a balance in its focus on popular stars and current feature films. Stories of local interest, by contrast, were few: visits to the Reserve Photoplay Company, news of Cleveland's Federated Women's Clubs' selection of films as part of the "Better Films" movement, profiles of local girls who enjoyed some success in the industry.[21]

In April, John DeKoven apparently took over editing the "Motion Picture Leader" after having written a column entitled "Greenroom Gleanings" containing "intimate whisperings" about the stars.[22] Local issues nearly disappeared, except for a brief photo profile of the Cleveland Screen Club's president, and "The Kwery Column" introduced in the fall.[23] Filling several pages

Motion Picture Leader

Cleveland, March 19, 1916

"Bondman," a Drama of Love and Hate

BY ARCHIE BELL.

WILLIAM FARNUM in Hall Caine's most interesting novel—via the film route—will be visible all this week at the Standard theater.

I had the privilege to see it privately last week, and in addition to being a most interesting photodrama it taught me several things which cannot fail to occur to all who see it. First, it shows that it is possible to make an unusual six reel film, one that will hold interest from start to finish, without an off color suggestion, without a flush that would cause a blush on the face of the most squeamish censor.

But, of course, Hall Caine wrote this story. And he wrote it at a time when he was giving us stories, instead of political and sociological opinions. He proved himself to be a master novelist, particularly when dealing with such passions as revenge, hate, and the kindred emotions of humanity.

These had full rein in "The Bondman." Also, Hall Caine was here writing about people with whom he was familiar. His characters were living to him, so he made them living to his readers. Caine has lately feasted at the tables of the aristocracy in London, drunk tea and listened to small talk. This later life reflects itself in his later writings.

"The Bondman" is brawn, muscle, almost primitive, for its scenes are laid in the Isle of Man and Iceland.

So a child could have picked the most appropriate actor on our stage to play the central part, or parts, for Mr. Farnum appears as both father, and son, by a trick of the camera. Farnum is a symbol of what is noble, brave, true. If he should play a villain, he would play him with so much gusto that he would not only make him convincing but fully half of the audience would vote in his favor. For once, in one drama, villainy would triumph.

Farnum is first seen as Stephen Orry, a large-limbed brute, fashioned like a Greek god, but withal as indolent and shiftless as any loafer. The people of Iceland have met for the annual festival on the Mount of Laws. Wrestlers have been competing for the championship belt.

After it has been awarded Stephen is discovered lounging near the festival. The winner tempts him to attempt his prowess as a wrestler. After considerable prodding, Stephen consents to go into the ring and, of course, almost breaks the back of the earlier winner, so that the daughter of the governor, Rachel Jorgensen, presents the belt to him. Their eyes meet and the drama has fairly started.

On his way home Stephen is overtaken by the man he has bested, with the result that man is left in the road with a broken back. Rachel leaves her home, banished by her father, and marries Stephen. He was a noble lover, but he makes a bad husband. He is too lazy to work and he abuses his wife, finally abandoning her and going away to the Isle of Man to live.

Years pass, and after much suffering and hardship Rachel dies, leaving a son, Jason (also played by Farnum). The son vows on his mother's death to find and kill his father for deserting the one he promised to love.

Fate brings Jason to the Isle of Man, on his quest of revenge, and

FIGURE 66. "Motion Picture Leader" cover, *Cleveland Sunday Leader,* March 19, 1916.

of each issue now were serializations: first *The Iron Claw,* then *The Secret of the Submarine.*[24] Along with the usual industry news briefs came articles by Harry A. Aitken (Triangle), James Kirkwood (Famous Players), and V.D. Horkheimer (Balboa), another on Brabant Film's experiment in making movies without scenery, and a short piece on Hugo Münsterberg's book and his psychological tests picked up in *Paramount Pictographs.*[25] Yet readers soon must have noticed even bigger changes. They could find more advice on writing scenarios, beginning with Alma Woodward's serial column on a "Mollie of the Movies" script and an excerpt from "Mary Pickford's Daily Talks" urging "college girls to write plots."[26] But what probably most caught their eyes was the attention given to stars, which aligned the magazine ever more closely with the "Motion Picture Mail." Along with DeKoven's front-page profiles was a "Gallery of the Gods" column and increasing numbers of stories in each issue.[27] Most of the latter were unsigned, but others were attributed to Sis Hopkins (Kalem's comic star) and Grace Darling.[28] While Pickford's "Daily Talks" remained a *Leader* feature during the other six days of the week, the *Sunday Leader* now added Beatriz Michelena's weekly column of "Heart to Heart Talks" to "Screen Struck Girls."[29] Perhaps most telling was the reduction of plot synopses for feature films in favor of a full-page photo gallery of a dozen stars that moviegoers could encounter that week "At the Film Theaters."[30]

Another Midwest newspaper, the *St. Louis Sunday Globe-Democrat,* came up with a novel supplement (fig. 67). In April, still without a named editor, the motion picture page expanded to two and then four pages. Several columns—A.H. Giebler's "Letters from a Correspondence School Actor" as well as "Answers to Motion Picture Fans"—carried over from before, but the first page now looked like a front cover, differently titled each week and filled with half a dozen star photos in an overlapping cluster, a brief column of gossip, and a bit of doggerel.[31] A serial episode of "The Mysteries of Myra" took up the middle pages. From June through September, the *Globe-Democrat* set off these pages as a "Motion Picture Section," with women filling most of the front-page "album" of stars.[32] A single, unsigned article usually dominated the last page, and most of these were devoted to stars such as Mary Pickford, Nell Shipman, Lottie Pickford, Sessue Hayakawa, and Tsura Aoki.[33] One exception was a reprint of Edward Lyell Fox's article for U.S. preparedness in the Great War; another highlighted the dangers courted by motion picture cameramen in location shooting.[34] In September the "Motion Picture Section" reverted to two pages, and in November to a single page retitled the "Motion Picture Forum" and folded into the Sunday magazine section.[35] During all this time, regular features included A.H. Giebler's columns

St Louis Sunday Globe-Democrat
Photoplay Forum
Motion Picture Stories
Answers to Fans
April 16, 1916.
For handsome men and bandits movie crowds are keen,
While others, if the truth were prefer a queen serene;
Yet on the swiftly changing film stars cannot tarry long,
They smile, they kill, they love, go, this kaleidoscopic throng.

FIGURE 67. "*St. Louis Sunday Globe-Democrat* Photoplay Forum" cover, April 16, 1916.

of stories—"Adventures in Movieland" and "Breaking into the Motion Pictures"—and the editor's answers to fans' questions.[36] What set off this supplement from nearly all others was its focus on stars, to the exclusion of any mention of specific films then playing in the city, and the absence of any picture theater ads or, with one exception, other signs of local interest.[37]

In early June of 1916, the *Seattle Times* began printing an "Amusements" section in the Sunday edition, with most of its eight pages devoted to motion pictures. Identified as head of the paper's "photoplay department," George

H. Bellman presumably edited this section, which slightly resembled the one in the *Philadelphia Evening Ledger*.[38] A major difference was the number of picture theaters that sponsored the section with ads, some of them large enough to take up half a page, and the *Times* claimed, perhaps rightly, to be "the pioneer in the matter of handling motion picture advertising in a big way."[39] Each week readers could find one or two photo profiles of stars, along with a few industry stories: for instance a brief bio of the scriptwriter C. Gardner Sullivan and advice from the scenario departments at Edison, Keystone, and Paramount.[40] Yet the bulk of the columns informed readers of the stars and feature films currently playing in the advertised theaters—likely supplied, as before, by theater managers. They also were treated to a unique column, "Who's Who in the Films," which named the cast of characters and actors for half a dozen current films. Rarely did the *Times* include anything of local interest: news of two Washington state girls as winners of the "Beauty and Brains" contest sponsored by *Photoplay* and World Film; a profile of the actress Seena Owen, from Spokane; and the founding of the Greater Features film exchange in the city.[41] Beginning in August, by arrangement with the *Chicago Sunday Herald,* the *Times* reprinted Louella Parsons's motion picture pages as a relatively regular feature. While many of these profiled stars such as the Talmadge sisters, Hayakawa and Aoki, or Edith Storey,[42] an equal number sketched a history of motion pictures in stories of the men and companies that pioneered its development—from Edison, Lumière, Lubin, Selig, and Spoor to Laemmle and Ince.[43]

This syndication arrangement came shortly after a transformation at the *Chicago Sunday Herald.* Whereas the *Chicago Sunday Tribune* continued to feature Mae Tinee's two pages, "Right Off the Reel" and "Latest News from Movie Land," in early June the *Sunday Herald* began printing a separate four-page "Motion Pictures" section, which followed Parsons's long-running "Confessions of a Movie Actress" page—with its serial story of a "film star's life" by Miss X, Parsons's own photo profile of a major star, and her "Answers to Movie Fans."[44] In the "Motion Pictures" section, Parsons signed a central column on the stars and feature films on offer that week, usually on the first page, flanked by a "Jitney Jim" story (now unsigned) and a "Chaplin's Own Story" chapter. Serial installments of *The Iron Claw, The Secret of the Submarine,* and *The Social Pirates* took up several other pages, and a directory of "Today's Moving Picture Programs at All the Leading Theaters in Every Neighborhood" filled the fourth.[45] Within a week, Parsons began to append more industry news briefs to her column, sometimes highlighting at least one with a subhead: "'Civilization' a Great Preparedness Play," "Drama Vs. the Movies," "Films and Music."[46] In August, the

"Confessions of a Movie Actress" page was retitled "The Real Romance of the Movies," with Parsons now writing not only star profiles and "Answers to Movie Fans" but also a series on the men and companies then considered responsible for developing motion pictures—reprinted in the *Seattle Sunday Times.*[47] In the "Motion Pictures" section, Parsons soon was stuffing two pages with industry news and gossip, reducing the serial installment to a single page and then adding two new serializations, "The Yellow Menace" and "The Crimson Stain Mystery."[48] And a writer with the pseudonym Bab kept readers abreast of a local "People's Movie Star Contest" aimed at choosing the cast for a proposed "great photoplay feature."[49]

In early October, the *Herald*'s "Motion Pictures" section expanded to eight pages, rivaling those of the *New York Evening Mail* and the *Cleveland Leader.* One or more star photos created a front-cover attraction, sometimes with an accompanying profile written by Parsons, the whole page set off by an abstract filmstrip border.[50] Columns from "The Real Romance of the Movies" now occupied inside pages, along with up-to-date reports on the movie star contest and industry news and gossip such as the cost of *Intolerance* (nearly $2 million) and Lois Weber's record-setting contract at Universal.[51] Serial episodes of "The Yellow Menace" and "The Crimson Stain Mystery" took up another two pages; and Parsons devoted the final page to a column about one or more stars or current films.[52] Finally, the directory of "Today's Programs in the Motion Picture Theaters in Every Neighborhood" was now so extensive that it covered two full pages. Hardly ever did the "Motion Pictures" section include anything on the local scene beyond the ubiquitous promotional pieces for the movie star contest, what films were playing in which picture theaters throughout the Chicago area, and Parsons's "Answers to Movie Fans." A rare exception was her appeal for moviegoers to tell their neighborhood managers what films they would like to see.[53] The *Sunday Herald*'s "Motion Pictures" section, in other words, could keep readers informed about one or more serials circulating in the region and perhaps help moviegoers decide which theaters to attend, but, with Parsons as a "go-between," it mainly seemed to serve as an inexpensive weekly summary of the industry's more costly monthly fan magazines and much less accessible trade press.

At least one other supplement appeared in late 1916: "The Moving Picture Item" published by the *New Orleans Sunday Item.* Ever since January 1916, the newspaper had been offering not one but two "Item Movie Pages" and a "Daily Movies" column, both edited by R. E. Pritchard.[54] In early November, readers suddenly found a separate Sunday section entitled "The Moving Picture Item" (in bold block letters) that, like the "Motion Pictures" section of the *Chicago Sunday Herald,* ran eight pages (fig. 68).

The MOVING PICTURE ITEM

AND we've all admired her so long, there's little wonder that she admires herself once in a while.

Edited by R. L. Pritchard

NOVEMBER 5, 1916

Vol. 1. No. 1

LASKY TELLS CHANGES MADE IN PRODUCING

Head of Big Film Company Contrast System of Present Day With the Haphazard Plans of Past

"ABOUT *The* PLAYERS"

SELZNICK GETS THE STUDIOS OF DEAD "BIO"

Clara Kimball Young, Norma Talmadge and Others to Produce in Plant Which Successes of the Past Built

MOVIES GOT BEGINNING IN HORSE FILM

Argument About Position of Equine's Hoop Resulted in First Picture Being Made in This Country

BY BEATRIZ MICHELENA

MARY PICKFORD.

THIS is the first of a series of high-grade pictures which will be printed in this frame each Sunday. You will get here the photographs of the players that you want, for the readers of The Item will select them for themselves. On account of the time that it requires to make these splendid cuts we have had to do the picking for this Sunday and next Sunday. Next week Lillian Walker will be shown.

But then we intend to print the picture of the star that the public wants—the one whose picture is requested by the most readers. Send in a note or postal saying, "Please print a picture of .... in the frame," and the actor or actress who gets the most votes up to a period of two weeks before the particular issue will be represented.

We Promise You:

FIRST, that this will be the poorest issue of the Moving Picture Item because this newspaper is going to bend every effort toward giving you the very best in moving pictures and to insure that you have a publication which will cover the entire field thoroughly and honestly.

In the confusion of starting an entire section, something entirely new, there are generally left undone some things that should be done, for the reason that the members of the staff have been compelled to devote a great share of their time to details and seemingly inconsequential matters that always have to be determined before the first issue of a publication can be made.

IN the first place, this magazine is being issued for your direct benefit, your benefit as a moving picture patron.

MOVING pictures had their beginning in the side-show class.

(To be continued next week.)

FIGURE 68. "The Moving Picture Item" cover, *New Orleans Sunday Item*, November 5, 1916.

As editor, Pritchard wrote an initial column making the following promises to readers.[55] They would find "the handsomest and newest pictures of all the players" and "the latest news of players and productions," all provided by the studios, as well as a "Moving Picture Directory" or chart listing the films to be shown each day of the week at nearly thirty movie houses—"to let you know in advance the goods [a theater] is asking you to buy."[56] Topping the column was a photo of Mary Pickford, "the first of a series of high-grade pictures which will be printed in this frame" each week, and chosen by readers as they were for the *Chicago Sunday Tribune.* That first page also included stories involving producers Lasky and Lewis J. Selznick, a column of brief star profiles, "About the Players," and a new series from Michelena on "the history of moving pictures." Other pages had stories signed by Helen Holmes and Coolidge W. Streeter (of *Paramount Pictographs*) and news of Fox ordering forty prints of *Daughter of the Gods* for showcase tours.[57] Complementing the directory were several pages of plot synopses for "the first-run pictures to be shown in New Orleans this week." In parallel with earlier supplements, there were serial installments of "Adventures of the Famous Beatrix Fairfax," "The Scarlet Runner," and "The Shielding Shadow," plus ads for two other serials, *Pearl of the Army* and *A Lass of the Lumberlands* (starring Holmes). Half a dozen theaters supported the "Moving Picture Item" with ads, and only the Boehringer Amusement Company's was large,[58] but Pritchard adopted a magnanimous tone, claiming that the *Item* "[did] not expect this [section] to be a paying proposition."[59]

5. Edna Vercoe's "Romance with the Movies"

If the story interests you so that you want to see it in the pictures, put it in your scrapbook.

Chicago Tribune, February 5, 1914

Reading through Mae Tinee's "Answers to Movie Fans" column in the spring of 1914, one can begin to gather a general notion of the number of movie fans in the Chicago area and some sense of their interests. Until recently, however, finding traces of what a single fan or even a small group of fans may have thought and felt about going to the movies has been extremely difficult. That changed during the Women and the Silent Screen conference held at Stockholm University in July 2008, when Barbara Hall (research archivist at the Margaret Herrick Library at the time) introduced a workshop on unexamined archive holdings. At one point, almost as an aside, she mentioned that the Herrick Library had just acquired a rare six-volume set of scrapbooks compiled by a teenager living in a suburb north of Chicago in the mid-1910s. If Hall had wanted to spark research interest, she certainly succeeded—amazed, some of us in the audience marveled that that kind of ephemera could survive from so early in cinema history![1] The following year I started perusing those scrapbooks—or "whatchamacallits" that don't fit neatly into archival taxonomies[2]—and came away even more amazed than expected. That experience led me to return twice to engage in more systematic study, with generous assistance from Hall and others, and then begin shaping my notes and selected photocopies into a text. As a senior scholar—and male—I may not be the person best able to see and think like a teenage girl living a hundred years ago, but her scrapbooks could hardly have been more crucial to the research that led to this book—and to this final chapter on the convergence of newspapers and the movies in the mid-1910s.

Each of the six scrapbooks contains 160 pages of relatively heavy paper, ten by seven inches in size, bound in deep-bronze alligator leather. The first volume is dated July 22, 1914; the second, August 12 and September 2,

1914; the third, September 14, 1914. The fourth and fifth volumes are not dated. The sixth has the more general date of January 1915. Each volume is titled "Moving Picture Pictorial," and the first four are inscribed with the author's name, Edna G. Vercoe or Edna G.B. Vercoe, with her address, 860 Sheridan Road, Highland Park, Illinois, a suburb north of Evanston and Chicago. Each also begins with several "contents" pages. Volume I, for instance, divides into three sections with boldface titles: "Perils of Pauline," "Lucille Love," and "Miscellaneous"—that last comprising an extensive list of two dozen stars and seven films, on pairs of verso/recto pages. Cut-out newspaper and magazine photos, graphic images, and printed material are pasted on most pages of each volume, often with small or large chunks of handwritten script in blue or black ink (fig. 69). In addition, the Margaret Herrick Library has collected miscellaneous material, correspondence (envelopes and letters or cards), and loose clippings in separate folders, some of it apparently having become detached from various pages that have blank spaces. According to Hall, these scrapbooks were acquired shortly before the Stockholm conference from a longtime collector of motion picture trade press issues and fan magazines, James W. Craig, who had donated parts of his collection to the library in the past.[3] He, in turn, may have purchased the scrapbooks at an estate sale, perhaps that of one of Edna Vercoe's nieces or a nephew-in-law.[4]

Discovering some biographical information about Edna Vercoe involved a bit of detective work, with efficient help from Highland Park librarian Julia Johnas.[5] Edna was a "New Year's baby," born on January 1, 1899, the fourth child and third daughter of Arthur W. and Edith M. Vercoe, who had come from Kent County, England, to Chicago in 1895–96. Arthur's father had been a Wesleyan minister. Together with his new wife, Arthur had shipped to South Africa to serve as a missionary in the early 1890s. In Chicago, according to an obituary, he was "associated" with the Rosehill Cemetery Company;[6] in 1911, he became president of the North Shore Trust Company, which specialized in real estate loans, and the family moved to the prosperous suburb of Highland Park.[7] The *Highland Park Press* described him as a "prominent citizen" who held several township and county offices from the mid-1910s on. When Edna began her "Motion Picture Pictorial" scrapbooks in the summer of 1914, she was fifteen years old and would graduate from Deerfield-Shields High School three years later in 1917 (fig. 70).[8] According to two postcards and one letter accompanying the scrapbooks, at least four of Edna's school friends—her sister Connie, "Floss" Schreiber, Ethel Hicks, and Josephine Faxon, who also had pen names such as Dody (for Josephine) and Edward or Nenna (for Edna

88

Mary Pickford.

M. L.: Recently a number of old films featuring Mary Pickford have been revived by companies not connected in any way with the Famous Players. It is probably in one of these you have seen the girl whom you think was Miss Pickford's double, but who is really Miss Pickford herself. She was just an amateur at the time these pictures were taken, which accounts for her acting disappointing you, who are, no doubt, accustomed to her splendid work of more recent days. You're welcome!

TAD: It would take me a whole day to tell Mary Pickford all the nice things you've said about her, wouldn't it? I think that if you will write to her in care of the Famous Players, inclosing a quarter for her photograph, she will send it to you. The Famous Players company is located at 213 West Twenty-sixth street, New York. You might ask her for her husband's, too, while you are about it.

JENNIE S.: Mary Pickford is 21 old. She has been with the Famous ers for a number of years. Pearl says she is not married.

Mary Pickford

MARY PICKFORD, one of Griffith's discoveries, who recently gave up her rôle in "A Good Little Devil" to return to the moving picture stage

FIGURE 69. Edna Vercoe scrapbook volume II: Mary Pickford. Margaret Herrick Library.

herself)—also loved the movies, collected photos and letters from lots of stars, and even had their own movie scrapbooks. In her December 1914 letter, written during a school study period, "Floss" refers to her own "Moving Album" and to a letter Edna has just received from "Little Mary" (Pickford) and another she is writing to Crane Wilbur, on whom both seem to have a

FIGURE 70. Edna Vercoe, Deerfield-Shields High School yearbook photo, 1917. Highland Park Public Library.

crush.[9] That letter and an August 1914 postcard from Edna to Josephine describe the two sisters as decorating their bedroom walls with movie star photos—present-day teenagers make similar choices from an expanded spectrum of stars and post them on both real and virtual walls.[10] Unfortunately, little is known of Edna after her high school years, other than that she never married, remained in Highland Park her entire life, and died in March 1984.

More detective work led me to the ever-widening range of sources on which Edna drew as she gathered material for her scrapbooks. Although nothing seems to have come from the local newspaper, she apparently collected publicity texts and photos from the Highland Park Theater, the only one in town, which had opened in early November 1913.[11] In her letter, "Floss," for instance, mentions that William Pearl, the owner-manager, "has never got the bulletins out" when she walks by the theater in the morning, so she couldn't save Edna from having to make "the trip down in the evening" to pick them up on her own. But Edna's family was well enough off that she could access resources beyond Highland Park. She definitely cut up pages from the *Chicago Tribune,* especially the Sunday editions, cut out an ad for "Pauline's 'Mummy' Puzzle Prize" in the *Chicago Sunday Examiner,* and may have taken some serial synopses from the *Chicago Sunday Herald.* Edna or one of her friends evidently subscribed to *Motion Picture Magazine* as well as *Photoplay,* the source of many clippings for her scrapbooks. She also was surprisingly enterprising: for instance writing to the *Chicago Tribune* asking for specific copies of the June 21 and August 22, 1914, issues.[12] She ordered movie star photos from the Film Portrait Company and movie star postage stamps from Theater Supply Postage Stamps, both of which advertised in the fan magazines.[13] She asked *Motography,* the trade journal with its main office in Chicago, to send her reviews of *The Perils of Pauline.*[14] Along with her friends, she mailed scores of letters to her favorite stars and received notes or even letters in return. Volume I, for instance, includes letters from Francis X. Bushman, Hughie Mack, and Ray Hanford, envelopes from Pearl White and Paul Panzer (*Pauline*'s villain), and a pencil drawing of Panzer on a motorcycle (fig. 71).[15] Volume III has signed photos from George Larkin, Sidney Bracy, Ray Gallagher, and Anna Little as well as a rare two-page letter from Romaine Fielding. Also in the latter volume is a postcard to "Little Lady" Edna from Lila Hayward Chester: responding to the teenage fan's apparent scrapbook efforts, she hopes "your collection will be quite complete shortly."[16] Perhaps most unusual, in August 1914, Edna contacted Universal, requesting specific copies of the company's bulletin, *Universal Weekly,* and those also provided material for her cutting and pasting.[17] In short, she was a good researcher.

The contents of these six scrapbooks offer a clear sense of what attracted Edna to the movies and made her an ardent fan. Only occasionally does she give space to a big feature film—Selig's *The Spoilers,* the French adaptation of *Les Misérables,* and the Italian epic *Cabiria*. That last, according to a ticket stub, she saw at a larger theater in Evanston; the other two, either there or perhaps in downtown Chicago.[18] A few other features and their stars receive scattered attention: in volume I, *Peg O' My Heart* (with Billie Burke) and *The Littlest Rebel* (with Mimi Yvonne); in volume III, *The Last Volunteer* (with Eleanor Woodruff); and in volume V, D.W. Griffith's *Judith of Bethulia* represented in a collage of production photos. The most frequent references are to Mary Pickford's features with Famous Players, but they come in tiny clippings for *Caprice, In the Bishop's Carriage, Tess of Storm Country,* and *Hearts Adrift* as well as tiny photos from *Such a Little Queen* and *The Eagle's Mate.*[19] Interestingly, there are nearly as many references to the star's earlier IMP one-reelers, which Universal was re-releasing in August-September 1914 to exploit Pickford's popularity. Perhaps because Universal supplied many of the films that played at the Highland Park Theater, IMP titles (with Pickford) such as *Mr. Burglar M.D.* and *In the Sultan's Garden* are among the scores that Edna listed, in volume III, as "plays I have seen" or "plays we have seen."

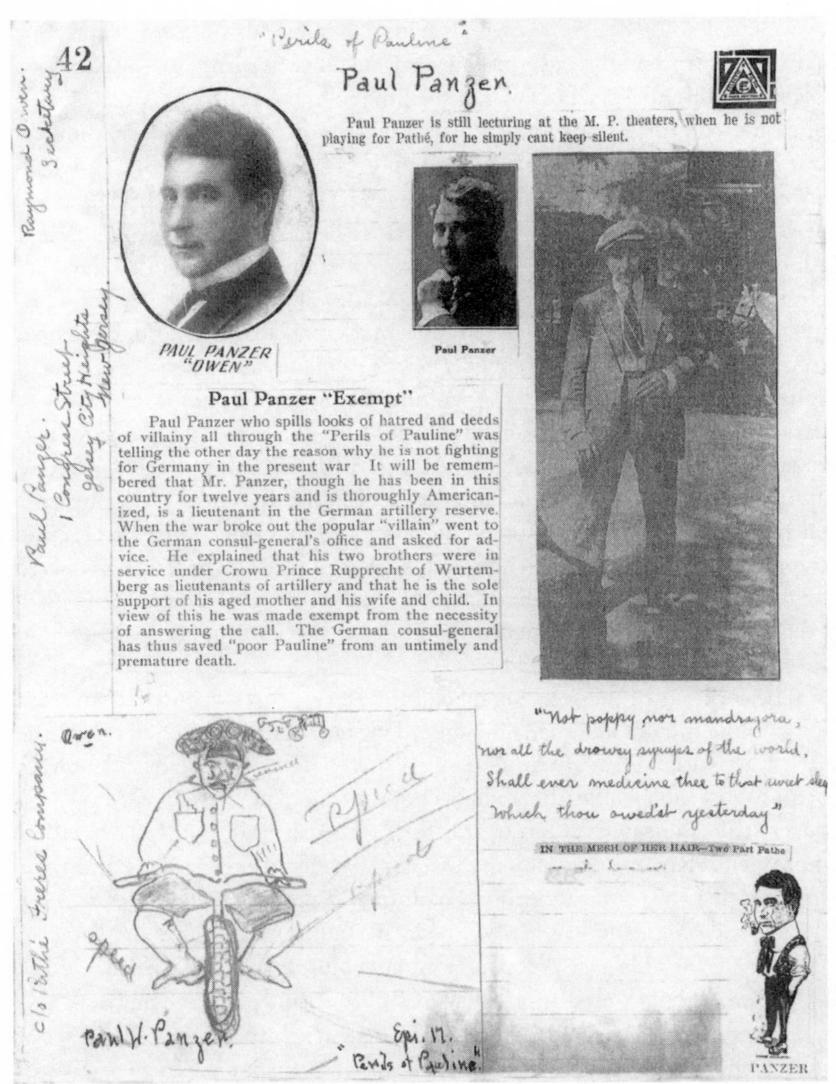

"Perils of Pauline"

42

Paul Panzen.

Paul Panzer is still lecturing at the M. P. theaters, when he is not playing for Pathé, for he simply cant keep silent.

PAUL PANZER
"OWEN"

Paul Panzer

Raymond Owen. Secretary

Paul Panzer. 1 Congress Street Jersey City Heights New Jersey

Paul Panzer "Exempt"

Paul Panzer who spills looks of hatred and deeds of villainy all through the "Perils of Pauline" was telling the other day the reason why he is not fighting for Germany in the present war It will be remembered that Mr. Panzer, though he has been in this country for twelve years and is thoroughly Americanized, is a lieutenant in the German artillery reserve. When the war broke out the popular "villain" went to the German consul-general's office and asked for advice. He explained that his two brothers were in service under Crown Prince Rupprecht of Wurtemberg as lieutenants of artillery and that he is the sole support of his aged mother and his wife and child. In view of this he was made exempt from the necessity of answering the call. The German consul-general has thus saved "poor Pauline" from an untimely and premature death.

Owen.

c/o Pathé Freres Company.

Paul W. Panzer.

Epi. 17.
"Perils of Pauline."

"Not poppy nor mandragora,
nor all the drowsy syrups of the world,
Shall ever medicine thee to that sweet sleep
Which thou owed'st yesterday"

IN THE MESH OF HER HAIR—Two Part Pathe

PANZER

FIGURE 71. Edna Vercoe scrapbook volume I: Paul Panzer. Margaret Herrick Library.

If Edna seemed less interested in feature films, she was nearly obsessed with the serials that enjoyed such popularity in 1914. In volume I, synopses and production photos of Pathé's *The Perils of Pauline* fill the first sixty pages; those of Universal's *Lucille Love* take up another thirty pages. In volume II, similar material on Universal's *The Trey O' Hearts* fills forty-five pages; *The Perils of Pauline* continues for twenty pages; and Thanhouser's *The Million Dollar Mystery* begins to appear in another twenty-five pages. Adopting the principle of seriality for her own purposes, Edna has all four titles run through the next three scrapbooks, while adding Universal's *The Master Key* for twenty pages in volume V and Pathé's *The Exploits of Elaine* for fifty pages in the last scrapbook, volume VI. Not only did she very likely see all of these serials at the Highland Park Theatre,[20] but her first scrapbook coincides almost exactly with a change in that theater's programming. In January 1914, manager Pearl limited vaudeville acts to Saturdays and began promoting serials such as Selig's *The Adventures of Kathlyn* and, in May, "*Lucille Love* Every Friday."[21] In July he dropped vaudeville entirely and instead promoted "*Perils of Pauline* Every Tuesday," continued to run *Lucille Love* on Fridays, and added *The Million Dollar Mystery* on Saturdays.[22] Throughout the rest of the year, Pearl highlighted this double or triple dose of serials in his ads, and the *Highland Park Press* even exploited their popularity by publishing John Fleming Wilson's fictional print version, "The Master Key," every Thursday, beginning on November 26, a day before the film would start its long run at the Highland Park Theatre.[23] In January 1915, the theater introduced *The Exploits of Elaine,* the serial that takes up so many pages in Edna's sixth and last scrapbook;[24] at the same time, however, the theater's programming began to change once more, and features such as *Threads of Destiny* (with Evelyn Nesbit Thaw), *The Daughters of Neptune* (with Annette Kellerman), and finally Paramount films rather than serials now received top billing.[25] That is when Edna abandoned work on her scrapbooks, or at least seemed to do so.

Edna's other obsession, of course, was with movie stars, and it is their photos, line drawings, gossip items, and other ephemera, together with her own marginalia, that fill most pages in all six scrapbooks. The number of stars included is huge and quite diverse, as evidenced initially by the "Contents" she compiled for each volume. Recurring in all of the scrapbooks are pages for Mary Pickford, Francis X. Bushman, Romaine Fielding, and Mary Fuller, with other stars such as Anita Stewart, Alice Joyce, and Florence Lawrence appearing in at least three. In addition, on the ad sheets for the Film Portrait Company in volume I, she underlines the names of twenty players whose photos she likely ordered. And in volume IV, she doubly underlines fifteen of the more than two hundred "Actors and Actresses I Know" (written out in three columns over two and a half pages), and marks twenty-eight others with single underlines. Most of those, as expected, occur frequently in the scrapbooks, but some well-known figures do not—G. M. Anderson, J. Warren Kerrigan, Hughie Mack, Anna Little, Clara Kimball Young, and Hazel Dawn—unlike many largely forgotten that do (Ella Hall, Harry Shumm, Clifford Bruce, Charles Manley). Among those doubly underlined is ten-year-old Joyce Fair, to whom Edna also devotes pages, along with other child actors: Lillian Walker, Matty Roubert, and Mlle. Fromat from *Les Misérables,* the only non-American actor so honored.[26] Apparently comedies did not appeal that much to Edna, as rising star Charlie Chaplin is nowhere to be seen. Her favorites were in the serials she followed so closely. Pearl White and Crane Wilbur, the stars of *The Perils of Pauline,* are especially prominent through all six scrapbooks, often occupy the initial pages, and always are given more than the usual two pages allotted to most others. Yet Grace Cunard and Francis Ford, the stars of *Lucille Love,* initially at least, receive almost as much attention, as do James Cruze, Marguerite Snow, and Florence LaBadie in *The Million Dollar Mystery,* and Cleo Madison and George Larkin in *The Trey O' Hearts.* Not only did Edna collect all kinds of photos and drawings of these and other stars, but she also amassed an immense number of short gossip items from fan magazines and newspapers, particularly from Mae Tinee's "Answers to Movie Fans" in the *Chicago Tribune.* In volume I, she pastes eight "Notes put in the paper" by her little "fan club" of friends and writes that Dody (Faxon) placed a query for E. H. (Ethel Hicks) about Clara Kimball Young. Moreover, she herself penned summary biographies of her favorites: Pearl White, Crane Wilbur, and Mary Fuller. In their fascination with stars, these scrapbooks, in other words, read like one teenage movie fan's attempt to create highly personalized monthly issues of a fan magazine in imitation of those published by the industry.

When Edna began composing her "Moving Picture Pictorial," she was working within a well-established historical tradition. Scrapbooks already had been an important part of middle-class American culture for decades, especially for girls and young women. They were a familiar mode of self-expression or self-narration, Tamar Katriel and Thomas Farrell write, in which the "author" gathered bits and pieces (or scraps) of significance to her everyday life and arranged them in a kind of "memory book" aesthetically organized according to the "rhetoric of display."[27] Jessica Helfand recently described these and other scrapbooks as "the original open-source technology . . . that celebrated visual sampling, culture mixing, and the appropriation and redistribution of existing media."[28] A popular example from the 1870s through the 1890s, according to Ellen Gruber Garvey,[29] was the trade card scrapbook that girls, often guided by instruction kits, made with chromolithographed cards distributed free by manufacturers to promote the brands of their mass-produced commodities—in the hopes, she adds, that the girls might become ardent consumers of those goods. Instead of trade cards, Edna cut up, rearranged, and pasted promotional material provided in one way or another by the new motion picture industry, sometimes for a cost. This leisure-time "work," likewise, served to stimulate the frequent habit of moviegoing that she shared with her girlfriends and to make the pleasures they enjoyed seemingly their own. So what can one say, without attributing too much artistic virtuosity to this teenager's creativity, about the "rhetoric of display" in Edna's scrapbooks and her appropriation and rearrangement of newspaper, magazine, and other ephemera about the movies?

One good example of Edna's compositional choices comes from her fascination with serials. Within each of the first five scrapbooks, she creates internally separate booklets devoted to at least three of her favorites. Each booklet includes synopses of the serial's chapters or episodes, production stills, and star photos. The synopses are usually cut out from a newspaper or magazine (occasionally they are handwritten) and arranged sequentially. She also takes the trouble to create covers for these booklets. In volume III, for instance, the "cover" for *The Perils of Pauline* includes its "author," title, and "publisher" (Pathé's trademark red rooster) taken from three different sources, the first page of a newspaper synopsis, and a rather heavily lined border anchored in all four corners by a logo for the serial's "distributor," Eclectic Films. Another, in volume IV, has a more simple cover design for *Lucille Love,* most notable for its small images of the serial's posters turned toward the background and arranged in a horizontal line below the bold title to give the impression of three-dimensionality, as if one were being positioned at a schematically replicated theater entrance. A third cover, in volume III, for *The Trey O' Hearts,* prints the title in two different typefaces and gives far more attention to the serial's stars, George Larkin and Cleo Madison. Volume IV has a more complicated cover for *The Perils of Pauline.* Although the border is quite similar to the earlier cover's, this one highlights the stars—Pearl White, Crane Wilbur, and Paul Panzer—in a fanlike design of symmetrically arranged photos that emphasizes the men's faces, especially Wilbur's, and in White's case her fashionable costume (fig. 72). The eight very different cut-out texts barely mention the serial's story and instead continue to focus attention on the three "leading stars" as well as the Pathé company and its studios in Jersey City. Finally, volume V has an intriguing cover for *The Trey O' Hearts* that resembles some surviving

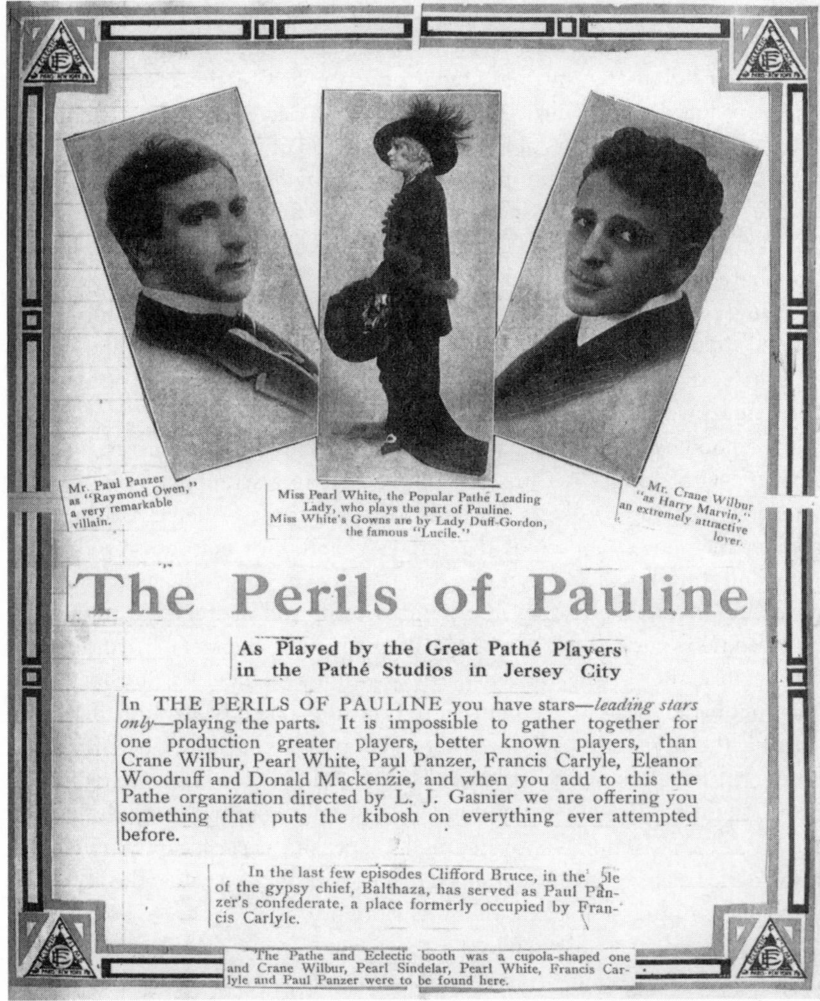

FIGURE 72. Edna Vercoe scrapbook volume IV: *The Perils of Pauline*. Margaret Herrick Library.

illustrated song slides in the way it embeds the serial's stars as small figures within what looks like the magnified petals of a rose.[30]

The scrapbook pages filled with Edna's favorite stars offer an even greater variety of compositional choices. She obviously devoted special attention to Pearl White and Crane Wilbur. A few pages include the two together, from volume I's collage of small photos, drawings, and brief texts to volume V's gendered fan "dreams" of the two, for instance Earl Simonson's doggerel, "To Pearl White / Pauline of the Perils," and the cartoon of a dinner table couple, with the woman gazing fondly at the dream "bubble" of Wilbur's face above her head. Most pages, however, present the stars separately, sometimes in adoring, large close-ups.[31] In volume I, for instance, one page frames a summary biography of Wilbur's career, cobbled together from blocks of text, with a peculiar assortment of images: a caricature drawing of a crane topped by the profile of his head,[32] a fictional will leaving "to my little friend, William Russell, my bottle of eyebrow producer and my guaranteed pompadour raiser" (fig. 73). The overall tone seems a bit tongue in cheek. Another page in volume VI has more flattering images, yet the snippets of text present a bewildering range of comments on the star: from fans' questions about whether or not he is still at Pathé and where he is living to a response to "Kitty C—You think Crane Wilbur the best of them all in spite of his mannerisms? And you love his pompadour and dense growth of eyebrows? How nice!" The pages devoted to White are far less ambiguous. In volume II, she appears solely in images of a woman capable of playing four different roles (one a cross-dressed figure at the wheel of an auto, fig. 74) and then in more disparate images (from a fashion model to an aeroplane pilot), either tagged by brief favorable texts or supported by a thumbnail bio into which one figure seems about to dive. In volume III, one page has diverse images of White surrounding an account of a near accident in filming (she was knocked out while jumping from a cliff into an Adirondack lake) and a brief bio in her own words, while the other can almost read as film frames in which she gazes intently at the viewer and then, in the other, smiles coquettishly.

Edna's interest in arranging an array of star images, with a minimum of text, is also noteworthy in the pages devoted to other female players. In volume I, for instance, are half a dozen images of Mary Fuller, who "love[s] all the girls and women I am called upon to play," recalling the photos of stars' faces registering "emotion" in the "Motion Picture Mail." In volume II, another half-dozen images demonstrate Fuller's versatility in "character studies," from a boyish youth and flower-garlanded girl to a heavily robed figure lifting a classical urn and a sullen mountain woman staring at the camera and clutching a rifle (fig. 75). A later page surrounds a centered, oval-shaped glamour photo of Grace Cunard with four smaller images depicting the different characters she played in *Lucille Love* and *Return of the Twin's Double*—and in the latter film she appeared as both sexes of twins (fig. 76).[33] In that same scrapbook also are two different pages presenting Hazel Dawn, the title of whose new film, "One of Our Girls," may also have implied her inclusion within this fan club of teenagers. While the glamour close-up of

6

Crane Wilbur.

Gallant, Crane Wilbur.

1907—Crane Wilbur caused many a flutter among female hearts as Frank Mason, that handsome protector of the distressed maiden, Lottie Love, in that pretty picture of the working girl's tribulations, "Lottie, the Poor Saleslady," which fairly had them yelling, at the Granby Theatre, Norfolk, Va.

Crane Wilbur

Crane Wilbur in Vaudeville

Crane Wilbur, popular Pathe star and hero of "The Perils of Pauline" series, has just concluded a most successful week's engagement at Dale's 116th Street Theater, New York City, a United Booking Office vaudeville theater. Mr Wilbur signed for a three weeks' engagement through the U. B. O. offices, one week at the aforementioned theater and one each at the Halsey and 5th Ave. Theaters in Brooklyn.

The engagement is a unique one inasmuch as these are regular vaudeville houses, giving two performances a day, whereas Mr. Wilbur appears in the evening only, devoting his days to protecting "Pauline" from further perils in and about the Pathe studios.

INQUIRER: Crane Wilbur is the actor who plays the part of the millionaire's son in Pathe's "The Perils of Pauline."

E. M. K.—I guess your drawing is of Crane Wilbur. Am I not clever?

He was made popular by Flossie C. P.—Crane Wilbur.

ARTHUR J. BUSCH.—The only rules I can give you are those contained in the magazine. A scenario of thirty or forty scenes usually make one reel, and twice that would make two. "With that wonderful frown and that look to bewilder, each one sighs when he comes 'round the incomparable Crane Wilbur." Milton ne'er equaled this, I'm sure. But Helen Beach is a competitor: "Then here's to Crane Wilbur, gloomy, sad and gay. If he weren't in the pictures, I'd surely stay away."

CRANE WILBUR. Pathé Star

CRANE WILBUR

"Say, wh-wh-who is that? Wait, I know him. It's m-m-m (business of trying to think) Oh, yes! It's Crane Wilbur!" The girl who quoted the above to her friend at the outer door of the Strand theater, New York City, last Sunday night, was about the only one of the hundred or more people waiting there who recognized in the dark young man purchasing a ticket at the box office, the Harry Marvin of "The Perils of Pauline" fame. The Mary Pickford "Behind the Scenes" picture was the theater's attraction.

I, Crane Wilbur, do leave to my little friend, William Russell, my bottle of eyebrow producer and my guaranteed pompadour raiser, hoping he will use them as freely as I have.

All Pathé players have been discharged, except Paul Panzer, Crane Wilbur and Pearl White, who will be paid for each piece they do.

Here's to Pearl White, so dainty and slight;
To Crane Wilbur, so handsome and brave;
To Sweet Alice Joyce, who is every one's choice—
Oh, long may her fame-banner wave!

H. E.: Crane Wilbur has been an actor in the movies for four years. Some of his late plays are "The Ghost," "The Couple Next Door," "Uncle John to the Rescue," and "Unmasked." Pearl White is not the mummy in "The Perils of Pauline."

FIGURE 73. Edna Vercoe scrapbook volume I: Crane Wilbur. Margaret Herrick Library.

Dawn's face dominates one page, eight different images highlighting her costumes and hairstyles in her recent stage success, *The Pink Lady,* fill the other. Finally, in volume V, eight cutouts of Viola Dana, whose Broadway success in *The Poor Little Rich Girl* led her to the movies, combine her off-screen figure with her on-screen appearances in Edison's *The Blind Fiddler.*

FIGURE 74. Edna Vercoe scrapbook volume II: Pearl White. Margaret Herrick Library.

What is striking about all of these displays is the strong sense that young women such as these have an unusual ability to play a great variety of roles, and sometimes even those of cross-dressed, gender-bending figures.

It would be rash to read too much into this one surviving set of scrapbooks from the mid-1910s. Yet the included postcards and letter suggest that, if

FIGURE 75. Edna Vercoe scrapbook volume II: Mary Fuller. Margaret Herrick Library.

Edna's circle of friends is in any way representative, many middle-class teenage girls were engaged in making movie fan scrapbooks and decorating their bedroom walls with star photos. If indeed other teenagers shared Edna's obsessions, as Leslie Midkiff DeBauche's research on slightly later high school "memory books" strongly suggests,[34] her scrapbooks offer an important reason why serials were so popular at the time and why

FIGURE 76. Edna Vercoe scrapbook volume II: Grace Cunard. Margaret Herrick Library.

stars already had become the movies' main attraction. In their playful range of agency, movie stars—and serial queens, for Edna, in particular—may well have served teenage girls as role models of self-fashioning as they explored their own sense of identity.[35] Finally, these scrapbooks demonstrate that newspaper and magazine ephemera arguably played a crucial role in the emergence of movie fan culture in the 1910s, and the "imagined community" of American film culture more generally. As an unusually motivated movie fan, Edna evidenced unusual skill in transforming "scraps," bits and pieces of everyday experience, into her own creative collaged displays. Ranging across a broad landscape of print material (from Chicago newspapers to fan magazines and even industry bulletins), she gathered snipped-out items or ingredients of special interest (particularly those about stars) and composed each volume not only following the "recipes" of earlier girls' scrapbooks, but also sometimes those of newspaper and fan magazine pages, and frequently personalized her pages with handwritten marginalia, from summary star profiles to long lists of the actors and actresses and films she had seen and "knew." In short, as a labor of love, she created what now reads as a fascinating record of her moviegoing experiences, a kind of "Menus for Movieland" compendium of her own that served as sustenance for the desires and tastes of a very localized community: that of her teenage movie fan friends.

This chapter, however, has to close with a puzzle. Did Edna Vercoe abandon her scrapbooks because her local theater was turning to feature films, or was that coincidence? And when precisely did she stop working on the last scrapbook, dated January 1915? One of its pages includes images of Ruth Roland in the Pathé serial *Who Pays?*, which was released in early May 1915 and played that summer at the Highland Park Theatre.[36] Was she collecting bits and pieces through 1915 and even into 1916, perhaps planning to continue her "memory books"? If she did, what happened to those additional volumes? Or did someone who inherited the scrapbooks tuck those loose "miscellaneous materials" into one or more surviving volumes? Along with postcards from Ella Hall and Edna Maison in volume VI, that envelope from Pearl White in volume I is dated February 1915. Similarly, one of Mary Pickford's pages in volume IV contains items referring to her Famous Players features released in the summer and fall of 1915. Among the loose clippings linked to the last two scrapbooks are at least three that can be identified as much later than the summer of 1915. One is William M. Henry's four-page article on Grace Cunard and Francis Ford, "Her Grace and Francis I," from the April 1916 issue of *Photoplay*. Another is a photo of Pickford sitting at a sewing machine, whose reverse side indicates that it came from *Film Fun* no. 327, dated June 1916. The third is an enchanting color watercolor portrait of Pickford that graced the November 1915 cover of *Photoplay*. Pickford's beguiling gaze accentuates the mystery.

DOCUMENT

"TODAY'S BEST MOVING PICTURE STORY," *CHICAGO TRIBUNE*, FEBRUARY 9, 1914

To more than a half million Chicagoans moving picture plays present the drama of daily life. A newspaper man has been assigned to THE TRIBUNE to view the films in advance of their release and to write for Tribune readers a daily short story of what he considers the best film to be shown each day. The story here presented will be shown in moving pictures in Chicago for the first time today. If the story interests you so that you want to see it in the pictures, put it in your scrap book. Then when it comes to your neighborhood you will have it.

DOCUMENT

POST CARD TO MISS JOSEPHINE FAXON, C/O ELNORE MASSON, N. SHERIDAN RD., WAUKEGAN, ILL., 5 AUGUST 1914

Dear Dody,

Three pictures of Hugo and 3 of Grace Cunard came today. Their not so good of Grace of pipins of Hugo. Connie put them over her bed. Course you know? We're going down now to see the pictures of Pauline tonight. We each got a photo from Marc McDermott. Hope you are having a good time and are finding packs of papers.

Edward

Afterword

> The writing of history, which does indeed come to conclusions and reach ends . . . actually moves forward through the implicit understanding that *things are not over,* that the story isn't finished, can't ever be completed.
>
> CAROLYN STEEDMAN, *Dust* (2002)

This book argues that, from 1913 to 1916, newspapers were instrumental in establishing and sustaining an increasingly ravenous popular American film culture. The menus they offered whetted movie fans' appetites through recurring weekend pages and sections as well as daily gossip columns and film reviews. If the industry gradually sought to assert a measure of control over what went into those menus through free publicity materials as well as direct advertising and, consequently, to construct a more or less homogeneous film culture, exhibitors and newspaper writers sometimes crafted those menu items to appeal to local or regional interests and tastes and, thus, support a film culture that could be relatively heterogeneous. Many newspaper writers and editors engaged in that crafting were young professional women—from Gertrude Price, Mae Tinee, Kitty Kelly, and Louella Parsons to Mary Anne Smith, Mary Leffler, Daisy Dean, Dorothy Day, and The Film Girl—and, given their rhetorical address, perhaps most of their readers also were women, among them young female movie fans such as Edna Vercoe and her teenage girlfriends. It was those writers who, even in the titles of their columns—referencing "Movie Land" and "Film Land"—did so much to create the imaginary discursive space of work and play (in parallel to Universal City) that would soon morph into an equally magical space, both here and nowhere, called Hollywood.

Rather than recapitulate the methodology and arguments developed in this book, which I trust already are laid out clearly and concisely in the prologue and introduction, let me explore, however briefly, several sets of questions that could encourage further research in at least three areas marking this stunningly transformative period of American cinema history.

Despite my best efforts, together with those of colleagues, to secure an extensive database of newspaper writing on the movies in the mid-1910s, that database certainly can be expanded greatly. How many columns, pages, and even supplements in other newspapers remain unexamined, not only in digital form at a growing number of websites but also on microfilm in public libraries and state historical society libraries? Do the newspaper columns, pages, and supplements described and analyzed in this book continue with little change in format and/or content, expand in certain ways, contract, or even disappear in the late 1910s and early 1920s?[1] And if so, how can the differences be explained? What further biographical information could be germane to knowing the backgrounds and future trajectories of all the newspaper professionals, especially women, writing about the movies in the mid- to late 1910s? And what was the state of newspaper film reviewing in the 1920s, given that, on the Advisory Council of the New York Film Arts Guild in 1926, seventeen of its twenty members were writers associated with newspapers, and seven of those were women, all but two from the Midwest?[2]

There also is much more to research in order to better understand the economic, political, social, and cultural context within which this newspaper writing flourished. Most generally, from a closer look at this and any extended database, how could a more thorough study of the patterns of movie circulation—what films and stars appeared where and when, in different regions of the country, in different cities and towns, and within the latter's different neighborhoods—expand and perhaps complicate this analysis of newspaper writers and their targeted readers/moviegoers? More specifically, what impact did the Great War have on the writers of those movie columns, pages, and supplements, before and after the United States eventually intervened in April 1917? To what degree was the newspaper writing dependent on the booming business of trade journals and fan magazines? Similarly, to what degree were the newspaper writers in league with publicity agents, scenario departments, and other branches of the motion picture industry? How did the newspaper writers position themselves in relation to city, state, and even national efforts to control motion picture distribution and exhibition through censorship? What else can this newspaper writing reveal about the relations between the movies and high culture (theater, opera, painting, music) and/or popular culture (pulp fiction, short stories, popular novels)? In what ways are the explicit and implicit principles that undergird this newspaper film criticism, along with those evidenced in the trade press, developed and extended in what we now accept as the earliest texts of film theory and criticism in the United States, France, and elsewhere?

Finally, there is the arduous task of puzzling out who went to the movies, where, when, how often, and what they thought and felt about their moviegoing experiences. Would a systematic analysis of various "Answers to Fans" columns in the newspapers reveal more or less distinct patterns of what attracted fans to the movies? Could movie scrapbooks other than Vercoe's survive somewhere in private or public collections, and might they complement hers or offer different insights about fans' fascinations? Could marginalia of one kind or another in the period's high school "memory books"[3] also offer evidence of student interests and tastes, especially those of teenage girls? Are there even diaries still extant that could hold jottings about the films or stars that one or more fans favored? And how would any of those research findings compare with the more familiar surveys that were organized by social reform groups and published in the trade press and special bulletins?

Whatever advances may come from this and other research in the future, let these words of the historian Arlette Farge be our motto: "We write history not just to tell it, but to anchor a departed past to our words and bring about an 'exchange among the living.'"[4]

APPENDIX

U.S. Newspapers

The following newspapers, arranged under city and town headings, contain motion picture pages, columns, and other materials that have been the subject of analysis in this book. Circulation figures come from the *Newspaper Annual and Directory* (Philadelphia: N.W. Ayer & Son, 1914) and *The Editor and Publisher and Journalist*, April 3, 1915, 880–92.[1] City population figures come from the *Thirteenth Census of the United States Taken in the Year 1910* (Washington, DC: Government Printing Office, 1913).

NEW YORK CITY, POP. 4,770,000

New York American, 277,000
New York Sunday American, 738,230
New York Herald, 109,200
New York Evening Mail, 157,050
New York Evening Tribune, 64,410
New York Times, 259,675
New York World, 391,950

CHICAGO, POP. 2,200,000

Chicago American, 380,080
Chicago Evening News, 350,550
Chicago Examiner, 240,000
Chicago Sunday Examiner, 530,000
Chicago Herald, 178,750
Chicago Sunday Herald, 219,500

Chicago Tribune, 303,315
Chicago Sunday Tribune, 459,725

PHILADELPHIA, POP. 1,550,000

Philadelphia Evening Ledger, 61,225
Philadelphia Sunday Ledger, 101,000
Philadelphia Times, 45,000

ST. LOUIS, POP. 690,000

St. Louis Morning Globe-Democrat, 116,975
St. Louis Sunday Globe-Democrat, 159,555
St. Louis Evening Post-Dispatch, 171,100
St. Louis Sunday Post-Dispatch, 304,520
St. Louis Morning Republic, 109,100

CLEVELAND, POP. 560,000

Cleveland Leader, 65,600
Cleveland Sunday Leader, 78,640
Cleveland Plain Dealer, 112,160
Cleveland Sunday Plain Dealer, 143,095
Cleveland Evening Press, 171,100

BALTIMORE, POP. 560,000

Baltimore Sunday News, 56,900
Baltimore Morning Sun, 92,325
Baltimore Sunday Sun, 81,945

PITTSBURGH, POP. 535,000

Pittsburgh Sunday Dispatch, 75,000
Pittsburgh Sunday Leader, 52,500
Pittsburg Sunday Press, 86,050

DETROIT, POP. 465,750

Detroit Free Press, 69,430
Detroit Sunday Free Press, 97,740

Detroit Evening News, 150,000
Detroit Tribune, 41,000
Detroit Sunday Tribune, 110,000

BUFFALO, POP. 425,000

Buffalo Courier, 52,150
Buffalo Sunday Courier, 88,620
Buffalo Evening News, 90,000
Buffalo Evening Times, 54,000
Buffalo Sunday Times, 52,000

SAN FRANCISCO, POP. 417,000

San Francisco Bulletin, 96,000
San Francisco Chronicle, 66,090
San Francisco Examiner, 107,120

MILWAUKEE, POP. 375,000

Milwaukee Evening Journal, 73,405
Milwaukee Sentinel, 45,935
Milwaukee Sunday Sentinel, 47,500

NEW ORLEANS, POP. 340,000

New Orleans Item, 57,055
New Orleans Picayune, 55,675
New Orleans Sunday Picayune, 69,625

WASHINGTON, DC, POP. 330,000

Washington Herald, 30,335
Washington Sunday Post, 45,000
Washington Star, 65,955
Washington Evening Times, 49,570

LOS ANGELES, POP. 320,000

Los Angeles Morning Examiner, 60,700
Los Angeles Sunday Examiner, 123,265

Los Angeles Evening Herald, 90,410
Los Angeles Evening Record, 42,630
Los Angeles Sunday Times, 86,150

MINNEAPOLIS, POP. 300,000

Minneapolis Evening Journal, 83,780
Minneapolis Morning Tribune, 98,345
Minneapolis Sunday Tribune, 149,310

KANSAS CITY, POP. 248,000

Kansas City Evening Star, 358,000
Kansas City Sunday Star, 174,135

SEATTLE, POP. 237,000

Seattle Times, 66,040
Seattle Sunday Times, 85,830

INDIANAPOLIS, POP. 234,000

Indianapolis Evening News, 107,065
Indianapolis Morning Star, 76,340
Indianapolis Sunday Star, 76,815

ST. PAUL, POP. 214,745

St. Paul Evening News, 70,010

PORTLAND (OREGON), POP. 207,000

Morning Oregonian, 55,035
Sunday Oregonian, 70,500

TOLEDO, POP. 170,000

Toledo Evening Blade, 42,175
Toledo Evening News-Bee, 69,865
Toledo Times, 19,000

ATLANTA, POP. 155,000

Atlanta Morning Constitution, 41,405
Atlanta Sunday Constitution, 44,100

OAKLAND, POP. 150,000

Oakland Evening Tribune, 46,030
Oakland Sunday Tribune, 39,000

SYRACUSE (NEW YORK), POP. 140,000

Syracuse Herald, 35,055
Syracuse Sunday Herald, 51,620

BIRMINGHAM (ALABAMA), POP. 133,000

Birmingham Age-Herald, 19,000
Birmingham Evening News, 34,050

OMAHA, POP. 125,000

Omaha World-Herald, 55,600
Omaha Sunday World-Herald, 41,000

GRAND RAPIDS, 112,000

Grand Rapids Evening Press, 63,700

SAN ANTONIO, POP. 100,000

San Antonio Light, 19,430

TRENTON (NEW JERSEY), 96,815

Trenton Times, 24,885

SALT LAKE CITY, POP. 92,775

Salt Lake Sunday Tribune, 28,010

DALLAS, POP. 92,000

Dallas Evening News, 49,000

DES MOINES, POP. 90,000

Des Moines Evening News, 40,375
Des Moines Register and Leader, 53,745
Des Moines Sunday Register and Leader, 38,895
Des Moines Evening Tribune, 27,825

DAYTON (OHIO), POP. 85,000

Dayton News, 30,470

DULUTH (MINNESOTA), POP. 78,500

Duluth Evening Herald, 28,015
Duluth News Tribune, 21,500

FORT WORTH, POP. 75,000

Fort Worth Star-Telegram, 25,480

FORT WAYNE (INDIANA), POP. 65,000

Fort Wayne Journal-Gazette, 25,145

AUGUSTA (GEORGIA), POP. 41,000

Augusta Sunday Chronicle, 9,125

MACON (GEORGIA), POP. 40,665

Macon News, 13,170

RACINE (WISCONSIN), POP. 38,000

Racine Journal-News, 6,455

HAMILTON (OHIO), POP. 35,000

Hamilton Journal, 6,615

CEDAR RAPIDS (IOWA), POP. 32,800

Cedar Rapids Republican, 14,770

LA CROSSE (WISCONSIN), POP. 30,500

La Crosse Tribune, 7,530

LIMA (OHIO), POP. 30,500

Lima News, 8,650

WATERLOO (IOWA), POP. 26,700

Waterloo Courier, 8,920
Waterloo Reporter, 7,845

SHEBOYGAN (WISCONSIN), 26,400

Sheboygan Journal, 3,500

MUSKOGEE (OKLAHOMA), POP. 25,275

Muskogee Times-Democrat, 10,876

OGDEN (UTAH), POP. 25,600

Ogden Standard, 3,925

COLUMBUS (GEORGIA), POP. 20,550

Columbus Morning Enquirer, 6,650

HUTCHINSON (KANSAS), POP. 16,360

Hutchinson Gazette, 7,240
Hutchinson News, 8,000

JANESVILLE (WISCONSIN), POP. 14,000

Janesville Evening Gazette, 5,780

BAKERSFIELD (CALIFORNIA), POP. 12,700

Bakersfield Californian, 5,000

GRAND FORKS (NORTH DAKOTA), POP. 12,500

Grand Forks Herald, 19,240

BOISE (IDAHO), POP. 17,360

Idaho Statesman, 22,000

RENO, POP. 10,865

Reno Evening Gazette, 3,500

ANACONDA (MONTANA), POP. 10,135

Anaconda Standard, 9,860

BISMARCK (NORTH DAKOTA), POP. 5,445

Bismarck Tribune, 6,000

Newspaper Abbreviations

For the purposes of space, the following acronyms are used for frequently cited sources from the period.

TRADE JOURNALS

EP	*Editor and Publisher,* then *Editor & Publisher and Journalist*
KK	*Kalem Kalendar*
M	*Motography*
MPM	*Motion Picture Magazine*
MPN	*Motion Picture News*
MPW	*Moving Picture World*
NYMT	*New York Morning Telegraph*
PM	*Photoplay Magazine*
UW	*Universal Weekly*

NEWSPAPERS

ALT	*Albert Lea Tribune*
AtC	*Atlanta Constitution*
AuC	*Augusta Chronicle*
AS	*Anaconda Standard*
BAH	*Birmingham Age-Herald*
BuC	*Buffalo Courier*
BE	*Buffalo Enquirer*
BN	*Baltimore News*
BST	*Buffalo Sunday Times*

CE	*Chicago Examiner*
CH	*Chicago Herald*
CL	*Cleveland Leader*
CN	*Chicago News*
CND	*Canton News-Democrat*
CPD	*Cleveland Plain Dealer*
CR	*Canton Repository*
CRH	*Chicago Record-Herald*
CRR	*Cedar Rapids Republican*
CSH	*Chicago Sunday Herald*
CSL	*Cleveland Sunday Leader*
CSPD	*Cleveland Sunday Plain Dealer*
CST	*Chicago Sunday Tribune*
CT	*Chicago Tribune*
DaN	*Dallas Morning News*
DFP	*Detroit Free Press*
DMN	*Des Moines News*
DMRL	*Des Moines Register and Leader*
DMT	*Des Moines Tribune*
DeN	*Detroit News*
DeNT	*Detroit News-Tribune*
DuNT	*Duluth News-Tribune*
FWJG	*Fort Wayne Journal-Gazette*
FWST	*Fort Worth Star-Telegram*
HN	*Hutchinson News*
HPP	*Highland Park Press*
JG	*Janesville Gazette*
KCS	*Kansas City Star*
LH	*Los Angeles Herald*
LCT	*La Crosse Tribune*
LN	*Lima News*
MO	*Morning Oregonian*
MST	*Minneapolis Sunday Tribune*
MT	*Minneapolis Tribune*
NOI	*New Orleans Item*
NOSI	*New Orleans Sunday Item*
NOTP	*New Orleans Times-Picayune*

NYEM	*New York Evening Mail*
NYT	*New York Tribune*
OS	*Ogden Standard*
OT	*Oakland Tribune*
OWH	*Omaha World-Herald*
PD	*Pittsburgh Dispatch*
PEL	*Philadelphia Evening Ledger*
PL	*Pittsburgh Leader*
PP	*Pittsburg Press*
RR	*Rockford Republic*
SAL	*San Antonio Light*
SFB	*San Francisco Bulletin*
SH	*Syracuse Herald*
SLGD	*St. Louis Globe-Democrat*
SLSGD	*St. Louis Sunday Globe-Democrat*
SLT	*Salt Lake Tribune*
SO	*Sunday Oregonian*
SPN	*St. Paul News*
SST	*Seattle Sunday Times*
ST	*Seattle Times*
TB	*Toledo Blade*
TNB	*Toledo News-Bee*
TT	*Toledo Times*
WH	*Washington Herald*
WR	*Waterloo Reporter*
WT	*Washington Times*

Notes

PROLOGUE

1. Richard Abel, *Americanizing the Movies and "Movie-Mad" Audiences, 1910–1914* (Berkeley: University of California Press, 2006), 215–26.

2. One claim came from "statistics . . . compiled by the Harriman National Bank of New York City." See "Press, Press Representative and the Picture—XVIII," *MPN* (February 12, 1916): 823.

3. Yvonne Spielmann, "History and Theory of Intermedia in Visual Culture," and Ursula Bertram, "What Is Intermedia?" in Hans Breder and Klaus-Peter Busse, eds., *Intermedia: Enacting the Liminal* (Dortmund, Germany: DortmundSchriften zur Kunst, 2005): 132 and 271, respectively. See also Dick Higgins, "Intermedia," *Leonardo* 34, no. 1 (2001): 49–54; and Ken Friedman, "Intermedia: Four Histories, Three Directions, Two Futures," in Breder and Busse, eds., *Intermedia*, 54.

4. Those regions, I argued, were crucial to the emergence of motion picture theaters because of the population concentrations in their urban centers and the extensive railway system linking them, and also because they were marked by differences in settlement history, ethnic immigration, and socioeconomic constituencies.

5. See certain key essays from the Chicago School of Sociology: Robert E. Park, "The Natural History of the Newspaper," *American Journal of Sociology* 29 (1923): 273–89; and Ernest W. Burgess, "The Growth of the City," in R.E. Park, E.W. Burgess, and R.D. MacKenzie, eds., *The City* (Chicago: University of Chicago Press, 1925), 47–62. For how this concept of daily newspapers' function can be applied to early cinema, see Paul S. Moore, "Everybody's Going: City Newspapers and the Early Mass Market for Movies," *City & Community* 4, no. 4 (December 2005): 339–57; Paul S. Moore, *Now Playing: Early Moviegoing and the Regulation of Fun* (Albany, NY: SUNY Press, 2008), 158–63; and Paul S. Moore, "Subscribing to Publicity: Syndicated Newspaper Features for Moviegoing in North America, 1911–1915," *Early Popular Visual Culture* 12, no. 2 (May 2014): 260–73.

6. Charles Taylor, "Modernity and Difference," in Paul Gilroy, Lawrence Grossberg, and Angela McRobbie, eds., *Without Guarantees: In Honour of Stuart Hall* (New York: Verso, 2000); and Charles Taylor, "Two Theories of Modernity," in Dilip P. Gaonkar, ed., *Alternative Modernities* (Durham, NC: Duke University Press, 2001). See also Dilip P. Gaonkar, "Toward New Imaginaries: An Introduction," *Public Culture* 14, no. 1 (2002): 10.

7. John Nerone and Kevin G. Barnhurst, "News form and the media environment: a network of represented relationships," *Media, Culture & Society* 25 (2003): 112, 121; and Benedict Anderson, *Imagined Communities: Reflections on the Origin and Spread of Nationalism*, 2nd ed. (London: Verso, 1991). At the time, John Baker Opdycke made the extravagant claim that the newspaper "is a school in and of itself. It instructs, not only the young, but the adult as well" in *News, Ads, and Sales: The Use of English for Commercial Purposes* (New York: Macmillan, 1914), 3.

8. With most others, I assume that newspapers published in languages other than English (aimed at ethnic immigrant communities) rarely included material concerned with motion pictures in these years—hence my exclusive focus on English-language newspapers. See, for instance, Judith Thissen's discovery of few references to early motion pictures in Yiddish newspapers in New York: "Jewish Immigrant Audiences in New York City, 1905–1914," in Melvyn Stokes and Richard Maltby, eds., *American Movie Audiences: From the Turn of the Century to the Early Sound Era* (London: BFI, 1999), 15–28. For exceptions, see Giorgio Bertellini, *Italy in Early American Cinema: Race, Landscape, and the Picturesque* (Bloomington: Indiana University Press, 2009), 252–53; Colin Gunckel, *Mexico on Main Street: Transnational Film Culture in Los Angeles before World War II* (New Brunswick, NJ: Rutgers University Press, 2015); Colin Gunckel, "'The War of Accents': Spanish Language Hollywood Films in Mexican Los Angeles," *Film History* 20, no. 3 (2008): 325–43; and Laura Isabel Serna, *Making Cinelandia: American Films and Mexican Film Culture Before the Golden Age* (Durham, NC: Duke University Press, 2014).

9. The term comes from Dilip P. Gaonkar and Elizabeth A. Povinelli, "Technologies of Public Forms: Circulation, Transfiguration, Recognition," *Public Culture* 15, no. 3 (2003): 389.

10. Admittedly, I have paid less attention to African American newspapers and journalists, which are closely analyzed in the first chapter of Anna Everett, *Returning the Gaze: A Genealogy of Black Film Criticism, 1901–1949* (Durham, NC: Duke University Press, 2001), 12–58. See also Mary Carbine, "'The Finest Outside the Loop': Motion Picture Exhibition in Chicago's Black Metropolis, 1905–1928," *camera obscura* 23 (1990): 9–41; and Jacqueline Najuma Stewart, *Migrating to the Movies: Cinema and Black Urban Modernity* (Berkeley: University of California Press, 2005).

11. Vachel Lindsay, *The Art of the Moving Picture* (New York: Macmillan, 1915); and Hugo Münsterberg, *The Photoplay: A Psychological Study* (New York: Appleton, 1916), reprinted as *The Film: A Psychological Study* (New

York: Dover, 1970). Lindsay's book is of particular interest because he claims that much of it "is proposed as a basis for photoplay criticism in America" (vii).

12. For studies of academic film culture's development, see Dana Polan, *Scenes of Instruction: The Beginnings of the U.S. Study of Film* (Berkeley: University of California Press, 2007); and Peter Decherney, *Hollywood and the Culture Elite: How the Movies Became American* (New York: Columbia University Press, 2005).

13. Charles Johanningsmeier, "The Devil, Capitalism, and Frank Norris: Defining the 'Reading Field' for Sunday Newspaper Fiction, 1870–1910," *American Periodicals* 14, no. 1 (2004): 93.

14. The 1910 census distinguished two categories of "whiteness": "native white" and "foreign-born white." See for instance "Color or Race, Nativity, and Parentage," *Thirteenth Census of the United States* (Washington, DC: Government Printing Office, 1913), 83. Prior studies usually describe nickelodeon audiences as largely comprised of women and children, immigrant and/or working class, but also inclusive of the non-immigrant middle class. See Kathy Peiss, *Cheap Amusements: Working Women and Leisure in Turn-of-the-Century New York* (Philadelphia: Temple University Press, 1986); Lauren Rabinovitz, *For the Love of Pleasure: Women, Movies, and Culture in Turn-of-the-Century Chicago* (New Brunswick: Rutgers University Press, 1998); Nan Enstad, *Ladies of Labor, Girls of Adventure: Working Women, Popular Culture, and Labor Politics at the Turn of the Twentieth Century* (New York: Columbia University Press, 1999); Richard Abel, *The Red Rooster Scare: Making Cinema American, 1900–1910* (Berkeley: University of California Press, 1999); Shelley Stamp, *Movie-Struck Girls: Women and Motion Picture Culture After the Nickelodeon* (Princeton, NJ: Princeton University Press, 2000); and Richard Abel, *Americanizing the Movies*, 89–95.

15. Mark Garrett Cooper, *Universal Women: Filmmaking and Institutional Change in Early Hollywood* (Urbana: University of Illinois Press, 2010); and Hilary Hallett, *Go West Young Women!: The Rise of Early Hollywood* (Berkeley: University of California Press, 2013). See also Shelley Stamp, *Movie-Struck Girls*. For further information on women working in the industry in the 1910s, see the Women Film Pioneers Project, wfpp.cdrs.columbia.edu/pioneer/ccp/.

16. Linda Nochlin, "Foreword: Representing the New Woman—Complexity and Contradiction," in Elizabeth Otto and Vanessa Rocco, eds., *The New Woman International: Representations in Photography and Films from the 1870s Through the 1960s* (Ann Arbor: University of Michigan Press, 2011), viii-ix.

17. Benjamin Lee and Edward LiPuma, "Cultures of Circulation: The Imaginations of Modernity," *Public Culture* 14, no. 1 (2002): 191–213.

INTRODUCTION

1. "Photo-Plays and Players," *CSL*, December 3, 1911, S.5.

2. "News of the Photoplays and Photoplayers," *OS*, February 22, 1913, 2; "News of the Photoplays and Photoplayers," *Hamilton Journal*, March 1, 1913,

4; "Motion Picture News," *FWJG*, March 9, 1913, 10; "News of the Photoplays and Photoplayers," *SAL*, March 23, 1913, 34.

3. "Right Off the Reel," *CST*, March 15, 1914, 5.3.

4. David Hochfelder, *The Telegraph in America, 1832–1920* (Baltimore: Johns Hopkins University Press, 2012), 40.

5. For an early history of the convergence between the telegraph and the railroads, see Alvin F. Harlow, *Old Wires and New Waves: A History of Telegraphy, Telephone, and Wireless* (New York: Appleton-Century, 1936).

6. James W. Carey, "Technology and Ideology: The Case of the Telegraph," *Communication as Culture: Essays on Media and Society*, rev. ed. (London: Routledge, 2009), 155. See also Menahem Blondheim, *News Over the Wires: The Telegraph and the Flow of Public Information in America, 1844–1897* (Cambridge, MA: Harvard University Press, 1994).

7. James W. Carey, "Technology and Ideology," 156.

8. Alfred McClung Lee, *The Daily Newspaper in America: The Evolution of a Social Instrument* (New York: Macmillan, 1947), 67.

9. David Hochfelder, *The Telegraph in America*, 86.

10. Benedict Anderson, *Imagined Communities: Reflections on the Origin and Spread of Nationalism*, 2nd ed. (London: Verso, 1991); and Michael Warner, *Publics and Counterpublics* (New York: Zone, 2005).

11. Guy S. Osborn, "Why Newspapers?" *EP*, May 6, 1911, 17.

12. Robert E. Park, "The Natural History of the Newspaper," *American Journal of Sociology* 29 (1923), summarized by Paul S. Moore in *Now Playing: Early Moviegoing and the Regulation of Fun* (Albany, NY: SUNY Press, 2008), 159.

13. Kevin G. Barnhurst and John Nerone, *The Form of News: A History* (New York: Guilford Press, 2001), 2.

14. Richard L. Kaplan, *Politics and the American Press: The Rise of Objectivity, 1865–1920* (Cambridge, England: Cambridge University Press, 2002), 125.

15. Paul S. Moore, "Advance Publicity for the Vitascope and the Mass Address of Cinema's Reading Public," in André Gaudreault. Nicolas Dulac, and Santiago Hidalgo, eds., *A Companion to Early Cinema* (Chichester, England: Wiley-Blackwell, 2012), 383–84.

16. Richard A. Schwartzlose, *The Nation's Newsbrokers, vol. 2: The Rush to Institution, from 1865 to 1920* (Evanston, IL: Northwestern University Press, 1990).

17. Alice Fahs, *Out on Assignment: Newspaper Women and the Making of Modern Public Space* (Chapel Hill: University of North Carolina Press, 2011), 36.

18. David Hochfelder, *The Telegraph in America*, 86, 160–61; and Roland Marchand, *Creating the Corporate Soul* (Berkeley: University of California Press, 1998), 48. In 1913–14, the threat of antitrust efforts forced AT&T to relinquish its control, but by then Western Union had a "revitalized organization and a much needed modernization program." David Hochfelder, *The Telegraph in America*, 163.

19. For information on E.W. Scripps, his newspaper chains, and the United Press Association, see Roy W. Howard, "The United Press Association," *EP*, April 26, 1913, 98; Elmo Scott Watson, *A History of Newspaper Syndicates in the United States, 1865–1935* (Chicago: Elmo Scott Watson, 1936); Alfred McClung Lee, *The Daily Newspaper in America;* Richard A. Schwartzlose, *The Nation's Newsbrokers, vol. 2;* and Gerald Baldasty, *E. W. Scripps and the Business of Newspapers* (Urbana: University of Illinois Press, 1999).

20. By 1900, evening newspapers outnumbered morning newspapers by a factor of three to one. Alfred McClung Lee, *The Daily Newspaper in America,* 64–67; and Gunther Barth, *City People: The Rise of the Modern City in Nineteenth-Century America* (New York: Oxford University Press, 1980), 79. See also the United Press ad, *EP*, April 29, 1911, 35. Scripps's wire service, by 1912, could offer ten to twelve thousand words per day (doubled on Saturdays, for the Sunday papers) to several hundred clients and a "pony service" of one to two thousand words daily for a larger number of small-town subscribers. Richard A. Schwartzlose, *The Nation's Newsbrokers, vol. 2,* 219–20.

21. Ibid., 219.

22. The *Chicago Day Book* consisted of thirty-two book-size pages, ran from November 1911 to July 1917, and had a circulation of twenty to thirty thousand. Duane C.S. Stolzfus, *Freedom from Advertising: E. W. Scripps's Chicago Experiment* (Urbana: University of Illinois Press, 2007), 3–4. See also Alfred McClung Lee, *The Daily Newspaper in America,* 188–89.

23. Elmo Scott Watson, *A History of Newspaper Syndicates in the United States, 1865–1935,* 55–56; Alfred McClung Lee, *The Daily Newspaper in America,* 539; and Richard A. Schwartzlose, *The Nation's Newsbrokers, vol. 2,* 229.

24. Elmo Scott Watson, *A History of Newspaper Syndicates in the United States, 1865–1935,* 57–58, 61; Alfred McClung Lee, *The Daily Newspaper in America,* 404, 594.

25. Richard A. Schwartzlose, *The Nation's Newsbrokers, vol. 2,* 237.

26. "Why Newspapers?" *EP*, May 6, 1911, 17.

27. Alfred McClung Lee, *The Daily Newspaper in America,* 68, 397. On February 7, 1909, a *Chicago Sunday Tribune* special edition honoring Abraham Lincoln ran 194 pages in fifteen sections. Lloyd Wendt, *Chicago Tribune: The Rise of a Great American Newspaper* (Chicago: Rand-McNally, 1979), 361.

28. Alfred McClung Lee, *The Daily Newspaper in America,* 69.

29. From *Universal Review* (September 1890), quoted in George H. Douglas, *The Golden Age of the Newspaper* (Westport, CT: Greenwood Press, 1999), 142. Others later described the Sunday edition as a "literary dime museum." John Baker Opdycke, *News, Ads, and Sales: The Use of English for Commercial Purposes* (New York: Macmillan, 1914), 62.

30. Paul Moore and Sandra Gabriele, "The American Sunday Newspaper Magazine: An Intermedial History, 1893–1900," Mapping the Magazine 3 conference, Cardiff University, July 8, 2011.

31. Reproductions of many Sunday-edition comics pages are collected in Nicholson Baker and Margaret Brentano, eds., *The World on Sunday: Graphic Art in Joseph Pulitzer's Newspaper (1898–1911)* (New York: Bulfinch Press, 2005). When newspapers were microfilmed, particularly en masse after World War II, and in black and white, most "original" copies were destroyed for storage reasons. Nicholson Baker, *Double Fold: Librarians and the Assault on Paper* (New York: Random House, 2001), 25–27.

32. Richard L. Kaplan, *Politics and the American Press*, 122.

33. Nathanial C. Fowler, "Woman as a Factor in Advertising" (a luncheon speech given to the Boston Women's Publicity Club), reported in "Women Buy for Men," *EP*, February 27, 1915, 755. See also "Sunday Paper for Women," *EP*, April 29, 1911, 35; and the *Chicago Daily News* ad extolling "Henrietta Chicago (nee Newyork), the sum of all the women readers of The Chicago Daily News . . .," *EP*, August 7, 1915, front cover.

34. Quoted in Richard L. Kaplan, *Politics and the American Press*, 128.

35. Gunther Barth, *City People*, 62.

36. Ibid., 80.

37. Paul S. Moore, "Subscribing to Publicity: Syndicated Newspaper Features for Moviegoing in North America, 1911–1915," *Early Popular Visual Culture* 12, no. 2 (May 2014): 262.

38. Charles Johanningsmeier, "The Devil, Capitalism, and Frank Norris: Defining the 'Reading Field' for Sunday Newspaper Fiction, 1870–1910," *American Periodicals* 14, no. 1 (2004): 94, 103. Frank Foxcroft describes a "typical" family reading scene on Sundays in "The American Sunday Newspaper," *Nineteenth Century* 62 (October 1907): 612.

39. Intriguingly, the President of Western Reserve University in Cleveland linked "the motion picture and the automobile . . . as modern agencies of civilization." Quoted by Gardner Mack, "Photoplays and Photoplayers: Pictures and Motor Cars as Twin Agents of Civilization," *WT*, September 20, 1915, 11.

40. Targeting women went along with the rise in the importance of consumption as a frequent, repeatable social activity, supported by advertising "for which women were conventionally more responsible than men." Michael Schudson, *Discovering the News: A Social History of the Newspaper* (New York: Basic Books, 1973), 100.

41. From colonial times on, women could be found in printing and newspaper offices; indeed, during the nineteenth century, "they were far better represented than they were almost everywhere else in the workforce." Quoted in George H. Douglas, *The Golden Age of the Newspaper*, 171. An 1889 issue of the *Journalist* profiled fifty women editors and reporters, the same year that the Women's Press Club formed in New York. See Marion T. Marzolf, *Up from the Footnote: A History of Women Journalists* (New York: Hastings House, 1977), 24.

42. Marion T. Marzolf, *Up from the Footnote*, 29.

43. Alice Fahs, *Out on Assignment*, 36, 171. For a fine study of the early "girl stunt reporters," see Jean Marie Lutes, *Front Page Girls: Women Journalists in*

American Culture and Fiction, 1880–1930 (Ithaca, New York: Cornell University Press, 2006), 12–38.

44. Ishbel Ross, *Ladies of the Press: The Story of Women in Journalism by an Insider* (New York: Harper & Brothers, 1936), 48–59; Marion T. Marzolf, *Up from the Footnote,* 23–24; and George H. Douglas, *The Golden Age of the Newspaper,* 178–82. As a reporter working for the *New York Tribune* in the early twentieth century, Ross knew many of these newspaperwomen.

45. Ishbel Ross, *Ladies of the Press,* 60–67; Marion T. Marzolf, *Up from the Footnote,* 33–34; George H. Douglas, *The Golden Age of the Newspaper,* 182–83.

46. Ishbel Ross, *Ladies of the Press,* 74–83; Marion T. Marzolf, *Up from the Footnote,* 36–37. See also A.C. Hasselbarth, "Women Writers of American Press," *EP,* October 4, 1913, 304.

47. Ishbel Ross, *Ladies of the Press,* 408–9; and "Woman Press Agent," *EP,* May 6, 1911, 15.

48. Marion T. Marzolf, *Up from the Footnote,* 32.

49. Alice Fahs, *Out on Assignment,* 1.

50. "The Moving Picture and the Press," *MPW,* May 6, 1911, 1006.

51. Ibid.

52. One exception was the "Moving Pictures and Vaudeville" column of block ads, which began to appear daily in the *St. Louis Times* in August 1909 and, within a month, was listing the brief programs of either licensed or "independent" films at more than two dozen cinemas, including some of the best downtown theaters, many suburban and neighborhood theaters, and even several airdomes. These ads disappeared the following summer, but exhibitors in other cities began to purchase newspaper ads on a regular basis. By fall 1911, four picture theaters in downtown Minneapolis were inserting small block ads among those for legitimate theaters and vaudeville houses on "The Stage" page of the *Sunday Journal.* At the same time, in Canton, Ohio, the Odeon competed with three vaudeville houses in ads for their Sunday movie programs in the *Sunday News.*

53. "In the Moving Picture World," *CSL,* September 3, 1911, B.6.

54. "Feature Photo Plays of the Week Edited by Ralph P. Stoddard," *CSL,* October 1, 1911, B.6. See also "Exclusive Sunday Leader Feature" ads, *CL,* October 3, 1911, S.1; October 24, 1911, 12; and November 3, 1911, 4.

55. "Film Makers Race for Flood Picture," "New Picture Fans Use Leader Coupon," and "Scenes from 'Colleen Bawn' Film Play Made in Ireland," *CSL,* October 8, 1911, B.6.

56. "New Educational Films," *CSL,* October 8, 1911, B.6; and "At the Leader Chain Houses This Week," *CSL,* October 15, 1911, B.6.

57. "Moving Picture Star Tells of the Thrills of Her Art," *CSL,* October 22, 1911, S.5, and October 29, 1911, S.5.

58. "Photo-Plays and Players," *CSL,* December 3, 1911, S.5.

59. "Splendid Picture Publicity," *MPW,* November 11, 1911, 473.

60. "Here You Are Folks! All About 'The Movies,'" *Chicago Day Book,* November 11, 1912, 11; "The Movies," *DMN,* November 11, 1912, 2; and *Cleveland Press,* November 11, 1912, 1.

61. "Today's Best Photo Play Stories," *CT*, February 11, 1914, 5.

62. "Today's Best Photo Play Stories," *CT*, March 4, 1914, 8.

63. "Today's Best Photo Play Stories," *CT*, March 18, 1914, 9.

64. "Today's Best Photo Play Stories," *CT*, March 25, 1914, 11.

65. "Today's Best Photo Play Stories," *CT*, April 22, 1914, 13.

66. Kitty Kelly, "Today's Best Photo Play Stories," *CT*, July 1, 1914, 13. In a photo of journalists traveling to Universal City, Kelly is described unflatteringly as a "pensive little mite." Ed Mock, "The Cruise of the Universal Special," *M*, May 1, 1915, 694.

67. "Today's Best Moving Picture Story," *CT*, February 6, 1914, 5. This idea came at the end of the *Tribune*'s short introduction to this daily column and ran for at least a week.

68. Vercoe's fascination with serials and their stars aligns closely with many "motion picture autobiographies" of women that Herbert Blumer collected in Chicago for the Payne Film Study in the late 1920s. Hilary Hallet, *Go West, Young Women!: The Rise of Early Hollywood* (Berkeley: University of California Press, 2013), 64–66.

69. "Social Affairs," *CR*, June 23, 1915, 7.

70. Advertisement, *CR*, November 7, 1915, 27.

CHAPTER 1. THE INDUSTRY GOES TO TOWN (AND COUNTRY)

1. "The Moving Picture and the Press," *MPW*, May 6, 1911, 1006. See the "special advertising matter" of "fifty different stories, written to fit every occasion" for *Homer's 'Odyssey.'*" Monopol Film ad, *MPW*, February 10, 1912, 504.

2. Epes Winthrop Sargent, "Advertising for Exhibitors," *MPW*, October 14, 1911, 111; February 24, 1912, 666; and August 31, 1912, 872. I follow Sargent in having "house organs" refer to the brochures or sheets, whether produced daily or weekly, that managers gave to their clientele. Sargent, "Advertising for Exhibitors," *MPW*, May 17, 1913, 696. Later the term also could refer to weekly or biweekly manufacturer bulletins. H. J. Streyckmans, "An Originator of House Organs," *MPW*, July 20, 1918, 340.

3. "The Moving Picture and the Press," 1006.

4. "'Spectator's' Comments," *NYDM*, February 28, 1912, 28. See also "Film Criticism and the Lay Press," *MPW*, May 20 1911, 1113; and "Film Criticism," *M*, August 1911, 56.

5. "'Spectator's' Comments," *NYDM*, February 28, 1912, 28.

6. "Facts and Comments," *MPW*, December 27, 1913, 1519. See also Julian T. Baber, "Efficient Publicity Work," *MPW*, May 30, 1914, 1270.

7. H.A.H., "One Year's Progress of Moving Pictures," *NYMT*, February 25, 1912, 4.2.1.

8. Robert Grau, *The Theatre of Science* (New York: Benjamin Blom, 1969), 315. Originally published in 1914.

9. "Views of the Reviewer," *NYDM*, October 9, 1912, 25.

10. Philip Mindl, "Publicity for the Pictures," *MPW*, July 11, 1914, 217. See also an interview with Joseph Brandt of Universal in Ernest A. Deuch, "Getting the Public to Ask for Universal Moving Pictures," *Judicious Advertising* 13, no. 11 (November 1915): 33.

11. Pamela Walker Laird, *Advertising Progress: American Business and the Rise of Consumer Marketing* (Baltimore: Johns Hopkins University Press, 1998), 260, 261, 266, 280–81; and Elspeth H. Brown, *The Corporate Eye: Photography and the Rationalization of American Commercial Culture, 1884–1929* (Baltimore: Johns Hopkins University Press, 2005), 168. See also Walter Dill Scott, *The Psychology of Advertising* (Boston: Small, Maynard, 1907), cited in Jackson Lears, *Fables of Abundance: A Cultural History of Advertising in America* (New York: Basic Books, 1994), 208.

12. Janet Staiger, "Announcing Wares, Winning Patrons, Voicing Ideals: Thinking About the History and Theory of Film Advertising," *Cinema Journal* 29, no. 3 (Spring 1990): 4.

13. I acknowledge the early interaction between American Mutoscope & Biograph (AM&B) and newspapers such as the *New York Journal* and *New York Sun* in which W.K.L. Dickson and Billy Bitzer provided news photos for publicity purposes and newspapers in turn informed AM&B of breaking news events. Paul Spehr, "The Public Wanted News: Programming the Biograph, 1896–1908," 8th International Seminar on the Origins and History of Cinema, University of Girona, Spain, March 31, 2011.

14. Richard Abel, *The Red Rooster Scare: Making Cinema American, 1900–1910* (Berkeley: University of California Press, 1999), 80–86.

15. "Vitagraph Press Announcements," *Vitagraph Life Portrayals* 1, no. 23 (June 1–15, 1912): 28, 30–31. Box 3, Hollywood Museum Collection, Margaret Herrick Library. This column exhorted exhibitors to cut out individual announcements and send them to their local papers.

16. The industry may have assumed that exhibitors would use their bulletins as raw material to devise their own publicity, much as newspaper editors used wire service dispatches to concoct their own stories. David Hochfelder, *The Telegraph in America, 1832–1920* (Baltimore: Johns Hopkins University Press, 2012), 74.

17. Epes Winthrop Sargent, "Advertising for Exhibitors," *MPW*, August 3, 1912, 440.

18. Epes Winthrop Sargent, "Advertising for Exhibitors," *MPW*, October 5, 1912, 139.

19. "Doings in Los Angeles," *MPW*, November 30, 1912, 870.

20. F. J. Beecroft, "Publicity Men I Have Met," *NYDM*, January 14, 1914, 48.

21. Robert Grau, *The Theatre of Science*, 320.

22. "At the American," *AS*, July 23, 1911, 11.

23. "At the Colonial," *NOI*, July 13, 1911, 12; "Film Shows Animals," *MO*, July 17, 1911, 14.

24. "'Captain Kate' at the American Today," *Columbus Enquirer*, August 30, 1911, 5. Folder 555: General Releases 1911, William Selig Papers, Margaret Herrick Library.

25. "'Captain Kate' at the Grand Theater," *Bellingham Herald,* August 2, 1911, 3.

26. "At the Leader Chain Houses This Week," *CL,* October 15, 1911, B.6; "Features in the Films," *CL,* October 22, 1911, S.5; and "Criticisms and Reviews," *CL,* October 29, 1911, S.5.

27. H.A.H., "One Year's Progress of Moving Pictures."

28. None of the newspaper ads or stories draw on the scathing review of the film in "Critical Reviews of the Licensed Films," *NYMT,* October 1, 1911, 4.2:5.

29. "Kate Claxton's 'Two Orphans' in Three Reels, Selig's Immortal Masterpiece at the Lyric Monday all Day," *Alton Telegraph,* October 21, 1911, 8. Folder 555, William Selig Papers, Margaret Herrick Library.

30. Selig ad, *NYDM,* September 6, 1911, 24; Grand Theatre ad, *Jonesboro Sun,* October 2, 1911, n.p.; Orpheum ad, *Titusville Herald,* February 22, 1912, 5.

31. "At the Colonial," *FWJG,* November 8, 1911, 12; and Unique ad, *Atlantic Telegraph,* December 22, 1911, 5. Neither ad mentions that Tom Mix plays a major character.

32. Unique ad, *Atlantic Telegraph,* October 31, 1911, 3; and The Ideal ad, *Stevens Point Journal,* December 30, 1911, 7.

33. Cosy Theater ad, *Aberdeen News,* November 10, 1911, 8.

34. "Comments on the Films," *MPW,* November 11, 1911, 468.

35. This eighteen-page booklet included a lecture for all three reels, written by Cecil Metcald, and a "musical program" of accompaniment arranged by Clarence E. Sinn of *Moving Picture World.* Folder 39, William Selig Papers, Margaret Herrick Library. Thanhouser released a one-reel *Cinderella* ten days prior to the Selig "feature." Thanhouser ad, *MPN,* December 9, 1911, 4; and "Cinderella," *MPN,* December 9, 1911, 43–44.

36. Selig ad, *NYDM,* December 6, 1911, 33; J. Willis Sayre, "Stone Practicing New Specialties," *ST,* January 4, 1912, 8; and "The Story of Cinderella in Picture at Imperial," *AS,* January 18, 1912, 2.

37. "At the Hippodrome," *Wilkes-Barre Times-Leader,* January 9, 1912, 16; and "See Cinderella as Guests of Mercury[;] This Paper to Be Hosts for Children," *San Jose Mercury,* January 11, 1912, 8.

38. "The Picture Theatres," *TNB,* March 9, 1912, 8. An earlier ad had only the head photo of Taliaferro. "At the Photo Plays," *TNB,* March 8, 1912, 6.

39. "Mercury Invites You to See Cinderella[;] Great Photoplay Free for Children," *San Jose Mercury,* January 12, 1912, 9.

40. "The Mercury Prepares a Treat for San Jose Youngsters," *San Jose Mercury,* January 9, 1912, 12.

41. New Boz Theatre ad, *Idaho Statesman,* January 21, 1912, 2. The Mission ad is from the *Salt Lake Herald-Republican,* December 29, 1911. Folder 39, William Selig Papers, Margaret Herrick Library.

42. Selig ad, *NYDM,* May 1, 1912, 30.

43. James S. McQuade, "The Coming of Columbus," *MPW,* May 4, 1912, 407–10; and "The Coming of Columbus," *M,* May 1912, 199–204.

44. "The Coming of Columbus," *M*, May 1912, 199; "Wonderful Moving Pictures," *CND*, June 16, 1912, n.p.; and *Muskogee Times-Democrat*, May 13, 1912, 3.

45. Colonial ads, *DMR*, May 19, 1912, 5; and *DMN*, May 19, 1912, 6. See also the Wigwam ad, *Muskogee Times-Democrat*, May 13, 1912, 10; and the Theatre Voyons ad, *Lowell Sun*, June 3, 1912, 5. The Odeon in Canton apparently drew on a Selig press sheet to write up a large ad that included a lengthy "cast of principal characters." Odeon ad, *CND*, June 2, 1912, 16.

46. "Masterpiece at American," *Iowa City Press*, May 7, 1912, 8; and "Theatre Voyons," *Lowell Sun*, June 3, 1912, 2.

47. Theatre Voyons," *Lowell Sun*, June 3, 1912, 2; "Pope Pleased with 'The Coming of Columbus,'" *MPW*, May 11, 1912, 521–22. Several Cleveland theaters also highlighted this endorsement. "Features of Many Theaters," *CL*, May 5, 1912, W.8; and "'Columbus' at Pearl," *CL*, June 9, 1912, W.6.

48. Epes Winthrop Sargent, "Advertising for Exhibitors," *MPW*, May 18, 1912, 623. According to an earlier ad for *Homer's Odyssey*, Monopol Film had recommended an essay contest for schoolchildren. Monopol Film ad, *NYDM*, February 14, 1912, 31.

49. Orpheum ads, *CND*, May 26, 1912, 14; June 2, 1912, 16; and June 9, 1912, 12.

50. *The Cowboy Millionaire* publicity is in folder 557, William Selig Papers, Margaret Herrick Library.

51. Grand Opera House ads, *CND*, March 16, 1913, 15; and June 6, 1913, 7. See also the Ark Theatre ad, *Logansport Journal-Tribune*, February 4, 1913, 10; and New Dome ad, *Youngstown Vindicator*, February 16, 1913, 1. Selig sold these ads to exhibitors at a rate of $0.90 to $1.50, depending on the column width.

52. Unique ad, *Anita Tribune*, February 6, 1913, 6, 12; and Isis Theater ad, *OS*, February 10, 1913, 6. These photos illustrate James S. McQuade's "The Millionaire Cowboy (Selig)," *MPW*, January 25, 1913, 344–45.

53. Princess ad, *Aberdeen News*, February 20, 1913, 6; and Grand Theatre ad, *Jonesboro Tribune*, February 27, 1913, 3. In nearby Lynn, the Olympia picked out the sensational moments "to see." Olympia ad, *Lynn Item*, February 15, 1913, 2.

54. Columbia Theater ad, *TNB*, February 1, 1913, 5; "At the Alhambra," *Wilkes-Barre Times-Leader*, February 4, 1913, 3; and Royal ad, *Mansfield News*, April 5, 1913, 11.

55. "What the Press Agents Say," *Colorado Springs Gazette-Telegraph*, March 16, 1913, 9. Other newspapers also noted the earlier film's popularity as a reason for the remake. "Week's Events in Pictureland," *CL*, February 9, 1913, W.4.

56. J. Willis Sayre, "In the Film World," *ST*, February 3, 1913, 9.

57. The *Pauline Cushman* publicity is in folder 345, William Selig Papers, Margaret Herrick Library.

58. Casino Theater ad, *DMRL*, March 23, 1913, 3; "Pauline Cushman, the Federal Spy," *Adams County Union Republican*, May 7, 1913, 10; Orpheum ad,

Titusville Herald, May 12, 1913, 5; "Amusements," *Mansfield News*, June 12, 1913, 4; and The Ideal ad, *Stevens Point Journal*, June 17, 1913, 4.

59. "Oakland Photo," *OT*, March 30, 1913, 6.

60. The Princess Theater ad, *AS*, April 6, 1913, 11; and Plaza ad, *Montgomery Advertising*, April 23, 1913, 6.

61. "Living Likeness of a Heroine," *Adams County Union Republican*, May 30, 1913, 2.

62. *Alone in the Jungle*'s publicity is in folder 160, William Selig Papers, Margaret Herrick Library.

63. "Alone in the Jungle Dreamland Wed'sd'y," *Oelwein Register*, October 7, 1913, 4.

64. "Did You Ever See a Lion Swim?" *Logansport Pharos-Reporter*, June 14, 1913, 8.

65. "Majestic," *Sheboygan Press*, July 3, 1913, 6.

66. "'Alone in the Jungle,'" *Portsmouth Times*, July 3, 1913, 13.

67. "Gaiety Audiences Held Spellbound," *FWJG*, June 17, 1913, 10.

68. "The Leap of Lioness in a Death Flurry" and "Did You Ever See a Lion Swim?" *Ada News*, August 20, 1913, 4.

69. *The Law and the Outlaw*'s publicity is in folder 293, William Selig Papers, Margaret Herrick Library. See also the Selig ad, *NYDM*, May 21, 1913, 31.

70. "Oakland Photo," *OT*, June 8, 1913, 9; Alcazar Theater ad, *AS*, June 15, 1913, 5; Palace ad, *CRR*, July 4, 1913, 3; Majestic ad, *Ada News*, August 1, 1913, 1; and The Ideal ad, *Stevens Point Journal*, September 3, 1913, 1.

71. "'The Law and the Outlaw' at Gem," *Oelwein Register*, August 11, 1913, 4.

72. "Remarkable Wild West Picture at Acme," *Olympia Record*, July 17, 1913, 2; and "All the World Loves a Lover," *LN*, August 17, 1913, 3.

73. Isis Theatre ads, *Ogden Examiner*, June 8, 1913, 6; and June 9, 1913, 6.

74. Majestic ad, *Ada News*, August 2, 1913, 1.

75. "Newspaper and Program Announcements," *KK*, July 1, 1913, 6, 12.

76. Tokyo ad, *Logansport Journal-Tribune*, July 4, 1913, 10; "The Grand," *FWJG*, July 13, 1913, 9; and Princess Theater ad, *Aberdeen News*, July 25, 1913, 8.

77. George Blaisdell, "Shenandoah," *MPW*, June 28, 1913, 1339–40; "'Shenandoah,' Three-Reel Feature," *Columbus Enquirer*, August 3, 1913, 4; and "'Shenandoah' at Hippodrome," *Gulfport Herald*, September 8, 1913, 4.

78. "The Latest Films," *RR*, July 9, 1913, 12; and "Dramatic Notes," *AS*, July 13, 1913, 2.

79. Arthur G. Stolte, "Motion Pictures," *WR*, June 28, 1913, 11; and The Family ad, *Adrian Telegraph*, July 14, 1913, 2.

80. A different example would be Selig's feature-length *The Spoilers* (April 1914), whose special promotion and dissemination Joel Frykholm analyzed in his dissertation, "Framing the Feature Film: Multi-Reel Feature Film and American Film Culture in the 1910s" (Stockholm University, 2009), 223–44.

81. Kalem promoted *The Hazards of Helen Railroad Series* with a new release "every Saturday" in a full-page ad in *MPW*, December 5, 1914, 1351.

82. "Newspaper and Program Announcements," *KK*, December 1, 1914, 28; and "Alice Joyce at the Star Theatre Tonight," *Chillicothe Constitution*, December 28, 1914, 1.

83. In 1914, very few women worked in the railroad industry, which made Helen an unusually modern role model. Nan Enstad, *Ladies of Labor, Girls of Adventure: Working Women, Popular Culture, and Labor Politics at the Turn of the Twentieth Century* (New York: Columbia University Press, 1999), 193–95.

84. "Newspaper and Program Announcements," *KK*, December 1, 1914, 34; "Indian Duo Will Amuse Ray Crowds," *MO*, January 6, 1915, 4; and Mary F. Laffler, "Flashes from Filmdom," *FWST*, February 22, 1915, 7. For an analysis of the *Hazards of Helen* series, see Nan Enstad, *Ladies of Labor, Girls of Adventure*, 193–99.

85. "Newspaper and Program Announcements," *KK*, December 1, 1914, 30; "Colonial Feature Saturday," *Rockford Register-Gazette*, January 22, 1915, 5; and "Current Theatrical Attractions," *Jackson Citizen-Patriot*, February 6, 1915, 5.

86. "Newspaper and Program Announcements," *KK*, December 1, 1914, 28; and "Helen to Thrill Grand's Crowds," *Reno Gazette*, January 23, 1915, 2.

87. "Newspaper and Program Announcements," *KK*, December 1, 1914, 36; and "The Escape on the Limited," *FWJG*, December 20, 1914, 2; and *Santa Fe New Mexican*, January 14, 1915, 4.

88. "The Wife's Story [Essanay]," *CT*, November 12, 1911, 7.7; and "The Inner Mind [Selig]," *CT*, December 3, 1911, 7.7.

89. These stories included Kalem's "Back to the Kitchen" and Edison's "Charlie's Reform," respectively, in the *Boston Evening Traveller*, February 24, 1912, 10A; and March 30, 1912, 10A.

90. American Film ad, *MPW*, March 16, 1912, 980–81. One of the earliest stories was "Where Broadway Meets the Mountains," *DMN*, January 27, 1912, 3.

91. "Edison-McClure," *MPW*, June 29, 1912, 1212. See also "Bushman Wins Big Contest," *MPW*, May 23, 1914, 1120–21. Apparently Edward A. McManus of the McClure company had the idea for this fictional tie-in. "Boosting Pathé Pictures," *MPW*, March 14, 1914, 1392.

92. Shelley Stamp, *Movie-Struck Girls: Women and Motion Picture Culture After the Nickelodeon* (Princeton, NJ: Princeton University Press, 2000), 137–39.

93. "Innovation," *M*, January 24, 1914, 54; and "Selig Resources for 'Kathlyn' Series," *MPN*, January 31, 1914, 20. See also the comments of E.B. Cappeller, general manager of the *Mansfield News*, in "Free Publicity," *EP*, June 13, 1914, 1097.

94. "Kathlyn" ads, *CT*, December 9, 1913, 4; December 11, 1913, 16; December 13, 1913, 18; December 16, 1913, 13; December 18, 1913, 16; and December 20, 1913, 17.

95. "Kathlyn" ads, *CT*, December 23, 1913, 10; and December 26, 1913, 7.

96. "Kathyln" ads, *CT*, December 27, 1913, 2; and December 29, 1913, 2.

97. Barbara Wilinsky, "Flirting with Kathlyn: Creating the Mass Audience," in David Desser and Garth S. Jowett, eds., *Hollywood Goes Shopping* (Minneapolis: University of Minnesota Press, 2000), 34–56.

98. The *Chicago Tribune*'s demographic comes from Lauren Rabinovitz, "Temptations of Pleasure: Nickelodeons, Amusement Parks, and the Sights of Female Sexuality," *camera obscura* 23 (May 1990): 73.

99. Barbara Wilinsky, "Flirting with Kathlyn," 34, 41, 44.

100. Sunday Tribune ad, *CT*, January 3, 1914, 15; and Harold McGrath, "The Adventures of Kathlyn," *CST*, January 4, 1914, 7.1–2.

101. "The Adventures of Kathlyn" ad, *Salt Lake Telegram*, January 1, 1914, 9; and *BT*, January 4, 1914, 51; "MacGrath's Latest to Greet Buffalo in Film and Story," *BT*, January 4, 1914, 50; Harold McGrath, "The Adventures of Kathlyn," *DFP*, January 4, 1914, Features, 8; *NOI*, January 4, 1914, 2; *FWST*, January 4, 1914, 2.28; *SH*, January 10, 1914, 10; *Youngstown Vindicator*, January 11, 1914, 4.8; "Kathlyn Story Appears Tomorrow," *Hamilton Republican-News*, January 23, 1914, 1; Harold MacGrath, "The Adventures of Kathlyn," *LN*, January 24, 1914, 2; and *CPD*, April 4, 1914, Magazine, 7–8. See also Jas. S. McQuade, "Chicago Letter," *MPW*, January 17, 1914, 270–71.

102. Casino ad, *DMRL*, January 11, 1914, 6; Casino ad, *LCT*, January 31, 1914, 2; and Colonial ad, *FWJG*, January 11, 1914, 18.

103. Tribune ads, *CT*, January 5, 1914, 11; January 6, 1914, 9; January 7, 1914, 7; January 8, 1914, 9; January 9, 1914, 9; and January 10, 1914, 15. See also the full-page Saturday ad, *CT*, January 17, 1914, 8.

104. "Kathlyn's Own Story" ad, *CST*, March 15, 1914, 5.8.

105. "Kathlyn" ads, *CT*, December 29, 1913, 2; and January 3, 1914, 15.

106. "Kathlyn" ad, *DFP*, January 10, 1914, 7.

107. "Kathlyn" ads, *CPD*, April 12, 1914, 2.4; and May 10, 1914, 2.6.

108. Other newspapers than those cited—for instance the *Boston American, San Francisco Examiner,* and *Deutsches Journal* (New York)—were listed in an Eclectic ad, *MPW*, March 21, 1914, 1546–47. Another reason for the serial's success was Pathé's decision to release a record number of prints of the first episode: 147 rather than the usual 25 to 30. See "Expediting Service," *MPW*, July 11, 1914, 284.

109. *New York Sunday American* ad, *Jersey Journal*, March 14, 1914, 2; and "The Perils of Pauline" ads, *AuC*, March 29, 1914, 26; *LAE*, May 1, 1914, 1.9; and May 2, 1914, 1.5. See also the full-page "The Perils of Pauline" ad, *PL*, April 5, 1914, 10; "The Perils of Pauline," *DeNT*, March 22, 1914, Financial, 8; "'The Perils of Pauline' for Times Readers," *New Brunswick Times*, April 21, 1914, 1; "The Perils of Pauline, an Amazing Novel by Goddard," *Columbus Ledger*, May 10, 1914, H.6; "The Perils of Pauline," *Cincinnati Enquirer*, May 17, 1914, 3.6; and "The Perils of Pauline," *CL*, June 7, 1914, Society, 10.

110. *New York Sunday American* ad, *New York Journal*, July 3, 1914, 4; and Blue Mouse ad, *SPN*, March 29, 1914, 6.

111. Pathé-Frères ad, *DeNT*, March 22, 1914, Financial, 8; and "Read and See 'The Perils of Pauline,'" *PL*, April 19, 1914, 1.5.

112. "Perils of Pauline" ads, *CL*, June 28, 1914, S.10; July 5, 1914, M.2; July 12, 1914, S.10; and July 26, 1914, M.11. See also "'Pauline' Reels Are Now Ready," *CPD*, May 3, 1914, Editorial/Dramatic, 3.

113. "Pauline" ads, *New York Journal*, July 6, 1914, 6; July 13, 1914, 9; July 20, 1914, 9; July 27, 1914, n.p.; and August 24, 1914, 8.

114. "Universal Syndicate Series," *MPW*, April 4, 1914, 47.

115. "Lucille Love, The Girl of Mystery" ad, *CL*, April 5, 1914, M.3; "Lucille Love, The Girl of Mystery," *CL*, April 12, 1914, N.4; *AtC*, April 12, 1914, n.p.; *NOTP*, April 12, 1914, 49; *SH*, April 12, 1914, 57; *OWH*, April 12, 1914, 20; *CH*, April 14, 1914, n.p.; *Columbus Enquirer-Sun*, April 19, 1914, 5; *SAL*, April 26, 1914, 22; *Lexington Herald*, April 26, 1914, 6; and *DuNT*, April 26, 1914, Magazine, 6.

116. Universal ads, *CL*, April 5, 1914, M.3; *CH*, April 12, 1914, 2.8; *AtC*, April 5, 1914, 68.

117. "Lucille Love, The Girl of Mystery" ad, *CL*, April 10, 1914, n.p.; "Lucille Love, The Girl of Mystery," *CL*, April 12, 1914, N.4; "Lucille Love, The Girl of Mystery" ad, *CL*, April 19, 1914, S.15; "Lucille Love, The Girl of Mystery" ads, *CH*, April 12, 1914, 2.8; and April 18, 1914, 5; and Universal ads, *CT*, May 2, 1914, 7; and May 6, 1914, 8.

118. "Where You May See 'Lucille Love,'" *CL*, June 14, 1914, S.10; July 12, 1914, S.10; and July 19, 1914, S.8.

119. Syndicate Film ad, *MPW*, April 25, 1914, 610. See also C.J. Hite on the Thanhouser campaign in "Advertising for the Exhibitor," *MPW*, July 11, 1914, 187.

120. "Million Dollar Mystery" ads, *BN*, June 21, 1914, 12; *SAL*, June 25, 1914, 5; and *CR*, June 28, 1914, 5; and Harold McGrath, "The Million Dollar Mystery," *CT*, June 29, 1914, 5.1; and *New Brunswick Times*, June 29, 1914, 6.

121. "The Million Dollar Mystery," *CPD*, July 5, 1914, Magazine, 6–7; *Tulsa World*, July 12, 1914, 2.2; and *Macon Telegraph*, July 26, 1914, 1.4.

122. Thanhouser ads, *CT*, June 8, 1914, 14; and June 17, 1914, 8; and *SAL*, June 10, 1914, 5.

123. Thanhouser ads, *CT*, June 20, 1914, 8; *BuC*, June 21, 1914, 78; and *SAL*, June 25, 1914, 5.

124. See the full-page Thanhouser ads, *CT*, June 22, 1914, 8; *BuC*, June 22, 1914, 9; and *OS*, June 27, 1914, 9. See also the contest ads, *CR*, June 28, 1914, 5, 17.

125. *Movie Pictorial* ad, *CT*, July 5, 1914, 7.9; and Mae Tinee, "The Agony of It! Harold MacGrath Is a Movie Actor and an Interviewee on the Same Day," *CT*, July 19, 1914, 5.4–5.

126. "Million Dollar Mystery" ads, *CPD*, July 5, 1914, Editorial/Dramatic, 8; and July 12, 1914, Editorial/Dramatic, 4. See also the graphed column ads, *CPD*, August 23, 1914, A.8; September 13, 1914, Editorial/Dramatic, 4; September 20, 1914, Editorial/Dramatic, 6; September 27, 1914, Editorial /Dramatic, 5; October 4, 1914, Editorial/Dramatic, 5; October 11, 1914,

Editorial/Dramatic, 8; October 18, 1914, Editorial/Dramatic, 4; and October 25, 1914, Editorial/Dramatic, 5.

127. Universal ad, *CL*, July 26, 1914, 1.4; Louis Joseph Vance, "Trey O' Hearts," *Iowa City Press*, August 4, 1914, 2; *Richmond Times-Dispatch*, August 10, 1914, 6; *NOTP*, August 23, 1914, 27; *AtC*, August 30, 1914, 41; *AuC*, August 23, 1914, 27; and *Aberdeen Sunday American*, August 30, 1914, 9. See also A. P. Robyn Syndicate ad, *MPW*, October 31, 1914, 585.

128. Victor Film Service ads, *CL*, August 2, 1914, S.10; August 9, 1914, S.8; August 16, 1914, M.2; August 23, 1914, M.2; and August 30, 1914, M.2.

129. Universal ads, *CL*, July 26, 1914, 1.4; *AtC*, August 16, 1914, M.9; and *Idaho Register* August 28, 1914, 6.

130. Universal ad, *AtC*, August 22, 1914, 12.

131. Trey O' Hearts ad, *NOTP*, August 23, 1914, 27.

132. Trey O' Hearts ads, *CL*, August 16, 1914, M.2; August 23, 1914, M.2; and September 13, 1914, M.7.

133. "The Trey O' Hearts" and "List of Theatres Showing Trey O' Hearts," *NYEM*, September 21, 1914, 11; October 5, 1914, 13; October 24, 1914, 4; and October 26, 1914, 11.

134. "Today's Best Moving Picture Story," *CL*, February 6, 1914, N.6.

135. "Today's Best Moving Picture Story," *CL*, February 6, 1914, N.6; February 9, 1914, 4; February 11, 1914, 11; and February 16, 1914, 10.

136. "Today's Best Moving Picture Story," *CL*, February 15, 1914, N.7.

137. "Today's Best Moving Picture Stories," *CL*, March 19, 1914, 10; April 4, 1914, 4; April 24, 1914, 12; and May 6, 1914, 13.

138. "Read the Story" ad, *CL*, June 7, 1914, S.8.

139. One newspaper I was unable to research is the *New York American*, which contracted with Pathé-Frères to print only that company's stories as "Today's Best Moving Picture Story" from February 7 to April 11, 1914. The February 9 page was reprinted, along with a half-page Pathé-Frères ad (naming five other newspapers), in the *NYDM*, February 18, 1914, 28. Accompanying each story was a list of two hundred theaters showing Pathé films in New York City and the surrounding region. Thanks to Paul Moore for much of this information. See also "Boosting Pathé Pictures," *MPW*, March 14, 1914, 1392.

140. "Here's Best Moving Picture Story," *TB*, February 14, 1914, 8.

141. "Today's Best Moving Picture Story," *CL*, February 14, 1914, 9.

142. See G.M. Anderson within "What's What and Who's Who in Moving Picture Shows," *TB*, March 21, 1914, 10; and Lillian Gish within "Gossip Concerning the Best Photoplays and Photoplayers," *TB*, April 4, 1914, 11.

143. The last column may be "Some New Film Play Stories," *TB*, July 15, 1914, 5.

144. "If You Like the Movies" ad, *Philadelphia Times*, February 23, 1914, n.p.; and *WT*, February 24, 1914, 1. Another similar ad appeared ten days later in the *Philadelphia Times*, March 5, 1914, n.p.

145. "Today's Best Photo Play Stories," *Philadelphia Times*, February 24, 1914, n.p.; "Today's Best Photo-Play Story," *WT*, February 27, 1914, 10.

146. See those stories with the column edited by Gardner Mack, "Photoplays and Photoplayers," *WT*, June 6, 1914, 6. See also "Best Photoplay Stories of the Day," *Philadelphia Telegraph*, April 2, 1914, n.p. Paul Moore's research provides the basis for this speculation about the Philadelphia newspapers.

147. Paul S. Moore, "Subscribing to Publicity: Syndicated Newspaper Features for Moviegoing in North America, 1911–1915," *Early Popular Visual Culture* 12, no. 2 (May 2014): 262.

148. "Today's Best Moving Picture Story," *CT*, February 5, 1914, 5.

149. "Stories of the Films and Where to See Them," *CT*, February 14, 1914, 7.

150. "Today's Best Photo Play Stories," *CT*, April 1, 1914, 13.

151. "Today's Best Photo Play Stories," *CT*, April 4, 1914, 10.

152. "Read This Story TODAY—Then See It in Moving Pictures," *CRH*, March 23, 1914, 7. The *New York Globe* also had an exclusive arrangement with Universal for daily film stories; see the large Universal ad, *New York Globe*, March 16, 1914, 6.

153. "Read This Story TODAY—Then See It in Moving Pictures," *CRH*, March 23, 1914, 7; and March 24, 1914, 7.

154. Universal ad, *CRH*, March 23, 1914, 7.

155. "Today's Picture Story," *CRH*, April 4, 1914, 7; and *CH*, August 8, 1914, 13; and "In the Picture Playhouses," *CH*, August 11, 1914, 11.

156. Universal ad for Vitagraph's *Regan's Daughter*, *CH*, September 29, 1914, 9.

157. "In the Picture Playhouses," *CH*, March 13, 1915, 6; and Louella O. Parsons, "Seen on the Screen," *CH*, March 19, 1915, 13.

158. For a short history of early motion picture brand names and trademarks, see Richard Abel, *The Red Rooster Scare*, 14–19.

159. Susan Strasser, *Satisfaction Guaranteed: The Making of the American Market* (New York: Pantheon, 1989), 34–35.

160. Richard Ohmann, *Selling Culture: Magazines, Markets, and Class at the Turn of the Century* (London: Verso, 1996), 139. See also Emily Fogg Mead, "The Place of Advertising in Modern Business," *Journal of Political Economy* 9 (March 1901): 234.

161. *Trade Marks, Trade-Names, Unfair Competition* (Washington, DC: Williams C. Linton, 1923), 2.

162. The first ad appeared in *CT*, February 6, 1910, 2.6; and *CRH*, February 6, 1910, 7.3.

163. "Pathé Pointers," *Film Index*, March 26, 1910, 6; and "Novel Advertising Campaign," *NYDM*, March 26, 1910, 20.

164. General Film Company ads, *CL*, December 10, 1911, S.5; and December 24, 1911, B.7.

165. Victor Film Service ad, *CL*, November 17, 1912, B.5; and the Lake Shore Film & Supply ad, *CL*, December 15, 1912, S.5.

166. Victor Film ad and "Advance Releases for the Week," *CSPD*, March 16, 1913, Editorial/Dramatic, 10.

167. General Film, Mutual, and Victor Film Service ads, *BT*, March 16, 1913, 67. These ads ran through much of the summer. In May 1913, regional exchanges for General Film, Mutual, Laemmle Film, and Warner's Features also briefly placed small ads in the *Minneapolis Journal*.

168. Universal, Mutual, and Famous Players ads, *OS*, April 19, 1913, 2; May 10, 1913, 2; and June 14, 1913, 2. At this stage, the Mutual trademark was an open eye. Other companies—Essanay, Reliance, and, briefly, Eclectic—also placed strip ads here, but without displaying their marks.

169. Universal, Mutual, and Famous Players ads, *DMRL*, April 27, 1913, 7; May 4, 1913, 7; and June 1, 1913, 9, respectively. See also the Universal, Mutual, and Famous Players ads, *SAL*, May 11, 1913, 31; and June 1, 1913, 34.

170. Universal, Mutual, and Warner's Features ads, *CPD*, November 16, 1913, 6; and March 8, 1914, 4.

171. Kinemacolor ad, *OS*, August 30, 1913, 2; and World Special Film ad, *OS*, December 11, 1913, 5.

172. "Thousands of Exhibitors Read These Ads!" *OS*, September 27, 1913, 2.

173. The Unique Theatre and Mutual Films ad, *DMN*, January 26, 1913, 6.

174. "Some Good Things Coming: Week's Gossip in Filmland," *CSL*, February 2, 1913, B.4.

175. New Royal ad, *SAL*, June 1, 1913, 34.

176. Mutual Film Corporation ad, *BST*, October 26, 1913, 62.

177. Columbia Theatre ad, *Cedar Rapids Evening Gazette*, November 25, 1913, 3.

178. Royal Theatre, Myers Theatre, and Lyric-Majestic ads, *Janesville Daily Gazette*, November 26, 1913, 4.

179. Dream Theatre ad, *Columbus Ledger*, December 12, 1913, 12; and Gamble Theatre ad, *Altoona Mirror*, December 31, 1913, 3.

180. Robert Grau, *The Theatre of Science*, 316–17.

181. General Film ads, *NYMT*, July 20, 1913, 4.2.3; July 27, 1913, 4.2.3; August 3, 1913, 4.2.4; and October 5, 1913, 4.2.3. Chester Beecroft was profiled in F. J. Beecroft [his brother?], "Publicity Men I Have Met," *NYDM*, January 14, 1914, 48. A later ad claimed that "$1,000,000" had been "spent in making [MPPC] brands famous throughout the world." General Film ad, *MPW*, December 20, 1913, 1378.

182. Mutual Movies ad, *KCS*, November 9, 1913, C.11; and *SPN*, November 15, 1913, 12.

183. Mutual Movies ads, *KCS*, November 23, 1913, C.11; December 7, 1913, C.10; and December 21, 1913, B.5. See also the Mutual Movie ad, *SPN*, November 29, 1913, 8.

184. Mutual Movies ad, *CT*, January 4, 1914, 1.8.

185. Philip Mindl, "Publicity for the Pictures," 217.

186. Ibid.

187. Ibid.

188. Ibid. Approximately twenty issues of *Reel Life* from 1914 survive at the Margaret Herrick Library.

189. Ibid.; and "'Our Mutual Girl,' Fifty-Two-Reel Serial Will Show All the Very Latest Fashions," *Sheboygan Press*, January 12, 1914, 8.

190. "Our Mutual Girl Weekly," *Reel Life*, May 30, 1914, 36.

191. Philip Mindl, "Publicity for the Pictures," 217.

192. "Our Mutual Girl Weekly," *Reel Life*, September 26, 1914, 4.

193. For short profiles of Robert H. Cochrane and Joseph Brandt, see F.J. Beecroft, "Publicity Men I Have Met," 48; Robert Grau, *The Theatre of Science*, 316; and "Universal Publicity Staff," *MPW*, September 26, 1914, 1756–57.

194. "Universal's National Advertising Campaign Creates a Sensation," *UW*, November 8, 1913, 3, 33.

195. "Moving Picture Stories" ad, *UW*, December 27, 1913, 18.

196. See the full-page ads in *UW*, February 7, 1914, 18; and February 14, 1914, 2.

197. Red Moon ad, *Baltimore News*, January 25, 1914, 11; and Myers Theatre ad, *Janesville Daily Gazette*, June 19, 1914, 4.

198. The Hippodrome ad, *Lebanon Daily News*, March 2, 1914, 5; and Faurot Opera House ad, *LN*, May 24, 1914, 8.

199. "Advertising Talks by the Chief," *UW*, December 19, 1914, n.p.

200. "Another Unique Universal Advertising Stunt, for Exhibitors," *UW*, December 12, 1914, 33.

201. In a later investigation, Famous Players may have exaggerated its national campaign. Federal Trade Commission vs. Famous Players-Lasky Corporation et al., docket 835, volume 2: 52. Adolph Zukor Collection, Margaret Herrick Library.

202. Michael Quinn, "Distribution, the Transient Audience, and the Transition to Feature Film," *Cinema Journal* 40, no. 2 (Winter 2001): 50. See also "Famous Players' Regular Releases," *MPN*, August 2, 1913, 31; "Famous Players to Put Out Regular Features," *NYMT*, August 3, 1913, 4.2.1; and the Famous Players ads, *MPW*, August 26, 1913, 854–55; and September 6, 1913, 1030–31.

203. Famous Players ad, *Boston Journal*, September 13, 1913, 5. See also the smaller ads, *Boston Journal*, November 1, 1913, 5; November 8, 1913, 5; November 15, 1913, 5; and November 22, 1913, 5.

204. Knickerbocker ads, *CL*, August 31, 1913, C.5; and September 14, 1913, M.2; Saxe's Lyric ad, *MT*, September 7, 1913, S.9; Talley's Broadway ad, *Los Angeles Times*, September 21, 1913, 3.3; and Grauman's Imperial ad, *San Francisco Chronicle*, September 21, 1913, 18.

205. Famous Players ad, *Boston Journal*, March 21, 1914, 7; and "The Pride of Jennico," *Boston Journal*, March 23, 1914, n.p.

206. See the last Famous Players ad, *Boston Journa*l, April 4, 1914, 7.

207. "Famous Players, Lasky, and Bosworth to release through Paramount," *NYMT*, May 24, 1914, 1; and "Feature Producers Affiliate," *MPW*, May 30, 1914, 1268.

208. Pre-Motion Pictures folder and General Film Corp. (1911–1913) folder, Hodkinson Collection 1171, Special Collections, UCLA Library.

209. Paramount Pictures ads, *NYMT,* July 5, 1914, 4.2.2; and July 19, 1914, 4.2.5; and "Paramount Pictures Corporation," *MPW,* July 11, 1914, 264. The first ad identified eleven district distributors: the five Famous Players Film exchanges, Wm. L. Sherry Feature Film (New York), Casino Feature Film (Detroit), Kansas City Feature Film, Notable Feature Film (Salt Lake City and Denver), and Progressive Motion Picture (San Francisco, Los Angeles, and Seattle). The second ad listed the specific film releases for August 31 through November 30. A slightly later ad listed the specific film releases through February 1915. Paramount Pictures ad, *MPW,* October 17, 1914, 368–69.

210. Correspondence B folder, box 11, Hodkinson Collection 1171, Special Collections, UCLA Library.

211. Paramount Pictures ad, *Saturday Evening Post,* September 5, 1914, 52–53.

212. All of those also featured in the two-page "Paramount Publicity" ad, *MPW,* September 5, 1914, 1318–19.

213. Paramount Pictures ad, *MPW,* September 12, 1914, 1458–59. A smaller version appeared in *NYMT,* September 6, 1914, 4.2.4. Endorsement letters from Rothapfel and Mastbaum also were reprinted in *Paramount Progress* 1, no. 1 (December 3, 1914): 11.

214. Paramount Pictures ads, *Saturday Evening Post,* October 3, 1914, 55; November 7, 1914, 55; December 5, 1914, 43; January 2, 1914, 23; and February 6, 1914, 28.

215. Ogden Theater ad, *OS,* September 3, 1914, 5; Crystal Theatre ad, *Cedar Rapids Tribune,* September 4, 1914, 3; Studebaker ad, *CT,* September 5, 1914, 5; Tally's ad, *LAE,* September 6, 1914, American Magazine, 4; Kozy Theatre ad, *Ludington Daily News,* September 6, 1914, 6; Lyric and Wm. Penn ads, *PD,* September 13, 1914, 4.6; and Broadway Theatre ad, *Muskogee Times-Democrat,* September 17, 1914, 3.

216. Knickerbocker ad, *CL,* September 6, 1914, Dramatic-Photoplay-Editorial-Real Estate, 5; and Wizard ad, *Baltimore News,* September 6, 1914, 10. The Ogden Theater not only called itself the "Home of Paramount Pictures" but also advised its patrons to "see this week's Saturday Evening Post." Ogden Theater ad, *OS,* October 3, 1914, 3. See also the Prudential Insurance ad, *Harper's Weekly,* December 19, 1896, 1256, reproduced in Roland Marchand, *Creating the Corporate Soul* (Berkeley: University of California Press, 1998), 37.

217. Orpheum ad, *Daily Northwestern,* October 13, 1914, 2; Owl Theatre ad, *Lowell Sun,* October 29, 1914, 2; Hippodrome ad, *Williamsport Gazette and Bulletin,* October 31, 1914, 5; Grand ad, *Massillon Evening Independent,* November 14, 1914, 8; Princess Theatre ad, *Moberly Morning Monitor,* December 13, 1914, 4; and Princess Theater ad, *Colorado Springs Gazette,* December 13, 1914, 10.

218. Moore's Strand Theater and Garden Theater ads, *Washington Post,* November 1, 1914, 59.

219. Bijou Theatre ad, *LCT,* October 31, 1914, 9.

220. "Editorial," *Paramount Progress* 1, no. 12 (February 18, 1915): n.p.

221. Paramount ad, *MPW*, January 16, 1915, 310; and *Ladies Home Journal* ad, *Saturday Evening Post*, December 26, 1914, 42.

222. Grogg's ad, *Bakersfield Californian*, January 6, 1915, 7; Grand ad, *Centralia Daily Chronicle-Examiner*, January 20, 1915, 4; "The New Theatre Opens Saturday, Jan. 23," *Portsmouth Herald*, January 21, 1915, 1; Regent Theater ad, *SH*, February 7, 1915, 17; and Plaza ad, *Waterloo Evening Courier and Reporter*, March 27, 1915, 7.

223. Faurot Opera House ad, *LN*, February 7, 1915, 15; Wigwam #1 ad, *SAL*, April 18, 1915, 21; and De Luxe ad, *HN*, June 17, 1915, 8.

224. "Photo Play Masterpieces at the New Davis," *PD*, May 23, 1915, 5.5.

225. "Editorial," *Paramount Progress* 1, no. 1 (December 3, 1914): n.p.

226. Ibid. See also Paramount ad for *Paramount Magazine* in *MPW*, January 30, 1915, 622.

227. Ibid.

228. "Paramount's Birthday," *NYDM*, May 26, 1915, 25.

229. General Film companies rarely relied on newspaper ads, except for series and serials. An exception was Lubin, which placed regular ads with its trademark Liberty Bell in one of its hometown Philadelphia newspapers beginning in late February 1915; within weeks those ads were running two lengthy columns down a page. Lubin ads, *PEL*, February 20, 1915, 5; and March 13, 1915, 5. A full-page Lubin ad also appeared in the special "Photoplay Section" of the *Ledger*, June 12, 1915, 16. These ads were different, however, in filling most of the space with a list of the company's principal stars and directors and drawing much less attention to a few new features. Other General Film companies soon joined Lubin with weekly ads—specifically, Vitagraph and Edison. They too simply listed their "prominent personages." Vitagraph ad, *PEL*, March 27, 1915, 7; and Edison ad, *PEL*, May 8, 1915, 7.

230. Schanze's ads, *Baltimore Sun*, December 27, 1914, 87; and January 3, 1915, 7. See also World Film ads, *PD*, May 31, 1914, 5.7; *AtC*, August 30, 1914, 14; and *AtC*, April 11, 1915, D.5.

231. Fox Film ads, *CL*, March 7, 1915, Dramatic, 7; and *PD*, June 27, 1915, 4.6. See also Fox Film ads, *PD*, February 28, 1915, 2.4; *AtC*, March 7, 1915, M.11; and *PEL*, May 1, 1915, 5.

232. Mutual ad, *Saturday Evening Post*, March 13, 1915, 71.

233. Mutual ads, *Saturday Evening Post*, March 20, 1915, 75; March 27, 1915, 56; April 3, 1915, 88; April 10, 1915, 87; April 24, 1915, 47; and May 8, 1915, 51.

234. Reliance ads, *Saturday Evening* Post, March 27, 1915, 75; and May 15, 1915, 43.

235. Alhambra ad, *PL*, March 21, 1915, Theatrical News, 5; Quality ad, *PD*, March 28, 1915, 5.5; "Mutual Master-Pictures Shown at Quality," *PL*, March 28, 1915, Theatrical News, 5; Dreamland ad, *CL*, April 11, 1915, Dramatic, 5; Strand ad, *AtC*, April 18, 1915, M.11; and Alhambra ad, *CPD*, April 25, 1915, Editorial/Dramatic, 5.

236. Ogden Theater ads, *OS*, April 10, 1915, 8; and June 12, 1915, 5; and Mutual ad, *Harrisonburg Daily News-Record*, May 26, 1915, 6.

237. Paramount ad, *MPW*, August 14, 1915, 1210; and William A. Johnston, "The Exhibitor and National Advertising," *MPN*, August 28, 1915, 35–36. Paramount also encouraged exhibitors to use more conventional publicity strategies of local advertising—billboards, streetcars, illuminated signs, electrotypes of stars, slides—and offered a "Publicity Book for Exhibitors of Paramount Pictures." Howard E. Spaulding, "Are You Telling Your People That You Show Paramount Pictures?" *Paramount Progress*, November 11, 1915, 5.

238. Paramount ad, *MPW*, August 21, 1915, 1266; and William W. Hodkinson, "Why National Advertising Is Necessary," *MPN*, December 25, 1915, 58.

239. Garden Theatre ad, *DMT*, September 2, 1915, 6; Paramount ad, *DFP*, September 2, 1915, 6; and "Strong Talk on Advertising," *Paramount Progress*, September 23, 1915, 5.

240. Paramount ads, *DFP*, September 9, 1915, 6; September 16, 1915, 6; September 23, 1915, 6; September 30, 1915, 6; November 11, 1915, 6; and November 29, 1915, 6; Paramount ads, *CT*, October 4, 1915, 12; October 10, 1915, 1.11; and October 11, 1915, 10; Paramount ads, *AtC*, October 18, 1915, 2; and November 1, 1915, 3; and Paramount ad, *Los Angeles Times*, November 8, 1915, 3.4. In Pittsburgh, one Paramount theater ad reproduced a photo of Blanche Sweet within a star-shaped frame at the same time that she was the subject of that week's national newspaper ad. Minerva Theater ad, *PD*, October 17, 1915, 6.6.

241. The *Des Moines Register* and *Des Moines Tribune* joined the downtown Garden theater (the primary venue for Paramount pictures) in such a contest. "Des Moines Papers and Exhibitor Conduct Novel Contest," *MPN*, November 27, 1915, 59.

242. Paramount ad, *Denver Post*, December 10, 1915, 17.

243. Paramount ads, *DFP*, December 9, 1915, 6; December 16, 1915, 6; December 23, 1915, 6; December 30, 1915, 6; January 6, 1916, 6; January 13, 1916, 6; January 20, 1916, 6; January 27, 1916, 6; and February 3, 1916, 6. See also Paramount ads, *CT*, November 15, 1915, 12; February 17, 1916, 12; and April 27, 1916, 8; and *Los Angeles Times*, April 27, 1916, 3.4.

244. Paramount ads, *CT*, May 11, 1916, 12; May 15, 1916, 5; and May 19, 1916, 10.

245. Bijou ad, *LCT*, September 16, 1916, 7; Lyric Theater ad, *AtC*, October 3, 1915, 39; Star Theatre ad, *Sandusky Register*, October 18, 1915, 10; Colonial ad, *Oelwein Register*, November 13, 1915, 4; and Iowa Theatre ad, *Emmetsburg Democrat*, January 26, 1916, 1. See also the Apollo Theatre ad celebrating its presentation of Paramount Pictures "for over a year," *Janesville Gazette*, January 28, 1916, 6.

246. Epes Winthrop Sargent, "Advertising for Exhibitors," *MPW*, May 22, 1915, 1252; Paramount Theatre ads, *Logansport Pharos-Reporter*, July 10, 1915, 4; and *CT*, October 2, 1915, 15; and Princess-Paramount Theatre ad, *TT*, February 27, 1916, 1.8.

247. Lyric Theatre ad, *AtC*, January 30, 1916, M.10.

248. Standard Theatre ad, *CL*, October 31, 1915, Dramatic, 6; and Palace Theatre ad, *CRR*, November 3, 1915, 2.

249. "Riots at Box Office When Theda Bara Goes on Stage," *Elyria Chronicle*, December 8, 1915, 6–7. Fox also sponsored smaller ads for *Carmen*. Alhambra ad, *Sandusky Register*, November 18, 1915, 8; and Fox ad, *ALT*, December 27, 1915, 4.

250. Paramount and Fox ad, *Bluefield Telegraph*, December 25, 1915, 9.

251. Paris Theatre ad, *Santa Fe New Mexican*, July 31, 1915, 6; and Metro Pictures ads, *DeNT*, November 21, 1915, 19; and *BT*, April 9, 1916, 54. Yet Richard A. Rowland, Metro's president, exhorted exhibitors to do more "LOCAL ADVERTISING." Rowland, "If I Were an Exhibitor," *MPN*, December 25, 1915, 57.

252. "'Sig,' $4,000,000 Production Company Is Launched," *MPN*, July 17, 1915, 87.

253. Rob King, "'Made for the Masses with an Appeal to the Classes': The Triangle Film Corporation and the Failure of Highbrow Film Culture," *Cinema Journal* 44, no. 2 (Winter 2003): 4–5.

254. Triangle Film ads, *CT*, September 15, 1915, 8; *SH*, September 20, 1915, 24; *NYT*, September 28, 1915, 3.4; *CT*, October 2, 1915, 14; and *OWH*, December 12, 1915, E.13. See also Frank Leroy Blanchard, "Photo-Play Makers Are Spending a Million a Year in Newspapers," *EP*, November 30, 1915, 529; and "Triangle Film Corporation Biographical Press Sheets," *MPN*, December 18, 1915, 77.

255. Empire Theater ad, *SAL*, October 24, 1915, 22; Liberty and Gordon Square ads, *CL*, October 31, 1915, Dramatic, 7; Willis Wood Theater ad, *Kansas City Times*, November 6, 1915, 8; Jefferson Theater ad, *Fort Wayne News*, November 24, 1915, 7; Palace Theatre ad, *BT*, December 5, 1915, 69; "Salt Lake City Pays Less Than New York to See Picture Plays," *SLT*, December 13, 1915, 44; Metropolitan ad, *CL*, December 19, 1915, Dramatic, 5; Temple ad, *Alton Tribune*, December 29, 1915, 7; and Colonial ad, *Kennebec Journal*, December 31, 1915, 8. By early 1916, Triangle was offering exhibitors a "press kit" of ten model ads for newspapers. "Live Wire Exhibitors," *MPN*, February 19, 1916, 987.

256. Rob King, "Made for the Masses," 15–16.

257. Triangle Film ads, *CT*, March 3, 1916, 8; March 10, 1916, 10; and March 17, 1916, 8.

258. "Triangle Plays" ads, *CT*, March 12, 1916, 1.7; and April 2, 1916, 8.3.

259. Liberty ad, *PD*, January 9, 1916, 4.7; Foto Play Theatre ad, *Grand Forks Herald*, January 9, 1916, 9; and Colonial Theatre ads, *CT*, February 25, 1916, 8; and February 26, 1916, 15.

260. Rob King, "Made for the Masses," 17.

261. "The Universal's Tremendous National Advertising Campaign," *UW* 6, no. 8 (February 20, 1915): 2. This campaign also included billboard advertising by Universal exchanges and promotional slides shown by Universal exhibitors. Ernest A. Deuch, "Getting the Public to Ask for Universal Moving Pictures," 33–36.

262. "Advertising Talks," *UW* 6, no. 4 (January 23, 1915): 32; and Epes Winthrop Sargent, "Advertising for Exhibitors," *MPW*, February 13, 1915, 975; and March 20, 1915, 1755.

263. "Are You Using These Ads?" *UW*, January 23, 1915, 36–37.

264. Those newspapers are listed in "The Universal's Tremendous Advertising Campaign," *UW* 6, no. 8 (February 20, 1915): 2.

265. Universal ads, *CT*, December 2, 1914, 15; and January 21, 1915, 7; and the Studebaker/Fine Arts ad, *CT*, January 27, 1915, 18.

266. Universal ads, *CT*, March 3, 1915, 9; and March 24, 1915, 9; *Indianapolis Star*, March 17, 1915, 4; *SAL*, April 7, 1915, 7; and April 28, 1915, 5; and *CSL*, May 10, 1915, Dramatic, 2.

267. Universal ads, *CSL*, May 2, 1915, Dramatic, 2; and *AtC*, May 5, 1915, 7.

268. For an astute, thorough analysis of Universal City in the mid-1910s, see Mark Garrett Cooper, *Universal Women: Filmmaking and Institutional Change in Early Hollywood* (Urbana: University of Illinois Press, 2010), 45–89.

269. Universal ads, *MPW*, September 26, 1914, 1716–21. See also "Universal's Chameleon City: The Most Remarkable Town Ever Built," *UW*, September 26, 1914, 4–5, 8–9, 37.

270. AT&T ad, *Telephone Review* 6 (January 1915 supplement): inside front cover. Reproduced in Roland Marchand, *Creating the Corporate Soul*, 69–70.

271. Ernest A. Deuch, "Getting the Public to Ask for Universal Moving Pictures," 36. Universal ads, *CT*, February 10, 1915, 10; and *SAL*, February 10, 1915, 12.

272. Universal ads, *SAL*, February 17, 1915, 12; and April 21, 1915, 5; *Indianapolis Star*, March 31, 1915, 15; and May 12, 1915, 5; *CSL*, May 7, 1915, Dramatic, 2; and *CT*, July 7, 1915, 14.

273. "The Strangest City in the World," *Elyria Evening Telegraph*, March 15, 1915, 6; "The Wonder City of Filmdom," *Galveston News Magazine Supplement*, April 4, 1915, 5; and "New Moving Picture City," *ALT*, April 6, 1915, 5; and *Greenville Weekly Democrat* (Mississippi), April 15, 1915, 6. See also "A City Built as a Background for Pictures," *CSL*, May 16, 1915, Feature, 7.

274. Walter H. Woods Co. ad, *Boston Sunday Globe*, March 28, 1915, 31. In a "follow up campaign," Universal kept a register of visitors to Universal City and notified them by mail "when a production which they had seen put on was ready for release." Ernest A. Deuch, "Getting the Public to Ask for Universal Moving Pictures," 36.

275. "Constitution's Beauty Contest" announcements and ads, *AtC*, March 28, 1915, F.3; March 29, 1915, 5; April 4, 1915, 35; and April 11, 1915, B.2. The winner, Alameda Holcombe, was announced in the *AtC*, May 16, 1915, n.p. See also "Universal's Nationwide Beauty Contest," *UW* 6, no. 14, April 3, 1915, 5.

276. Kitty Kelly, "Flickerings from Filmland," *CT*, March 6, 1915, 11. In July 1915, William Selig organized an even larger "movie special" train of fourteen cars that left Chicago for the Selig Jungle-Zoo and Selig studio in Los Angeles and whose patrons and entertainments were filmed by newsreel cameramen for the *Hearst-Selig Pictorial News*. See Kia Afra's analysis of this Selig tour in

"'Seventeen Happy Days' in Hollywood: Selig Polyscope's Promotional Campaign for the Movies Special of July 1915," *Film History* 22 (2010): 199–218.

277. Kitty Kelly, "Flickerings from Filmland," *CT*, March 8, 1915, 12; March 13, 1915, 15; and March 15, 1915, 14.

278. Kitty Kelly, "Flickerings from Filmland," *CT*, March 17, 1915, 14.

279. Kitty Kelly, "Flickerings from Filmland," *CT*, March 20, 1915, 12; and May 5, 1915, 12.

280. "Theodore N. Vail and G.E. Farland Visit," *OWH*, December 5, 1915, E.10.

281. The term comes from Michael Schudson's *Advertising, the Uneasy Persuasion* (1984), quoted and extended in Janet Staiger, "Announcing Wares, Winning Patrons, Voicing Ideals," 21.

282. Grand Theatre, Theatre Royal, Foto Play Theatre, and The Met ads, *Grand Forks Sunday Herald*, September 5, 1915, 9.

283. Frank H. Spearman, "The Girl and the Game: A Story of Mountain Railroad Life," *CSL: Fiction Magazine*, December 26, 1915, 2–3; and the Bijou Dream ad, *CSL*, January 2, 1916, Dramatic, 5. See also "The Girl and the Game" ads, *BC*, December 25, 1915, 7; and January 1, 1916, 5.

284. Studebaker, La Salle Opera House, Castle, Strand, and Colonial ads, *CT*, March 6, 1916, 17.

285. William W. Hodkinson, "Why National Advertising Is Necessary," *MPN*, December 25, 1915, 58. Hodkinson specifically singled out the "9,891 native white families" in his example of Grand Rapids, Michigan (population 112,571). He also cited the precise subscription figures of how many national magazines and Chicago and Detroit newspapers (all with Paramount ads) were sent to these families. The term "native white" comes from the racial/ethnic categories used by the U.S. Census Office.

ENTR'ACTE: LOCAL AND REGIONAL NEWSREELS

1. See the Pathé Weekly ads, *CL*, January 28, 1912, W.8; February 4, 1912, S.6; February 11, 1912, S.6; and February 18, 1912, B.6. See also Colonial ad, *DMRL*, April 23, 1912, 2.

2. Film Man, "Comments and Suggestions," *NYDM*, October 30, 1912, 25.

3. Crescent ad, *CL*, April 14, 1912, S.6; and Mall ad, *CL*, May 26, 1912, S.6. I have not found further information about the *Cleveland Animated Weekly*.

4. "Moving Pictures of Woodland Races," *Woodland Daily Democrat*, September 3, 1913, 1; and "Pantages," *OT*, December 3, 1913, 5. I have not found further information about this local newsreel, either.

5. "Hearst Following Lead of the Item," *NOI*, February 20, 1914, 2. The *Item* unabashedly claimed credit for instigating a new "national weekly," the *Hearst-Selig News*, first released a few weeks later.

6. "Item Animated Weekly to Show Ball Pictures," *NOI*, February 22, 1914, 2.8; "First Item Movies Feature Carnival," *NOI*, March 1, 1914, 12; "Newcomb

Students in Motion Pictures," *NOI*, March 26, 1914, 2; "Item Animated Weekly to Show War Pictures," *NOI*, April 27, 1914, 7; "Track Meet Film Record Among Best," *NOI*, June 17, 1914, 4; and "Police Chief and His 'Family' on Film," *NOI*, June 28, 1914, 4.

7. Ibid. Also "The Item 'Movies' Magnet for Throng . . . at the Trianon," *NOI*, March 6, 1914, 3.

8. Ray H. Leek, "Here Are the First 'Herald Movies,'" *CSH*, July 5, 1914, 5.1.

9. Apparently none of these films survive, except for strips of frame stills reproduced along with Leek's story.

10. *Chicago Herald Movies* ad, *CSH*, July 12, 1914, 2.4; and *CH*, July 22, 1914, 11; and July 27, 1914, 7.

11. *Chicago Herald Movies* ad, *CSH*, July 12, 1914, 2.4; and *CH*, July 27, 1914, 7.

12. *Chicago Herald Movies* ad, *CH*, July 15, 1914, 11.

13. *Chicago Herald Movies* ad, *CH*, July 16, 1914, 3; July 20, 1914, 7; July 22, 1914, 11; July 28, 1914, 12; and July 29, 1914, 13.

14. *Chicago Herald Movies* ad, *CH*, July 30, 1914, 13; and *CSH*, August 2, 1914, 2.4.

15. "Chicago Herald Movies," *CSH*, August 9, 1914, 2.4.

16. *Chicago Herald Movies* ad, *CH*, August 11, 1914, 11.

17. *Chicago Herald Movies* ad, *CSH*, August 9, 1914, 2.4; *CH*, August 11, 1914, 11; August 13, 1914, 14; August 31, 1914, 11; and September 7, 1914, 15. One issue had "Miss Madelene" team up with "Prince, the dog detective"; another had her wear "$250,000 worth of real gems" at a local jewelers' convention.

18. *Chicago Herald Movies* ad, *CH*, September 22, 1914, 12.

19. *Chicago Herald Movies* ad, *CH*, December 4, 1914, 11.

20. *Chicago Herald Movies* ad, *CH*, December 8, 1914, 13; December 14, 1914, 13; December 15, 1914, 13; December 21, 1914, 12; and December 28, 1914, 10.

21. For a month, ads for the Old Mill did include an "extra feature—*The Times Herald Weekly*, an animated review of Dallas." Old Mill ads, *DN*, December 27, 1914, 1.2; January 10, 1915, 2; and January 22, 1915, 9. I have yet to find further information about the *Times Herald Weekly*.

22. *Animated Weekly* ad, *CT*, June 4, 1915, 9.

23. Kitty Kelly, "Flickerings from Film Land," *CT*, June 7, 1915, 14.

24. *Animated Weekly* ad, *CT*, June 19, 1915, 15.

25. *Animated Weekly* ad, *CST*, July 18, 1915, 1.10.

26. *Animated Weekly* ad, *CT*, June 30, 1915, 11; July 7, 1915, 15; July 8, 1915, 15; July 9, 1915, 15; and July 10, 1915, 15.

27. *Animated Weekly* ad, *CST*, July 18, 1915, 1.10; September 5, 1915, 2.2; and September 12, 1915, 2.2. For further information on the *Tribune* war pictures and Edwin Weigle, see Richard Abel, "Charge and Countercharge: 'Documentary' War Pictures in the USA, 1914–1916," *Film History* 22, no. 4 (2010): 366–88; and Cooper C. Graham and Ron van Dopperen, "Edwin F.

Weigle: Cameraman for the *Chicago Tribune," Film History* 22, no. 4 (2010): 389–407.

28. *Animated Weekly* ad, *CST*, August 1, 1915, 2.2.

29. Central Film Company ad, *CT*, July 27, 1915, 11.

30. The *Northwest Weekly*'s first issue may have appeared earlier, in April or May of 1915, according to "Northwest Movies at Orpheum Weekly," *Bismarck Tribune*, October 15, 1915, 4. In early August, the *Northwest Weekly* offered footage of the Eastland Disaster, perhaps excerpted from the *Herald Movies*. Ideal Theatre ad, *Grand Rapids Leader* (Wisconsin), August 2, 1915, n.p.

31. "Reel Newspaper for Duluthians," *DuNT*, September 5, 1915, 12; "Twin City Movie Man Films Choice Scenes of City," *LCT*, September 23, 1915, 10; "Northwest Movies at Orpheum Weekly," *Bismarck Tribune*, October 15, 1915, 4; and "Tribune's Northwest Weekly," *ALT*, November 6, 1915, n.p.

32. "Tells How Night Outdoor 'Movie' Films Are Made," *DuNT*, October 3, 1915, 5; and "How 'Movies' Are Made," *ALT*, October 29, 1915, 3.

33. "Twin City Movie Man Films Choice Scenes of City," *LCT*, September 23, 1915, 10.

34. The Royal Theatre ad, *ALT*, October 30, 1915, n.p.; and "Albert Lea in Movies," *ALT*, November 5, 1915, 4.

35. "Northwest Weekly," *Bismarck Tribune*, November 9, 1915, 4; and "Grandstand Collapse in Northwest Weekly," *Bismarck Tribune*, December 11, 1915, 4.

36. Royal Theatre ads, *ALT*, October 23, 1915, 4; and October 30, 1915, 4; and "Bismarck Daily Tribune Northwest Weekly," *Bismarck Tribune*, November 24, 1915, 2.

37. "Will Make Debut in Moving Picture Field," *Charlotte Observer*, August 13, 1915, 6.

38. "N.O. to Appear in Movies Every Week," *NOI*, October 9, 1915, 2; "World Series Games Shown on Films Here," *NOI*, October 16, 1915, 2; and "Orange Day Scenes on Item Universal Film," *NOI*, December 4, 1915, 5.

39. *Indianapolis Star-Universal Animated Weekly* ads, *Indianapolis Star*, October 19, 1915, 9; October 20, 1915, 9; October 25, 1915, 9; October 26, 1915, 6; October 28, 1915, 9; October 30, 1915, 9; and November 1, 1915, 4.

40. "Amusements," *NOI*, October 30, 1915, 2.

41. *Charlotte Daily Observer's Universal Animated Weekly* ads, *Charlotte Observer*, September 20, 1915, 9; September 30, 1915, 10; and October 21, 1915, 10.

42. "Will Make Debut in Moving Picture Field," *Charlotte Observer*, August 13, 1915, 6.

43. "Where the Evening Ledger-Universal Weekly Can Be Seen," *PEL*, June 17, 1916, Amusement Section, 3. Most theaters were in Philadelphia, but others were located in Hamilton; Lancaster; and Atlantic City, New Jersey.

44. "Paramount Pictographs" announcement in "Item's Daily Movies," *NOI*, February 11, 1916, 7.

45. "Selig-Tribune Showing Today," *CT*, January 3, 1916, 2.1.

46. For a full menu of each *Selig-Tribune* issue, see the listings that begin in "Stories of the Films," *MPW*, January 22, 1915, 656. The *Chicago Tribune* ads continued throughout 1916, although they became weekly in June and then smaller, with fewer frame stills. "Selig-Tribune—Bi-Weekly" ad, *CST*, June 11, 1916, 8.3; and "The Selig-Tribune—Semi-Weekly" ad, *CST*, November 26, 1916, 7.3.

47. "Selig-Tribune Today," *CT*, January 6, 1916, 2.1; and "Today—Selig-Tribune," *CST*, January 9, 1916, 2.12.

48. *Ford Animated Weekly* also debuted about this time. Produced by Edison, this newsreel was distributed free through Ford "branch offices" or dealerships. "Edison Company in Detroit," *MPW*, October 30, 1915, 769. For this reference I thank Katy Peplin, a doctoral student in Screen Arts & Cultures at the University of Michigan.

49. Selig-Tribune ad, *CST*, January 9, 1916, 2.12.

50. Selig-Tribune ad, *CST*, January 16, 1916, 2.13.

51. One can find local newsreels, however, at least into the 1920s. Individual stories from the *Detroit News Weekly* survive at the Wayne State University Library.

52. Selig-Tribune ad, *CST*, March 5, 1916, 7.6.

CHAPTER 2. "NEWSPAPERS MAKE PICTURE-GOERS"

The phrase in the chapter title comes from F. E. Simmons, manager of the Dreamland, in a speech to the Cleveland League of Motion Picture Exhibitors. "Exhibitors Hear That Newspaper Advertising Pays," *CSL*, February 22, 1914, S.12.

1. This chapter revises and greatly expands the survey of newspaper discourse in Richard Abel, "Entr'acte 5: Trash Twins," in *Americanizing the Movies and "Movie-Mad" Audiences* (Berkeley: University of California Press, 2006), 215–26; and "'Zip! Zam! Zowie!': A New Take on Institutional American Cinema's History Before 1915," *Historical Journal of Film, Radio, and Television* 29, no. 4 (December 2009): 421–32.

2. J. Willis Sayre, "Bernhardt Comes in Fear and Trembling," *ST*, September 6, 1911, 7.

3. "A Glimpse at the Menus in the Local Theaters," *Minneapolis Journal*, September 17, 1911, 4.

4. "Week in Moving Pictures," *Youngstown Vindicator*, September 3, 1911, 17; "Silent Actors in New Roles at the Odeon" and "Great Interest Being Shown in 'The Crusaders,'" *CND*, September 24, 1911, 24.

5. "At the Photoplays," *TNB*, November 8, 1911, 15; and January 20, 1912, 9.

6. Notice of the *Republic*'s column of reviews appeared in "Motion Pictures and the Press," *NYDM*, June 7, 1911, 29. See also "Film Criticism by the St. Louis Republic," *NYMT*, October 8, 1911, 4.2.

7. "The Press, the Press Representative and the Picture 1," *MPN*, October 16, 1915, 41–42. This misconception was due not only to ignorance but also to

newspapers' increasing reliance on regional and even national, as well as local, advertising for their circulation, "selling their space and the readership it represented to advertisers." Michael Schudson, *Discovering the News: A Social History of the Newspaper* (New York: Basic Books, 1973), 93. Partly responsible for rationalizing the relationship between newspapers and advertisers was the American Newspaper Publishers Association, founded in 1887, initially concerned with regulating newspapers' business with advertising agencies such as N.W. Ayer and Son.

8. William A. Johnston, "The Newspaper vs. the Trade Paper," *MPN*, October 16, 1915, 39. See also Russell E. Smith, "Best Film Ad Medium," *EP*, September 6, 1913, 239; and Frank Webb, "Motion Picture Ads," *EP*, January 3, 1914, 560.

9. Gene Morgan, "Moving Pictures and Makers," *CT*, November 19, 1911, 2.2.5. Weeks later, Morgan likely became the anonymous Reel Observer for "In the Moving Picture World," *CT*, December 3, 1911, 2.2.5.

10. "Photo-Plays and Players," *CSL*, December 3, 1911, S.5. Yet the shift from "In the Moving Picture Field" to "Photo-Plays and Players" began a week earlier when nine picture theaters and one state rights distributor (Feature & Educational Film) advertised in a prototype half-page. "Review of Photo-Plays[;] News of Picture Theaters," *CSL*, November 26, 1911, S.5. In Cleveland, the *Leader* had a circulation well below those of the *Press, Plain Dealer*, and *News*.

11. "Photo-Plays and Players," *CSL*, February 4, 1912, S.6.

12. "Presbyterian Church Survey" and "American Films Popular Abroad: Foreigners Like Cowboy and Indian Pictures Best of All," *CSL*, February 11, 1912, S.6; "Better Pay for Writers," *CSL*, March 17, 1912, S.6; "Kalems Everywhere," *CSL*, March 31, 1912, S.8.

13. "Crescent Shows Cleveland Weekly," *CSL*, April 7, 1912, S.8; "New West Side Theater Opens to Big House," *CSL*, June 23, 1912, n.p.

14. "Newest Theater Model of Beauty," *CSL*, October 27, 1912, M.7; Samuel Bullock, "The Modern Moving Picture Theater, and Its Relation to the Social Center Movement," *CSL*, November 10, 1912, B.5; "'Superior' Rises from Small Start" and "Manager of Victor Is Good Organizer," *CSL*, December 8, 1912, B.7; "Some 'Flickers' in the Film Business," *CSL*, December 22, 1912, S.5; and "He Is Veteran in Film Renting Trade," *CSL*, June 1, 1913, C.4.

15. "New Year's Week Finds Big Attractions at Photo-Play Theaters," *CSL*, December 29, 1912, Theatergoers Section, 4–5; and "Here's Way to See Films Free[;] News of Photoplay Theaters," *CSL*, January 6, 1912, Theatergoers Section, 6–7.

16. Ralph P. Stoddard, "Aladdin's Wonderful Lamp Eclipsed," *CSL*, February 2, 1913, B.4; and March 16, 1913, M.10.

17. "Amusements and Places of Entertainment," *CSL*, November 16, 1913, Society Section, 10.

18. "'Bill' Wright Writes About Movie Pages," *CSL*, December 7, 1913, S.12.

19. "What City's Best Photoplay Theaters Are Showing," *CSL*, March 22, 1914, S.12; and "What Cleveland's Photoplay Theaters Are Showing," *CSL*, July 5, 1914, M.2.

20. "What Cleveland's Photoplay Theaters Are Showing," *CSL*, October 25, 1914, M.5.

21. "Film Exhibitors See Rosy Future for Houses Here," *CSL*, January 4, 1914, S.10; "Improves Picture by Screen Setting," *CSL*, January 25, 1914, S.12; and "You May Risk One Eye Here on Scenes from Photoplays Cut Out by Ohio Censors," *CSL*, February 8, 1914, S.12.

22. "Now Splitting Up Motion by the Use of Cinematography to Aid Athlete Training," *CSL*, February 1, 1914, S.12; Ralph F. Stoddard, "Sugar Coating Classics in Motion Pictures to Make Them Inviting," *CSL*, March 1, 1914, S.12; and "Aitken at Head of $1,000,000 Film Firm," *CSL*, April 5, 1914, S.12.

23. "Gossip of the Players In and Out of the Studio," *CSL*, August 23, 1914, M.2; "What Do You Want to Know?" *CSL*, November 29, 1914, M.11; "Whose Picture Do You Want?" *CSL*, June 28, 1914, S.10; and Movie Star Photo Coupon ad, *CSL*, March 28, 1915, S.9.

24. "How the Movie Queen Makes Up," *CSL*, January 24, 1915, Feature, 1.

25. In early 1912, the *Springfield News* (Illinois) and *Pittsburgh Leader* reportedly began printing weekly columns devoted to motion pictures. "Correspondence," *MPW*, March 16, 1912, 976; and March 30, 1912, 1185. In June 1912, the *Philadelphia Times* established a daily block ad of picture theater programs and then a Sunday page of "local picture theatre and film industry news." Paul S. Moore, "Subscribing to Publicity: Syndicated Newspaper Features for Moviegoing in North America, 1911–1915," *Early Popular Visual Culture* 12, no. 2 (May 2014): 264–65. In late 1912, the *Baltimore News* also introduced a Sunday page that, with its many local picture theater ads and columns of brief film synopses likely supplied by house managers, looked like a collective advertisement. "In the Moving Picture Field," *Baltimore Sunday News*, November 3, 1912, 14; and April 13, 1913, 12; and "Best Film Ad Medium," *EP*, September 6, 1913, 239.

26. Ona Otto, "In the Land of Photoplays and Players," *SFB*, December 23, 1911, 4.

27. Otto is identified as a young woman in "Ona Otto Talks of Photographs and Motor Cars," *SFB*, May 18, 1912, 1. See also Epes Winthrop Sargent, "Advice to Exhibitors," *MPW*, January 20, 1912, 198.

28. For information on *flaneur* reporters encountering motion pictures, especially in the nickelodeon period, see Jan Olsson, *Los Angeles Before Hollywood* (Stockholm: National Library of Sweden, 2008), 80–87, 166–68.

29. Ona Otto, "In the Land of Photoplays and Players," *SFB*, December 30, 1911, 7; January 6, 1912, 7; January 13, 1912, 8; January 20, 1912, 18; and January 27, 1912, 12.

30. The February and March issues of the *San Francisco Bulletin* are missing from the microfilm I consulted.

31. Ona Otto, "Window Shopping," *SFB,* January 30, 1912, 8. Most of Otto's other pieces appeared in the *Bulletin*'s "Automobile and Real Estate Section." In late 1913, Otto also was identified as a scenario writer for *The Christmas Waking of Snugs and Hugs,* a local movie starring a toy dog named Kinks. "'Kinks' Makes Hit, 'Snugs and Hugs' Show Dog's Ability," *San Francisco Call & Post,* December 15, 1913, 5.

32. The trade press noticed a gradual change in newspapers' attitudes toward motion pictures around this time. "Facts and Comments," *MPW,* February 8, 1913, 548. W. Stephen Bush also noted that "some of the dailies in the Midwest have begun to take the motion picture seriously." "The Moving Picture and the Press," *MPW,* March 8, 1913, 975. In March 1913, Hearst's *Chicago American* reportedly introduced a weekend page edited by Tom Bourke. Jas. S. McQuade, "Chicago Letter," *MPW,* April 5, 1913, 32.

33. "Times Man Will Be Studio Guest," *SST:* "Amusements," June 25, 1916, 1.

34. J. Willis Sayre, "In the Film World," *ST,* January 24, 1913, 9; January 27, 1913, 9; and January 29, 1913, 9.

35. J. Willis Sayre, "In the Film World," *SST,* February 2, 1913, 16; and *ST,* February 24, 1913, 9. The *Times* also claimed, rather myopically, to be the first paper outside of New York City "to establish a Sunday photoplay section."

36. J. Willis Sayre, "In the Film World," *SST,* February 16, 1913, 14.

37. George H. Bellman, "In the Film World," *ST,* March 4, 1913, 9; and *SST,* March 9, 1913, 22; and March 16, 1913, 27. J. Willis Sayre, "New Bills at Film Theatres," *SST,* April 6, 1913, n.p.; J. Willis Sayre, "Photoplay Happenings," *SST,* April 20, 1913, 23; and Sayre, "Moving Picture News," *SST,* July 6, 1913, 25.

38. J. Willis Sayre, "Film World Happenings," *SST,* June 8, 1913, 21; and Sayre, "Moving Picture News," *SST,* June 15, 1913, 21.

39. J. Willis Sayre, "News of Photoplays," *SST,* May 26, 1913, 5.

40. J. Willis Sayre, "In the Picture Houses," *SST,* September 14, 1913, 22.

41. Occasional articles also appeared in the magazines section. Robert Grau, "The Highest Paid Woman in the World," *SST,* February 25, 1915, 59.

42. "'Movie' Makers Seek Drama's Stars," *CPD,* February 16, 1913, C.4; and "Picture Theatres," *CPD,* February 23, 1913, Editorial/Dramatic, 6. The *Plain Dealer* had the largest circulation of Sunday editions, although lower than the *Cleveland Press*'s daily circulation.

43. "The Movies," *CPD,* November 9, 1913, Editorial/Dramatic, 4; and November 16, 1913, Editorial/Dramatic, 6.

44. "A Cash Prize for Telling What Movie You Liked Best Last Week," *CPD,* November 23, 1913, Editorial/Dramatic, 4; and "What Movie?" *CPD,* November 30, 1913, Editorial/Dramatic, 4.

45. "Moving Pictures Beat Detectives" and "Tour Teams in Movies," *CPD,* November 30, 1913, Editorial/Dramatic, 4; "U.S. Exports Films," *CPD,* December 7, 1913, Editorial/Dramatic, 4; and "Boy Scouts," *CPD,* February 1, 1914, Editorial/Dramatic, 6.

46. Charles Henderson, "Something About the World's Greatest Motion Picture Drama Up to the Present Day and About the Somewhat Weird Italian Genius Who Penned the Book," *CPD*, July 26, 1914, Editorial/Dramatic, 1; and Henderson, "The Man Who Has Made More People Laugh Than Any Living Person Says He Has Succeeded Because He Regarded Fun-Making as a Serious, Painstaking Study," *CPD*, September 20, 1914, Editorial/Dramatic, 1.

47. "Family Album Gives Way to Moving Picture Machine," *CPD*, October 11, 1914, Editorial/Dramatic, 8; "Can You Look Scared?" *CPD*, 25, October 1914, Editorial/Dramatic, 5; "Hands to the Photo Play Actors Are Like Food to the Starving," *CPD*, November 1, 1914, Editorial/Dramatic, 4; and "It's Hard to Be a Film Actress, Says Mary Fuller," *CPD*, November 8, 1914, 4.

48. "Cleveland Scenario Writer Was Big Vaudeville Star" and "A Cat That's a Movie Fan," *CPD*, October 11, 1914, Editorial/Dramatic, 8; "Fiddles and Photo Plays—There's Really a Very Intimate Connection Between Them," *CPD*, October 18, 1914, Editorial/Dramatic, 4; "Running Picture Theater Is Dull Work for Him," *CPD*, November 1, 1914, Editorial/Dramatic, 4; and "He Conducts Film Theater That Stands for 'Class,'" *CPD*, November 15, 1914, Editorial/Dramatic, 4.

49. "Thousands Take Advantage of Leader's Great Offer," *PL*, February 23, 1913, Classified, 24. The "Independent" *Pittsburgh Leader* apparently had no relation to the "Republican" *Cleveland Leader*. The *Leader* also tied with the *Chronicle Telegraph* for third in circulation after the *Press* and *Gazette Times*.

50. "Where You Can See *REAL MOVING PICTURES*[;] *Leader Coupons Redeemed*," *PL*, February 23, 1913, Classified, 24.

51. "REAL MOVING PICTURES," *PL*, September 14, 1913, Classified, 31.

52. "The Movie Lorelei," *PL*, July 27, 1913, Classified, 31.

53. "Exceptional Motion Picture Treats Free to Leader Readers," *PL*, March 2, 1913, Theatrical & Society, 23; and "Attractive Photoplay Entertainment Provided for Leader Readers," *PL*, March 9, 1913, Sporting, 15.

54. "Motion Picture News," *BST*, March 9, 1913, 43. In Buffalo, the *Times* tied with the *Courier* for second in circulation after the *News*.

55. Intriguingly, that Sunday the *Fort Wayne Journal-Gazette* displayed the same banner on its motion picture page, yet the contents differed not only in the program descriptions (and ads) for nine local picture theaters, but also in two added columns: "Photoplay Stars in Next Week's Pictures" and "The Motion Picture's Place in the World's Work and Play." "Motion Picture News," *FWJG*, March 9, 1913, 10.

56. "Pathé Weekly Camera Operators Must Be Johnny on the Spot," *BST*, March 9, 1913, 43.

57. "William J. Burns, Famous Detective, Is Latest Feature" and "Motion Pictures Are 17 Years Old," *BST*, March 9, 1913, 42.

58. Warner's Feature Film and Fuller Feature Film Exchange ads (the latter featuring Helen Gardner and her films) and the star photos of Augustus Carney, Guy Combs, May Buckley, and Gardner, *BST*, March 30, 1913, 63.

59. "The Movie Editor by Raye," *BST*, September 28, 1913, 72. In later issues, the writer briefly became "Miller" and then simply "Himself."

60. "Leading Theater Programs Appear Only in the Times," *BST*, April 20, 1913, 49.

61. "With Film and Screen," *BST*, March 8, 1914, 52; "Motion Picture News," *BST*, March 8, 1914, 53; and "The Silent Drama," *BST*, April 5, 1914, 54; and June 7, 1914, 72.

62. "Mutual Movie Star Meets Prominent Suffragettes," *BST*, March 8, 1914, 53; "'Mutual Actress Perfect Blonde,' Says Belasco," *BST*, March 15, 1914, 60; and "Universal 'Movie' City Will Move to New Site in San Fernando," *BST*, April 5, 1914, 54.

63. "Buffalo Delegates Play Lead Part in New York Session," *BST*, June 14, 1914, 72; "The Regent—Theater Beautiful—Greets Buffalo Today," *BST*, September 27, 1914, 54; and "New Ariel—Buffalo's Latest Photo-Play Temple Delights Thousands," *BST*, November 22, 1914, 74.

64. "Movie Men Endorse Kathlyn Series as Big Drawing Card," *BST*, March 8, 1914, 52; "Kathlyn Plays Make Good in Photo-Play Houses of Buffalo," *BST*, March 15, 1914, 60; and "Buffalo Delegates Declare Serial Film Most Popular Feature," *BST*, June 14, 1914, 72.

65. "Five Buffalo Churches to Use Movies During Big Biblical Campaign," *BST*, August 30, 1914, 59; and "Free to School Children" ad, *BST*, September 20, 1914, 49.

66. "The Movie Man Says," *BST*, March 15, 1914, 60; and March 22, 1914, 60; "The Movie Editor by Himself," *BST*, April 5, 1914, 54; and "Exposition Flashes by Miller," *BST*, June 14, 1914, 72.

67. "Buffalo Theaters and Movie News," *BST*, December 13, 1914, 97.

68. "The Craze to Act in the Movies," *BST*, December 13, 1914, All Feature Section, n.p.

69. "Toledo to Be Picture Play Authority of Middle West," *TB*, May 17, 1913, 7. The *Blade* had the second-largest circulation in the city after the *News-Bee*.

70. Ibid.; and "New Alhambra Most Elegant," *TB*, May 31, 1913, 8.

71. "Quo Vadis Shows Merit of Picture Drama[;] David Belasco's Brother a Movy Director," *TB*, October 1, 1913, 12.

72. "News of the Moving Pictures," *TB*, January 3, 1914, 12.

73. No copies of the *Toledo Times* survive prior to early January 1914, but the Sunday page probably appeared in the fall of 1913.

74. "News of the Photoplays and Photoplayers," *TT*, January 4, 1914, 6; and January 11, 1914, 6. The *Times* had the lowest circulation (nineteen thousand) of the city's three newspapers.

75. "With the Photoplays and Players," *TT*, January 11, 1914, 11; and "Scenes from 'Creation' Photo-Drama of Passing Ages," *TT*, February 8, 1914, 3.

76. "Ruin of Temple Completes Film" and "Jacob Adler Appears in Motion Pictures," *TT*, March 1, 1914, 8; and "Motion Picture Men Invade Mexico," *TT*, March 15, 1914, 6.

77. "Reel News of Photo Plays and Players," *TT*, July 19, 1914, 2.

78. "In 'Movie' Land," *SPN*, October 26, 1913, 5; and November 2, 1913, 5.

79. "In Movie Land," *SPN*, December 28, 1913, 5; and January 18, 1914, 5. See also Gertrude Price, "Refugee from Mexico Becomes 'Movie' Star," *SPN*, January 25, 1914, 5; and "She Braves Death for Movie Films," *SPN*, February 1, 1914, 8.

80. "In Movie Land," *SPN*, March 8, 1914, 4; and March 29, 1914, 6.

81. "The Following Theaters Are Members of the Motion Picture Exhibitors' Association of St. Paul" ad, *SPN*, March 8, 1914, 4; and April 19, 1914, 4.

82. "Arthur Leslie," *MPW*, August 1, 1914, 686. Leslie claimed that Syndicate Film Publishing was formed in fall 1912, but newspapers seem not to have used the service until early 1913.

83. Syndicate Publishing ads, *Altoona Mirror*, September 16, 1903, 9; *Washington Post*, November 1, 1911, 9; *Racine Journal-News*, January 23, 1914, 2; *Des Moines Capital*, March 20, 1914, 11; and *SH*, September 27, 1914, 14.

84. "Mrs. Leslie's Bequest Attacked in Court," *AtC*, December 13, 1914, B.12; and "Mrs. Frank Leslie Said to Be Daughter of Negro," *SH*, December 23, 1914, 11.

85. Jas. S. McQuade, "Chicago Letter," *MPW*, April 19, 1913, 265.

86. Ibid.

87. "At the Moving Picture Playhouses," *DMRL*, February 9, 1913, 7; and "Motion Picture News," *Columbus Enquirer*, February 16, 1913, 3. In an early Sunday page, the *Cleveland Plain Dealer* printed two short paragraphs copyrighted by Syndicate Publishing, but its subsequent industry news or gossip does not match that of newspapers supplied by Leslie's service. "News and Moves in Film World," *CPD*, February 23, 1913, Editorial/Dramatic, 6.

88. "Motion Picture News," *FWST*, February 14, 1913, 2.33; *OS*, February 22, 1913, 2; and *Hamilton Journal*, March 1, 1913, n.p.

89. "News of Photoplays and Photoplayers," *OS*, March 8, 1913, 2; *Hamilton Journal*, March 8, 1913, n.p.; "Motion Picture News," *MST*, March 16, 1913, Society, 10; and *FWJG*, March 16, 1913, 18. For differing compilations of syndicated material, see "Motion Picture News," *The State* (Columbia, South Carolina), March 2, 1913, 29.

90. "Motion Picture News," *FWJG*, March 9, 1913, 10. The Fort Wayne paper puzzlingly copied the "Indian picture" banner from the *Buffalo Sunday Times*. Other papers soon adopted the second Syndicated Film banner for their columns. "News of Photoplays and Photoplayers," *SAL*, March 23, 1913, 64.

91. "News of Photoplays and Photoplayers," *OS*, April 19, 1913, 2; and June 14, 1913, 2.

92. "News of Photoplays and Photoplayers," *OS*, March 22, 1913, 2; April 19, 1913, 2; July 5, 1913, 2; July 12, 1913, 2; August 2, 1913, 2; and September 6, 1913, 4.

93. "With the 'Movies' Here and There, as Well as Everywhere," *WR*, March 29, 1913, 19; and "Motion Pictures," *WR*, May 24, 1913, 13. This page appeared on Saturdays.

94. Arthur G. Stolte, "Motion Pictures," *WR*, June 21, 1913, 11.

95. "Passed by the National Board of Censorship," *WR*, May 10, 1913, 15; "Kinemacolor Plays to 'Show' Exhibitors Some New Things," *WR*, June 28, 1913, 11; and "Kinemacolor Secures Pictures of Well Known Theatre People," *WR*, July 12, 1913, 11.

96. "Moving Picture Factory in Iowa," *WR*, May 24, 1913, 13; Arthur G. Stolte, "An Afternoon with Don Meaney at the Essanay Motion Picture Studio," *WR*, November 1, 1913, 10; and "Iowa Exhibitors Meet in Annual Gathering," *WR*, December 6, 1913, 10.

97. "Motion Picture News" ad, *WH*, April 10, 1913, 1; and "Motion Picture News," *WH*, April 11, 1913, 12.

98. "Motion Picture News," *WH*, April 11, 1913, 12.

99. "Motion Picture News," *WH*, April 12, 1913, 11.

100. "Motion Picture News," *WH*, April 14, 1913, 11; April 17, 1913, 13; and May 27, 1913, 13; and "Motion Pictures as Method of Teaching," *WH*, April 19, 1913, 13.

101. "Motion Picture News," *WH*, April 12, 1913, 11; April 16, 1913, 13; and April 19, 1913, 13.

102. "Moving Picture Patrons" ads, *WH*, April 19, 1913, 13; and May 5, 1913, 5; and "The Motion Picture as an Agency of Evangelization," *WH*, June 20, 1913, 9.

103. "Motion Picture News," *WH*, April 13, 1913, 8.

104. "Motion Picture News," *WH*, May 27, 1913, 13; and July 19, 1913, 13.

105. As far as I know, no business records survive from either Syndicate Publishing or Syndicate Film Publishing.

106. "News of Photoplays and Photoplayers," *SAL*, May 11, 1913, 31; and *DMRL*, July 7, 1913, 7; and "Motion Picture News," *MST*, July 6, 1913, Society, 7. Both the *Tribune* and the *Light*, however, continued to pick up items from Leslie's service to include, along with local ads, in Sunday pages devoted to theater and photoplays.

107. B.V. La Frances, "Motion Pictures," *DuNT*, May 27, 1913, Magazine, 8; and June 8, 1913, Magazine, 5. The first page reproduced Edison's declaration that motion pictures "will revolutionize education," yet later pages adopted a format closer to those of the Cleveland, Pittsburgh, Buffalo, and Minneapolis newspapers.

108. "News of Photoplays and Photoplayers," *Lexington Herald*, March 23, 1913, 48; and "Motion Picture News," *Frederick Post*, June 7, 1913, 3. Paul Moore reports that the *Pittsburgh Post*'s "News of Photoplays and Photoplayers" page began on March 16, 1913, and the *Milwaukee Sentinel*'s "Motion Picture News" column on March 22, 1913. A "News of Photoplays and Photoplayers" page also appeared in the *Eau Claire Sunday Leader* (Wisconsin), February 22, 1914, 3.

109. Arthur Leslie was even named as editor for the last two columns of "News of Photoplays and Photoplayers," *OS*, April 30, 1914, 8; and May 1, 1914, 8.

110. Arthur G. Stolte, "Motion Pictures," *WR*, March 7, 1914, 10; and "Miss Rose Graves and Arthur Stolte Married in Chicago Wedding a Surprise Affair," *Waterloo Times-Tribune*, July 12, 1914, 7.

111. "Going Gossip About Photo Plays and Photo Players," *AS*, January 18, 1914, 3.7; and "About Photo Plays and Photo Players," *AS*, February 1, 1914, 3.7.

112. Arthur Leslie ad, *NYMT*, December 13, 1914, 7. See also the Leslie ad, *NYMT*, September 13, 1914, 2. Syndicated Film claimed to distribute the story version of Thanhouser's serial *The Million Dollar Mystery* to as many as two hundred newspapers. Syndicate Film ad, *MPW*, April 25, 1914, 610.

113. The subtitle of this section draws from the "The Great Central Market" ad (full page), *CT*, June 23, 1915, 13.

114. "For Big 'Movie' Studio," *CN*, February 5, 1914, 4. The *News* had the largest circulation of the city's daily newspapers.

115. Early stars included Francis X. Bushman, Ruth Stonehouse, and Arthur V. Johnson. "A 'Movie' Favorite," *CN*, February 10, 1914, 4; "Ruth Stonehouse," *CN*, February 14, 1914, 4; and "A 'Movie' Favorite," *CN*, February 19, 1914, 4.

116. "Big 'Movie' Shows Are to Be the Rule," *CN*, February 19, 1914, 4; "'Squaw Man' Here in Moving Pictures," *CN*, February 16, 1914, 14; and "'Hearts Adrift' Told in 'Movie' Pictures," *CN*, February 19, 1914, 4.

117. "Movie Shows for Week," *CN*, February 9, 1914, 16.

118. W.K. Hollander, "New 'Movie' Bills at Theaters Next Week," *CN*, March 18, 1916, 9.

119. "Special Programs for Today, Thursday and Friday at High-Class Moving Picture Theaters," *CT*, February 18, 1914, 9; and "Special Programs for Today, Sunday, Monday and Tuesday at High-Class Moving Picture Theaters," *CT*, February 21, 1914, 7.

120. See the full-page ad, *CST*, February 22, 1914, 8.6.

121. "Right Off the Reel" may have first appeared as the title of a weekly column in *Exhibitors' Times*, beginning on May 24, 1913. The writer was T.B. or Thomas Bedding.

122. "In the Frame of Public Favor," *CST*, March 1, 1914, 5.3. In the early 1910s, a gilded frame was still "the most common method of situating the screen in an auditorium." William Paul, "Screens," in Richard Abel, ed., *The Encyclopedia of Early Cinema* (London: Routledge, 2005), 573.

123. Susan Stewart, *On Longing: Narratives of the Miniature, the Gigantic, the Souvenir, the Collection* (Durham, NC: Duke University Press, 1993), 101.

124. Such picture-player popularity contests first appeared in the *New York Morning Telegraph* in September 1911, and over the next two years were taken up by *Motion Picture Story Magazine*, *Ladies' World*, and eventually several metropolitan newspapers.

125. The alleged popularity of the stars "in the frame of public favor" was never based on more than twenty-five hundred votes, at least for the month that the *Tribune* published the vote count.

126. "Answers to Movie Fans," *CST*, April 12, 1914, 5.3.

127. Mae Tinee, "Babes in the Movie Zoo," *CST*, April 12, 1914, 5.3; and "Mae Tinee Writes from New York," *CST*, April 19, 1914, 5.3.

128. "Answers to Movie Fans by Mae Tinee," *CST*, May 31, 1914, 5.3; "Gossip of the Movie Plays and Players," *CST*, July 12, 1914, 8.5; and Mae Tinee, "Gossip of the Movie Plays and Players," *CST*, August 2, 1914, 8.5.

129. Mme. Qui Vive, "The Love Affairs of Peggy," *CST*, July 5, 1914, 7.12. The anonymous serial story of Peggy ran until early December 1914.

130. "The Voice of the Movie Fans," *CST*, September 20, 1914, 8.4; September 27, 1914, 8.5; and October 4, 1914, 8.4.

131. "In Movieland," *CST*, September 27, 1914, 8.5; November 22, 1914, 8.11; November 29, 1914, 8.4; and December 9, 1914, 8.9.

132. "Adventures of the Silly Gal-Lilies in Movie Land," *CST*, December 20, 1914, 8.7.

133. "Right Off the Reel by Mae Tinee," *CST*, January 31, 1915, 5.3.

134. "In the Frame of Public Favor," *CST*, January 3, 1915, 8.7. Whether or not this profile of Frances Peck (aka Mae Tinee) is accurate, an early biographical note claims she was the daughter of a Denver evangelist, served as a cub reporter on the *Denver Republican*, and, after a failed marriage, moved to Chicago to join the *Chicago Tribune*. See Ishbel Ross, *Ladies of the Press: The Story of Women in Journalism by an Insider* (New York: Harper & Brothers, 1936), 411–12.

135. "Right Off the Reel by Mae Tinee," *CST*, April 4, 1915, 5.3; and "Latest News from Movie Land by Mae Tinee," *CST*, April 4, 1915, 8.8.

136. Mae Tinee, "The Waiter's Tip or A Discovery," *CT*, April 17, 1915, 8; and Mae Tinee, "What Saved the Day for Mrs. Lansing," *CT*, May 1, 1915, 12.

137. "Tomorrow's Sunday Tribune" ad, *CT*, May 22, 1915, 14; and July 17, 1915, 5.

138. "$10,000 for 100 Words," *OS*, June 22, 1914, 5; *FWST*, June 28, 1914, 4; and *CPD*, September 6, 1914, X.2; "The Million Dollar Mystery," *SAL*, June 26, 1914, Women's Clubs/Society, n.p.; *Lincoln Sunday Star* (Nebraska), September 27, 1914, n.p.; and *CR*, November 8, 1914, 14. See also "Another $10,000 Offered for Photoplay Solution," *FWST*, March 28, 1915, 27; "Mission Canyon Scene of 'Diamond From the Sky,'" *FWST*, April 4, 1915, 19; and "The Diamond in the Sky," *Trenton Times*, August 5, 1915, 12; and August 26, 1915, 4.

139. "Right Off the Reel," *AuC*, from March 8, 1914, C.8, to January 3, 1915, C.8; "Right Off the Reel," *BC*, from March 15, 1914, 55, to January 3, 1915, 52; and "Right Off the Reel," *OT*, March 29, 1914, 12, and June 14, 1914, 12. By September 1914, the *Augusta Chronicle* was reprinting only "In the Frame of Public Favor" and "The Love Affairs of Peggy" and filling the rest of the page with three or four large picture theater ads. *AuC*, September 20, 1914, C.8.

140. "Today's Features at the Movies," *CRH*, March 23, 1914, 10; and March 24, 1914, 11.

141. "Reel Drama," *CRH*, March 29, 1914, 2.5. The circulation of the *Sunday Record-Herald* nearly equaled that of the *Sunday Tribune*.

142. Moya Luckett, *Cinema and Community: Progressivism, Exhibition, and Film Culture in Chicago, 1907–1917* (Detroit: Wayne State University Press, 2013), 158.

143. Ray H. Leek, "Reducing 'The Spoilers' to Film" and "La Salle to Become Film Theater," *CRH*, March 29, 1914, 2.5; "'Dope' Fiends in the Making" and "The Studebaker Now Film House," *CRH*, April 5, 1914, 2.5; and "Gossip of the Photoplay Theaters and Occupants," *CRH*, April 19, 1914, 2.5.

144. An "Extra Girl," "How the 'Extra Girl' Breaks Into Movie Acting—for a While," *CRH*, May 24, 1914, 2.5.

145. "Art, Religion, and Other Causes Aided by 'Movies,'" *CRH*, May 31, 1914, 2.5; and "You Just Can't Kill a Movie Actor; Richard Travers Has Proved This," *CRH*, June 7, 1914, 2.4.

146. "In the Picture Playhouses," *CH*, August 11, 1914, 11. The *Chicago Record-Herald* became the *Chicago Herald* in mid-June 1914. "History of the Four Papers That Are Now the Herald," *CSH*, June 14, 1914, 1.6.

147. The "Extra Girl," "How Beery Came to Be a Lady," *CSH*, September 13, 1914, 2.4; "On the Outside Watching an Ade Photoplay," *CSH*, September 20, 1914, 2.4; and The "Extra Girl," "Novelli Loves Conflict of Either Weapons or Hearts," *CSH*, November 22, 1914, 6.6.

148. See the full-page ad for Parsons's column, *CSH*, December 13, 1913, Magazine, 8; Louella O. Parsons, "How to Write Photo Plays," *CSH*, December 13, 1914, 6.8; December 20, 1914, 6.6; December 27, 1914, 6.8; and January 3, 1915, 6.6. For further information on Parsons, see Samatha Barbas, *The First Lady of Hollywood: A Biography of Louella Parsons* (Berkeley: University of California Press, 2005) and Hilary Hallet, *Go West, Young Women!: The Rise of Early Hollywood* (Berkeley: University of California Press, 2013), 71–99.

149. Gene Morgan, "Where Are Chicago's Big Shoes? Charles Chaplin, Movie Laugh Maker, Asks You," *CSH*, January 10, 1915, 6.6.

150. "Come to Our Movies," *CSH*, January 17, 1915, 6.6; "In the Picture Playhouses," *CSH*, January 24, 1915, 6.6; and January 31, 1915, 6.7; and "From Filmland," *CSH*, February 7, 1915, 6.6.

151. Rosemary Grey, "His Hobby [Francis X. Bushman]," *CSH*, January 24, 1915, 6.6; "Findings from Filmland," "Answers to Movie Queries," and "Advice to Would-Be Movie Comedians," *CSH*, January 31, 1915, 6.6; and Gene Morgan, "Clipping Film with Censors," *CSH*, February 7, 1915, 6.6.

152. See the large ad in *CSH*, March 28, 1915, 1.4; and the initial strip, "Introducing Charley Chaplin's Comic Capers," in *CH*, March 29, 1915, 16. See also the large ad in *CH*, January 2, 1915, n.p.; and the initial strip, "Movies: Featuring Haphazard Helen in Her Desert Love," *CSH*, January 3, 1915, 4.2.

153. Caroline Carr, "Ruth Roland Breezily Mixes Tea and Business," *CSH*, April 18, 1915, 6.6; Carr, "Pretty Grace Darmond, Who Rides, Swings, Acts," *CSH*, April 25, 1915, 5.6; and Carr, "Hard World and Luck Help Miss Bayne," *CSH*, May 2, 1915, 5.6.

154. Gene Morgan, "Mr. Jitney Jim Yearns to Break Into Reel Drama," *CSH*, May 9, 1915, 5.2; "What Fans Want to Know," *CSH*, April 11, 1915, 6.6; "Late

News for Film Fans," *CSH*, April 18, 1915, 6.7. One could still read Morgan's Jitney Jim stories through late 1915. Gene Morgan, "Jitney Jim Tells Myrtle the Secret of Winning Praise from Critics," *CSH*, November 28, 1915, 5.4.

155. "The Story of My Life by Charley Chaplin," *CSH*, July 4, 1915, 5.6, and "My Adventures in Movieland by Charley Chaplin," *CSH*, August 8, 1915, 5.6.

156. "Chicago Sunday Herald's Gallery of Moving Picture Stars—Seven Faces You See Most Every Day," *CSH*, June 20, 1915, 9.4; and "Pictures of Movie Stars Whom You All Know," *CSH*, June 27, 1915, 9.4.

157. Louella O. Parsons, *How to Write for the Movies* (Chicago: McClurg, 1915).

158. Louella O. Parsons, "The Story of Lillian Gish—Most Beautiful Blonde in the World," *CSH*, July 11, 1915, 6.5; and Parsons, "Here's Ideal Film Personality—Clara Kimball Young Is Playful Child and Brainy Woman," *CSH*, July 18, 1915, 6.6.

159. See the large ad, *CH*, September 16, 1915, 7; and Louella O. Parsons, "How to Become a Movie Actress," *CSH*, September 19, 1915, 6.1.

160. Louella O. Parsons, "How to Become a Movie Actress," *CSH*, September 19, 1915, 6.1, September 26 1915, 6.1; October 3, 1915, 6.1; and October 10, 1915, 6.1.

161. Louella O. Parsons, "How to Become a Movie Star," *CSH*, October 3, 1915, 6.3; October 10, 1915, 6.6; October 17, 1915, 6.4; November 7, 1915, 5.1; November 14, 1915, 5.6; November 21, 1915, 5.4; and November 28, 1915, 5.4.

162. Sunday Herald ad, *CH*, February 18, 1915, 12.

163. "From Filmland" Sunday pages in the Boise *Idaho Statesman*, April 18, 1915, n.p.; and *OT*, April 25, 1915, 31; and October 17, 1915, 13.

164. Gardner Mack, "Photoplays and Photoplayers" and "What Sort of a Play Does the Public Want to See?" *WT*, March 17, 1914, 8.

165. "What Do You Want to See Mr. and Mrs. Public?" *WT*, March 20, 1914, 10.

166. Gardner Mack, "Every Modern Film Story a Style Show for Women," *WT*, June 3, 1914, 10.

167. Gardner Mack, "Motion Picture Has Become Great Boon of the Shopper," *WT*, December 31, 1914, 7.

168. Gardner Mack, "Class of Program to Which Objection Could Not Be Raised," *WT*, April 7, 1914, 10.

169. Gardner Mack, "When Getting People Into a Theater Is a Species of Con Game," *WT*, March 30, 1914, 6.

170. Gardner Mack, "Exhibitors Who Help Regular Patrons Are Helping Themselves," *WT*, March 17, 1914, 8; and Mack, "What the Photoplay Department of the Times Supports," *WT*, May 26, 1914, 6.

171. Gardner Mack, "Quality Not Quantity First on the List of the Public's Demands," *WT*, March 19, 1914, 6; and Mack, "Yellow Film Hurts More Exhibitors Than It Helps," *WT*, March 27, 1914, 10.

172. Gardner Mack, "One Theater Manager to Give Public What It Wants," *WT*, March 28, 1914, 8.

173. Gardner Mack, "Ten Thousand People Prove Demand for Cleaner Kinds of Films," *WT*, April 3, 1914, 10; and Mack, "Class of Program to Which Objection Could Not Be Raised," *WT*, April 7, 1914, 10.

174. Gardner Mack, "Class of Program to Which Objection Could Not Be Raised," *WT*, April 7, 1914, 10.

175. Gardner Mack, "Quality Not Quantity First on the List of the Public's Demands," *WT*, March 19, 1914, 8.

176. "Marguerite Snow Was Leading Woman Here Before Becoming Screen Star," *WT*, January 7, 1915, 9; "Scenario Writers of District Form an Inquest Club," *WT*, January 10, 1915, 9; and "Wild Riding Cowgirl Is Native of the District of Columbia," *WT*, June 19, 1915, 7.

177. "What Children Want Most to See in the Motion Pictures," *WT*, February 5, 1915, 13; "What Length of Film Do You Like Best, Mr. and Mrs. Public," *WT*, March 2, 1915, 14; and "Recreation Survey Develops Some Surprises as to Films," *WT*, March 3, 1915, 7. To introduce the March 2 survey, Mack quoted extensively from a current article in the *New York Dramatic Mirror*.

178. "Progressive Motion Picture Party Is Newest Social Function," *WT*, May 10, 1915, 9.

179. "Press Club and the Government Will Begin Showing Photoplays," *WT*, August 9, 1915, 10.

180. In highlighting Paramount's new policy of newspaper advertising, Mack implicitly acknowledged a model for his own column's efforts. "Patrons of Films to Be Given More News About the Plays and Players," *WT*, May 19, 1915, 7.

181. "Special Service to Supply Film to Churches and Schools," *WT*, March 11, 1915, 7; and "Interpret Laws with Free Picture Shows in Municipal Playgrounds," *WT*, July 30, 1915, 12.

182. "Harold Lockwood One of Actor Types Screen Play Develops," *WT*, January 14, 1915, 9; "Experience Teaches Stage Star How Film Actors Must Work," *WT*, February 2, 1915, 9; "Managers to Prevent Stage Stars Being Featured in the Films," *WT*, February 18, 1915, 9; "Fostering Spirit of Antagonism Toward Stage Will Not Help Films," *WT*, April 8, 1915, 6; "Do Pictures Aid or Injure the Drawing Power of Great Stage Stars?" *WT*, April 29, 1915, 6; "Exhibitor Believes Motion Picture Stars Are Best Actors," *WT*, July 17, 1915, 7; "Battle Between the Stage and Screen Has Reached an Acute State," *WT*, July 26, 1915, 9; and "Stock Companies Are Training Schools for the Motion Pictures," *WT*, July 31, 1915, 5.

183. "Expert Gives Advice as to How Not to Write Picture Scenarios," *WT*, February 6, 1915, 7; "E. Phillips Oppenheim Writing Series of Detective Tales for the Film," *WT*, February 10, 1915, 11; "Advice From Sargent as to How to Find Good Plots for Scenarios," *WT*, April 9, 1915, 7; "What Constitutes a Good Scenario as Outlined by Experts," *WT*, April 23, 1915, 11; "How Scenario Editor Plays Important Part in Every Photoplay," *WT*, April 24, 1915, 7; and "Sargent Designs an Ideal School to Train Writers for Schools," *WT*, September 28, 1915, 11. The *Times* heavily advertised Oppenheim's serial *The Black Box*.

184. "Picture Play Can No Longer Depend on Made-to-Order Thrills," *WT*, February 16, 1915, 9; "Evolution of Film Makes Photoplay an Art and Not an Industry," *WT*, March 10, 1915, 7; "Circus, Not the Film, Is the Place for Hair Raising Feats to Be Shown," *WT*, April 17, 1915, 7; and "Expert Bewails the Tendency to Star 'Punch' Instead of the Story," *WT*, May 29, 1915, 15.

185. "Tucker Tells About Use of Dialogue in Making of Photoplays," *WT*, January 5, 1915, 9; "What and Why Speech Is Necessary in the Making of Film Plays," *WT*, January 21, 1915, 7; "Men Employed to Cut and Edit the Film Often Make or Mar a Play," *WT*, January 23, 1915, 7; "Props Are Important Element in Making of the Film Drama," *WT*, February 9, 1915, 9; and "Actress in Pictures Knows Real Worry of Designing Costumes," *WT*, July 7, 1915, 7.

186. "Actress Tells Girls Who Want to Be Screen Stars 'Don't,'" *WT*, February 20, 1915, 9; and "Film Industry Gives Same Opportunity to Women as It Gives to Men," *WT*, June 3, 1915, 6. Mack also continued to praise actresses as fashion models for women. "Screen Stars Become Fashion Models for Women Patrons," *WT*, March 13, 1915, 7; and "Photoplay Fashions First Aid to the Fair Students of Style," *WT*, June 11, 1915, 18.

187. "Making War Films an Undertaking More Dangerous Than Making War," *WT*, January 28, 1915, 9; "Motion Pictures Are Used in Training Europe's Army Recruits," *WT*, February 3, 1915, 11; and "European Armies Are More Friendly to Motion Picture Cameraman," *WT*, June 12, 1915, 9.

188. Anna Held, "Film Work Both a Revelation and a Revolution for Anna Held," *WT*, February 19, 1916, 12; "Photoplay Mahomet Attracts Mountain of Stage Producers," *WT*, May 1, 1916, 9; and "Today's Best Films by Gardner Mack," *WT*, May 26, 1916, 14. Ads from at least eight city picture theaters supported the Saturday page. As the *Times* reduced its Saturday page to an unsigned column in late 1916, another paper began to fill the gap. Frank P. Morse, "Speaking of the Silent Drama," *Washington Post*, October 1, 1916, MT2.

189. "In the World of Films," *PD*, May 3, 1914, 4.8. "Pittsburg" was an accepted variant of "Pittsburgh" at the time. The *Dispatch* had the second-highest circulation in the city.

190. George M. Downe, "Movie Men Are Joyful Over Trade Prospects," *PD*, May 3, 1914, 4.8.

191. World Film and Warner's Features ads, *PD*, May 31, 1914, 5.7; Fort Pitt Film ad, *PD*, June 14, 1914, 5.7; George M. Downe, "Wonders of Antiquity Shown on the Screen [*Antony and Cleopatra*]," *PD*, May 10, 1914, 5.8; Downe, "'Our Mutual Girl' Rescues Her Protégee's Brother," *PD*, May 24, 1914, 5.8; and Downe, "Pittsburgers Progress," *PD*, June 28, 1914, 5.7. Fort Pitt Film produced short films of local events for "educational purposes" as well as other "commercial work."

192. Box Office Attractions ad, Feature Film and Calcium ad, and "Gossip of the Studios," *PD*, September 6, 1914, 4.7.

193. "With Local Film Folk" and "Steady Rise to Top [A.A. Weiland]," *PD*, September 20, 1914, 4.6; and George M. Downe, "Films in Demand," *PD*, October 25, 1914, 2.7. Weiland Film was an important regional distributor of non-affiliated films, including *Atlantis* and many nonfiction "war pictures."

Abel (no relation, as far as I know) was the manager of Continental Feature Film, another regional rental exchange.

194. *"The Virginian," PD,* September 6, 1914, 4.7; *"Atlantis," PD,* September 13, 1914, 4.6; *"Love Everlasting," PD,* October 25, 1914, 2.7; and *"The Wishing Ring," PD,* November 8, 1914, 4.6.

195. "Stars Elevating Status of Photo-Play," *PD,* November 15, 1914, 5.1; and Charles B. Frost, "A Look at the Future; A Glance at the Past," *PD,* November 22, 1914, 4.8.

196. Charles B. Frost, "In Newspapers Lies Best Solution of Movie Censorship," "Heard in the Managers' Offices," and "Newsy Items from Local Filmland," *PD,* December 13, 1914, 6.4; and Frost, "Details of Producing Picture Play Are Great," *PD,* December 27, 1914, 4.4.

197. "When Cold Chills North Scenario Writers Bask in Sun of California," *SO,* April 12, 1914, 5.8.

198. Mary Anne Smith, "News of the Photoplays and Stars of Movies Told by Miss Smith," *SO,* May 3, 1914, 3.10. She specifically mentioned *Moving Picture World, New York Dramatic Mirror, New York Morning Telegraph,* and *Motography.*

199. Ibid.

200. Mary Anne Smith, "Movies Teach Columbia Students How to Be Newspaper Reporters," *SO,* June 21, 1914, 3.9; Smith, "Pullman Car Movies Show Scenery Travelers Miss on Night Rides," *SO,* June 28, 1914, 4.2; and Smith, "Educational and Cultural Films Aim of New Paramount Company," *SO,* August 2, 1914, 3.8. That last column included a summary of William W. Hodkinson's plans for the Paramount Film Corporation.

201. Mary Anne Smith, "At the Motion Picture Theaters," *SO,* October 11, 1914, 4.4; and Smith, "At the Photo-Play Theaters," *SO,* November 8, 1914, 4.4. The theaters included the Majestic, Columbia, Peoples, Sunset, National, Star, and occasionally the Globe.

202. Mary Anne Smith, "At the Motion Picture Theaters," *SO,* November 29, 1914, 4.4; and February 2, 1915, 4.4.

203. Mary Anne Smith, "At the Motion Picture Theaters," *SO,* November 8, 1914, 4.4.

204. "Right Off the Reel by Mae Tinee," *SO,* August 22, 1915, 6; and July 16, 1916, 7.

205. Gertrude P. Corbett, "Society News," *MO,* May 5, 1915, 10; "Society News," *MO,* June 24, 1915, 8; and "Baby Rivals Will Be Shown at Fair," *MO,* September 18, 1915, 7.

206. "The Ft. Worth Sunday Sandwich," *FWST,* August 2, 1914, 6; and August 23, 1914, 4.

207. According to its editorial page, the *Star-Telegram* was a member of the Associated Press, so some industry items could have come from its telegraph service.

208. "News for 'Movie' Fans" ad and "Questions of 'Movie' Fans," *FWST,* October 25, 1914, 21.

209. "Margarita Fisher's Stage Career Began at Age of 8," *FWST*, October 25, 1914, 21.

210. "Doings of the Week in Theaters and Picture Houses," *FWST*, December 20, 1914, 35.

211. "Girl of 17 Made Good Start as Film Actress," *FWST*, January 3, 1915, 12; and Mary B. Leffler, "Tillie's Punctured Romance Is Scream," *FWST*, January 10, 1915, 14.

212. Mary B. Leffler, "Movie Stars in Private Life," *FWST*, January 31, 1915, n.p.; Leffler, "Do You Prefer Single or Multiple Reel Pictures?" *FWST*, February 14, 1915, 30; Leffler, "Fans Voting Heavily for Multiple Reel Pictures," *FWST*, February 21, 1915, 23; and Leffler, "Climax of Photoplay Serials in 'The Goddess,'" *FWST*, April 25, 1915, 22.

213. Mary B. Leffler, "In the Photoplay World," *FWST*, May 16, 1915, 16; and May 23, 1915, 30.

214. "The Constitution's Moving Picture Page," *AtC*, August 23, 1914, B.4. Although the *Birmingham News & Age Herald* may have had a motion picture page months earlier, I could only research the Sunday page beginning in March 1916.

215. "Cleo Madison Makes Friends with the Kids," *AtC*, August 23, 1914, B.4; and "Barrymore to Star in Famous Players' 'Man From Mexico,'" *AtC*, August 30, 1914, 14.

216. "Local Society Folks to Aid in 'Movie' for Buy-a-Bale Movement," *AtC*, September 20, 1914, 33; "Mrs. Starr Teaches Mayor Role of Movie Performer; Also Brother Art of Love," *AtC*, October 11, 1914, M.11; "W.C. Brandon Joins Warner Features Co.," *AtC*, September 27, 1914, M.10; "Big Business Reported by Arthur S. Hyman [World Film manager]," *AtC*, October 11, 1914, M.11; and "'Al' Fowler [Alpha manager]," *AtC*, October 25, 1914, A.11.

217. *The Trey O' Hearts* coupon ad, *AtC*, August 23, 1914, B.4; Savoy and Alpha ads, *AtC*, September 27, 1914, M.10; "Author Crystalized by an Earthquake," *AtC*, October 18, 1914, 34; and Savoy and Alpha ads, *AtC*, December 13, 1914, M.12.

218. "Answers to Movie Fans," *AtC*, November 1, 1914, M.11; November 8, 1914, A.11; and November 29, 1914, A.13.

219. "News and Notes of the Film World, Conducted by L.E. Winchell," *AtC*, February 28, 1915, M.9.

220. Universal ads, *AtC*, February 28, 1915, M.9; and March 21, 1915, M.11; "Two Famous Stars Now in the Movies," *AtC*, February 28, 1915, M.9; and "A Group of Stars in the Silent Drama," *AtC*, March 7, 1915, M.11.

221. "Behind the Scenes with Britt Craig," *AtC*, February 28, 1915, M.9.

222. The *New York Tribune* opened a Sunday page in mid-March, but it took a "high art" attitude toward motion pictures, initially concerned about the "invasion of Broadway" by feature films. Supported by very few ads, the page ended abruptly in early August, and nothing followed until a tiny "Feature Films" column three months later in the arts and amusements pages. "Photo Plays and Players," *NYT*, March 15, 1914, 3.9; "Feature Films," *NYT*, December

13, 1914, 3.6; and "Feature Films," *NYT,* May 23, 1915, 4.8. According to Paul Moore, in February 1913, "Zit," the vaudeville editor of the *New York Evening Journal,* began to integrate motion picture material into his vaudeville page.

223. "Motion Picture News by THE CENSOR," *NYEM,* October 3, 1914, 4; and October 10, 1914, 7. The *New York Evening Mail* had a circulation of just half that of the *New York American* and *New York Times.*

224. "Motion Picture News by THE CENSOR," *NYEM,* October 10, 1914, 7.

225. Ibid. "The Films and Film Folk by 'Wid,'" *NYEM,* December 5, 1914, 12.

226. "Motion Picture News by THE CENSOR," *NYEM,* October 10, 1914, 7.

227. "News of Motion Pictures by THE CENSOR," *NYEM,* November 7, 1914, 4.

228. "News and Comments of the Motion Picture World by THE CENSOR," *NYEM,* November 14, 1914, 7.

229. "The Films and Film Folk by 'Wid,'" *NYEM,* December 5, 1914, 12.

230. "We Have with Us This Evening," *NYEM,* December 5, 1914, 12; and "The Films and Film Folk by 'Wid,'" *NYEM,* December 7, 1914, 8.

231. "Gossip of Films and Film Folk by 'Wid,'" *NYEM,* December 5, 1914, 15; and "The Films and Film Folk," *NYEM,* December 26, 1914, 10.

232. "The Films and Film Folk by 'Wid,'" *NYEM,* December 12, 1914, 12; December 26, 1914, 10; and January 16, 1915, 6.

233. "The Films and Film Folk by 'Wid,'" *NYEM,* December 7, 1914, 8; January 30, 1915, 4; and February 17, 1915, 13.

234. "Gossip of Films and Film Folk by 'Wid,'" *NYEM,* December 7, 1914, 15; and "The Films and Film Folk by 'Wid,'" *NYEM,* January 9, 1915, 6; January 16, 1915, 6; February 8, 1915, 11; and February 13, 1915, 4.

235. "Screen Results," *NYEM,* November 14, 1914, 7; and "Review of Photo-Play Features by 'Wid,'" *NYEM,* December 5, 1914, 12; and December 12, 1914, 6.

236. "The Films by 'Wid,'" *NYEM,* April 27, 1915, 5; and July 29, 1915, 7.

237. "The Films and Film Folk by 'Wid,'" *NYEM,* March 10, 1915, 11; and July 30, 1915, 7; and "The Films by 'Wid,'" *NYEM,* June 5, 1915, 5.

238. "The Films by 'Wid,'" *NYEM,* March 27, 1915, 5; and July 10, 1915, 10.

239. "The Films by 'Wid,'" *NYEM,* March 6, 1915, 6; March 20, 1915, 6; and April 3, 1915, 5. The editor singled out was Mitt Hoffman of World Film.

240. "The Films and Film Folk by 'Wid,'" *NYEM,* March 3, 1915, 6.

241. "The Films by 'Wid,'" *NYEM,* April 24, 1915, 5; May 19, 1915, 6; and August 7, 1915, 4.

242. "The Films and Film Folk by 'Wid,'" *NYEM,* July 20, 1915, 11; and July 26, 1915, 11.

243. "The Films and Film Folk by 'Wid,'" *NYEM,* July 8, 1915, 13.

244. "The Films and Film Folk by 'Wid,'" *NYEM,* July 26, 1915, 11.

245. "The Films by 'Wid,'" *NYEM,* May 22, 1915, 5. See also the disgust Ida Dudley Dale, a social activist, showed for "how fine girls were selected, like animals" for ushers. Phillip Papas and Lori Weintraub, *Images of America: Port Richmond* (Charleston, SC: Arcadia, 2009), quoted in Richard Koszarski,

"Richard Hoffman: A Collector's Archive," in André Gaudreault et al., eds., *A Companion to Early Cinema* (Chichester, England: Wiley-Blackwell, 2012), 502.

246. "The Films and Film Folk by 'Wid,'" *NYEM*, March 13, 1915, 6; and April 17, 1915, 6.

247. "Films and Film Folk by 'Wid,'" *NYEM*, March 8, 1915, 11.

248. "The Films by 'Wid,'" *NYEM*, July 24, 1915, 5.

249. From July 1916 on, a number of writers were assigned to write about motion pictures, none for more than two or three months, for instance Stanley Olmsted, T.E. Oliphant, and Frederick James Smith.

250. "DRAMA, the Stage, the Screen," *NYEM*, September 1, 1915, 7.

251. George F. Worts, "But What of the Scenario?," *NYEM*, February 26, 1916, 5.

252. George F. Worts, "That Scenario of Yours," *NYEM*, March 4, 1916, 7.

253. George F. Worts, "The Case of the Million Lorettas," *NYEM*, March 11, 1916, 5.

254. George F. Worts, "The Two Dollar Picture Show to Be or Not to Be," *NYEM*, January 15, 1916, 7.

255. For a broader analysis of these war pictures, see Richard Abel, "Charge and Counter-Charge: 'Documentary' War Pictures in the USA, 1914–1916," *Film History* 22, no. 4 (2010): 366–88.

256. G.F.W., "German War Pictures Draw a Mob; Riot Calls Bring Police in Army," *NYEM*, September 21, 1915, 5.

257. "War of the War Pictures Is On," *NYEM*, November 23, 1915, 7.

258. "Impartial Applause for Mail's War Films," *NYEM*, January 18, 1916, 5.

259. "Near Fist Fight Caused by Conflicting Patriotism at Showing of War Film," *NYEM*, January 25, 1916, 4.

260. "Photo Plays," *PEL*, November 28, 1914, 12.

261. These ads appeared in *PEL*, November 14, 1914, 13; November 21, 1914, 13; and November 28, 1914, 13. The column for November 21 briefly described the films playing in a dozen picture theaters.

262. "Today's Photoplay Calendar," *PEL*, January 22, 1915, 5; "Questions and Answers," *PEL*, February 6, 1915, 5; and "Answers to Correspondents," *PEL*, February 13, 1915, 5.

263. "Original 'Movie' Film Machine a Local Invention," *PEL*, November 21, 1914, 13; "The Original Studio," *PEL*, December 5, 1914, 13; "Sarcasm," *PEL*, January 9, 1915, 5; and "Suffrage Film at the Victoria," *PEL*, February 13, 1915, 5.

264. "More War Photography," *PEL*, November 21, 1914, 13; "Women as Camera Men," *PEL*, December 5, 1914, 13; "Photo Plays," *PEL*, December 12, 1914, 13; "Where the Motion Picture Holds Interesting Sway," *PEL*, January 2, 1915, 5; "Five Reasons Why Photoplays Are Popular," *PEL*, January 9, 1915, 5; and "Photo Plays," *PEL*, March 6, 1915, 5.

265. Lubin ads, *PEL*, March 13, 1915, 5; and March 20, 1915, 5.

266. *Photo-Play Review* ads, *PEL*, April 10, 1915, 5; April 17, 1915, 5; and April 24, 1915, 6.

267. "Photo Plays," *PEL*, February 20, 1915, 5; "Latest News of Movieland Filmed in Two Feature Reels—Number One," *PEL*, April 17, 1915, 4; "Griffith on Poe," *PEL*, April 17, 1915, 5; "Blanche Sweet Speaks," *PEL*, April 24, 1915, 7; the Movie Actors' Ass'n ad, *PEL*, May 15, 1915, 6; and *Technique of the Photoplay* ad, *PEL*, May 22, 1915, 7.

268. "Verbal and Pictorial Films Depicting Filmland's News and Gossip," *PEL*, April 3, 1915, 6; and "Vogue of Motion Picture Industry Shown in Figures," *PEL*, April 10, 1915, 6.

269. "Motion Pictures in Medical Schools," *PEL*, May 15, 1915, 7.

270. "Photoplay Section," *PEL*, June 12, 1915. Macgowan later recalled that he "covered dramas and books as well as the movies" for the *Ledger* and even claimed he "was the Photoplay Editor," but only in this special section is he mentioned at that time. Kenneth Macgowan, *Behind the Screen: The History and Techniques of the Motion Pictures* (New York: Delta, 1965), 184–85.

271. P.R. Plough, "Demand for Film News in Dailies Increasing," *MPN*, December 25, 1915, 61.

272. "Amusement Section," *PEL*, October 14, 1915, 1–4; and November 13, 1915, 6.

273. "Are Movies Dangerous Trash or a Great Art in Its Infancy?" *PEL*, October 23, 1915, Amusement, 1; "Teaching the College Man How to Movie," *PEL*, December 4, 1915, Amusement, 1; and "Enter the Silhouette Movie," *PEL*, December 11, 1915, Amusement, 1.

274. "Tully Marshall on the Movies," "Sing Sing Convict Wins Photoplay Contest," and "The New Broadway of the Movies," *PEL*, October 23, 1915, n.p.

275. "Theatrical Baedeker" and "Prominent Photoplay Presentations," *PEL*, October 30, 1915, n.p.

276. "The Photoplay Man-About-Town," *PEL*, October 23, 1915, n.p.; and "With the Exhibitors," *PEL*, October 30, 1915, n.p.

277. Forrest ad, *PEL*, October 30, 1915, n.p.; Metropolitan and Garden ads, *PEL*, December 4, 1915, 8, 10; and Lubin and Pathé Exchange ads, *PEL*, December 11, 1915, 3, 10.

278. Grace Kingsley, "Los Angeles the Globe's Moving Picture Center," *Los Angeles Times*, January 1, 1915, V146. A theater reviewer and interviewer at the time, Kingsley later became the *Times*'s chief reporter on motion pictures.

279. *The Perils of Pauline* contest ads, *LAE*, May 1, 1914, 1.9; and May 2, 1914, 1.5; Charles Goddard, "The Perils of Pauline," *LAE*, May 3, 1914, Editorial/Dramatic, 2; "'Pauline' Reels Are Now Ready," *LAE*, May 3, 1914, Editorial/Dramatic, 3; *The Exploits of Elaine* ad, *LAE*, January 1, 1915, 2.5; Arthur B. Reeve, "The Exploits of Elaine," *LAE*, January 3, 1915, 9.1–2; and *The Exploits of Elaine* ad, *LAH*, February 12, 1915, 2.13.

280. "Loyalty," *LAH*, May 1, 1914, Magazine, 1; and "War," *LAH*, May 11, 1914, Magazine, 1.

281. "Little L.A. Girl Is Queen of Juvenile Motion Picture Co.," *LAH*, May 1, 1914, 2.1; "Queen of Filmdom to Dare Border Perils," *LAH*, May 11, 1914, 2.1; and "Southland Glories in Childhood Film," *LAH*, June 22, 1914, 2.1.

282. Otheman Stevens, "Theatres Photo Plays," *LAE*, August 30, 1914, American Magazine, 5; and September 6, 1914, American Magazine, 5.

283. Tally's Broadway and Clune's Auditorium ads, *LAH*, September 6, 1914, American Magazine, 4.

284. "Motion Plays and Pictures," *LAH*, February 27, 1915, 11.

285. Guy Price, "Facts and Fables of the Foyer," *LAH*, May 7, 1914, 17; and "'Showmen' Great Aid to Movies," *LAH*, February 27, 1915, 11.

286. *LAH*, January 8, 1915, 14, quoted in Jan Olsson, *Los Angeles Before Hollywood*, 32.

287. "With the Local Photoplay Houses," *BAH*, January 3, 1915, 17.

288. "Colley Is Now the Owner of Princess," *BAH*, January 3, 1915, 17; "Photoplay Houses Will Be Open Today," *BAH*, January 31, 1915, 15; Ellis C. Hollums, "Commission to Act on Petition to Have 'Movies' on Sunday," *BAH*, February 7, 1915, 16; and "Majestic Theatre to Open Monday," *BAH*, March 7, 1915, 32.

289. "Why Mary Pickford Remained with the Famous Players Co.," *BAH*, January 10, 1915, 8; "Pearl White, Pathe Star, Got Her Start by Chance," *BAH*, January 31, 1915, 15; and "V. L. S. E. Company to Release Great Feature Films," *BAH*, May 2, 1915, Editorial, 1.

290. Reliance ad, *BAH*, January 31, 1915, 15; and the Movie Actors Ass'n ad, *BAH*, May 2, 1915, Editorial, 1.

291. Richard F. Lussier, "A Travelog in Local Filmdom," *BAH*, October 24, 1915, 1.8; and Lussier, "Footlights and Screen," *BAH*, October 25, 1915, 5.

292. Richard F. Lussier, "Film Love Casts," *BAH*, November 7, 1915, 10.

293. "At the Photoplay Houses," *BAH*, October 27, 1915, 2.

294. Richard F. Lussier, "Footlights and Screen," *BAH*, October 28, 1915, 2. *Damaged Goods* "made such an impression" that the following week the film returned to the Strand, lectured by the "city's health officer," Dr. R.M. Cunningham, and shown to women only one Saturday morning and afternoon and men only that same night. Lussier, "Footlights and Screen," *BAH*, November 2, 1915, 2; November 3, 1915, 2; November 4, 1915, 2; and November 5, 1915, 7.

295. Richard F. Lussier, "Footlights and Screen," *BAH*, November 9, 1915, 7.

296. Richard F. Lussier, "Footlights and Screen," *BAH*, November 29, 1915, 5; and November 30, 1915, 2.

297. Richard F. Lussier, "Footlights and Screen," *BAH*, December 27, 1915, 8; and December 30, 1915, 2.

298. Richard F. Lussier, "Footlights and Screen," *BAH*, January 18, 1916, 2; and January 20, 1916, 2.

299. Richard F. Lussier, "Footlights and Screen," *BAH*, December 11, 1915, 2.

300. Richard F. Lussier, "Footlights and Screen," *BAH*, January 27, 1916, 2.

301. Richard F. Lussier, "Footlights and Screen," *BAH*, January 22, 1916, 2; and January 24, 1916, 2.

302. "With the Photoplays and Players," *AuC*, March 7, 1915, 7.

303. "With the Photoplays and Players," *AuC*, March 28, 1915, 12; April 4, 1915, 10; and April 25, 1915, 8.

304. "A Remarkable Crowd," *AuC*, March 28, 1915, 12; "Public Appreciates Masterpiece," *AuC*, April 25, 1915, 8; "'Hypocrites' Called Back By Request," *AuC*, June 6, 1915, 8; and "Motion Pictures for Children Huge Success," *AuC*, June 27, 1915, 8.

305. "Motion Picture an Event in Stage History," *AuC*, March 28, 1915, 12; and "Smalleys Favor Newspaper Craft," *AuC*, April 25, 1915, 8.

306. "In Movie Land," *AuC*, March 25, 1915, 10; March 26, 1915, 10; May 11, 1915, 10; and June 15, 1915, 12.

307. "Any of These Productions Are Well Worth Seeing," *NOI*, April 14, 1915, 1.14; and "Some of Filmdom's Biggest Features Here This Week," *NOI*, May 5, 1915, 1.13.

308. "When and Where the Photoplays Are Showing This Week," *NOI*, May 12, 1915, 1.13; and "Item's Moving Picture Directory," *NOI*, May 19, 1915, 1.12.

309. "Real Reel Features Promised 'Movie Fans' in Orleans This Week," *NOI*, July 4, 1915, 2.9; and "The Item's Page of News and Gossip of the Moving Picture World," *NOI*, July 18, 1915, 2.4.

310. "The Item's Movie Page," *NOI*, July 25, 1915, 2.5; and August 8, 1915, 2.14.

311. "'Movies' and the Item," *NOI*, November 14, 1915, 1.8.

312. "The Item Movies Pages," *NOI*, January 16, 1916, 1.10–11; and February 25, 1916, 2.12–13.

313. "Says the Movie Editor, by R.E. Pritchard," *NOI*, January 16, 1916, 1.11.

314. "Item to Give Rotogravures of Photo Players Sundays," and the Sunday Item ad, *NOI*, April 9, 1916, 3.7 and 3.8.

315. "Orleans Picture Lovers Given Chance to Aid in Bringing Makers Here," *NOI*, April 23, 1916, 2.4.

316. "Fancies and Features of the Films," *SLT*, November 14, 1915, n.p.

317. The Rex and American theaters, for instance, each supplied separate synopses of three different films on that week's programs.

318. "About Players, Pictures and Everything," *SLT*, November 14, 1915, n.p; and "Melange of the Movies," *SLT*, January 16, 1916, n.p. "Who's Who in the Movies," *SLT*, December 12, 1915, n.p.; and December 26, 1915, n.p.

319. "Thus Does the Debate About the Drammer and the Screen Go On," *SLT*, December 26, 1915, n.p.; George E. Carpenter, "Admission Prices and the Modern Feature Film," *SLT*, January 16, 1916, n.p.; and "Play Soft Music, Says DeMille," *SLT*, February 6, 1916, n.p.

320. "Features of the Sunday Tribune," *SLT*, December 11, 1915, 20. The page ranked sixth out of twelve features, yet above the comics and sports.

321. "What's Doing in the World of Footlights, Spotlights, Photoplays," *OS*, May 15, 1915, 8–9.

322. "'Movie' Jokes from Photoplay Magazine," *OS*, May 15, 1915, 8. The advertising theaters included the Ogden, Orpheum, Alhambra, Rex, Oracle, Isis, and sometimes the Lyceum.

323. "How Pearl White Became a Star," *OS*, June 5, 1915, 8; "Lasky to Release Many Productions," *OS*, June 19, 1915, 8; and "Pathe 'Who Pays' Series Big Success," *OS*, June 19, 1915, 9.

324. "With the Movies," *OS*, September 18, 1915, 10. The weekly programs were listed for the Orpheum, Alhambra, Lyceum, Oracle, and Ogden.

325. "Biography of Anita Stewart," *OS*, September 18, 1915, 11; "Francis Ford Tells How He Achieved Fame," *OS*, October 30, 1915, 8; and "Dustin Farnum Triangle Star," *OS*, January 1, 1916, 5.

326. "Stage and Film Gossip of Interest to Theatre Goers," *OS*, January 8, 1916, 8; and "Photoplay Forum," *OS*, January 8, 1916, Magazine, 15.

327. "The Most Beautiful Blond," *OS*, January 8, 1916, Magazine, 15; "Whooping Up Motion Pictures," *OS*, January 22, 1916, Magazine, 15; and "An Indian Writes Indian Photoplays," *OS*, May 22, 1915, 8. See also "Answers to Fans" and "As to Photoplay Writing," *OS*, January 22, 1916, Magazine, 15; A. H. Giebler, "Letters from a Correspondence School Actor," *OS*, from January 8, 1916, Magazine, 15, to April 29, 1916, Magazine, 20; and A. H. Giebler, "Breaking Into Motion Pictures," *OS*, from September 2, 1916, Magazine, 21, to December 2, 1916, Magazine, 23.

328. "News of the Photoplays," *NOTP*, November 16, 1915, 9.

329. "News of the Photoplays," *NOTP*, November 18, 1915, 21.

330. "Photo Plays," *NOTP*, November 21, 1915, C.4; and November 28, 1915, C.4; and "News of the Photoplays and the Photoplayers," *NOTP*, December 12, 1915, A.18.

331. "News of the Photoplays," *NOTP*, November 21, 1915, C.4.

332. Ibid.; "Public Opinion Turning Toward Shorter Films and Is Tiring of Features," *NOTP*, November 28, 1915, C.4; "Adolph Zukor, President of Famous Players Film Company, Sets Value on Locations," *NOTP*, December 12, 1915, A.18; "Features in the Week," *NOTP*, December 19, 1915, B.12; and "Motion Pictures' Power to Carry Impressive Lessons Recognized by Church and School," *NOTP*, December 26, 1915, C.7.

333. "Youngest Photoplay Star Before the Screen Is Native Louisianian Born in Alexandria," *NOTP*, December 12, 1915, A.18; and "Irene Fenwick, Born in New Orleans, Is One of the Hardest Working Actresses," *NOTP*, December 19, 1915, C.7. See the Crescent (an exclusive Paramount theater) and Triangle Theatre ads, *NOTP*, January 16, 1916, C.13; and the nine picture theater ads, *NOTP*, February 6, 1916, C.13.

334. "Official of Fox Film Corporation Pays High Tribute to Judgment of People of the South," *NOTP*, February 27, 1916, C.12; and "Popular New Orleans Film Exchange Managers," *NOTP*, February 27, 1916, C.13. At the same time, in Florida, the *Jacksonville Times-Union* began running Sunday pages sponsored by local exhibitor ads, not only with two pages bannered "What's New at the Movies," but also with lengthy stories of local production studios. "What's New at the Movies," *Sunday Times-Union*, January 2, 1916, 16–17; "Scenes of Action in the Thanhouser Plant," *Sunday Times-Union*, January 16, 1916, 8; and "Jacksonville's Film Colony," *Sunday Times-Union*, February 6, 1916, 9.

335. In October 1914, the *Cedar Rapids Republican* (Iowa) began publishing a Sunday page seemingly modeled on those already running in the *Buffalo Times* and *Toledo Times*. Three months later, a similar Sunday page appeared in the *Grand Forks Herald* (North Dakota). The following summer, the *Grand Rapids Press* (Michigan) also began printing a Saturday half-page bannered "Happenings in Photoplay Land," which had a very local orientation: Half a dozen of the city's twenty-two theaters contributed ads, and several of the stars profiled—for instance "Our Own Vivian Martin" and Marguerite Snow—had lived in the city or frequently performed there. "What Is Being Done in the Big Moving Picture World," *CRR*, October 18, 1914, 19; and November 8, 1914, 23; "With the Film Stars," *Grand Forks Herald*, January 31, 1915, 7; and "Happenings in Photoplay Land," *Grand Rapids Press*, August 28, 1915, 7; and September 4, 1915, 7; "Our Own Vivian Martin Is Photoplay Star," *Grand Rapids Press*, August 28, 1915, 7; and "Dainty Star Once Trod Boards in Grand Rapids," *Grand Rapids Press*, September 4, 1915, 7.

336. N.D. Tevis, "Week's Offering in Movieland as Seen in La Crosse," *LCT*, February 12, 1915, 10. The middle initial stands for "Dean." Later stories congratulated Tevis as a new father and celebrated his scoop on a tornado story. "Dean's a Daddy," *LCT*, April 26, 1915, 3; and "How N.D. Tevis Beat the 'Jinx' to Storm Scoop," *LCT*, June 16, 1915, 1.

337. "Week's Offerings in Movieland," *LCT*, March 5, 1915, 8; March 19, 1915, 11; and April 30, 1915, 9.

338. The Dome, a picture theater located on the north side, was managed by two men who apparently were part of a Syrian community of sixty families. "Week's Offerings in Movieland," *LCT*, December 10, 1915, 9; and "Silk Weavers from Orient Turn to Good Americans in Melting Pot of La Crosse," *LCT*, January 29, 1916, 7.

339. "Week's Offerings in Movieland," *LCT*, March 5, 1915, 8. Five months later, Pickford's *Dawn of a Tomorrow* "broke all records for attendance at the Bijou." "Week's Offerings in Movieland," *LCT*, August 13, 1915, 7.

340. "Week's Offerings in Movieland," *LCT*, October 22, 1915, 8; and November 12, 1915, 9.

341. "Week's Offerings in Movieland," *LCT*, January 8, 1916, 8.

342. "Week's Offerings in Movieland," *LCT*, February 19, 1916, 9; and March 11, 1916, 9.

343. "Week's Offerings in Movieland," *LCT*, May 20, 1916, 9; May 27, 1916, 11; and June 3, 1916, 10.

344. "Week's Offerings in Movieland," *LCT*, April 15, 1916, 9. Not until late July 1916 did the six picture theaters in La Crosse begin to advertise their current programs on the same page with Tevis's "Weekly Offerings."

345. "The Silent Drama: Photo Play News for the Motion Picture Lover," *MST*, April 25, 1915, 9. After dropping the Syndicated Film Publishing service, the *Tribune* printed only the weekly synopses of three or four picture theater programs.

346. "The Silent Drama," *MST*, May 2, 1915, 9.

347. Vachel Lindsay, "An Epitaph for John Bunny," *MST*, May 9, 1915, 9; "Minister Scenario Writer Approves of the Movies," *MST*, May 30, 1915, 9; and "Geraldine Farrar, Prima Donna, to Play 'Carmen' in Pictures," *MST*, June 20, 1915, 9.

348. "Clara Kimball Young Rehearsing for 'Marrying Money,' New 'Movie' Play," *MST*, July 18, 1915, 9; "Marguerite Clark to Appear First Under Lyric's New Policy," *MST*, August 1, 1915, 9; "Mary Pickford to Play in 'Rags' Which Edith Delano Wrote for Her," *MST*, August 8, 1915, 9; and "Fannie Ward to Play in Comedy That Has Made the World Smile," *MST*, August 22, 1915, 8.

349. "Film Men Will Mix Business and Pleasure in Minneapolis Convention," *MST*, May 2, 1915, 9; "Summer Movies for Children Are Planned by Club Women," *MST*, May 2, 1915, 10; "Motion Picture Men's Convention a Success," *MST*, May 9, 1915, 9; "Minneapolis Movie Managers Give Their Ideas on Proposed Board of Censorship of Films," *MST*, May 16, 1915, 9; "Motion Pictures in Public Schools," *MST*, June 13, 1915, 9; "Children the Real Movie Fans / Should Pictures Be Censored for Them? / League Formed to Regulate Films," *MST*, July 25, 1915, 9; and "Do Movies Hurt the Eyes? Local Specialists Say 'No,'" *MST*, August 22, 1915, 9.

350. "Local Movies to Be Shown at the Strand," *MST*, May 30, 1915, 9; "Northwest Weekly," *MST*, July 4, 1915, 9; "Northwest Rowing Races Featured in Pictures," *MST*, August 1, 1915, 9; and "Northwest Weekly" ads, *MST*, August 29, 1915, 9; September 5, 1915, 9; September 12, 1915, 9; September 19, 1915, 9; and September 26, 1915, 9.

351. "Movies," *MST*, August 29, 1915, 9; and "Movie Menu," *MST*, October 10, 1915, 9.

352. "Gossip of Film Favorites," *MST*, September 12, 1915, 11; "Bits of News for Movie Fans," *MST*, October 10, 1915, 9; and "What You Can See This Week" and "The Press Agents Say," *MST*, December 19, 1915, 11.

353. "Movies," *MST*, December 19, 1915, 11; "At the Movie Houses," *MST*, February 20, 1916, 10; and "Movieland," *MST*, May 14, 1916, 9.

354. "CINEMAS," *MST*, June 25, 1916, 10. Variations appeared over the next few months. "THE CINEMAS," *MST*, July 2, 1916, 7; "Cinema Offerings," *MST*, July 16, 1916, 6; "At the Cinemas," *MST*, August 6, 1916, 6.

355. "Startling Gowns Worn by Louise Glaum in Photoplay Attraction, 'The Wolf Woman,'" *MST*, July 16, 1916, 6; "David Belasco on the Movies," *MST*, July 23, 1916, 6; and "Little Stories of the Movies," *MST*, May 28, 1916, 10; June 4, 1916, 10; and June 25, 1916, 10. Early on, the stars profiled in "Little Stories" included Anita Stewart, Alice Brady, Viola Dana, Norma Talmadge, Mr. and Mrs. Sidney Drew, and Olga Petrova.

356. "Women Engaged in Motion Picture Industry Coming to Minneapolis for Big May Exposition," *MST*, April 2, 1916, 10. This article singled out four small-town exhibitors in Minnesota, plus Mrs. Myrtle Vinton (of Bridger, Montana), "a vice-president of the Motion Picture Exhibitors associations of the Northwest."

357. "Motion Picture Committee of Federated Women's Clubs to Work for Better Movies," *MST*, June 25, 1916, 8.

358. "Screenings by Anna Mait," *MST*, March 19, 1916, 11; March 26, 1916, 12; May 21, 1916, 10; May 28, 1916, 10; July 2, 1916, 7; July 9, 1916, 8; July 16, 1916, 7; and August 20, 1916, 8. Several of these columns appeared on the "Vaudeville" page.

359. "Motion Pictures by Philip H. Welch," *MST*, August 21, 1916, 9; August 23, 1916, 3; August 25, 1916, 7; August 26, 1916, 4; and August 27, 1916, 10.

360. Archie Bell, "Wall Street Invests $4,000,000 in Films," *CSL*, June 13, 1915, D.2; Bell, "Ohio Censors Bar Film Masterpiece," *CSL*, June 27, 1915, D.2; Bell, "Theaters Hit Hard, W.A. Brady Admits," *CSL*, August 15, 1915, D.3; and Bell, "'Best Sellers' Are Now Seen, Not Read," *CSL*, August 29, 1915, D.2.

361. "SOCIETY by Mary B. Miller / THEATERS by Archie Bell / CLUBS by Louise Graham," *CL*, October 1, 1915, 7; and October 7, 1915, 7. Graham also had dabbled in writing industry news articles on several Sunday pages. Louise Graham, "Now Operatic Stars Shine on the Films," *CSL*, July 4, 1915, D.2; and "'Right of Way' Picture Cost $50,000," *CSL*, July 11, 1915, D.2.

362. "Movie Talent Contest" ad, *CSL*, June 27, 1915, D.6; "Ask Any Girl—'When Are You Going into the Movies?,'" *CSL*, July 11, 1915, D.1; and "Notice to Leader Movie Girls!" ad, *CL*, November 16, 1915, 9.

363. Archie Bell, "Two Most Ambitious Actors Have a Long Fight for Fame," *CSL*, July 25, 1915, D.3; John D. Raridan, "Valeska's Ultra Raiment Colors First Photoplay," *CSL*, October 17, 1915, D.5; Bell, "Riots at Box Office When Theda Bara Goes on Stage," *CSL*, October 24, 1915, D.1; Bell, "It's Carmen, Carmen, Carmen on the Lips and in the Thoughts of All the City's Host of Movie Fans," *CSL*, October 31, 1915, D.5; "'Queen Mary,' as Jap Girl, Proves Screen Versatility," *CSL*, November 7, 1915, D.7; and "Beverly a Water Nymph in Return to Bushman," *CSL*, November 14, 1915, D.7.

364. Anita Stewart, "No. 1—The Road to Fame in the Movies," *CL*, November 26, 1915, 8; "Art and the Films," *CSL*, December 5, 1915, R.2; and "They Entertain Thousands from One End of the Country to the Other Every Day and Night in Films," *CSL*, December 5, 1915, 5.3.

365. "Exhibitors Asked to Discuss Problems" and "Editor's Question Box," *CPD*, January 3, 1915, Editorial/Dramatic, 5; and "Photo Play Editor Kept Busy with Hundreds of Letters," *CPD*, January 10, 1915, Editorial/Dramatic, 5.

366. "Your New Theater—The Liberty Is Ready for You," *CPD*, April 14, 1915, Editorial/Dramatic, 4; "Introducing Miss Marguerite Clark, Full Fledged Ohioan," *CPD*, April 25, 1915, Editorial/Dramatic, 4; and "Who Is Your Favorite Movie Actor—and Why?" *CPD*, May 9, 1915, Editorial/Dramatic, 3.

367. "In the Frame of Public Favor [Ethel Clayton]" and "Whose Picture Do You Want Here?" *CPD*, July 4, 1915, Editorial/Dramatic, 3; "In the Frame of Public Favor [Anita Stewart]," *CPD*, July 11, 1915, Editorial/Dramatic, 3; and "In the Frame of Public Favor [Lillian Lorraine]," *CPD*, August 29, 1915, Editorial/Dramatic, 3.

368. *CPD*, September 5, 1915, Editorial/Dramatic, 4; September 19, 1915, Editorial/Dramatic, 4; and September 26, 1915, Editorial/Dramatic, 4.

369. E. Arthur Roberts, "Ohio Censorship Fight May Be Carried to the Courts" and "Question Box," *CPD*, August 29, 1915, Editorial/Dramatic, 3; Roberts, "Cleveland Takes Place Among Leading Photo Play Cities," *CPD*, September 5, 1915, Editorial /Dramatic, 6; Roberts, "It's Hard Work for Theda to Play 'Vampire' Roles," *CPD*, September 19, 1915, Editorial/Dramatic, 4; and Roberts, "Glaring Errors Ruin Many Photo Plays," *CPD*, October 3, 1915, Editorial/Dramatic, 4.

370. "News of Photo Plays and Players, Edited by E. Arthur Roberts," *CPD*, January 17, 1916, 6.

371. "Right Off the Reel by Mae Tinee," *SLGD*, June 6, 1915, Sunday Magazine, 7; July 4, 1915, Sunday Magazine, 6; and July 11, 1915, Sunday Magazine, 3.

372. "The Photoplay Forum: What's What and Who's Who in Movie Land," *SLGD*, August 15, 1915, Sunday Magazine, 3. The next two months are missing from the microfilm copies at the Library of Congress.

373. "The Photoplay Forum," *SLGD*, from October 10, 1915, Sunday Magazine, 2, to November 7, 1915, Sunday Magazine, 5.

374. "The Photoplay Forum," *SLGD*, October 10, 1915, Sunday Magazine, 2; and October 24, 1915, Sunday Magazine, 4.

375. "The Photoplay Forum," *SLGD*, October 17, 1915, Sunday Magazine, 4; and October 31, 1915, Sunday Magazine, 4.

376. The *St. Louis Globe-Democrat* ran Giebler's "Letters from a Correspondence School Actor" from December 19, 1915, Sunday Magazine, 3, to July 2, 1916, Sunday Magazine, 4.

377. "War on the Film Censors Is Begun by Producers," *SLGD*, November 14, 1915, Sunday Magazine, 7; "Motion Picture Kisses Measured by the Foot Rule," *SLGD*, November 21, 1915, Sunday Magazine, 3; "Shadow Lovers," *SLGD*, December 12, 1915, Sunday Magazine, 3; and "Motion Pictures Creating a New Race," *SLGD*, December 28, 1915, Sunday Magazine, 4. An added feature story was "Unusual Photos of Motion Picture Players," *SLGD*, December 5, 1915, Sunday Magazine, 5.

378. "Queen of the Cowboy Movies," *SLGD*, February 6, 1916, Sunday Magazine, 5; "Putting 'Pep' in Motion Pictures," *SLGD*, February 20, 1916, Sunday Magazine, 5; and "A Flash in Motion Pictures," *SLGD*, April 2, 1916, Sunday Magazine, 5. See also another story about the current debate over movie comedy, "Refined Comedy Versus the Slapstick in Motion Pictures," *SLGD*, March 5, 1916, 5.

379. An exception was a story about "Umbrella Bill" in an animated serial "Made-in-St. Louis." "St. Louis the Birthplace of the New Movie," *SLGD*, January 9, 1916, Sunday Magazine, 1.

380. "The Reel Players," *DFP*, September 2, 1915, 6; September 9, 1915, 6; and September 16, 1915, 6.

381. "The Reel Players," *DFP*, November 11, 1915, 6.

382. "The Screen," *DFP*, December 19, 1915, 3.10.

383. "The Movies," *DeNT*, August 29, 1915, 13.

384. "The Movies," *DeNT*, September 5, 1915, 11.

385. "Photoplays," *DeNT*, September 12, 1915, 13.

386. "Photoplays," *DeNT*, September 26, 1915, 17. The specific examples come from "Photoplays," *DeNT*, November 7, 1915, 18–19.

387. George W. Stark, "Motion Picture Comments," *DeNT*, November 7, 1915, 18; November 14, 1915, 18; November 28, 1915, n.p.; and December 19, 1915, 16.

388. "The Dignity of the Wild West as Seen by Picture Star Who Lived the Life," *DeNT*, November 7, 1915, 18; "Gives Convicts Chance in Movies," *DeNT*, November 21, 1915, 18; "Sing Sing Convicts Call Her the Most Popular Film Star," *DeNT*, December 5, 1915, 19; "Youngest Star in Filmdom," *DeNT*, December 5, 1915, 21; and "Appears in New Film," *DeNT*, December 19, 1915, Society, 18.

389. "Master Exhibitor Will Speak Here," *DeNT*, November 14, 1915, 18; "Urges Picture Men to Advertise" and "The Photo Music Drama Is Big Picture Feature of the Future, Declares Composer," *DeNT*, November 28, 1915, n.p.

390. "Right Off the Reel / Facts for Movie Fans," *OSWH*, October 3, 1915, E.9.

391. Latest Reels and What's at the Theaters This Week" and "All the News About the Moving Pictures," *OSWH*, October 31, 1915, E.6–7. See also Ross H. Chamberlen, "Some Putts and Drives Made at the 19th Hole," *OSWH*, October 10, 1915, S.4.

392. "Our Policy in This Department," *OSWH*, October 3, 1915, E.9.

393. "The Advance Agent," *OSWH*, October 24, 1915, E.7; and "The Photoplay Guide," *OSWH*, October 31, 1915, E.6.

394. "Organize Class in Scenario Writing," *OSWH*, October 24, 1915, E.6.

395. Laemmle Film Service ads, *OSWH*, October 24, 1915, E.6; and November 21, 1915, E.7; Triangle-Strand ads, *OSWH*, December 12, 1915, E.13; and January 2, 1916, E.12; and Metro Pictures ad, *OSWH*, December 26, 1915, E.6.

396. "An Editorial," *OSWH*, December 12, 1915, E.14; and February 13, 1916, E.6.

397. "The Query Box," *OSWH*, from October 24, 1915, E.6, to January 23, 1916, E.9.

398. "The Film and the Farm; Social Life," *OSWH*, October 10, 1915, E.11; and "'Movie Man's Friend' Is a Helpful Volume," *OSWH*, December 19, 1915, E.13.

399. "Another Newspaper That Is Doing Its Duty by the Exhibitors of Its City," *MPN*, November 13, 1915, 56.

400. "The Press, Press Representative and the Picture—IX," *MPN*, December 11, 1915, 55.

401. "A Boost for the World-Herald," *OSWH*, December 12, 1915, E.13.

402. See the M section, *DuNT*, October 10, 1915; October 17, 1915; November 21, 1915; and November 28, 1915, n.p.

403. A.H. Giebler, "As to Photoplay Writing," *DuNT*, November 21, 1915; and November 28, 1915, n.p.; and "Reel Facts About Reel Folk," *DuNT*, December 5, 1915, M.13.

404. "Close-Ups of Film Favorites [Marguerite Clark]," *DuNT*, December 5, 1915, M.13.

405. "Two Producers Warn Against Plunge," *DuNT*, December 26, 1915, M.8; John R. Freuler, "Americans Should Object to Censorship of Movie," and "Theda Warns Ambitious Girls," *DuNT*, March 12, 1916, D.4; and George Stark, "Chaplin and Pickford Sign Contracts, World Wags On," *DuNT*, March 19, 1916, D.5.

406. "Critic Says Walthall Leads," *DuNT*, January 23, 1916, M.8. Lyceum ads, *DuNT*, November 21, 1915, M.10; and December 5, 1915, M.14.

407. "News of the Movies," *DMT*, August 17, 1915, 3; September 2, 1915, 6; and September 29, 1915, 14.

408. "News of the Movies," *DMT*, September 9, 1915, 12; October 7, 1915, 8; and November 15, 1915, 5. Another brief story, however, made fun of World Film's plan to send out "free press agents" who would instruct local exhibitors on how to get free advertising in newspapers. "News of the Movies," *DMT*, September 29, 1915, 14.

409. "News of the Movies," *DMT*, August 19, 1915, 6; September 25, 1915, 2; October 23, 1915, 5; and October 26, 1915, 3; "Music at the Garden to Fit the Pictures," *DMT*, November 3, 1915, 10. A later news item reported that Essanay and other companies no longer were accepting "amateur scenarios." "News of the Movies," *DMT*, November 16, 1915, 3.

410. "News of the Movies," *DMT*, August 20, 1915, 8; August 21, 1915, n.p.; and August 26, 1915, 2.

411. "Flickerings and Flashes from Filmland," *DMT*, November 10, 1915, 9. See the similar, unbannered page, *DMT*, November 3, 1915, 10. One month later, the *Des Moines Register and Leader* introduced a similar Sunday page and then briefly adopted the same banner. "The Week at the Moving Picture Houses," *DMRL*, December 26, 1915, 5; and "Flickerings and Flashes from Filmland," *DMRL*, January 23, 1916, 7.

412. "Flickerings and Flashes from Filmland," *DMT*, December 1, 1915, 4; December 29, 1915, 8; and January 5, 1915, 4. In a survey, however, William Fox found that most exhibitors opposed the idea of presenting a series of Shakespeare films. "News of the Movies," *DMT*, December 2, 1915, 3.

413. Majestic ad for Dustin Farnum in Triangle's *The Iron Strain, DMT*, November 17, 1915, 9; Majestic ad for Douglas Fairbanks in Triangle's *The Lamb, DMT*, November 24, 1915, 9; and Garden Theatre ad for Francis X. Bushman and Beverly Bayne in *Pennington's Choice, DMT*, December 15, 1915, 10.

414. "Theda Bara Says She Is Not the World's Wickedest Woman," *DMT*, January 5, 1916, 4; "Anita Stewart Tells Girls How to Be Successful and Happy," *DMT*, January 12, 1916, 10; and "News of the Movies," *DMT*, January 17, 1916, 5.

415. "News of the Movies," *DMT*, October 4, 1915, 11; and October 30, 1915, 2; and "Triangle Pictures Will Be Shown in Majestic Sunday," *DMT*, November 17, 1915, 9. See the Majestic ads, *DMT*, November 17, 1915, 9; November 24, 1915, 9; December 1, 1915, 4; December 8, 1915, 10; and December 15, 1915, 10.

416. YMCA ad, *DMT*, November 17, 1915, 9; and "Film Club Formed by Movie Patrons," *DMT*, December 22, 1915, 11.

417. "News of the Movies," *DMT*, January 24, 1916, 4; and January 25, 1916, 3.

418. "News of the Movies," *DMT*, February 2, 1916, 4; and February 3, 1916, 16.

419. Gottlieb probably was a friend of the A.H. Blank family. A year before her first column appeared, she and Mrs. Blank won top prizes in a card game involving forty players. "This Page of Special Interest to Women," *Des Moines Capital*, September 14, 1914, 8. She went on to head the public relations department of A.H. Blank's circuit of cinemas in the 1920s and of Central States Theater Corporation from 1933 to 1950. See *Variety Obituaries, vol. 6, 1964–1968* (New York: Garland, 1988), n.p.

420. "What Do You Want to Know About Movies? By Dorothy Day" *DMT*, February 25, 1916, 3; "Arbuckle Weighed 16 Pounds at Birth; Grown Some Since by Dorothy Day," *DMT*, February 26, 1916, 5; "Men and Women Take Lives in Their Own Hands by Dorothy Day," *DMT*, February 29, 1916, 9; and "Today and Thursday at the Movies by Dorothy Day," *DMT*, March 1, 1916, 9.

421. "Mountain Thriller at Casino—Mollie King in Film Bow," *DMT*, March 31, 1916, 2.1; and "News of the Movies by Dorothy Day," *DMT*, April 13, 1916, 11.

422. "Short Sighted Policy of Many Newspapers Regarding Motion Pictures Pointed Out by Spedon," *MPN*, October 16, 1915, 42.

423. "The Press, the Press Representative and the Picture" and "Live Wire Exhibitors" columns in *Motion Picture News*, from October 1915 through April 1916.

424. Email correspondence from Paul Moore, March 30, 2010.

425. In one of her first "Seen on the Screen" columns, Caroline Carr raised the question "Shall 'Movies' Be Discarded as Nickname for Film Plays?" and confessed that she thought it sensible "to say 'movies'" because the nickname was "a sign of comradeship." Carr, "Seen on the Screen," *CH*, March 15, 1915, 11.

ENTR'ACTE: NEWSPAPER MOVIE CONTESTS

1. Announcement, *NYMT*, September 24, 1911, 4.6. "Florence E. Turner Wins First Prize in Popularity Contest," *NYMT*, December 17, 1911, 8.1; and "Popular Player Contest," *MPM* (January 1912): 133 and (June 1912): 139. For further information on these contests, see Richard Abel, *Americanizing the Movies and "Movie-Mad" Audiences* (Berkeley: University of California Press, 2006), 236–37.

2. More puzzling is the *New York American*'s equally complicated contest in early 1916 that awarded expensive gifts to movie actresses garnering the most votes, but fans who "secure[d] the largest number of votes" for their favorites were invited to a "Movie Ball" and promised autographed photographs. "Movie Votes in Series 'A' End To-day," *New York American*, January 22, 1916, 6; "Thousands Applaud Movie Contest; First Series 'C' Coupon To-Day," *New York American*, January 23, 1916, M.7; and "Movie Leaders Through Series 'C' Winners to Be Announced Feb. 17," *New York American*, February 13, 1916, L.8.

3. Announcement, *NYMT*, August 18, 1912, 4.2.1; "Martha Russell Voted the Most Popular Moving Picture Player," *NYMT*, December 29, 1912, 4.2.1; "Prize Puzzle Contest," *MPM* (September 1912): 111–12; and "A Tale of the French Settlers," *MPM* (December 1912): 129. See also Richard Abel, *Americanizing the Movies*, 239–40.

4. *Ladies' World* (August 1912): 4 and (September 1912): 1, cited in Nan Enstad, *Ladies of Labor, Girls of Adventure: Working Women, Popular Culture, and Labor Politics at the Turn of the Twentieth Century* (New York: Columbia University Press, 1999), 174.

5. "Popular Player Contest," *MPM* (March 1913): 141, (April 1913): 117–18, (June 1913): 113, and (October 1913): 109; and "Photoplay Magazine's Great Popularity Contest," *PM* (July 1913): 61.

6. "Ladies World Contest," *MPW*, January 3, 1914, 56.

7. "Bushman Wins Big Contest," *MPW*, May 23, 1914, 1120–21.

8. Announcement, *TB*, February 18, 1911, 1. For a week, others followed daily and thereafter once or twice a week through March 10, 1912.

9. "First Offering of Blade Picture Show Critics," *TB*, February 25, 1911, 15; "Here Are Prize Winning Moving Picture Criticisms," *TB*, March 4, 1911, 24; "Picture Show Critics Do Better This Week," *TB*, March 11, 1911, 12; and "Moving Picture Criticism Winners," *TB*, March 18, 1911, 13. See photos of the winning girls, along with brief interviews, in "Moving Picture Criticism Winners," *TB*, February 27, 1911, 7.

10. "Mirror Review Contest," *NYDM*, January 24, 1912, 35; February 7, 1912, 32; February 14, 1912, 27; and February 21, 1912, 26.

11. "Results of Review Contest #2," *NYDM*, March 6, 1912, 27; "Fourth Review Contest," *NYDM*, March 20, 1912, 27; "Review Contest Results," *NYDM*, May 8, 1912, 27; "Winning Reviews for May," *NYDM*, June 12, 1912, 27; and "Winning Reviews," *NYDM*, July 10, 1912, 33.

12. Epes Winthrop Sargent, "Advertising for Exhibitors," *MPW*, May 18, 1912, 623.

13. Orpheum ads, *CND*, May 26, 1912, 14; June 2, 1912, 16; and June 9, 1912, 12. In July, Selig distributed to the Chicago Press Club "a booklet of prize essays" probably collected from exhibitors who adopted the scheme. Epes Winthrop Sargent, "Advertising for Exhibitors," *MPW*, July 27, 1912, 339.

14. "1,200 Theater Tickets Given Away Every Week," *CSL*, November 17, 1912, B.5; and "Six Leader Readers Will Get Six League Theater Tickets Free," *CSL*, December 1, 1912, B.5.

15. "Motion Picture News," *WH*, April 13, 1913, 11; and April 15, 1915, 13.

16. "A Cash Prize for Telling What Movie You Liked Best Last Week," *CPD*, November 23, 1913, Editorial/Dramatic, 4; and "What Movie?" *CPD*, November 30, 1913, Editorial/Dramatic, 4.

17. Minnie Gordon, "Liked This Movie Best," *CPD*, December 7, 1913, Editorial/Dramatic, 4; Daisy Downey, "Best 'Movie Applause,'" *CPD*, December 14, 1913, Editorial/Dramatic, 6.

18. Julia Bates, "This Week's Best Movie," *CPD*, January 4, 1914, Editorial/Dramatic, n.p.

19. "Prize Movie Contest," *TB*, January 24, 1914, 11.

20. "This Week's Best Movie" and "Here's Best Moving Picture Story," *TB*, February 14, 1914, 8.

21. "Latest News from Movie Land by Mae Tinee," *CST*, April 25, 1915, 8.3.

22. "Who Is Your Favorite Movie Actor—and Why?" *CPD*, May 9, 1915, Editorial/Dramatic, 3.

23. Selig ad, *CT*, May 8, 1915, 26; and Ziegfeld ad, *CT*, May 31, 1915, 15. Adapted from the stage play *The Nigger, The New Governor* received "much adverse criticism" that the Ziegfeld's manager, Alfred Hamburger, "believed to be unwarranted." The Chicago censor's approval of *The New Governor* led Kitty Kelly to lobby for its permission to let *The Birth of a Nation* be screened in the city. At the same time, just outside Philadelphia, the Globe Theatre offered cash prizes for the best essay "reviewing *Hypocrites!* from any angle or viewpoint." Richard Koszarski, "Richard Hoffman: A Collector's Archive," in André Gaudreault et al., eds., *A Companion to Early Cinema* (Chichester, England: Wiley-Blackwell, 2012), 517.

24. "Write Your Opinion of Solution of the 'Outcast' Problem," *BAH*, November 5, 1915, 7; and "Letter Contest Extended One Day," *BAH*, November 7, 1915, A.10.

25. *The Million Dollar Mystery* ads in *CT*, June 22, 1914, 8; *BC*, June 22, 1914, 9; *SAL* June 25, 1914, 5; *OS*, June 27, 1914, n.p.; and *CR*, June 28, 1914, 17. See also "$10,000 for 100 Words," *OS*, June 22, 1914, 5; *FWST*, June 28, 1914, 4; and *CPD*, September 6, 1914, X.2; and "The Million Dollar Mystery," *SAL*, June 26, 1914, Women's Clubs / Society, n.p., and *Lincoln Sunday Star* (Nebraska), September 27, 1914, n.p.

26. "The Solution of 'The Million Dollar Mystery,'" *CST*, February 21, 1915, 7.1.

27. Universal ads, *CSL*, July 26, 1914, 1.4; and *AtC*, August 22, 1914, 12.

28. "Write Movie Play; Win $25," *FWST*, July 5, 1914, 21; "Are You Writing Movie Play?" *FWST*, July 12, 1914, n.p.; and "Scenarios Must Be in by 6 P.M. Saturday," *FWST*, July 17, 1914, 11.

29. Bettie Braun, "'Get in Action' Last Tip to Scenario Writers," *FWST*, July 9, 1914, 5; and "Make Your Synopsis Clear," *FWST*, July 15, 1914, 9.

30. "Will You Accept Five Hundred Dollars?" *CST*, November 8, 1914, 8.9.

31. "A Word in Your Ear About Our Two (2) Scenario Contests!" *CST*, December 13, 1914, 8.8. See also "Another $10,000 Offered for Photoplay

Solution," *FWST*, March 28, 1915, 27; "Mission Canyon Scene of 'Diamond From the Sky,'" *FWST*, April 4, 1915, 19; and "The Diamond in the Sky," *Trenton Times*, August 5, 1915, 12; and August 26, 1915, 4.

32. American Film ads, *CT*, April 27, 1915, 8; and May 3, 1915, 12. In some cities this contest was still running prior to screenings of the "concluding chapters." Richard F. Lussier, "Footlights and Screen," *BAH*, November 23, 1915, 2.

33. *Technique of the Photoplay* ad, *PEL*, May 22, 1915, 7; "The Moving Picture Bookshelf," *PEL*, February 19, 1916, Amusement Section, 3.

34. "Here Is Chance for Scenario Writers to Gain Lasting Fame—and $50 Reward" and "How to Write Photoplay Stories," *OWH*, February 6, 1916, E.7.

35. "100 Scripts Sent in Photoplay Contest," *OWH*, March 1, 1916, 1.

36. Harry O. Hoyt, "Beginning the Evening Ledger Lessons in Scenario Writing—A Course of Practical Instruction," *PEL*, June 3, 1916, Amusement Section, 1, 3; Hoyt, "Evening Ledger Scenario Lessons," *PEL*, June 10, 1916, 1, 3; Hoyt, "Evening Ledger Scenario Lessons 12 and 13," *PEL*, June 17, 1916, 1, 2; Hoyt, "Scenario Lesson Seventeen," *PEL*, June 24, 1916, 1, 2. Hoyt was on the scenario staff of Metro Pictures.

37. The contest's judges were Stanley V. Mastbaum, president of the Stanley Booking Company, and Max Karger, director general of Metro Pictures.

38. William Courtney, "Evening Ledger Prize Scenario Contest Opens with Model Script of Produced Photoplay," and Harry O. Hoyt, "How to Prepare Your Character List and Your Scene Plot," *PEL*, July 1, 1916, 1. The entry blank was first printed in the *Ledger*, July 8, 1916, 1. Another contest soon followed: "Evening Ledger Photoplay Cast Contest Opens with Entry List," *PEL*, July 15, 1916, 1.

39. "Have You Met the Herald Movie Girl?" *CSH*, August 30, 1914, F.2.

40. Allen C. Rankin, "Who Will Be Sue?" *CSH*, December 6, 1914, 6.7; and Rankin, "Time for Submitting Pictures for 'Sue' Contest Ends Tuesday," *CSH*, December 20, 1914, 6.6.

41. Allen C. Rankin, "Judges Announce Selections in 'Sue' Contest," *CSH*, December 27, 1914, 6.8; and Rankin, "Voting Is Heavy in Sue Contest," *CSH*, January 3, 1915, 6.6. Judges included Bushman, James McQuade of *Moving Picture World*, the local Exhibitors' Association president, the *Herald*'s "Photoplay Editor," and Lorado Tuft, "the world famous sculptor."

42. "Miss Warshauer Choice as 'Sue,'" *CSH*, March 7, 1915, 2.1.

43. "Movie Talent Contest" ad, *CSL*, June 27, 1915, D.6; and "Ask Any Girl—'When Are You Going into the Movies?,'" *CSL*, July 11, 1915, D.1.

44. "Notice to Leader Movie Girls!" ad, *CL*, November 16, 1915, 9.

45. Helen Osborne, "Girl Who Wins Charley Chaplin Prize Tells How She Did It," *CSL*, June 27, 1915, D.5.

46. "Which of Film Stars Do You Look Most Like?" ad, *CL*, November 24, 1915, 7.

47. "Look Like Mary Pickford? Tell the Movie Editor," *DMN*, February 26, 1916, 2. In April, the *Minneapolis Tribune* staged a similar contest: "Are You a Twin Sister of a Moving Picture Star?" *MST*, April 2, 1916, 10; and "Contest Winners to Be Announced Tuesday Morning," *MST*, April 30, 1916, 12.

48. See the ads for this contest, *NOPT*, February 13, 1916, A.13; February 20, 1916, C.2; and February 27, 1916, C.3.

49. "News of the Photoplays," *NOPT*, December 4, 1916, 9; and the *Cupid and Contraband* ad, *NOPT*, December 10, 1916, A.22.

50. "Press Affords Opportunity to Any Pittsburger to Become Moving Picture Star," *Pittsburg Press*, August 8, 1916, 1.1–2; and "Winners in the Big Movie Contest Are to Get Added Prizes," *Pittsburg Press*, August 29, 1916, 1.6.

51. "People's Movie Star Contest" ad, *CH*, October 5, 1916, 7; and "Chief Winners in Herald Movie Contest," *CSH* Motion Pictures supplement, December 10, 1916, 7.1.

52. "Film Fans to Become Associate Editors," *CSH*, May 2, 1915, 6.6.

53. See also "Fun from the Films," *CSH*, May 9, 1915, 6.7; and June 6, 1915, 6.7.

54. "Contributions from the Film Fans," *CSH*, May 23, 1915, 6.7.

55. "One Dollar Laughs from Our Film Readers," *CSH*, May 30, 1915, 6.7.

56. "Fun from the Films," *CSH*, May 16, 1915, 6.7.

57. "You Know Who This Is. Prizes for You" ad, *DMT*, March 23, 1916, 5–6; and "Do You Know This Movie Star?" ad, *DMT*, March 31, 1916, 6–7.

CHAPTER 3. "IN MOVIE LAND, WITH THE FILM STARS"

1. "Gallery of Picture Players," *MPM* (April 1911): 1–8. In September 1911, *Photoplay Magazine* began printing its own "Gallery of Picture Stars," drawn, unlike *Motion Picture Story Magazine*, exclusively from the "Independents."

2. "Gallery of Picture Players," *MPM* (March 1912): 1–16.

3. "Answers to Inquiries," *MPM* (August 1911): 144–46.

4. "Answers to Inquiries," *MPM* (February 1912): 149; and (March 1912): 146.

5. "Chats with the Players," *MPM* (February 1912): 136.

6. "Calcium Flashes," *CSL*, September 3, 1911, B.6; "Francis X. Bushman," *CSL*, September 24, 1911, B.6; and "Edith Storey," *CSL*, October 1, 1911, B.6.

7. "Moving Picture Star Tells of the Thrills of Her Art," *CSL*, October 22, 1911, S.5; "Everyone Laughs to See This Man in Film," *CSL*, October 29, 1911, S.5; and "'The Solax Kid' Magda Foy," *CSL*, November 12, 1911, S.5.

8. "Questions Pour in from Picture Fans," *CSL*, November 26, 1911, S.5; and "Answering Questions," *CSL*, January 14, 1912, S.5.

9. "Santa Claus' Stationary Portraits of Moving Picture Stars," *CSL*, December 24, 1911, Copperplate Pictorial Section, 3.

10. "Leader's Gallery of Popular Photo Players," *CSL*, January 14, 1912, S.5; "The Girl with the Smile Who Cheers Vitagraph Plays," *CSL*, March 10, 1912, S.6; and "Lubin Comedian Is Popular Photoplayer," *CSL*, April 28, 1912, W.8.

11. "Work of Picture Actor Is Not a Life of Ease," *CSL*, November 17, 1912, B.5; and "Beautiful Actress Appears Before Thousands," *CSL*, December 1, 1912, B.5.

12. "Watch Picture Shows This Week; Get Free Tickets," *CSL*, December 1, 1912, B.5; and "1,200 Free Theater Tickets to Picture-Goers Who Can Tell What Photo-Plays These Scenes Are From," *CSL*, December 8, 1912, S.7.

13. Mabel Condon, "Sans Grease Paint and Wig," *M*, October 12, 1912, 207; and December 7, 1912, 435–36.

14. "The Movies" appeared simultaneously in the *Chicago Day Book*, November 11, 1912, 11; *DMN*, November 11, 1912, 2; *TBN*, November 11, 1912, 1.6; *Cleveland Press*, November 11, 1912, 1.4; and others, from the *St. Paul News* to the *New Orleans Statesman*. It is difficult to estimate how many read Price's syndicated stories, but the combined readership of Scripps-McRae newspapers and United Press subscribers was likely at least several million.

15. Gerald Baldasty, *E. W. Scripps and the Business of Newspapers* (Urbana: University of Illinois Press, 1999).

16. E.W. Scripps to Robert F. Paine, February 26, 1906, cited in Gerald Baldasty, *E. W. Scripps and the Business of Newspapers*, 147.

17. Quotation from Minutes of Conference Between E.W. Scripps, E.B. Scripps, and George Putnam, August 17, 1902, cited in Gerald Baldasty, *E. W. Scripps and the Business of Newspapers*, 104.

18. The *Des Moines News*, for instance, was especially interested in the Socialist Party's political triumph in Milwaukee, Wisconsin. Dorothy Dale, "The Rule of the Socialists in Milwaukee and What They Are Doing," *DMN*, July 21, 1910, 4.

19. R.F. Paine to W.D. Wasson, January 27, 1906. Cited in Gerald Baldasty, *E. W. Scripps and the Business of Newspapers*, 141.

20. Gerald Baldasty, *E. W. Scripps and the Business of Newspapers*, 143.

21. John Brigham, *History of Des Moines and Polk County, Iowa*, vol. 1 (Chicago: S.J. Clarke, 1911), 558.

22. "Des Moines Women Found in All Fields of Labor," *DMN*, July 7, 1907, 9; and "Women Are Rapidly Taking the Jobs That Belong to Men," *DMN*, October 6, 1907, Sunday Supplement, 3. Years later, the *News* was still promoting this "special attention," but now with a featured "Women's Page." Front-page ad, *DMN*, June 24, 1914, 1.

23. The *Cleveland Leader* several times supported the continuing protest in the trade press against using "movies" because "it harms the business." "Photo-Plays and Players," *CL*, December 10, 1911, S.5; "Protest Against Use of Name, 'Movie,'" *CL*, October 20, 1912, S.5. See also "'Spectator's' Comments," *NYDM*, May 15, 1912, 25; and Sargent, "Advertising for Exhibitors," *MPW*, August 31, 1912, 872. For an analysis of this nomenclature debate, see Gregory Waller, "Photodramas and Photoplays, Stage and Screen, 1909–1915," in Leonardo Quaresima and Laura Vichi, eds., *The Tenth Muse: Cinema and the Other Arts* (Udine, Italy: Forums, 2001), 575–85.

24. Most explicitly in drama critic Walter Pritchard Eaton's "The Menace of the Movies," *American Magazine* 86 (September 1913): 60.

25. Gertrude Price, "Dolores Cassinelli of Essanay," *DMN*, November 12, 1912, 8; Price, "King Baggot Detests Sentimental Stuff; Longs to Be Regular

Dyed-in-the-Wool Rip Roarin' Jake," *DMN*, December 7, 1912, 2; Price, "Mary Fuller? Why, Of Course, You've Met Mary! And Such a Deep-Dyed Pessimist Is This Slip-of-a-Girl Who Likes Witches, Old People and Poor Folks Most," *DMN*, December 28, 1912, 4; Price, "Funniest, Fattest Man in the Movies Is John Bunny Who Plays 'Mr. Pickwick,'" *DMN*, December 29, 1912, 4; "The Airman's Hoodoo Is What Mabel of the Movies Calls Her Pretty Self," *DMN*, March 4, 1913, 7; and "'Dimples' Costello Writes Name on Thousands of Pictures for Dear Public," *DMN*, April 11, 1913, 12.

26. Gertrude Price, "Everybody Writes to Pretty Helen, Starlet of the Flying A," *DMN*, February 23, 1913, 4; Price, "This Boy Acts, Travels, Studies; But Success Has Not Spoiled Him," *DMN*, June 2, 1913, 2; and Price, "Movie Industry Is Great New Field for 'Natural' Actors, Girls and Boys," *DMN*, October 8, 1913, 6. W. Stephen Bush later would "pay a well-deserved tribute" to child actors in a column that first appeared as "The Screen Children's Gallery," *MPW*, February 28, 1914, 1066.

27. Aunt Gertie, "A Little Personality About a Great Big Man [Thomas Edison]," *DMN*, June 3, 1913, 3.

28. "The Dustman, as Told by Aunt Gertie," *DMN*, June 9, 1913, 5; and "The Little Mermaid, as Told by Aunt Gertie," *DMN*, June 26, 1913, 7.

29. Aunt Gertie, "Just Think—This Real Princess Loves to Go to the Movies," *DMN*, May 25, 1913, 3.

30. "He's the Matinee Idol of the Movies," *TNB*, December 11, 1912, 2; "Movie Stars Who Play Leads in Western Dramas at Unique Theater," *DMN*, December 12, 1912, 7; Gertrude Price, "The Great Spirit Took Mona, But in This Girl She Still Lives," *DMN*, February 6, 1913, 12; Price, "Would You Guess That This Cowboy Is a New York Actor?" *DMN*, February 15, 1913, 2; and Price, "Picturesque Indian Maid Is Fearless-Ambitious-Clever!" *DMN*, April 27, 1913, 4. See also Price on Louise Lester and her "Flying A" series: "Everyone Is for Busy Ann, 'Calamity' Ann You Know!" *DMN*, April 29, 1913, 10.

31. "Runs, Rides, Rows," *DMN*, April 16, 1913, 6.

32. Early in 1912, the *News* was one of fifty dailies across the country that published "'Flying A' stories." Although only three stories ever appeared, they suggest that "Flying A" films may have been popular in Des Moines, although no theater ever advertised them. American Film ad, *MPW*, March 16, 1912, 980–81; and the first story, "The Grub Stake Mortgage—A Moving Picture Short Story of Western Life," *DMN*, January 17, 1912, 10.

33. "Here They Are! Snapshots from 'Wounded Knee,' Where Our 'Movie' Experts Are," *DMN*, October 23, 1913, 4; and Gertrude Price, "Indian Braves Adopt Heap Big 'Movie' Man and Call Him 'Wanbli Wiscasa,'" *DMN*, November 2, 1913, 4. For further information on this film's production, see Charles J. Ver Halen, "Bringing the Old West Back," *MPN*, November 22, 1913, 19–20.

34. James McQuade, "Chicago Letter," *MPW*, February 7, 1914, 660; and March 14, 1914, 1388–89; "'Buffalo Bill' Picture Shown," *MPW* (March 1913): 1370; and "Great Picture of Indian Wars Is Coming Here," *DMN*, April 18,

1914, 5. For a good discussion of this film's production, distribution, and exhibition, see Joy S. Kasson, *Buffalo Bill's Wild West: Celebrity, Memory, and Popular History* (New York: Hill & Wang, 2000), 257–63.

35. Gertrude Price, "'Movie' Queen Beards Tigers," *Cleveland Press*, November 13, 1912, 10; Price, "Stunning Mary Pickford—Only 19 Now!—Quits $10,000 'Movies' Career to Shake Her Golden Locks as a Belasco Star," *DMN*, January 9, 1913, 7; "Movie Queen Is Alice Joyce," *DMN*, March 1, 1913, 1; and "Live With Flowers and Grow Beautiful, Says Girl," *DMN*, November 29, 1913, 5.

36. "Bored by World, Actress Goes to 'Movies' to Get Thrills!" *DMN*, March 17, 1913, 8.

37. "She Reads Balzac, Likes Baseball, and Is Pretty," *DMN*, April 9, 1913, 4.

38. "Face Is Fortune of Tallest Picture Player Who Sheds Real Tears for Sake of Art," *DMN*, March 25, 1913, 4.

39. Gertrude Price, "No One Will Ride Pinto but Dainty, Daring Clara," *DMN*, March 27, 1913, 6.

40. "Daring Girl Rider Coming," *DMN*, July 27, 1912, 3; and "Summer Amusements," *DMN*, July 28, 1912, 12.

41. Gertrude Price, "Charming Little Woman Runs 'Movie' Business by Herself, and Makes Big Success," *DMN*, February 9, 1913, 2; "Lucky Thirteen Word Proves to Be a New Money Making Position," *DMN*, May 15, 1913, 8; and Price, "Sad Endings Are All Right, Says This Woman Director," *DMN*, September 27, 1913, 5.

42. Gertrude Price, "Here's a Story for Kiddies; 10-Year-Old Movie Star Draws $100 a Week," *DMN*, December 30, 1912, 1.

43. "'Most Engaged Girl' In All America Is Miss Adrienne Kroell; She's Proposed to Nearly Every Day—And by a Different Man!" *DMN*, November 14, 1912, 12.

44. Perhaps so many of Price's stories appeared in the *Des Moines News* because Sue McNamara, the dramatic editor and special feature writer, was especially partial to "personality sketches." A. C. Hesselbarth, "Women Writers of American Press," *EP*, December 27, 1913, 476.

45. Edison ad, *NYMT*, January 25, 1914, 5:2; and "Important Films of the Week," *NYMT*, February 1, 1914, 5:5.

46. "Suffragettes See Parade Picture," *DMN*, June 25, 1912, 5; and "*Votes for Women* in Picture Play," *DMN*, June 27, 1912, 5. For more information on *Votes for Women*, see Shelley Stamp, *Movie-Struck Girls: Women and Motion Picture Culture After the Nickelodeon* (Princeton, NJ: Princeton University Press, 2000), 175–79. Also a strong advocate of women's suffrage, the *Cleveland Leader* often heralded the "new woman" in articles on athletic figures, such as "A Modern Race of Amazons," *CL*, August 6, 1912, C.1; in full-page ads for the Ohio Woman Suffrage Party, such as "Her Job," *CL*, September 1, 1912, M.4; and in stories such as "The Stick-Up Girl: A True Story of an Uncaught Outlaw," *CL*, March 16, 1913, Feature Section, 1.

47. Gertrude Price, "A Day with General Jones and Her Army of 'Hikers' on Their Way to the Capitol," *DMN*, February 23, 1913, 3.

48. "Western Girl You Love in the 'Movies' is a Sure Enough Suffrager," *DMN*, February 11, 1913, 3. The 101 Ranch Wild West "cowgirls" also were linked with the suffrage movement. "Girls with Wild West Show to Help Women Gain Equal Suffrage," *TB*, August 17, 1912, 7.

49. Gertrude Price, "Only Movie Players Live in this Town," *TNB*, January 6, 1914, 13. Mark Cooper argues that the political elections in Universal City were largely a publicity stunt promoting that "Land of Make-Believe." Mark Garrett Cooper, *Universal Women: Filmmaking and Institutional Change in Early Hollywood* (Urbana: University of Illinois Press, 2010), 50–52.

50. Gertrude Price, "Sees the Movies as Great New Field for Women Folk," *TNB*, March 30, 1914, 14. The article includes a headshot of Price herself, as one of those "women folk." A month later, *Motion Picture Magazine* published a long article on professional women working as scenario editors in the industry, including Marguerite Bertsch (Vitagraph), Louella Parsons (Essanay, Chicago), Josephine Rector (Essanay, Niles), and several "graduates of Beta Breuil's 'scenario class'" at Vitagraph. Edwin M. La Roche, "A New Profession for Women," *MPM* (May 1914): 83–88.

51. Parsons is quoted in Rosalind Rosenberg, *Beyond Separate Spheres: Intellectual Roots of Modern Feminism* (New Haven, CT: Yale University Press, 1982), 172. I have taken that quote from Susan A. Glenn, *Female Spectacle: The Theatrical Roots of Modern Feminism* (Cambridge, MA: Harvard University Press, 2002), 5.

52. "Chats with the Players," *MPM* (February 1912): 135–38; and (March 1912): 133–36.

53. "Chats with the Players," *MPM* (February 1912): 135–36.

54. "Chats with the Players," *MPM* (March 1912): 133–34.

55. "Miss Mabel Condon" ad in *M*, September 6, 1913, 10.

56. Mabel Condon, "Sans Grease Paint and Wig," *M*, February 15, 1913, 111.

57. "Intimate Interview Behind the Scenes with a 'Picture' Idol," *OS*, May 10, 1913, 2.

58. "Danger and Death Faced by Screen Artists on Land and Sea," *OS*, March 22, 1913, 2; and *Lexington Herald*, March 23, 1913, 4.8; "Aeroplaning for Motion Pictures 'Twixt Heaven and Earth," *OS*, April 19, 1913, 2; and "A New Constellation of Stars Twinkling in Amusement Firmament," *OS*, August 30, 1913, 2.

59. "Amusing Love Notes to Photoplay Stars from Ardent Admirers," *OS*, March 22, 1913, 2; and *Lexington Herald*, March 23, 1913, 4.8.

60. "In the Frame of Public Favor," *CST*, March 1, 1914, 5.3.

61. "In the Frame of Public Favor," *CST*, March 15, 1914, 5.3.

62. "In the Frame of Public Favor," *CST*, March 8, 1914, 5.3; March 22, 1914, 5.3; March 29, 1914, 5.3; and April 5, 1914, 5.3.

63. "In the Frame of Public Favor," *CST*, March 8, 1914, 5.3; April 16, 1914, 5.3; May 10, 1914, 5.3; and June 21, 1914, 8.3.

64. "Gossip of the Silent Players," *CST*, March 1, 1914, 5.3.

65. "Answers to Questions," *CST*, March 15, 1914, 5.3; "Answers to Movie Fans by Mae Tinee," *CST*, April 12, 1914, 5.3; and April 19, 1914, 5.3.

66. "Answers to Movie Fans by Mae Tinee," *CST*, March 22, 1914, 5.4.

67. "Answers to Movie Fans by Mae Tinee," *CST*, June 7, 1914, 5.3.

68. "Answers to Movie Fans by Mae Tinee," *CST*, June 21, 1914, 8.5.

69. "The Slave in 'Cabiria,'" *CST*, July 12, 1914, 8.5; and "Gossip of the Movie Plays and Players," *CST*, July 19, 1914, 8.5.

70. "Will You Take Your Star Married or Single?" *CST*, August 9, 1914, 6.8; and August 23, 1914, 7.8.

71. "The Voice of the Movie Fans," *CST*, September 20, 1914, 8.4.

72. "In Movieland," *CST*, October 4, 1914, 8.4; and November 15, 1914, 8.7.

73. Full-page advertisement, *CT*, February 27, 1915, 7.

74. Mae Tinee, "Charles Chaplin, a Modest Violet, Scared to Death of Publicity," *CST*, January 10, 1915, 8.7.

75. "A Little About 'Little Mary,'" *CST*, February 28, 1915, 5.3; "Girls, Why Do We 'Fall' for Francis X.?" *CST*, March 7, 1915, 5.3; and "Alice Joyce, the Star with the Charm," *CST*, March 14, 1915, 5.4.

76. "Vive Notre Maurice Costello!" *CST*, March 21, 1915, 5.6; and "'Thanhouser's Florence' Picture Today," *CST*, March 28, 1915, 5.4.

77. Mae Tinee, "Latest News from Movie Land," *CST*, February 7, 1915, 8.5.

78. Mae Tinee, "Latest News from Movie Land," *CST*, May 9, 1915, 8.3; and May 23, 1915, 8.3.

79. Mary B. Leffler, "What Is Doing in the 'Movies,'" *FWST*, May 31, 1914, 17; and Leffler, "Flashes from Filmdom," *FWST*, June 14, 1914, 5. "Flashes from Filmdom" bannered the column through late December.

80. "Gossip of the Film World," *FWST*, May 31, 1914, 17.

81. "Gossip of the Film World," *FWST*, July 1, 1914, 16; and July 5, 1914, 21; and Harold MacGrath, "The Million Dollar Mystery," *FWST*, July 5, 1914, 22.

82. "Gossip of the Film World," *FWST*, July 15, 1914, 9.

83. "Film Actress Who Won First Place in Paper Contest," *FWST*, July 12, 1914, n.p; "Gossip of the Film World," *FWST*, July 17, 1914, 11; July 22, 1914, 5; and August 4, 1914, 5.

84. "Gossip of the Film World," *FWST*, July 9, 1914, 5. Was this another sign that the Fort Worth newspaper was aligned with the *Chicago Tribune*?

85. "Answers of 'Movie' Fans," *FWST*, October 25, 1914, 21; and "News for the 'Movie' Fans" ad, *FWST*, October 25, 1914, 21.

86. "Girl of 17 Made Good at Start as Film Actress," *FWST*, January 3, 1915, 12; "Gossip of the Film World," *FWST*, January 15, 1915, 12; and Mary B. Leffler, "Movie Stars in Private Life" and "Mary Pickford to Be Seen in 'Cinderella,'" *FWST*, January 31, 1915, n.p.

87. "Film Gossip," *FWST*, February 14, 1915, 30.

88. "Extracts from the Diary of Mary Fuller" and "Autobiography of J. Warren Kerrigan," *MPM* (July 1914): 82–83 and 97–99, respectively; and "Extracts from the Diary of Crane Wilbur," *MPM* (September 1914): 83–85.

89. Jean Darnell, "Ruth Roland, the 'Kalem Girl,'" and Russell E. Smith, "Lillian Gish: 'The Most Beautiful Blonde' in the World," *MPM* (August 1914): 84–85 and 89–91, respectively.

90. "Brief Biographies of Popular Players," *MPM* (September 1914): 86–88; and "How I Became a Photoplayer," *MPM* (October 1914): 104–7.

91. Esther Hoffman, "'Drowning' Is Pleasant!" *DMN*, July 25, 1914, 1; and Hoffman, "Shyest Man in the Movies," *DMN*, July 25, 1914, 2. Days earlier, however, Stonehouse had signed a very different article, "Only One Woman in 10,000 Can Wear the Extreme Clothes," *DMN*, July 20, 1914, 3.

92. Idah M'Glone Gibson, "Would You Have a Pleasing Personality?" *DMN*, July 10, 1914, 5; and Gibson, "Don't Attempt the Venus Slouch Unless You Have the Proper Lines Says Beverly Bayne," *DMN*, July 11, 1914, 5.

93. "Most Beautiful Blond in World of Movieland," *DMN*, September 6, 1914, 5; Esther Hoffman, "This Little Movie Star Is Good Friend of Princess of Portugal," *DMN*, September 9, 1914, 5; and Hoffman, "The Girl with the Curl—She's Most Winsome Miss of the Movies," *DMN*, September 23, 1914, 5.

94. Esther Hoffman, "Who's Who on the Films," *DMN*, October 13, 1914, 7; October 19, 1914, 7; November 14, 1914, 6; December 5, 1914, 3; and Hoffman, "Who's Who on the Films," *Los Angeles Record*, January 13, 1915, 8.

95. Esther Hoffman, "He's Thankful for His Face—The Funny Bunny Face You've Seen at the Movies," *DMN*, November 25, 1914, 1; and Hoffman, "Sends 50 Dolls to War Orphans," *Reno Evening Gazette*, December 12, 1914, 5.

96. Contest ad, *DMN*, October 24, 1914, 1; "Help Find Most Beautiful 'Phone Girl in America!" *DMN*, October 30, 1914, 10; "They're Waiting for Dorothy," *DMN*, November 13, 1914, 5; "Pretty Irene Hough, Omaha, Neb., Chose for 'Dorothy!' Nineteen-Year-Old Blond," *DMN*, November 27, 1914, 1; and Casino ad, *DMN*, December 30, 1914, 6.

97. Esther Hoffman, "Beautiful Ella Hall of Film Fame Designs Her Own Frocks and Hats," *DMN*, November 7, 1914, 5; "Margarita Fischer Hits Formula for Harrison Beauty, Model 15," *DMN*, November 11, 1914, 3; "'Looking Glass Never Fibs,' Says Movie Actress Who Studies Mirror," *DMN*, November 11, 1914, 10; and "Filmy Fabrics for Film Favorite," *DMN*, November 22, 1914, 3.

98. Esther Hoffman, "How to Be Beautiful," *Reno Evening Gazette*, June 29, 1915, 4; and July 3, 1915, 4; and Hoffman, "Lillian Gish's Talk on Beauty," *LN*, July 15, 1915, 8.

99. Gertrude M. Price, "New Star, Maybe, in Movie Ranks; Newspaper Woman Lands Job," *Los Angeles Record*, January 18, 1915, 1; Price, "Gertrude Price Turned into Spanish Girl by Actress; Tells How to Use Rouge," *Los Angeles Record*, January 19, 1915, 1–2; and Price, "'Putting Comedy Over' in Movies / Famous Comediennes Tell You How," *Reno Evening Gazette*, September 6, 1915, 5.

100. Gene Morgan, "What Tyrone Power Thinks of Himself and the Celluloid Drama," *CSH*, January 17, 1915, 6.6; Morgan, "Auburn Haired Personality in Film," *CSH*, January 31, 1915, 6.7; and Morgan, "In Reel Life But Not in Real Life," *CSH*, March 7, 1915, 6.6.

101. Gene Morgan, "Here's Chicago's Best 'Movie Fan'; She Loves Film Drama and Writes It," *CSH*, January 24, 1915, 6.6; Morgan, "Clipping Film with Censors," *CSH*, February 7, 1915, 6.6; and Morgan, "Kill Movie? 'Never' Say Fans," *CSH*, March 14, 1915, 6.6.

102. Gene Morgan, "Mr. Jitney Jim Yearns to Break Into Reel Drama," *CSH*, May 9, 1915, 5.15; Morgan, "Jitney Jim Talks of New Uses for Celluloid Dramas," *CSH*, May 16, 1915, 5.2; and Morgan, "Jitney Jim Outwits the Hardened Film Censors of Kansas," *CSH*, June 6, 1915, 5.2.

103. Rosemary Gray, "His Hobby [Francis X. Bushman]," *CSH*, January 24, 1915, 6.6; and Gray, "Her Hobby [Kathlyn Williams]," *CSH*, January 31, 1915, 6.6. Later this column would adopt more conventional graphics.

104. Caroline Carr, "Ruth Roland Breezily Mixes Tea and Business," *CSH*, April 18, 1915, 5.6; Carr, "Pretty Grace Darmond, Who Rides, Swims, Acts," *CSH*, April 25, 1915, 5.6; and Carr, "Essanay Star Says Movies Will Only Take Professionals," *CSH*, May 2, 1915, 5.6.

105. Advertisement, *CH*, March 25, 1915, 13; and "Charlie Chaplin, The Movie Man—Who Can Say He's a Stranger!" *CSH*, March 28, 1915, Rotogravure, 4. See also the final installment of "My Adventures in Movieland—By Charley Chaplin," *CSH*, August 15, 1915, 5.6.

106. "What the Fans Want to Know," *CSH*, April 11, 1915, 5.6; April 25, 1915, 5.6; and May 2, 1915, 5.6; "To Correspondents," *CSH*, April 11, 1915, 5.6; and "Answers to Queries," *CSH*, April 25, 1915, 5.6.

107. "Film Fans to Become Associate Editors," *CSH*, May 2, 1915, 6.6.

108. Louella O. Parsons, "Seen on the Screen," *CSH*, March 20, 1915, 14.

109. Louella O. Parsons, "Seen on the Screen," *CH*, March 22, 1915, 14; March 24, 1915, 7; and March 26, 1915, 10.

110. Louella O. Parsons, "Seen on the Screen," *CH*, April 1, 1915, 12; and May 10, 1915, 8. She usually interviewed local industry leaders, for instance Aaron Jones, Alfred Hamburger, George K. Spoor, and Winfield R. Sheenan (Fox Film). Parsons, "Seen on the Screen," *CH*, April 9, 1915, 8; May 12, 1915, 10; June 2, 1915, 8; and June 4, 1915, 10.

111. Louella O. Parsons, "Seen on the Screen," *CH*, May 7, 1915, 8.

112. Louella O. Parsons, "Seen on the Screen," *CH*, May 5, 1915, 10.

113. Louella O. Parsons, "Seen on the Screen," *CH*, April 12, 1915, 8; and May 20, 1915, 8; and Parsons, "Girls All Eager for Chance to Become 'Movie' Actresses," *CH*, May 24, 1915, 8.

114. Louella O. Parsons, "Seen on the Screen," *CH*, April 19, 1915, 8.

115. "Here's $62 Talk by Miss Farrar," *CH*, June 9, 1915, 2.1; Louella O. Parsons, "Seen on the Screen," *CH*, June 11, 1915, 8; June 18, 1915, 8; and July 10, 1915, 8. Parsons also interviewed Samuel Goldfish, on his own way from Los Angeles to New York, and Adolph Zukor, who was visiting the downtown offices of the Jones, Linick & Schaefer Company. Parsons, "Seen on the Screen," *CH*, June 17, 1915, 8; and July 3, 1915, 8.

116. "The Story of My Life by Kathlyn Williams," *CSH*, June 13, 1915, 5.2; "The Story of My Life by Edna Mayo," *CSH*, June 20, 1915, 5.6; "The Story of

My Life by Marguerite Clark," *CSH,* June 27, 1915, 5.6; Louella Parsons, "The Story of Lillian Gish—'Most Beautiful Blonde in the World,'" *CSH,* July 11, 1915, 6.5; and Parsons, "Here's Ideal Film Personality—Clara Kimball Young Is Playful Child and Brainy Woman," *CSH,* July 18, 1915, 6.6.

117. "Pictures of Movie Stars That Are Worth Saving," *CSH,* July 18, 1915, 9.4.

118. "The Story of My Life by Charley Chaplin," *CSH,* July 4, 1915, 5.6; and August 8, 1915, 5.6. See also *Charlie Chaplin's Own Story* (Indianapolis: Bobbs-Merrill, 1916).

119. Louella Parsons, "How to Become a Movie Actress," *CSH,* September 19, 1915, 6.1; and September 26, 1915, 5.6; Parsons, "How to Become a Movie Star," *CSH,* October 3, 1915, 6.3; October 10, 1915, 6.6; October 17, 1915, 6.4; October 24, 1915, 6.3; and October 31, 1915, 6.3.

120. "Behind the Screens with Britt Craig," *AtC,* February 28, 1915, M.9.

121. Advertisement, *AtC,* March 5, 1915, 6.

122. Sidney Ormond, "Ziegfeld's Follies Scored Big Hit at the Atlanta Theater," *AtC,* March 13, 1914, 3; Britt Craig, "Rejuvenation of Aunt Mary (at the Lyric)," *AtC,* May 26, 1914, 9; and "Does Britt Craig Know?" *AtC,* August 1, 1914, 1.

123. Britt Craig, "Behind the Screens," *AtC,* February 28, 1915, M.9.

124. "Behind the Screens with Britt Craig," *AtC,* March 7, 1915, M.11; and March 21, 1915, M.11.

125. "Behind the Screens with Britt Craig," *AtC,* March 14, 1915, B.3; and March 21, 1915, M.11.

126. "Behind the Screens with Britt Craig," *AtC,* February 28, 1915, M.9.

127. "Behind the Screens with Britt Craig," *AtC,* February 20, 1916, B.11.

128. George F. Worts, "News and Views of Filmland," *NYEM,* December 24, 1915, 7.

129. In the *Birmingham Age-Herald,* Richard F. Lussier also, if less frequently, circulated short star profiles. Lussier, "Footlights and Screens," *BAH,* December 11, 1915, 2; December 13, 1915, 5; and January 11, 1916, 2.

130. George F. Worts, "Chas. Chaplin's Press Agent Is Heard but Never Seen," *NYEM,* December 4, 1915, 4; and "Chaplin Is Center of Film Fight of Dollars," *NYEM,* February 8, 1916, 7.

131. George F. Worts, "Mary Pickford Neglected? Not If Mother Knows It," *NYEM,* November 27, 1915, 6; and Worts, "Hundred Year Old Ghost Stalks," *NYEM,* January 22, 1916, 6.

132. George F. Worts, "Clara Kimball Young Returns from Cuba to Win Contest and Lead a Ball," *NYEM,* February 19, 1916, 7.

133. A week of daily columns signed by Bernhardt appeared in the *Boston Globe.* Announcement, *Boston Globe,* October 6, 1912, 51. The Scripps-McRae chain syndicated Burke's column, which ran almost daily in the *Des Moines News* from June through September 1912. "Billie Burke," *DMN,* July 7, 1912, 3; July 10, 1912, 3; July 23, 1912, 5; August 14, 1912, 5; and August 19, 1912, 5.

134. Idah M'Glone Gibson, "Would You Have a Pleasing Personality?" *DMN*, July 10, 1914, 5; Gibson, "The Eyes Reveal What You Are," *DMN*, July 15, 1914, 5; Gibson, "Beverly Bayne Dispels Beauty Beliefs," *DMN*, July 16, 1914, 5; "It's Hard to Be a Film Actress, Says Mary Fuller," *CPD*, November 8, 1914, Editorial/Dramatic, 4; and "Blanche Sweet Speaks," *PEL*, April 24, 1915, 7.

135. "Talks with Screen-Struck Girls [Series Two, No. 3]," *CRR*, February 20, 1915, 17; Beatriz Michelena, "Talks with Screen-Struck Girls," *Trenton Sunday Times-Advertiser*, February 6, 1916, 3.1; Michelena, "Talks with Screen Struck Girls," *Riverside Enterprise*, February 12, 1916, 2; and Michelena, "Talks with Screen Struck Girls," *Idaho Statesman*, February 12, 1916, 9. This second series allegedly was carried by hundreds of newspapers. "500 Newspapers Will Use Second Series Beatriz Michelena 'Talks,'" *MPN*, January 29, 1916, 549.

136. "Mary Fuller Tells How to Break Into the Movies!" *PP*, May 3, 1915, 14; "Going Into Movies Is Becoming Fad Says Mary Fuller," *Sault Ste. Marie Evening News*, May 15, 1915, 6; "Mary Fuller Says Dressing for the Movies Is Problem," *Sault Ste. Marie Evening News*, May 22, 1915, 6; and "Mary Fuller Says 'Movie' Actress Is Ahead of Styles," *Sault Ste. Marie Evening News*, May 29, 1915, 6.

137. "Anita Stewart Tells Girls How to Achieve Success and Happiness," *CSL*, November 26, 1915, 8; "Action Is the Spice of Life, Says Helen Holmes," *OWH*, December 26, 1915, E.7; "Kerrigan Tells How He Happened Into the 'Movies,'" *OWH*, January 2, 1916, E.13; "Blanche Sweet Tells How She Got Her First Job in Movies," *MST*, January 30, 1916, 11; and "Theda Warns Ambitious Girls," *DNT*, March 12, 1916, D.4.

138. "Grace Darling Talks to Girls," *MST*, March 5, 1916, 10; March 12, 1916, 12; March 19, 1916, 11; and April 2, 1916, 11.

139. Biographers have only glanced at Pickford's newspaper column: Cari Beauchamp, *Without Lying Down: Frances Marion and the Powerful Women of Early Hollywood* (Berkeley: University of California Press, 1997), 53; and Eileen Whitfield, *Pickford: The Woman Who Made Hollywood* (Lexington: University of Kentucky Press, 1997), 152–53. Two papers at recent Women and the Silent Screen conferences have drawn more critical attention to the column: Anke Brouwers, "If It Worked for Mary . . . Mary Pickford's Daily Talks with the Fans," in Monica Dall'Asta, Victoria Duckett, and Lucia Tralli, eds., *Researching Women in Silent Cinema* (Bologna: University of Bologna, 2013), 197–219; and Katje Lee, "No, OUR Mary: (Re)Claiming Mary Pickford for Canada," Women and the Silent Screen VII, University of Melbourne and Victorian College of Arts and Music, October 1, 2013.

140. McClure Newspaper Syndicate ad, *EP*, October 23, 1915, 508–9. See also Alfred McClung Lee, *The Daily Newspaper in America: The Evolution of a Social Instrument* (New York: Macmillan, 1947), 586; and George H. Douglas, *The Golden Age of the Newspaper* (Westport, CT: Greenwood Press, 1999), 141–42.

141. "Daily Talks by Mary Pickford," *CT*, November 8, 1915, 15; *BE* November 8, 1915, 5; *CR*, November 8, 1915, 5, *DaN*, November 8, 1915, 9;

NOTP, November 8, 1915, 6; and *Macon Telegraph* (Georgia), November 8, 1915, 3.

142. Advertisements, *BE*, October 31, 1915, 33; *WH*, November 7, 1915, 10; and *CR*, November 7, 1915, 27. "Daily Talks by Mary Pickford," *CR*, December 10, 1915, 8.

143. "Beauty Chats by Edna Kent Forbes," *NOTP*, December 13, 1915, 6; "Table Talks by May DeWitt Talmadge," *NOTP*, January 3, 1916, 6; and "By Laura Jean Libbey," *CN*, March 1, 1916, 10. See also "Daily Talks by Mary Pickford," *CR*, November 24, 1915, 5; *DN*, December 3, 1915, 26; and *SH*, December 27, 1915, 20; and "Mary Pickford Says," *Galveston Daily News*, March 1, 1916, 6. In at least three newspapers, "Daily Talks" also appeared on the Editorial page. *AS*, December 20, 1915, 4; *DNT*, January 24, 1916, 6; and *Bakersfield Californian*, March 1, 1916, 12.

144. Advertisements, *Lima Times-Democrat* (Ohio), January 3, 1916, 8; and *New York American* (for the *New York Globe*), January 23, 1916, W.2.

145. "Daily Talks by Mary Pickford," *Saginaw Daily News* (Michigan), October 4, 1916, 4; and *DaN*, October 10, 1916, 10.

146. Not shared, of course, was that she was born Gladys Louise Smith in Toronto on April 8, 1892, not 1893.

147. "Daily Talks by Mary Pickford," *BE*, November 8, 1915, 5; *CR*, November 11, 1915, 9; *Macon Daily Telegraph*, November 15, 1915, 3; and *SH*, December 1, 1915, 2.24.

148. "Daily Talks by Mary Pickford," *CR*, December 16, 1915, 13; *SH*, December 27, 1915, 20; *CR*, January 10, 1916, 8; *Marion Daily Star* (Ohio), January 10, 1916, 5; and *NOTP*, February 28, 1916, 6.

149. "Daily Talks by Mary Pickford," *NOTP*, December 13, 1915, 6; *CR*, December 22, 1915, 10; January 17, 1916, 7; and January 24, 1916, 7; *DaN*, January 3, 1916, 9; *Flint Daily Journal*, January 17, 1916, 8; *DeNT*, January 24, 1916, 6.

150. "Daily Talks by Mary Pickford," *CR*, January 20, 1916, 8.

151. "Daily Talks by Mary Pickford," *DNT*, February 28, 1916, 6; *DaN*, February 28, 1916, 9; *CN*, March 1, 1916, 10; *Bakersfield Californian*, March 1, 1916, 12; *CN*, March 2, 1916, 10; March 6, 1916, 10; and *AS*, March 6, 1916, 6.

152. "Daily Talks by Mary Pickford," *SH*, December 2, 1915, 2.2; *NOTP*, December 13, 1915, 6; *DuNT*, February 7, 1916, 6; *DaN*, February 14, 1916, 11; and *CN*, April 1, 1916, 10. This interest, according to family members, may have been the result of an abortion that, early in her marriage to Owen Moore, left Pickford unable to bear children. Scott Eyman, *Mary Pickford: America's Sweetheart* (New York: Donald I. Fine, 1990), 80–81.

153. "Daily Talks by Mary Pickford," *NOTP*, December 20, 1915, 8; and *DNT*, May 15, 1916, 4.

154. "Daily Talks by Mary Pickford," *DNT*, April 10, 1916, 6.

155. "Daily Talks by Mary Pickford," *DaN*, May 8, 1916, 13.

156. "Daily Talks by Mary Pickford," *DNT*, May 29, 1916, 6.

157. "Daily Talks by Mary Pickford," *CR*, February 9, 1916, 10.

158. "Daily Talks by Mary Pickford," *CR*, February 16, 1916, 7.

159. "Daily Talks by Mary Pickford," *CN*, March 8, 1916, 10.

160. "Daily Talks by Mary Pickford," *DNT*, April 24, 1916, 6.

161. "Daily Talks by Mary Pickford," *DaN*, January 31, 1916, 9; *DNT*, January 31, 1916, 6; *Saginaw Daily News*, January 31, 1916, 5; and *AS*, January 31, 1916, 6.

162. "Daily Talks by Mary Pickford," *CR*, December 15, 1915, 10; *DNT*, March 13, 1916, 6; and *CN*, April 28, 1916, 10.

163. "Daily Talks by Mary Pickford," *CN*, March 9, 1916, 10; and *AS*, March 20, 1916, 6.

164. "Daily Talks by Mary Pickford," *DaN*, June 12, 1916, 11; *NOTP*, June 19, 1916, 7; and *DaN*, June 20, 1916, 11. "Daily Talks by Mary Pickford," *DaN*, June 26, 1916, 9; *NOTP*, June 26, 1916, 8; *AS*, July 1, 1916, 6; *NOTP*, July 4, 1916, 6; *DaN*, July 4, 1916, 9; *AS*, July 4, 1916, 4; July 5, 1916, 6; *DaN*, July 5, 1916, 13; *DNT*, July 17, 1916, 6; *DaN*, July 31, 1916, 11; and September 30, 1916, 10. The column ended within weeks of Frances Marion's collapse from exhaustion and grief over her sister's suicide in early September 1916. Cari Beauchamp, *Without Lying Down*, 64.

165. For analyses of Pickford's poor, orphan characters in the 1910s, see Hilary Hallett, *Go West Young Women!: The Rise of Early Hollywood* (Berkeley: University of California Press, 2013), 54–55; and Victoria Sturtevant, "'The Poor Little Rich Girl': Class and Embodiment in the Films of Mary Pickford," in Cynthia Lucia, Roy Grundmann, and Art Simon, eds., *The Wiley-Blackwell History of American Film I: Origins to 1928* (Chichester, England: Wiley-Blackwell, 2012), 207–27.

166. Daisy Dean, "News Notes from Movieland," *CR*, January 6, 1916, 12; and "Listen! Movie Fans," *LCT*, January 10, 1916, 1. See also Dean, "News Notes from Movieland," *Albuquerque Journal*, March 4, 1916, 3; and March 20, 1916, 3.

167. "Amusements," *SAL*, July 31, 1915, 8. Where Daisy Dean was located remains uncertain, although someone with that name is mentioned, about that same time, as having "left this morning for a trip to the Pacific Coast" from a town near Janesville, Wisconsin. "Avalon," *Janesville Gazette*, August 5, 1915, 8.

168. "News Notes from the Movies," *LCT*, January 11, 1916, 3.

169. Daisy Dean, "Newsy Notes from Movieland," *HN*, February 19, 1916, 13. This newspaper may have been the only one to rename the column "Newsy Notes."

170. Daisy Dean, "News Notes from Movieland," *CR*, April 1, 1916, 10.

171. Daisy Dean, "Newsy Notes from Movieland," *HN*, June 10, 1916, 14.

172. Daisy Dean, "Newsy Notes from Movieland," *HN*, March 18, 1916, 16; and May 24, 1916, 6.

173. Daisy Dean, "Newsy Notes from Movieland," *HN*, April 15, 1916, 11; and August 15, 1916, 10.

174. Daisy Dean, "News Notes from Movieland," *CR*, April 10, 1916, 11.

175. Daisy Dean, "Newsy Notes from Movieland," *HN*, February 14, 1916, 12.

176. Daisy Dean, "Newsy Notes from Movieland," *HN*, February 9, 1916, 12; June 8, 1916, 8; August 16, 1916, 10; and October 9, 1916, 4.

177. Daisy Dean, "Newsy Notes from Movieland," *HN*, May 26, 1916, 14; July 8, 1916, 11; and October 13, 1916, 4. For a sustained analysis of these and other women working at Universal during this period, see Mark Garrett Cooper, *Universal Women*.

178. Daisy Dean, "Newsy Notes from Movieland," *HN*, November 22, 1916, 4.

179. The "Questions and Answers" column was announced in "Flickerings and Flashes from Filmland," *DMRL*, January 23, 1916, 7.

180. Dorothy Day, "Questions and Answers," *DMT*, February 24, 1916, 3.

181. Dorothy Day, "What Do You Want to Know About Movies," *DMT*, February 25, 1916, 3.

182. Dorothy Day, "Arbuckle Weighed 16 Pounds at Birth; Grown Some Since," *DMT*, February 26, 1916, 5.

183. "Anita King, 'The Paramount Girl,' Appearing in 'The Race' at the Garden Theatre Friday and Saturday, Tells of Her Famous Trip and Machine," *DMT*, April 20, 1916, 8.

184. Ishbel Ross, *Ladies of the Press: The Story of Women in Journalism by an Insider* (New York: Harper & Brothers, 1936), 412–13. Underhill died of tuberculosis in 1928.

185. Harriette Underhill, "Petrova of the Pictures," *NYT*, November 19, 1916, 4.4.

186. Harriette Underhill, "Nance O'Neil, Filmist," *NYT*, December 10, 1916, 4.4.

187. Harriette Underhill, "In Re Marjorie Rambeau," *NYT*, December 17, 1916, 4.4.

188. Harriette Underhill, "Mr. Keenan Now Speaking," *NYT*, December 31, 1916, 4.4.

ENTR'ACTE: CARTOONS AND COMIC STRIPS

1. Donald Crafton, *Before Mickey: The Animated Film, 1898–1928* (Cambridge, MA: MIT Press, 1982). See also Peter Krämer, "Bad Boy: Notes on a Popular Figure in American Cinema, Culture and Society, 1895–1908," in John Fullerton, ed., *Celebrating 1895, The Centenary of Cinema* (Sydney: John Libbey, 1998), 117–30.

2. Stephen Bottomore, ed., *I Want to See This Annie Mattygraph: A Cartoon History of the Movies* (Pordenone, Italy: Le Giornate del cinema muto, 1995). Many of these cartoons come from magazines and trade journals, however, and also from Great Britain. See also Richard Abel, ed., *Early Cinema*, vol. IV (London: Routledge, 2013), 383–426.

3. "In the Movies in Real Life," *DMT*, September 15, 1913, 6.

4. "And Now You May Learn Tango from Movie Film!" *DMN*, January 16, 1914, 3; and "Movie Murders Harm Digestion, Says Health Board Doctor, Advises Comics," *DMN*, January 23, 1914, 1.

5. "Gossip of the Movie Plays and Players," *CST*, July 29, 1914, 8.5.

6. "Real Reporter Breaks Into Movies," *CT*, August 17, 1915, 1; and "Mayor Thompson Real Movie Hero," *CST*, August 29, 1915, 2.1.

7. "Many Nickels Make Mr. Movieman a Statler Swell. Yes. Reelly," *CSL*, January 19, 1913, M.1.

8. "Sane Fourthing in Three Reels," *DMN*, July 4, 1914, 4.

9. Hugh Fullerton, "Johnny Poe—The College Hero—A Movie Picture in Thirteen Reels," *DMN*, December 14, 1914, 8.

10. Joshua Lambert, "'Wait for the Next Pictures': Intertextuality and Cliffhanger Continuity in Early Cinema and Comic Strips," *Cinema Journal* 48, vol. 2 (Winter 2009): 4.

11. Ibid., 7, 10.

12. Ibid., 13–14.

13. Ibid., 14. This "Desperate Desmond" strip appeared on August 10, 1910. Libbey was a very successful working-girl fiction writer and later a newspaper advice columnist.

14. Ibid., 12–13.

15. In researching early newspaper comic strips, Lambert found this "bad boy" comic strip in microfilm of *Varheit* and shared some half a dozen individual strips.

16. "Osgar Cleverly Saves a Historic Film by His Presence of Mind," *DMN*, May 4, 1913, 13; "A Heroic Wild West Film That Turned Out a Disappointment," *DMN*, May 5, 1913, 6; and "Osgar Pirates the Death Scene in 'Queen Elizabeth,'" *DMN*, May 14, 1913, 6.

17. "Oscar and Adolph at Their Gay Pranks," *DMN*, December 20, 1914, 13.

18. "Diana Dillpickles in a 4-Reel 'Screecher' Film," *DMN*, March 31, 1914, 8.

19. "Diana Dillpickles . . .," *DMN*, April 16, 1914, 10.

20. "Adventures of the Silly Gallillies in Movie Land," *CST*, December 20, 1914, 8.7.

21. "Adventures of the Silly Gallillies . . .," *CST*, December 27, 1914, 8.7; and February 21, 1915, 5.3.

22. "Adventures of the Silly Gallillies . . .," *CST*, January 24, 1915, 5.3.

23. "Adventures of the Silly Gallillies . . .," *CST*, January 10, 1915, 8.7; January 31, 1915, 5.3; February 7, 1915, 5.3; and March 28, 1915, 5.4.

24. "Adventures of the Silly Gallillies . . .," *CST*, May 16, 1915, 5.3.

25. "Adventures of the Silly Gallillies . . .," *CST*, October 10, 1915, 5.3.

26. For further information on *The Motion Picture Girls* series (1914–16) and Ruth Fielding, who became unusually successful in the movies through a long-running series of novels (1913–34), see Anne Morey, "Acting Naturally: Juvenile Series Fiction About Moviemaking," in *Hollywood Outsiders: The*

Adaptation of the Film Industry, 1913–1934 (Minneapolis: University of Minnesota Press, 2003), 35–69.

27. "Adventures of the Silly Gallillies . . .," *CST*, February 13, 1916, 31.

28. "Haphazard Helen" ad, *CH*, January 2, 1915, 9.

29. "Haphazard Helen in Luck and Love (First Installment)," *CSH*, February 21, 1915, 4.2. By the second installment, plot and pictures were attributed to Carothers, and verse, to J. P. McEvoy. "Haphazard Helen," with plot and pictures now by Burroughs and verse by McEvoy, was still running under the head "Movies" in *CSH*, December 5, 1915, 4.2.

30. "Haphazard Helen as the Girl Detective," *CSH*, April 4, 1915, 4.2.

31. "MOVIES Featuring Haphazard Helen in Her Desert Love," *CSH*, January 3, 1915, 6.1; "Haphazard Helen in a Romance of the Air," *CSH*, January 25, 1915, 4.2; and "When Haphazard Helen Rode Nitro Glycerine," *CSH*, February 7, 1915, 4.2.

32. "The Lost Treasures of the Incas," *CSL*, February 7, 1915, Dramatic, 8. Several of these full-page comics were divided into single strips printed daily in the *Washington Times* from March 4, 1915, to March 20, 1915.

33. "When Fate Frowned," *CSL*, February 14, 1915, Dramatic, 8.

34. "Advice to Would-Be Movie Comedians," *CSH*, January 31, 1915, 6.7; "Advice to Would-Be Stars in Motion Picture Drama," *CSH*, February 7, 1915, 6.6; and "Advice to Would-Be Movie Actors," *CSH*, February 14, 1915, 6.6.

35. "How to Become a Camera Man," *CSH*, March 7, 1915, 6.6.

36. "It Never Occurs to Film Directors," *CSH*, March 21, 1915, 6.6.

37. "How to Write a Scenario, with Apologies to Our Teacher," *CSH*, February 28, 1915, 6.6.

38. "How to Become a Film Star Without Leaving the Flat," *CSH*, April 4, 1915, Magazine, 6.

39. "Our Sport Movies (A Thrill an Inch) . . . Passed by the Board of Nonsenseship," *CH*, March 15, 1915, 11; and March 16, 1915, 11.

40. "If the Movie Man Had Only Lived in Those Days," *CSH*, May 9, 1915, 5.2.

41. "Charley Chaplin's Comic Capers" ads, *CSH*, March 28, 1915, 1.4; and *CH*, March 29, 1915, 11.

42. "Introducing Charley Chaplin's Comic Capers," *CH*, March 29, 1915, 4. This strip also was signed initially by the "Carothers Co."

43. "Charley Chaplin's Comic Capers," *CH*, March 30, 1915, 16.

44. "Charley Chaplin's Comic Capers," *DMT*, May 13, 1915, 12.

45. "Charley Chaplin's Comic Capers," *CH*, April 1, 1915, 16.

46. "Charley Chaplin's Comic Capers—A Wordless Tragedy," *CH*, August 23, 1915, 4.

47. "Charley Chaplin's Comic Capers—Maybe Charley Dreamed He Was Dead," *DMT*, May 13, 1915, 12.

48. "Charley Chaplin's Comic Capers," *CSH*, December 5, 1915, 4.1.

49. "Charlie Chaplin's Comic Capers—Even the Lowest Specimen of Human Life Believes in Preparedness," *CH*, June 29, 1916, 16.

CHAPTER 4. "FILM GIRLS" AND THEIR FANS IN FRONT OF THE SCREEN

1. Richard Abel, *The Red Rooster Scare: Making Cinema American, 1900–1910* (Berkeley: University of California Press, 1999), 85–86.

2. Alice Fahs, *Out on Assignment: Newspaper Women and the Making of Modern Public Space* (Chapel Hill: University of North Carolina Press, 2011), 32.

3. Ishbel Ross, *Ladies of the Press: The Story of Women in Journalism by an Insider* (New York: Harper & Brothers, 1936), 427–28.

4. Full-page advertisement, *CST*, January 3, 1915, 8.3. See also Ishbel Ross, *Ladies of the Press*, 407–8; and Alice Fahs, *Out on Assignment*, 89–90.

5. Charles Johanningsmeier, "Understanding Readers of Fiction in American Periodicals, 1880–1914," in Christine Bold, ed., *Oxford History of Popular Print Culture 6: US Popular Print Culture, 1860–1920* (Oxford: Oxford University Press, 2011), 601. He also stresses the importance of "school training," in which students were "exhorted to see in literary works models for good, moral behavior" for defining "national character." That many schools were beginning to use motion pictures as "educational" tools by the early and mid-1910s requires further research on another possible practice of "school training."

6. The questions concerning authority and authenticity derive in part from Eric Schocket's essay "Undercover Explorations of the 'Other Half,' or the Writer as Class Transvestite," *Representations* 64 (Autumn 1998): 111.

7. "At the Leader Chain Houses This Week," *CSL*, October 15, 1911, B.6; "Features in the Films," *CSL*, October 22, 1911, S.5; and "Criticisms and Reviews," *CSL*, October 29, 1911, S.5.

8. Ralph P. Stoddard, "Films All Should See," *CSL*, November 5, 1911, S.5.

9. Ralph P. Stoddard, "Films All Should See," *CSL*, November 12, 1911, S.5.

10. "Cinderella Is a Splendid Film," *CSL*, January 7, 1912, B.7; "Films Worth Seeing," *CSL*, January 14, 1912, S.5; and "Features in Films Are Shown Here," *CSL*, February 4, 1912, S.6.

11. "Reo Stadt" could have served as a pseudonym, of course, for Stoddard himself.

12. "Reviews of Films by Reo Stadt," *CSL*, March 31, 1912, S.8.

13. "Bernhardt Film a Hit" and "'Personal'—First Hit," *CSL*, April 14, 1912, S.8. The latter story voiced the opinion of R.H. McLaughlin, the Colonial Theater's manager. See also the lengthy story of a private exhibition of Selig's *Coming of Columbus*: "Famous Historic Film Completed," *CSL*, April 28, 1912, W.8.

14. "Today's Best Moving Picture Story," *CT*, February 5, 1914, 5.

15. Moya Luckett, *Cinema and Community: Progressivism, Exhibition, and Film Culture in Chicago, 1907–1917* (Detroit: Wayne State University Press, 2013), 149.

16. "Today's Best Moving Picture Story," *CT*, February 11, 1914, 5.

17. "Today's Best Photo Play Stories," *CT*, February 14, 1914, 7. The *Tribune* claimed that "a staff of trained story writers" was producing these synopses after seeing the films; the language, however, is similar to that later signed by Kitty Kelly.

18. "Today's Best Photo Play Stories," *CT*, March 28, 1914, 6.

19. "Today's Best Photo Play Stories," *CT*, May 23, 1914, 11.

20. "Today's Best Photo Play Stories," *CT*, June 13, 1914, 13; and June 20, 1914, 9.

21. "Today's Best Photo Play Stories," *CT*, May 20, 1914, 11; June 10, 1914, 11; and June 13, 1914, 13.

22. "Today's Best Photo Play Stories," *CT*, June 27, 1914, 9.

23. "Today's Best Photo Play Stories," *CT*, April 18, 1914, 10.

24. "Today's Best Photo Play Stories," *CT*, April 1, 1914, 13.

25. "Today's Best Photo Play Stories," *CT*, June 17, 1914, 11.

26. "Today's Best Photo Play Stories," *CT*, June 17, 1914, 11; June 20, 1914, 9; and June 27, 1914, 9.

27. "Today's Best Photo Play Stories," *CT*, April 11, 1914, 10.

28. "Today's Best Photo Play Stories," *CT*, April 29, 1914, 11.

29. "Today's Best Photo Play Stories," *CT*, May 16, 1914, 9.

30. "Today's Best Photo Play Stories," *CT*, June 8, 1914, 14; and Kitty Kelly, "Photoplay Stories and News," *CT*, July 11, 1914, 11.

31. Kitty Kelly, "Photoplay Stories and News," *CT*, July 15, 1914, 8.

32. "Today's Best Photo Play Stories," *CT*, April 25, 1914, 12.

33. Kitty Kelly, "Today's Best Photoplay Stories," *CT*, July 1, 1914, 13; and Audrie Alspaugh, "Mr. Wells on the Novel of the Future," *CT*, August 1, 1914, 11. Kelly also wrote at least one scenario. See the Essanay ad, *MPW*, March 13, 1915, 1551.

34. Kitty Kelly, "Photoplay Stories and News," *CT*, July 8, 1914, 11.

35. Kitty Kelly, "Today's Best Photoplay Stories," *CT*, July 1, 1914, 13.

36. Kitty Kelly, "Photoplay Stories and News," *CT*, August 13, 1914, 11.

37. Kitty Kelly, "Photoplay Stories and News," *CT*, August 29, 1914, 11.

38. Kitty Kelly, "Photoplay Stories and News," *CT*, July 22, 1914, 11.

39. Ibid.

40. Kitty Kelly, "Photoplay Stories and News," *CT*, August 8, 1914, 11. After the authorities issued a permit, *Traffic in Souls* finally began running at the downtown Princess Theater, and Carl Laemmle exhorted "young girls" and "daughters" to see this "great moral drama." Universal ad, *CT*, August 13, 1914, 11.

41. Kitty Kelly, "Photoplay Stories and News," *CT*, August 5, 1914, 11.

42. Kitty Kelly, "Photoplay Stories and News," *CT*, July 18, 1914, 11; and August 15, 1914, 9; "In Celluloid Land with Kitty Kelly," *CT*, September 19, 1914, 11; and Kelly, "Flickerings from Film Land," *CT*, December 23, 1914, 10.

43. Kitty Kelly, "Photoplay Stories and News," *CT*, August 1, 1914, 15; and Kelly, "Flickerings from Film Land," *CT*, November 11, 1914, 11.

44. Kitty Kelly, "Photoplay Stories and News," *CT*, September 16, 1914, 9.

45. Kitty Kelly, "Photoplay Stories and News," *CT*, August 13, 1914, 11; and October 17, 1914, 11. She also noted that *The Girl of the Open Road* (Edison)

was "written for Mabel Trunnelle's purposes by Mrs. Woodrow Wilson." Kelly, "Flickerings from Film Land," *CT*, December 2, 1914, 14.

46. Studebaker ad, *CT*, September 2, 1914, 11.

47. Kitty Kelly, "Photoplay Stories and News," *CT*, September 22, 1914, 9.

48. Kitty Kelly, "Flickerings from Film Land," *CT*, September 30, 1914, 9.

49. Kitty Kelly, "Flickerings from Film Land," *CT*, September 26, 1914, 9.

50. Kitty Kelly, "Photoplay Stories and News," *CT*, October 10, 1914, 17; and Kitty Kelly, "Flickerings from Film Land," *CT*, November 28, 1914, 15.

51. "In Celluloid Land with Kitty Kelly," *CT*, September 19, 1914, 11; and "Flickerings from Film Land by Kitty Kelly," *CT*, September 26, 1914, 9. The column's title actually continued to fluctuate for the next month and finally settled on "Flickerings from Film Land by Kitty Kelly" on October 28, 1914.

52. "Right Off the Reel," *CST*, September 27, 1914, 8.3.

53. Advertisement, *CST*, January 3, 1915, 8.3. Most prominent, of course, were cartoonists, drama and music writers, sports writers, and humorists.

54. "The Film of the Week," *CSPD*, February 15, 1914, Editorial/Dramatic, 6; February 22, 1914, Editorial/Dramatic, 4; and March 22, 1914, Editorial /Dramatic, 4.

55. "The Film of the Week," *CSPD*, April 19, 1914, Editorial/Dramatic, 4; May 31, 1914, Editorial/Dramatic, 4; and August 30, 1914, Editorial/Dramatic, 3.

56. "The Film of the Week," *CSPD*, March 15, 1914, Editorial/Dramatic, 4; and May 24, 1914, Editorial/Dramatic, 4.

57. "The Film of the Week," *CSPD*, February 22, 1914, Editorial /Dramatic, 4.

58. "The Film of the Week," *CSPD*, March 22, 1914, Editorial/Dramatic, 4.

59. "The Film of the Week," *CSPD*, July 5, 1914, Editorial/Dramatic 4; and August 9, 1914, Editorial/Dramatic, 6.

60. "The Film of the Week," *CSPD*, May 24, 1914, Editorial/Dramatic, 4.

61. "The Film of the Week," *CSPD*, July 12, 1914, Editorial/Dramatic, 4.

62. "Minutes 'Mong the Movies by Ruth Vinson," *CSPD*, July 19, 1914, Editorial/Dramatic, 4.

63. "Minutes 'Mong the Movies by Ruth Vinson," *CSPD*, July 26, 1914, Editorial/Dramatic, 3.

64. "Minutes 'Mong the Movies by Ruth Vinson," *CSPD*, August 9, 1914, Editorial/Dramatic, 6.

65. "Minutes 'Mong the Movies by Ruth Vinson," *CSPD*, July 26, 1914, Editorial/Dramatic, 3; August 9, 1914, Editorial/Dramatic, 6; and August 30, 1914, Editorial/Dramatic, 3.

66. "Minutes 'Mong the Movies by Ruth Vinson," *CSPD*, August 16, 1914, Editorial/Dramatic, 3; and August 30, 1914, Editorial/Dramatic, 3.

67. "Minutes 'Mong the Movies by Ruth Vinson," *CSPD*, September 20, 1914, Editorial/Dramatic, 6.

68. "Minutes 'Mong the Movies by Ruth Vinson," and "The Film of the Week," *CSPD*, October 4, 1914, 5.

69. Mary Leffler, "Flashes from Filmdom," *FWST*, June 14, 1914, 5. The very first column was actually titled "What Is Doing in the 'Movies,'" *FWST*, May 31, 1914, 17.

70. Mary Leffler, "Flashes from Filmdom," *FWST*, June 25, 1914, 13; and June 26, 1914, 9.

71. Mary Leffler, "Flashes from Filmdom," *FWST*, July 5, 1914, 21. *Quo Vadis?* also came in for praise, but the film playing at the city's Airdome apparently was the three-reel version released to exploit the popularity of Cines's epic. The listed producer was Kline or Cline rather than Kleine.

72. Mary Leffler, "Flashes from Filmdom," *FWST*, June 18, 1914, 10; and July 1, 1914, 16.

73. Mary Leffler, "Flashes from Filmdom," *FWST*, July 1, 1914, 16; July 9, 1914, 5; and July 21, 1914, 14.

74. Mary Leffler, "Flashes from Filmdom," *FWST*, July 12, 1914, n.p.

75. "Screen Results," *NYEM*, November 14, 1914, 7; and "Review of Photoplay Features," *NYEM*, November 21, 1914, 5. The *New York Times* printed scattered unsigned reviews in 1913–14. Weekly or biweekly reviews, still unsigned, began to appear in the fall of 1915, but even then, most of these engaged with films adapted from stage plays or imported epics, or with stage actors who turned to film acting. *The New York Times Films Reviews I: 1913–1931* (New York: New York Times & Arno Press, 1970).

76. "The Films and Film Folk by 'Wid,'" *NYEM*, November 28, 1914, 12.

77. "Screen Results," *NYEM*, November 14, 1914, 7.

78. "The Films and Film Folk by 'Wid,'" *NYEM*, November 28, 1914, 12.

79. "The Films and Film Folk by 'Wid,'" *NYEM*, December 12, 1914, 6; and December 19, 1914, 13.

80. "The Films and Film Folk by 'Wid,'" *NYEM*, December 5, 1914, 12; and December 12, 1914, 6.

81. "The Films and Film Folk by 'Wid,'" *NYEM*, December 19, 1914, 13.

82. Mary Leffler, "Flashes from Filmdom," *FWST*, March 18, 1915, 5.

83. Mary Leffler, "Flashes from Filmdom," *FWST*, March 22, 1915, 11. Five years earlier, Max Linder had directed himself in a similar story of his "audition" for Pathé-Frères in *Les Débuts de Max Linder au le cinématographe.*

84. Mary Leffler, "Flashes from Filmdom," *FWST*, March 22, 1915, 11; and April 25, 1915, 22.

85. Mary Leffler, "Flashes from Filmdom," *FWST*, April 13, 1915, 9; April 18, 1915, 32; and May 2, 1915, 25.

86. Mary Leffler, "Flashes from Filmdom," *FWST*, March 21, 1915, 25; and April 4, 1915, 19.

87. Mary Leffler, "Flashes from Filmdom," *FWST*, April 4, 1915, 19.

88. Mary Leffler, "Flashes from Filmdom," *FWST*, March 21, 1915, 25; and March 28, 1915, 27.

89. Mary Leffler, "Flashes from Filmdom," *FWST*, May 16, 1915, 16.

90. "The Films and Film Folk by 'Wid,'" *NYEM*, December 19, 1914, 1.3. Later he expanded these criteria to distinguish Lighting and Camera Work from

Photography and moved Direction to the top of his graphs. "The Films and Film Folk by 'Wid,'" *NYEM*, June 5, 1915, 5.

91. "Worth-While Feature Films Recommended by 'Wid,'" *NYEM*, February 13, 1915, 4.

92. "Worth-While Feature Films Recommended by 'Wid,'" *NYEM*, April 3, 1915, 5.

93. "Worth-While Feature Films Recommended by 'Wid,'" *NYEM*, January 23, 1915, 6.

94. "Worth-While Feature Films Recommended by 'Wid,'" *NYEM*, April 10, 1915, 5.

95. "Worth-While Feature Films Recommended by 'Wid,'" *NYEM*, May 8, 1915, 6.

96. "Worth-While Feature Films Recommended by 'Wid,'" *NYEM*, July 17, 1915, 8.

97. "'Close Ups' Are Very Important," *NYEM*, January 9, 1915, 5; and "Worth-While Feature Films Recommended by 'Wid,'" *NYEM*, January 2, 1915, 6; and February 27, 1915, 6. Münsterberg describes actors' facial expressions in close-up, and their psychological effect, in "Movies the Great Art of America, Says Dr. Munsterberg," *CSH*, April 30, 1916, 7.1. He also discusses "the close up" in terms of objects or gestures in "Why We Go to the Movies," *Cosmopolitan*, December 15, 1915, reprinted in Allan Langdale, ed., *Hugo Münsterberg on Film* (New York: Routledge, 2002), 176–77. See also Münsterberg, *The Film: A Psychological Study* (New York: Dover, 1970), 38–39. Lindsay never uses the term and, discussing the "triangular ground plan" of the film frame, describes what we now would call a mid-shot or American shot. Vachel Lindsay, *The Art of the Moving Picture* (New York: Macmillan, 1915), 19–20.

98. "Worth-While Feature Films Recommended by 'Wid,'" *NYEM*, June 19, 1915, 5; and "Feature Films as Wid Sees Them," *NYEM*, July 23, 1915, 5.

99. "Worth-While Feature Films Recommended by 'Wid,'" *NYEM*, April 17, 1915, 6. Rarely did "Wid" include such a one-reel film in his recommendations.

100. "Worth-While Feature Films Recommended by 'Wid,'" *NYEM*, February 20, 1915, 4.

101. "Worth-While Feature Films Recommended by 'Wid,'" *NYEM*, January 30, 1915, 4.

102. "Worth-While Feature Films Recommended by 'Wid,'" *NYEM*, March 13, 1915, 6.

103. "Worth-While Feature Films Recommended by 'Wid,'" *NYEM*, May 15, 1915, 5; May 22, 1915, 5; June 5, 1915, 5; and July 17, 1915, 8.

104. "Films and Film Folk by Wid," *NYEM*, August 4, 1915, 7.

105. "Worth-While Feature Films Recommended by 'Wid,'" *NYEM*, May 1, 1915, 6; and July 3, 1915, 4.

106. "Worth-While Feature Films Recommended by 'Wid,'" *NYEM*, March 13, 1915, 6.

107. "Films and Film Folk by Wid," *NYEM*, July 13, 1915, 7. For further information on this "epilogue" film that "was not screened in many places," see Melvyn Stokes, *D.W. Griffith's The Birth of a Nation* (Oxford: Oxford University Press, 2007), 144–45, 225.

108. "Worth-While Feature Films Recommended by 'Wid,'" *NYEM*, May 15, 1915, 5. Lindsay composed an unusually lengthy analysis of *Ghosts*, partly to counter the literati's denunciation of the film but also to explain how and why he thought the adaptation succeeds or does not. Vachel Lindsay, *The Art of the Moving Picture*, 152–56.

109. "Worth-While Feature Films Recommended by 'Wid,'" *NYEM*, May 22, 1915, 5; and July 10, 1915, 10.

110. "Worth-While Feature Films Recommended by 'Wid,'" *NYEM*, May 22, 1915, 5.

111. "Worth-While Feature Films Recommended by 'Wid,'" *NYEM*, January 16, 1915, 6.

112. Kitty Kelly, "Flickerings from Film Land," *CT*, January 6, 1915, 10.

113. Kitty Kelly, "Flickerings from Film Land," *CT*, January 26, 1915, 14.

114. Kitty Kelly, "Flickerings from Film Land," *CT*, February 1, 1915, 12.

115. Kitty Kelly, "Flickerings from Film Land," *CT*, March 11, 1915, 8.

116. Kitty Kelly, "Flickerings from Film Land," *CT*, February 2, 1915, 10.

117. Kitty Kelly, "Flickerings from Film Land," *CT*, January 19, 1915, 10.

118. Kitty Kelly, "Flickerings from Film Land," *CT*, February 24, 1915, 12.

119. Kitty Kelly, "Flickerings from Film Land," *CT*, February 13, 1915, 13; February 15, 1915, 10; and March 2, 1915, 10.

120. Kitty Kelly, "Flickerings from Film Land," *CT*, January 11, 1915, 10.

121. Kitty Kelly, "Flickerings from Film Land," *CT*, January 16, 1915, 11.

122. Kitty Kelly, "Flickerings from Film Land," *CT*, January 22, 1915, 10.

123. Kitty Kelly, "Flickerings from Film Land," *CT*, February 12, 1915, 14. This second reference to Northwestern suggests that Kelly may have had some affiliation with the university, but not as a former student; in a belated wedding announcement, she was described as "a graduate of the University of Iowa." Jas. J. McQuade, "Chicago News Letter," *MPW*, November 13, 1915, 1286.

124. Kitty Kelly, "Flickerings from Film Land," *CT*, February 23, 1915, 10.

125. Kitty Kelly, "Flickerings from Film Land," *CT*, February 5, 1915, 8.

126. Kitty Kelly, "Flickerings from Film Land," *CT*, January 28, 1915, 14.

127. Kitty Kelly, "Flickerings from Film Land," *CT*, March 4, 1915, 8. Kelly later used similar terms to call her readers' attention to Bushman's appearance at the downtown Studebaker. Kelly, "Flickerings from Film Land," *CT*, August 17, 1915, 10.

128. One week, for instance, she accompanied a large Lasky company crew into the desert in Southern California for filming on *The Arab* and later reported on the activities of the Photoplay Authors League, its officers, and its "little magazine called The Script." Kitty Kelly, "Flickerings from Film Land," *CT*, April 21, 1915, 12; and April 28, 1915, 14.

129. Kitty Kelly, "Flickerings from Film Land," *CT*, May 24, 1915, 14. Earlier Kelly had alluded to the daunting task of a "professional picture see-er" by appending brief reviews to half a dozen titles as "Filmoids" in several columns. Kelly, "Flickerings from Film Land," *CT*, February 13, 1915, 13; and February 19, 1915, 10.

130. Kitty Kelly, "Flickerings from Film Land," *CT*, May 3, 1915, 18.

131. Kitty Kelly, "Flickerings from Film Land," *CT*, May 25, 1915, 18.

132. Kitty Kelly, "Flickerings from Film Land," *CT*, April 26, 1915, 10.

133. Kitty Kelly, "Flickerings from Film Land," *CT*, May 18, 1915, 14.

134. Kitty Kelly, "Flickerings from Film Land," *CT*, May 4, 1915, 14.

135. Kitty Kelly, "Flickerings from Film Land," *CT*, May 27, 1915, 12. For further information on efforts to ban or permit screenings of *The Birth of a Nation* in Chicago, see Melvyn Stokes, *D.W. Griffith's The Birth of a Nation*, 150–153; and Anna Everett, *Returning the Gaze: A Genealogy of Black Film Criticism, 1901–1949* (Durham, NC: Duke University Press, 2001), 85–88.

136. Everett analyzes Lester A. Walton's critique, in the *Chicago Defender*, of such "free speech" supporters of *The Birth of a Nation*'s screening. Anna Everett, *Returning the Gaze*, 78–81.

137. Kitty Kelly, "Flickerings from Film Land," *CT*, September 28, 1915, 13.

138. Kitty Kelly, "Flickerings from Film Land," *CT*, May 3, 1915, 18.

139. Kitty Kelly, "Flickerings from Film Land," *CT*, May 20, 1915, 12.

140. Kitty Kelly, "Flickerings from Film Land," *CT*, July 21, 1915, 12.

141. Kitty Kelly, "Flickerings from Film Land," *CT*, July 13, 1915, 12.

142. Kitty Kelly, "Flickerings from Film Land," *CT*, August 10, 1915, 12; and September 6, 1915, 14.

143. Kitty Kelly, "Flickerings from Film Land," *CT*, August 3, 1915, 12; August 10, 1915, 12; and August 23, 1915, 14.

144. Kitty Kelly, "Flickerings from Film Land," *CT*, July 26, 1915, 18.

145. The first, for Universal's *The Garden of Lies*, appeared on July 12, and the credit box became a regular feature by July 19.

146. Kitty Kelly, "Flickerings from Film Land," *CT*, July 16, 1915, 12.

147. Kitty Kelly, "Flickerings from Film Land," *CT*, August 18, 1915, 10.

148. Kitty Kelly, "Flickerings from Film Land," *CT*, April 23, 1915, 16.

149. Kitty Kelly, "Flickerings from Film Land," *CT*, July 2, 1915, 14.

150. Kitty Kelly, "Flickerings from Film Land," *CT*, July 6, 1915, 18.

151. Kitty Kelly, "Flickerings from Film Land," *CT*, July 21, 1915, 12.

152. In an "Author's Note," Carr described her first experience of motion pictures as "a very awed little girl," apparently in the 1890s. Caroline Carr, *The Art of Photoplay Writing* (New York: H. Jordan, 1914), 4.

153. Caroline Carr, "Seen on the Screen," *CH*, March 16, 1915, 11. In another column, she argued that it was "sensible" to accept "movies" as "a purely American . . . term of endearment" used by fans, especially children. Carr, "Seen on the Screen," *CH*, March 15, 1915, 11.

154. Louella O. Parsons, "Seen on the Screen," *CH*, March 19, 1915, 13.

155. Louella O. Parsons, "Seen on the Screen," *CH*, March 20, 1915, 11; and March 22, 1915, n.p. Cast lists already had appeared in several anonymous reviews: "In the Picture Playhouses," *CH*, January 1, 1915, 13; and January 4, 1915, 13.

156. Louella O. Parsons, "Seen on the Screen," *CH*, March 22, 1915, n.p.

157. Louella O. Parsons, "Seen on the Screen," *CH*, March 27, 1915, 8; and April 3, 1915, 12. She also devoted one column to visiting the local Selig studio. Parsons, "Seen on the Screen," *CH*, April 2, 1915, 10.

158. Louella O. Parsons, "Seen on the Screen," *CH*, March 24, 1915, 7.

159. Louella O. Parsons, "Seen on the Screen," *CH*, April 16, 1915, 8; April 21, 1915, 8; and May 3, 1915, 10.

160. Louella O. Parsons, "Seen on the Screen," *CH*, April 5, 1915, 10; and April 17, 1915, 8.

161. Louella O. Parsons, "Seen on the Screen," *CH*, April 14, 1915, 8.

162. Louella O. Parsons, "Seen on the Screen," *CH*, April 22, 1915, 10; May 4, 1915, 8; and May 11, 1915, 8.

163. Louella O. Parsons, "Seen on the Screen," *CH*, May 18, 1915, 8.

164. Louella O. Parsons, "Seen on the Screen," *CH*, April 10, 1915, 8; and May 12, 1915, 10.

165. Louella O. Parsons, "Seen on the Screen," *CH*, October 15, 1915, 8.

166. Louella O. Parsons, "Seen on the Screen," *CH*, April 7, 1915, 10; April 28, 1915, 8; April 30, 1915, 8; May 1, 1915, 12; and May 19, 1915, 8. In an intriguing note, she viewed *The Unbroken Road* (Life Film) "flashed on a small piece of cardboard and projected by a house machine." Parsons, "Seen on the Screen," *CH*, May 13, 1915, 8.

167. Louella O. Parsons, "Seen on the Screen," *CH*, June 15, 1915, 10.

168. Louella O. Parsons, "Seen on the Screen," *CH*, August 3, 1915, 8.

169. Louella O. Parsons, "Seen on the Screen," *CH*, August 10, 1915, 8.

170. Louella O. Parsons, "Seen on the Screen," *CH*, August 7, 1915, 4.

171. Louella O. Parsons, "Seen on the Screen," *CH*, July 13, 1915, 10.

172. Louella O. Parsons, "Seen on the Screen," *CH*, October 22, 1915, 8.

173. Louella O. Parsons, "Seen on the Screen," *CH*, October 16, 1915, 8.

174. Louella O. Parsons, "Seen on the Screen," *CH*, November 10, 1915, 8. Yet, in reviewing *Rags* (Famous Players), Parsons earlier concluded, "Mary is the picture." Parsons, "Seen on the Screen," *CH*, August 4, 1915, 10.

175. In January 1916, Juanita Gray replaced Currie, with little change in subject matter, made explicit when her column was renamed "Motion Pictures: News of the Plays and Players, Gossip of the Theatres," *CE*, August 28, 1916, 6.

176. James Warren Currie, "The Turn of the Reel," *CE*, June 13, 1915, 4.8.

177. James Warren Currie, "The Turn of the Reel," *CE*, August 11, 1915, 6.

178. James Warren Currie, "The Turn of the Reel," *CE*, November 20, 1915, 12.

179. James Warren Currie, "The Turn of the Reel," *CE*, November 3, 1915, 6.

180. "Photoplays of the Week," *CE*, October 24, 1915, 5.9; and James Warren Currie, "Turn of the Reel," *CE*, November 29 1915, 10.

181. G. F. W., "Mary Pickford Breaks Record in 'Esmeralda,'" *NYEM*, September 6, 1915, 8.

182. G. F. W., "Blanche Sweet Is a Capable Becky," *NYEM*, September 13, 1915, 7; and "Turnbull's First Film a Psychological Story," *NYEM*, September 14, 1915, 7. The scenario was by Herbert Turnbull, "formerly dramatic editor of the New York 'Tribune.'"

183. G. F. W., "Seeing 'The Old Homestead' the First Time," *NYEM*, December 29, 1915, 15.

184. G. F. W., "Ridgley-Reid Team Does Well in 'Golden Chance,'" *NYEM*, January 18, 1916, 5; and "What Good Direction Can Do for a Film," *NYEM*, January 25, 1916, 9.

185. G. F. W., "Theda Bara's Carmen Is a Decided Vampire," *NYEM*, November 2, 1915, 8. Burns Mantle, by contrast, wrote an enthusiastic review of Lasky's *Carmen*, surprised by the unexpected acting ability of "Gerry" Farrar, especially in "close ups." Burns Mantle, "'Gerry' Farrar's Carmen Is Alluringly Physical," *NYEM*, November 1, 1915, 10.

186. G. F. W., "Fairbanks a Knockout in Five Fast Reels," *NYEM*, February 1, 1916, 11.

187. G. F. W., "One Reason Why Films Should Be Censored," *NYEM*, February 7, 1916, 9.

188. B. M., "'Maciste' of 'Cabiria' Returns to the Screen," *NYEM*, March 20, 1916, 4; and "'Ramona' a Master Picture of Sentiment and Atmosphere," *NYEM*, April 6, 1916, 6.

189. Richard F. Lussier, "Footlights and Screens," *BAH*, November 4, 1915, 2.

190. Richard F. Lussier, "Footlights and Screens," *BAH*, December 4, 1915, 2.

191. Ibid.

192. Richard F. Lussier, "Footlights and Screens," *BAH*, December 28, 1915, 7; and January 1, 1916, 2.

193. Richard F. Lussier, "Footlights and Screens," *BAH*, January 11, 1916, 2.

194. "Seen on the Screen by The Film Girl," *SH*, June 17, 1915, 11. The Film Girl's name—Miss Marjorie Dunmore Tooke—finally was revealed when she was appointed a YMCA secretary in overseas service and set sail for France. "Herald 'Film Girl' for Overseas Duty," *SH*, October 13, 1918, 1; and "Sails for France," *SH*, December 11, 1918, 3. *Motion Picture News* took special note of this "young lady of education and refinement who attends the showing of all pictures in the downtown section and gives her unbiased criticism of every program" and sometimes travels to New York "to attend advance showings of the bigger and better pictures." "The Press, Press Representative and the Picture—VI," *MPN*, November 20, 1915, 46.

195. "Seen on the Screen by The Film Girl," *SH*, November 20, 1915, 7.

196. "Seen on the Screen by The Film Girl" and "Daily Talks by Mary Pickford," *SH*, November 10, 1915, n.p.

197. "Seen on the Screen by The Film Girl," *SH*, June 22, 1915, 9; and October 15, 1915, n.p.

198. "Seen on the Screen by The Film Girl," *SH*, July 14, 1915, 14; September 10, 1915, 10; September 29, 1915, 9; and October 22, 1915, n.p.

199. "Seen on the Screen by The Film Girl," *SH*, July 27, 1915, 11; August 17, 1915, 5; and November 20, 1915, 7.

200. "Seen on the Screen by The Film Girl," *SH*, July 15, 1915, 11.

201. "Seen on the Screen by The Film Girl," *SH*, September 15, 1915, 4.

202. "Seen on the Screen by The Film Girl," *SH*, November 22, 1915, 9.

203. "Seen on the Screen by The Film Girl," *SH*, July 8, 1915, 11.

204. "Seen on the Screen by The Film Girl," *SH*, July 22, 1915, 19.

205. "Seen on the Screen by The Film Girl," *SH*, October 16, 1915, 7. *Tess of Storm Country* was shown during "Mary Pickford week at the Strand." "Seen on the Screen by The Film Girl," *SH*, November 15, 1915, 13; and November 16, 1915, 11.

206. "Seen on the Screen by The Film Girl," *SH*, June 29, 1915, 11.

207. "Seen on the Screen by The Film Girl," *SH*, August 20, 1915, 12; and September 25, 1915, 7.

208. "Seen on the Screen by The Film Girl," *SH*, September 21, 1915, 11.

209. "Seen on the Screen by The Film Girl," *SH*, August 17, 1915, 8; December 10, 1915, 14; and December 29, 1915, 4. In that last column, surprisingly, she even described *The Painted Lady*, despite Blanche Sweet's presence, as "a punk picture."

210. "Seen on the Screen by The Film Girl," *SH*, August 14, 1915, 7.

211. "Seen on the Screen by The Film Girl," *SH*, August 5, 1915, 11; November 13, 1915, n.p.; and November 26, 1915, 21.

212. "Seen on the Screen by The Film Girl," *SH*, August 11, 1915, 10; October 5, 1915, 11; November 27, 1915, 6; and November 29, 1915, 2.

213. "Seen on the Screen by The Film Girl," *SH*, June 28, 1915, 7; and December 28, 1915, 5.

214. "Seen on the Screen by The Film Girl," *SH*, November 29, 1915, 9.

215. "Seen on the Screen by The Film Girl," *SH*, July 17, 1915, 27; September 11, 1915, 7; and December 18, 1915, 5.

216. "Seen on the Screen by The Film Girl," *SH*, November 29, 1915, 9. Those subtitles or intertitles were written by Anita Loos.

217. "Seen on the Screen by The Film Girl," *SH*, September 28, 1915, 11; October 30, 1915, n.p.; and November 2, 1915, 11.

218. "Seen on the Screen by The Film Girl," *SH*, August 14, 1915, n.p.; October 30, 1915, n.p.; and November 5, 1915, 11.

219. "Seen on the Screen by The Film Girl," *SH*, October 6, 1915, n.p.

220. "Seen on the Screen by The Film Girl," *SH*, July 28, 1915, 11.

221. "Seen on the Screen by The Film Girl," *SH*, September 14, 1915, 9.

222. "Seen on the Screen by The Film Girl," *SH*, October 15, 1915, n.p.

223. "Seen on the Screen by The Film Girl," *SH*, November 2, 1915, 11; and November 6, 1915, 9.

224. "Seen on the Screen by The Film Girl," *SH*, October 5, 1915, 11.

225. "Seen on the Screen by The Film Girl," *SH*, December 11, 1915, 5.

226. "Seen on the Screen by The Film Girl," *SH*, July 12, 1915, 9; July 19, 1915, 11; July 26, 1915, 7; and August 9, 1915, 7.

227. "Seen on the Screen by The Film Girl," *SH*, December 15, 1915, 11.

228. "Seen on the Screen by The Film Girl," *SH*, July 2, 1915, 15. She also called attention to the *Motion Picture News*'s campaign to promote newspaper advertising. "Seen on the Screen by The Film Girl," *SH*, September 17, 1915, 11.

229. "Seen on the Screen by The Film Girl," *SH*, July 17, 1915, 27; and August 7, 1915, 6.

230. "Seen on the Screen by The Film Girl," *SH*, August 7, 1915, 6.

231. "Seen on the Screen by The Film Girl," *SH*, September 11, 1915, 7; September 13, 1915, 9; and December 1, 1915, 17.

232. "Seen on the Screen by The Film Girl," *SH*, August 13, 1915, 33.

233. "Seen on the Screen by The Film Girl," *SH*, November 30, 1915, 11.

234. "News of the Movies," *DMT*, September 22, 1915, 9.

235. Ibid.

236. "News of the Movies," *DMT*, August 24, 1915, 12; and September 24, 1915, 5.

237. "News of the Movies," *DMT*, February 14, 1916, 5.

238. "Fairbanks Rises to Film Favoritism; New Play a Scream," *DMT*, March 1, 1916, 9.

239. Dorothy Day, "News of the Movies," *DMT*, April 13, 1916, 11.

240. Dorothy Day, "Real Fire, Thrilling Escapes, Give This Film Real Thrills," *DMT*, March 21, 1916, 4.

241. Dorothy Day, "News of the Movies," *DMT*, August 26, 1916, 5.

242. Dorothy Day, "News of the Movies," *DMT*, June 2, 1916, 5.

243. Dorothy Day, "News of the Movies," *DMT*, September 26, 1916, 9.

244. Dorothy Day, "News of the Movies," *DMT*, August 26, 1916, 5.

245. Dorothy Day, "News of the Movies," *DMT*, October 30, 1916, 7.

246. Dorothy Day, "News of the Movies," *DMT*, January 28, 1916, 11.

247. Dorothy Day, "News of the Movies," *DMT*, June 2, 1916, 5.

248. Dorothy Day, "William Farnum Is Some Scrapper in 'Fighting Parson,'" *DMT*, March 2, 1916, 3.

249. Dorothy Day, "News of the Movies," *DMT*, September 13, 1916, 6; and November 4, 1916, 5.

250. Dorothy Day, "News of the Movies," *DMT*, May 1, 1916, 10.

251. Dorothy Day, "News of the Movies," *DMT*, July 10, 1916, 9; and September 18, 1916, 2.

252. Dorothy Day, "News of the Movies," *DMT*, May 1, 1916, 5.

253. Dorothy Day, "News of the Movies," *DMT*, August 3, 1916, 9.

254. Philip H. Welch, "Motion Pictures," *MST*, September 3, 1916, 8.

255. Philip H. Welch, "Motion Pictures," *MT*, September 20, 1916, 14.

256. Philip H. Welch, "Motion Pictures," *MST*, October 22, 1916, 9.

257. Philip H. Welch, "Motion Pictures," *MT*, September 9, 1916, 5; and November 11, 1916, 11.

258. Philip H. Welch, "Motion Pictures," *MT*, September 9, 1916, 11.

259. Philip H. Welch, "Motion Pictures," *MT*, September 25, 1916, 8.

260. Philip H. Welch, "Motion Pictures," *MT*, November 2, 1916, 17.

261. Philip H. Welch, "Motion Pictures," *MST*, September 24, 1916, 13.11; and *MT*, November 8, 1916, 17.

262. Philip H. Welch, "Motion Pictures," *MT*, October 4, 1916, 8.

263. Philip H. Welch, "Motion Pictures," *MT*, August 25, 1916, 7.

264. Philip H. Welch, "Motion Pictures," *MT*, September 1, 1916, 8.

265. Philip H. Welch, "Motion Pictures," *MT*, September 12, 1916, 9.

266. Philip H. Welch, "Motion Pictures," *MT*, October 21, 1916, 22.

267. Philip H. Welch, "Motion Pictures," *MT*, October 26, 1916, 9; and November 8, 1916, 17. Intriguingly, a year earlier the *Tribune*'s Sunday motion picture page had printed an unsigned article quoting from Hugo Münsterberg's *The Photoplay* and highlighting his emphasis on "the close up which focuses the attention and reveals the inner life of the mind." "Foremost Psychologist in U.S. Foresees New Art in the Movies," *MST*, November 28, 1915, 12.9–10.

268. Philip H. Welch, "Motion Pictures," *MT*, October 27, 1916, 11. A similar "sense of pictorial story telling" marked Ralph Ince's *The Sins of the Mother*. Philip H. Welch, "Motion Pictures," *MT*, November 17, 1916, 4.

269. Philip H. Welch, "Motion Pictures," *MT*, September 13, 1916, 16.

270. Philip H. Welch, "Motion Pictures," *MT*, October 23, 1916, 5.

271. Philip H. Welch, "Motion Pictures," *MST*, October 29, 1916, 13.11.

272. Philip H. Welch, "Motion Pictures," *MT*, October 25, 1916, 8.

273. Ibid.

274. "Seen on the Screen by The Film Girl," *SH*, December 11, 1915, 5.

275. "Seen on the Screen by The Film Girl," *SH*, December 4, 1915, 5.

276. "Seen on the Screen by The Film Girl," *SH*, January 7, 1916, 19.

277. "Seen on the Screen by The Film Girl," *SH*, January 21, 1916, 12.

278. "Seen on the Screen by The Film Girl," *SH*, January 15, 1916, 7.

279. "Seen on the Screen by The Film Girl," *SH*, February 3, 1916, 14; and November 10, 1916, n.p.

280. "Seen on the Screen by The Film Girl," *SH*, November 18, 1916, 7.

281. "Seen on the Screen by The Film Girl," *SH*, December 28, 1915, 5.

282. "Seen on the Screen by The Film Girl," *SH*, January 7, 1916, 19; March 2, 1916, 9; and August 12, 1916, 4.

283. "Seen on the Screen by The Film Girl," *SH*, April 3, 1916, 7.

284. "Seen on the Screen by The Film Girl," *SH*, January 22, 1916, 7.

285. "Seen on the Screen by The Film Girl," *SH*, December 27, 1915, 7.

286. "Seen on the Screen by The Film Girl," *SH*, January 13, 1916, 9.

287. "Seen on the Screen by The Film Girl," *SH*, January 15, 1916, 7.

288. "Seen on the Screen by The Film Girl," *SH*, January 4, 1916, 15; and September 22, 1916, n.p.

289. "Seen on the Screen by The Film Girl," *SH*, January 21, 1916, 12.

290. "Seen on the Screen by The Film Girl," *SH*, February 2, 1916, 9.

291. "Seen on the Screen by The Film Girl," *SH*, February 18, 1916, 10.

292. "Seen on the Screen by The Film Girl," *SH*, June 26, 1916, 9.

293. Louella O. Parsons, "Seen on the Screen," *CH*, November 30, 1915, 8; and August 2, 1916, 4.

294. Louella O. Parsons, "Seen on the Screen," *CH*, February 1, 1916, 10.

295. Louella O. Parsons, "Seen on the Screen," *CH*, December 8, 1915, 10. Thomas Ince also got the star treatment with an interview. Parsons, "Seen on the Screen," *CH*, June 24, 1916, 9.

296. Louella O. Parsons, "Seen on the Screen," *CH*, May 12, 1916, 13; and June 27, 1916, 9. See also Parsons, "Seen on the Screen," *CH*, February 10, 1916, 6.

297. Louella O. Parsons, "Seen on the Screen," *CH*, July 20, 1916, 4.

298. Louella O. Parsons, "Seen on the Screen," *CH*, February 4, 1916, 8; March 22, 1916, 8; and March 11, 1916, 4.

299. Louella O. Parsons, "Seen on the Screen," *CH*, February 18, 1916, 6; February 25, 1916, 6; and March 25, 1916, 8.

300. Louella O. Parsons, "Seen on the Screen," *CH*, July 4, 1916, 9; and July 8, 1916, 9.

301. The *Herald* printed a one- or two-page "Convention Daily," sponsored by large ads, during the week of July 12–17. Most of the articles were unsigned, but those reporting on convention news were written by Harlan. E. Babcock.

302. Louella O. Parsons, "Throng Flocks to Herald Booth to Get Alice Brady's Advice," *CH*, July 15, 1916, 9.

303. Louella O. Parsons, "Here's Good News for Herald Fans: Alice Brady on Way to Meet Them," *CH*, July 13, 1916, 8; Parsons, "Clara Kimball Young Arrives to Greet 'Fans' at Exposition," *CH*, July 13, 1916, 9; Parsons, "Edith Storey Is Outdoors 'Fan,'" *CH*, July 17, 1916, 8; and Parsons, "Stars—4 of 'Em All in Cluster," *CH*, July 18, 1916, 8.

304. Louella O. Parsons, "Seen on the Screen," *CH*, January 10, 1916, 7.

305. Louella O. Parsons, "Seen on the Screen," *CH*, June 23, 1916, 9. A little later, Vachel Lindsay shared his review of *The Wild Girl of the Sierras*, which exemplified his own concept of film as "sculpture in motion." Parsons, "Seen on the Screen," *CH*, July 29, 1916, 4.

306. Louella O. Parsons, "Seen on the Screen," *CH*, July 24, 1916, 4. A year earlier, W. Stephen Bush urged exhibitors to cast a more critical eye on what he defined as "punch": "If such be our definition of a strong climax or an highly emotional scene or a hair-raising accident [it] is all right in its place, but it is not half as important as the proper balancing of a program." Quoted in Gardner Mack, "Photoplays and Photoplayers," *WT*, May 29, 1915, 15.

307. Louella O. Parsons, "Seen on the Screen," *CH*, January 26, 1916, 14; and May 3, 1916, 8.

308. Louella O. Parsons, "Seen on the Screen," *CH*, March 7, 1916, 6; July 13, 1916, 10; August 1, 1916, 9; and November 7, 1916, 12.

309. Louella O. Parsons, "Seen on the Screen," *CH*, August 9, 1916, 7.

310. Louella O. Parsons, "Seen on the Screen," *CH*, January 31, 1916, 6.

311. Louella O. Parsons, "Seen on the Screen," *CH*, January 18, 1916, 6.

312. Louella O. Parsons, "Seen on the Screen," *CH*, February 23, 1916, 12.

313. Louella O. Parsons, "Seen on the Screen," *CH*, March 23, 1916, 8.

314. Louella O. Parsons, "Seen on the Screen," *CH*, June 12, 1916, 7.

315. Louella O. Parsons, "Seen on the Screen," *CH*, August 8, 1916, 4.

316. Louella O. Parsons, "Seen on the Screen," *CH*, March 10, 1916, 8; March 22, 1916, 8; and August 15, 1916, 4. She reprinted a Buffalo professional musician's letter, which listed blatant continuity mistakes in half a dozen films, including Chaplin's *The Fireman*. Parsons, "Seen on the Screen," *CH*, July 26, 1916, 7.

317. Louella O. Parsons, "Seen on the Screen," *CH*, June 25, 1916, n.p.; June 28, 1916, 9; and July 28, 1916, 4.

318. Louella O. Parsons, "Seen on the Screen," *CH*, August 8, 1916, 4.

319. Louella O. Parsons, "Seen on the Screen," *CH*, July 5, 1916, 49.

320. Louella O. Parsons, "Seen on the Screen," *CH*, May 8, 1916, 8.

321. Louella O. Parsons, "Seen on the Screen," *CH*, December 21, 1915, 8.

322. Louella O. Parsons, "Seen on the Screen," *CH*, April 19, 1916, 4.

323. Louella O. Parsons, "Seen on the Screen," *CH*, July 7, 1916, 4.

324. Louella O. Parsons, "Seen on the Screen," *CH*, July 11, 1916, 6.

325. Louella O. Parsons, "Seen on the Screen," *CH*, July 29, 1916, 4.

326. Louella O. Parsons, "Seen on the Screen," *CH*, July 31, 1916, 7. Although Parsons expected the film to be unprofitable, *Where Are My Children?* ran for twelve straight weeks at the nine-hundred-seat LaSalle theater in the Loop. In Boston, the Majestic Theatre manager distanced himself from the Allison Birth Control League that leased his theater one night to use the film to defend a doctor accused of "disseminating obscene literature—i.e., pamphlets concerning birth control." Boston Photoplay ad, *Boston Globe*, July 28, 1916, 4.

327. Louella O. Parsons, "Seen on the Screen," *CH*, February 26, 1916, 6; and June 25, 1916, 9.

328. Louella O. Parsons, "Seen on the Screen," *CH*, August 10, 1915, 8. See also Moya Luckett, *Cinema and Community*, 141–42.

329. Louella O. Parsons, "Seen on the Screen," *CH*, February 12, 1916, 8. The Castle had only three hundred seats. Moya Luckett, *Cinema and Community*, 165.

330. Louella O. Parsons, "Seen on the Screen," *CH*, January 10, 1916, 7; and March 1, 1916, 8.

331. Louella O. Parsons, "Seen on the Screen," *CH*, March 6, 1916, 6. She had praised the Strand earlier for its "bits of the tuneful opera" that accompanied the screening of *Carmen*. Parsons, "Seen on the Screen," *CH*, January 22, 1916, 6.

332. Louella O. Parsons, "Seen on the Screen," *CH*, December 12, 1915, 10.

333. Louella O. Parsons, "Seen on the Screen," *CH*, July 17, 1916, 9.

334. Louella O. Parsons, "Seen on the Screen," *CH*, March 13, 1916, 6.

335. Louella O. Parsons, "Seen on the Screen," *CH*, January 28, 1916, 6; June 30, 1916, 9; July 21, 1916, 4; and November 8, 1916, 4.

336. Louella O. Parsons, "Seen on the Screen," *CH*, June 16, 1916, 9.

337. Kitty Kelly, "Flickerings from Film Land" and "Motion Picture Directory," *CT*, July 7, 1916, 11.

338. Kitty Kelly, "Flickerings from Film Land,"*CT*, October 23, 1915, 10.

339. Kitty Kelly, "Flickerings from Film Land," *CT*, March 2, 1916, 10; and March 11, 1916, 14.

340. Kitty Kelly, "Flickerings from Film Land," *CT*, October 19, 1916, 19. A week later she interviewed "Fatty" Arbuckle, who was leaving Keystone to form his own company, Comique Film. Kelly, "Flickerings from Film Land," *CT*, September 27, 1916, 17.

341. Kitty Kelly, "Flickerings from Film Land," *CT*, July 19, 1916, 11.

342. Kitty Kelly, "Flickerings from Film Land," *CT*, October 18, 1915, 12.

343. Kitty Kelly reported early on how small the audiences were at the Studebaker. Kelly, "Flickerings from Film Land," *CT*, October 20, 1915, 14. For an analysis of Triangle's expensive, exclusive exhibition strategy, see Rob King, "'Made for the Masses with an Appeal to the Classes': The Triangle Film Corporation and the Failure of Highbrow Film Culture," *Cinema Journal* 44, no. 2 (2005): 3–33.

344. Kitty Kelly, "Flickerings from Film Land," *CT*, March 6, 1916, 16.

345. Kitty Kelly, "Flickerings from Film Land," *CT*, February 28, 1916, 14.

346. Kitty Kelly, "Flickerings from Film Land," *CT*, April 20, 1916, 18.

347. Kitty Kelly, "Flickerings from Film Land," *CT*, February 15, 1916, 14; February 23, 1916, 14; March 16, 1916, 14; and March 23, 1916, 14.

348. Kitty Kelly, "Flickerings from Film Land," *CT*, March 20, 1916, 16.

349. Kitty Kelly, "Flickerings from Film Land," *CT*, October 23, 1915, 10; and February 29, 1916, 14.

350. Kitty Kelly, "Flickerings from Film Land," *CT*, February 16, 1916, 16. That summer the Orchestra Hall became a "summer resort" with its new "air washing, cooling, and ventilating plant." Kelly, "Flickerings from Film Land," *CT*, July 13, 1916, 15.

351. Kitty Kelly, "Flickerings from Film Land," *CT*, March 4, 1916, 14; and August 7, 1916, 15.

352. The Cosmopolitan (an Ascher Brothers house) was at 7938 South Halsted; the Boulevard was at Ashland and Garfield. Kitty Kelly, "Flickerings from Film Land," *CT*, March 25, 1916, 14.

353. Kitty Kelly, "Flickerings from Film Land," *CT*, November 6, 1915, 14.

354. Kitty Kelly, "Flickerings from Film Land," *CT*, July 1, 1916, 14; August 10, 1916, 15; and September 6, 1916, 13.

355. Kitty Kelly, "Flickerings from Film Land," *CT*, July 20, 1916, 15. She reproduced a letter from a man who, taking her advice, found *Hypocrites* "a corking good picture" and in no way "improper." Kelly, "Flickerings from Film Land," *CT*, July 22, 1916, 11.

356. Kitty Kelly, "Flickerings from Film Land," *CT*, July 31, 1916, 11. Earlier she had worried that Chicagoans would not see *Where Are My Children?* because the National Board of Review had "turn[ed] up its toes in aesthetic

hesitation and disapprove[d] of it." Kelly, "Flickerings from Film Land," *CT*, April 8, 1916, 18. Kelly's review was reprinted in full in *FWJG*, November 20, 1916, 15.

357. Kitty Kelly, "Flickerings from Film Land," *CT*, July 14, 1916, 19.

358. Kitty Kelly, "Flickerings from Film Land," *CT*, May 22, 1916, 16.

359. Kitty Kelly, "Flickerings from Film Land," *CT*, June 21, 1916, 18.

360. Kitty Kelly, "Flickerings from Film Land," *CT*, September 20, 1916, 13.

361. Kitty Kelly, "Flickerings from Film Land," *CT*, January 22, 1916, 14.

362. Kitty Kelly, "Flickerings from Film Land," *CT*, January 25, 1916, 22.

363. Kitty Kelly, "Flickerings from Film Land," *CT*, March 8, 1916, 16; September 6, 1916, 13; and September 13, 1916, 15.

364. Kitty Kelly, "Flickerings from Film Land," *CT*, January 4, 1916, 14; February 1, 1916, 20; February 18, 1916, 14; June 8, 1916, 21; July 21, 1916, 11; and September 20, 1916, 13.

365. Kitty Kelly, "Flickerings from Film Land," *CT*, June 7, 1916, 20; June 8, 1916, 21; and August 3, 1916, 11.

366. Kitty Kelly, "Flickerings from Film Land," *CT*, October 16, 1915, 14.

367. Kitty Kelly, "Flickerings from Film Land," *CT*, December 15, 1915, 19.

368. Kitty Kelly, "Flickerings from Film Land," *CT*, January 31, 1916, 8.

369. Kitty Kelly, "Flickerings from Film Land," *CT*, February 15, 1916, 14.

370. Kitty Kelly, "Flickerings from Film Land," *CT*, March 8, 1916, 16.

371. Kitty Kelly, "Flickerings from Film Land," *CT*, January 15, 1916, 14.

372. Kitty Kelly, "Flickerings from Film Land," *CT*, June 6, 1916, 20; and October 9, 1916, 21.

373. Kitty Kelly, "Flickerings from Film Land," *CT*, April 20, 1916, 18. For a revealing study of American film intertitles, especially in translation, see Laura Isabel Serna, "Translations and Transportation: Toward a Transnational History of the Intertitle," in Jennifer M. Bean, Anupama Kapse, and Laura Horak, eds., *Silent Cinema and the Politics of Space* (Bloomington: Indiana University Press, 2014), 121–45.

374. Kitty Kelly, "Flickerings from Film Land," *CT*, April 28, 1916, 18.

375. Kitty Kelly, "Flickerings from Film Land," *CT*, July 29, 1916, 11.

376. Kitty Kelly, "Flickerings from Film Land," *CT*, February 18, 1916, 14.

377. Kitty Kelly, "Flickerings from Film Land," *CT*, April 6, 1916, 12.

378. Kitty Kelly, "Flickerings from Film Land," *CT*, May 22, 1916, 16.

379. Kitty Kelly, "Flickerings from Film Land," *CT*, June 9, 1916, 23.

380. Kitty Kelly, "Flickerings from Film Land," *CT*, September 22, 1916, 15.

381. Kitty Kelly, "Flickerings from Film Land," *CT*, June 26, 1916, 14.

382. Kitty Kelly, "Flickerings from Film Land," *CT*, February 7, 1916, 14. Later she described *Diana's Inspiration* as so "soporific narratively" as to "baffle analysis." Kelly, "Flickerings from Film Land," *CT*, August 1, 1916, 19.

383. Kitty Kelly, "Flickerings from Film Land," *CT*, March 13, 1916, 14.

384. Kitty Kelly, "Flickerings from Film Land," *CT*, April 24, 1916, 20. She frequently faulted films such as *The Conqueror* for being too slow and prolonged. Kelly, "Flickerings from Film Land," *CT*, January 5, 1916, 14.

385. Kitty Kelly, "Flickerings from Film Land," *CT*, June 13, 1916, 18.

386. Kitty Kelly, "Flickerings from Film Land," *CT*, July 20, 1916, 15. Weeks earlier, incensed by Thomas Dixon's jingoistic *Fall of a Nation,* she summed up its tempestuous action in a similar phrase—"So things go"—and felt relief at "not being a New York millionaire . . . obliged to live in their Dixonized dwellings." Kelly, "Flickerings from Film Land," *CT*, July 4, 1916, 16.

387. Kitty Kelly, "Flickerings from Film Land," *CT*, September 7, 1916, 11. Similarly, she described *The Dark Silence,* in which Clara Kimball Young "sobs and sighs, but doesn't die," as "a picture of the old school of heart-wringing sentimentalism." Kelly, "Flickerings from Film Land," *CT*, September 18, 1916, 13.

388. Kitty Kelly, "Flickerings from Film Land," *CT*, August 8, 1916, 15; and October 9, 1916, 21.

389. Kitty Kelly, "Flickerings from Film Land," *CT*, February 14, 1916, 14; and March 7, 1916, 12.

390. Kitty Kelly, "Flickerings from Film Land," *CT*, April 5, 1916, 18.

391. Kitty Kelly, "Flickerings from Film Land," *CT*, April 22, 1916, 16. Downtown Chicago theaters, Kelly reported, mainly used "photographs and stills" to draw audiences.

392. Kitty Kelly, "Flickerings from Film Land," *CT*, October 14, 1916, 17.

393. Kitty Kelly, "Flickerings from Film Land," *CT*, April 29, 1916, 16.

394. Jas. S. McQuade, "Chicago News Letter," *MPW*, December 2, 1916, 1310. Whether any conflict between Kelly and Mae Tinee factored into this reassignment is unclear.

395. Kitty Kelly, "Flickerings from Filmland," *CE*, April 10, 1917, 9. The announcement circulated widely in the trade press: "Kitty Kelly with Chicago Examiner," *M*, March 24, 1917, 649; "Chicago Examiner Gets Kitty Kelly as M.P. Critic," *MPN*, March 31, 1917, 1988; and Jas. J. McQuade, "Chicago News Letter," *MPW*, March 31, 1917, 2085. Soon she joined Mae Tinee and Parsons as both a writer and editor with a page titled "The Screen." The *Examiner* merged with the *Herald,* which was bought by Hearst in 1918, and Kelly, rather than Parsons, continued writing about the movies there into the early 1920s. For a few months, Kelly also contributed film reviews to *Photoplay*. See Randolph Bartlett and Kitty Kelly, "The Shadow Stage," *Photoplay* (December 1917): 67, 120, 122–23.

396. Mae Tinee, "Flickerings from Film Land," *CT*, October 16, 1916, 21; and "Right Off the Reel by Mae Tinee," *CT*, October 19, 1916, 13. Her column accompanied the *Tribune*'s "Motion Picture Directory" on Sundays.

397. "Right Off the Reel by Mae Tinee," *CT*, November 18, 1916, 10; and Mae Tinee, "Nazimova Makes Her Screen Debut," *CT*, December 6, 1916, 10.

398. Mae Tinee, "Flickerings from Film Land," *CT*, October 17, 1916, 15; October 23, 1916, 19; and October 24, 1916, 15.

399. "Right Off the Reel by Mae Tinee," *CT*, October 20, 1916, 19.

400. "Right Off the Reel by Mae Tinee," *CT*, October 28, 1916, 15.

401. "Right Off the Reel by Mae Tinee," *CT*, November 14, 1916, 19.

402. "Right Off the Reel by Mae Tinee," *CT*, October 24, 1916, 15; and November 21, 1916, 12.

403. "Right Off the Reel by Mae Tinee," *CT*, November 13, 1916, 17.

404. "Right Off the Reel by Mae Tinee," *CT*, October 20, 1916, 19.

405. "Right Off the Reel by Mae Tinee," *CT*, November 1, 1916, 21. Bessie Barricale "impersonate[s] a man" in this Irish comedy.

406. "Right Off the Reel by Mae Tinee," *CT*, December 5, 1916, 20; and December 14, 1916, 16.

407. "Right Off the Reel by Mae Tinee," *CT*, November 10, 1916, 19.

408. "Right Off the Reel by Mae Tinee," *CT*, November 6, 1916, 23.

409. "Right Off the Reel by Mae Tinee," *CT*, November 8, 1916, 15.

410. Mae Tinee, "Flickerings from Filmland," *CT*, October 16, 1916, 21.

411. "Right Off the Reel by Mae Tinee," *CT*, October 19, 1916, 13.

412. "Right Off the Reel by Mae Tinee," *CT*, November 20, 1916, 14.

413. "Right Off the Reel by Mae Tinee," *CT*, November 4, 1916, 17.

414. "Right Off the Reel by Mae Tinee," *CT*, November 25, 1916, 14.

415. "Right Off the Reel by Mae Tinee," *CT*, December 7, 1916, 14.

416. "Right Off the Reel by Mae Tinee," *CT*, October 22, 1916, 19.

417. Mae Tinee, "Flickerings from Film Land," *CT*, October 17, 1916, 15.

418. "Right Off the Reel by Mae Tinee," *CT*, November 29, 1916, 14. Intriguingly, the Chicago Motion Picture Owners' Association later would protest her "frivolous treatment" of motion pictures. "Latest News of Chicago," *M*, February 16, 1918, 328.

419. Santiago Hidalgo defines the "interpretive framework" created by trade press journalists as follows: "a *collectivity* of individuals, who produce *regular* comments, *extending* over a period of many years, and which display a diverse *use* of language." Hidalgo, "Early American Film Publications: Film Consciousness, Self Consciousness," in André Gaudreault et al., eds., *A Companion to Early Cinema* (Chichester, England: Wiley-Blackwell, 2012), 217.

420. Four years earlier, Louis Reeves Harrison and Epes Winthrop Sargent had noted the usefulness of relatively close shots, but in technical advice for screen actors and scenario writers. Harrison, "Eyes and Lips," *MPW*, February 18, 1911, 348–49; and Sargent, "Technique of the Photoplay," *MPW*, August 5, 1911, 282. Janet Staiger has argued that such close shots likely had an effect on acting style and editing practices, particularly eye-line matches and shot/reverse shots. "The Eyes Are Really the Focus: Photoplay Acting and Film Form and Style," *Wide Angle* 6, no. 2 (1985): 21–22.

421. Vachel Lindsay, *The Art of the Moving Picture*, 178–79.

422. Hugo Münsterberg, *The Photoplay: A Psychological Study* (New York: Appleton, 1916), reprinted as *The Film: A Psychological Study* (New York: Dover, 1970), 38–39. See also "Movies the Great Art of America, Says Dr. Munsterberg," *CSH*, April 30, 1916, 7.1. Yet his attitude toward women may have kept him from saying anything specific about close-ups, especially of women's faces. See Hilary Hallett, *Go West, Young Women!: The Rise of Early Hollywood* (Berkeley: University of California Press, 2013), 42.

423. Louis Delluc, "La beauté au cinema," *Le Film* 73 (August 6, 1917): 5, translated as "Beauty in the Cinema" in Richard Abel, *French Film Theory and Criticism I, 1907–1929* (Princeton, NJ: Princeton University Press, 1987), 139.

424. Jean Epstein, "Grossissement," in *Bonjour Cinéma* (Paris: Editions de la sirene, 1921), 93–94, translated by Stuart Liebman as "Magnification" in Richard Abel, *French Film Theory and Criticism I*, 235–36.

425. One of the first novels about making movies in Los Angeles was Margaret Turnbull's *The Close Up* (1918), which told the story of a working girl from New York who succeeds in becoming a studio office manager and eventually a movie star.

426. See the ten intense examples from cinema history, beginning with Gina Manès in Epstein's *Coeur fidèle* and Renée Falconetti in Carl Dreyer's *Passion de Jeanne d'Arc*. Mark Cousins, "The Face of Another," *Sight & Sound* (December 2012): 47–50.

427. Orpheum ad, *RR*, August 25, 1915, 4.

428. "Things Theatrical Here at Home," *Waterloo Courier and Reporter*, October 11, 1915, 8.

429. "Triangle Pictures to be Shown at Queen," *Galveston News Magazine Supplement*, October 17, 1915, 32.

430. Magnet ad, *Lincoln Sunday Star*, February 24, 1916, 7.

431. Majestic Theater ad, *Fort Wayne News*, June 24, 1916, 4.

432. Kitty Kelly, "Flickerings from Film Land," *CT*, August 30, 1916, 11.

433. "Right Off the Reel," *OT*, June 12, 1914, 12; and "Theatrical," *Trenton Times*, August 5, 1915, 12.

434. Bijou ad, *Racine Journal News*, September 26, 1916, 6.

435. Happy Hour ad, *SH*, January 28, 1917, 9.

436. Pastime Theatre ad, *Sheboygan Press*, April 29, 1915, 2; and Garden Theater ad, *Muskegon Chronicle*, May 22, 1915, 6. For an earlier example in the trade press, see the Photo Play Productions ad, *MPN*, August 15, 1914, 8; and *M*, August 22, 1914, 3.

437. Orpheum ad, *RR*, August 26, 1915, 4.

438. Bijou ad, *Racine Journal News*, October 29, 1915, n.p.

439. "At the Jefferson," *Fort Wayne Sentinel*, October 30, 1915, 15; and Palm ad, *RR*, November 10, 1915, 9.

440. "City in Brief," *Waterloo Courier and Reporter*, November 22, 1915, 9.

441. "Kitty Kelly Boosts 'Grex of Monte Carlo,'" *Rockford Register-Gazette*, December 23, 1915, 5; and "With the Film Stars," *RR*, January 24, 1916, 5. The latter reprinted her praise of Pickford in *The Foundling*.

442. Whatever internal disputes provoked this unusually public upbraiding remain to be uncovered, but it certainly was framed as a gendered matter of taste, registering pleasure or displeasure at the transformation in Keystone's comedies in late 1915, as the company became an important component of Triangle programs. For an astute, persuasive analysis of this change, see Rob King, *The Fun Factory: The Keystone Film Company and the Emergence of Mass Culture* (Berkeley: University of California Press, 2009), 143–209.

443. Rex ad, *DNT*, November 28, 1915, 15; and "Great Newspaper Is Opposed to Its Critic," *Iowa City Citizen*, January 24, 1916, 7. In its early November bulletin, Triangle quoted the *Tribune* editorial to boost its programs. Rob King, "'Made for the Masses with an Appeal to the Classes,'" 24. Arguably what irked Kelly most was the unfulfilled promise of Triangle's expensive programs, with only a few fine features and good Keystones.

444. Kitty Kelly, "Flickerings from Film Land," *CT*, October 20, 1915, 14; and October 27, 1915, 10.

445. Kitty Kelly, "Flickerings from Film Land," *CT*, October 20, 1915, 14; January 5, 1916, 14; January 25, 1916, 22; and February 11, 1916, 14.

446. Magnet ad, *Lincoln Sunday News*, February 24, 1916, 7.

447. "All-Feature Day at the Victoria," *The Patriot* (Harrisburg, Pennsylvania), March 25, 1916, 8; "*Police* at the Colonial," *RR*, May 29, 1916, 4; and "As to *The Count*," *RR*, September 9, 1916, 12.

448. Kitty Kelly, "Moving Picture Combine to Rule Main Producers," *Ludington News* (Michigan), March 28, 1916, 1; "Misleading Lady Called Artistic by Kitty Kelly," *Jonesboro Tribune* (Arkansas), April 25, 1916, 4; and Broadway ad, *ALT*, August 2, 1916, 4.

449. "What Whack for Brady," *Idaho Statesman*, June 4, 1916, 6.

450. Strand ad, *CRR*, May 15, 1916, 18; Bijou ad, *Aberdeen Sunday American*, June 25, 1916, 7; "Excellent Program at the Jefferson," *FWJG*, June 16, 1916, 17; and "Garden," *Muskegon Chronicle*, July 15, 1916, 5.

451. "Amusements," *Fort Wayne News*, June 20, 1916, 4; *Ann Arbor Times*, June 24, 1916, 2; Majestic Theatre ad, *FWJG*, June 25, 1916, 36; Columbia ad, *KCS*, August 4, 1916, 17; Family Theatre ad, *Elkhart Review* (Indiana), August 11, 1916, 2; and Columbia ad, *Portsmouth Times* (Ohio), October 31, 1916, 3.

452. "Flickerings from Filmland," *Marble Rock Journal*, December 1, 1915, 2; and June 15, 1916, 6. A rare half-page ad soliciting investors for a new production company reproduced Kelly's full column on a proposed feature, *Mama's Angel Child*. American Standard Motion Picture Corporation ad, *Rockford Register-Gazette*, March 24, 1916, 8.

453. Kitty Kelly ad, *CST*, April 30, 1916, 7.4. One year later, trade press accolades accompanied her return, as "one of the foremost motion picture critics," to film reviewing in the *Chicago Examiner*, with testimonials from such luminaries as Chicago exhibitor Aaron J. Jones, D.W. Griffith, William S. Hart, Charles Ray, and Norma Talmadge. Jas. J. McQuade, "Chicago News Letter," *MPW*, March 31, 1917, 2085; and "Chicago Examiner Gets Kitty Kelly as M.P. Critic," *MPN*, March 31, 1917, 1988.

ENTR'ACTE: MOTION PICTURE WEEKLIES

1. "The Motion Picture Mail" ad, *NYEM*, September 7, 1915, 4.

2. The only existing copies of "Motion Picture Mail" are on microfilm at the New York Public Library.

3. Facial expression images had been a staple of theatrical acting guides and manuals at least since the eighteenth century.

4. H.H. Van Loan, "Are the Movies Safe for Respectable Girls?," "Motion Picture Mail," January 29, 1916, 3, 15.

5. "Candid Reviews of Current Features," "Motion Picture Mail," June 17, 1916, 22.

6. In July 1916, the *Ledger* reduced its coverage of motion pictures in the Amusement section to little more than one page, with much smaller ads from the Stanley Booking Company. This reduction carried through the rest of the year, with the exception of large ads for Pathé's serials *The Shielding Shadow* and *Pearl of the Army*, Metro's *Romeo and Juliet* and *The Great Secret* (with Francis X. Bushman and Beverly Bayne), Fox's *A Daughter of the Gods* (with Annette Kellermann), and Ince's *Civilization*.

7. "Editorial," *PEL*, January 1, 1916, Amusement section, 2; Edwin Arden, "Photoplay the Greatest Critic," *PEL*, January 22, 1916, 1; "Do Stage or Films Inspire Actor Most?" *PEL*, January 29, 1916, 4; Mme Bertha Kalich, "The Art of the Photoplay," *PEL*, March 4, 1916, 1; Robert Warwick, "Movies as a Help to the Stage Actor," *PEL*, April 15, 1916, 3; and "If William Shakespeare Had Known the Photoplay," *PEL*, April 22, 1916, 1.

8. "Muensterberg in the Movies," *PEL*, February 26, 1916, 1, 4.

9. Hugh Ford, "Life Is a Stage and the World Its Setting," *PEL*, February 4, 1916, 1; "How Griffith, the Wizard, of the Photoplay Works," *PEL*, April 8, 1916, 1; "Police Whistle Directs Work of New Pictures [Herbert Brenon]," *PEL*, April 22, 1916, 4; Jesse L. Lasky, "Why the Movies Are No Longer Making Progress," *PEL*, May 27, 1916, 4; John R. Freuler, "What Happens from Scenario to Screen," *PEL*, June 17, 1916, 1; and William A. Brady, "The Future Now Secure for Play and Photoplay," *PEL*, June 24, 1916, 1.

10. Cecil B. DeMille, "The Lighting of the Photoplay," *PEL*, January 29, 1916, 1, 2; DeMille, "What Makes a Real Success in Photoplaydom?" *PEL*, March 4, 1916, 1; and "Lighting Is to the Movie What Music Is to the Drama," *PEL*, March 18, 1916, 4.

11. Edward Bok, "Merion's Model School Takes Up the Movies," *PEL*, January 8, 1916, 1; "The Child and the Movie; A Problem in Sociology," *PEL*, March 11, 1916, 1, 4; and "A Vaudeville of the Movies," *PEL*, March 25, 1916, 4. See also Dr. Francis Trevelyan Miller, "Photoplays the Educational Force of the Future," *PEL*, May 6, 1916, 1.

12. "Which Are the Six Greatest Photoplays?" and "Your Favorite Movies" ads, *PEL*, April 1, 1916, 1, 3; and "The Six Greatest Photoplays," *PEL*, April 8, 1916, 2. This contest apparently was prompted by Arthur Brisbane's challenge to members at a Motion Picture Board of Trade dinner.

13. For just two months, from late November 1915 to late January 1916, the *Dayton News* also inserted an eight-page supplement bannered "Motion Picture News" in its Sunday edition. Sponsored by ads from nearly a dozen local picture theaters, this supplement included a balance of industry stories and news of local interest, along with a regular "Motion Picture Directory"

listing the city's forty picture theaters and ten others in surrounding towns and a "Questions and Answers" column. One story acknowledged how important suburban picture theaters were for families in residential areas. "Dayton Suburban Theaters Occupy Important Field," *Dayton Sunday News* "Motion Picture News" supplement, December 12, 1915, 2. Another on local church screenings implied that the unnamed editor was a woman. "Used Movies in Church for Quite a Season," *Dayton Sunday News* "Motion Picture News" supplement, January 2, 1916, 6.

14. "Society by Mary B. Miller / Photoplay by Archie Bell / Clubs by Louise Graham," *CL*, February 6, 1916, 7. Bell also edited the columns on theater and music. "The Motion Picture Leader" ad, *CL*, February 5, 1916, 12. In the bottom-right corner of several later weekday issues reminding readers of the Sunday supplement was a small ad of a society woman holding a wide parasol in a boldly stylized "modernist" design.

15. "Motion Picture Leader's Gallery of Stars—Vivian Martin," *CLS* "Motion Picture Leader," February 6, 1916, 1; Archie Bell, "Mary Pickford Is Most Charming 'Peppina,'" *CSL* "Motion Picture Leader," February 27, 1916, 1–2; "The Movie Fan," *CSL* "Motion Picture Leader," March 19, 1916, 1.

16. Advertisers other than local theaters included William Fox, Bluebird Photo Plays, Red Feather Photo Plays, Pathé Exchange, Powers Cameragraph, and Jontzen Printing.

17. "Mary Pickford's Daily Talks" ad, *CSL* "Motion Picture Leader," February 6, 1916, 10. The *Leader* was quite late in contracting with McClure for these columns; other newspapers had been printing the column since November.

18. Although the banner for these pages sometimes read "Reviews of Feature Photo-Plays," the texts always were plot synopses.

19. Archie Bell, "Moving Pictures Real Reformer of the Stage," *CSL* "Motion Picture Leader," February 6, 1916, 2; Louise Graham, "Olga Petrova Rises at 3 to Meet Sol, Who's Fickle," *CSL* "Motion Picture Leader," February 20, 1916, 2; Graham, "Men Folks Just Cannot Help Humming of Kisses," *CSL* "Motion Picture Leader," February 27, 1916, 5; Bell, "'Bondman,' A Drama of Love and Hate," *CSL* "Motion Picture Leader," March 19, 1916, 1–2; and Bell, "'Ne'er-Do-Well,' Film of the Hour," *CSL* "Motion Picture Leader," March 26, 1916, 1–2.

20. Anita Stewart, "Anita Stewart Talks to Girls," *CSL* "Motion Picture Leader," February 20, 1916, 6; Pearl White, "Daring Girl Tells Life Story," *CSL* "Motion Picture Leader," March 19, 1916, 4; Bertha Kalich, "Movies Will Create Great Literature," *CSL* "Motion Picture Leader," March 26, 1916, 7; and Pearl White, "Gosh! Pearl White Wants to Eat 'Em Alive," *CSL* "Motion Picture Leader," April 16, 1916, 12.

21. Winifred Van Duser, "Making a Comedy Film Is No Laughing Matter," *CSL* "Motion Picture Leader," February 6, 1916, 3; "Scene in Movie Studio as Photoplay Is Being Made," *CSL* "Motion Picture Leader," February 20, 1916, 3; "Club Women Enthuse Over Better Film Move," *CSL* "Motion Picture Leader,"

February 20, 1916, 6; "Akron Girl Stars in Film Play, One Day," *CSL* "Motion Picture Leader," March 5, 1916, 6; "Cleveland Girl Is Authoring Star and Producer," *CSL* "Motion Picture Leader," March 5, 1916, 12; "Women to Pick Films Today," *CL*, March 31, 1916, 7.

22. John DeKoven, "Greenroom Gleanings," *CSL* "Motion Picture Leader," March 19, 1916, 5; and March 26, 1916, 5; and DeKoven, "Keenan Slyly Sheds Two-Reel Tears," *CSL* "Motion Picture Leader," April 16, 1916, 1–2.

23. "First President of Screen Club," *CSL* "Motion Picture Leader," July 2, 1916, 5; and "The Kwery Column," *CSL* "Motion Picture Leader," November 19, 1916, 4.

24. "The Iron Claw, 13th Episode," *CSL* "Motion Picture Leader," May 21, 1916, 10–11; "The Secret of the Submarine, 7th Installment," *CSL* "Motion Picture Leader," July 2, 1916, 8–9.

25. "Movies to Be Made Without Scenery Now," *CSL* "Motion Picture Leader," May 21, 1916, 2; "Munsterberg Tells Film Power," *CSL* "Motion Picture Leader," May 21, 1916, 6; H.A. Aitken, "Screen Morals in Hands of Women," *CSL* "Motion Picture Leader," August 20, 1916, 5; James Kirkwood, "What Material to Put in a Photoplay," *CSL* "Motion Picture Leader," November 19, 1916, 6; and V.D. Horkheimer, "Ouch! Who Is He Hitting?" *CSL* "Motion Picture Leader," November 19, 1916, 7.

26. Alma Woodward, "Mollie of the Movies," *CSL* "Motion Picture Leader," March 26, 1916, 3; April 16, 1916, 3; and November 19, 1916, 7; "Mary Urges College Girls to Write Plots," *CSL* "Motion Picture Leader, July 2, 1916, 11; and Will M. Richey, "Here's the Right Way to Start a Story for a Movie Play," *CSL* "Motion Picture Leader," August 20, 1916, 4.

27. "Gallery of the Gods #6: Hobart Bosworth," *CSL* "Motion Picture Leader," March 19, 1916, 6; "Gallery of the Gods #7: Harold Lockwood," *CSL* "Motion Picture Leader," March 26, 1916, 5; "Gallery of the Gods #10: Maurice Costello," *CSL* "Motion Picture Leader," April 16, 1916, 7; John DeKoven, "New Film Star Can Cry Over Chops," *CSL* "Motion Picture Leader," July 2, 1916, 1–2; and DeKoven, "When Mollie King Registers a Kiss," *CSL* "Motion Picture Leader," August 20, 1916, 1–2.

28. Sis Hopkins, "Sum Advice on Etikket, Makes Easy Things Hard," *CSL* "Motion Picture Leader," May 21, 1916, 6; and Grace Darling, "Grace Darling's Dream Comes True—in Movies," *CSL* "Motion Picture Leader," August 20, 1916, 8.

29. "Beatriz Michelena to Talk to Screen Struck Girls Here," *CSL* "Motion Picture Leader," March 26, 1916, 10; Beatriz Michelena, "Talks with Screen-Struck Girls," *CSL* "Motion Picture Leader," April 16, 1916, 4; Michelena, "Film Actress Must 'Feel' the Passion," *CSL* "Motion Picture Leader," July 2, 1916, 3; and Michelena, "This Is the Price Girls Pay to Land Places in Movies," *CSL* "Motion Picture Leader," August 20, 1916, 4.

30. "At the Film Theaters," *CSL* "Motion Picture Leader," November 19, 1916, 3. Feature film plot synopses now were reduced to just six, over two pages.

31. "Photoplay Forum / Motion Picture Stories / Answers to Fans," *SLSGD*, April 16, 1916, 1, 4; "Motion Picture News / Fiction / Answers to Fans," *SLSGD*, April 23, 1916, 1, 4.

32. "Motion Picture Section," *SLSGD*, June 4, 1916, 1, 4.

33. "Real Dainties in the Movies," *SLSGD* "Motion Picture Section," July 2, 1916, 4; "Handicapped by Their Famous Names," *SLSGD* "Motion Picture Section," July 9, 1916, 4; "A Beautiful Girl of Motion Pictures," *SLSGD* "Motion Picture Section," July 16, 1916, 4; and "Japanese in Motion Pictures," *SLSGD* "Motion Picture Section," July 23, 1916, 4.

34. "A Moving Picture Editorial by Edward Lyell Fox," *SLSGD* "Motion Picture Section," June 11, 1916, 4; and "The Cameraman in Motion Pictures," *SLSGD* "Motion Picture Section," July 30, 1916, 4.

35. "Motion Picture Forum," *SLSGD* "Magazine Section," November 12, 1916, 6.

36. A.H. Giebler, "Adventures in Movieland," *SLSGD* "Motion Picture Section," July 23, 1916, 4; and Giebler, "Breaking into Motion Pictures," *SLSGD* "Motion Picture Section," October 8, 1916, 1.

37. "Motion Picture Stars to Be Photographed in St. Louis for 'The Crisis Film,'" *SLSGD*, April 9, 1916, 1. Because my research was limited, it's possible that some material on motion pictures could be found elsewhere in either the Sunday edition or one or more daily editions each week.

38. "Times Man Will Be Studio Guest," *SST* "Amusement" section, June 25, 1916, 1.

39. See the block statement, *SST* "Amusement" section, June 4, 1916, 6. The principal advertisers were the Coliseum, Liberty, Alhambra, Rex, Strand, Clemmer, Colonial, and Mission.

40. "About C. Gardner Sullivan," *SST* "Amusement" section, June 18, 1916, 2; "Photoplay Writing Method Employs Chance," *SST* "Amusements" section, August 6, 1916, 1; "Film Editor Gives Some Advice to Writers," *SST* "Amusement" section, August 13, 1916, 1; and "Writing Scenario Is Artist's Work," *SST* "Amusement" section, August 27, 1916, 3.

41. "Seattle Girl Is Winner of Prize," *SST* "Amusement" section, June 4, 1916, 2; "Film Exchange Is Formed Here," *SST* "Amusement" section, June 11, 1916, 1; and "Washington Girl Tells Why She Is Actress," *SST* "Amusement" section, July 9, 1916, 1.

42. Louella O. Parsons, "Bond of Sisterhood Unbroken by Stage Triumphs," *SST*, August 6, 1916, 6; and Parsons, "The Real Romance of the Movies," *SST* "Amusement" section, August 27, 1916, 6; and December 10, 1916, 6.

43. Louella O. Parsons, "The Real Romance of the Movies," *SST* "Amusement" section, August 13, 1916, 6; August 20, 1916, 6; August 27, 1916, 6; September 3, 1916, 6; October 1, 1916, 6; October 8, 1916, 6; October 29, 1916, 6; and December 10, 1916, 6.

44. "Confessions of a Movie Actress," *CSH*, June 4, 1916, 5.4.

45. "Motion Pictures," *CSH*, June 4 1916, 7.1–4; June 11, 1916, 7.1–4; and June 18, 1916, 7.1–4.

46. Louella O. Parsons, "Cinema Masterpieces Playing in Chicago This Week," *CSH* "Motion Pictures," June 18, 1916, 7.3; Parsons, "Is It a Movie or Not? Take Your Choice," *CSH* "Motion Pictures," June 25, 1916, 7.3; and Parsons, "Notable Cinema Dramas in Chicago This Week," *CSH* "Motion Pictures," July 2, 1916, 7.3.

47. Louella O. Parsons, "The Real Romance of the Movies," *CSH*, August 13, 1916, 5.4. The *Herald* also introduced a new comic strip with kids, *Back-Yard Movies*, to pair with "Charlie Chaplin's Comic Capers," *CSH*, August 13, 1916, 4.2 and 4.

48. Louella O. Parsons, "Last of Big Movie Spectacles Moves Out of Chicago" and "The Secret of the Submarine," *CSH* "Motion Pictures," August 13, 1916, 7.1, 7.3; "The Crimson Stain Mystery" and "The Yellow Menace," *CSH* "Motion Pictures," September 3, 1916, 1, 2.

49. "Be a Movie Star!" announcement, *CSH* "Motion Pictures," September 10, 1916, 7.1; Bab, "200 in Movie Star Race; Get First Coupon Today," *CSH* "Motion Pictures," September 17, 1916, 6.1; and Bab, "Another Week to Join Herald Movie Star Contest," *CSH* "Motion Pictures," October 1, 1916, 7.1. Doggerel identifies Bab as Harlan E. Babcock. "How Prudy Parr Becomes a Star," *CSH* "Motion Pictures," October 22, 1916, 7.3; "The Magic of the Movies," *CSH* "Motion Pictures," October 29, 1916, 7.3.

50. Louella O. Parsons, "Did You Ever Wonder What Becomes of the Screen Children? [Adele De Garde]" *CSH* "Motion Pictures," October 22, 1916, 7.1; and Parsons, "Why the Photodrama Ranks High as an Art [Nazimova]," *CSH* "Motion Pictures," December 3, 1916, 7.1.

51. Louella O. Parsons, "Figures Prove Griffith's 'Intolerance' More Than 'Million Dollar Spectacle,'" *CSH* "Motion Pictures," December 24, 1916, 7.2; and Parsons, "Lois Weber Secures Record Contract as Director for the Universal," *CSH* "Motion Pictures," December 24, 1916, 7.6.

52. For the latter, see Louella O. Parsons, "Why E.H. Southern Appears on the Screen," *CSH* "Motion Pictures," October 8, 1916, 7.8; Parsons, "'Romeo and Juliet' Pictures Fulfill Idealists' Dream," *CSH* "Motion Pictures," October 15, 1916, 7.8; Parsons, "At the Picture Theaters," *CSH* "Motion Pictures," October 29, 1916, 7.8; and Parsons, "How Mary Pickford Makes Good as Manager," *CSH* "Motion Pictures," December 10, 1916, 7.8.

53. Louella O. Parsons, "Tell Manager Kind of Film You Like," *CSH* "Motion Pictures," November 5, 1916, 7.8.

54. R.E. Pritchard, "Says the Movie Editor," *NOSI* "Item Movie Pages," January 16, 1916, 1.

55. R.E. Pritchard, "We Promise You," *NOSI* "The Moving Picture Item," November 5, 1916, 1.

56. "Pictures for the Week at the Movie Houses," *NOSI* "The Moving Picture Item," November 5, 1916, 5. A smaller directory of daily bills was printed on page 5.

57. "Helen Holmes Tells Stories of 'Thrills,'" *NOSI* "The Moving Picture Item," November 5, 1916, 5; Coolidge W. Streeter, "Babies Life Made Easy in

Studios" and "40 Prints of 'Daughter of Gods' to Tour," *NOSI* "The Moving Picture Item," November 5, 1916, 8.

58. Boehringer Amusement Company ad, *NOSI* "The Moving Picture Item," November 5, 1916, 8.

59. R.E. Pritchard, "We Promise You," *NOSI* "The Moving Picture Item," November 5, 1916, 1. By the end of the year, "The Moving Picture Item" was running six pages, with more industry stories, more local picture theater ads, and a column answering fans' questions.

CHAPTER 5. EDNA VERCOE'S "ROMANCE WITH THE MOVIES"

1. Another teenager's movie memorabilia from the same period does survive in the Richard Hoffman Collection at the Museum of the Moving Image. Richard Koszarski, "Richard Hoffman: A Collector's Archive," in André Gaudreault et al., eds., *A Companion to Early Cinema* (Chichester, England: Wiley-Blackwell, 2012), 498–523. That collection, however, largely comprises theater programs, posters, and photographs, yet it shares with Vercoe a "handwritten database" listing the films and stars Hoffman saw in Staten Island, New York City, Philadelphia, and Germantown theaters between late 1913 and late 1916. Unlike Vercoe, he showed no interest in serials.

2. The slang term comes from Ronald and Mary Zboray, "Is It a Diary, Commonplace Book, Scrapbook, or Whatchamacallit? Six Years of Exploration in New England's Manuscript Archives," *Libraries and the Cultural Archives* 44, no. 1 (2009): 101–23. Thanks to Leslie Midkiff DeBauche for drawing my attention to this essay.

3. Craig's name is inscribed on the inside front cover of the fourth volume, near a small photo of Thomas Edison.

4. In her obituary, Vercoe is named as the aunt of Jane (David) Harris, Muriel G. Engle, and Mary B. Venning. *CT*, March 18, 1984, n.p.

5. Johnas gathered this information from "The Harris/Davis/Callum/Vercoe Families Home Page" at Geneology.com, the Twelfth (1900) and Fourteenth Census (1920) of the United States, and "Arthur W. Vercoe Prominent Citizen Passes Away Sunday," *HPP*, February 4, 1937, 1.

6. Edna Vercoe was buried in the Rosehill Cemetery, apparently in the family plot.

7. North Shore Trust Company ad, *The Highland Park Press and The Lake Forester, Souvenir Edition 1923,* n.p.

8. "The Class of 1917," *The Deerfield V,* Deerfield-Shields High School, 1917, 9.

9. The December 1914 letter ("I don't know" the day, she writes) from "Floss" to "Nenna" is included in the "Miscellaneous" folder related to volume II.

10. The August 25, 1914, postcard from "Edward" to Josephine Faxon is included in the "Miscellaneous" folder related to volume I. The front of this postcard has a photo of the "N.W. University Gymnasium," an apparent refer-

ence to Northwestern University. In her letter, "Floss" hopes that Edna will tell Crane Wilbur that she pounded her thumb trying to find space for his photo on her bedroom wall.

11. Highland Park Theatre ads, *HPP*, October 30, 1913, 4; and November 6, 1913, 4. Nan Enstad analyzes the "active consuming gaze" of young working women for movie posters and movie star photographs, who probably did not have the money and time to collect scrapbooks, in *Ladies of Labor, Girls of Adventure: Working Women, Popular Culture, and Labor Politics at the Turn of the Twentieth Century* (New York: Columbia University Press, 1999), 179–82.

12. The September 24, 1914, letter from "L. H. Rose, Country Circulator" is included in volume I.

13. There are two ad sheets and a brochure from the Film Portrait Company included in volume I. The brochure is intriguing, as it advertises the company's eleven-by-fourteen-inch pictures "for a post card album or the walls of a 'den' or smoking room."

14. The October 19, 1914, letter from *Motography*, which announces that it is sending Edna its review of *The Perils of Pauline*, episodes 9–13, is included in volume I.

15. The page devoted to Paul Panzer also includes handwritten lines from act 3, scene 3, of *Othello*, the sole reference to Shakespeare in the scrapbooks: "Not poppy nor mandragora, nor all the drowsy syrups of the world, Shall ever medicine thee to that sweet sleep which thou owed'st yesterday." Spoken by Iago as a lead-in to the scene in which he begins to persuade Othello of Desdemona's alleged betrayal, the lines not only are aptly pinned to Panzer's villain but also raise intriguing questions: Could students be reading *Othello* in a tenth-grade class in 1914, and, if not, why would Edna have been reading the play on her own or with her girlfriends?

16. This postcard, dated September 19, 1914, is included in the "Correspondence" folder related to volume III.

17. The August 14 and September 10, 1914, letters from Universal are included in volume I. The second letter confirms that the company is sending her the *Universal Weekly* issue of August 29, 1914.

18. Inserted into the second scrapbook is a loge ticket stub for *Cabiria* at the Evanston Theatre, dated the evening of November 21. It would have been relatively easy for Edna, especially with family or friends, to travel south to Evanston by train on the North Shore Line or sometimes take the elevated train from Evanston to Chicago. See the 1915 brochure of the Chicago and Milwaukee Electric, including a map of the stations: northshoreline.com/ptt15.html. On December 13, 1914, *Cabiria* did play for one Sunday afternoon and evening at the Highland Park Theatre. See the Highland Park Theatre ad, *HPP*, December 10, 1914, 6.

19. *Such a Little Queen* and *The Eagle's Mate* were released in 1915, which suggests that Edna inserted these tiny photos later in volume IV.

20. Edna's postcard to Josephine Faxon mentions that she will be seeing an episode of *The Perils of Pauline* that night.

21. Highland Park Theatre ads, *HPP*, January 29, 1914, 7; and May 7, 1914, 6.

22. Highland Park Theatre ads, *HPP*, July 16, 1914, 6; and July 23, 1914, 6.

23. "New Moving Picture Serial to Start," *HPP*, November 12, 1914, 1; "The Master Key" ad, *HPP*, November 12, 1914, 6; and "Read the first installment of the 'Master Key' in this issue. See the picture at the Highland Park Theatre Friday night," *HPP*, November 26, 1914, 1.

24. Highland Park Theatre ad, *HPP*, January 7, 1915, 7.

25. Highland Park Theatre ad, *HPP*, January 7, 1915, 5; and April 29, 1915, 6, 7.

26. In volume II, the second set of pages devoted to *Cabiria* does include a newspaper photo of Maciste.

27. Tamar Katriel and Thomas Farrell, "Scrapbooks as Cultural Texts: An American Art of Memory," *Text and Performance Quarterly* 11, no. 1 (January 1991): 2.

28. Jessica Helfand, *Scrapbooks: An American History* (New Haven: Yale University Press, 2008), xvii.

29. Ellen Gruber Garvey, "Readers Read Advertising Into Their Lives: The Trade Card Scrapbook," in *The Adman in the Parlor: Magazines and the Gendering of Consumer Culture, 1880s–1910s* (New York: Oxford University Press, 1996), 16–50.

30. For further information on such illustrated song slides and the popularity of illustrated songs at least through 1913–14, see Richard Abel, *Americanizing the Movies and "Movie-Mad" Audiences* (Berkeley: University of California Press, 2006), 127–35.

31. In volume I, a large photo of Wilbur comes from Mae Tinee's "Right Off the Reel" page, *CST*, July 29, 1914.

32. The caricature is clipped from the September 1914 issue of *Motion Picture Magazine.*

33. In volume IV, the two pages devoted to *Return of the Twin's Double,* excised from the August 29, 1914, issue of *Universal Weekly,* include one photo of a cross-dressed Cunard with a fake mustache.

34. One such "memory book," Helen Schloss's "School Friendship Book," completed upon her graduation from Detroit's Liggett School in 1917, suggests how this teenager and her girlfriends appropriated, sometimes in playful parody, Theda Bara and "vamping" in their everyday lives. See Leslie Midkiff DeBauche and Sally Key DeBauche, "Doing Women's Film History, Thinking Like an Archivist," Doing Women's Film History conference, University of East Anglia, Norwich, England, April 2–4, 2014.

35. For a theoretical discussion of such collecting more broadly as "a socially creative and recuperative act," see Janet Staiger, "Cabinets of Transgression: Collecting and Arranging Hollywood Images," *Participations* 1, no. 3 (February 2005), http://www.participations.org.

36. *Who Pays?* ad, *CH*, May 5, 1915, 10; and Highland Park Theatre ad, *HPS*, July 8, 1915, 12.

AFTERWORD

1. Paul Moore, for instance, draws my attention to a rotogravure section, "Motion Play Magazine," that appeared in at least a dozen newspapers from 1917 through 1922. Email correspondence, August 19, 2014.

2. This information comes from research shared by Kaveh Askari on a panel at the Society for Cinema and Media Studies conference in Chicago, March 8, 2013.

3. Leslie Midkiff DeBauche and Sally Key DeBauche, "Doing Women's Film History, Thinking Like an Archivist," Doing Women's Film History conference, University of East Anglia, Norwich, England, April 2–4, 2014.

4. Arlette Farge, *The Allure of the Archives,* trans. Thomas Scott-Railton (New Haven: Yale University Press, 2013 [1989]), 124.

APPENDIX

1. *Newspaper Annual and Directory* became a standard reference work in the early twentieth century. Its publisher, N.W. Ayer & Son, had been for decades one of the more important advertising agencies. Ralph M. Hower, *The History of an Advertising Agency: N. W. Ayer & Son at Work* (Cambridge, MA: Harvard University Press, 1939), 105–6.

Selected Bibliography

NEWSPAPERS, SCRAPBOOKS, AND OTHER SOURCES

American Newspaper Annual and Directory. Philadelphia: N.W. Ayers & Son, 1914–16.

Baldasty, Gerald. *E.W. Scripps and the Business of Newspapers.* Urbana: University of Illinois Press, 1999.

Barnhurst, Kevin G., and John Nerone. *The Form of News: A History.* New York: Guilford, 2001.

Barth, Gunther. "Metropolitan Press." In *City People: The Rise of Modern City Culture in Nineteenth-Century America,* 58–109. New York: Oxford University Press, 1980.

Carey, James W. "Technology and Ideology: The Case of the Telegraph." In *Communication as Culture: Essays on Media and Society,* rev. ed. London: Routledge, 2009.

Douglas, George H. *The Golden Age of the Newspaper.* Westport, CT: Greenwood Press, 1999.

Editor and Publisher, 1911–16.

Fahs, Alice. *Out on Assignment: Newspaper Women and the Making of Modern Public Space.* Chapel Hill: University of North Carolina Press, 2011.

Gaonkar, Dilip Parameshwar. "Toward New Imaginaries: An Introduction." *Public Culture* 14, no. 1 (2002): 1–19.

Helfand, Jessica. *Scrapbooks: An American History.* New Haven, CT: Yale University Press, 2008.

Hockfelder, David. *The Telegraph in America, 1832–1920.* Baltimore: Johns Hopkins University Press, 2012.

Johanningsmeier, Charles. "The Devil, Capitalism, and Frank Norris: Defining the 'Reading Field' for Sunday Newspaper Fiction, 1870–1910." *American Periodicals* 14, no. 1 (2004): 91–112.

Kaplan, Richard L. *Politics and the American Press: The Rise of Objectivity, 1865–1920.* Cambridge, England: Cambridge University Press, 2002.

Katriel, Tamar, and Thomas Farrell. "Scrapbooks as Cultural Texts: An American Art of Memory." *Text and Performance Quarterly* 11, no. 1 (January 1991): 1–17.

Laird, Pamela Walker. *Advertising Progress: American Business and the Rise of Consumer Marketing.* Baltimore: Johns Hopkins University Press, 1998.

Lee, Alfred McClung. *The Daily Newspaper in America: The Evolution of a Social Instrument.* New York: Macmillan, 1947.

Lutes, Jean Marie. "Into the Madhouse with Nellie Bly: Girl Stunt Reporting in Late Nineteenth-Century America." *American Quarterly* 54, no. 2 (June 2002): 217–53.

Marchand, Roland. *Creating the Corporate Soul.* Berkeley: University of California Press, 1998.

Marzolf, Marion T. *Up from the Footnote: A History of Women Journalists.* New York: Hastings House, 1977.

Ohmann, Richard. *Selling Culture: Magazines, Markets, and Class at the Turn of the Century.* London: Verso, 1996.

Otto, Elizabeth, and Vanessa Rocco, eds. *The New Woman International: Representations in Photography and Film from the 1870s through the 1960s.* Ann Arbor: University of Michigan Press, 2011.

Park, Robert E. "Natural History of the Newspaper." *American Journal of Sociology* 29 (1923): 273–89.

Ross, Ishbel. *Ladies of the Press.* New York: Harper & Brothers, 1936.

Schudson, Michael. *Discovering the News: A Social History of the Newspaper.* New York: Basic Books, 1973.

Schwartzlose, Richard A. *The Nation's Newsbrokers, vol. 2: The Rush to Institution, from 1865 to 1920.* Evanston, IL: Northwestern University Press, 1990.

Stewart, Susan. *On Longing: Narratives of the Miniature, the Gigantic, the Souvenir, the Collection.* Durham, NC: Duke University Press, 1993.

Stolzfus, Duane C. S. *Freedom from Advertising: E. W. Scripps's Chicago Experiment.* Urbana: University of Illinois Press, 2007.

Strasser, Susan. *Satisfaction Guaranteed: The Making of the American Market.* New York: Pantheon, 1989.

Thirteenth Census of the United States. Washington, DC: Government Printing Office, 1913.

Trade Marks, Trade-Names, Unfair Competition. Washington, DC: Williams C. Linton, 1923.

Warner, Michael. *Publics and Counterpublics.* New York: Zone Books, 2002.

Watson, Elmo Scott. *A History of Newspaper Syndicates in the United States, 1865–1935.* Chicago: Elmo Scott Watson, 1936.

Wendt, Lloyd. *Chicago Tribune: The Rise of a Great American Newspaper.* Chicago: Rand-McNally, 1979.

Zboray, Ronald and Mary. "Is It a Diary, Commonplace Book, Scrapbook, or Whatchamacallit? Six Years of Exploration in New England's Manuscript Archives." *Libraries and the Cultural Archives* 44, no. 1 (2009): 101–23.

STUDIES IN AMERICAN SILENT CINEMA HISTORY

Abel, Richard. *Americanizing the Movies and "Movie-Mad" Audiences, 1910–1914.* Berkeley: University of California Press, 2006.

———. "The Movies in a 'Not So Visible Place': Des Moines, Iowa, 1911–1914." In *Hollywood in the Neighborhood: Historical Case Studies of Local Moviegoing,* 107–29. Edited by Kathryn Fuller-Seeley. Berkeley: University of California Press, 2008.

———. "Zip! Zam! Zowie!: A New Take on Institutional American Cinema's History Before 1915." *Historical Journal of Film, Radio and Television* 29, no. 4 (December 2009): 421–32.

Afra, Kia. "'Seventeen Happy Days' in Hollywood: Selig Polyscope's Promotional Campaign for the Movie Special of July 1915." *Film History* 22, no. 2 (2010): 199–218.

Allen, Robert C. "Relocating American Film History: The 'Problem' of the Empirical." *Cultural Studies* 20, no. 1 (2006): 48–88.

Aronson, Michael. *Nickelodeon City: Pittsburgh at the Movies, 1905–1929.* Pittsburgh: University of Pittsburgh Press, 2008.

Barbas, Samantha. *First Lady of Hollywood: A Biography of Louella Parsons.* Berkeley: University of California Press, 2005.

Bean, Jennifer M. "The Imagination of Early Hollywood: Movie-Land and the Magic Cities, 1914–1916." In *Early Cinema and the National,* 332–41. Edited by Richard Abel, Giorgio Bertellini, and Rob King. New Barnet, England: John Libbey, 2008.

Bean, Jennifer M., ed. *Flickers of Desire: Movie Stars of the 1910s.* New Brunswick, NJ: Rutgers University Press, 2011.

Beauchamp, Cari. *Without Lying Down: Frances Marion and the Powerful Women of Early Hollywood.* Berkeley: University of California Press, 1997.

Bottomore, Stephen, ed. *I Want to See This Annie Mattygraph: A Cartoon History of the Movies.* Pordenone, Italy: Le Giornate del cinema muto, 1995.

Brower, Jordan, and Josh Glick. "The Art and Craft of the Screen: Louis Reeves Harrison and the *Moving Picture World." Historical Journal of Film, Radio, and Television* 33, no. 4 (2013): 533–55.

Cooper, Mark Garrett. *Universal Women: Filmmaking and Institutional Change in Early Hollywood.* Urbana: University of Illinois Press, 2010.

deCordova, Richard. *Picture Personalities: The Emergence of the Star System in America.* Urbana: University of Illinois Press, 1990.

Dall'Asta, Monica, Victoria Duckett, and Lucia Tralli, eds. *Researching Women in Silent Cinema.* Bologna, Italy: University of Bologna, 2013.

Enstad, Nan. *Lades of Labor, Girls of Adventure: Working Women, Popular Culture, and Labor Politics at the Turn of the Twentieth Century.* New York: Columbia University Press, 1999.

Everett, Anna. *Returning the Gaze: A Genealogy of Black Film Criticism, 1909–1949.* Durham, NC: Duke University Press, 2001.

Fuller, Kathryn. *At the Picture Show: Small-Town Audiences and the Creation of Movie Fan Culture.* Washington, DC: Smithsonian Institution Press, 1996.

Grau, Robert. *The Theatre of Science.* New York: Benjamin Blom, 1914.

Hallett, Hilary A. *Go West, Young Woman! The Rise of Early Hollywood.* Berkeley: University of California Press, 2013.

Hildago, Santiago. "Early American Film Publications: Film Consciousness, Self Consciousness." In *A Companion to Early Cinema,* 202–23. Edited by André Gaudreault, Nicolas Dulac, and Santiago Hildago. Chichester, England: Wiley-Blackwell, 2012.

Hulfish, David S. *Motion-Picture Work.* Chicago: American Technical Society, 1915.

Keil, Charlie, and Ben Singer, eds. *American Cinema of the 1910s: Themes and Variations.* New Brunswick, NJ: Rutgers University Press, 2009.

Keil, Charlie, and Shelley Stamp, eds. *American Cinema's Transitional Era: Audiences, Institutions, Practices.* Berkeley: University of California Press, 2004.

King, Rob. *The Fun Factory: The Keystone Film Company and the Emergence of Mass Culture.* Berkeley: University of California Press, 2009.

______. "'Made for the Masses with an Appeal to the Classes': The Triangle Film Corporation and the Failure of Highbrow Film Culture." *Cinema Journal* 44, no. 2 (Winter 2003): 3–33.

Koszarski, Richard. "Richard Hoffman: A Collector's Archive." In *A Companion to Early Cinema,* 498–523. Edited by Gaudreault et al. Chichester, England: Wiley-Blackwell, 2012.

Lindsey, Vachel. *The Art of the Moving Picture.* New York: Macmillan, 1915.

Lucia, Cynthia, Roy Grundmann, and Art Simon, eds. *American Cinema 1: Origins to 1928.* Chichester, England: Wiley-Blackwell, 2012.

Luckett, Moya. *Cinema and Community: Progressivism, Exhibition, and Film Culture in Chicago, 1907–1917.* New York: Columbia University Press, 2013.

McLean, Adrienne L. "'New Films in Story Form': Movie Story Magazines and Spectatorship." *Cinema Journal* 42, no. 3 (2003): 3–26.

Melnick, Ross. *American Showman: Samuel 'Roxy' Rothafel and the Birth of the Entertainment Industry.* New York: Columbia University Press, 2012.

Moore, Paul S. "Advance Publicity for the Vitascope and the Mass Address of Cinema's Reading Public." In *A Companion to Early Cinema,* 381–97. Edited by André Gaudreault et al. Chichester, England: Wiley-Blackwell, 2012.

______. "Everybody's Going: City Newspapers and the Early Mass Market for Movies." *City & Community* 4, no. 4 (December 2005): 229–57.

______. "The Social Biograph: Newspapers as Archives of the Regional Mass Market for Movies." In *Explorations in New Cinema History: Approaches and Case Studies,* 263–79. Edited by Richard Maltby et al. Chichester, England: Wiley-Blackwell, 2011.

______. "Subscribing to Publicity: Syndicated Newspaper Features for Moviegoing in North America, 1911–1915." *Early Popular Visual Culture* 12, no. 2 (2014): 260–73.

Morey, Anne. "Acting Naturally: Juvenile Series Fiction about Moviemaking." In *Hollywood Outsiders: The Adaptation of the Film Industry, 1913–1934*, 35–69. Minneapolis: University of Minnesota Press, 2003.

Münsterberg, Hugo. *The Photoplay: A Psychological Study.* New York: Appleton, 1916.

Olsson, Jan. *Los Angeles Before Hollywood: Journalism and American Film Culture, 1905–1915*. Stockholm: National Library of Sweden, 2008.

Peiss, Kathy. *Cheap Amusements: Working Women and Leisure in Turn-of the-Century New York.* Philadelphia: Temple University Press, 1986.

Polan, Dana. *Scenes of Instruction: The Beginnings of the U.S. Study of Film.* Berkeley: University of California Press, 2007.

Quinn, Michael. "Paramount and Early Film Distribution, 1914–1921." *Film History* 11, no. 1 (1999): 98–113.

Rabinovitz, Lauren. *For the Love of Pleasure: Women, Movies, and Culture in Turn-of-the-Century Chicago.* New Brunswick, NJ: Rutgers University Press, 1998.

Sargent, Epes Winthrop. "Newspaper Advertising." In *Picture Theatre Advertising*, 82–93. New York: Chalmers, 1915.

Singer, Ben. *Melodrama and Modernity: Early Sensational Cinema and Its Contexts.* New York: Columbia University Press, 2000.

Staiger, Janet. "Announcing Wares, Winning Patrons, Voicing Ideals: Thinking About the History and Theory of Film Advertising." *Cinema Journal* 29, no. 3 (Spring 1990): 3–31.

______. "The Eyes Are Really the Focus: Photoplay Acting and Film Form and Style." *Wide Angle* 6, no. 2 (1985): 14–23.

Stamp, Shelley. "Lois Weber at Rex: Performing Femininity Across Media." In *Performing New Media, 1890–1915*, 13–21. Edited by Kaveh Askari, Scott Curtis, Frank Gray, Louis Pelletier, Tami Williams, and Joshua Yumibe. New Barnet, England: John Libbey, 2014.

______. *Movie-Struck Girls: Women and Motion Picture Culture After the Nickelodeon.* Princeton, NJ: Princeton University Press, 2000.

Stokes, Melvyn. *D. W. Griffith's* The Birth of a Nation: *A History of "The Most Controversial Motion Picture of All Time."* Oxford, England: Oxford University Press, 2007.

Waller, Gregory A. *Main Street Amusements: Movies and Commercial Entertainment in a Southern City, 1896–1930.* Washington, DC: Smithsonian Institution Press, 1995.

______. "Photodramas and Photoplays, Stage and Screen, 1909–1915." In *The Tenth Muse: Cinema and the Other Arts*, 575–85. Edited by Leonardo Quaresima and Laura Vichi. Udine, Italy: Forums, 2001.

Whitfield, Eileen. *Pickford: The Woman Who Made Hollywood.* Lexington: University of Kentucky Press, 1997.

Wilinsky, Barbara. "Flirting with Kathlyn: Creating the Mass Audience." In *Hollywood Goes Shopping*, 34–56. Edited by David Desser and Garth S. Jowett. Minneapolis: University of Minnesota Press, 2000.

Index